INTO TA

INTO TA
A Comprehensive Textbook on Transactional Analysis

Edited by

*William F. Cornell,
Anne de Graaf,
Trudi Newton, and
Moniek Thunnissen*

LONDON AND NEW YORK

First published 2016 by Karnac Books Ltd.

Published 2018 by Routledge
2 Park Square, Milton Park, Abingdon, Oxon OX14 4RN
52 Vanderbilt Avenue, New York, NY 10017, USA

Routledge is an imprint of the Taylor & Francis Group, an informa business

Copyright © 2016 by William F. Cornell, Anne de Graaf, Trudi Newton, and Moniek Thunnissen for the edited collection, and to the individual authors for their contributions.

The rights of the contributors to be identified as the authors of this work have been asserted in accordance with §§ 77 and 78 of the Copyright Design and Patents Act 1988.

All rights reserved. No part of this book may be reprinted or reproduced or utilised in any form or by any electronic, mechanical, or other means, now known or hereafter invented, including photocopying and recording, or in any information storage or retrieval system, without permission in writing from the publishers.

Notice:
Product or corporate names may be trademarks or registered trademarks, and are used only for identification and explanation without intent to infringe.

British Library Cataloguing in Publication Data

A C.I.P. for this book is available from the British Library

ISBN-13: 9781782202066 (pbk)

Typeset by V Publishing Solutions Pvt Ltd., Chennai, India

CONTENTS

INTRODUCTION vii

ABOUT THE EDITORS AND CONTRIBUTORS xi

PART I: THEORY

CHAPTER ONE
Ego states 3

CHAPTER TWO
Strokes 39

CHAPTER THREE
Transactions 59

CHAPTER FOUR
Games 85

CHAPTER FIVE
Script 115

CHAPTER SIX
Passivity and discounting 159

CHAPTER SEVEN
Contracts 189

CHAPTER EIGHT
Groups and organisations 211

CHAPTER NINE
Ethics 237

CHAPTER TEN
Supervision   259

PART II: PRACTICE

CHAPTER ELEVEN
Psychotherapy   279
*Articles by William Cornell, Jo Stuthridge, Mark Widdowson,
    Michele Novellino & Moniek Thunnissen*

CHAPTER TWELVE
Counselling and coaching   311
*Articles by Patrizia Vinella, Sylvie Monin, Mich Landaiche,
    Liselotte Fassbind-Kech & Jan Grant*

CHAPTER THIRTEEN
Management and organisational development   341
*Articles by Anne de Graaf, Maarten Kouwenhoven, Anita Mountain,
    C. Suriyaprakash, Mil Rosseau & Rik Rosseau*

CHAPTER FOURTEEN
Learning and personal development   381
*Articles by Giles Barrow, Trudi Newton, Evelyne Papaux,
    Karen Pratt & Jan Ruigrok*

INDEX   413

OVERVIEW OF IMPORTANT WEBSITES   425

INTRODUCTION

Transactional analysis

Transactional analysis (TA) has been enjoying an increase in interest ever since its inception, now more than sixty years ago, by the Canadian-American psychiatrist Dr. Eric Berne. It has proven itself to be an extremely effective model used by professionals working in a variety of contexts and fields, such as psychotherapy, coaching and counselling, management and organisational development, or learning and personal development. TA combines a highly accessible theory on the development of people and systems with a highly practical approach, centred on the possibilities of growth and development.

The personality model used in TA is based on the three ego states: Parent, Adult, and Child. (In order to distinguish these from actual parents, adults, or children, TA professionals write these words with a capital letter when discussing ego states.) Communications between individuals are referred to in TA as "transactions". From each of the three ego states, people always and everywhere engage in transactions with others. This results in a means to evaluate the numerous options within daily communication, as either more or less effective. The models of ego states and transactions can also be used to better understand—and thus also to better manage or guide—groups, teams, and organisations.

TA works on the assumption that all human beings "write" the script of their own story from the very beginning of their lives. Innate predisposition, all life experiences—positive and negative, the messages that a child picks up from caregivers, all contribute to this script. The script indicates the direction and the manner in which life develops. In everyday life, the script often becomes visible in the games that people play. A game is a specific series of transactions with an ulterior motive on a psychological level that is out of awareness. With the help of TA, people can become more aware of the healthy and defensive elements in their life script. They can then utilise and improve its strength, while changing the more restrictive parts of the script.

Berne based TA on a humanistic principle. Important characteristics within this are consciousness, free will, and self-actualisation. The humanistic movement was a response, on the one hand, to the dominance of psychoanalysis which, at that time, saw a human being as determined by inner drives, and on the other hand, as a correction to behaviourism, which saw a human as a kind of machine whose behaviour is an object of study. The need for personal development, according to humanistic psychology, is a fundamental aspect of human nature.

Therefore, three resulting core statements within the philosophy of TA are:

- I'm OK/You're OK.
- Everyone can think.
- Change is possible.

The apparently simple statement, "I'm OK, you're OK" is truly a colloquial summary of TA's underpinning philosophy. It combines an awareness of being in the world with others as independent but connected human beings, with a belief in a positive aspiration to trust and respect each other and ourselves (Sills & Hargaden, 2007). The background of the three core statements is a belief in the core self as valuable, in the importance of self, of mutual acceptance, and of the capacities of being human. Professionals in TA use a mutual working relationship defined by contracts. In the advanced theory parts of this book more will be said about the depth of these statements.

I'm OK/You're OK is a fundamental premise within TA: every human being has value and dignity. When a child is born, he (or she, of course, but we will use the one for simplicity) has this basic or existential position: I'm OK/You're OK. Experiences acquired will lead people to behave according to one of the other three life positions: I'm Not OK/You're OK, I'm OK/You're Not OK, or I'm Not OK/You're Not OK. Most people know all four of these existential positions and for a large part of the time find themselves in their preferred position. Positive experiences in life can easily help people get from one of the three negative positions into the I'm OK/You're OK position.

Everyone, with the exception of people with serious brain damage, has the ability to think for himself. And everyone has responsibility for the quality of his own life. Obviously, you do not always have control over what happens to you. But you do have control when it comes to how you then deal with what has happened. This often requires thinking, which each one of us is capable of.

TA offers an optimistic theory and a practical methodology centred on growth and development. Children often make "survival decisions", based on early experiences in life. This may be the best strategy available at the time, to survive in a sometimes hostile, neglectful, or cold world. But they often apply the same outdated strategies in adulthood, which may then lead to problems. Within TA, we work on the premise that people have the choice to change their script at any time in their life, in order to give a positive twist to their existence. This applies to people who, because of complaints or problems, have sought help from a psychologist or psychiatrist, but also to people who have a happy and fulfilling life and wish to develop further. After all, you do not need to be sick to want to get better!

The goal of *Into TA* is to help both beginners and more experienced readers to further open the treasure trove of TA. Those who are just starting their journey into TA will find all the basic models neatly presented in a sequence. In this way, knowledge and experience of TA can be traced and developed from its foundations onward to more depth and complexity. For those who have previously spent time in this room of treasures, this book offers the opportunity to deepen the knowledge and experience they have already acquired. We have also chosen to highlight the relationship with related theories, so that the development of TA can be understood within the broader perspective of the theory and practice of social-psychological care.

We have written this book with the thousands of students, at the various TA training centres all over the world, in mind. In addition, we have also had in mind the many professionals who make use of TA concepts in their work and who may require a book that can serve as a reference guide as well as a source to further deepen their knowledge. In essence, we have written this book for all professionals who, like us, are convinced that the quality of the relationship between the professional and her (or his) client is the main ingredient in the necessary or desired growth and development.

After all, people acquire—often in the first years of their life—"the scratches on their soul" in their relationships with other people. So it is precisely the relationships with other people—often later in life—that hold the key to the process of healing, of becoming whole.

Within TA, we repeatedly deal with reacquiring or increasing autonomy. Autonomy is a quality that becomes apparent in the deployment of three capacities: awareness, spontaneity, and intimacy. Autonomy involves feelings, thoughts, and behaviour which are responsive to the here and now, instead of to convictions from the there and then (which are fed by "script").

Structure of the book

The book consists of two parts. Part I: Theory and Part II: Practice.

Part I comprises ten chapters in which the theory of TA is presented. Each chapter has the following structure:

Basic theory: a general overview of the basic concepts of TA. This is generally consistent with the content of the TA 101, an introductory two-day TA training course, which has the same content internationally.

Further theory: the background of concepts is addressed and various theories are compared and positioned in relation to one another. This theory is dealt with during ongoing TA courses.

Furthermore: specific aspects of the theory are further highlighted for those who can't get enough.

Related theories: TA concepts are discussed in relation to other theories from psychotherapy, organisational development, and education.

In Part II, a number of TA professionals from all over the globe discuss the application of TA within their specific area of work. Chapters Eleven through Fourteen deal successively with the fields of psychotherapy, coaching and counselling, management and organisational development, and education and personal development.

At the back of the book there is an overview of some websites. These are sites of the ITAA (International Transactional Analysis Association) and of the PSD and IBOC (Professional Standards Division and the International Board of Certification).

The ITAA website offers the opportunity to find regional TA associations such as EATA (European Association for Transactional Analysis), ALAT (Asociación Latinoamericana de Análisis Transaccional), USATAA (United States of America Transactional Analysis Association), SAATA (South Asian Association of Transactional Analysts), and more. The website of EATA enables visitors to find national TA associations in Europe.

Lastly, at the back of the book we have included a web link to a list of articles that have been awarded an Eric Berne Memorial Award (EBMA).

This book could not have been written without the help and support of a number of people. We would like to thank in particular Ria van Elten for helping us prepare all the artwork. And Publishing Company De Tijdstroom who ventured the publication of the Dutch version of this book.

Finally, we are enormously grateful, in terms of both our professional and personal development, to our patients/clients, students, and colleagues. Without sharing their experiences in life and learning, as well as their feedback and reflection, we would never have been able to write this book.

William F. Cornell (USA), TSTA
Anne de Graaf (NL), TSTA
Trudi Newton (UK), TSTA
Moniek Thunnissen (NL), TSTA

As regards the terms "professional", "client", and "patient": when referring to a TA professional, we have used the word "professional", unless it clearly concerns a teacher, a coach, a therapist, or an organisational consultant. We use the word "client" unless it is clear that we are referring to a person with an indicated psychiatric disorder. In this case, we use the term "patient".

Reference

Sills, C., & Hargaden, H. (2007). *Ego States. Key Concepts in Transactional Analysis*. London: Worth.

ABOUT THE EDITORS AND CONTRIBUTORS

Giles Barrow

Giles Barrow is a teaching and supervising transactional analyst (TSTA) in the education field and based in the UK. He works with children, young people, parents, and professionals in adult and community education as well as schools. He has written widely on school culture, leadership in learning, and applying TA in the context of education. The power of TA for him is the apparent simplicity of language and concepts which make accessible the complexity of human experience and psychology. It remains the most useful way of making sense of the relational aspects of teaching and learning. Most importantly, it informs the installation of hope and the possibility for flourishing.

Giles can be reached at giles.barrow@virgin.net.

William Cornell

William F. Cornell, MA, TSTA-P, studied behavioral psychology at Reed College in Portland, Oregon and phenomenological psychology at Duquesne University in Pittsburgh, PA, following his graduate studies with training in transactional analysis and body-centred psychotherapy. Since those trainings, Bill has studied with several mentors and consultants within psychoanalytic perspectives. Bill has published numerous journal articles and book chapters, many exploring the interface between TA, body-centred and psychoanalytic modalities, and has edited several books. He is co-editor of the *Transactional Analysis Journal*. Bill is the author of *Explorations in Transactional Analysis: The Meech Lake Papers* and the forthcoming *Somatic Experience in Psychoanalysis and Psychotherapy: In the Expressive Language of the Living*, and a contributing author of this volume, INTO TA. He is a recipient of the Eric Berne Memorial Award. For him the power of TA is in its flexibility to work with individuals and groups at both conscious and unconscious levels of experience.

Bill can be reached at wfcornell@gmail.com.

Liselotte Fassbind-Kech

Liselotte Fassbind-Kech is a TSTA in the field of counselling. Her first professional activity was physiotherapy. That is one of the reasons she still emphasises the importance of the client's physical signals in counselling. From 2004 till 2010 she was co-leader of the Eric Berne Institute in Zürich. She now runs a private counselling practice and loves to teach TA occasionally in various settings in Italy and in the French part of Switzerland. She is a member of the Swiss Association of Counselling (SGfB) and of the examining commission for the Swiss Federal Diploma of Counsellor in the psychosocial field. The power of TA for her is in its philosophy including the assumption that people can think and decide what gives them the potency to change their lives in significant ways.

Liselotte can be reached at lf@beratung-fassbind.ch.

Anne de Graaf

Anne de Graaf, MSc, is a TSTA in the field of management and organisational development. For many years he worked for a large (TA based) consultancy firm in the Netherlands. Currently he is co-owner and teacher/supervisor at one of the largest TA training institutes in the world, TA Academie, Soesterberg, the Netherlands. He is the co-author of the successful TA management book *Einstein and the Art of Sailing*. The power of TA for him lies in the strong emancipatory tendency of the thinking behind TA, that is, TA empowers people!

Anne can be reached at anne@ta-academie.nl.

Jan Grant

Jan Grant, BEd, MEd. (Adult Ed.), is a TSTA in education and counselling, and a certified imago relationship therapist. Jan started her professional career as a primary teacher. She worked for many years for the NSW Health Department as a community educator. It was here that she saw the power of group work. She started counselling individuals after completing her certification in TA. She has been in private practice for thirty years, where she sees individuals, couples, and supervisees. Jan lives and works in Sydney and divides her time between her private practice and her teaching and supervising at the Australian College of Applied Psychology. For her the power of TA is the integrative theory that covers how individuals work, how relationships work, and how groups work.

Jan can be contacted at jangrant@optusnet.com.au.

Maarten Kouwenhoven

Maarten Kouwenhoven is a psychologist and the first TSTA in the Netherlands. He is one of the founders of the European Association for Transactional Analysis and worked for twenty years with TA in a mental hospital. In this hospital, working with borderline patients, he developed the theory of problem solving sanctioning. Then he spent ten years as a consultant at KPMG and constructed his theory of strategic coaching. He now develops the theory of three-dimensional leadership based on ego states, which is also applied in forensic mediation in the Netherlands by lawyers. He has written more than thirty articles and books on TA in different languages. The power of TA for him lies in connecting people by knowledge which can be understood by everybody.

Maarten can be reached at maartenkouwenhoven@planet.nl.

Mick Landaiche

N. Michel Landaiche, III, PhD, is a licensed mental health counsellor employed as a staff psychotherapist and training supervisor for the student counselling centre at Carnegie Mellon University in Pittsburgh, PA. In addition, he serves as a faculty member teaching Bowen family systems theory for the Western Pennsylvania Family Center. He works regularly with the TA communities in Lyon, France and Bucharest, Romania. He has also authored seven articles and co-authored two others that have been published in the *Transactional Analysis Journal*. For him, the power of TA is its applicability across disciplinary boundaries and fields of practice, with the attention paid by the TA community to the processes of training and supervision being particularly central to his ongoing professional growth. He is especially grateful for the TA concept of aspiration.

Mick can be reached at mlandaiche@gmail.com.

Sylvie Monin

Sylvie Monin is a PTSTA in counselling and has a Swiss Federal Diploma of Counsellor in the psychosocial field. She runs a private practice in Geneva working with both individuals and groups. She is a partner and a member of the teaching and supervising team of the TA-Center, Geneva, where she is in charge of the counselling curriculum. She has authored articles on TA counselling, been a guest editor of the *Transactional Analysis Journal* for the January 2013 issue dedicated to counselling, and is now a co-editor of the *TAJ*.

For her, the power of TA lies in the simple language that describes rich, complex and in-depth theories that can be applied to different fields and the stance that human beings are OK, that all have the capacity to think, that people can decide their destiny, and that these decisions can be changed.

Sylvie can be reached at sylvie.monin@bluewin.ch.

Anita Mountain

Anita Mountain, MSc, is a TSTA (with organisational and psychotherapy specialties), FITOL, certified PCM trainer, certified PCM coach, and accredited AC executive coach. Anita works nationally and internationally with a wide variety of professionals from top teams. She is iconoclastic in the way she uses her TA knowledge and runs a successful organisational TA programme in the UK where her passion is to enable the TA student to *be* a transactional analyst rather than *do* TA. Anita is co-author of *Working Together; Organizational Transactional Analysis and Business Performance*, which has been referred to as the "best business book". The power of TA for her lies in the philosophical underpinning of OK-ness. If we get to really *know* that we have a right to be in the world and be respected and this goes for others too, then we will have less conflict and greater peace.

Anita can be reached at ta@mountain-associates.co.uk.

Trudi Newton

Trudi Newton is a TSTA in education and discovered transactional analysis about twenty-five years ago. Since then she has used it in all areas of life and has enjoyed introducing others to its delights and benefits through training, supervision, and personal connection. Now a writer, researcher, and consultant working with other educators to facilitate radical learning and community development, she previously delivered TA training in Cambridge and London, and in other countries including Russia and South Africa. She has written several books including *TACTICS* (with Rosemary Napper), which looks in detail at the process of learning and teaching. For her, the power of TA lies in its accessibility, its coherence of philosophy, theory, and practice, and the difference it has made to so many people's understanding of themselves and others.

Trudi can be reached at trudi.newton@btinternet.com.

Michele Novellino

Michele Novellino, MD, is a psychiatrist and psychologist, and TSTA in psychotherapy and counselling. He works in private practice as a psychotherapist, trainer, and supervisor, and is director of the Eric Berne Institute in Rome. He is a founder member and past president of three Italian TA associations (AIAT, IAT, SIAT), and founder of the TA psychodynamic approach with Carlo Moiso and of transactional psychoanalysis, and was awarded the 2003 Eric Berne Memorial Award for his work on unconscious communication. He is author of more than twenty books on TA and various other psychology issues, and of more than 150 papers. His last books are: *Sognando con Bosch* (*Dreaming with Bosch*), *Seminari berniani* (*Bernean Seminars*), and *Dizionario Didattico di Analisi Transazionale* (*Teaching Dictionary of Transactional Analysis*). The power of TA for him is to present a flexible methodology useful both in an in-depth psychotherapy as in a brief focused psychotherapy, counselling, and consultation.

Michele can be reached at m.novellino@libero.it.

Evelyne Papaux

Evelyne Papaux is a TSTA in the educational field. For years she has been working with children and their families in various environments, with babies, children with special needs, in multicultural environments, in day care centres, and in homecare. She has always considered the quality of the relationship to be the core of the educational process: being with, growing with, learning with the other in various contexts but with the same enthusiasm and care. As a TA practitioner in education her conviction is that TA is a significant means of promoting prevention and/or resilience.

The power of TA for her is its philosophy that supports an ethical thinking and attitude and its models that keep inviting her to reflect on her practice.

Evelyne can be reached at evelynepapaux@bluewin.ch.

Karen Pratt

Karen Pratt is a teaching transactional analyst (TTA) living in South Africa. She works as a coach, trainer, facilitator, and supervisor. She has a passion for enabling learning and is most alive working within the rich diversity of people in Africa and internationally. She believes in the power of authentic connection within which new meaning can be made. The power of TA for her is that people can easily relate to the models both to understand themselves and their patterns of communication, and to develop new life-giving ways of growing within families, communities, and organisations.

Karen can be reached at info@tamatters.co.za.

Mil Rosseau

Mil Rosseau is PTSTA-E. His TA training was clinical with the first generation trainers such as Raymond Hostie, Bob and Mary Goulding, George Thomson, Jacqui Schiff, Salomon Nasielski, and Richard Erskine. While running TA therapy groups with his wife Sonja, he translated clinical TA into his second area of work: higher education. From 1985 on, he introduced TA in the business world, supporting companies in mergers, cultural integration, personal growth, and change management. As a business consultant, Mil travels the globe, discovering time and again the power of TA as the "Swiss Army knife" for people-based challenges. Recently, with his sons Rik and Pablo, he founded BIRD: Business Institute for ReDecision. Mil invests his experience collected over the years into the TA community, starting the TA Academy Belgium with the help of his Dutch colleagues. The power of TA for Mil is best represented by the wonderful epithet expressed by George Thomson: "We know how to live!"

Mil can be reached at mil@ta-academie.com.

Rik Rosseau

Rik Rosseau holds a bachelor's degree as a civil engineer and architect. During his employment in retail, his main focus was on customer experience. In 2009 he set up his company, Home-Made, where he assists people in coming home. He combines TA-based coaching with residential real estate advice. As an independent trainer he facilitates personal development as an essential part of organisational growth. He teaches, and uses and shows basic TA and redecision therapy. He is co-founder of BIRD, the Business Institute for Redecision. Rik is writing his CTA-O exam and lives with his wife and two daughters in a quiet village in Flanders. The power of TA for him is its unyielding drive for health and simplicity. TA is serious fun.

Rik can be reached at rik@home-made.be.

Jan Ruigrok

Jan Ruigrok has a background as a teacher and works as a self-employed trainer and coach within his company, Rigardus. He is, among other things, in charge of the project *ECHO*, which stands for Centre for Restorative Justice in Education. Restorative justice is based on the self-regulatory way ancient societies functioned, fleshing out a healthy living, learning, and working environment. Restorative justice in Dutch education uses TA because it provides a unique way to structure intuition. In addition, Jan works as a provocative coach. His purpose here is to make people feel so uncomfortable regarding their destructive behaviour that they convert automatically into constructive behaviour. Provocative coaching for him is a unique way of coaching and counselling, drawing from the natural child and reaching intimacy. Jan is the author of many books on these topics. The power of TA for him is the chance it offers to deal with things life has in store.

He can be reached via jan@rigardus.nl.

Jo Stuthridge

Jo Stuthridge MSc, NZAP is a TSTA (psychotherapy) and a registered psychotherapist in New Zealand. She maintains a private psychotherapy practice in Dunedin and is director of the Physis Institute, which offers training in TA. She has published several articles on transactional analysis and has a special interest in working with trauma. Jo is a teaching and research associate with the Department of Psychotherapy and Counselling at Auckland University of Technology. She is also a current co-editor of the *Transactional Analysis Journal*. For her, the power of TA is that it offers a theory for understanding both intrapsychic and interpersonal human experience within a humanistic value system.

Jo can be reached at jstuthridge@xtra.co.nz.

C. Suriyaprakash

C. Suriyaprakash, MBA, PhD, is a TSTA (organisational) and works as professor of human resources, Jansons School of Business, Coimbatore, India. He is co-founder and facilitator, Relations Institute of Development, specialising in organisational development training, coaching, and counselling based on TA. Currently he is a member of the faculty of Asha Counselling and Training Services, Coimbatore, president elect of the International Transactional Analysis Association (ITAA) and secretary, South Asian Association of Transactional Analysts (SAATA). He is recipient of the Muriel James Living Principles Award of the ITAA for the year 2013. His research interests are on personality and leadership studies from the Indian philosophical perspective. The power of TA for him lies in its versatility to encompass the whole spectrum of human relationships spanning the individual, interpersonal, group, and organisational levels, with an integrative approach based on humanistic, psychodynamic, and behavioural perspectives.

Suriya can be reached at suriya.sunshine@gmail.com.

Moniek Thunnissen

Moniek Thunnissen, MD, PhD, is TSTA in psychotherapy. She is a psychiatrist working in her own company for treatment, supervision, consultation, and training. In the TA Academy in Soesterberg she developed the TA psychotherapy programme. As a psychiatrist-psychotherapist she worked in the Psychotherapeutic Centre De Viersprong for sixteen years and there did her PhD research on the long-term results of the TA programme for patients with personality disorders. Later she was director of training for psychiatrists in a mental hospital, GGZWNB, in Bergen op Zoom. She is the author of seven books and numerous articles on TA, psychotherapy, and psychiatry. She was vice president of research and innovation of the ITAA and is part of the editorial board of *TAJ*. The power of TA for her is that TA works with cognitions, behavior, and emotions, and helps people to take responsibility for the quality of their life.

Moniek can be reached at m.thunnissen@ziggo.nl.

Patrizia Vinella

Patrizia Vinella is a TSTA (counselling) and a registered psychotherapist and counsellor. She is a teacher and supervisor for the Performat Institute (Pisa, Catania, and Rome) and is vice-president of Istituto di Analisi Transazionale (IAT). Patrizia has a private practice as a psychotherapist and counsellor in Apulia, where she lives. The power of TA for her is to provide a simple way to explain to people the complexity of human beings and offer useful instruments for all helping professions.

Patrizia can be reached at pvinella@centroaleph.it.

Mark Widdowson

Mark Widdowson, PhD, is a TSTA (psychotherapy) and a UKCP registered psychotherapist. He is the author of *Transactional Analysis: 100 Key Points and Techniques* and *Transactional Analysis for Depression: a Step-by-step Treatment Manual*, both published by Routledge. He is an active researcher, and has written many articles on TA research, and was awarded the 2014 silver medal by the European Association for Transactional Analysis for research and his contributions to the evidence base for TA. He lives in Manchester, where he has a small therapy practice, and is a lecturer in counselling and psychotherapy at the University of Salford. He is continuing to develop his model of transactional analysis for depression. For him, the power of TA is in its theories which are simple, elegant, and easy to understand and yet have much depth, complexity, and versatility.

Mark can be reached at mark.widdowson1@btinternet.com.

PART I

THEORY

CHAPTER ONE

Ego states

1.1 Basic theory
    1.1.1 Intuition
    1.1.2 Functional analysis
    1.1.3 Egogram
    1.1.4 First-order structural analysis
    1.1.5 Diagnosis
1.2 Further theory
    1.2.1 Second-order structural analysis
    1.2.2 Child ego state (C_2)
    1.2.3 Parent ego state (P_2)
    1.2.4 Adult ego state (A_2)
    1.2.5 Integrated and integrating Adult
    1.2.6 Pathology
    1.2.7 Decontamination
1.3 Furthermore
    1.3.1 Red and blue
    1.3.2 Representing the ego states
    1.3.3 Functional fluency
    1.3.4 Ego stages
    1.3.5 Social-cognitive TA
    1.3.6 Neurobiology
    1.3.7 The personality of an organisation
1.4 Related theories
    1.4.1 Origins
    1.4.2 Drive, ego, object, self and mentalising
    1.4.3 Differences and similarities
    1.4.4 Behavioural therapy, cognitive therapy, and schema therapy
    1.4.5 Humanistic approaches
    1.4.6 The neurotic organisation
References

1.1 Basic theory

Three circles, each one above the other, containing the words "Parent", "Adult", and "Child"—this has been the iconic image and central concept of transactional analysis (TA) since its inception by Eric Berne. The circles indicate the three ego states by which every complex of thought, feeling, and action of an individual can be categorised. The basic model of the ego states is used within TA in two ways: structural analysis reveals an image of the development of a person's personality structure (the inside). Functional analysis attempts to further study and understand the communicative behaviour of people (the outside). Given its centrality to TA, this first chapter is primarily focused on this concept.

1.1.1 Intuition

Eric Berne (1910–1970), the founder of transactional analysis, developed his initial ideas on ego states during his work as a psychiatrist in the United States army. During the Second World War, he was given just one minute to perform a "psychiatric analysis" of new recruits. He assessed approximately 25,000 soldiers in four months. The two questions that Berne asked each recruit were: "Are you nervous?" and "Have you ever been to a psychiatrist?" He noted that if he tried to answer these questions intuitively, before the recruits gave their answer, that he was surprisingly often correct. He then went a step further. For a number of days, he also tried to guess the profession of all the recruits he saw (more than 300). It turned out that he was right in about half the cases. Berne later analysed how he had used his intuition. He concluded that he mainly looked at the eyes and gaze of the recruit in order to estimate their attitude to reality. In particular, he looked at the lower part of the face and neck to get an impression of their instinctive functioning. This marked the beginning of his thinking on the model of ego states as a way to describe someone's personality. He reported his findings in eight articles, published between 1949 and 1962. These articles tell the story of the early development of his thinking in the direction of transactional analysis. After his untimely death at the age of sixty in 1970, these articles were compiled and published as a book with the title *Intuition and Ego States: The Origins of Transactional Analysis* (1977).

After the war Berne began his training as a psychoanalyst and was deeply influenced by the theories of ego psychology developed by Erik Erikson and Paul Federn. Ultimately, Berne identified three ego states in which all of a person's thoughts, feelings, and actions can be categorised: Parent, Adult, and Child. Since a person can switch an ego state at any point in time (there are in fact an infinite number of ego states that are brought together within the "sets" Parent, Adult, and Child), Berne defined an ego state phenomenologically as a coherent system of feelings related to a given subject, operationally as a coherent set of behavioural patterns, or pragmatically as a system of feelings which motivates a related set of behavioural patterns (1961, p. 17). The Adult functions as that which seeks connection with current reality, the Parent appears in the likeness of parental figures, and the Child contains remnants from one's childhood. Each person eventually develops an individual, consistent pattern of behaviour. This pattern is based on a person's characteristic mix of current and past feelings and experiences. Interestingly, in Berne's early definitions, there is an absence of types of cognition or thinking.

Heathcote (2010) outlines the evolution of Eric Berne's conceptualisation of ego states from his first use of the term in 1957 in his papers on intuition through to his more complete theory presented in 1961. Initially influenced by the psychoanalysts Paul Federn and Erik Erikson, psychiatrist Eugen Kahn, and neurosurgeon Wilder Penfield, Berne's understanding of ego states continued to develop over the course of his writing.

The basic model of ego states is used in two ways.

- Structural analysis: what is the background of the behaviour of a person? Which past experiences and insights underlie a person's actions? This involves peeking into a person's "inside", so to speak.
- Functional analysis: which ego state is directing a person's feelings, thoughts, and actions in the here and now? What can be observed about a person's "outside"?

Since in everyday life, one initially encounters a person's "outside", we will begin our exploration of the ego states model with a discussion of functional analysis.

In order to make a distinction between the concepts Parent, Adult, and Child and the daily use of the words "parent", "adult" and "child", transactional analysis employs the use of capital letters for the concepts Parent, Adult, and Child.

1.1.2 Functional analysis

Our first encounter with TA usually consists of learning to work with the ego states Parent, Adult, and Child. These recognisable modes, in one's own behaviour and that of others, form the basis for a functional analysis. With functional analysis, observable behaviour is classified and patterns in this behaviour are made visible. Emphasis is placed on external social behaviour (the outside), and not yet on the intrapsychic frame (the inside). The latter, as mentioned earlier, is the subject matter of structural analysis. We distinguish the following functional ego states:

- The Structuring Parent (SP), in its positive mode, can be instructive; it can offer useful structure and limitations and/or be powerful. In its negative mode it can be dominant, bossy, and/or punitive.
- The Nurturing Parent (NP), in its positive mode, can be caring, supportive, understanding, and/or loving. In its negative mode it can be patronising, suffocating, and/or too lenient.
- The Adult (A) thinks and acts logically. The Adult can also appear aloof.
- The Natural Child (NC) can be spontaneous, authentic, high-spirited, and/or curious in its positive mode. In its negative mode it can be egocentric, reckless, boundless, and/or immature.
- The Adapted Child (AC) can be cooperative, obedient, and friendly, and/or complaisant. In its negative mode it may be submissive, rebellious, complaining, and/or over-adapted.

Berne—an exemplar of his time—was sometimes rather judgemental in his choice of words. This is evident in his use of terms such as Critical Parent and Free Child. This has been cause for debate among TA professionals for quite some time. In this textbook, we have opted for more neutral terms: Structuring Parent instead of Critical Parent and Natural Child instead of Free Child.

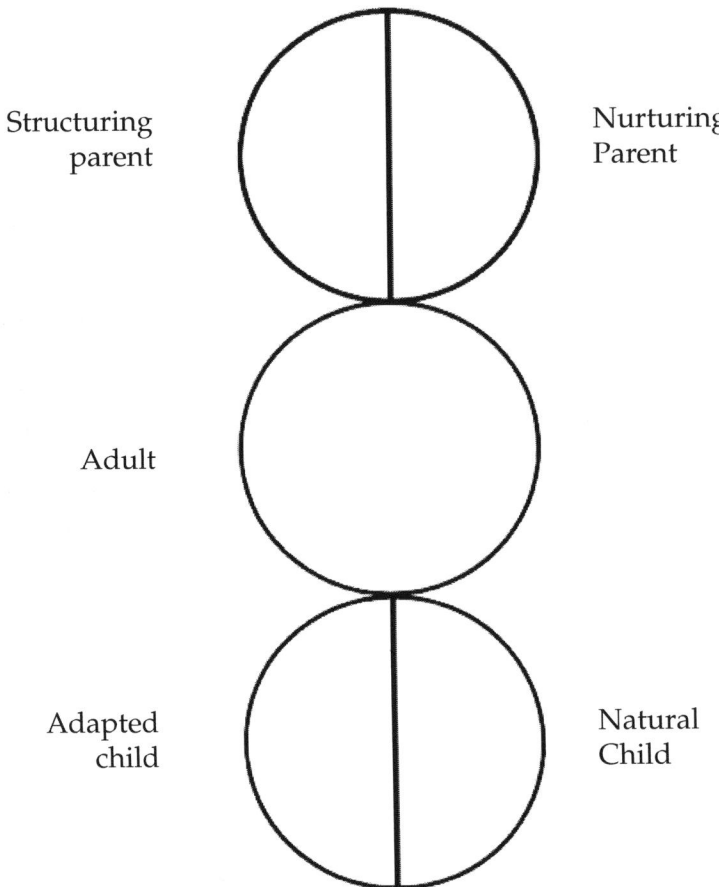

Figure 1.1. Functional ego states.

Each ego state has a plus and a minus side. It seems that if too much of the quality of the plus side is deployed, the minus side begins to act up. Too much of a good thing becomes itself the problem! Indeed, if the Nurturing Parent provides too much care, this will quickly be seen to be patronising. The excessively spontaneous Natural Child will soon go on record as egocentric—as lacking consideration for others. Cooperation by the Adapted Child may sometimes be a necessary quality. Submission, however, is never helpful. The negatively Adapted Child has several manifestations. The rebel feels, thinks, and acts as if there is freedom. In reality there is only resistance (by the child) against what another (a parent) wants. The over-Adapted Child is too focused on what the other wants. He no longer checks if this is actually what the other expects.

Berne described the ego states Parent, Adult, and Child as observable behaviour. The ego states of transactional analysis are phenomenological realities, visible in direct interaction (Berne, 1961). Parent, Adult, and Child represent real people who currently exist or once existed, who have a name and an identity, a shoe size, and a phone number. Everyone is always in one of the ego states, but switches frequently to another, often without realising it. This is a major difference between the ego states and the concepts developed by Freud—the id, ego, and superego—which are unobservable abstractions (also see section 1.4.3).

1.1.3 Egogram

Often, patterns can be identified in people's behaviour that can be traced directly to the way the five functional ego states are "loaded". These behavioural patterns make people unique as well as predictable. Dusay (1972) developed the "egogram" in order to bring these patterns into focus. The egogram is a graphical representation of the degree in which a person makes use of the different functional ego states. Hay, in her book *TA for Trainers* (1992), speaks about the egogram as a "communication style". This makes sense, when one considers that someone with a good dose of Nurturing Parent in their behaviour communicates differently from someone who predominantly applies the Natural Child. An egogram is preferably made by a third person, not by the person under analysis. It is an intuitive snapshot of this person as experienced by others. There are also questionnaires enabling oneself (or another) to make an egogram within certain contexts.

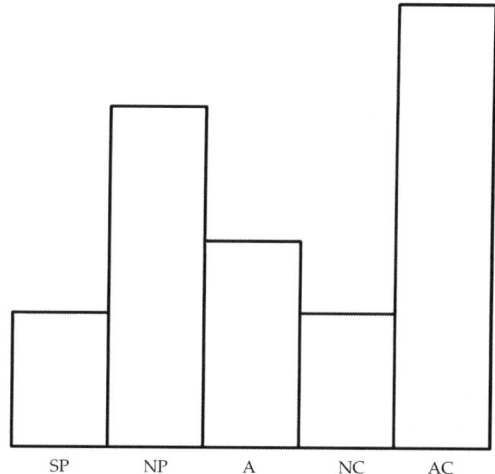

Figure 1.2. Mary's egogram.

As the eldest daughter of a large family, Mary's egogram shows a predominance of the Nurturing Parent (NP). She has the responsibility of caring for her younger brothers and sisters and takes over many tasks from her ailing mother. Her Structuring Parent (SP) is significantly less developed. She follows more than she directs. She rarely sets boundaries of her own volition. Her Adult (A) scores higher than

> her Structuring Parent. In the tension between the expectations of her role in the family and those of the outside world, she has learned to exhibit deliberate and adequate behaviour. Her Natural Child (NC) scores as poorly as her Structuring Parent. She is reluctant to spontaneously show her emotions. It is not surprising that her Adapted Child (AC) ultimately has the highest score, given that she allows the needs of others to prevail over her own.

In Mary's egogram above, A is in the middle, with NP and NC on either side. These are the ego states that are most central to a person's core self. Since SP and AC are mainly developed under the influence of the outside world, they are placed on the furthest sides of the egogram. When making an egogram, more attention is given to the relative picture (the relationships or ratio between the bars in the chart) than to their measure (the height of the bars in the chart). It is preferable to first determine the most and the least powerful ego state, followed by the other ego states. Drawing an egogram is not a scientific method. Most people intuitively know what their egogram will look like. However, discussing the egogram with others often reveals that someone has blind spots (in communication), whereby, for example, they experience themselves as Adapted Child, while others see much more of the Structuring Parent. As a result of this feedback someone may decide to change their behaviour if it has proven to be ineffective.

Dusay introduced the "constancy hypothesis", which closely resembles Pascal's law of communicating vessels: the total available amount of energy a person has for the different ego states is constant. In other words, if someone invests more energy in one ego state, this will automatically decrease the energy available for the others. So, for example, if someone invests more energy into the Nurturing Parent, he will notice that less energy remains for the Structuring Parent. This provides a powerful way to change. It is easier to increase the use of an ego state that you rarely use than it is to decrease the use of a heavily represented ego state. Therefore, the recommendation for change is as follows: go ahead and use your underutilised ego states more often and the other ego states will naturally become smaller. The egogram is an effective instrument by which a person can measure desired changes over a given period of time (Dusay, 1972).

Mary can continue to develop by taking her own needs more seriously and, if necessary, by setting limits to the requests or demands made by others. Her Natural Child and Structuring Parent would grow and the amount of energy devoted to her Adapted Child would decrease.

The egogram, in the way Dusay developed it, makes no distinction between the positive and the negative aspects of each ego state. It's all about the net balance of scores. By and large, the highest scoring ego state will have both positive and negative implications. A change in the egogram can therefore mean a shift towards applying the positive aspects of the ego state more frequently. For example, the Structuring Parent can set boundaries more often and offer constructive criticism, instead of blaming or nagging someone. And the Adapted Child: can cooperate from a sense of loyalty more often, instead of sulking and complaining.

Barrow, Bradshaw, and Newton (2001) proposed working with an organisation egogram. Drawing up such an egogram helps to better understand the organisational culture. Just as any individual, organisations have a unique history which determines what was possible in the past as well as what is acceptable in the present. The organisational culture facilitates and limits all those who work in or with the organisation in question. If there is a strong Natural Child evident in the egogram of the organisation, then this might give all those in the organisation permission to have fun, and be creative and enterprising. If, at the same time, the Adult is small, then this can put the brakes on the necessity for thoughtful or efficient work.

1.1.4 First-order structural analysis

Structural analysis is the graphical display of one's basic psychological structure (the "inside"). When you look at the body of an individual, you do not see a skeleton. And yet you know it's there. Likewise, you also know that there is an internal structural pattern to the way you think, feel, and act. The basic model of the ego states (first-order structural model) is represented in Figure 1.3.

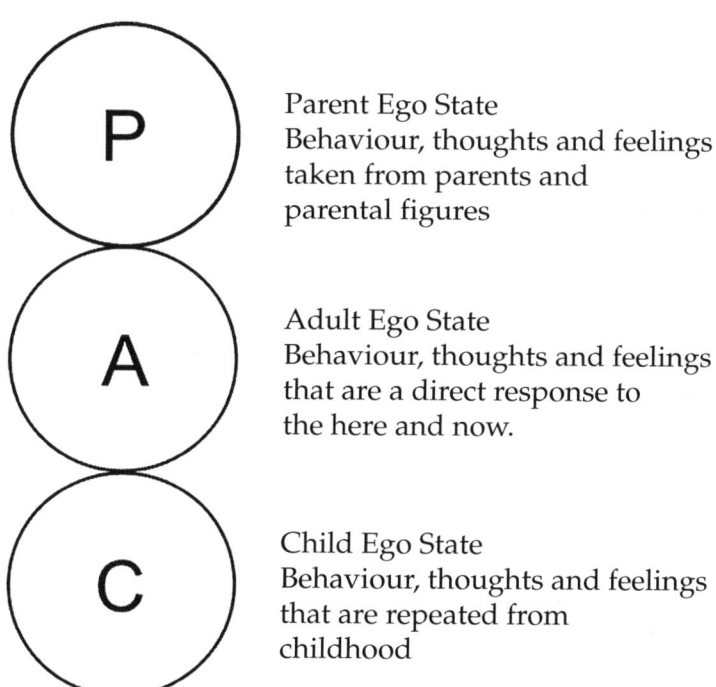

Figure 1.3. First-order structural analysis.

- When mental energy flows to the Child ego state, a person connects to characteristic thoughts, feelings, and behaviour, which have at their core: happiness, sadness, anger, or fear. These are thoughts, feelings, and behaviour that are congruent with the current situation: joy in achieving a good grade in an exam, or anger if you discover that someone has driven a dent in your car. In addition, the Child ego state contains memories of situations from childhood. These may be happy memories, such as being given a bath or being read to at bedtime. But it may also be that thoughts, feelings, and behaviour are activated and reproduced from a period in youth when one may have had to stand one's ground during complex or embarrassing situations. For example: when Bas peed in his trousers as

a six-year-old boy and was embarrassed in front of the class, he was so ashamed that he decided to never again cry in public.
- If one's thoughts, feelings, and behaviour resemble those of parents, educators, or other persons of authority from one's early years of development then energy has passed into the Parent ego state. These thoughts, feelings, and behaviour are then often loaded with norms, values, and moral convictions. Sometimes, all of a sudden, verbally or non-verbally, when a father or mother corrects a child's behaviour, he or she will hear their own father or mother speaking through them, as it were. The way in which a person commits to work, or grumbles at the way others cut corners, etc., also often reveals a similar attitude in this person's parents.
- If the Adult ego state is engaged, then you can assess current situations and behaviour in a way that is appropriate to precisely this situation. Facts are connected to each other and behaviour is focused on tackling problems. When an adult person is functioning effectively, his or her Adult ego state is "in charge". The Adult uses information from the situation at hand, in addition to information from the Parent and the Child ego state. There is the capacity for reflection between impulse and action.

The norms and values that someone has inherited from home or elsewhere belong to the Parent ego state. Experiences are a component of the Child ego state. Both ego states can stimulate or prevent someone from thinking clearly or strategically about taking a successful approach to a given situation. The result is often that someone uses the same approach, which may be more or less effective, time and time again.

An "internal" egogram, also known as a psychogram, can only be done by the person in question. This is where the internal measure of ego states is brought into view. Hay (1992) speaks of "styles of thought", in contrast to the "communication styles" that others attribute to a person in an egogram. In this way it becomes clear how people often view themselves very critically, while others mainly see adapted behaviour. Therefore, in the externally defined egogram, the Adapted Child scores high, while the negatively Structuring Parent is strongly present in an internally experienced egogram. The way in which mental energy is internally distributed among the internal ego states greatly affects how someone "thinks" about something. This thinking does not always fall in line with the way a person deals with things. Speculating about someone's "inside", based solely on what someone reveals on the "outside", is therefore not recommended.

1.1.5 Diagnosis

Someone who observes and analyses behaviour well will create ways in which to influence this behaviour. The ego states model is particularly suitable for better understanding communication as well as for making it more efficient. The analysis of ego states therefore starts with the observation (often intuitively) of a person's behaviour, which forms the basis for a hypothesis on the nature of the observed ego states.

These hypotheses can then be verified with the use of the four methods of diagnosis formulated by Berne (1961).

- Behaviour diagnosis. This mainly involves the careful observation of words, intonation, gestures, postures, and facial expressions. If all the information is consistent (congruent), then the diagnosis will be unambiguous. If there is a discrepancy between what is said and how it is said, then the diagnosis becomes more complex ("I am not angry!" he shouted, while his eyes spewed fire).
- Social diagnosis. In this case, the response of others is used. For instance, when the recipient of a communicative message feels intimidated and fearful (Child ego state), this may indicate that the transmitter is in the Parent ego state.
- Historical diagnosis. This is a diagnosis on the basis of information obtained from the person/client, and possibly from his environment, by which the origin of displayed experience and its corresponding behaviour is revealed. For example, a client may be sitting stiffly straight, staring sourly ahead, and hardly responding. One may have the impression that the client is in a Parent ego state. However, further enquiry reveals that this person feels like a child of nine who has just been harshly scolded for doing something wrong.
- Phenomenological diagnosis. With this form of diagnosis, a there and then situation is mentally, emotionally, and physically experienced as a here and now experience. For example, a mother hears herself shouting at her son: "I'm done with this. That's it, no more!" Subsequently, she realises in a flash that this is an exact repeat of what her father used to shout at her when he was angry.

Berne made use of a prevalent view at the time of what communication is and how it works. Communication was a matter of sending and receiving, of stimulus and response. However, this model discounts the context in which (a part of) the meaning of this communication is grounded. In addition, there is an even greater drawback to this model of communication. It is too linear a view of the way communication takes place. Anyone who only looks at their own behaviour will indeed only see linear causality: "I'm reacting from my Parent because you are positioning yourself in your Child." However, cybernetics and system theory have taught us that communication can only be understood within a model that examines the way things are interconnected. Communication knows no beginning or end. It is a matter of continuous mutual influence, and the transmitter cannot unilaterally determine what his own behaviour means for the other. This is why White (2011) proposed a fifth diagnostic perspective: contextual diagnosis.

- Contextual diagnosis. This form of analysis includes the broad context in which communication takes place. What happens when people step over the threshold of a system? For example, what is the impact of a restrictive organisational culture on employees? Or: what if a person has to work in an operating room under high pressure? What effect does current tension in a country or in the world have on the immediate behaviour of people and their environment?

In contextual diagnosis there are always three main relevant questions:

- What do I do that makes the other do what they do? Example: "I communicate from my Adult, so the other also has his or her Adult available."

- What does the other do that makes me do what I do? Example: "The other speaks to me from their Parent, so my energy flows to my Child."
- What do others do, in a broad context, whereby I do this and the other does that? In a highly hierarchical culture, much of the communication—certainly between executives and employees—will take place in an exchange between Parent (executive) and Child (employee).

Berne stated that for a full analysis, all four (or five) of the perspectives should be used and weighed against each other to formulate the final diagnosis. In practice, however, one usually works with the behaviour diagnosis and the social diagnosis. For more complex situations, you might also apply the historical and phenomenological diagnoses. The contextual diagnosis is a valuable addition in all cases.

1.2 Further theory

One of the advantages of TA is that complex intra—and interpersonal processes can be described in an accessible way. Berne had, among other things, the emancipation of psychiatric patients in mind when he further developed TA. Already in 1947, he published the book *The Mind in Action*, which was rereleased more than ten years later (1959) under the name *A Layman's Guide to Psychiatry and Psychoanalysis*. The subtitle on the cover was: "A Total Handbook for Understanding Yourself". Long before a large number of self-help books appeared in bookshops, Berne put knowledge in the hands of patients (lay men), in order that they could understand themselves and change their own lives. Describing insights into human motives and behaviour in an accessible way has been one the main characteristics of TA from the outset.

1.2.1 Second-order structural analysis

As stated earlier, the functional analysis of ego states can make the functioning of ego states visible on "the outside". Structural analysis concerns the content of ego states, their "inside".

Transactional analysis theory identifies three levels of structural analysis: structural analysis of the first, second, and third order. Each order attempts to understand personality at a deeper level. In this way, the inside begins to reveal its secrets. Structural analysis of the first order, described in Section 1.1.4, is the simplest. Here the models of Parent, Adult, and Child, and their respective tasks are described, without further subdivision. In second-order structural analysis, Parent and Child are subdivided on the basis of the way in which they have developed since birth. Third-order structural analysis further subdivides the Child according to experiences acquired during the earliest years of life.

Second-order structural analysis, the subject of this section, explores the influences that make people who they are. During the time that people grow up, they build up the means by which they retain experiences as well as reflections on these experiences. This is how one's personality develops.

In second-order structural analysis, the first-order structural analysis from Section 1.1.4 is then further subdivided. We refer to the comprehensive ego states as P_2, A_2, and C_2.

- The Parent P_2 is composed of parents and parental figures the person has had first-hand experience with up till now, whereby the experience of the total person of the other—the Parent, Adult, and Child of the other—is introjected into P_2. To distinguish the introjected P, A, and C, we call them P_3, A_3, and C_3.
- The Adult A_2 is not further subdivided.
- The Child is subdivided into:
  - The Somatic Child (C_1), which is present from birth and represents individual predispositions and congenital temperamental characteristics.
  - The Little Professor (A_1), which harbours strategies which the child possesses for solving problems: intuition and pre-logical thinking.
  - The Magical Parent (P_1), in which messages from the environment during childhood, as well as the fantasies about them, are stored.

Second-order structural analysis is sometimes compared with an archive, a storage system. The developing person stores memories of thoughts, feelings, and behaviour (of themselves in the Child and of others in the Parent) in different categories. According to the structural model of the second order, direct experiences are stored in the Child, while the impressions gained by the child of the feelings, thoughts, and behaviour of important others, are stored in the Parent. Enquiry and exploration into the content of a person's inner archive gives insight into their personality structure and motivations. What drives this person, for instance, to pay weekly visits to elderly parents or to practise the piano for an hour every day? How does this person hinder herself by continuing to smoke, or by still arguing with her ex-husband after many years? What does this person do to reach a decision? How does this person react under pressure?

But the archive metaphor does have its limitations. The image of the filing cabinet is "true" because many experiences from the distant and recent past are stored in the ego states. But

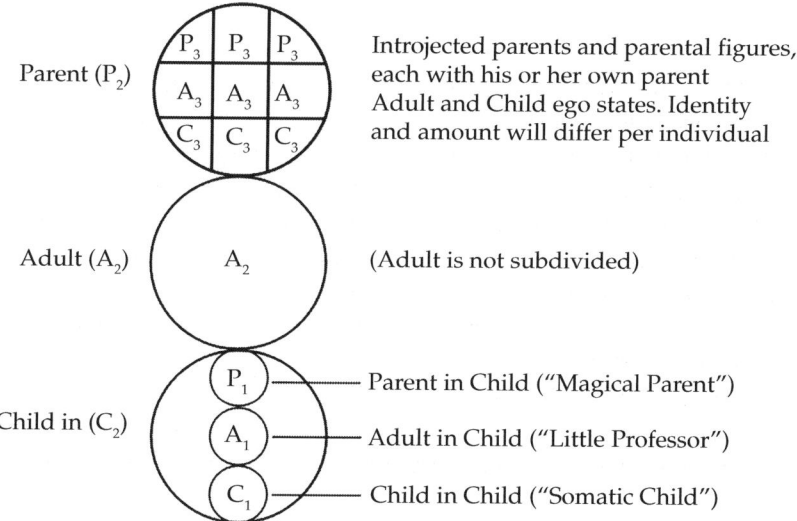

Figure 1.4. Second-order structural analysis (Stewart and Joines, 1987, p. 31).

the image is "not true" because—in contrast to a static filing cabinet, where nothing changes without direct outside intervention—ego states are in fact much more dynamic than this. Neurocognitive research shows that memories are not neatly lined up alongside each other in archives, but that new memories influence old memories in many different ways. Draaisma (2001) contends that people rewrite their memories and that one memory can even overwrite the other. When people become a father or mother themselves, their memories of their upbringing also change. This revision can be so radical that old memories are no longer accessible in their old form. It was Sigmund Freud who first observed that our memories are not cast in stone. Quite to the contrary, Freud realised that current life experiences actually alter the nature and meaning of memories. The human brain is not a mechanical device but a living, growing organ. As described by researchers Satel and Lilienfeld, "Almost nothing is static in the brain. The organ continuously rewires itself in response to experience and learning by altering the strength of connections countless times every second" (2013, p. 16). There is not simply a linear causality between experiences (stored in the Child) and introjections (stored in the Parent) and that which a person thinks, feels, or does in the here and now. Let us use another metaphor: the model of the ego states is like a map, not the area itself. Whoever blindly follows the map will easily get lost!

1.2.2   Child ego state (C_2)

The development of the Child ego state (C_2) is as when a nut from a beech tree falls to the ground and then sprouts into a fresh sapling. In principle, everything is already contained within that little nut. Needs, aspirations, and feelings such as hunger, thirst, pleasure, anger, and fear, are all present at birth. These grow to become more complex feelings and needs as a person gets older. Each year, a new growth ring is added, in which the experiences of that year are gathered (Hay, 1993). These experiences consist of positive experiences that give the child the conviction that he is welcome: "You're an okay person! You're allowed to experiment! Cry, laugh, get angry and make mistakes. You're allowed to think! You, the other and the world will understand." And then there are experiences which are negatively coded by the developing child: "Don't be so stupid! Don't touch that! Behave! Watch out!" These experiences can lead to anxious, negative, and/or defensive behaviour. These experiences and the interpretation the child gives them are like knots in the growth rings. The tree continues to grow, but the traces of positive experiences and the scars of negative ones will remain present. The moment an individual has an experience in the here and now that he associates with the past and the knots formed then, the experiences, feelings, and behaviours related to this past can be activated.

> A client who is sent to a coach because of her noisy and disturbing behaviour at her place of work discovers that as the youngest child in a family of five older brothers (then and there), she had "decided" that she had to be noisy to be seen and heard. In her life and work at the moment (here and now), this behaviour is disturbing to her colleagues and often dysfunctional. She is more often ignored than seen and heard.

Many writings on TA emphasise the historical, fixated, and regressive nature of the Child ego state. One of the questions this raises is the age to which the ego state develops. Does it stop forming at the age of five, eight, or eighteen? Or does it continue throughout life? Cornell (2009) sees the Child as an ego state that undergoes lifelong development and which has both fixed as well as free components.

As said before, C_2 is subdivided into C_1, A_1, and P_1. A newborn baby is mainly geared towards experience and functions somatically (C_1). Very soon the baby develops a basic mode of rational thinking and can translate sensory experiences into actions. For instance, a three-day-old baby can recognise the scent of its own mother's milk (Stern, 1985, 1990). This is the beginning of the Adult in the Child (A_1). The Parent in the Child (P_1) also develops within the first year. The Parent in the Child (P_1) contains the do's and don'ts accumulated from the environment in which the child grows up, as well as the fantasies that the child has developed associated with these do's and don'ts. These messages therefore often acquire a more threatening or absolute form than originally intended by the parents or guardians.

In the earlier example of the noisy client, the experience of not being heard is stored in C_1. In P_1, the noisy brothers are present as introjects, after which A_1 draws the conclusion as the "Little Professor" that she can get attention by crying or by making noise.

Bradshaw (1990) gives a number of characteristics of childlike "thinking" which is illuminating for the way C_2 forms and informs itself.

- Children think in absolute terms and make use of an all-or-nothing polarity: if my father is unreliable, then all men are unreliable!
- Children think emotionally instead of logically: if I feel guilty, then I must be a bad child!
- Children think egocentrically and take everything personally: if mum has no time for me, then I must be doing something wrong or something is wrong with me!

If you keep the following in mind, in addition to the idiosyncrasy of children's thinking, then you won't be surprised about the private world that the child creates in C_2.

- Children have limited power. They grow up as "dwarves", with often little power and influence, in a world of "giants".
- Children have little skill in handling stress. They often grab at the first straw that offers security.
- Children have limited access to information. They do not see the whole picture of the world in which adults live.

The young child experiments with conclusions drawn from what he has seen, heard, and felt. And the child experiments with convictions based on these conclusions. Developmental psychologist Alison Gopnik (1999) and her colleagues show in their book *The Scientist in the Crib* how the young child does this in an almost scientific manner. The child builds hypotheses which are subsequently tested in practice. Tenable "theories" are stored as permanent guidelines in A_1, which is also why this ego state is often referred to as the "Little Professor". The child who extends his hand to the electrical socket, while simultaneously watching the parents, is conducting an important psychological experiment. The reaction of the parents—alarmed, angry, or gently rebuking—is registered by the child and this contributes to the way in which the child interacts with the world in the future. The driving force of a growing child is the need to chart and measure the world into which he has been born. The development of the Child ego state continues all through a person's life.

Ego state theory in transactional analysis is a living, breathing, evolving set of ideas.

1.2.3 Parent ego state (P_2)

The Parent ego state (P_2) can be described as the stored collection of thoughts, feelings, and behaviour that the child has taken over from caregivers and other educators during his early years. The whole personality of the mother or father is taken in at that time: the behaviour, the statements made, but also non-verbal and emotional aspects. In psychology, these are referred to as introjects: values and standards that are included in the structure of the personality of a human being. In the here and now, associations with conclusions and beliefs of then and there can lead to behaviour that can be characterised as a repetition of the behaviour patterns of the child's caregivers and authority figures.

> A client grew up in an environment with a lot of water surrounding the house. All the ditches, ponds, and small lakes meant that his mother often spoke to him with an admonishing tone. "Don't do that," she called out, when he even so much as looked in the direction of all those exciting things around the house. Even to this day, he can hear that voice if he wants to explore an area outside his direct comfort zone. The voice keeps him "in check" each time he wants to tackle something new.

A very young child does not consciously select but retains almost all his experience with his caregivers and authority figures—simultaneously within the Child ego state (in C_1 as direct experience and in P_1 as fantasy about how best to deal with this experience) and in the Parent ego state P_2. Over time some of these introjects are reinforced and confirmed in the child's experience, while others fall away in their influence. Thus, gradually, a frame of reference is formed that will increasingly function as an organising and limiting structure. Even in a grown-up person the Parent ego state continues to fill up with messages that that person considers to be reliable and appropriate. For one person this might be a message from a boss or supervisor about how to deal with problems at work, while for another person it might be messages from a politician who seems to offer a solution to social problems.

In the more primitive, childlike P_1, one therefore finds the raw emotional reactions of parents, coloured by fantasies and distortions, and set at an age in which the child still saw the world through a magical lens. In the developed P_2, one finds the revised messages that have proven their value in the practice of everyday life. If the child grows up in a confidence-building and supportive environment, the content of the messages in P_1 and P_2 will be that other people and the world can be trusted in principle. The child develops a corresponding frame of reference. However, if the child grows up in an environment in which there is neglect, abuse, or misuse, then the messages in P_1 and P_2 will have a different colour. The world is then a more dangerous place, where other people are not to be easily trusted. Be on your guard! From this frame of reference, other people and the world will be met with fear and mistrust. This proves, time and again, to be a self-fulfilling prophecy.

Some authors (such as Stewart & Joines, 1987, p. 31, see Figure 1.4) suggest further dividing P_2 into P_3, A_3, and C_3. P_3 is then the storage facility of all the messages from parents, educators, and authority figures. A_3 is the collection of statements about reality that a person hears from parental figures and which he has then registered or copied. Many of these claims may be objectively true. But others will be based on misunderstandings or fantasies these parental figures have about the world. Finally, C_3 is the collection of memories of the parental figure's Child ego state. For example, Mark's experience of his father grumbling about being too busy; in answer to a question by Mark, the father answers: "Why are you bothering me with this now?!" As a manager, Mark discovers that he sometimes uses exactly the same words with his employees who ask him questions when he has a lot of work to do. While the words seem to be from the Parent, they are in fact more the expression of his father's Child ego state.

1.2.4 Adult ego state (A_2)

In the Adult ego state (A_2), you register reality from the most objective perspective possible. The Adult records what is happening in the inner world and in the outside world. Using the aggregation of all of this data, the Adult makes choices with regard to appropriate and effective functioning in the here and now. If the Adult is "turned on", you evaluate signals from the environment, combined with information from the Parent and the Child ego state, before you react. If the Adult is functioning properly, you continuously make decisions about what you want to do. Of course, this happens in a fraction of a second. The Adult harbours a significant amount of intuitive understanding (from A_1, the Little Professor). Engaging the Adult ego state requires an active decision that increases in strength with practice. If we place a definition of "free will" next to this information about the Adult ego state, you will notice that they are an extension of each other.

Fennis (2009) defines free will as "the ability to weigh up all the available information in order to make a choice". He adds: "Practising free will guzzles energy. Free will is like a battery that runs empty surprisingly quickly" (translated for this edition).

For many clients, the exercise for creating "a moment of reflection between impulse and action" turns out to be very beneficial. The impetus for taking action often stems from the Parent or the Child. The Adult can be actively engaged in order to delay a response to an impulse. The age-old advice to count to ten in situations of anger or annoyance is not a bad idea! Exercising with meditation (via mindfulness training, for example) helps the Adult to gain strength.

The first years of childhood are crucial in a person's development. However, it has become evident that people develop throughout their lives. Especially one's resilience and the way one learned as a child how to deal with setbacks, affect the quality of one's later life (Cornell, 2009).

1.2.5 Integrated and integrating Adult

Just as peace is more than the absence of war, health is also more than the absence of disease. "You don't have to be sick to get better!" The ideal, for Berne (1961), is the realisation of what he called "an integrated Adult". With an integrated Adult one can more readily access whatever is valuable in the Parent and the Child ego state. Everything that is connected to limiting experiences and is stored within these ego states can be overcome and no longer has control over one's thoughts, feelings, or actions. This means that one can respond more autonomously, entirely within the here and now, to what is going on inside and outside, without the script intervening. TA works on the assumption that everyone, already at a young age, develops a story, the script, which has three basic functions:

- It helps to give meaning to your past.
- It provides guidance for addressing issues that you encounter in the present.
- It "predicts" the future.

In Chapter Five, on the script, we will go into detail on this central TA concept.

The Adult ego state ensures that you can deal with the here and now. This ego state registers, interprets, and concludes. The Adult absorbs information from the outside world in the here and now, through the five senses. The Adult also takes note of how the Child reacts and examines whether this response is relevant in the here and now. The Adult also looks at whether there are ideas in the Parent that can be valuable in the here and now. Berne's description of the integrated Adult delineated three properties (1961):

- Pathos: personal sensitivity, attractiveness, and responsiveness (qualities from the Child integrated in the Adult).
- Logos: processing of objective data (A_2 in strict sense).
- Ethos: moral qualities and ethical responsibilities (Parental qualities integrated into the Adult).

The integrated Adult is the last stage in the development of the Adult ego state. This is when all the valuable content from the Parent and the Child ego state is assimilated and integrated into the Adult ego state. For Berne (1961, p. 195) this was the desired final outcome of a person's psychological development:

> "Certain people when functioning qua adult, have a charm and openness of nature which is reminiscent of that exhibited by children. [...] On the other hand, there are also moral qualities, which are universally expected of people who undertake grown-up responsibilities. [...] Transactionally, this means that anyone functioning as an Adult should ideally exhibit three kinds of tendencies: personal attractiveness and responsiveness, objective data processing and ethical responsibility; representing respectively archeopsychic, neopsychic, and exteropsychic elements integrated into the neopsychic ego state."

The appropriate and functional attributes of the Child and the Parent are included in the Adult.

Keith Tudor (2010, 2014) has undertaken both a critique of traditional ego state theories and an expansion of our thinking about the capacities of the Adult ego state. While not dismissing the rational/cognitive functions of the Adult, Tudor describes the maturational capacities

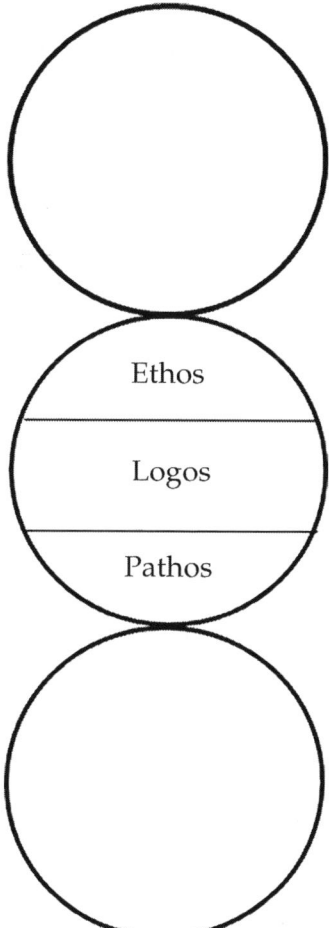

Figure 1.5. Integrated Adult.

of the Adult as including awareness of relational needs, reflective and critical consciousness, motivational strivings, and imagination (2014, pp. 47–54). He suggests the therapeutic slogan, "Assume Adult—until proven otherwise" (2014, p. 60) and describes a process of "expanding the Adult" in which the therapist seeks to facilitate a working relationship to support the client's Adult functioning alongside patterns of transferential relating.

In her "Functional Fluency" model, Susannah Temple (1999) introduced the concept of "the integrating Adult", thereby highlighting that this aspect of the Adult is not static but a continuous process of integration. For more information, see Section 1.3.1.

1.2.6 Pathology

Berne was a medical doctor and this coloured his view of human functioning. His frame of mind was that of "health and disease". He spoke of non-optimally functioning ego states in terms of pathology. Although "pathology" may sound a bit heavy in this context, if people do not or are not able to optimally make use of their integrated Adult, then we may speak of this being pathological. When people make unwise choices or repeatedly fall into unhealthy patterns, either at work or in relationships, and they fail to understand why this is so, then there can be reason to speak of a pathology of the ego states: contamination, constancy, or exclusion (Woollams & Brown, 1978). "Contamination" means that the boundaries between ego states are too permeable, whereby the Adult becomes contaminated with material from the Parent (P_2) or the Child (C_2). We use the term "constancy" when someone only makes use of one ego state, while the other two are ignored. When only two ego states are used, the third undergoes "exclusion".

Contamination

Berne (1961) defined contamination as follows: "Contamination is the standardised intrusion of a part of one ego state into another ego state." Hay (1992) contends that material from the Parent or the Child "leaks" into the Adult ego state. The metaphor is striking because, in the case of contamination, there is indeed too much permeability of the boundaries between the ego states. The strategy against contamination—"decontamination"—involves making the boundaries of the Adult ego state more robust, so that decisions made by the Adult are not tainted, distorted, or cropped by either the Child or the Parent.

A common example of Parent-Adult contamination (Figure 1.6a) are prejudices, which often reflect stereotyping and overgeneralisation, opinions which are not based on facts. However, the person thinks that it is an Adult-fact and not a Parent-opinion. Some examples are prejudices such as "All Dutch people are stingy!", but also convictions like "If I call in sick for even one day, I will be fired," or "Before we can go on vacation the whole house must be clean and tidy."

In the case of a Child-Adult contamination (Figure 1.6b), (fearful) experiences of then and there are used to measure and evaluate the here and now. Suspicion, superstition, paranoia, and phobia are experienced as reality and are taken as truth. There are hotels without a thirteenth floor and without room thirteen. "Nobody wants to stay there!" it is assumed. A Child-Adult contamination can also be recognised in statements such as "When push comes to shove, no one can really be trusted," or "Something terrible will happen if you go out alone."

There is the risk of complete confusion when we're faced with a "double contamination" (Figure 1.6c). The view on reality is distorted because content from both Parent and Child are seen as representing the truth. This double contamination is the most common form of contamination. So, if the Parent dictates a certain preconception ("real men don't cry"), the Child may respond with fear (when their eyes well up with tears).

Constancy

Sometimes it seems as if a person completely resides and functions within one ego state. Only one ego state is utilised while the other two are ignored. A constant Parent can be an

EGO STATES 21

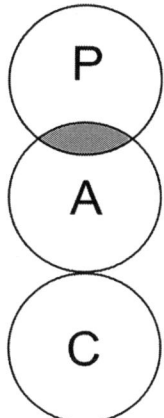

Figure 1.6a. Parent-Adult contamination.

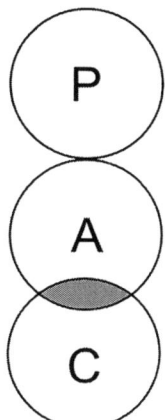

Figure 1.6b. Child-Adult contamination.

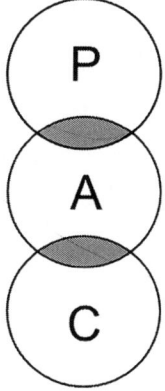

Figure 1.6c. Double contamination.

authoritarian teacher who does not have fun with the students and is not open to reason, who enforces rules but does not facilitate thinking. A constant Child is a Peter Pan, the eternal youngster who always wants to have fun without having to take responsibility or think about the effects of behaviour. A constant Adult puts rationality on autopilot and is often far removed from opinions and feelings.

Exclusion

The difference to constancy is that with exclusion a person uses two ego states and excludes one. A person with an excluded Parent will be in a poor position to provide for himself and others. A lack of responsible standards and values can lead such a person into trouble. Whoever excludes the Child will find it impossible to feel pleasure, excitement, or curiosity. And misery and sorrow are also excluded. Nobody can live or work with a completely excluded Adult. Such a person is a danger to himself and his surroundings. With bipolar disorders in the manic phase, it is the Child that is mostly engaged: overconfidence, spending a lot of money, no need for sleep. In the depressive phase, the Parent takes revenge and the person is wracked with self-reproach, and the Child responds with guilt and helplessness.

1.2.7   Decontamination

Decontamination—the alleviation of contamination—is an essential technique in TA. Often people are not aware of the fact that they distort their reality, nor the extent to which they do so. For them, their frame of reference is a logical and natural part of who they are. Faced with contamination or exclusions, one should realise that no one just contaminates (or excludes) accidentally or arbitrarily. At some time in the past this was probably the best option or the only available view of reality. Therefore, a compassionate and respectful response is called for. People learn at some point to "act mad" in order not to go mad. To bring about change, it is often desirable and usually necessary that the professional first joins before adding another point of view. If people feel understood, they will be more likely to walk with you.

In Berne's view (1977), the ultimate aim of decontamination is to achieve an integrated Adult, which is not infringed upon by confusing, unprocessed experiences from the past, or by the non-integrated ego states of significant others from one's history. It is important that the confusion between the different ego states is examined and faced. Eventually, the Adult can take over the reins, so that it can assume full responsibility over one's thoughts, feelings, and behaviour.

In the work of the TA professional, decontamination already commences when drawing up the contract (see Chapter Seven). During the process of decontamination, there is often a shift in the frame of reference, not infrequently accompanied by a sense of relief over letting go of certain fixations. Energy returns to the here and now because it is not being drawn to the then and there as much.

1.3 Furthermore

The concept of ego states has been and still is the most debated and most criticised of all TA concepts. Some TA professionals have aimed to change and/or improve this concept for a variety of reasons. We'll touch on a few of them.

1.3.1 Red and blue

One of the first to criticise the ego state concept was the American corporate trainer Abe Wagner. In his book *The Transactional Manager* (1981) and later in his *TAJ* article "Blue ego states for effective communication" (1994), he went in search of a practical and easily accessible way to work with TA concepts. His main objective was to attract the attention of the Child in the other. Wagner believes that there are effective, blue ego states, and ineffective, red ego states. "Stay blue and people will respond to you. Turn red and it's better not said." The effective ego states, according to Wagner, are: the Nurturing Parent, the Adult, and the Natural Child. These ego states communicate the message "I'm OK, you're OK", through content, tone, posture, and facial expression. In the Introduction we discussed in detail the concept of the "existential position" or "life position", to which "I am OK/not OK" and "You are OK/not OK" refer. In contrast, ineffective ego states, like the Structuring Parent communicate "You are not OK", while the Adapted Child communicates "I am not OK" in the compliant mode, and "You are not OK" in the rebellious mode.

Both the blue and the red ego states provoke the equivalent ego state in the other, which Wagner calls co-dependency: "Co-dependency is very prevalent in the organisational world and it can be overcome by engaging in OK complementary transactions." Breaking this symbiotic chain, which Wagner calls "bicycle management", is a task for any TA professional who works in a company or organisation. Imagine the following: A CEO mainly directs from the Parent, so that the director primarily reacts from the Child. And now the director mainly directs from the Parent whereby the manager reacts from the Child, and so on. A picture emerges of "a series of bikes in a row". When consultants also approach directors (or other employees) primarily from the Parent, they confirm the symbiotic chain and they impede the healthy development of autonomous workers. It is more effective to persist with cross transactions (see Chapter Three) which break through the symbiotic chain.

1.3.2 Representing the ego states

Van Beekum (1996) has noted that there is often confusion about the structural and the functional model of the ego states. He maintains that this confusion is partly caused by the fact that both models are graphically displayed in the same way. He is researching the idea of using circles in the structural model while the functional model is displayed using squares. He then combines this in one graphic (see Figure 1.7) and shows how one can view the relationship between the structural and the functional model.

This model clearly shows how there are five possibilities for functioning within the here and now. This graph, as proposed by Van Beekum, makes it possible, as he says, to "see the differences between both models".

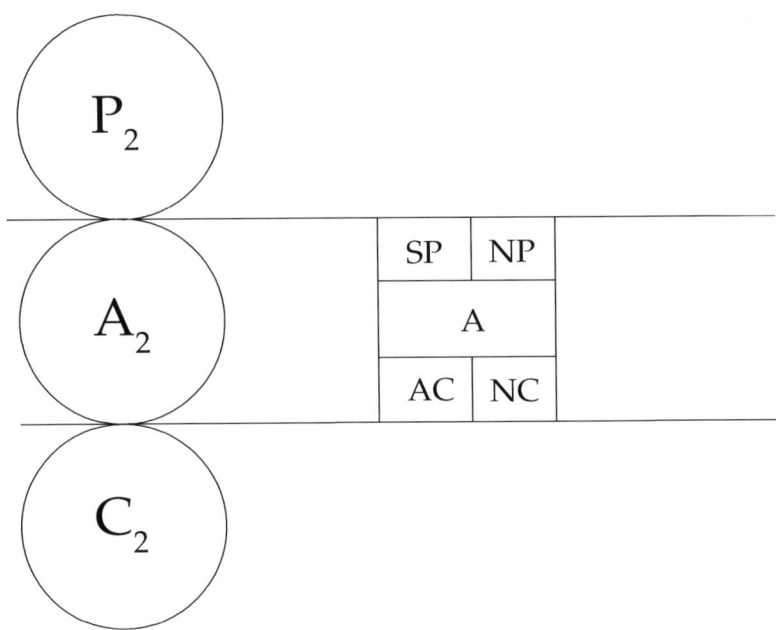

Figure 1.7. Relationship between the structural and functional model (van Beekum, 1996).

1.3.3 Functional fluency

The functional fluency model (Temple, 1999, 2004) shows the integrated Adult in action. Moreover, Temple prefers the term "integrating Adult" because it is not a static Adult ego state, but an ego state that is continuously developing, as more content from the relevant parts of the Parent and Child ego states is assimilated and integrated in a constructive manner.

The functional fluency model is not so much a model of ego states, but more a model of human functioning, informed by ego state theory as well as by other theories (Temple, 2004, p. 198). This is why Temple uses stacked squares in her drawing instead of circles, and avoids the words Parent, Adult, and Child. She created new terms, linked to various categories of human existence and functioning, with both positive and negative aspects:

1. The Parent ego state is linked to the function of social responsibility: the use of energy for the benefit of others and yourself. This works in the following two ways:
   - By giving direction and control, in a structuring, inspiring, well-organised, and firm manner (structuring mode), or in a dominant, bossy, punitive manner (dominating mode).
   - By taking care, in a nurturing, accepting, involved, and sympathetic manner (nurturing mode), or in a patronising, inconsistent, and pampering manner (marshmallowing mode).
2. The Adult ego state is associated with the function of reality assessment: the use of energy for collecting and interpreting information as well as for an awareness of the here and now. The Adult is alert, aware, grounded, rational, investigative, and evaluative (accounting mode).
3. The Child ego state is associated with the function of self-actualisation: the use of energy for one's own benefit. Again, this can be done in two ways:

- By entering into social relationships with others in a cooperative, friendly, and assertive manner (cooperative mode) or in an overly adapted, anxious, subordinate, or rebellious manner (compliant/resistant mode).
- By doing things in a natural, unique, and spontaneous manner and by being creative, expressive, and energetic (spontaneous mode), or by behaving in an immature, egocentric, ruthless, and selfish way (immature mode).

The five central modes of structuring, nurturing, accounting, cooperative, and spontaneous offer a positive range and combination of ways of responding effectively. The four negative modes are less effective ways of responding and can be explained as manifestations of contaminated aspects of Adult functioning. All nine modes are manifestations of an integrating Adult ego state (Temple, 2004, p. 200). A questionnaire has been developed for conducting research using this model, the Temple Index of Functional Fluency (TIFF) (www.functionalfluency.com), the validity of which is currently being examined.

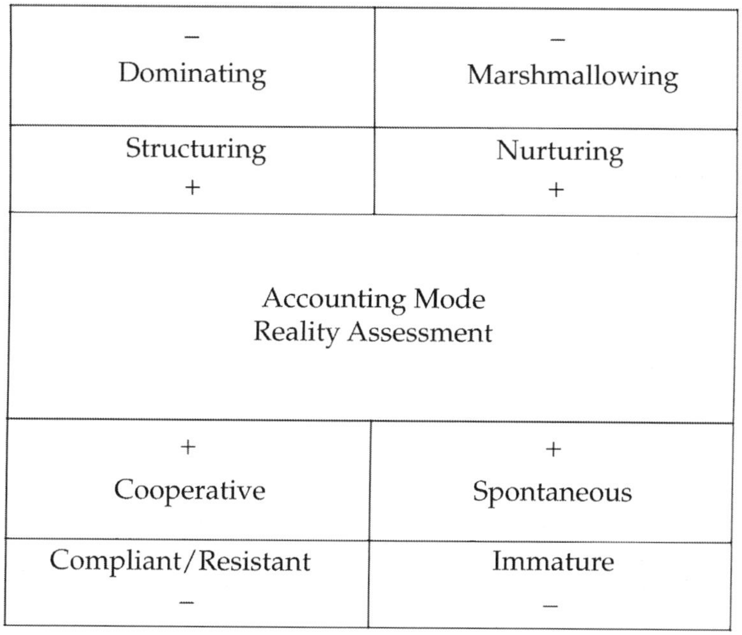

− Dominating	− Marshmallowing
Structuring +	Nurturing +
Accounting Mode Reality Assessment	
+ Cooperative	+ Spontaneous
Compliant/Resistant −	Immature −

Figure 1.8. Behavioural modes on the functional fluency model.

1.3.4 Ego stages

Maria Teresa Romanini (1991, 1996) offers some interesting and rather challenging alternatives to the Bernian model of ego states. Writing and publishing in Italian, her work has not gained broad recognition or consideration the wider TA community, but more recently, Alessandra Pierini (2008, 2014), publishing in English, has brought attention to Romanini's innovations. Romanini introduces the concept of the "real" ego or "ego stages" in contrast to Berne's descriptions of ego states as intrapsychic structures. In part informed by their work with children, Romanini and Pierini argue that one needs to account for the actual, objective state (i.e., developmental stage) of the person, a combination of the individual's actual chronological age, self-perception, and the external, social perception of the person. So, for example, "… a 7-year-old child … is recognized by the external world and by himself as a child, irrespective of the ego state he or she is using at any given moment" (Pierini, 2014, p. 105). A child may be seven years old in his actual stage of ego development, while functioning predominantly from his Parent ego state in his intrapsychic experience of himself. While appearing to others as a young boy, he may be functioning frequently from his Parent ego state.

To further reflect the lived realities of children, Romanini offered an alternative diagram to Berne's familiar stacked circles with Parent at the top, Adult in the middle, and Child at the base. Romanini and Pierini suggest that it is sometimes more accurate to place the Child ego state at the centre of the diagram, with Parent on top and Adult below.

It is customary in TA to think of how the Adult ego state can be contaminated by the Child (or Parent), but Romanini argues that for the developing ego stage of a child, the Child ego state may, in fact, be contaminated by the Adult ego state:

> When a child finds it too laborious to play or use his imagination, he or she may be blocked by a parental judgment. I view this as a contamination of the Child ego state by the Parent ego state. The Adult ego state contaminates creativity by excessive rationality … . (Pierini, 2014, p. 106)

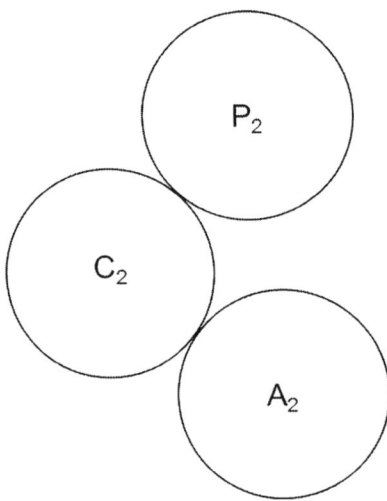

Figure 1.9. Child ego stage of real ego in the child.

1.3.5 Social-cognitive TA

A fascinating addition to Berne's model of the ego states is the socio-cognitive approach of an Italian research group led by Professor Pio Scilligo, who passed away in 2009 (Bastianelli & Ceridono, 2012; De Luca & Tosi, 2011; Scilligo, 2011). Scilligo's research relied on, among others, the interpersonal model, Structural Analysis of Social Behaviour (SASB), put forward by Lorna

Smith Benjamin (1996). Benjamin arranged all interpersonal behaviour in two dimensions: love-hate and autonomy-control. The combination of these poles gives rise to the following four configurations:

- Free: a combination of love and independence, whereby you give power to yourself and/or others in a loving way.
- Protective: a combination of love and control, whereby you take power from yourself and/or others in a loving way.
- Rebellious: a combination of hatred and autonomy, whereby you give power to yourself and/or others in a hateful, negative way.
- Critical: a combination of hatred and control, whereby you take power from yourself and/or others in a hateful, negative way.

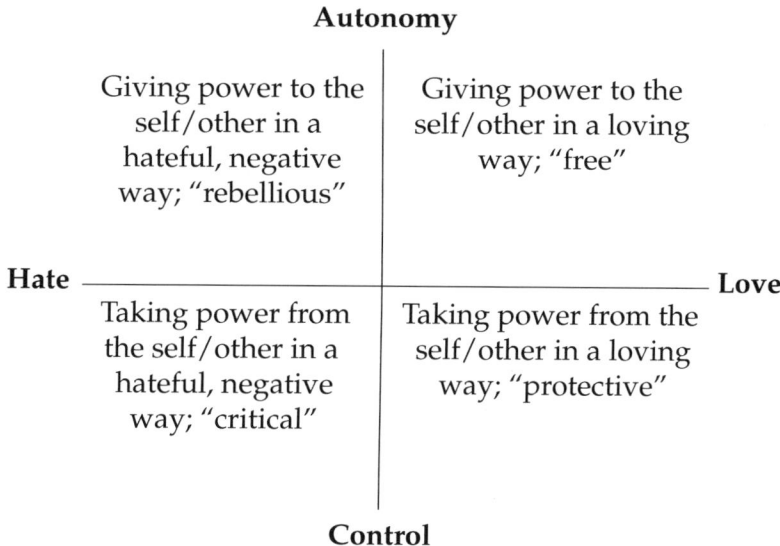

Figure 1.10. Dimensions in social cognitive TA.

Scilligo and his colleagues investigated the psychotherapeutic relationship with the following question: "Which ego states are more effective, and which are less effective?" They combined all three ego states (Parent, Adult, and Child) with the four aspects mentioned above (free, protective, rebellious, and critical). This gives the following four combinations:

- With the Parent: the Free Parent, the Protective Parent, the Rebellious Parent, and the Critical Parent.
- With the Adult: the Free Adult, the Protective Adult, the Rebellious Adult, and the Critical Adult.
- With the Child: the Free Child, the Protective Child, the Rebellious Child, and the Critical Child.

The strength of this model is that it has been extensively studied in research. Scilligo introduces the concept of an "integrated self", which significantly alters the understanding of "self" as described by Berne. Scilligo defines the integrated self as "a web of potential meanings, values, and norms of action with emotional valence, creatively emerging from experience, in view of a core tendency of the person who projects self into the future …" (2009, p. 64). While ego states are seen as states of mind formed and based in experiences of the past, Scilligo argues that the self has an innate sense and orientation towards the future. He underscores the agency of the self as an active, dynamic force rather than as a reflective state of mind. Scilligo's research has indicated that free and protective ego states are most associated with an integrated self. These are the ego states that appear in Scilligo's research studies to increase after psychotherapy, while the rebellious and critical ego states decrease (De Luca & Tosi, 2011).

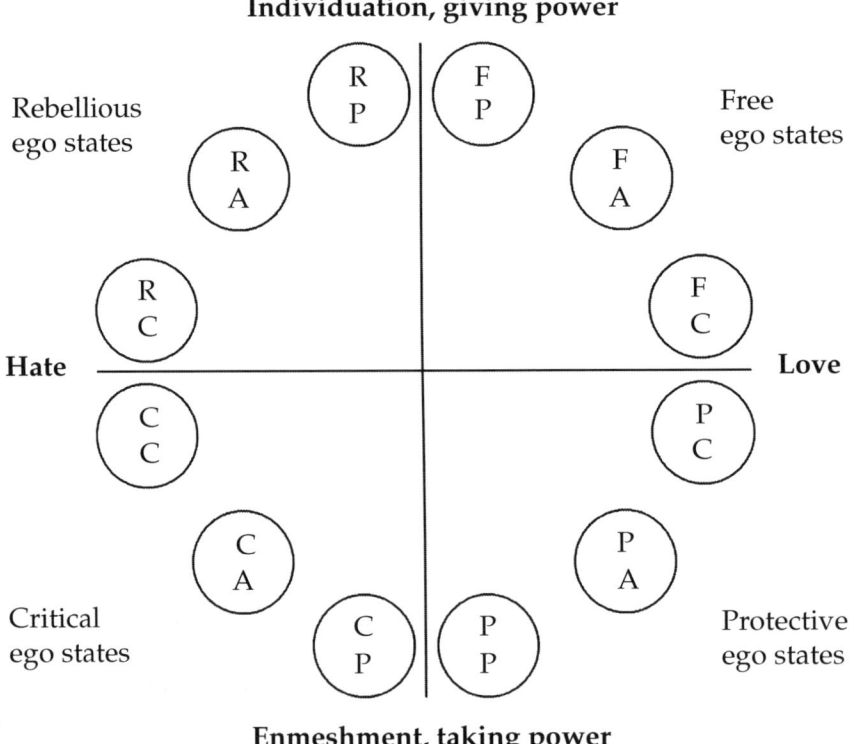

Figure 1.11. The circumplex model of ego states.

1.3.6 Neurobiology

When Berne developed the theory of ego states in the 1960s, he hoped that eventually specific brain areas ("psychic organs") would be found, corresponding to the Parent, Adult, and Child (Berne, 1961). He used the following terms:

- Exteropsyche, which functions with norms and values acquired from others.
- Neopsyche, which has the function of processing data and evaluating reality.
- Archaeopsyche, which reacts on the basis of pre-logical thinking and poorly differentiated perceptions.

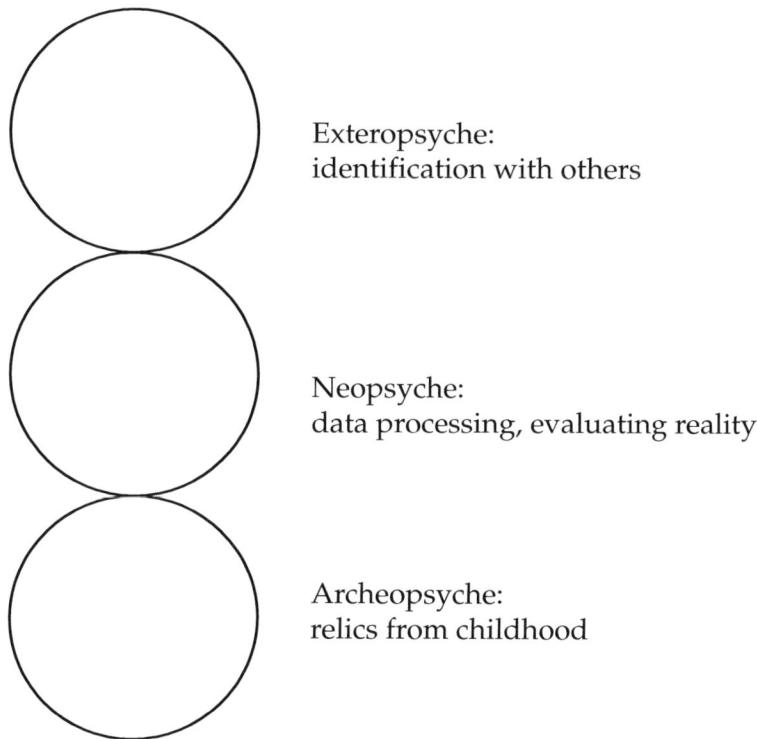

Figure 1.12. The "psychic organs" according to Berne.

From neurobiological research that has been done over the past decades, it is becoming increasingly clear that there are no specific functions linked to specific brain areas. Rather, the different functions in the brain are performed by neural networks, which, due to repeated activation, form a larger network; "neurons that fire together, wire together". This creates a pattern of thinking, feeling, an emotional tone, behaviour, memory, and internal models by which a person defines and experiences himself and his own frame of reference (Gilbert, 2003; Hine, 1997; Thunnissen, 2007).

The Adult ego state is the function that is mainly located in the cerebral cortex, especially the medial-orbital prefrontal cortex, where working memory and the integration between memory and emotional valuation are located and from where one's mood is regulated. Furthermore, the function of the Adult is located in the dorsolateral prefrontal cortex, which harbours a "switching station" between input from the senses and output in terms of motor skills. In addition, spatial working memory is situated here.

The Parent ego state develops from birth, first by direct, non-verbal intuitive communication between the parent and the child, whereby both mainly use their right brain. In this way, a baby learns to regulate his needs and emotions. The baby develops a sense of self based on the unconditional positive stimuli received from the parents. If the environment does not provide sufficient developmental experiences, too few neuronal connections will be established between the older, primitive parts of the brain and the newer parts of the brain, principally the neocortex. This person will then be inclined to respond with "primitive" or impulsive behaviour instead of thinking before acting. In short, the Parent ego state and the Adult are insufficiently developed.

At birth, the Child ego state is most present. The right brain hemisphere is dominant and experiences are stored in the implicit, unconscious memory. From around the second year—simultaneously with the development of speech and an increasing integration between the left and right hemispheres—the child begins to develop explicit autobiographical memory (in the hippocampus). In the first years of life, the baby learns to regulate his attention and emotions and to communicate with his environment, based on his affective relationships with his significant others. If these capacities are insufficiently developed, due, for example, to affective neglect or because the baby has a sensory impairment, then language and cognition will not develop as normal. The Child ego state remains too dominant and is not sufficiently corrected or regulated by the Adult and the Parent (Schore, 1994). In terms of neural networks, the principle "use it or lose it" applies. Connections which are frequently activated are retained while others are pruned (Allen & Allen, 2005).

1.3.7 The personality of an organisation

Organisations can seem to have a "personality"—the outward expression of the organisational ethos, the sense that people both within the organisation and outside it have of how it operates, what it cares about, and so on. Is the organisation described as "welcoming", "businesslike", "high-achieving"? Originally developed for schools, to enable staff to get a picture of their school's culture, the egogram assessment tool (EAT) uses the ego state metaphor to describe the behaviours of an organisation and how these in turn communicate meaning to others (Barrow, Bradshaw, & Newton, 2001 p. 104). The aim is to build up a sense of what the organisation does that reflects its capacity to draw on specific ego states. The EAT itself is a graded questionnaire, to be completed by as many employees as possible, that also invites respondents to give evidence for their scoring. When the scores are collated a profile of the organisation's "personality" is generated. By observing the balance of ego states in the resulting egogram, staff can appreciate their achievements and observe "gaps" or "preferred" ego states and potential for change. Each EAT can be designed to take account of the organisation's history and vision, as well as its unique context and local and national features that have an impact (ibid, p. 121).

1.4 Related theories

1.4.1 Origins

Berne based his theory of ego states on publications by various thinkers. Penfield, a well-known neurologist from the 1950s, showed (1952) that during epileptic seizures as well as with direct electrical stimulation of the temporal cortex, people received spontaneous memories, whereby they thought, felt, and behaved just the same as during the original situation. In the same period, psychologists Federn and Weiss introduced the term "ego state" (Federn, 1952), which they used to describe a process during hypnosis, dreaming, or a psychosis, whereby an internal conflict or traumatic event is recalled. However, Berne made the ego states the core of his theory, not only in pathological situations, but at all moments throughout life.

The "discovery" of the ego states by Berne was revolutionary. For the first time, a clear relation was established between intrapsychic and interpersonal phenomena. Sadly, Berne passed away in 1970 at the relatively young age of sixty. One is left wondering whether he would have been able to further develop and construct his theory if he had lived longer. His contemporaries, like Aaron Beck and Albert Ellis, the founders of behavioural therapy and rational emotive therapy (currently REBT), were granted rather more time: Beck was born in 1920 and is still active in 2015. Ellis died in 2007 at the age of ninety-three. Both witnessed the developments in the science of psychology since the 1960s, during which time an ever-increasing importance has been placed on cognition, research, and evidence-based approaches.

In the same decade in which Berne developed his theory, there was also criticism from various angles on the then dominant model of psychoanalysis. This led to various schools of thought within psychoanalysis (see 1.4.2), behavioural therapy, cognitive therapy, and schema therapy (see 1.4.5) as well as the humanistic approaches (see 1.4.6). The following is a brief description of the above, in relation to the ego states as used in TA.

1.4.2 Drive, ego, object, self and mentalisation

During the period of time that Berne was developing transactional analysis, other approaches like ego psychology, object relations theories, and the self psychology model were also developing, each seeking to provide alternatives to the classical psychoanalytic model. Each of these theories belongs within the psychodynamic approaches, which seek to understand all aspects of the relationship between the individual and the environment, both internally and externally. The various models emphasise different aspects of human functioning and they partially overlap each other (Gabbard, 2005; Pine, 1990; Sills & Hargaden, 2007).

Freud, the founder of psychoanalysis, was the first at the end of the nineteenth century to draw a link between mental disorders and childhood experiences. He claimed that psychopathology in adults was the result of unresolved conflicts about sexuality and aggression. While Freud emphasised the great influence of (what he called) "drives", later schools of thought placed the emphasis on different areas of the psyche (Pine, 1990).

- Ego psychology (Hartmann, Cumming & Cumming, and others) highlights the role of the ego as the agency that maintains a balance between the drives and the outside world. Psychological problems arise when the ego fails in the maintenance of a harmonious interaction between the various components of the psyche. In this theory, the influence of the environment plays a greater role than in the model of classical psychoanalysis.
- Object relations theory (Klein, Winnicott, Mahler, Kernberg, and others) suggests that the psyche of the child develops through early experiences with caregivers. The novelty of this theory is that it was partially developed by observing healthy children in a nursery. How

do these children interact with their mother? What happens when the mother goes away, or if another child takes away their toys? Based on these observations, object relations theory suggests that early relations between the caregiver (object), the child (subject), and their corresponding affects, form the building blocks of the psyche. If these early relationships were inadequate, or if there was abuse or neglect, a person carries these dynamics unconsciously within him, projects them on to others, and thus recreates the early childhood relationships with people in his current life.

- Self-psychology, developed by Kohut, also recognises the importance of early relationships: parents are essential to the self-confidence and self-esteem of the child. When parents don't "mirror" their child enough (when they don't give the individuality of the child enough space and fail to give him enough unconditional affirmation, as well as appropriate limits), children can develop a pathological sense of self—whether narcissistic, inflated, or inferior, and often a combination of these.
- In addition to the three psychological schools of thought described by Pine, recent years have seen the development of a fourth: mentalisation theory (Fonagy & Bateman, 2006). This theory reserves a central place for the ability of people to correctly assess their own and others' mental states. People develop this ability via "attachment", the proximity of an involved adult (Bowlby, 1988). This is how children develop their social intelligence and a system of attributing meaning. This is not so much about the internalisation of representations of experiences, which Berne emphasises within the development of the Child ego state, and Kernberg in his object relations theory. Rather, mentalisation theory concerns the development of a mechanism that can process and interpret new interpersonal experiences. The person is not a repository of historical relations, but an individual who is able to understand, regulate, and monitor his own affects (Gabbard, 2005).

In conclusion we can say that the theory shifts from the theory of drives to the notion that people are driven by the need for attachment and relationships. The building blocks of the psyche—objects, self, and their associated affects, as described in the object relations theory—can be recognised in TA's description of the structural analysis of Parent and Child.

1.4.3 Differences and similarities

Although Berne also introduced a trichotomy within TA—namely the Parent, Adult, and Child—he emphasised the differences with the psychoanalytic format: the Parent, the Adult and the Child are not constructs, like the *Über-Ich*, *Ich*, and *Es* (superego, ego, and the id), but phenomenological realities. It may seem that by doing so Berne paid little attention to unconscious processes (which according to psychoanalysis mostly take place in the id, but also partly in the ego and the superego). However, the drives and the unconscious do indeed have a place in the theory of the ego states. The Child is where authentic feelings, needs, and desires have their place. The Parent is not the same as the superego, but an internalisation of authentic parental figures as well as larger systems in the outer world with their socialising influence. The function of the Parent includes the conservation of energy and the reduction of anxiety, since the person learns to make certain decisions automatically after a period of time. This saves a lot of energy and the individual develops a relatively stable and clear, but sometimes also a considerably unshakable, frame of reference. This conception of the Parent is not inconsistent with the theory of drives, and it corresponds particularly closely with object relations theory. Although TA does not work primarily with such psychoanalytic techniques as free association and dream analysis, Berne described the importance of intuition in his early works, emphasising the role of the unconscious of both the therapist and the patient.

TA is closely related to ego psychology. Terms such as adaptation, reality testing, autonomy, and responsibility are key concepts in TA's working language. Object relations theory is also recognisable in the definitions of ego states and the script. Particularly, second-order structural analysis can be seen as a working model of object relations. Berne borrowed the concept "existential position" from Melanie Klein, who viewed existential life positions as an intrapsychic function. Later, Harris, Ernst, and Steiner changed the concept "I'm OK, you're OK" into an interpersonal process. Though Berne did not place a lot of emphasis on the concept of the self, more attention has been given to self-experience and the development of a personal identity and sense of self within TA over the last decades (Cornell & Hargaden, 2005; Erskine & Trautmann, 1996; Hargaden & Sills, 2002). This is implicit in TA's conception of how children make early decisions. The process of decontamination and thus of questioning one's own familiar frame of reference basically comprises the advancement of the mentalising capacity of the client or patient.

1.4.4 Behavioural therapy, cognitive therapy, and schema therapy

Beck and Ellis developed, respectively, behavioural therapy and rational emotive therapy (RET). These schools lay emphasis on externally observable behaviour and thought. Thinking is primary, for this forms the basis from which people direct their emotions. Behavioural theory was initially limited to visible behaviour. Later, invisible behaviour, thinking, gained an important place in this theory, which was then named cognitive behavioural therapy (CBT). At the beginning of the twenty-first century, when it became clear that patients with persistent problems were often difficult to treat with only a behavioural or RET approach, the therapeutic relationship gained an increasingly important position in cognitive behavioural therapy (Gilbert & Leahy, 2007).

Though Berne was not so explicit about it, there is common ground between TA and behavioural therapy. Berne believed in reinforcement and repetition. The theory of strokes (see Chapter Two) is based on learning principles. In the case of games (Chapter Four) we see recognition and reinforcement through predictable strokes: the repetition of "old" behaviours with the aim of validation, which will be confronted in therapy (Clarkson, 1992, p. 66).

An approach based on cognitive behavioural therapy, which has become popular in recent years and which has a lot in common with TA, is schema therapy (Muste, Weertman, & Claassen, 2009; Young, Klosko, & Weishaar, 2003). In the last decade of the previous century, Young developed this form of therapy for people with personality disorders who had not benefited from a symptom-targeted treatment. Schema therapy includes elements of cognitive theory, behavioural theory, psychodynamic theory, attachment theory, and Gestalt theory. The therapeutic relationship receives explicit attention and the therapist takes on a caring role in relation to the patient, using the technique of limited reparenting.

Schema therapy assumes that people develop poorly adapted "schemas" if their basic needs are not met. Schemas are deeply entrenched implicit beliefs about one's self, others, and the world, which are experienced as irrefutable and self-evident, very much as TA understands script decisions and beliefs. In addition to the schemas, there are "modes", or states of mind: the Vulnerable (Abandoned, Abused, Disappointed, Rejected) Child, the Angry Child, the Impulsive Child, and the Happy Child; the Adapter, the Detached Protector, and Over-Compensator; the Punitive Parent, and the Demanding Parent; the Healthy Adult. In a Dutch comparative study (Giessen-Bloo et al., 2006) it was shown that schema therapy achieved better results in patients with borderline personality disorder than the psychodynamic approach, or transference-focused therapy. It is more or less certain that schema therapy drew from a number of the key concepts in TA, such as the ego states and scripts. However, there is no mention by Young and his colleagues of this influence.

1.4.5 Humanistic approaches

Rogers (1951) was the first to popularise the term "unconditional positive regard". Together with "accurate empathy" and "congruence", these form the basic conditions that people need in order to express themselves and to grow. Rogers's approach has been elaborated upon in the client-centred method (Lietaer, Vanaerschot, Snijders, & Takens, 2008). This is person-oriented rather than symptom-oriented, whereby the person is his own expert who strives towards personal growth, self-reflection, and self-awareness. In Gestalt theory (Perls, Hefferline, & Goodman, 1951; Van Praag, 1987), contact with one's self and with others became the basis for both the theory and therapy.

In psychosynthesis (Assagioli, 1965; Gendlin, 1978; Van Cuilenburg, 2008), a humanistic and transpersonal school of psychology, place is reserved for the soul, the imagination, and for personal as well as transpersonal growth. Assagioli, the founder of psychosynthesis, reserves a central place in his theory for a person's (free) will. This is essential for the functioning of personality and as a guiding mechanism for making choices and attributing meaning. Important aspects of psychosynthesis are self-realisation and the realisation that one can be blocked by pain from the past and/or present and by the inability to exploit one's qualities to the full. The awareness of motives residing in the lower unconscious, and of qualities such as joy and wisdom from the higher unconscious, hereby function with healing effect.

Within TA, especially Bob and Mary Goulding, with their redecision therapy, further elaborated upon the humanistic school of thought (McClure Goulding & Goulding, 1978, 1979). Further examples of the humanistic perspective in TA are concepts such as "autonomy" and the dimensions of "awareness, spontaneity, and intimacy", which form the basic capacities for growth (Berne, 1964) as well as the concept of "I'm OK, you're OK" by Ernst (1971).

Generally speaking, within the humanistic approaches there is more space for the healthy, positive sides of humankind, in contrast with the emphasis on psychopathology in the psychoanalytic and behavioural approaches. In this regard, TA is placed within the humanistic school of thought.

1.4.6 The neurotic organisation

The theory of ego states is also used within the field of management and organisational development, to analyse the organisation as a whole. The concept of ego states can be used to create a better understanding of a healthy and more often of a pathological corporate culture. At an organisational level one can see that organisations have a tendency to use preferred ego states. Contaminations of ego states can create a culture that prevents organisations from being as effective and as efficient as they can be. In Chapter Thirteen a view is presented in which leadership is held highly responsible for what is called the organisational climate, which can be seen as another metaphor to name corporate culture. This is in line with what corporate neurosis expert Manfred Kets de Vries (1984) holds to be true about the role of leadership. Organisations, he argues, tend to reflect the personalities of their leaders. He analyses dysfunctional organisational behaviour in terms of accepted psychoanalytic types and arrives at some genuine insights into why some companies are healthier than others. Kets de Vries argues that the fantasies, beliefs, and aspirations of managers in an organisation have an all-permeating influence on the culture of their organisation. Above all he is fascinated by the relation between fantasies, decision-making, and factual behaviour of leadership in organisations. He argues that managers in organisations may exhibit paranoid, obsessive-compulsive, theatrical, depressive, or schizoid styles (or a combination of all). They can thereby give rise to the existence of myths, stories, and common beliefs in the culture of the organisation. If the dominant style is dysfunctional (rigid and/or extreme), this can lead to "symptoms of disease" within the whole organisation. This is not about blaming managers in any way, but this is about assessing and developing corporate culture in an effective way.

References

Allen, J. R., & Allen, B. A. (2005). *Therapeutic Journey: Practice and Life*. Oakland, ME: TA Press.
Assagioli, R. (1965). *Psychosynthesis. A Collection of Basic Writings*. Wellingborough, UK: Turnstone.
Barrow, G., Bradshaw, E., & Newton, T. (2001). *Improving Behaviour and Raising Self-Esteem in the Classroom: A Practical Guide to Using TA*. London: David Fulton.
Bastianelli, L., & Ceridono, D. (2012). Drivers and self ego states in social cognitive TA. *Paper 2e, EATA Research Conference*, November.
Beekum, S. van (1996). The graphics of ego states. Paper presented at the Advanced Working Conference, *Ego States in Transactional Analysis*, Amsterdam, March.
Benjamin, L. S. (1996). *Interpersonal Diagnosis and Treatment of Personality Disorders*. New York: Guilford Press.
Benjamin, L. S. (1996). Interpersonal theory of personality disorders. In: M. F. Lenzenweger & J. F. Clarkin (Eds.), *Theories of Personality Disorders* (pp. 157–230). New York: Guilford Press.
Berne, E. (1947). The Mind in Action. New York: Simon & Schuster.
Berne, E. (1959). *A Layman's Guide to Psychiatry and Psychoanalysis*. New York: Ballantine, 1973.

Berne, E. (1961). *Transactional Analysis in Psychotherapy*. New York: Grove Press.
Berne, E. (1964). *Games People Play*. New York: Grove Press.
Berne, E. (1977). *Intuition and Ego States: The Origins of Transactional Analysis*. San Francisco, CA: TA Press.
Bowlby, J. (1988). *A Secure Base: Clinical Applications of Attachment Theory*. London: Routledge.
Bradshaw, J. (1990). *Homecoming. Reclaiming and Championing your Inner Child*. New York: Bantam.
Clarkson, P. (1992). *Transactional Analysis Psychotherapy. An Integrated Approach*. London: Tavistock/Routledge.
Cornell, W. F., & Hargaden, H. (2005). *From Transactions to Relations: The Emergence of a Relational Tradition in Transactional Analysis*. Chipping Norton, UK: Haddon Press.
Cornell, W. F. (2009). *Explorations in Transactional Analysis. The Meech Lake Papers*. Pleasanton, CA: TA Press.
Cuilenburg, P. van (2008). *De stille plek in jezelf. Meditatie in de psychosynthese*. (The Silent Spot within Yourself.) Haarlem, Netherlands: De Toorts.
Draaisma, D. (2001). *Waarom het leven sneller gaat als je ouder wordt*. (Why Life Goes Faster when You Get Older.) Groningen, Netherlands: Historische Uitgeverij.
Dusay, J. (1972). Egograms and the constancy hypothesis. *Transactional Analysis Journal*, 2(3): 37–41.
Ernst, F. (1971). The OK Corral: The grid for get-on-with. *Transactional Analysis Journal*, 1(4): 33–42.
Erskine, R., & Trautmann, R. (1996). Methods of an integrative psychotherapy. *Transactional Analysis Journal*, 26(4): 316–328.
Federn, P. (1952). *Ego Psychology and the Psychoses*. New York: Basic Books.
Fennis, B. (2009). Reclamejongens weten het allang: de rede doet er niet zoveel toe. *Trouw*, November 22.
Fonagy, P., & Bateman, A. W. (2006). Mechanisms of change in mentalisation-based treatment of borderline personality disorder. *Journal of Clinical Psychology*, 62: 411–430.
Gabbard, G. O. (2005). *Psychodynamic Psychiatry in Clinical Practice*. Washington, WA: American Psychiatric Press.
Gendlin, E. T. (1978). *Focusing*. Toronto: Bantam.
Giessen-Bloo, J., Dyck, R. van, Spinhoven, P., Tilburg, W. van, Dirksen, C., Asselt, T. van, Kremers, I., Nadort, M., & Arntz, A. (2006). Outpatient psychotherapy for borderline personality disorder: Randomized trial of schema-focused therapy vs. transference-focused psychotherapy. *Archives of General Psychiatry*, 63: 649–658.
Gilbert, M. (2003). Ego states and ego state networks: Some questions for the practitioner. In: C. Sills & H. Hargaden (Eds.), *Ego states* (pp. 232–246). London: Worth.
Gilbert, P., & Leahy, R. L. (Eds.) (2007). *The Therapeutic Relationship in the Cognitive Behavioural Psychotherapies*. New York: Routledge.
Gopnik, A. (1999). *The Scientist in the Crib. What Early Learning Tells Us About the Mind*. New York: Perennial.
Hargaden, H., & Sills, C. (2002). *Transactional Analysis. A Relational Perspective*. Hove, UK: Brunner-Routledge.
Hay, J. (1992). *TA for Trainers (2nd edition)*. Watford, UK: Sherwood, 2009.
Hay, J. (1993). *Working It Out At Work: Understanding Attitudes and Building Relationships*. Watford, UK: Sherwood.
Heathcote, A. (2010). Eric Berne's development of ego state theory: Where did it all begin and who influenced him? *Transactional Analysis Journal*, 40: 254–260.

Hine, J. (1997). Mind structure and ego states. *Transactional Analysis Journal*, 27(3): 278–289.
Kets de Vries, M. F. R. (1984). *The Neurotic Organisation: Diagnosing and Changing Counterproductive Styles of Management*. London: Karnac.
Lietaer, G., Vanaerschot, G., Snijders, J. A., & Takens, R. J. (2008). *Handboek gesprekstherapie. De persoonsgerichte experiëntiële benadering*. (Comprehensive Textbook of Person-centred Experiential Psychotherapy.) Utrecht, Netherlands: De Tijdstroom.
Luca, M. L. de, & Tosi, M. T. (2011). Social-cognitive transactional analysis: An introduction to Scilligo's model of ego states. *Transactional Analysis Journal*, 41: 206–220.
McClure Goulding, M., & Goulding, R. L. (1978). *Changing Lives through Redecision Therapy*. San Francisco, CA: TA Press.
McClure Goulding, M., & Goulding, R. L. (1979). *The Power is in the Patient*. New York: Brunner/Mazel.
Muste, E., Weertman, A., & Claassen, A. (2009). *Handboek klinische schematherapie*. (Comprehensive Testbook of Schema Focussed Therapy.) Houten, Netherlands: Bohn Stafleu van Loghum.
Penfield, W. (1952). Memory mechanisms. *Archives of Neurology and Psychiatry*, 67: 178–198.
Perls, F., Hefferline, R., & Goodman, P. (1951). *Gestalt Therapy. Excitement and Growth in the Human Personality*. New York: Penguin.
Pierini, A. (2008). Has the unconscious moved house? *Transactional Analysis Journal*, 38: 110–118.
Pierini, A. (2014). Being a transactional analysis child therapist: How working with children is different. *Transactional Analysis Journal*, 44: 103–117.
Pine, F. (1990). *Drive, Ego, Object and Self: A Synthesis for Clinical Work*. New York: Basic Books.
Praag, D. van (1987). *Gestalttherapie. Een procesbenadering*. (Gestalt Therapy, a Process Approach.) Amersfoort, Netherlands: Acco.
Rogers, C. (1951). *Client-Centered Therapy. Its Current Practice, Implications, and Theory*. Boston, NJ: Houghton Mifflin.
Romanini, M. T. (1991). Io reale. (The real ego.) In: *Atti del Congresso Italiano di Analisi Transazionale, A.T. teorica e applicata: Stato dell'arte* (pp. 93–122). Rome: Associazione Italiana di Analisi Transazionale and Societa Italiana di Metodologie Psicoterapeutiche ed Analisi Transazionale.
Romanini, M. T. (1996). Bambino: Stadio dell'io e stato dell'io. (The child: Ego stage and ego state.) *Rivista Italiana di Analisi Transazionale e Metodologie Psicoterapeutiche*, XVI(31): 7–24.
Satel, S., & Lilienfeld, S. O. (2013). *Brainwashed: The Seductive Appeal of Mindless Neuroscience*. New York: Basic Books.
Schore, A. N. (1994). *Affect Regulation and the Origin of the Self*. Hillsdale, NJ: Lawrence Erlbaum.
Scilligo, P. (2009). *Analisi Transazionale socio-cognitiva*. (Social-cognitive Transactional Analysis.) Rome: LAS.
Scilligo, P. (2011). Transference as a measurable social-cognitive process: An application of Scilligo's model of ego states. *Transactional Analysis Journal*, 41: 196–205.
Sills, C., & Hargaden, H. (2007). *Ego States. Key Concepts in Transactional Analysis*. London: Worth.
Stern, D. N. (1985). *The Interpersonal World of the Infant*. New York: Basic Books.
Stern, D. N. (1990). *Diary of a Baby*. New York: Basic Books.
Stewart, I., & Joines, V. (1987). *TA Today (2nd edition)*. Melton Mowbray, UK: Lifespace, 2012.
Temple, S. (1999). Functional fluency for educational transactional analysis. *Transactional Analysis Journal*, 29(3): 164–174.
Temple, S. (2004). Update on the functional fluency model in education. *Transactional Analysis Journal*, 34(3): 197–204.

Thunnissen, M. (2007). *Begrijpen en veranderen. Theorie en Toepassingen van de Transactionele Analyse.* (To Understand and to Change. Theory and Applications of Transactional Analysis.) Halsteren, Netherlands: DGW.

Tudor, K. (2010). The state of the ego: Then and now. *Transactional Analysis Journal, 40*: 261–277.

Tudor, K. (2014). The neopsyche: The integrating Adult ego state. In: K. Tudor & G. Summers (Eds.), *Co-Creative Transactional Analysis: Papers, Responses, Dialogues, and Developments* (pp. 29–68). London: Karnac.

Wagner, A. (1981). *The Transactional Manager. How to Solve People Problems with Transactional Analysis.* Dora, FL: TA Communications.

Wagner, A. (1994). Blue ego states for effective communication. *Transactional Analysis Journal, 24*(4): 282–284.

White, T. (2011). *The contextual diagnosis of ego states.* Retrieved from http://admin99.wordpress.com/2011/07/25/the-contextual-diagnosis-of-ego-states/. Accessed 20 October 2015.

Woollams, S., & Brown, M. (1978). *Transactional Analysis.* Huron Valley, MI: Institute Press.

Young, J. E., Klosko, J. S., & Weishaar, M. E. (2003). *Schema Therapy. A Practitioner's Guide.* New York: Guilford Press.

CHAPTER TWO

Strokes

2.1 Basic theory
    2.1.1 Introduction
    2.1.2 Hungers
    2.1.3 Classification of strokes
    2.1.4. Structuring time
2.2 Further theory
    2.2.1 Emotionally skilled
    2.2.2 Stroke profile
2.3 Furthermore
    2.3.1 A fourth hunger
    2.3.2 Autonomy extended: integrity
    2.3.3 Nurture and structure
    2.3.4 Strokes in organisations
2.4 Related theories
    2.4.1 Maslow's hierarchy of needs
    2.4.2 Affect regulation and mentalisation
    2.4.3 Pride matters more
    2.4.4 Assertive discipline and appreciative inquiry
    2.4.5 Moral leadership
References

In the previous chapter, we were introduced to the basic concept of ego states. We described how personality develops with regard to structure and function. In this second chapter we will describe the drives that underlie this development: what motivates people to develop themselves, in either a constructive or sometimes a destructive way? Here, the concept of "strokes" plays an important role. Any kind of attention is a form of recognition by the other. Recognition is therefore a central theme in TA. Recognition for who you are and recognition for what you do. Every person needs this. This chapter is about how recognition and attention (in TA this is designated by the concept "strokes") can be used to guide and motivate. How and in what people choose to invest their time is therefore a crucial issue within TA. There is a huge difference between a choice that yields few strokes (such as "withdrawing") and a choice that provides intensive strokes (such as "having a meaningful encounter"). The stroke climate in a family, a team, or in a company or organisation has a major impact on the health and happiness of people. Healthy and happy people get more done in their lives.

2.1 Basic theory

2.1.1 Introduction

One important question lies at the centre of many psychological theories: what motivates people? What drives people to do things that are unhealthy for them? Why do some people smoke or commit suicide, or hit their children or make their partner's life miserable? But also, why do others look after their dying mother for years, or enjoy raising their disabled son or daughter, or enjoy working hard, or refuse further treatment in the terminal stage of cancer?

Within TA this question is essential. Berne, who attached great importance to simple and engaging language, suggests that human behaviour is determined by various kinds of "hungers", basic needs which, if not satisfied, lead to the disorganisation of one's personality (1961, 1970). The choice for the powerful word "hunger", instead of the less impacting word "need", appears to have been motivated by the fact that hunger is (literally) a matter of survival.

If you don't feed your hunger, you ultimately die. If you do not get what you need, this doesn't necessarily have a direct consequence for the survival of the organism. The English language contains an additional nuance: there is a difference between a "need" and a "want". This is an important theme within the educational debate. "Parents should always give children what they need and think about if they should give their children what they want." Those who don't know how to make that distinction contribute to a society in which consumerism and ad hoc gratification appear to be a life necessity: "I want it all and I want it now!"

At birth, there is physical hunger: a baby cries when he is hungry and goes to sleep satisfied after feeding. The baby still lives according to the so-called pleasure/pain principle. But almost immediately, another hunger is added to the mix: the hunger to be touched. And after a few years there will be the hunger to give structure to one's time: a toddler is rarely bored, while a six year old is often bored stiff!

Within TA we describe these various needs and desires as types of hunger at different levels.

- At the biological level, the hunger for stimuli: food, stimulation of the senses, and physical pleasure. Without stimuli, the physical organism atrophies.
- On a psychological level, the hunger for recognition of who you are and what you do. Without recognition, the mental organism atrophies.

Mountain and Davidson (2011) are of the opinion that the hunger for recognition pertains to a hunger for specific stimuli. They distinguish these stimuli from general stimuli, such as the warmth from the sun, or pleasurable music, or light shining in one's eyes. A stroke (= unit of recognition) is received from a specific person and is specifically intended for a person. They therefore propose to call the second hunger the "hunger to belong".

- On a social level, there is a hunger for structure. According to which patterns do you structure your time? Without structuring time, the ability to make contact atrophies.

There is an interaction between these three levels, whereby a dynamic system of motivation is created. Any disruption in one of the hungers causes an overcompensation in at least one of the others. Erskine composed an integrative theory of motivation by introducing the concept of relationship hunger, the drive for intimacy. Satisfaction of relationship hunger depends on the awareness of relational needs (internal stimulus), what the individual believes about self and others in the interpersonal relationships (structure), and the behaviour of the other person in the relationship (external stimulus) (1998, p. 137).

> George receives little attention and recognition in his private life. He focuses diligently on his favourite sport, basketball, and ends up playing in ever higher-ranked teams. As a result, he also needs to train more and monitor his diet carefully. The lack of attention at home is replaced by recognition on the basketball court as well as with the structure of training and competing. When he is unexpectedly not chosen for the top team and doesn't need to train as much, he falls into a slump. Only then does it become clear how much he compensated for his lack of recognition with his sport.

2.1.2 Hungers

Eric Berne conceptualised transactional analysis as a social psychiatry, meaning a model of human development that was based on interpersonal interactions. Berne emphasised that people can only keep their ego states intact and coherent when they are in continuous interaction with the outside world. Then the boundaries between the ego states remain permeable and there is a healthy functional balance between the ego states. TA theory places great importance on the quality of recognition among people as fundamental to healthy psychological development. Berne used the informal term "stroke" to indicate "units of recognition" between people. "Stroke" does not easily translate into other languages, but he chose the word to suggest and evoke a sense of being "touched" by the recognition of others. He meant to evoke the bodily importance for babies and young children to be touched, caressed, held, "stroked" to feel and know their value to others.

The lack of interpersonal interaction and recognition is the primary reason that solitary confinement is perhaps the worst possible punishment, and why healthy people may start to hallucinate during a long, lonely journey in the mountains or at sea. Even babies need stimulation, in the form of food and touching, from the first day of their lives (according to some, even when in the womb). Spitz (1945) examined the situation of young children in orphanages during the war and found that these children often weren't growing and flourishing enough, despite receiving enough nurturing. He concluded that a lack of physical contact and attention led to this "failure to thrive". Shortly after the fall of the Iron Curtain (1989), images appeared on television of children who were growing up in orphanages in countries like Romania. The dead look in the eyes of these children shocked the world. They received food and drink every day, but there was no one who spoke to them lovingly, let alone to pick them up and hold them.

Sensory deprivation doesn't only lead to psychological changes, but also organic decay. Since most essential sensory stimuli are derived from social interaction and physical intimacy, Spitz preferred to speak of emotional rather than sensory deprivation. With babies this mostly involves physical stimuli, such as touching; symbolic stimuli, a smile or a compliment, raised eyebrows or a reproach, become increasingly necessary later on. If babies are not touched enough, they can die. If people are not recognised, respected, or feel seen, they become depressed, may become addicted to alcohol or cease to take care of themselves. Ultimately, this too can lead to death.

Somewhat less extreme: the resident in the nursing home, the scientist working completely alone in the study, or the person making the schedule, working late in an empty school; all such situations may offer too few stimuli whereby they may become isolated and depressed.

From experiments conducted by Harlow and Harlow (1962) with rhesus monkeys, it was shown that monkeys raised alone—without a mother—became social misfits: they had short lives and they could not hold their own when they were later placed in a colony with other monkeys. If they are brought up without a mother, but are in contact with peers, they do slightly better. But they fail to raise their own offspring. If they are allowed to choose between a "mother" made of iron wire with a feeding bottle and a "mother" made of wire covered with soft cloth but without food, they prefer the soft mother and only rush over to the iron mother in order to drink, after which they return to firmly cling to the safe soft cloth mother. Within TA, this hunger for stimuli is referred to as the need for a "stroke", which in English can mean both "caress" and "slap". The definition of stroke is a unit of social recognition. It is also important to stress that the recipient determines the meaning of the stroke, of course in a social-cultural context. Meaning giving is never an individual thing.

> Tom has never been happy in school—or in fact anywhere. He receives little affection at home, and mostly tries to stay out of the way of his father and older brother because when they do notice him it usually means they shout at him for doing or not doing something or sometimes hit him. In school he isn't badly behaved, just withdrawn and tries not to be noticed. Eventually he finds himself in a special education unit because, unknown to him, his teachers are concerned about him. Here, Anna, a well-intentioned and affectionate care worker touches him on the shoulder as she talks to him. She really wants to help Tom by giving him genuine strokes but to Tom it feels awful—it is a new and unexpected experience that he can't manage.

2.1.3. Classification of strokes

We distinguish between different types of strokes:

- Conditional: for something the other does ("Good job! You got an eight for that test!"), and unconditional: for what the other is ("You're a wonderful person")
- Positive: "You've done that very well", and negative "I think that was a dirty trick you pulled"
- Verbal: through words, and non-verbal: through facial expressions, touch, and the like
- Living: in the here and now, and preserved: in the past (letters, photographs, recordings of someone's voice, memories)
- Direct: "We are proud of you!", and indirect: "We are so proud of our Alex!"
- Authentic: honest, sincere, and inauthentic (plastic): content and tone may be contradictory ("Um, that's a very interesting new hairstyle that you have now"), or it is clear that the other does not really mean it: "Oh, darling, how nice to see you, we should meet again soon", after which she drifts back to someone else at the party
- "Target": a stroke that moves, that brings tears to your eyes.

Table 2.1. Conditional and unconditional strokes.

	Positive	*Negative*
Conditional	You did that very well!	That was a dirty trick.
Unconditional	You're a star!	You're good for nothing.

Strokes are usually categorised according to Table 2.1.

Children are basically programmed which types of strokes are acceptable and which are not. The Little Professor (A_1) tries all sorts of behaviour to find out which ones yield the strokes the child needs. If a certain behaviour results in a stroke, then it's likely that the child will repeat that behaviour. Moreover, as a rule: anything is better than no strokes at all. If it appears there are not enough positive strokes to provide for the different types of hunger in the child, then he will go in search of negative strokes that will work. If a child receives too little attention, he will do all sorts of things in order to attract attention. The child may distract the mother with a series of questions, or he will begin to act out or do dangerous things so that the mother will be forced to respond. Unconditional negative strokes are generally harmful, especially during childhood. Children who are regularly told "You're such a brat", or "I wish you were never born", run the risk of developing a negative self-image and allowing their behaviour to be determined by these messages. On the other hand, if someone says to you: "I can't stand the sight of you", then it is also clear that a change in behaviour on your part will have little meaning or effect. You might be better off by no longer investing energy in this relationship (Stewart & Joines, 1987).

In many transactions we see a combination of positive and negative, conditional and unconditional strokes. A statement such as "This is poor behaviour for someone of your stature" is a combination of a negative conditional and a positive unconditional stroke (McCormick, 1977). And if your manager says, "You did a fine job—finally for once", this is a confusing mix of a positive conditional and a negative, perhaps even an unconditional negative stroke.

These confusing combinations are shown in Table 2.2 (Haimowitz & Haimowitz, 1976).

Table 2.2. Confusing stroke combinations.

	Positive	*Negative*
Positive	Warm fuzzies	Warm pricklies
Negative	Cold fuzzies	Cold pricklies

In the case of "warm pricklies" (sweet and sour), the other's remark appears at first friendly. But the devil is in the tail: "Ah, nice! So you've finally combed your hair!" With "cold fuzzies" (sour-sweet), after something negative there is still a little niceness to follow: "It's nice that for once you finished that report on time".

As time passes, each individual gradually builds up a stroke economy, a way of dealing with strokes, based on their own tendencies (a child with an introverted disposition likes to play alone and has a different set of needs and ways to attain strokes from a child with an extroverted disposition), and on early experiences with caregivers and the conclusions that he has drawn from them. For instance: Mary is taking steps towards becoming a scientist. She spends her days alone behind the computer yet receives an adequate supply of strokes from the incidental contact she has with her supervisor or fellow researchers. Bernard is a teacher and thrives on the daily contact with his students to whom he can directly offer his knowledge and experience.

Sometimes people experience a deficiency of certain strokes in their childhood; they become emotionally neglected, expressing emotions is not tolerated, or only in a certain way (for example, anger is allowed but not sadness). To ease the pain of this, they have learned to ignore certain needs, which increases the chance of having problems with social interaction and intimate relationships as adults. (We will discuss this in more detail in Chapter Five). Every social system has its own stroke climate, though there are general patterns that can be highlighted.

In schools, it is generally the case that those who perform above or below the average, the "over- and underachievers", receive the most strokes. Brilliant and troublesome students can count on getting the full attention of the teaching staff. The average student is often neglected. This can lead to students, who do not have the ability to be brilliant, to begin to exhibit difficult behaviour, if only to arrive at their quota of strokes. As a result, the number of underachievers increases. A considerable sense of calm can be created in the classroom if teachers give the average students enough strokes. And what is true in schools also applies to many office environments.

Everyone wears a particular pair of coloured glasses: pink, black, or with plain glass. This is the stroke filter. It ensures that strokes are admitted which match the existing self-image. Thus, while one person will dilute the positive message—"What a nice dress you're wearing" receives the response, "Oh, it's just a hand-me-down from my sister"—another is a master at warding off negative strokes—"I'm really annoyed that you're late" receives the response, "How nice that you've been waiting for me". Many people have difficulty accepting conditional negative strokes and to hear them for what they are. They react defensively. For example, if someone says, "You cannot smoke here", this person can count on receiving a response like "Get lost!" or "Mind your own business". At other times, people make a negative stroke much larger. A remark such as "This report is really too long, could you reduce it to ten pages?" they convert into "I suck at this job". By whether or not you acknowledge certain strokes, you can control your own frame of reference. Ideally speaking, you would accept unconditional positive strokes and ward off unconditional negative strokes. Conditional strokes, both positive and negative, can be used as incentives or as feedback. Neurobiologically, stroke patterns are recorded in the brain. It is therefore understandable that it is sometimes difficult to break a pattern of negative strokes. If people are accustomed to a poor "stroke climate" (the thermostat is low), they need to gradually get used to a larger dose of strokes. A professional who accompanies and guides such people may at times scare them off by giving (unconditional) positive strokes too soon.

It is tempting to think positive strokes are (always) better than negative ones. However, this is not the case. It is all about the intention and the manner in which the stroke is delivered. By giving or withholding a stroke, you can either validate or inhibit behaviour. This is an important theoretical principle on which behavioural therapy is based. A negative conditional stroke is a warning that someone does not appreciate certain behaviour. Positive conditional strokes can make one feel competent. If the environment is too polite to let a person know that they have bad breath, or that it would be better if they didn't go to that job interview wearing casual clothes, then this could clearly be to their disadvantage.

Excessive compliments or pampering, for example by giving predominantly unconditional positive strokes, can actually be just as harmful as neglect. A child will then not learn to take others into account or to adapt his behaviour. Such a person may develop an "inflated ego" or false self, and then expect that he will receive respect and recognition without having to do anything for it. An excess of positive strokes can also have a detrimental effect on one's experience of autonomy and the right to a person's self-evaluation. If everyone, or a significant other, ascribes certain qualities to you, this may in fact deprive you of the space to appreciate yourself differently. An excess of positive strokes is also a pitfall in many TA environments. Criticism may be stifled because only positive strokes should be exchanged. But people often learn the most from their mistakes!

In section 2.3.3, we will return to the importance of nurturing and structure in education.

In a stroke-poor environment, you learn in a different way. In the setting of group relations, a methodology which has been developed at the Tavistock Centre in London and which is based on psychoanalytical thought (including Bion's theory of groups, see section 8.4.7 in Chapter Eight), a research setting is deliberately created in which people are not actively stroked. During a conference lasting several days, groups are formed and are given the task to examine the development of authority, roles, and organisation within the group, between the groups, and within the institution as a whole. In this way, a space is created in which the need for and the resulting patterns of strokes of each participant can be examined. The unstructured design of these small and large groups often evokes fear. Participants experience first-hand how they tend to distort reality and how they select, interpret, and manipulate strokes, and thus how they maintain their own frame of reference. This teaches participants to reduce their fear of negative strokes and to value complex situations as a learning and working environment.

2.1.4 Structuring time

Besides the hunger for stimuli and strokes, Berne identified a third hunger: how do you structure your time in such a way that you can exchange enough strokes so as to give your individuality and that of others enough room to flourish? If someone lands up in a lonely situation, they not only lack strokes but also face the question, "What will I do with all this time?" When Robinson Crusoe was shipwrecked and landed up on a desert island, he investigated the island and built himself a shelter. In the true story, transcribed in the novel Un Uomo (1979) by Oriana Fallaci (English translation: Fallaci, 1981), Alex Panagoulis—a resistance fighter against the junta in Greece at the time—was captured and put in solitary confinement. By constantly attempting to escape, by challenging the guards in all kinds of ways, and by playing mental chess and writing poems, he was able to provide himself with enough stimuli during his four years of captivity. In this way, he supplied his own need for strokes. He held his morale and it stopped him from going insane.

Berne's theory (1961) of the hunger for structuring time examined the common ways people spend their time together, linking the level of interpersonal risk to the quality and intimacy of personal recognition. He distinguished between six forms by which people structure time according to the increase in the intensity of strokes.

Children learn "social programming" from their parents: the way in which time is structured within their social system.

1. *Withdrawal*. The need to withdraw is an essential hunger. By resting, meditating, sleeping, or closing yourself off from stimuli, you restore the balance after a period in which you received too much stimuli. You can organise your thoughts and bring about a new balance between experiences, needs, and feelings. This withdrawal can be physical; alone in your home or in your room. But it can also be mental. You remain in the company of others, but you're in your own little world. If people do not withdraw enough, this can be because they struggle to reflect on their experiences. They avoid embarrassing or confrontational thoughts and this prevents them from facing and confronting the reality of their unfulfilled needs or desires. Some people often withdraw because they have difficulty sharing their experiences with others. They avoid the strokes they could be receiving, whether these are positive or negative. They do this in order to avoid comparing their frame of reference with those of others, thereby convincing themselves of their own image of reality. They then proceed to act based on their untested imagery, as if it were the "definitive reality".

    When people withdraw as a pattern of repetition from behaviour learned in early life, there may be a question of dysfunctional withdrawal. It then doesn't have the function of restoring the balance of autonomy, but to repeat once functional but now dysfunctional patterns. Withdrawal provides few strokes. This may eventually lead to a deficiency.

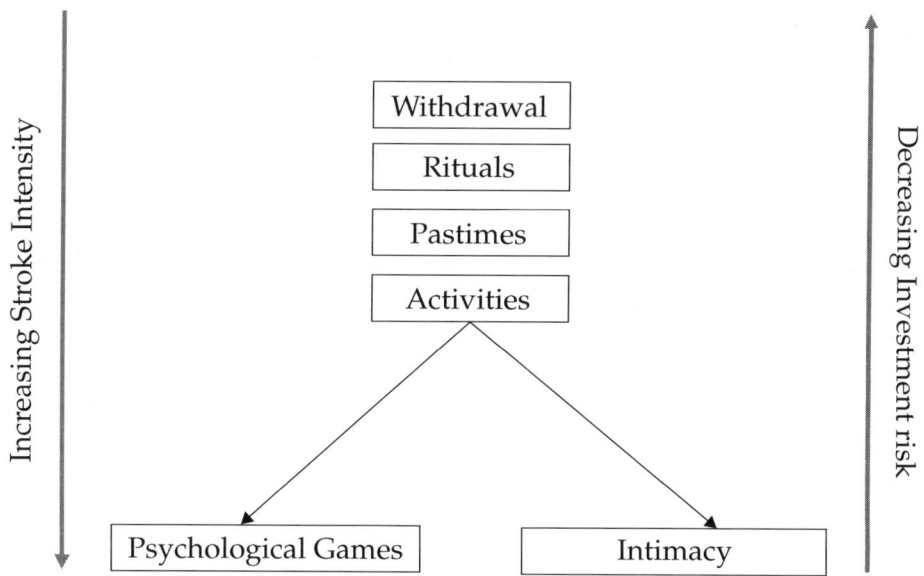

Figure 2.1. The six forms of structuring time.

2. *Rituals*. Rituals consist of a predictable, socially defined exchange of strokes. For example, "Hey, hello, how are you?" "Fine. And you?" "Oh just fine too. Nice weather eh?" "Yeah, well we really needed it, a little sun after all that rain".

    This predictability provides a degree of security and structure that, if the exchange does not take too long, can give one a pleasant feeling. You know what's coming and you can feel at home with it. Additionally, rituals provide structure and security in certain circumstances: the church service at a funeral, the reception at a wedding, the meeting with colleagues from another office, the washing ritual before surgery or the instrument check in an aircraft prior to the flight.

    Rituals can be brief and may be comprised of just a few sentences, or involve a whole Christmas Day with relatives. Rituals provide strokes that are predictable and usually not very profound or personal. But certain religious, initiation, or hazing rituals can be very powerful. Berne described rituals as the "grease" of human relations, that is, rituals keep things moving but they don't allow people to get very close. Rituals are comfortable and impersonal (1964, p. 52).

3. *Pastimes*. When people are gathered together with the primary aim of having a "nice" time together, we then speak of this as pastime. More often than not, people will exchange pleasant positive strokes without much risk of closeness and intimacy. Subjects discussed are devoid of depth, they often have a ritual character, but there is more space and time for exchange and for variation, both in terms of subject matter and mood. However, there is an unspoken agreement that it should remain "fun". It's often about "there and then" rather than matters that concerns the "here and now". At a party, for instance, you may find a "pastime" discussion about the youth of today, and in another corner about the politics of the

current government, or a discussion about the last and/or next vacation. The sole purpose is to engage in non-committal discussions about certain things: "They raised a glass, took a leak, and all remained just as it was". It can provide a way of "checking out" other people before deciding if we want to become more intimate.

Many pastimes in social contexts, as in companies and organisations, have a psychologically more binding or less informal function. "Social assessment" is taking place. Employees discuss, while passing the time in the coffee lounge or the cafeteria, the affairs of the company or organisation. During this pastime, the interlocutors are continually evaluating whether their thoughts expressed in words actually fit within the community at hand. The central question is, "Can what I'm thinking be thought here?" If this is not the case, then employees will think themselves straight out of the company or organisation. Most people want to prevent this from happening. "Belonging" is an important factor when it comes to what motivates people.

If one of the participants during a pastime moment becomes personal and begins, for instance, to talk about her despair concerning the drug addiction of her son, or if she wants to take political action against certain government plans, this would generally give rise to an uncomfortable or embarrassing situation, because it is not the purpose of a pastiming exchange. To become too personal would be a transgression of this time structure and its interpersonal function of comfortable but not intimate ways of being with others. The desperate mother will have to go somewhere else to find someone who will listen, and the political activist will have to adapt, or organise a course of action with other people.

The exchange of photos on mobile phones and sharing the latest apps are examples of new, technology-driven pastimes.

4. *Activities*. When stroke exchange is aimed at a shared task or goal, then we speak of activities. This can range from launching a new product on the market, preparing a meal, playing a football match, conducting a protest, or following a training schedule. Activities can be about work, about hobbies or household affairs. What is central is that people want to achieve a goal (together). Activities generate a lot of strokes, mainly conditional positive or conditional negative, which are focused on the action and the result, not the person. In activities, the Adult ego state is active: thinking, feeling, and doing in the here and now.

The energy is focused on external sources of recognition. This time structure is easily interchangeable with other time structures. For example, at work the most important time structure is activity, but there are also rituals that take place, like the chat over a cup of coffee at the start of the working day, or following rules and procedures before workers in a laboratory can begin their work. During the break, it's about pastimes, when TV shows from the previous day are criticised, for example. Psychological games and intimacy might also take place during work.

5. *Psychological games*. Psychological games are characterised by a series of transactions that often yield a predictable, negative result for at least one, but usually for all players of the game. Initially it involves transactions with an ulterior motive, of which people are not

aware. Berne saw psychological games as the replay of early childhood dynamics and defences that were consciously intended to be self-protective and make relationships predictable, but that then typically left both people feeling disappointed or frustrated by the outcome. In Chapter Four we will return to a detailed discussion of games and game analysis.

Elisabeth has been abandoned for the third time by a man who was initially quite charming, and who took her out to dinner and gave her flowers. After a few months, she began to support him financially because he was temporarily going through a difficult period. Eventually he took off to the horizon while she remained behind, several thousand euros poorer, with the feeling that no man can be trusted, and with the question why she keeps falling into the same trap.

6. *Intimacy*. Within this form of structuring time, people exchange strokes freely, without a hidden agenda or manipulation. They are aware of the mutual implications and they are open to each other's frame of reference (Adult). There is also room for loyalty and care (Parent), and there is space for one's own feelings and those of the other (Child). Intimacy yields an in-depth, although less predictable exchange of strokes. Even if what the other person says might be painful for the recipient, it is intended as honest information for the purpose of growth and equal exchange. Intimacy can lead to physical proximity and sexuality, but also to anger or tears. When there is intimacy, the social and psychological layers of communication come together. It is an open relationship without games and without mutual exploitation. Intimacy meets the deep need in every human being to feel comfortable and safe with another person, with all one's positive and negative aspects.

One of Eric Berne's early co-workers, Dr. Stephen Karpman, writes in the centenary *Transactional Analysis Journal* theme issue about the originator of transactional analysis (2010): "Intimacy may be called Eric Berne's 'unfinished symphony'. Although Berne placed intimacy at the top of his time structuring list of how people can spend time together, he privately believed that true intimacy occurred only at rare moments in a person's life." In an attempt to continue where Berne stopped, Karpman suggests a TA intimacy theory called "the intimacy scale" applicable to all those who want to understand and improve the quality of their relationships. The scale runs from silence (S), via talking about things, objects, and places (T.O.P.), and about people, ideas, psychology, issues, philosophy, interests (P.I.), to talking about me and you (M/Y), heading towards talking about us (U). In other words it runs from isolation via friendship to intimacy.

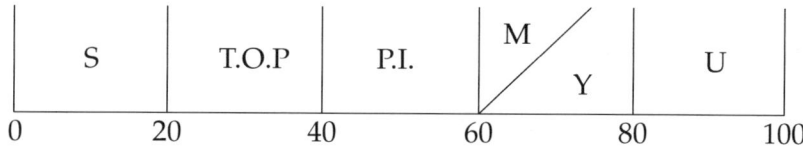

Figure 2.2. Intimacy scale.

2.2 Further theory

2.2.1 Emotionally skilled

Steiner (1971, 1984) has written extensively on the importance of strokes. He developed the concept of stroke economy. Analogous to the market economy, which is based on the assumption that a shortage of goods leads to hoarding and to an increase in prices, it seems that an economic way of thinking has crept into the way strokes are handled. Children may unwittingly learn family or socially acceptable rules about strokes, for example:

- Don't just give away strokes! Just casually giving a compliment to someone can lead to obligations or expectations.
- Don't ask for strokes! Even if you feel the need for them. A stroke you receive after asking for it is not worth very much. The only valuable strokes are those that are given freely.
- Don't accept strokes! When you receive a stroke, your response should be humble: "Oh, it was a small effort", or "Well, I'm sure you would have done a much better job".
- Don't reject any strokes! Even if you do not want them. A beautiful woman who constantly gets compliments on her appearance cannot just all of a sudden say that she no longer appreciates this and would prefer to receive a stroke for her intelligence.
- Don't give strokes to yourself! "Self-praise is no recommendation". You don't want to be thought of as arrogant.

Steiner argues that these rules mean that the infinite supply of strokes available in the world is restricted to a small amount. These strokes would only be exchanged under certain conditions, for example, between parents and children or in an intimate relationship. In this way, children are controlled and trained to behave according to the wishes of their parents or educators. According to Steiner, by giving or withholding, intensifying or minimising positive and negative or conditional and unconditional strokes, parents or caregivers stimulate or inhibit the child's development of autonomy in various areas.

This affects one's ability to love, the capacity to think, and the potential to enjoy. If five-year-old Ben says he loves his teacher, it matters if his mother then fondly smiles or disapprovingly says "But you love your mommy the most, don't you?". It matters whether seven-year-old Farida's questions about how the world works are dismissed with the words "You don't need to worry yourself with such thing yet, dear", or whether her questions are taken seriously.

It makes a difference whether ten-year-old Chantal is allowed to enjoy a day at the theme park or whether her father repeats five times that such a day out is very expensive, and that he was never taken to do fun things with his parents. Children benefit from educators who give their strokes in such a way that it promotes the children's autonomy so that they are later able to enter into effective relationships and to be able to solve problems independently and to enjoy their lives and their work. Adults also often unconsciously obey the rules of a stroke economy learned within their family and social systems and then spend their lives in a state of partial stroke deprivation. Steiner (2003) developed a programme called "emotional literacy", by which people relearn how to be emotionally skilled and to regain their capacity for spontaneity and intimacy.

2.2.2 Stroke profile

McKenna (1974) designed a diagram, analogous to the egogram, to chart the way people deal with strokes: the stroke profile. The stroke profile is a tool to help people recognise and evaluate their beliefs and patterns for getting and giving recognition.

Do you ever ask for strokes? And do you also sometimes refuse to give strokes if the other requests one? The stroke profile examines these questions for both positive and negative strokes.

People suffering from depression often exhibit a remarkable pattern in their stroke profile. They give few strokes. They hardly accept and barely ask for positive strokes, but they accept negative strokes quite easily (Thunnissen, 2007).

> Anita, a twenty-two-year-old woman, has been suffering from anorexia nervosa for six years. Her eating problems started when her mother was admitted because of symptoms of depression. Both Anita's eating problems and her mother's depression have a function in the family, where being ill was the only accepted way to express feelings and to get attention. Father has an inoperable lung tumour. Chances are he will die within a year. Mother, in her fear and sadness, asks a lot from Anita.
>
> Anita is an only child, born after an older sister was stillborn after eight months of pregnancy. She describes her father as a man who finds it hard to express his feelings. Mother is a very caring woman, but often ill. She has been repeatedly admitted to hospital in connection with depression. The family was very closed and was characterised by conflict avoidance and over-concern. It seems that Anita had been given the task to make up for the loss of her stillborn sister. This made it impossible for her to take the step towards being a teenager and to extract herself from the family. Anita has become extremely anxious and anorexic—a symbolic refusal to grow up.
>
> Anita was later admitted to a psychotherapeutic centre, where she took part in an intensive three-month programme with TA as a treatment model. This programme works with contracts by which Anita, together with her therapists and other group members, formulate the goal of her treatment. Anita's contract says, "I will break out of my cocoon and I'm going to become a butterfly." When she decided, after several weeks of treatment, to break loose from the symbiosis with her mother, she was overcome by an overwhelming sense of negativity. She did not fully understand where this came from. It was decided that Anita's stroke profile should be created. It soon became clear that she predominantly accepted and requested negative strokes, while she mostly gave positive strokes. At a glance it became clear how negativity was dominant, whereby she created her own basic negative feelings and had this confirmed over and over again. Then and there, she practised asking for positive strokes, while she was continually monitored to see whether she indeed accepted the strokes. This became the leitmotif of the treatment. She went to work on many areas, including strokes, being a woman, body image, and sexuality. Eventually she left with a fulfilled contract. She is settling down in a new city, finishing her education, starting hobbies, and making friends.

People have an intuitive idea of how they perceive themselves. In a group, it is useful to have the participants share their views of each other. Often, but not always, you will find in their stroke profile that people who easily give out positive strokes find it harder to give out negative strokes and vice versa. Depressed people often absorb negative strokes like a sponge, while they hardly even hear a positive stroke when it is given to them. Many people hardly ever ask for positive strokes. Asking for negative strokes often occurs indirectly and unconsciously: John is surprised at the fact that he himself elicits negative strokes from others by often arriving a little late or by forgetting appointments.

Refusing to give strokes also often happens unconsciously. Many people automatically react disapprovingly of someone who does something annoying, instead of asking themselves if this is an effective response.

It is clear that negative strokes have a much greater impact than positive ones. If the stroke profile reveals that someone mostly gives, receives, and asks for negative strokes, then this is something that calls for serious attention. Often the person does not realise himself how he is creating his own solitude.

2.3 Furthermore

2.3.1 A fourth hunger

Fanita English is a creative thinker within TA. She invented a number of new concepts that we have found to be important contributions to TA theory. One of her contributions concerns the theory of another type of hunger (1972). In addition to the need for stimuli, recognition, and structuring time, she also sees a need for the satisfaction of curiosity, which is independent of the need for strokes from others. She is referring to the specifically human urge to discover things and to understand how the world works.

With babies, this is visible in their need to put everything in their mouths and to literally taste them. With adults, it can be seen in their creativity, their urge to create or to invent, or to discover uncharted territories. If this need is wisely encouraged by parents, the child will learn to also enjoy playing and taking risks as an adult—one of the necessary conditions for intimacy! English situates this hunger in the Adult in the Child, A_1, the Little Professor. She uses her own words for the disctinction within the Child ego state:

- *Sleepy*, C_1: the earliest part of the Child which depends to a high degree for his survival on the environment. By sucking and crying, Sleepy shows his survival instinct. But with insufficient stimuli from outside, death lies in wait. This means, according to English, that C_1 also harbours a regressive tendency. If children are not actively kept alive with strokes, they lapse into passivity or they die.
- *Spunky*, A_1: the passionate, creative part; the hero of myths and fairy tales, who grabs issues by the horns, is curious, and doesn't avoid taking risks.
- *Spooky*, P_1: the ability to internalise and symbolise. This helps the baby to learn to perceive and understand symbolic strokes such as smiling, frowning, or verbal expressions, in addition to physical strokes. Spooky does not make choices and therefore absorbs positive, destructive or confusing strokes in equal measure. For example, the child takes his first cautious steps and falls. Mother picks up the crying toddler and says, while smiling, "But you can't do that yet."

Spunky is eventually decisive for subsequent decisions for the script, for what your life will look like, and how you are going to satisfy your needs. Spunky mediates between Spooky's demands and Sleepy's regressive needs.

2.3.2 Autonomy extended: integrity

Ken Mellor (2008) sees integrity, in relation to wholeness, morality, and ethics, as central to autonomy and a freeing force in people's lives. Mellor defines integrity as the capacity for achieving oneness with everything. Awareness, spontaneity, and intimacy, Berne's original idea about three autonomy-defining capacities, continue to play a profound role in understanding autonomy. Mellor just adds integrity as another important capacity. Everyone has this quality to some extent, he argues. "The more integrated we are, the more integrity we have and the more abundant the flow of life energy through us because our systems are more open … for a maximum of aliveness we need a maximum of integrity" (p. 194). Mellor concluded his article with: "People with a developed capacity for autonomy are integrated, aware, spontaneous, and intimate to a high degree. Their experience of their 'selves' in the here and now is expanded greatly, perhaps far beyond the reaches of most people. Interestingly, associated with this, the more autonomous people become, the more the time-space-entity range in which they live extends."

Julie Hay recently (2014) suggested adding "responsibility" or "accountability" to Berne's (1964) version of autonomy, defined as accepting responsibility for our own behaviour, recognising that we act based on our own decisions (and that we can change previous decisions). Drego (2006, p. 90) wrote that Berne's (1972) three-handed position of "I'm OK, you're OK, they're OK" envelops both individual and social freedom. It spans both individual wholeness and mutual responsibility between individuals and between groups.

2.3.3 Nurture and structure

The American educator Jean Illsley Clarke (Clarke & Dawson, 1989) explains the theory of hunger on the basis of two dimensions: care and structure. With assertive and supporting care, the needs of the child are recognised and the child is encouraged to think and do what he is capable of. Too much care carries the risk of abuse, whereby the child is used to satisfy the emotional or physical needs of the parents. Not enough care harbours the risk of conditional care, whereby the child must meet the expectations and requirements of the parents in order to receive strokes. Neglect and pampering are both forms of abuse.

Regarding the dimension of structure, negotiable rules are central. These are the rules that ensure safety, order, and structure. Some rules ("Be honest") may be non-negotiable within a family. Others (for example, rules about bedtime or alcohol use) grow or change along with the development of the child. Through these rules, children learn to think clearly and to solve problems, or to negotiate and argue with their parents. On the one hand, there is rigidity, enforcing obedience through fear, and criticism, which put the self-image of the child under pressure. On the other hand, there are "marshmallow rules", as flexible as soft pink sweets, whereby a child doesn't know where he's at, with irresponsibility, helplessness, and hopelessness as a possible consequence. And finally, there is the total absence of rules, abandonment, whereby children learn that their parents are not available. This model enables clients and educators to question whether or where they have veered away from their beliefs about nurturing and structure, which patterns this has produced, and how this continues to influence their private and professional lives.

2.3.4 Strokes in organisations

Following the merger of two schools, discontent was growing among the (in many cases) redeployed staff. Initially it seemed that the merger would mostly mean a profit. Both schools, each with a wide range of education on offer, would probably not have been able to keep their heads above water without the merger, given the shrinking market demand. The school's neighbourhood was beyond its growth period. Not everyone had been applauding the decision, of course. But a large majority of the staff understood the necessity as well as the opportunities this merger would bring. After a good start, the working climate at one of the sites began to rapidly deteriorate. Initially, there were minor disagreements about schedules, classrooms, tasks during break time, and so on. The disagreements became so prevalent that the managing director had little time for normal daily tasks. She constantly had to extinguish small fires or herself became embroiled in semi-conflictual conversations.

The external consultant who engaged with this rapidly deteriorating situation used TA stroke theory in order to understand what was going on. A lot of post-merger stress, as she knew, was caused—often without those involved being aware of it—by the dissolution of the stroke pattern of too many people. Most people who feel happy at their work, owe part of that satisfaction to their having been able to acquire their daily portion of positive strokes. They feel they have been seen and heard. They know that their efforts are appreciated by colleagues and management. Replenishing the stroke stock goes largely unnoticed, through the daily "Hello" and the cup of coffee with the janitor upon arrival, to the formal recognition during meetings, as when those present are thanked for their contributions. In the new (post-merger) situation, many of these patterns had been heavily disrupted. The shortage of positive strokes was being increasingly supplemented by the elicitation of negative strokes. The working environment was obviously not getting any better.

The consultant wrote a short report for the manager, in which she made clear what she thought was missing in the newly merged school. Although the manager looked upon this analysis with some scepticism, she was willing to go along with the plan that the consultant presented. The plan predominantly consisted of practical stroke experiments, in addition to training the staff and management on basic TA theory.

2.4 Related theories

2.4.1 Maslow's hierarchy of needs

The American psychologist Maslow (1954) proposed a hierarchy of five different human needs, in the form of a pyramid.

One can recognise several of the types of "hunger" within the structure of this pyramid. First, the need for physical strokes, followed by strokes related to structure and safety. From a secure base, people can enter into contact with others, feel valued and recognised, and develop themselves socially, emotionally, intellectually, and spiritually. In situations when physical needs or the need for security are not or only barely being supplied (as in the case of war or natural disasters), "neurotic symptoms" often surprisingly diminish. People are so busy with survival and self-preservation that they are distracted from all their aches and pains.

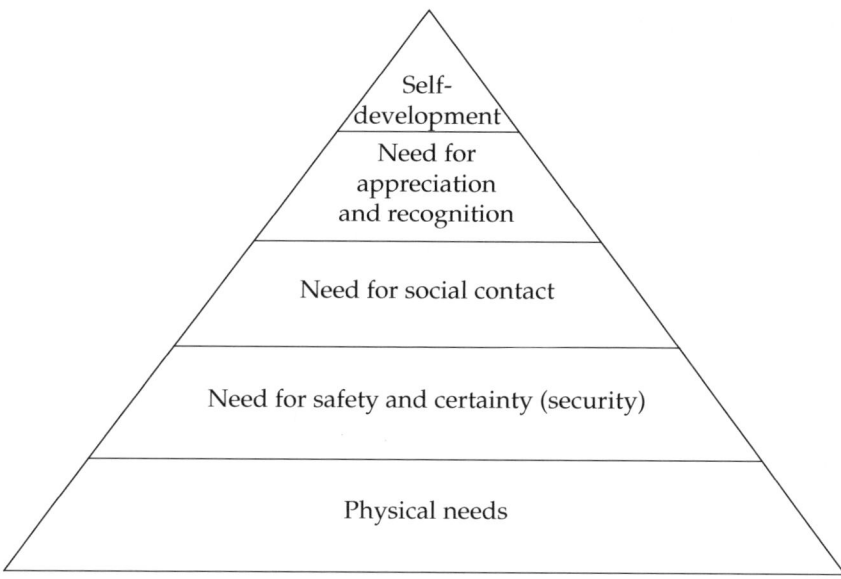

Figure 2.3. Maslow's pyramid.

> A taxi driver in New Orleans told me how he had experienced the situation after Hurricane Katrina in 2005, when a large part of the old town was flooded: "It was the best time of my life! Everyone was helpful and nice to each other, there was much less crime than usual." And with a wink, he added "And the entire public transport system was down, so I never did better business with my cab than I did then."

Sometimes it is too easily assumed that the base is in order. But if the basic needs for safety and security have not been adequately met, then all the energy invested in service of the "higher" needs will lead to unsatisfactory results. In organisations where it is insufficiently safe for employees, self-development groups and other courses will not be of optimal benefit.

2.4.2 Affect regulation and mentalisation

One fascinating area of research in recent decades is that of infant research (see, for instance, Daniel Stern, 1990, 1995), whereby little babies, sometimes only a few days old, are the subject of all kinds of research. A well-known test involves placing two gauze pads on either side of a five-day-old baby's head. One gauze pad is infused with milk from the baby's own mother, the other with the milk of another mother. The baby turns its head unfalteringly toward the smell of the milk of its mother.

At such a young age, little babies can already distinguish and focus on the familiar smell of their own mother. From this and other research it has become very clear how early the attachment—and thus the exchange of strokes—develops. Young babies learn to handle their own emotions through the strokes from those to whom they are attached. They discover that strong feelings like hunger, pain, coldness, anger, and sadness can be calmed by the nurturing and comfort provided by the mother and father. Gradually, they learn to regulate their affects. In other words, this is how they begin to learn how to deal with their emotions.

From the perspective of evolution, the function of early attachment relationships is to provide the baby with an environment in which to develop a maximum understanding of the mental state of himself and others. In this way, self-reflection gradually emerges; the ability to think about himself and others. Mentalising (Fonagy, Gergely, Jurist, & Target, 2002) is a core feature in this whole process, and can be defined as the capacity to read one's own "spirit" and those of others, in order to develop an adequate response. You create a concept of your own convictions, feelings, hopes, expectations, and plans, as well as those of others. Mentalising is an important activity in self-organisation: the set of cognitive, affective, and behavioural capabilities, whereby you can function adequately or less adequately in the world. Uncertainty in attachment relationships can lead to a restriction in the ability to mentalise.

2.4.3 Pride matters more

Consciously working with strokes as a powerful tool in guiding management is one of the most underrated interventions in companies and organisations. The old aphorism of the gardener—"what you pay attention to will grow!"—is a truism that is unfortunately ignored in many companies and organisations. If the daily commitment by the team or organisation is not seen or heard enough, then people will find other ways to satiate their hunger for recognition, either by complaining or gossiping, by cutting corners, or by taking a few days' sick leave.

A pioneering study by management consultancy McKinsey (Katzenbach, 2003) shows that, ultimately, most people do not actually work for money. McKinsey contradicts the notion that people need bonuses to make them run faster. "Money is not the motivator people think it is: pay-for-performance programmes result in self-serving behaviour and skin-deep organisational commitment." Money motivates people only superficially and for only a very short time. A new job can certainly be attractive, because you can climb a few steps up the salary ladder. However, the pay cheque is not that important in the long term when it comes to forming a bond between people and their company or organisation. Katzenbach reveals clearly that employees who receive recognition for their own performance and are proud of their company or organisation offer a more significant contribution to that company or organisation. Pride matters more than money!

2.4.4 Assertive discipline and appreciative inquiry

In schools, assertive discipline and appreciative inquire are two modalities that employ recognition but in very different ways. Assertive discipline, a very popular method for managing pupil behaviour, works by negative and positive recognition, for, hopefully, reinforcement of desirable behaviour. It is clearly explainable to pupils, it gives control and authority to teachers and it has a stated system of rewards and sanctions. But it is unconcerned with needs, personal history, or motivation (like Skinner's "black box") and, maybe for this reason, it doesn't always work—about 5–10% of pupils are immune to the offered rewards and don't care about being handed the sanctions (such as exclusion from school). There is more emphasis on the desired compliance by pupils than on understanding, sometimes with the result that the "sanctions" are seen as rewards by pupils.

Appreciative inquiry on the other hand emphasises resource, success, and positive possibilities—it uses personal and group experience of what works well and starts future planning from that base. This approach recognises that everyone has some successful strategies to draw on and works by affirming good and memorable experiences of "getting it right". Similarly, many psychologists specialising in educational settings such as Thomas Gordon (a colleague of Carl Rogers) and Nel Noddings promote acceptance and care of the individual child as the basis for effective learning. In writing on the ethics of care in education Noddings shows concern for the real needs of students, including emotional needs, and the potential for schools to be supportive communities (2005). Gordon, too, promotes empathic listening and respect for pupils as the basis of teacher-learner relationships that will have positive outcomes (1975).

2.4.5   Moral leadership

Another way to motivate people is to connect them to a higher purpose. As Antoine de Saint-Exupéry (1948) put it: "If you want to build a ship, don't drum up the men to gather wood, divide the work, and give orders. Instead, teach them to yearn for the vast and endless sea."

An impressive example of motivating with desire and vision is the leadership of Nelson Mandela. The movie *Invictus* by the director Clint Eastwood shows how Mandela stimulated the then almost completely white South African rugby team to win the rugby World Cup in their own country in 1995. Mandela was convinced that the rugby team could play an important role in connecting white and black in a racially torn South Africa. The coach of the team understood this vision and took the role of bridge builder upon himself. He had the players visit Robben Island, where Mandela had been imprisoned for nearly thirty years, and he had them give rugby lessons to black kids living on the street. In this way, the players became connected to the country they represented. It became clear that mutual contact and stroke exchange between the various population groups was a powerful weapon against ignorance, helplessness, and hatred. When the rugby team indeed won the World Cup, it united the different population groups who had hated each other for decades—in a way that a politician would never have been able to.

References

Berne, E. (1961). *TA in Psychotherapy*. New York: Grove Press.
Berne, E. (1964). *Games People Play—The Basic Hand Book of Transactional Analysis*. New York: Ballantine.
Berne, E. (1970). *Sex in Human Loving*. London: Penguin.
Berne, E. (1972). *What Do You Say After You Say Hello?* New York: Grove Press.
Clarke, J. I., & Dawson, C. (1989). *Growing Up Again (2nd edition)*. Center City, MN: Hazelden, 1998.
Drego, P. (2006). Freedom and responsibility: Social empowerment and the altruistic model of ego states. *Transactional Analysis Journal*, 36(2): 90–104.

English, F. (1972). Sleepy, Spunky and Spooky. *Transactional Analysis Journal*, 2(2): 64–67.
Erskine, R. (1998). The therapeutic relationship: Integrating motivation and personality theories. *Transactional Analysis Journal*, 28(2): 132–142.
Fallaci, O. (1981). *A Man.* Feltham, UK: Hamlyn.
Fonagy, P., Gergely, G., Jurist, E., & Target, M. (2002). *Affect Regulation, Mentalization, and the Development of the Self.* New York: Other Press.
Gordon, T. (1975). *Teacher Effectiveness Training*, New York: Crown.
Haimowitz, M. L., & Haimowitz, N. R. (1976). *Suffering is Optional!* Evanston, IL: Haimowoods Press.
Harlow, H. F., & Harlow, M. K. (1962). Social deprivation in monkeys. *Scientific American*, 207(5): 136–146.
Hay, J. (2014). Extending the donkey bridge for autonomy. *IDTA Newsletter*, 9(1): 8.
Karpman, S. B. (2010). Intimacy analysis today: The intimacy scale and the personality pinwheel. *Transactional Analysis Journal*, 40(3): 224–242.
Katzenbach, J. R. (2003). *Why Pride Matters More than Money. The Power of the World's Greatest Motivational Force.* New York: Crown Business.
Maslow, A. (1954). *Motivation and Personality.* New York: Harper.
McCormick, P. (1977). *Social Transactions.* Stockton, NJ: Vanguard Press.
McKenna, J. (1974). Stroking profile. *Transactional Analysis Journal*, 4(4): 20–24.
Mellor, K. (2008). Autonomy with integrity. *Transactional Analysis Journal*, 38(3): 182–189.
Mountain, A., & Davidson, C. (2011). *Working Together, Organizational Transactional Analysis and Business Performance.* Farnham, UK: Gower.
Noddings, N. (2005). What does it mean to educate the WHOLE child? *Educational Leadership*, 63(1): 8–13.
Saint-Exupéry, A. de (1948). *Citadelle.* Paris: Gallimard.
Spitz, R. (1945). Hospitalism, genesis of psychiatry. Conditions in early childhood. *Psychoanalytic Study of the Child*, 1: 53–74.
Steiner, C. (1971). The stroke economy. *Transactional Analysis Journal*, 1(3): 9–15.
Steiner, C. (1984). *Scripts People Live. Transactional Analysis of Life Script.* New York: Grove Press.
Steiner, C. (2003). *Emotional Literacy. Intelligence with a Heart.* Fawnskin, CA: Personhood Press.
Stern, D. (1990). *Diary of a Baby.* New York: Basic Books.
Stern, D. (1995). *The Motherhood Constellation.* New York: Basic Books/HarperCollins.
Stewart, I., & Joines, V. (1987). *TA Today (2nd edition).* Melton Mowbray, UK: Lifespace, 2012.
Thunnissen, M. (2007). *Begrijpen en veranderen. Theorie en toepassingen van de transactionele analyse.* (To Understand and to Change. Theory and Applications of Transactional Analysis.) Halsteren, Netherlands: DWG.

CHAPTER THREE

Transactions

3.1　Basic theory
　　3.1.1　Introduction
　　3.1.2　Social and psychological level
　　3.1.3　Crossed transactions
　　3.1.4　Transactions with an ulterior motive
　　3.1.5　Rules
　　3.1.6　An effective relationship
3.2　Further theory
　　3.2.1　Forms of complementary transactions
　　3.2.2　Forms of crossed transactions
　　3.2.3　Forms of transactions with an ulterior motive
　　3.2.4　Specific forms of transactions
　　3.2.5　Metacommunicative transactions
　　3.2.6　Non-verbally covert messages
3.3　Furthermore
　　3.3.1　Projection and communication
　　3.3.2　Transference, countertransference, and projection
　　3.3.3　Relational TA
　　3.3.4　The alleged simplicity of TA
3.4　Related theories
　　3.4.1　Watzlawick and colleagues
　　3.4.2　Solution focused approach
References

In the previous two chapters, we discussed the structure of personality using ego states and the human need for strokes and structure. The next step in the analysis is to describe the communication between people: the analysis of transactions. Berne made a conscious decision to use the term "transaction", in order to indicate that a transaction is a unit within the communication between people. By speaking of transactions, TA clearly indicates that people invest something of themselves in communication … and expect something in return. The art of effective communication is, among other things, to allow the exchange of transactions that you wish to maintain and to bring an end to those transactions that you want to stop. This third chapter is concerned with the rules and patterns of communication that TA sees in this process. They are recognisable to everyone and immediately usable. Ultimately, the TA theory of transactions concerns the question whether and how people mutually (positively) influence each other.

3.1   Basic theory

3.1.1   Introduction

Transactions are a core concept in transactional analysis, so much so that TA has been named after it. Why have transactions been assigned such a central place?

Interactional analysis?

In response to the question whether a transaction is the same as an interaction, Berne says in an interview (YouTube, "Games People Play", interview in 1966): "Interaction is a somewhat cowardly word compared with transaction." Interaction lacks commitment and is more a description. "Transaction means people get something in return", he continues. This goes back to the fundamental question of all social psychology: why do people talk to each other? They invest something (of themselves) and expect that this investment will yield something!

Transactions form the bridge between the interpersonal (outside) and intrapsychic (inside). After all, transactions are what take place within the social domain, while they are also a reflection of the internal world of the participants in a transaction. In a series of transactions, the preferred ego states of each of the parties involved in the communication often become clear. Do you tend to react mainly from the perspective of Parent: dominant, critical, or caring? Or is Child the main ego state: where pleasure is more important than completing tasks or taking responsibility? Also, your frame of reference, the view you have of yourself, others, and the world, shines through in your transactions. Do you see yourself as someone who needs to be on your guard against others, as someone who will get the job done, as someone who generally knows better than others, or as a person who tackles tasks with confidence?

Strictly speaking, the function of transactional analysis is the identification of specific ego states involved in a transaction. People who are aware from which ego state they and others communicate increase their choices and thus their personal effectiveness (Karpman, 1971).

In Berne's time, terms such as "sending and receiving" dominated thinking on communication. It was a way of thinking which adhered to linear causality; there is a stimulus and there is a response; there is one cause and all that follows is the result. However, as soon as people are involved, linear causality no longer applies. What we have is circular cohesion, or rather, an infinite coherence. When it comes to communication, you often do not know where it begins and on what the outcome or the result depends. Whatever the case, the effect of communication is strongly influenced by attribution of meaning, which is coloured by your gender, your age, your history, and your position. People are unique attributors of meaning.

Communication is therefore continually a matter of subjective attribution of meaning to selective perception. This ensures that communication is both fascinating and complicated. One of the principles in the more systemic view of communication is that you cannot understand communication by attempting to control it, but by examining its limits. Human relations and communication are indeed very complex phenomena. Someone who is aware of the possibilities and impossibilities of human communication can better understand how to optimally exercise influence. TA is a powerful tool when it comes to developing a broader and deeper understanding of the (im)possibilities in communication.

Transactions are the building blocks of communication. Those who study the general aspects of communication (communication theory) and the more personal characteristics of individual communication (communication practice) can greatly increase their efficacy in many areas of their lives, both at home and at work. After all, it is via communication that people influence each other.

When you are emotional, you often think and act in terms of linear causality. Anna is angry. She thinks that Jack does not take good care of her, yet he still wants to have sex with her. Jack feels misunderstood because sex is a way for him to show that he loves her. For both of them, psychic energy is being directed from the Adult to the Parent or Child. The Adult becomes contaminated.

3.1.2 Social and psychological level

A transaction is a unit of social exchange consisting of a stimulus and a response, which simultaneously serves as the stimulus for the next response (McCormick, 1977). The term "transaction" was deliberately chosen because each person receives something from the interaction, such as recognition, confirmation of their position in life, or enhancing their frame of reference and/or psychological and somatic well-being. Each stroke is in fact a transaction and vice versa (see the previous chapter). After all, a stroke is a unit of recognition, and can only be given by way of a transaction.

The simplest transaction is the complementary transaction, in which the response comes from the ego state that was addressed by the stimulus. The arrows of the transaction run parallel (Figure 3.1a). Such a transaction may resemble the following example:

JOHN (FROM ADULT): "What time is it?"
ANNETTE (FROM ADULT): "Ten o'clock."

62 INTO TA

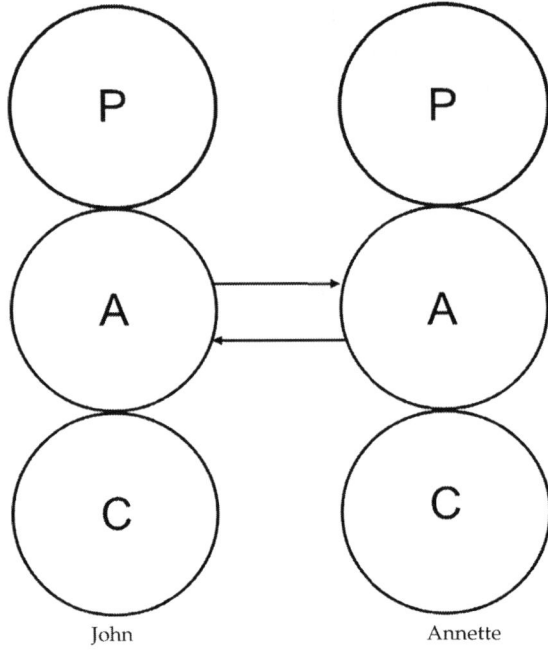

Figure 3.1a. Simple complementary transaction.

Another possibility is the following complementary transaction (Figure 3.1b):

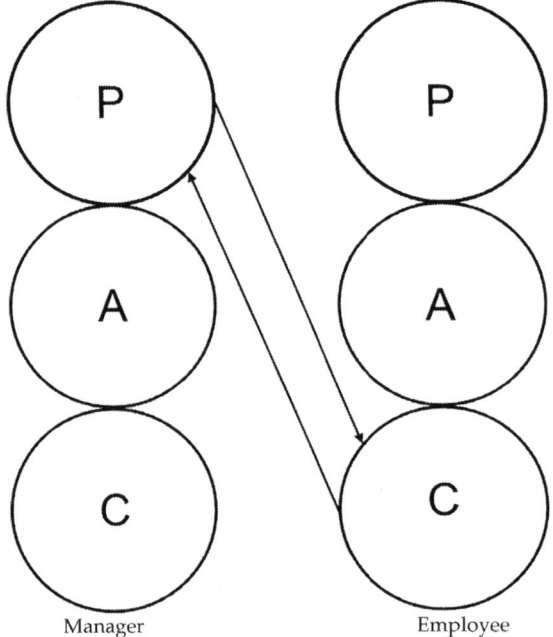

Figure 3.1b. Simple complementary transaction.

MANAGER (FROM PARENT): "You must have that report completed and handed in by Monday."
EMPLOYEE (TIMID, FROM CHILD): "I'll do that."

However, upon closer inspection, even the simplest transaction is complex. There are almost always several ego states involved, on a social as well as psychological level (Figure 3.2). The social level is the level of content, the psychological level that of the relation.

At the social level, the same thing happens as in Figure 3.1a:

JOHN (FROM ADULT): "What time is it?"
ANNETTE (FROM ADULT): "Ten o'clock."

On a psychological level, however, the following may be happening:

JOHN (FROM CHILD): "I'll be late soon!"
ANNETTE (FROM PARENT): "Yes, indeed, so why did you sit around wasting time this morning?"

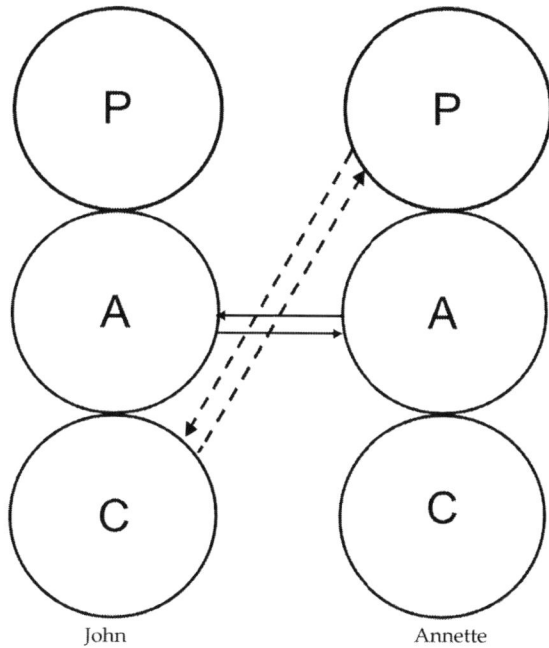

Figure 3.2. Transaction on social and psychological level.

Even if this is not made explicit, the psychological level gives a certain colour to the A-A communication; by the tone of voice, for example. Upon careful observation, most single transactions turn out to be multiple transactions. This is because, usually unconsciously, there is always a hint of Parent or Child being acted out within a transaction (McCormick, 1977). The Adult's reaction is thus influenced by enthusiasm or dislike from the Child, and approval or disapproval from the Parent.

Along with the information from the Adult, communication often takes place via non-verbal signals, and with concern, sympathy, tension, lack of interest, curiosity, anger, pleasure, or any other kind of emotion. This is usually not a problem. Thus, mothers love taking care of their children and children are usually all too happy to be coddled. Partners know each other's weaknesses and complement or support each other, often without realising they're doing so.

A manager and an employee usually work with a set of unspoken expectations. As long as both their expectations correspond during communication, and the social and psychological levels are congruent and fit together logically, then there's not a cloud in the sky. However, if their expectations do not correspond, then they may be dealing with transactions with an ulterior motive, which involve a discrepancy between the social and the psychological level. For more information on this, see section 3.1.4.

3.1.3 Crossed transactions

An effective way to guide communication is via crossed transactions. In a crossed transaction, someone does not respond from the addressed ego state and often does not focus on the ego state from where the stimulus came. Consider the following situation:

An employee complains, "I won't be able to have this report done on time." This elicits either a critical response from the manager ("Why not? Did you get started on it too late?") or a caring response ("That's a pity. How much time will you need to get it done?").

However, if the manager chooses not to respond with the expected Parent–Child transaction, and instead addresses the employee with the Adult, then we have a crossed transaction. For example, by saying "What have you done so far to address the issue?" Or, "I would like the report on my desk by Monday next week. What can you do to make sure this will be achieved?" This transaction is graphically represented in Figure 3.3.

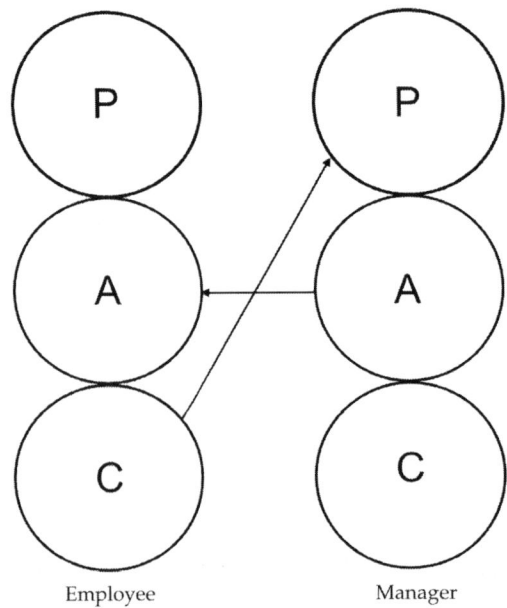

Figure 3.3. Crossed transaction: stimulus C → P receives reaction A → A.

In Figure 3.3, the manager deliberately chooses to apply a crossed transaction and thereby alters the direction of the communication. Crossed transactions can also occur unexpectedly. They can lead to conflicts or blockages in communication. Annette might, when being asked for the time in the previous paragraph for example, express her psychological level message openly:

JOHN (FROM ADULT TO ADULT): "What time is it?"
ANNETTE (FROM PARENT TO CHILD): "Are you late again? Then why did you sit around wasting time this morning?"

Instead of a neutral answer to the question about the time, John receives a reproach (see figure 3.4). The most logical reaction from John would be that he repeats the question: "I asked what time it is. I didn't ask for feedback on my performance." Chances are, however, that John will defend himself: "Well, it was a late night last night" or he in turn challenges Annette: "Waste time? You always make a mess of the kitchen, which I have to clean up and then I run out of time."

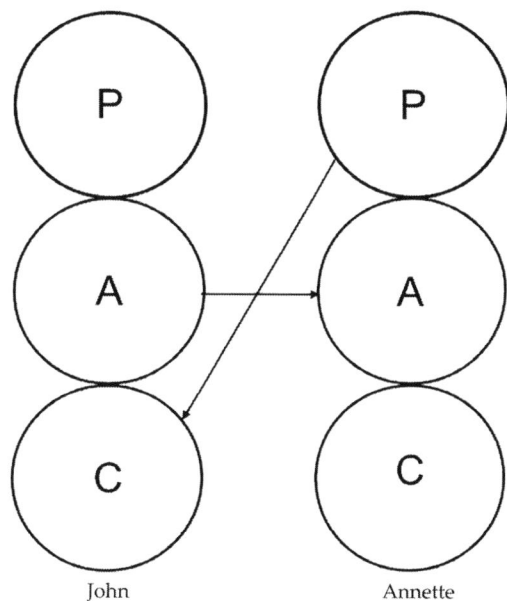

Figure 3.4. Crossed transaction: stimulus A → A yields reaction P → C.

These are the crossed transactions whereby A-A communication unexpectedly turns into a P-C or C-P communication. Further analysis shows that a psychological, hidden level of communication suddenly comes to the surface, by way of buried or hitherto unspoken reproaches, frustrations, or expectations.

3.1.4 Transactions with an ulterior motive

As mentioned, most transactions contain a message simultaneously on the social and psychological levels. As long as these levels are congruent, all will go well. If this is not the case, problems may arise. Consider the following situation:

> Ahmed and Farida meet each other as colleagues and like each other. They get to know each other well, since they work together on a number of projects and eventually they express their feelings for each other. They begin a relationship with each other.

In this situation, the social and the psychological levels are congruent. No problems in communication arise. It would be different if the social and psychological levels contradict each other or begin to contradict each other over time, as in the following scenario:

> Ahmed and Farida get to know each other as colleagues and like each other. Ahmed does his best to cooperate with Farida on a project and Farida enjoys his attention. She doesn't tell Ahmed that she has been in a relationship with Salem for a long time. Over dinner after a long day at work, Ahmed tells her about his feelings. Farida responds somewhat mockingly and triumphantly: "Don't you know that I'm in a relationship?" Ahmed feels rejected and humiliated and no longer wants to work together with Farida.

In this case, the series of transactions resulted in a psychological game. More on this in Chapter Four. In another example, if a manager, wringing his hands and with a loud voice, announces that "We are going to reorganise, but this won't result in any serious cutbacks," then this message will almost certainly be received with derisory laughter by the employees. For they know very well, from the newspapers and from others, that this is not how it will go in reality, and certainly not if the message is delivered in this manner.

Since research conducted by Mehrabian in 1971, much has been said and written about the role that non-verbal expressions play in the whole of communication. Mehrabian claimed that 55% of communication is visual (body language, such as posture and gestures), 38% is vocal (tone, hard or soft) and 7% verbal (content). According to this analysis, 93% of all communication is non-verbal. For years it has been claimed that it is not "what" you say but "how" you say it. Obviously, "how" is a significant factor. Mehrabian's research, however, focused on the question of what happens when people communicate with each other about their feelings. In that case, non-verbal communication is dominant. When it comes to business or content-heavy exchange, then the content is of greater importance. Moreover, a lot of research conducted after 1967 (including Burgoon, Buller, & Woodall, 1996) shows that context is of enormous influence on the role of non-verbal factors. Who says what, where, and when?

3.1.5 Rules

Berne (1961, 1964) discovered that much communication develops according to three rules or laws:

1. *Complementary transactions can continue indefinitely.* A-A (exchange of information), P-P (discussions), C-C (pleasure), or P-C (care for the other or chastising the other) can produce

an endless exchange of transactions. If you want to change the communication, then a crossed transaction is often the preferred method.
2. *Where communcation stops, it is often because of a crossed transaction.* The application of crossed transactions is an effective way to guide communication. If there is a sudden conflict or confusion in communication, chances are that one of the two interlocutors has made use of a crossed transaction. If you are suddenly put off-balance by something the other person says and you ask yourself, confused, "What on earth is happening?", then it is highly likely that a crossed transaction has occurred. The other does not respond from the expected ego state, but from a different one, and "forces" you to review your reaction. Do you also change your ego state, do you repeat your previous transaction from the same ego state, or do you deliberately choose an option that allows you to direct the communication in your desired direction? Or is there an ulterior motive at the psychological level, in which case rule 3 applies?
3. *The result of the transaction is usually determined by the psychological level.* For more on the various forms of transactions with ulterior motives, see section 3.2.3, and Chapter Four on games.

People are often barely aware of the psychological level of communication. In therapy groups and coaching sessions, it can occur that a man sitting with clenched fists and a tightened jaw is told that he is very angry. If he really lets this message penetrate, it may be that the penny suddenly drops and he lets out a liberating chuckle that makes clear that he had not yet realised this fact.

Intuitively, people usually react with a mixture of Adult skills, Child feelings, and Parental care or values. If they manage to avoid unwanted emotional reactions (from P or C) within themselves or others, they function from the perspective of an integrated Adult; see Chapter One.

3.1.6   An effective relationship

With a relationship diagram it is fairly easy to analyse whether a relationship—whether at work or private—is effective or whether there are serious shortcomings. In a relationship oriented towards connection, the following transactions are essential.

1. P-P: both agree on norms and values, can consult with each other concerning the goals of the team, or concerning the children's education or life in general.
2. A-A: both can jointly run a company or household, draw up a contract or plan, and execute it.
3. C-C: both can experience fun together, argue, party, play, do something fun, have sex, or experience intimacy.
4. P-C: one can take care of the other, provide constructive criticism, and set limits.
5. C-P: one can ask and receive care from the other and learn from the other's criticism.

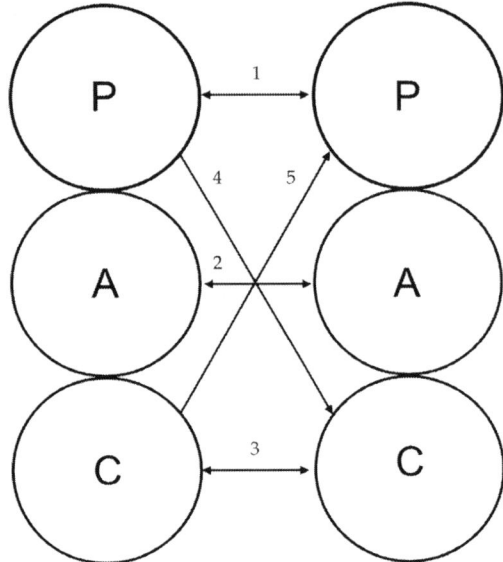

Figure 3.5. Effective relationship.

> Patrick and Ann go to relationship therapy. With the help of the therapist, they draw their three ego states and the transactions between them: their relationship diagram. Their arguments are often about one or the other not honouring agreements—according to the other. They have "agreed" that there should be no nibbling or drinking behind the laptop, but Patrick repeatedly finds empty chip bags or dirty glasses next to the keyboard. When he gets upset about this, Ann goes into defence mode or challenges him in return. Also, agreements about outings and vacations, the finances, or the division of household chores, often end up in conflict or disagreement. There is little A-A connection.
>
> On the P-P level, there are also many differences of opinion. Patrick has difficulty with the spiritual courses Ann is taking, while she thinks that he is developing in a very materialistic direction, now that he has become a high-earning entrepreneur.
>
> Their connection is strongest on the C-C level. They are good at parties together and are still passionate in their lovemaking. Ann still finds Patrick to be "the most attractive man on earth".
>
> From the beginning of their relationship, they have argued a lot. Very often there has been blaming back and forth, in increasingly harsh tones, until one of the two angrily walks away. These are escalating P-C transactions over and over again. And on the other hand, there is little complementary P-C communication. Time and again, they fail to take care of one another and they find it difficult to accept criticism from each other (see figure 3.6).

3.2 Further theory

3.2.1 Forms of complementary transactions

As discussed in section 3.1, the complementary transaction is the least complex form of transaction. In theory, there are nine possible complementary transactions:

- From Parent to Parent, Adult or Child of the other.
- From Adult to Parent, Adult or Child of the other.
- From Child to Parent, Adult or Child of the other.

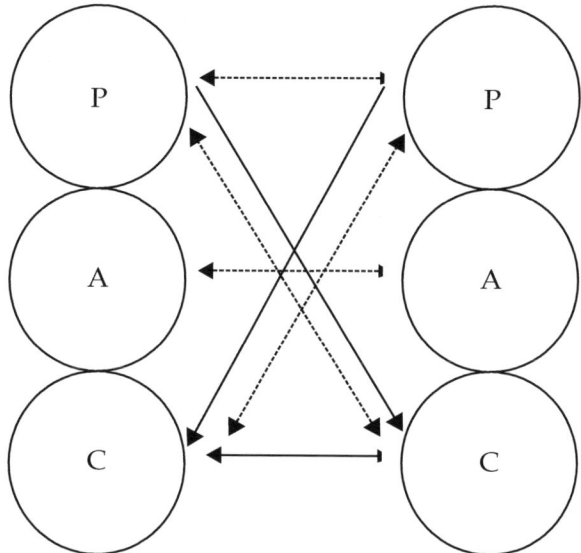

Figure 3.6. Relationship diagram of Patrick and Ann.

From the perspective of functional analysis (where the Parent is divided into the Structuring and Nurturing Parent, and the Child into the Natural and Adapted Child; see Chapter One), this number increases to twenty-five possibilities: from each of the five functional ego states to each of the five functional ego states of the other. In practice, however, certain transactions are more common and others less. The following transactions occur frequently.

1. Complementary transactions whereby both partners in communication use the same ego state.

    • 1a Parent–Parent:

STIMULUS: "Youth nowadays ... Children just sit behind their computers!"
RESPONSE: "Yeah. It's not for nothing that so many children have ADHD nowadays; they simply don't play outside enough!"

    • 1b Adult–Adult:

STIMULUS: "What are we having for dinner tonight?"
RESPONSE: "Noodles with fish."

    • 1c Child–Child:

STIMULUS: "Shall we have a nice evening together?"
RESPONSE: "Yeah, sure. I'm in the mood for that."

2. Complementary transactions whereby one uses the Parent ego state and the other the Child ego state.

    • 2a Parent–Child:

STIMULUS (PARENT): "And now you're going to turn off the computer and go play outside!"
RESPONSE (CHILD): "Okay."

- 2b Child–Parent:

STIMULUS (CHILD): "I'm in the mood to just laze about tonight and I don't feel like doing any household chores. Is that okay?"
RESPONSE (PARENT): "Yes, that's fine; you worked very hard this week."

3. Less frequent are transactions in which one partner uses Parent or Child and the other partner responds from the Adult.

- 3a Parent–Adult:

STIMULUS (PARENT): "The youth nowadays ... Children just sit behind the computer all day! They get ADHD from that, you know?"
RESPONSE (ADULT): "I read somewhere that the percentage of children diagnosed with ADHD hasn't increased in recent years."

- 3b Child–Adult:

STIMULUS (CHILD): "I'm in the mood to just laze about tonight, and you?"
RESPONSE (ADULT): "I promised myself to prepare everything for work tomorrow."

Understanding these patterns of communication helps to use more options when communicating. In practice, when it comes to complementary transactions, you will mostly deal with the transactions described in 1 and 2 of this subparagraph.

3.2.2 Forms of crossed transactions

There are many possible combinations of crossed transactions, especially if you not only consider the structural but also the functional analysis view of communication.

> Hans says to Samuel, "Don't you also think it's ridiculous that we have to work so much overtime?" (Stimulus from the Structuring Parent, SP, focused on Samuel's SP). Hans expects approval from Samuel's SP, so that they can join in a round of mutual complaint. Samuel responds differently, however: "It sounds like this is bothering you a lot. Are you perhaps becoming a bit strung out?" (Response Nurturing Parent—Adapted Child). Samuel thinks Hans is actually asking for compassion rather than support.

These are the most common crossed transactions, which Berne called type 1 and type 2.

1. *Type 1, crossed transaction: from $A \rightarrow A$ to $C \rightarrow P$*
   Stimulus (A-A) from Louis: "Where's the corkscrew?" Response (C-P) Sacha: "I can't always think of everything, you know?" Apparently Sacha doesn't experience Louis' question as an

Adult request for information but as a surreptitious reproach ("You must have misplaced the corkscrew") or as an expectation ("You should know where the corkscrew is"). This form of crossed transaction also occurs with a *transference reaction* whereby the other does not adequately respond in the here and now, but as if the interlocutor is an authority figure (Parent) for whom you should hide in your shell.

Doctor (A-A): "How much do you weigh?" Patient (C-P): "Yes, I know I eat too much." The patient hears the doctor's question as coming from the Parent, and responds from the Child rather than the Adult. If the doctor doesn't realise this, she will be inclined to automatically react from the Parent.

Doctor (P-C): "Yes, it would indeed be a good idea if you watched your weight a little bit." Thus, an A-A communication has turned into a P-C communication, which makes it difficult for both parties to take responsibility for their own lives. The tendency arises to pass on responsibility (by the patient) or to take over responsibility (by the doctor).

In case of a transference reaction, a person often experiences the other as "someone from their own past". The patient responds from the Child to a question from the Adult of the doctor as if the doctor is a father, mother, or another authority figure from the past. Managers often speak to their employees from the Parent as if they are still the children in the family in which they grew up. While Freud once thought that transference takes place on a "blank screen", it is now known that it is usually a far more subtle phenomenon. A metaphor will help to clarify. A hunter is walking through the woods with the intention of killing a rabbit. Suddenly he thinks he spots one. He aims and shoots, but the bullet ricochets off a stone. The hunter probably mistook the stone for a rabbit. The question is whether this particular stone was "rabbit-like", which led to the misunderstanding. What did the doctor do to make it possible for the patient to not hear the question as coming from the Adult? What did the employees do that perhaps caused the manger to direct his message to their Child? in them? And to make it even more complex: what are the societal images of doctors and patients, and of managers and employees, which invite such transferences?

2. *Type 2, crossed transaction: from $A \to A$ to $P \to C$*
Stimulus (A-A) from Louis: "Where's the corkscrew?" Response (P-C) Sacha: "Well, you lost it". In this case, Sacha experiences Louis' question again as a surreptitious reproach, but now she goes on the counterattack. This is the prototype of the countertransference reaction. Patient (A-A): "I weigh a hundred kilos." Doctor (SP-C): "That's too much; you really should do something about it." Or, patient (A-A): "I weigh a hundred kilos." Doctor (NP-C): "Well, you really wouldn't think so, you know?" The doctor hears the stimulus as coming from the Child of the patient rather than from the Adult, and so reacts from the Structuring or from the Nurturing Parent. For more information about transference and countertransference, see section 3.3.2.

Crossed transaction from $C \to P$ or $P \to C$ to $A \to A$

Two other common crossed transactions are those in which the stimulus comes from the Parent or from the Child and the other switches to the Adult. As mentioned, this can be an effective way to redirect communication and to make the step from complaining or blaming to problem-solving behaviour.

- Stimulus (C-P): a woman complains to her friend in frustration and anger about her husband who drinks too much: "Why is this happening to me again now?" Response (A-A): "You're married to an alcoholic." The woman feels the need to throw out a complaint and is expecting compassion or possibly criticism from the other, but not a reality check.
- Stimulus (P-C) from a manager (angry): "Why are you making such a mess of things again? That report was long overdue!" Response (A-A) from the employee: "I will give it priority as of now. I can tell you that it will be ready by Monday." Again, the person lower in rank does not respond in the expected manner, from the Child (Adapted: "I'll do my best," or Rebellious: "I don't care about your tasks"), but instead proposes to solve the problem.

3.2.3   Forms of transactions with an ulterior motive

In almost all transactions, there is, as mentioned, both a social and psychological level. These become transactions with an ulterior motive when the social and psychological levels are not congruent. According to the third rule of communication, the psychological level determines the outcome of the transactions. Another definition is that transactions with an ulterior motive involve more than two ego states. If three ego states are involved, we speak of an angular transaction. If four are involved, then we have a duplex transaction.

1. *Angular transaction*

    Angular transactions are used professionally by salespeople, advertisers, politicians, teachers, therapists, and anyone whose income depends on persuading or convincing others. The stimulus comes from one ego state while addressing two ego states in the other.

    Car salesman (A-A): "This car costs 40,000 euros. That may be beyond your budget." Simultaneously on a psychological level (A-C): "You don't look like you can afford that much for a car."

    The client responds (A-A). "I'll take it."

    After all, on a psychological level the following is being "said" (C-A): "Of course I can afford it!"

    Often the message in an angular transaction is aimed at the "greedy" Child. "This is the last one in stock! This is a one-time offer!"

    Another example is the teacher who says to the student in a high school graduating class who is cutting corners: "You know, you'll never pass the exam, forget it."

    The message at the social level (A-A) is: "With these grades you won't succeed."

    At the same time, on a psychological level (A-C) it is: "I see that you get failing grades and I think you can do much better."

    It may be that on a psychological level, the Child of the student is triggered: "Damn, I'll show them that I can make it!"

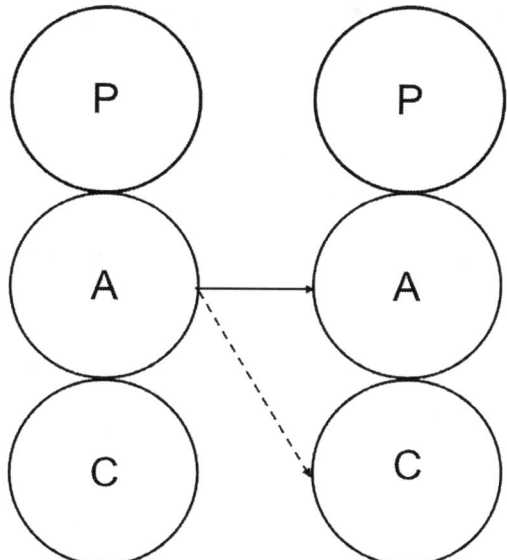

Figure 3.7. Angular transaction: stimulus A → A and simultaneously A → C.

2. *Duplex transaction*

In this case, four ego states are involved. For example:

At a social level (A-A): "Would you like to see my room?" "Yes, sure."

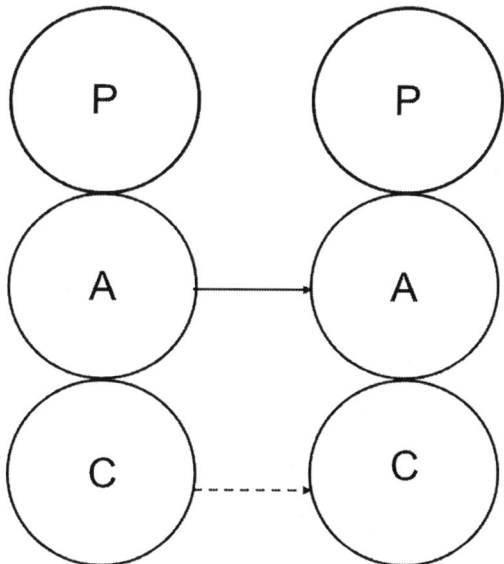

Figure 3.8. Duplex transaction: stimulus A → A and simultaneously C → C.

On a psychological level (C-C): "I would like to be alone with you, and who knows what might happen!" "Yes, that would be great ..."

In a duplex transaction, the ego states are congruent at the social and psychological level. If there is a contradiction at the social and psychological level, then we are dealing with a game. More on this in Chapter Four.

3.2.4 Specific forms of transactions

Blocking transactions

People use blocking transactions especially if the stimulus is perceived as a threat to their own frame of reference (the sum of thoughts, feelings, and behaviours that someone uses to map the world), or when they do not want to address a question and wish to redirect the conversation. Those who use a blocking transaction are actually redefining the situation. Politicians are masters at this. A journalist asks, "Aren't you terribly angry with the Prime Minister?" "It depends on what you consider angry", the Member of Parliament answers. In everyday life you will also regularly encounter blocking transactions. "Do you love me?" "Oh, what is 'love'?" or: "Why are you ignoring me?" "I'm not doing that at all, I'm thinking". A well-known example of a blocking transaction is when a mother asks "Who here is making a mess?" and the child replies "Not me!"

Tangential transactions

Tangential transactions have the purpose of keeping one's own frame of reference intact. In this case, there is really a situation of "talking past each other"! Everyone seems to be having his or her own conversation.

Mary tells Ann that a lump was discovered in her breast and that she has an appointment at the hospital in about three weeks. Instead of addressing Mary's concern, Ann talks about her neighbour who was in the same situation, which ultimately turned out to be a false alarm. It would have been less pleasant if Ann had told her the story of her aunt, who had to go to hospital and then had a breast amputation within three days. It is often easier to talk about other people than to address each other directly and to share concern, compassion, and sorrow.

At work, such a transaction may look like this. The manager asks, "When will the budget be ready?" To which the controller replies: "Have you heard what happened in the city council debates?" Here the controller avoids a clear answer to the question. It is tempting to go along with tangential transactions and then to think afterwards, "But hold on, just when will the budget be ready?"

A component of media training of politicians is to learn how to strategically insert tangential transactions in order to elegantly avoid answering questions when they don't want to.

Bull's eye transactions

A "bull's eye transaction" is a constructive transaction from the (integrating) Adult which addresses all three ego states of the other. The bull's eye transaction is successful if the other reacts from the (integrating) Adult. A mother says to her sixteen-year-old daughter who is getting poor results at school and wants to go out with a group of older friends at the weekend, "I know you want to go out (C), and you will think that I shouldn't interfere in your business (P), but would you mind still talking to me about it (A)?" The daughter responds: "I do find it annoying, actually, but I'll talk about it." Sometimes a bull's eye transaction can achieve its goal with just one word:

> During coaching sessions, Liesbeth tells how her father used to sit her down on the piano stool when she had received her school report, and then run through all her grades, particularly her failing grades, and give her recommendations for improvement. She would feel small and inferior. When at one point she said how she felt when she was summoned by her boss, her coach responded "So you were back on that piano stool." Suddenly she realised from P, A, and C which pattern of repetition she was falling into.

A bull's eye transaction can also be observed when both the jury and the audience are emotionally moved by the audition of people like Paul Potts, Susan Boyle, or Emmanuel Kelly on talent shows on TV (www.youtube.com/watch?v = W86 jlvrG54o). The Parent evaluates the performance: "You have a beautiful voice!" The Adult determines that the participant meets the criteria to proceed to the next level. "Programs like *X-Factor* were invented for people like you." The Child is moved by the fact that someone unexpectedly gives such a powerful performance: "I have a lump in my throat."

Bull's eye transactions are especially effective because they let the other know that all ego states are being taken seriously. It contains the implicit invitation for the other to do the same. This facilitates an effective problem-solving approach!

3.2.5 *Metacommunicative transactions*

Widdowson (2008) describes the metacommunicative transaction as a special transaction, effective in the unfolding therapeutic relationship. A metacommunication is an intervention that utilises the therapist's countertransference in the here and now of the therapy exploring the relational significance for the client of what is occurring in the therapy. The use of metacommunicative transactions can be highly effective in following Woollams and Brown's (1978) "Four Rules of Therapy" (pp. 265–267):

(a) emphasis on the OK position of the therapist both during and after therapy,
(b) the therapist deals with the structure of the therapeutic relationship,
(c) and with issues of transference and countertransference,
(d) with here and now problems between the participants in the therapy and other major life events, before dealing with the content of the contract.

The therapist uses metacommunicative transactions in different ways. The therapist stimulates awareness in the client by questions like "What are you experiencing right now?" or "What are you aware of in your body as you say that?" The therapist cultivates an attitude of curiosity in the sessions and invites the client to view his experiences from multiple perspectives. With a focus on the here and now of the therapeutic relationship the therapist uses the material that becomes clear within the session: subjective experiences of the client, feelings, thoughts, and impulses the therapist might have in relation to the clients story. Metacommunicative transactions can be intensely intimate and risky; being honest with clients can feel shameful or scary. However, saying as a therapist "I feel stuck right now and I am not sure where to take this" can be liberating and open up a new avenue of exploration.

Metacommunicative transactions stimulate the Adult of therapist and client, and help to "deconfuse" the client's ego states.

3.2.6 Non-verbally covert messages

Vandra (2009) suggests that ulterior transactions are not only transmitted by non-verbal signals. Based on the communication theory of Buda (1988), he states that there are six alternative mechanisms for transmission of ulterior transactions by verbal messages and actions. These six are:

1. Presuppositions: If we make a statement or ask a question, we often make presuppositions that are transmitted by the message behind its content.
2. Situation: The situation is defined by the participants and influenced by the physical environment (in which the message occurs), the social environment (who else is present), the relationship and its dynamic (how the participants are related).
3. Historical context: The historical context is the history of the relationship, the history of similar communicative situations (what has happened in other cases), and the history of the moment (each message is a reaction to a former action or a former message).
4. Meta-language or communication by allusions: Meta-language is described as a communication that is the consequence of social rules that oblige us to play roles or forbid us to express our sincere opinion or to have open discussions about many things. It is communication that is using allusions instead of naming the terms.
5. Actions: Actions can potentially transmit messages that can be a substitute for verbal communication. Action-transmitted messages represent an independent communication channel.
6. Non-actions (discounting): One cannot do nothing because "doing nothing" is also an action. Even if somebody is doing nothing, he or she is staying, waiting, sleeping, and so on. One cannot *not* communicate.

Although these mechanisms exist independently of non-verbally transmitted covert messages, in most cases, covert messages transmitted by verbal and action mechanisms are accompanied and reinforced by non-verbal signals.

3.3 Furthermore

3.3.1 Projection and communication

In the book *TA after Berne* (Barnes, 1977), Vann Joines explores the boundaries of Berne's thinking. He argues for an integrated view of transactions in which the complex relationship between the intrapsychic, interpersonal, and systemic dimensions of reality are kept in mind. He hereby makes use of the psychoanalytic concept of "projection". People often have the illusion of being in contact with the other, while communication actually takes place between the projected archaic ego states of those involved.

Each person sees the other and reality through the lens of their own frame of reference built up during the course of his life. Without being aware of it, you often relive early childhood experiences which you project on the other. When someone is aware of these projections he may occasionally stop and ask himself, "Am I reacting to the effect that the other is intending to have on me, or am I reacting to what I am imagining as their intention? Am I hearing the intention of the other or am I listening to the whispers of my script?"

> When she saw on the screen of her mobile phone that her boss was trying to reach her, she hesitated to accept the call. She also often delayed reading and responding to his emails. "What is going on with me?" she wondered. Whenever her boss spoke to her, she noticed that she was startled. She tried to reassure herself by thinking that he often approached her rather directly and unexpectedly. He would then air his opinion, before he had properly informed himself of the facts. But was this a reason to be so jumpy in her response? After all, she was no longer a child! It seemed as if she had difficulty seeing the man as he really was. One day, when she showed her sister a picture made during a business trip, the sister exclaimed, "Gosh, your boss looks so much like our Dad." Suddenly, all the pieces of the puzzle fell into place. She was feeling like the ten year old who could never do well enough.

3.3.2 Transference, countertransference, and projection

> After the death of their mother, the four adult children are together to divide the inheritance. In no time, there is a tense, irritable mood and everyone falls back into the old family patterns. Yvonne, the eldest, begins putting things in order and concerning herself with the others. Martin already starts collecting the things he wants to have. Vincent is not all there and plays with his phone. Liesbeth, the youngest, acts the clown and tries to break the tension.

During childhood, the ego states are filled with experiences acquired from relationships within the family, extended family, and the larger social environment. The patterns learned in this time often influence subsequent friendships, romantic relationships, and social and peer contacts. You think you are open to others, but often you repeat the early relationships you had with your parents, siblings, and other important people from your past. This mechanism of projection plays a role in all relationships, and is a source of love and attraction on the one hand and of conflict and tension on the other. The analysis of the ego states and transactions can help to maintain good communication and smooth out rough communication patterns.

Projection is the mechanism by which the complex psychoanalytic phenomena of transference and countertransference take place. Within TA, we describe transference as the repetition of early relationships (often with parents and significant others) in the relationship with professionals such as teachers, trainers/coaches, therapists, or managers. Usually it involves Child–Parent transactions.

Countertransference is both the response of the professional to the transference of the other (often Parent–Child transactions) as well as her own repetition of early relationships in the relationship with the other (this can also be Parent–Child, but also Child-Child or Child–Parent). It may be that a teacher, given her past, needs the care of the pupil just as much as the pupil needs that of the teacher.

In their book *Co-creative Transactional Analysis* (2014) Tudor and Summers propose to use the word "co-transference" instead of either transference or countertransference. With "co-transference" they describe the psychological field, co-created by the archaic or introjected ego states of both the therapist and the client. In their view, co-transference is created and perpetuated by the input of both client and therapist who create a dyad which is a repetition of relationships from the past of either of them. Both therapist and client experience an intrapsychic conflict or impasse which is projected onto the other. In this way the internal conflict gets enacted in an external relationship (p. 205). The therapist works in a partnership with the client, offers corrective experiences, is active engaged in a reciprocal and mutual relationship with the client, and acknowledges the place of the external world in therapy. The therapist works with what is present and is aware of the influence of the past in the present. The aim of the therapy is to expand the neopsychic functioning of the client or, in other words, the integrating Adult of the client.

Transference and countertransference are encountered everywhere and often form an explanation for phenomena which are difficult to understand. Why, for instance, does someone submit herself to be a secretary for a manager who barely sees or appreciates what she does for him? Why does a man persist in an ugly divorce battle, preferring to spend thousands of dollars on lawyers than in making sure his ex-wife is financially secure?

The analysis of processes of transference and countertransference is one of the main "active ingredients' of coaching, counselling and therapy, where it is one of the main "active ingredients". By eliciting the client's feelings of transference, the professional can better understand what deficits or neglected elements are present within the client's Child ego state. This may contribute to the empathy the professional can feel for the client.

Likewise, the coach, counsellor, or therapist can use her countertransference (for example wanting to care for the client or be cared for by the client, or to be admired by the client or secretly admiring the client) in order to better understand the client or to help him to develop further. If coaches, counsellors, and therapists, as well as teachers, trainers, and managers, are not aware of how much they need the client for their own unmet needs, this can be detrimental to efficacy and professionalism. Many clients—and this also applies to students, supervisees, and employees—effortlessly feel the needs of others and tend to offer their care or concern, often at their own expense.

Richard Erskine (2005) believes that transference is not driven by the need for repetition, but by the hope that things will be different or better this time. The employee who has a distrustful and suspicious attitude towards life may adjust the image of himself, others, and the world in which he lives in the here and now, based on the positive experiences gained from a highly reliable leader. In this way, the here and now continues to offer the opportunity to create distance between origin and future.

Berne emphasised that the goal of psychotherapy is "the decontamination of the Adult". However, for some clients, this is not sufficient. For them, it is also necessary to disentangle the Child ("deconfusion of the Child"). In the latter situation, the therapist allows herself to be "used" by the client, to some extent; a "reparative" relationship is initiated whereby the client can experience and process old, rejected feelings (Cornell & Hargaden, 2005; Hargaden & Sills, 2002). The client projects feelings and experiences onto the therapist, in the hope that the therapist can transform these feelings and can give them back in a form that is now manageable.

Early experiences in school can lead to ongoing transferential relationships occurring in any learning situation in adulthood. Children enter school having already made some decisions about how they relate to others and either adapt, reinforce, or revise these through their encounters with teachers and pupils. Teachers may do this too! So the scene is set for transference and countertransference as we recreate early symbiotic relationships. Later, as students or adult learners people may project onto their tutors unconscious (or semi-conscious) beliefs and assumptions originating in their school experience: learning is hard work, I never was any good at maths, school was boring, Teachers are out to get you; or, alternatively: teachers look after you, schooldays are the best days of your life; or, from the part of teachers: you have to be strict, they won't like me if I give them too much homework. Aware teachers and educators at all stages will address the potential symbiotic learning relationship by encouraging thinking and refusing invitations to "learn it for me" or censure.

Awareness also is the key tool to help a manager to detect transferential invitations from his employees. If he is also aware of his own possible countertransferential responses, he has the opportunity to promote autonomous behaviour, instead of creating a symbiotic chain (Holdeman, 1989) on the shop floor over and over again. Symbiosis occurs between two people who are not fully utilising all of their ego state possibilities. In the symbiotic chain the manager communicates from Parent mostly, while the employee uses his Child ego state most of the time. Transference often is the mechanism that starts this ineffective, growth-preventing pattern. The manager and/or the employee both project beliefs onto each other originating from their experiences with the relationships in their family of origin—"If I don't tell them, it won't happen" or "I'm not supposed to have too much ideas of my own"—relationship in their family of origin.

3.3.3 Relational TA

An exciting development within TA in recent years is that of relational transactional analysis (Cornell & Hargaden, 2005; Hargaden & Sills, 2002). In this approach, much emphasis is placed on handling transference and countertransference. Although Berne already stated in 1960 that the quality of the therapeutic relationship is crucial to the success of psychotherapy, he did not develop this issue further.

Moreover, he dealt with a different type of client than do contemporary therapists (more anxious and neurotic rather than those suffering from addictions and personality disorders). In the 1960s many people sought help because they felt constrained by the demands of their script. It was often sufficient to decontaminate their Adult, so that they could clearly distinguish between their wants and desires on the one hand, and their responsibilities and moral standards on the other, and thereby make informed choices. Berne preferred to work cognitively with clients, to help them make conscious choices.

However, he indicated that decontamination was not sufficient for a number of clients. In these cases, decontamination should be followed by deconfusion; the disentanglement of the Child ego state from the emotional beliefs and forces of the past. This process examines which early (sometimes preverbal) needs have been insufficiently met or even damaged. Here, the quality of the therapeutic relationship and especially understanding the language of the unconscious is essential. The therapist works with her and the client's images, fantasies, and feelings which are called up during the transference relationship.

Good teachers or coaches will not knowingly invite regression, but will sometimes repair the student's or client's deficits by their attitude and approach. De Haan (2008) is of the opinion that relational coaching is about looking at the relationship between coach and coachee from the perspective of the coachee. In developing that relationship, the issue is not so much what the coach says or does. It is much more about how the coachee experiences and values the relationship.

The relational educator becomes engaged in and affected by the learning rather than being a detached, unchanging director of the process. The capacity for personal contact, connectedness, playfulness, openness, authenticity, vulnerability, and self-awareness becomes part of the description of an effective teacher, along with the ability to hold authority while maintaining an "equal but asymmetric" relationship with learners. The teacher is someone who creates a facilitating environment and is able to stand back and let the learning happen without imposing herself but nevertheless remains totally engaged.

3.3.4 The alleged simplicity of TA

Anyone who mentioned in the 1970s that they worked with concepts from TA, would often be told that TA has far too simple a view of the complex reality of humankind. To the allegation that TA oversimplifies the view of things, Berne always answered "I'd rather over-simplify things than over-complexify them!" The global bestsellers that put TA on the map, such as Berne's *Games People Play* (1964) and Thomas Harris's *I'm OK–You're OK* (1967), paved the way for the many psychology books for the layman which have since appeared. Now if you walk into a bookshop or visit an internet bookshop, you can choose from innumerable publications that make insights from the behavioural sciences understandable for the interested layman using accessible language. TA has the honour of being a forerunner in this development. The professionals (the medical establishment of psychiatrists and psychotherapists) had to get used to the fact that their field of expertise had been made accessible to lay people who wanted to understand more of themselves, others, and the world in which they lived and worked. In those years, TA was accused of popularising psychological insight too much, being so-called pop-psychology. These reproaches sometimes still echo today. Those who truly dig into what TA has developed in the decades since Berne and Harris, both theoretically and practically, know better. While Berne was best known for *Games People Play*, several of his other books, including *Transactional Analysis in Psychotherapy* and *Principles of Group Treatment*, offer serious perspectives on the nature of psychotherapy and human development. The *Transactional Analysis Journal* has been in publication for more than forty years, devoted to exploring and expanding transactional analysis theory and techniques and deepening the interface with other theoretical models. The four decades since the books that "popularised" TA have seen the publication of many TA texts within the psychotherapy, counselling, educational, and organisational fields of application. It was part of Berne's vision that TA would find practical applications in the places where people actually live, learn, and work; the development of TA in the fields beyond psychotherapy has been the actualisation of Berne's vision.

Those who work with TA must, of course, be careful not to discount the complexity of personality, the complexity of intrapsychic reality, and the often ambiguous nature of interpersonal communication. On the other hand, one needs so-called "complexity reducers" in order to make the complex reality of living and working manageable. To find one's way in a certain area, after all, it helps if one has a map—as long as one realises that the main aim of models such as that of the ego states and transactions is to reduce the complexity of reality to a more orderly and transparent area.

3.4. Related theories

3.4.1. Watzlawick and colleagues

A groundbreaking book about interpersonal communication is *Pragmatics of Human Communication*, by Watzlawick, Beavin, and Jackson (1967). The authors, affiliated to the Mental Research Institute in Palo Alto, California, investigated fundamental characteristics of interpersonal communication. One of their central arguments is that it is impossible *not* to communicate. Additionally: all behaviour is communication.

By applying the principles of cybernetics, such as homeostasis and feedback, to interpersonal systems, the authors made clear that "disturbed behaviour" sometimes functions to maintain system stability. A marijuana-smoking and alcohol-drinking adolescent acts as a lightning conductor for his arguing parents who forget their own problems in order to deal with his.

In healthy, spontaneous relationships, it is usually not necessary to articulate the psychological goings on of a relationship. Conversely, "sick" relations are characterised by a constant struggle regarding the nature of the relationship, while the actual content of the communication becomes increasingly irrelevant. Watzlawick and colleagues were the first to make a clear distinction between the content and the relationship level. They unravelled how a poor distinction between these levels can lead to paradoxes, impasses, and ambiguities. A sign in a restaurant that says "If you think our waiters are rude, talk with our manager" can be understood in at least two very different ways: the manager is the person to whom you can voice your complaints or the manager is himself the superlative of rudeness. In addition, communication problems often involve punctuation problems. Does the woman complain because the man is hiding behind his newspaper, or does he hide himself because she complains so much? Circular thinking (at a given moment there is no cause or effect, but constant interaction) helps to break the discussion about punctuation. Watzlawick and his colleagues argue, like Berne, that the relation at the psychological level, is more important than the content at the social level.

Because communication often takes place in a series or a pattern, each behaviour is simultaneously stimulus, response, and reinforcement. This allows participants in communication to use a different punctuation. The rat may think, "I have trained my researcher, every time I press the lever, he gives me food." Or, the married couple who argue for years about the fact that he retreats as the only possible defence against her nagging (according to him), while she claims that she only nags because he is always so passive. This is how rigid patterns of transactions arise, whereby both partners communicate mainly from the Parent or the Child, and end up playing games instead of becoming intimate. Disagreement over meaning in a series of events lies at the root of much conflict in human relations. Only when people succeed in communicating about the patterns that each of them sees in the interaction (meta-communication), can change take place.

Communication theory summarises a symptom as a non-verbal message: I am not to blame as the one who doesn't act, for it is something that is beyond my power: it's my nerves, my illness, my poor eyes, alcohol, education, the communists, or my wife.

Change is possible if people are willing to take responsibility for their symptoms, and to see that they themselves have a stake in their disease, the education of their children, or the relationship with their partner. In systems theory (see for instance, Minuchin, 1974; Willi, 2005) it has been explained how interactions within families or couples can strengthen each other in a destructive way, but can also be reshaped to lead to positive communication.

3.4.2. Solution focused approach

A recent approach, which makes clear communication, a respectful approach, and especially problem solving a priority, is the solution focused method. Berne's aim of making therapy as short as possible and to focus on healing and change, instead of remaining stuck in the analysis of the obstacles to change, is clearly elaborated in the solution focused method.

> Suppose you go to a restaurant and you are very hungry. After waiting a while, the waiter arrives and introduces himself. Then he begins to ask you how hungry you are, why you are so hungry, how long you've been hungry, if you also used to be hungry before, what role hunger played in the family home, and which disadvantages and, possibly also, which benefits hunger has. If you then, even hungrier, ask whether you can finally order, the waiter asks that you first fill out some questionnaires about hunger (and perhaps about other matters that are important to the waiter). After all this, you then get presented with a meal which you do not choose yourself, but which the waiter says is good for you and has also helped other hungry people. What are the chances that you will leave this restaurant satisfied? (Bannink, 2006, p. 11; translated for this edition).

This restaurant parody is unfortunately applicable in many mental health institutions, but may also be recognisable in education and in organisations: it is not the wish of the customer and the solution to the problem that are paramount, but a detailed exploration of the problem, establishing a diagnosis, and prescribing a treatment by an expert.

The solution focused approach sees the problem as a challenge, offers hope as an important contribution to success, and places the vision of the client in a central position. The role of the professional is primarily to assist in finding solutions, and a small change is often enough to change the course of the client's life. The focus is on the future. Solution focused questions include:

- "Has there been any improvement between registering for therapy and the first meeting? If so, tell me."

- "Can you find exceptions to the problem described, situations where the problem did not occur or was less severe? If so, tell me."
- "Is it possible to formulate a hypothetical solution: in behavioural terms, can you describe what would be different if the problem were (adequately) resolved?"
- And the miracle question: "Imagine that you wake up in the morning and a miracle has happened: your problem is solved! What would be the first sign that this has happened? And how would others notice that the problem had been solved?"

The solution focused approach is often short-term and seen as cost-effective. And because the client is "put to work", this approach can also prevent overload or burnout for the professional (Bannink, 2006; de Shazer, 1985).

References

Bannink, F. (2006). *Oplossingsgerichte vragen. Handboek oplossingsgerichte gespreksvoering.* (Solution-focused questions. Comprehensive Textbook of Solution-focused Therapy.) Amsterdam: Pearson.
Berne, E. (1961). *Transactional Analysis in Psychotherapy.* New York: Grove Press.
Berne, E. (1964). *Games People Play.* New York: Grove Press.
Buda, B. (1988). A közvetlen emberi kommunikáció szabályszerűségei (The regularities of direct human communication) [electronic version]. Magyar Elektronikus Könyvtár [web page]. Retrieved 1 November 2005 from http://mek.oszk.hu/02000/02009/02009.htm.
Burgoon, J., Buller, D., & Woodall, J. (1996). *Non-Verbal Communication: The Unspoken Dialogue.* New York: McGraw-Hill.
Cornell, W. F., & Hargaden, H. (Eds.) (2005). *From Transactions to Relations.* Chipping Norton, UK: Haddon Press.
Erskine, R. (2005). Transference and transactions. In: W. F. Cornell & H. Hargaden (Eds.), *From Transactions to Relations* (pp. 75–96). Chipping Norton, UK: Haddon Press.
Haan, E. de (2008). *Relational Coaching. Journeys towards Mastering One-To-One Learning.* Chichester, UK: John Wiley & Sons.
Hargaden, H., & Sills, C. (2002). *Transactional Analysis. A Relational Perspective.* Hove, UK: Brunner-Routledge.
Harris, T. A. (1967). *I'm OK–You're OK.* New York: Harper & Row.
Holdeman, Q. L. (1989). The symbiotic chain. *Transactional Analysis Journal, 19*(3): 137–140.
Joines, V. (1977). An integrated systems perspective. In: G. Barnes (Ed.), *Transactional Analysis after Berne* (pp. 257–272). New York: Harper & Row.
Karpman, S. (1971). Options. *Transactional Analysis Journal, 1*(1): 79–87.
McCormick, P. (1977). *Social Transactions.* San Francisco, CA: Transactional Publications.
Mehrabian, A. (1971). *Silent Messages.* Belmont, CA: Wadsworth.
Minuchin, S. (1974). *Families and Family Therapy.* Cambridge, MA: Harvard University Press.
Shazer, S. de (1985). *Keys to Solution in Brief Therapy.* New York: W. W. Norton.
Tudor, K., & Summers, G. (2014). *Co-creative Transactional Analysis.* London: Karnac.
Vandra, A. (2009). Mechanisms for transmission of ulterior transactions. *Transactional Analysis Journal, 39*(1): 46–60.

Watzlawick, P., Beavin, J. H., & Jackson, D. D. (1967). *Pragmatics of Human Communication.* New York: W. W. Norton.

Widdowson, M. (2008). Metacommunicative transactions. *Transactional Analysis Journal, 38*(1): 58–71.

Willi, J. (2005). *Couples in Collusion.* Northvale, NJ: Jason Aronson.

Woollams, S., & Brown, M. (1978). *Transactional Analysis.* Ann Arbor, MI: Huron Valley Press.

CHAPTER FOUR

Games

4.1　Basic theory
    4.1.1　Introduction
    4.1.2　The game prototype
    4.1.3　The drama triangle
    4.1.4　Degrees of games
    4.1.5　Why play games?
    4.1.6　Instead of a game?
    4.1.7　Games and enactment
    4.1.8　Assertiveness
    4.1.9　The compassion triangle
    4.1.10　The role of the bystander
4.2　Further theory
    4.2.1　Berne and games people play
    4.2.2　Games categorised according to the switch
    4.2.3　Substitute feelings
    4.2.4　Type 1 and type 2
4.3　Furthermore
    4.3.1　Fairy tales, stories, and the drama triangle
    4.3.2　Patterns of substitute feelings
    4.3.3　Games and addictions
    4.3.4　Games in the classroom
    4.3.5　Games in teams and organisations
4.4　Related theories
    4.4.1　Cognitive behavioural therapy
    4.4.2　Emotionally focused therapy
    4.4.3　The neglected organisation
References

Chapter Two described the need to give structure to time as one of our three basic "hungers". One of the six ways of structuring time is the psychological game. A game involves transactions between people whereby there is a difference between the overt social and the covert psychological level. A game is characterised by repetitive transaction and stroke patterns, a predictable course of development, an ulterior motive, and ultimately a switch in the actual meaning of the transactions. Eric Berne described these patterns in the book that gave TA its worldwide recognition. This book, which mainly focuses on examining ineffective communication, was entitled *Games People Play*. Since its publication, TA uses the term "psychological game" to examine and have a (positive) influence on the "fuss" that goes on between partners, colleagues, friends, parents, and children, between managers and employees as well as between therapists and their clients. The point of every game is that all participants seek to have their beliefs—about themselves, about others and about the world in which they live—reinforced. Game analysis helps to break down the (often painful) "I-told-you-so" tendencies.

4.1   Basic theory

4.1.1   Introduction

> Anna has a new job and therefore moves to another place of residence. She feels uncomfortable in the new environment where she knows no one. She reaches out to her colleagues, but this doesn't seem to be working. Most have a family, are busy, or do not seem to have much need for social contact. During the lunch break she has a conversation with Jamie, one of her colleagues. She says she often feels alone at weekends. Jamie feels some compassion for his young colleague's situation and then realises that he and his wife sometimes find it difficult to find a babysitter when they go out on the weekends.
>
> Would Anna like to do that on occasion? A few weeks later, Jamie and his wife want to go out for the night and he asks if Anna is busy the next Saturday. She isn't and so he asks her if she would like to babysit for them that night. There is a short silence until Anna responds, annoyed, "I'm not a high school student who you can just ask to babysit!" Jamie feels put in his place, and he is confused and angry. He only wanted to help her. And Anna is offended and indignant. She expected him to invite her for dinner to introduce his new colleague to his wife, and now he asked her as a babysitter! Does she really give such a pathetic impression?

The situation between Anna and her colleague is an example of a game such as those that can take place in daily life between partners, colleagues, and friends, between parents and children, between managers and their employees, and between therapists and their clients. Games have a number of characteristics (Stewart & Joines, 1996).

1. Repetition. Everyone plays an habitual game over and over again. The players and circumstances may differ, but the pattern remains the same.
2. Beyond Adult consciousness. Games are played beyond Adult consciousness. Only in the final stage, after the switch, people sometimes wonder what is taking place and why the same thing always seems to happen to them. Often they do not realise what their own role is in these events.

3. Ulterior motives. Games always involve two levels of communication, one at the overt level, the other being secret or obscured from direct communication. It is the ulterior, hidden message that is the real communication. When the ulterior message emerges, one or both "players" end up feeling confused or upset.

People always find others who are willing to play their familiar psychological game with them. It seems as if everyone is wearing a T-shirt bearing the logo of his or her game-invitation. On the front is the overt text and on the back, the secret message. For example, a social worker always gets clients who seem to ask for help, but end up not accepting it. This T-shirt says "I'll help everyone" on the front, and "From the frying pan into the fire" on the back.

The woman who continues to meet men who try to seduce her at first but then treat her like rubbish later, wears a T-shirt which says "I'm a great woman" on the front, and "Until you get to know me better … I'm a huge disappointment" on the back. The manager has one that says "We will work together to achieve success" on the front and on the back "And then I'm going to run off with the profit". As discussed in Chapter Two, games are a form of structuring time with a high level of pseudo-intimacy, with a fixed course of development and a predictable outcome, whereby players end up feeling badly about themselves or each other.

4.1.2   The game prototype

Berne (1961) states that the most common game in groups and organisations is the "Why don't you do …?"—"Yes, but" game. It is a social game with an unlimited number of participants. One of the players presents a seemingly insoluble problem and the other players contribute solutions under the motto "Why don't you …?" to which another player responds with "Yes, but". An experienced "Yes, but" player can withstand a whole group or a whole team until everyone gives up and the player "wins". "Winning" in this case means being proven right about one's unconscious belief that this problem (and probably most others) has no solution.

It seems as if the one playing "Yes, but" is looking for an Adult solution to a problem. However, this only applies to the social, overt level. On a deeper psychological level, a number of transactions are taking place that are a repetition of an earlier situation in which a frightened child searched in vain for reassurance from a parental figure. Eventually the player "proves" that no one can help him: "I told you so!" The motto of this game is "The parent (in the here and now this can be the manager, partner, therapist, or teacher) can never help me."

Just like chess or football, a psychological game adheres to certain rules that ensure that all follows a predictable course. Each game, according to Berne, contains the following formula:

Con + Gimmick = Response => Switch => Cross-up => Pay-off (C + G = R => S => X => P)

Take the game of "Schlemiel", for example, whereby the player constantly does or says awkward things, and the players forgive him after the word "sorry". Until the cup is full.

> Con: Albert spills coffee on the white tablecloth of his hostess Lydia.
> Gimmick: Lydia hides her annoyance and smiles faintly as Albert says "Oh, sorry".
> Response: this game can last a night, but also weeks, months, or years, in which Albert forgets appointments, causes a small fire during a barbecue, loses a borrowed book, and is forgiven each time by Lydia, who keeps herself under control with difficulty. Both derive sufficient strokes from the situation: Albert can vent his childlike aggression and receives forgiveness. Lydia feels mature and sensible. Until a switch occurs.
> Switch: Albert goes to visit Lydia but has had too much alcohol and accidentally drives over her dog. For Lydia, this is inexcusable. Finally she is openly furious. She doesn't only release her anger concerning this incident, but also about all the other incidents with Albert, by saying: "I've had it with you".
> Cross-up: Albert is confused. So far, Lydia has always forgiven him, but now, all of a sudden, not any more? Lydia also feels confused about the wave of pent-up anger that she suddenly feels.
> Pay-off: Eventually both withdraw into what seems to be their repetitive bad feeling, Lydia in a sense of anger and Albert in a "feeling" of being misunderstood and unjustly accused.

As long as the switch has not occurred, the function of the game is the preservation of the familiar frame of reference. The world remains predictable and familiar. In this way, the psychological balance is preserved. In the example, Albert is the irresponsible, charming buffoon and Lydia has the comfortable position of being the sensible, forgiving friend.

After the switch, and the pay-off, intense feelings are temporarily laid bare: anger, frustration, triumph, inferiority, and despair. Suddenly, the theme of one's life can be made clear. For Albert, this theme is making a mess of things until everyone gives up on him. For Lydia, this theme is enjoying the lonely ivory tower of her anger. With any pay-off of a game, your life plan (script) develops further and the answer to the question of how your life will end becomes clearer. More on this follows in Chapter Five on script.

Hine (1990) drew attention to the bilateral nature of games: both partners carry responsibility for the game and have their own separate intrapsychic reasons for the game which interlock with the reasons of the other and leads to the ongoing and cumulative nature of games.

4.1.3 The drama triangle

Stephen Karpman (1968) developed a diagram called the drama triangle as another way of understanding the dynamics of games. The drama triangle makes a kind of innate sense and has become widely popular (Figure 4.1). Karpman argues that people always take on one of the following three roles in a game: Rescuer, Persecutor, or Victim, and that a role change occurs at the switch. For example, in a game, when in a situation of providing care or help, the client may assume the role of Victim and the caregiver the role of Rescuer. This may last some time (weeks, months, or years) until a switch occurs. The client is unhappy with the care offered and changes from Victim to Persecutor. The bewildered caregiver suddenly changes from Rescuer to Victim.

The Persecutor knows everything better than everyone else, belittles others, and considers them as inferior, not OK. The Persecutor wants to score and discounts the value and dignity of others.

The Rescuer also sees others as inferior, as not OK, and offers assistance from a position of superiority. The Rescuer seeks glorification for helping, discounts the ability of others to think for themselves and act independently, and overestimates her own capabilities.

The Victim sees himself as inferior and incompetent, not OK, and seeks either a Rescuer or a Persecutor. The Victim wants attention, fails to recognise his own competence, and sees himself as someone who deserves rejection or needs the help of others to make decisions or to act.

If we analyse the game "Why don't you?"—"Yes, but" with the drama triangle, one player starts as the Victim looking for a Rescuer. For a while this can yield complementary transactions, whereby the Rescuer makes all kinds of suggestions, which the Victim routinely rejects. Until one of the two has had enough, and this is the moment of the "switch" when the roles change. The Rescuer switches to the Persecutor: "You don't want to be helped at all," or the Victim reproaches the Rescuer: "Oh, you are no help at all." In the first case, the Victim remains the Victim and at most changes the tone of expression from sad and submissive to belittled and ashamed. In the second case, the original Rescuer becomes the Victim after the switch. In either case, the switch "lets the cat out of the bag" and it becomes clear what was written on the back of the T-shirt. The covert level of the previous transactions is revealed. This initially provides confusion for all of the players. After some time, however, short or long, the players resume their original positions. The Victim goes in search of a new Rescuer (or starts a second round with the same person), and the Rescuer gathers herself and goes in search of new Victims (or responds again to the game invitation of the same Victim).

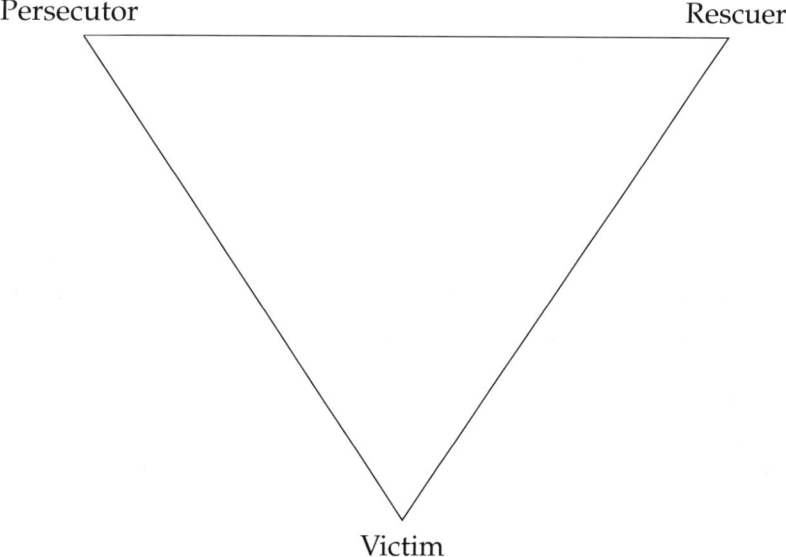

Figure 4.1. Drama triangle.

4.1.4 Degrees of games

The degree to which people play games may differ.

- First degree games: These games are socially acceptable. They provide a juicy story at the pub, at the kitchen table, or around the coffee machine at work.
- Second degree games: The consequences are such that not everyone can be allowed to know about them. They involve intense feelings such as shame, depression, resentment, sadness, or anger.
- Third degree games: These games are serious and can end up in the hospital, the courtroom, or the morgue. The emotions run so high that the game degenerates into explosions of anger, helplessness, or sadness, abuse, formal charges, suicide attempts, manslaughter, or murder.

Sometimes acts of individual people have a great influence on world events, for instance Hitler on the Second World War, or the banker Madoff on the credit crisis. These too, could be called a game, but a game "hors catégorie", a game that goes beyond the normal categories.

People often continue playing their games at the same level and merely look for different players over the course of time. Sometimes games degenerate and gradually slide from first degree to third degree games. Gerben Hellinga, a Dutch psychiatrist, applied the theory of game-levels to diagnose personality disorders (1993). Instead of game, he uses the term "I-told-you-so-ism" (translated for this edition), and describes three steps of self-fulfilling prophecies, by which people fall in the hole they have dug themselves. Through selection, interpretation, and manipulation (SIM), people maintain their frame of reference. Selection is a mechanism everybody uses to prevent becoming crazy in the abundance of stimuli around us. Interpretation of stimuli is the next step which discloses more about our frame of reference and our earlier experiences. For example, if somebody broke into your house recently, you will react with more fear to strange noises in the first weeks after this event. Manipulation is a third step and means that unconsciously we are setting up familiar games and seduce others to play with us. In this way everybody creates his own SIM card to navigate through life. This SIM card helps us to affirm our opinions about ourselves, others, and the world: I told you so!

4.1.5 Why play games?

As stated earlier, children often learn not to openly ask for what they need or to say what is troubling them. For many people it is therefore threatening to show their vulnerability to others. It is safer and more predictable to receive strokes through games, with their fixed course and outcome. Initially these are positive, but ultimately negative. Moreover, stroke exchanges in games are intense and provide a lot of attention. By the end of the game people confirm their existential position. For example: "My son is so difficult, I'm a good mother!" (+/−). Or: "It's probably my fault. Other mothers would know better what to do with such a son" (−/+). Or: "My son is so difficult, and that's my fault" (−/−).

In a game we use outdated strategies, which may have proved useful in childhood (then and there), but are no longer effective in the here and now. If a child grows up in a family where everyone responds to setbacks with rage or by falling ill, then this will be the frame of reference by which he will behave as an adult. It may be that he chooses the role of the Rescuer and becomes a doctor who is at patients' beck and call day and night. Or he chooses the role of Victim and calls in sick when there are conflicts at work. The role of Persecutor means that he becomes angry at the world and blames the environment for every misfortune in life.

The analysis of games that people play in the present can reveal what beliefs from childhood they still carry around with them now, and how they use these games to justify their current behaviour. To an outside observer, a game often appears to be both illogical and obviously unproductive. But from the inside, games provide important, compelling behaviours that recreate early family dynamics. So these ulterior communication patterns reflect a fundamental reality within the Child ego state, which can be far more compelling than Adult reason. Games often serve as important defences against the failures, shame, and pains of childhood. Game analysis is an effort to bring Adult awareness and choice into the motivations of the Child, which are typically operating out of awareness. According to Berne (1961), games have biological, psychological, social, and existential benefits (see section 4.2.1 in this chapter). The biggest advantage is probably that games keep relationships predictable, allowing one to avoid the vulnerability and often threatening time structure of intimacy (Cornell, 2009). People play a game out of fear of a genuine encounter.

4.1.6 Instead of a game?

Because games are a way of structuring time and yield intensive stokes, it is not easy to stop playing them. Many people will hang onto their trusted games. A game is, paradoxically, both an approach to intimacy and a way to avoid it. If the "threat" of intimacy becomes real, you can always get a game going. It is often fear for the genuine encounter that makes people grasp for a game. For anyone who wants to investigate this, consider what happened "just before the quarrel broke out" or "just before the conflict escalated". Very often you will discover that there was indeed a threat of intimacy. The fear of letting someone know what is really going on, what you really need, or what you would really like to say, takes over.

> Marian drives home after a tough working week. She hopes that Paul cleaned up the house and will welcome her home with a glass of wine. She has a lot to tell him. When she arrives home, Paul is still busy in the kitchen. Too bad, she thinks. She sits down on the couch and waits until Paul has finished in the kitchen and has time for her. The waiting lasts forever. Marian becomes irritated and frustrated. His hobby, cooking dinner, is once again more important than her story about her job. After twenty minutes on the couch, she stands up, strides into the kitchen, and shouts "There's no need anymore, you know ... you can keep your dinner!" This forms the beginning of a tumultuous weekend with many more game moments.

Essential for a good understanding of games, is to know that they are played unconsciously, without Adult involvement. Vann Joines (workshop TA conference Bilbao, 2011) has argued that those who have loaded their Adult ego state sufficiently (with psychic energy) always recognise a game invitation. Engaging your Adult is always necessary for you to be aware that a game is lying in wait and to determine how you can break through it. "What do I really need from the other person at this time?" is the question that can help in this process. Also engaging your Natural Child often keeps you from getting caught up in a game. Humour, a joke, and a smile ("Here we go again") often allow a game to stagnate, decline, or wane. The Adult and the (positive) Natural Child are two ego states that are not interested in the roles of the drama triangle. They are helpful in preventing or breaking through game behaviour.

An environment where there is room for authentic feelings and vulnerability provides the conditions for game-free communication. Thus, life itself offers opportunities for the correction and repair of previously learned inhibiting patterns. Sometimes people go into therapy or look for coaching or counselling to change persistent patterns. Even then there are ambivalent motives. On the one hand, they genuinely want to change, and on the other hand they are attached to the security of the familiar strokes and roles provided within the drama triangle.

It may therefore be the case that a client, through a game such as Wooden Leg or Millstone ("What can you expect from someone who has had such a messed-up childhood as me?") will try to keep things the way they are or were. This can lead to endless discussions trying to understand how all this came about, based on the illusion that only then things can change. TA is an active form of therapy. This means that the steps towards change are more important than the analysis of the problem. Analysis can always be done later.

In game analysis the first step towards change is what Berne called social control. The person recognises the bait or the weak spot and decides with the Adult to not get involved in the game. Immediately, the following questions will present themselves: "What then? How do I structure my time now, if I no longer use the roles of Victim, Rescuer, or Persecutor to relate to others? Am I capable of intimacy, of a genuine encounter?" Or, as Berne says in the title of one of his books: "What do you say after you say hello?" (1972).

If you no longer need games to interact with others, the Child is given the space to express itself in a more natural and constructive manner. Insight into how games function and what games you are sensitive to, gives you the opportunity to stop playing games. Ask yourself what cons you set and what your weaknesses are. The experience that it is more pleasant to be authentic with each other than to play games can also lead to behavioural change.

According to Dusay (1966), we can deal with games in five ways, with Adult awareness:

- Unmasking. This is the most common option. From your Adult ego state you make it clear that you do not want to play, but want to communicate in a different way.
- Ignoring. You can pretend not to hear the bait. You can start on something else, give a humorous reaction, walk away, and so on.
- Providing alternatives. Immediately address the underlying question and the authentic needs.
- Switch to a different time structure (for example, activity or intimacy). Determine with the other person what options he or she has for stroke exchanges.
- "Playing Along". This requires doing so with full Adult awareness. For example, someone asks you if you would like to visit. You know she has just moved and that there is a lot of clutter in the house. She would love it if you help out. But she doesn't ask you this directly. Since you have no problem helping, you enthusiastically agree to the invitation for coffee, knowing that you will be enlisted to unpack boxes. If you know from the beginning what's going

on, then no game is being played. Sometimes, however, you get involved in a game that is already well advanced. Then there is often no stopping it. Stopping is not an option. Letting the game play itself out is then the only way to go. The goal is then limiting the damage. In this case, refusing the pay-off is a great option!

When breaking out of a game, the following questions are important: "What did I not say? What did I keep to myself, which has begun to live a life of its own beneath the surface?" Learning to deal with uncertainty, openness, and vulnerability helps to considerably reduce the level of game playing in your life.

4.1.7 Games and enactment

Any reading of the contemporary TA literature will reveal that the term "game" rarely appears any more. Has the concept of games, once at the foundation of TA, actually disappeared? No, it has been gradually replaced by other ways of understanding the process that Berne saw as a primary mechanism of defence and of failure and frustration in many of our personal relationships. In the analysis of games as developed by Berne, the primary focus of attention for the therapist, counsellor, group leader, or consultant was on the external transactions between the "players" which could be diagrammed and then interpreted. Games were seen first and foremost as persistent patterns of defence in which people maintained high levels of psychological investment, even though the results were often negative.

Over the past two decades, the understanding of games has evolved—such that attention to "games" has not actually disappeared in transactional analysis, but the understanding and ways of intervening have significantly evolved. Models of transference and countertransference are now used with increasing frequency to describe the interpersonal patterns that Berne called games. From this perspective, there is a fundamental understanding that aspects of games are unconscious, and that "games" are forms of communication as well as defence. In the traditional model of game analysis, the therapist positioned herself outside the game process whenever possible so as to identify, diagram, and/or confront the game. Hargaden and Sills, as one example, summarise a more contemporary understanding of games this way: "The therapist was required to *play* the game and not to confront it at this stage of the therapy. … when the therapist allows himself to be moulded by the interpersonal pressure, and if he is able to observe the changes, this is a rich source of data about the patient's internal world" (2002, p. 80; italics in original).

Games, in other words, while defensive in their function, also provide important doors of understanding to the internal conflicts and vulnerabilities of the client, student, or supervisee. The way in which the professional listens to the game is of enormous importance to the levels of understanding that can unfold.

The concept of *enactment* (Gowling & Agar, 2011; Shadbolt, 2012; Stuthridge, 2012) has offered further developments in our understanding of games and their meanings. Central to the concept of enactment are those experiences either from the past or emergent in the present for which a person has no words. What is present in the room cannot be spoken, so the initial form of communication is action, that is, a way of being or a pattern of doing that exerts palpable pressure on the working relationship. What cannot be told in the moment is shown, done, enacted, and these enactments have powerful, usually unconscious impacts on the professional partner. Writing about the experiences of rupture and repair over the course of psychotherapy, Carole Shadbolt observes, "Whether we refer to ruptures as script, enactments, evidence of a co-created impasse, an interpersonal or co-created game or an existential reality, it is when rupture either bursts through dramatically into awareness or emerges half consciously that is at the heart of the therapeutic opportunity for change" (2012, p. 11). Transactional analysts have learned to listen to and understand games quite differently from the ways first proposed by Berne.

In the more traditional approaches to games, primary attention was paid to the behaviour and motivation of the "identified patient". In our more contemporary understandings of games and enactments, it can be rather difficult to say clearly who is the "patient". The professional's own vulnerabilities from the past or in the present are seen as contributing to the likelihood of games and enactments. The therapist has an ongoing responsibility to monitor her own emotional reactions and unconscious sensitivities. Jo Stuthridge has provided an eloquent summary:

> Enactments in therapy provide an opportunity to discover the lost parts of oneself for both client and therapist. When we remain stuck in these interpersonal fault lines, we risk reinforcing trauma and rigid script patterns. When we manage to haul ourselves out of these chasms, we create a more flexible script and new possibilities for intimacy. (2012, p. 249)

Game theory is alive and well in transactional analysis, although the concepts and meanings have changed and matured. A theme issue of the *Transactional Analysis Journal*, "Games and Enactments" (2015, pp. 41–42) is devoted to the current state of countertransference. Models of transference, countertransference, and enactment will be central concepts to that discussion.

4.1.8 Assertiveness

All positions in the drama triangle are at odds with the characteristics of assertive behaviour (De Graaf & Kunst, 2010). Assertiveness is based on:

- Respect for yourself.
- Respect for the other.
- Respect for the communication.

The chance that assertive people get caught up in a game is not so great. Assertive people are able to say what they feel, think, and want, in a way that respects the other's dignity. Assertive communication is positive, direct, connecting, and real. In the drama triangle, personal responsibility is avoided (in the role of Victim as well as Persecutor) or exaggerated (in the role of the Rescuer). Assertive behaviour takes on responsibility in an Adult way (Choy, 1990).

- Instead of Rescuing from the negative Nurturing Parent, you can offer your help from the positive Nurturing Parent. Use your own thoughts, feelings, and behaviours and do not fill in the blanks for the other.

- Instead of becoming the helpless Victim (the negative Adapted Child), you can say what you need. If you want something, ask for it and expect from others that they will ask for what they need (the positive Natural Child).
- Instead of Persecuting (the negative Structuring Parent), you can give an assertive response (the positive Structuring Parent). Express your needs and boundaries in a healthy way.

Although it seems logical to represent the alternative to the roles of the drama triangle also in the shape of a triangle, this is somewhat confusing. Karpman chose a triangle as a dynamic model, in which the changing of roles (the switch) is made clearly visible by placing the roles in the corners of a triangle. But for effective behaviour, this is different. It does not involve the dynamics of changing roles. The trick is to not allow yourself to be "lured" into any one of the corners. A good strategy is as follows: use your Adult, stand in the centre of the triangle, and feel how the corners "pull", then choose your own reaction.

By refusing the role of the Victim, the Rescuer, or the Persecutor, and by staying in the centre of the triangle, you take the "fun" out of a game invitation. From the centre, you make use of elements from all three corners: SP + assertive limit setting; NP + responsible caring and NC + the power of vulnerability. See Figure 4.2.

A powerful prevention against game behaviour is to ensure that your family, your circle of friends, or your company or organisation, has a healthy stroke climate. In *Climate Change in Organisations* (De Graaf & Levy, 2008) it says that:

> People need—in the workplace and elsewhere—to be taken note of. Being taken note of does not mean that you have to agree with what co-workers say or do. It does mean that, as a manager, you see and mention their input (which can appear in many, sometimes strange, disguises). A lot of withdrawal behaviour, frustration and cynicism—with all of its consequences—is rooted in the feeling of not mattering, of not knowing how to make a meaningful contribution. (translated for this edition)

Transactional analysis can help to gain insight into this phenomenon and provides tools to make a change for the better. In the preface of Claude Steiner's book (2009) Terry Berne (son of Eric Berne) states: "I have always thought that the aim of Transactional Analysis necessarily implied a vision beyond the establishment or search for individual well-being ... the basic paradigm of TA extends to an individual's entire circle of active contacts and everyday dealings with the world at large, including family, friends, acquaintances and co-workers."

4.1.9   The compassion triangle

Steve Karpman, the originator of the drama triangle, suggests in his book, *A Game Free Life* (2014), that a very rewarding way to avoid or stop game-playing is using the compassion triangle. The core of this compassion triangle is the use of empathy. Karpman suggests that by observing closely, we can notice that every player involved takes all the three roles in the drama triangle at the same time. This can become clear by asking questions like: if I am a Victim and feel trapped, how am I Rescuer and Persecutor too?; if the other person is a Rescuer, how is she a Victim and a Persecutor at the same time? Karpman gives some very

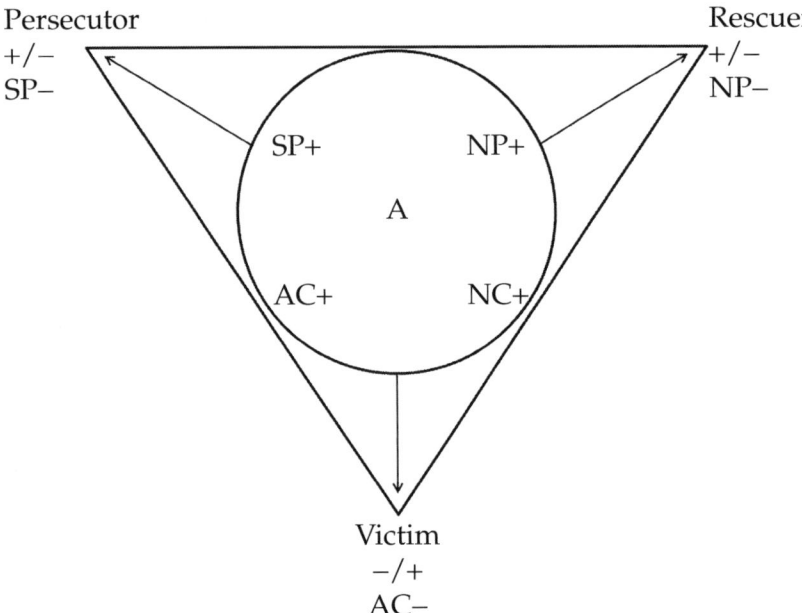

Figure 4.2. Assertive behaviour.

practical instructions about how to observe the other and the self from the perspective of the compassion triangle:

Starting with the other:
Observe the Victim, give sympathy, and say things like: I see that you feel hurt, trapped in a situation that seems unsolvable. I am really sorry!
Observe the Rescuer, give appreciation, and say things like: I know you are trying to help, but it doesn't seem to be working, so you will be left feeling unappreciated no matter what you try. Sorry about that. Thanks for trying to help out!
Observe the Persecutor, give feedback, and say things like: I can't handle the way you're talking and that frustrates me. I get confused and nasty sometimes. Sorry!

Looking at the self:
Having taken the role of Persecutor, apologise and say things like: I apologise for shouting when I can't think of anything else to do. I can see it scares you sometimes. I am really sorry about that!
Having taken the role of Victim, sympathise and say things like: I feel helpless and confused to handle you getting mad at me. Then I get stubborn and refuse to apologise. I am sorry!
Having taken the role of Rescuer, appreciate and say things like: I am really trying to make things better. That was my intention at least. Can we discuss what would be another way of helping out?

Working with the compassion triangle, all feelings from the six roles (Victim, Rescuer, and Persecutor for each person) get validation, not just one or none. The game stops. Intimacy becomes a possibility again.

4.1.10 The role of the Bystander

Clarkson (1987, 1996) argues for the expansion of the drama triangle and game analysis with the often unnoticed role of the Bystander.

The term "bystander behaviour" was coined in New York, where a young woman was murdered within sight and earshot of dozens of people, all of whom did nothing. A bystander is someone who stands to the side while others need help.

When people remain silent during a meeting, this does *not* mean that they have nothing to say. There may be many reasons why they do not participate in verbal conversation, very good ones at that! An inadequate reason is that someone has plenty to say outside the meeting room, but "chooses" not to participate in the conversation during the meeting. This kind of behaviour can render a system (a group or an organisation) weak and powerless. Many organisations have a long tradition of looking the other way, of members taking cover, playing hide and seek, looking for (and finding) scapegoats, and of misplaced office humour. These game patterns drain away the energy an organisation needs to achieve success and results.

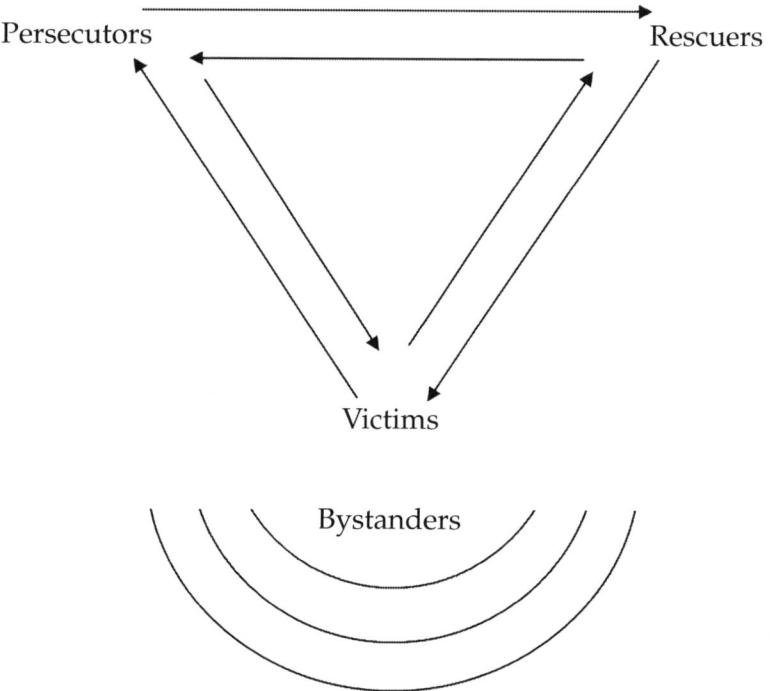

Figure 4.3. The role of the bystander.

Bystander behaviour can be recognised by the following characteristics:

- People are aware that something is going on.
- They do not take responsibility, either for change, or for maintaining the situation.
- They can flawlessly explain why they had no choice.
- They discount (this is an unconscious process) their ability to exert influence.

Bystanders often make use of the following slogans (Clarkson, 1996):

- It's not my problem.
- It is much more complicated than it seems.
- I don't have the whole picture.
- I do not want to burn my fingers.
- It's their own fault.
- Let sleeping dogs lie.
- I mind my own business.
- I just do what is asked of me.
- Neutrality is the best option.
- I can't make a difference anyway.
- The truth lies somewhere in the middle.
- I can only judge things from my own point of view.

Clarkson is not suggesting you poke your nose into every issue, let alone become a Rescuer. She does note, however, that you are already involved simply by being part of the group or system, whether you like it or not. You cannot *not* be involved. Even if you do nothing, you exert your influence, for good or bad, positive or negative. After all, you cannot not communicate. In this context, it is interesting to read what the psychoanalyst Viktor Frankl has to say. Frankl argues that people can always choose how they want to relate to what they experience. "It is the last of all human freedoms." Even Auschwitz and Dachau offered "every day, every hour, the opportunity to decide whether to surrender to the forces that threatened to rob you of your inner freedom" (Frankl, 1969, pp. 65–66).

Coming down off the audience platform has its advantages! On a personal level, it gives the satisfaction of grabbing the bull by the horns and putting your energy into addressing issues, instead of sleepless nights, bouts of worry, or developing ulcers and heart problems. By giving your energy to what the organisation or group represents, the organisation or group will gradually become stronger and more powerful. Organisations and groups benefit from employees and members who use their freedom and autonomy in order to contribute to the greater good of the organisation.

4.2   Further theory

4.2.1   Berne and games people play

To his own surprise, Berne became instantly famous in the United States with the publication of his book *Games People Play* in 1964, which sold more than five million copies. Many people recognised themselves in the descriptions of the various games. It was even fashionable for a time within TA to devise catchy or humorous names for as many games as possible.

In *TA in Psychotherapy* (1961), Berne already gave a first overview of games. He presented the story of a phobic woman who accused her husband of not allowing her to participate in any social or sporting activities (Figure 4.4). In the course of therapy, the man softened. She enrolled in swimming and dance classes. And guess what? She panicked in the pool, was terrified on the dance floor, and withdrew from both activities. Marriage to this dominant man and the game that developed within this marriage had provided her with a few benefits:

- Internally psychological: The game holds her convictions in place. She can blame him for not doing anything on her own, instead of facing her own fears directly.
- Externally psychological: Because of the game, she can avoid certain anxiety-causing situations which challenge her frame of reference. Moreover, she binds her husband to herself, since she is afraid to venture alone.
- Internally social: The mutual game between partners structures time and creates pseudo-intimacy. Her accusations give her power and control within their sex life.
- Externally social: She can fill her time with the game "If it weren't for you" with her friends and helpers. She can complain about her domineering, unreasonable husband. And she plays "If it weren't for you" with him. En passant, she teaches her children how this game is played.
- Biological: Games provide intensive strokes and are an effective antidote to feelings of loneliness and isolation. This is also the case for the woman in this example.
- Existential: She reaffirms her life position: −/+ or −/− (and sometimes +/−).

Not only does she look for a dominant husband, but he also selects a phobic woman. He also has his reasons for this:

- Internally psychological: He can express his "sadistic" impulses in this relationship.
- Externally psychological: He protects her from the evil outside world.
- Internally social: He avoids sexual intimacy.
- Externally social: He can complain to his friends and get the freedom to go his own way.
- Biological: He receives intensive strokes.
- Existential: The game reaffirms his life position: +/− (and sometimes −/+ and −/−).

The game analysis with the transaction diagram makes clear how the partners accuse each other on the social level, but protect each other on the psychological level.

On the social level:

- He (Parent): "You stay at home and take care of the household."
- She (Child): "If it weren't for you, I could do all sorts of things and have fun!"

On the psychological level:

- He (Child): "You must always be here when I get home. I'm terrified that you'll leave me."
- She (Child): "OK—if you'll help me avoid situations I'm afraid of."

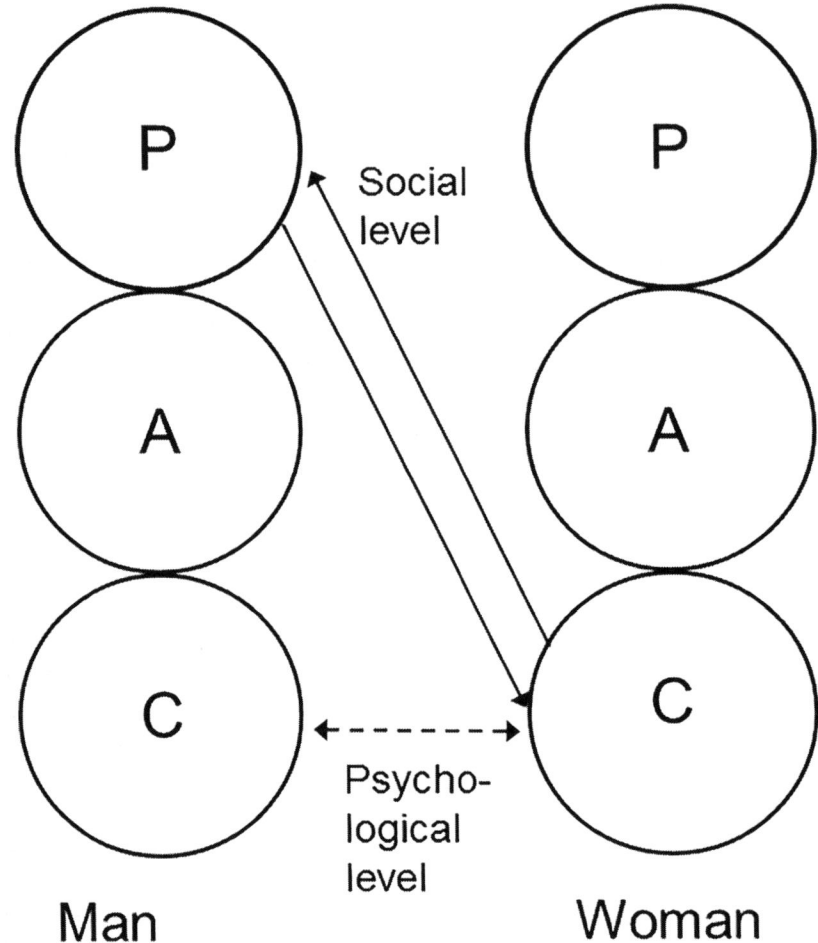

Figure 4.4. The game "If it weren't for you".

Since there is no crossed transaction, neither at the social nor psychological level, this game can go on endlessly, perhaps for a lifetime, as long as the hidden motive of "not facing fear" remains intact. If the complementary transactions are broken, for example, because one of them takes on a hobby and spends more time outside the house, or because the couple goes into therapy, the underlying fear is made explicit. It can then go in three directions: the couple takes refuge in the safety of avoidance, they both face their fears and their relationship acquires more depth and excitement, or one of them recoils and the other does not, with divorce as a possible consequence.

4.2.2 Games categorised according to the switch

It can be useful to describe games according to the type of switch that occurs.

- From the Persecutor to the Victim.

> Alma arrived in the Netherlands as a young Moroccan woman and has since had four children. She is very often angry, with her husband who earns so little, with her children who ask for too much attention, with the doctors who can't find the cause of her physical symptoms, and with Dutch society as a whole. If only she could return to Morocco. Then she would be able to enjoy a carefree old age. But now everything and everyone is making this impossible. Her husband lets himself be chastised and is afraid of her tantrums. When he finally qualifies for an early pension, he suggests they return to Morocco. He expects that Alma will perk up, but she suddenly changes like a leaf on a tree. She becomes frightened as a mouse and no longer dares to leave the house, let alone return to Morocco.

The game begins with an accusation. The wife complains to her husband that he is never at home, the employee complains to the manager that he is assigned too many tasks, the mother complains to her children that they prevent her from developing. The covert, unconscious motive of the player is not to change the situation, but rather to reinforce the internal belief that the player is not entitled to a caring partner, a manageable set of tasks, or personal development. So when the husband takes more time off from work and suggests taking dancing lessons together, his wife suddenly comes up with all sorts of reasons why it's not possible, until finally her husband gets angry and switches from Victim to Persecutor and the wife finds herself switching from the role of Persecutor to Victim. Or the supervisor blames his employee for a lack of effort, and the employee calls in sick. The children become teenagers and rebel against their overprotective mother. And instead of spending more time on her hobbies, the mother lies awake at night, anxiously waiting for her children to arrive home safely. And so the Persecutor switches to the role of Victim, thus proving that he or she has failed or doesn't deserve to be rejected.

- From Victim to Persecutor.

    In the game "Yes, but" someone first asks, often non-verbally, for help or advice which he then rejects. After the switch, he chooses the reproachful role: "See, you too can't help me."

    Another example is the game "Rapo". This can start with a sexually enticing signal after a first encounter at a party: "Will you take me home, then we can enjoy a cup of coffee at my place?" When the other person, once there, reacts with a sexual advance, the first player rejects this indignantly: "What are you thinking, pervert" or "In the end, all men want the same thing." The front of the T-shirt of the first player more or less states "I'm available", yet adds "But not for you" on the back. Even without sexual overtones, this game is often played: Marie plans to help her poor neighbour by doing the groceries for her, but soon feels that she is being used to do many more things. When at a certain point she decides to set a limit, the neighbour becomes angry: "I knew you would leave me here alone."

    It regularly happens that the switch occurs at the moment someone, for example in the role of coach or therapist, confronts the other player with his Victim behaviour. So long as this person receives strokes as the Victim, he remains in this role. If he is invited to think for himself and to do things, however, then in a game he becomes angry and accuses the other: "I should have known that I can't really expect you to help me."

- From Rescuer to Victim.

    This switch is common among caregivers who get caught up in the game "I'm only trying to help you". If the hidden motive of the counsellor is not that the client becomes able to stand on his own two feet and take responsibility, but rather that she is needed or even indispensable to the client, then the counsellor can end up in the role of Victim and end up with a burnout. The same pattern can come into play with teachers who become too involved in the lives of their students, or with employees who "live for their work".

Colleagues often know perfectly well which people to ask to take on an extra job or to take over a task for them. The Rescuer receives strokes for the willingness to help out, but discovers in time, and to her astonishment, that colleagues don't invite her for a fun outing or that she is overlooked for a promotion. At this point a switch can take place to the role of Victim: "You see, I don't belong. They don't even see me. No one returns my care."

- From Victim to the Rescuer.

  Just as some clients have learned as children to take care of their parents, so it may happen that they are very sensitive to the needs and requirements of their therapist or coach. When the therapist or coach, for example, becomes overworked, falls sick and thus switches from the role of Rescuer to that of Victim, the client can take on the role of Rescuer.

  It turns out that children, even though they have suffered abuse or emotional neglect by their parents, often show a deep loyalty towards their parents and continue to defend them to the detriment of themselves. Also the Stockholm syndrome (or capture-bonding), which acquired its name from the place where a hostage situation took place, is a case of role reversal: the hostage defends the hostage takers and generally has positive feelings towards them.

- From Rescuer to Persecutor.

  This is a possible switch which can occur among professionals who can't tolerate their help being rejected or when clients draw up their own plan: "After all I've done for you, this is what I get?! Well then, figure it out for yourself." Or consider the employee who feels increasingly misused because he is always ready to do the dirty work or jumps in to perform unexpected tasks: "I'm always the one who has to clean up the mess around here! You think I'm an idiot?" He then withdraws indignant, alone in his resentment or cynicism.

- From Persecutor to Rescuer.

  This variant is rare. An example could be that students who have always bullied and tormented a teacher offer him a bottle of wine at their graduation party or reunion. "He always meant well, and we really gave him a hard time, poor guy."

  Learning to recognise the moment of the switch can be very useful in interrupting the flow of the game. If we can hold a person's attention at the point of the switch, he can often bring the internal conflict into Adult awareness and then consciously choose to switch out of the game rather than complete it.

4.2.3 Substitute feelings

In a game, people experience intense feelings that are often not authentic. Authentic feelings are feelings that are appropriate and effective in a given situation, such as fear when in danger, sadness when you are abandoned, and anger when you are inhibited or blocked from doing something you want to do. Children often learn in their families that certain feelings are acceptable while others are not, and they also receive, often unspoken, messages. Examples of this are:

- "Boys don't cry."
- "You do not have to be angry about this. Mommy will buy a new one."
- "You be the wise one. You're the oldest here."
- "You look like a hag when you get so angry."
- "Afraid? Aren't you a real man?"

In this way, children learn to replace their authentic feelings with substitute feelings, which are accepted: anger or guilt instead of sadness, feeling pathetic instead of fearful, and triumph instead of anger. The term "substitute feeling" is defined as: a familiar emotion, taught and encouraged in youth, which is experienced in many different stressful situations and which is inadequate for solving problems in a mature way (Stewart & Joines, 1996, p. 310). More on this in Chapter Five.

Berne used the term "racket" instead of substitute feeling in his writings about games. The word "racket" comes from the world of the Mafia and literally means "extortion", "deceit", or "treachery". By paying the "protection racket" the owner would get his business protected by the Mafia. In a similar way "racket feelings" protect us from the risk of the authentic feeling being punished or denied by caregivers. Berne chose this word to indicate the manipulative character of racket feelings. However, because rackets are deployed out of Adult consciousness, and because children often make use of them as a survival strategy within the family, the term is not very appropriate. That's why we propose in this book to avoid the word racket completely and use substitute feelings instead.

Fanita English pointed out that people themselves suffer from the falseness and ineffectiveness of their substitute feelings. She stressed the fact that in many families some feelings are not acceptable and children are punished or shamed for expressing them. Thus children learn to substitute acceptable feelings for the unacceptable ones (1976).

Children find that they can get attention and recognition from others with substitute feelings. The result is that, as adults, when things get tough, they take refuge within these feelings that were accepted in the family, and unconsciously use them to control their environment and protect themselves.

> René withdraws behind his desk when he really comes under pressure at his job. When his colleagues then still "keep nagging at him", which is how he experiences things, he takes a few days' sick leave. His colleagues know this by now and so treat him carefully. If there are additional tasks that need to be done, they won't be quick to ask him to do them.

It is often not easy to distinguish an authentic feeling from a substitute feeling.

Thomson (1983) suggests distinguishing between functional and non-functional feelings. Functional feelings play a key role in identifying and solving problems. Feelings are functional if they are accompanied by functional behaviour. Non-functional feelings do cause discomfort, but provide little or no awareness about the nature of the problem, let alone contribute to any problem-solving activity. Fear, anger, and grief are Child ego state reactions to the threat of danger (fear), to not getting what you want (anger), and to the experience of loss (grief). When it comes to functional feelings, Thomson says, fear, anger, and sadness have a "specific temporal quality".

Fear has to do with the future, with that which might happen to you. Anger is about the present, in which someone does something you do not like and which you want to change. Sadness is related to the past and is accompanied by learning to accept a loss you have already incurred. If feelings are "out of temporal order", they cannot be functional: being afraid of the past, sad for the future, or angry about the past. As Thomson explains, in such cases we may talk of "substitute feelings".

Unfortunate events that clients have had to go through often have a connection with their past, their present, and their future. It is common for clients to feel caught in one of these three feelings, while being unaware of other feelings or believing them to be unacceptable. It is the job of the professional to make clients aware of the hidden components of this complex of feelings. Working with one of the feelings in which the client is stuck will always mean that it is necessary to investigate the other two.

Authentic feelings like anger, sadness, and fear can all become inauthentic, substitute feelings that cover other feelings that are more vulnerable or that had been problematic in the family of origin. If this happens, the expression of the feeling offers no relief or solution to the situation. You will also see that when someone exhibits a substitute feeling the other usually does not show empathy but rather embarrassment, discomfort, or confusion. For example, crying can be both authentic or a substitute feeling. "Substitute crying" often elicits exaggerated sympathy, aloofness, or irritation. Authentic crying receives respectful silence and the person feels relieved afterwards. "Substitute anger" may provoke smiling or irritation. After real anger, the person often cries.

4.2.4 Type 1 and type 2

In his first definitions of the term game, Berne did not yet use the concepts of "switch" or "cross-up". He spoke instead of a series of transactions with ulterior motives, aimed at a weak spot and leading to a precisely defined pay-off (Stewart & Joines, 1996). As the theory of TA developed, the switch became essential within the game. Yet it often happens that the switch fails to take place and a person remains stuck in transactions from, for example, the role of the Rescuer or the Victim. This does lead to unpleasant feelings, but not to a switch or a pay-off.

Fanita English has published a number of illuminating articles on this topic (1972a, 1972b, 1976). She calls this form of structuring time "racketeering": a series of transactions with ulterior motives which take place outside Adult consciousness, accompanied by unpleasant, substitute feelings among the participants. English argues that the players are concerned with receiving strokes through the familiar roles in the drama triangle. The players remain in their roles so the switch doesn't take place. According to English, a game—including the switch and the pay-off—occurs only when the ongoing exchange of substitute feelings fails and the players are not receiving sufficient strokes to satisfy their needs. English distinguishes two types of patterns of substitute feelings, namely:

- Type 1, from the Child ego state, helpless or rebellious (Victim position).
- Type 2, from the Parent ego state, being too helpful or too critical (Rescuer or Persecutor position).

As long as these two types find each other, all can go well for quite a while. Only when this doesn't yield enough strokes, then one of the two will switch and a game will briefly come into play. Type 1 becomes type 2: the Victim becomes the Persecutor ("Now I've got you!"). Or type 2 becomes type 1: the Persecutor or the Rescuer becomes the Victim ("Kick me"). Often each player only remains in this position for a short while and quickly returns to the familiar position again, either with the same person or with a new player. The purpose of these substitute patterns is not to reach the pay-off, as with a game, but to actually reinforce the familiar pattern.

If a person becomes aware of this pattern—which may exist for many years—then there is the possibility of deep feelings of doubt or despair. In therapy or counselling, type 1 presents himself as helpless or bemused. But the therapist or counsellor should be aware that this attitude can suddenly turn into criticism and negativity. The client might also suddenly stay away and seek another therapist. Type 2, in particular the Rescuer type, often seems competent, gives out many strokes, and is a cooperative client. However, a deep despair may occur after the switch, even with suicide as a possible outcome.

4.3   Furthermore

4.3.1   Fairy tales, stories, and the drama triangle

Why does the story of Oedipus still captivate our imagination after more than 2,000 years? According to the predictions made by the Oracle of Delphi, Oedipus would murder his father and marry his mother. His parents, the king and queen of Thebes, therefore gave him up as a foundling. Oedipus was indeed found by a shepherd and grew up at the court of the king of Corinth. When he then heard of the prophecy of the Oracle of Delphi, he left Corinth for Thebes. On the way, he fell into an argument and killed his opponent, who turned out to be King Laius of Thebes, Oedipus' father. He then solved the riddle of the Sphinx and, as a reward, was given permission to marry the queen-widow Jocasta, his mother.

Agonisingly, the public watch the hero heading towards his demise. First he gets into a fight with an unknown passer-by, and in the battle that follows, the other loses his life. Then he helps a queen in the defence of her realm and is rewarded by entering into marriage with her. As an unsuspecting spectator, you might think: look, he knew the Oracle's prophesy, so what could be easier than to make at least these two resolutions: don't murder anyone and don't marry a woman who is more than ten years older than himself. It is precisely the predictability of this ominous outcome that evokes pleasure among the spectators. As well as recognition, for they too regularly get into situations where they afterwards say "If only I had ...". Once again, they have become ensnared in a game and they haven't been able to resist the temptation of the drama triangle.

This pattern can also be seen in fairy tales like Little Red Riding Hood. At first glance, the moral of this tale is that it is dangerous for little girls to walk alone in the forest. On closer inspection it turns out to be rather different. Little Red Riding Hood starts out as the Rescuer of her grandmother, but then, just like her grandmother, she becomes the Victim of the wolf. Then the hunter arrives at the scene as the Rescuer of Little Red Riding Hood and the Persecutor of the wolf. Ultimately, the wolf becomes the Victim and pays with his life.

It is more correct to say that the moral of the story is that it is very dangerous for wolves when there are little girls wearing red bonnets walking around in the forest. Professor of psychology and psychiatry, Bruno Bettelheim, in his book *The Uses of Enchantment* (1976), describes how children derive meaning from fairy tales. Fairy tales describe inner drives in a way children unconsciously understand, and they provide examples of solutions to pressing problems.

4.3.2 Patterns of substitute feelings

Practitioners in caregiving professions are not immune to the drama triangle. Freudenberger (1975) described a specific form of burnout that occurs in people in these professions, characterised by a loss of interest for clients and colleagues, and by physical and emotional exhaustion whereby professionals can no longer muster up positive feelings, sympathy, or respect for their clients. He distinguished three types of professionals who are susceptible to this form of burnout. Clarkson (1992) developed this theory further and linked it to the existential position and role in the drama triangle:

- The overly dedicated and driven professional.
  These professionals can't say "no". They easily feel guilty and inadequate, and always put the interests of their clients first. They feel that they have to earn the respect of the other. They largely identify themselves with the victimisation of the other: the sexually abused girl, the mistreated wife, or the unemployed spouse. By caring for others, they are actually also caring for the wounded, lost child within themselves. They offer the understanding to others that they never experienced themselves. Unconsciously, they hold out hope that if they do this long enough, their grateful clients or "the world" will do something for them in return. They are not able to maintain satisfying relationships with others. Their life position is: "I'm not OK and you're OK." Their role in the drama triangle is first that of the Rescuer and later that of the Victim.
- The overly involved, chaotic professional overwhelmed in work.
  With these professionals, work is the only source of strokes. There's no longer a boundary between work and private life. For example, these professionals live in the orphanage where they work, they work double shifts at the crisis intervention centre, or have ex-clients living in their home. They actually do not believe that clients are or can become independent and autonomous individuals. Individuation and separation are not processes they want to promote. Sharing the misery and poverty of clients gives a sense of intimacy and relieves their own loneliness. They therefore seek out clients who have few options for friendship and little chance of improvement. After all, if the clients would stand on their own feet, they would lose their jobs, status, and legitimacy. There is an underlying sense of despair whereby sharing each other's misery is the highest that can be achieved. Their life position is: "I'm not OK and you are not OK." The role in the drama triangle is initially often the Persecutor and later that of the Victim.
- The authoritarian bossy professional.
  These professionals believe that no one can do the job better than them. They want to keep the control and overview of everything, because nobody is as intelligent, well educated, powerful,

and talented as they are. Their conviction is that "If the world would only listen to me and follow my instructions, then we'd all be happy. And if anything goes wrong, it's the fault of others." There is an underlying sense of fear, the fear that no one knows the real answers and that they themselves will one day be unmasked. Their life position is: "I'm OK and you're not OK." The role in the drama triangle is that of Persecutor and ultimately that of Victim.

Most people recognise elements from one or more types. By taking your own development seriously and by continuing to find pleasure and inspiration in what you do, you can ensure that you do not slip into one of the three patterns just mentioned. It is also important to indicate if you are in danger of getting stuck and to then make new decisions. Be open to feedback from colleagues and make sure that work is not the only important aspect of your life.

4.3.3   Games and addictions

The theory on games is very useful in the analysis of the psychological and social aspects of mental and physical problems. Within TA, the theory of games has mainly been developed for addictions to alcohol (Steiner, 1984). With addictions to drugs, eating, or work, as well as with physical illnesses and disabilities, the drama triangle also often plays a role.

In recent years, much has been discovered about the neurobiological mechanisms that play a role in addiction. The tendency for addiction has a strong genetic component and is associated, among others things, with a congenitally reduced dopamine level in the brain. This is similar to colour blindness. Just as those with colour blindness don't see green or red, people with reduced dopamine levels experience their feelings less intensely. There is a sort of haze hanging over their emotional life. It is the job of educators to teach the growing child how to live with this condition.

It often goes well, but with some people things are less bright. This becomes evident when they consume alcohol, nicotine, or drugs for the first time. Suddenly a whole new world is opened up to them! They feel better than they've ever felt before and suddenly they understand what others mean when they talk of intensely enjoying music, nature, sex, or intimacy. However, their pleasure is short-lived. As soon as the effect of the drug wears off, they fall back into their usual level of emotion, or they even experience a lower sense of feeling, or "rebound effect". This makes the craving to use the drug again almost irresistible.

By focusing on the neurobiological perspective, the psychological and social aspects of addiction are in danger of being overlooked. For not everyone with susceptibility to addiction becomes an alcoholic or a junkie. Though it is more difficult for those with a congenital tendency to addiction to uphold their personal responsibility and freedom of choice, it remains every individual's personal responsibility to figure out how to deal with the possibilities and deficits in life. Steiner (1984) described three different games in alcoholics: Drunk and proud, Lush, and Wino. The general game of "Alcoholic" has five roles: the alcoholic in the role of Victim, the partner in the role of Persecutor, and the caregiver as the Rescuer.

In addition, there is often a Dummy, the straw man or fool who time and again gives the Victim the benefit of the doubt. This is often the mother of the alcoholic. And finally, there is the Connection, the bartender or dealer. In the initial phase, the spouse often fulfils all the roles. She helps her husband to bed when he comes home drunk in the middle of the night and justifies his behaviour. Sometimes she is also the Persecutor who accuses him, or the Rescuer who begs him to change his behaviour. The crux of this game is receiving forgiveness for drinking and everything that goes with it. Therapy will therefore need to focus on how the alcoholic wallows in self-torture (Berne, 1964). As long as the surrounding benefits from the game (the wife as Rescuer "I'm only trying to help you", or as the Persecutor "Look at what you're doing to me", and the mother in dummy behaviour "See what a good mother I am"), the alcoholic will not have much incentive to stop drinking. Because the game "Alcoholic" yields many intensive strokes, both from the psychological benefits of the game and from the effect of the alcohol, it is often not easy to stop.

4.3.4   Games in the classroom

TA's theory of games is also useful in educational settings. Teachers may be experiencing stress from administrative overload on top of teaching and other responsibilities; pupils may be bringing unhappy experiences or learned patterns of behaviour from home. When they meet in the classroom the scene is set for games. School cultures can also subtly allow games if the staff room is a place where teachers complain about their jobs and their pupils and feel unsupported by the senior management. Or if the stroke level in the school is generally low, if strokes are only exchanged for achievement or behaviour, or if negative strokes are the norm.

"I don't get it", especially when it is communicated with a certain tone, is one of the most common game invitations in the classroom. This seemingly innocuous statement from the Adult of the student is in reality, on a psychological level, often an invitation from the Child to be rescued. "You need to try again to make it clear to me!" The teacher who—instead of addressing the Adult of the student with the question "What don't you understand?"—tries from the Parent to do his best to explain things to the student, is entering into a game that can last a school year or longer. To put it in a more exaggerated way: the more the teacher allows herself to be tempted to do most of the work, the less energy the student will put into examining what he does not understand.

Newell and Jeffery (2002) suggest that there are several reasons a pupil may play games in class: to defend against feelings he doesn't want to feel, such as inadequacy (which might show up as angry reactions to demands); because the game moves are familiar (the end result might be bad but at least he knows what to do); or simply that the pupil doesn't know any other way to behave when scared or uncertain because he has never been shown different options at home or at school. All these reasons, though with different behavioural manifestations, can also be true of teachers. Because of the inherent structure of education systems, and the perceived power differential between teachers and pupils, teachers may seem to usually take on the Parent role in the game. The psychological level, however, will reveal a Child need for reassurance or affirmation.

Education is most effective when the teacher's Adult is at the helm within the teaching environment. The teacher's Child ego state adds interest, curiosity, and enthusiasm. The teacher's Parent ego state ultimately gives approval and acceptance, and offers support. For this to happen, and be sustained, the organisational games and substitute feelings in the school will need to be addressed as well as increasing the teacher's awareness.

The drama triangle turns out to also be a powerful tool in detecting games within education. The Hungarian teacher Attila Vandra (2007) argues that the large number of psychological games evident in education seriously affects the mental health of people working in this profession. His research shows that the probability that the teacher takes on the role of Rescuer is very high. Rescuer behaviour in many educational contexts is a source of unnecessary conflict. After all, the teacher who teaches and educates from the role of Rescuer invites the students to take on the role of Victim. Students who refuse this begin to see the Rescuer as Persecutor and thus often find themselves taking the position of Rebellious Child.

Vandra wonders why many professionals in supporting occupations, under which he also classifies the teaching profession, have mental health problems. His assumption is that "They are trying to rescue the helpless child they once were, who had no support." That makes these professionals more susceptible to the pitfalls of the Rescuer position and ultimately that of the Victim.

Classroom involvement in games prevents the development of the desired proactive, problem-solving behaviour in pupils. When a student says, "I have a question about how best to tackle this issue" (instead of "I don't get it"), or "I made a mistake and now I know how I can do differently next time" (instead of "I'm no good at this") we know that a healthy, effective learning climate is in place.

4.3.5 Games in teams and organisations

People often work in organisations or participate in groups where they can play their favourite games.

> Maria works as a social worker in a youth organisation where it is commonplace that the employees are overworked and feel they fall short. This fits perfectly with her pattern of being an over-involved, overworked Rescuer. Eventually she ends up at home with burnout and receives sickness benefits.
>
> Bas has explicit political views and conveys these views as the Persecutor. He works as a teacher at an experimental school where there is a lot of room for creativity and expression, and where in the staffroom a lot of time is devoted to criticising the policies of the government and to all the bureaucratic rules. Until the school gets a visit from quality control and is threatened with closure if things are not changed within three months.

The question is whether it is primarily the games of the employees that form the culture in an organisation, or whether the organisation itself generates its own games. Increasing bureaucracy and regulations can rapidly decrease the pleasure in one's work. If police officers, nurses, or doctors have to spend 50% or more of their time behind the computer filling out forms to prove their accountability to directors, financiers, regulators, or insurers, the meaning and passion with which they exercise their profession can disappear.

In the TA book, *Climate Change in Organisations* (*Klimaatverandering in organisaties*) (2008) Yvonne Burger states that

> It's about the development of personal leadership: to become aware of your own resources, fears, insecurities, motivations and barriers, in order to be more effective and at the same time to be able to offer more to the organisation—and beyond. Personal leadership requires courage or fearlessness. Fearlessness does not mean that you no longer have any fear, but that you have the ability to recognise, to feel and to use this fear as a launching pad from which to grow. Whatever you have to contribute to the organisation—or the world—is obviously different for each individual, depending on whatever moves you the most. (translated for this edition)

Personal leadership acts as an antidote to a working environment in which the game level is high. Leadership is an inside job. It starts with questioning yourself!

4.4 Related theories

4.4.1 Cognitive-behavioural therapy

The elements of "repetition" and "circumventing the Adult consciousness" are also part of the theory of conditioning in educational psychology and (cognitive) behavioural therapy. Classical conditioning studies explore how behaviour becomes predictable. Pavlov's dog kept hearing a bell and received food afterwards. After a short time, the dog would begin salivating at the sound of the bell, and not only when the food was in front of his nose. Through such conditioning, people learn which situations are dangerous and better avoided, and where food and fun can be found. This healthy mechanism can also become derailed. For a person with the eating disorder bulimia, seeing or even thinking of a pastry shop becomes the predictor of an eating binge. And for someone who suffers from panic attacks, light-headedness can be the harbinger of a panic attack (Mineka & Zinbarg, 2006). These associations are largely unconscious.

While the model of classical conditioning stresses the impact of the environment on the person, people also actively exert their influence on this environment. This involves the principle of operant conditioning: behaviour that leads to positive consequences is reinforced and becomes more frequent. Behaviour that has negative consequences will disappear. This principle is reflected in the idea that both positive and negative strokes significantly influence and guide behaviour (see Chapter Two on strokes). Games involve a complex case of operant conditioning, whereby people are reinforced in their harmful or destructive behaviour. In recent decades, the concepts of "cognition" and "emotions" have come to play an increasingly important role within behavioural therapy. The area of overlap between cognitive-behavioural therapy and TA has therefore become even larger.

4.4.2 Emotionally focused therapy

A movement within systemic therapy, developed by Sue Johnson (2008), emotionally focused therapy (EFT) has gained recognition in recent years. Johnson studied hundreds of recordings of interviews with married couples. She wondered what the reason was that some couples stayed together while others did not. Her conclusion was that in marital conflicts there is often a fear of attachment and closeness, which was usually created by previous attachment traumas, either in this relationship or in previous intimate relationships.

Partners are afraid of being hurt (again) and would rather withdraw or cloak their pain with an attack on the other than show that they are hurt. This creates "demon dialogues" between partners, which can also be described as games in TA theory. From within the despair over the loss of connection with their partner, they both become ensnared in increasingly negative interactions. Just as Berne did in his time, Johnson gives these dialogues intriguing names:

- Finding the Bad Guy: Taking turns, the partners attack each other. They accuse and judge one another. Both feel they need to protect themselves from the other. They do not see how their own behaviour provokes the next attack.
- Protest Polka: One partner is critical and aggressive, the other defensive and aloof. Every word by one of them evokes negative reactions and emotions from the other. The more one partner blames the other partner, the more he or she withdraws and the sharper the attacks of the first partner become.
- Freeze and Flee: Both partners withdraw into an ivory tower. There is only a deathly silence. Both partners feel powerless to restore their unity and are coldly polite or indifferent towards each other.

Johnson's approach is based on the attachment theory of Bowlby (1979), which stressed that a secure attachment is one of the primary requirements for a healthy (mental) development of the child. In order to survive, children are extremely dependent on the care (Nurturing Parent) and protection (Structuring Parent) of others. The majority of people (60–70%) appear to be securely attached. A small group is insecurely attached, whether anxious or avoidant or disorganised (a combination of anxious and avoidant). The attachment style is often transmitted from parent to child, but can be influenced or changed. Under stress, securely attached people can also fall into an anxious, avoidant, or disorganised attachment style.

During EFT treatment, the basic need for connectedness and the fear of losing this connectedness are discussed in a number of steps. Partners learn to reach out to each other and to (re)connect. The accessibility, responsiveness, and commitment ("ARC") of both partners is encouraged. Partners learn to engage in conversations in which they avoid and prevent the "diabolical dialogues".

4.4.3 The neglected organisation

In recent years, more and more attention has been paid to the question of how game patterns in organisations hinder executives and their staff in the optimal realisation of organisational objectives or company results. It is clear that a non-optimal stroke climate may result in a strong tendency to provide for one's own stroke requirement through game behaviour (Mountain & Davidson, 2011).

Research into ineffective patterns in organisations (Emrys Lamé, 2008) makes use of the orthopedagogical metaphor. Like parents, who help their child to develop into an autonomous adult by being caring, accessible, and responsive, managers do the same—if all is well—in the relationship with their employees. In neglected organisations, defined as organisations which do not meet the physical, emotional, normative, and educational needs of the employees (Van Hekken, 1992), people appear to behave like neglected children. The dynamics in such an organisation have high levels of game-based interactions, just like the dynamics involved for a neglected child, his parents, and the wider environment. Neglect is sometimes caused, and always followed, by a disturbed relationship between the manager and the employee, with lots of game playing and few real encounters.

The Australian management consultant, Anthony Sork (2007) works with the hypothesis of the "critical attachment period". Employees who after 120 days do not experience the place in which they work as a place where they are accepted for who they are, as a place that is reliable and secure, and as a place where they belong, will not give the best they have to offer. Underachievement and absenteeism become the norm. In order to explore, experiment, and innovate in the workplace, people need a secure attachment.

References

Berne, E. (1961). *TA in Psychotherapy*. New York: Grove Press.
Berne, E. (1964). *Games People Play*. New York: Grove Press.
Berne, E. (1972). *What Do You Say After You Say Hello?* New York: Grove Press.
Bettelheim, B. (1976). *The Uses of Enchantment: the Meaning and Importance of Fairy Tales.* London: Thames & Hudson.
Bowlby, J. (1979). *The Making and Breaking of Affectional Bonds*. London: Tavistock/Routledge.
Burger, Y. (2008). *Klimaatverandering in organisaties. Leiderschap maakt het verschil.* (Climate Change in Organisations. Leadership Makes the Difference.) Amsterdam: SWP.
Choy, A. (1990). The winner's triangle. *Transactional Analysis Journal*, 20(1): 40–46.
Clarkson, P. (1987). The bystander role. *Transactional Analysis Journal*, 17(3): 82–87.
Clarkson, P. (1992). *Transactional Analysis Psychotherapy. An Integrated Approach*. London: Tavistock/Routledge.
Clarkson, P. (1996). *The Bystander. An End to Innocence in Human Relationships?* London: Whurr.
Clarkson, P. (2003). *The Therapeutic Relationship*. London: Whurr.
Cornell, W. (2009). *Explorations in Transactional Analysis. The Meech Lake Papers*. Pleasanton, TX: TA Press.
Dusay, J. (1966). Response to games in therapy. *Transactional Analysis Bulletin*: selected articles from volumes 1–9. San Francisco, CA: TA Press.
Emrys-Lamé, M. (2008). *Verwaarloosde organisaties. Een onderzoek naar hechtingsstijlen tussen medewerkers en leidinggevenden.* (Neglected Organisations. A Survey of Attachment Styles between Employees and Leaders.) Utrecht, Netherlands: Universiteit Utrecht.
English, F. (1972a). The substation factor. Rackets and real feelings. Part I. *Transactional Analysis Journal*, 1(4): 27–33.
English, F. (1972b). The substation factor. Rackets and real feelings. Part 2. *Transactional Analysis Journal*, 2(1): 23–25.
English, F. (1976). Racketeering. *Transactional Analysis Journal*, 6(1): 76–81.
Frankl, V. (1969). *Man's Search for Meaning*. London: Hodder & Stoughton.
Freudenberger, H. (1975). The staff burn-out syndrome in alternative institutions. *Psychotherapy: Theory, Research and Practice*, 12(1): 35–45.

Gowling, D., & Agar, J. (2011). The importance of experience. In: H. Fowlie & C. Sills (Eds.), *Relational Transactional Analysis: Principles in Practice* (81–90). London: Karnac.

Graaf, A. de, & Kunst, K. (2010). *Duurzaam leidinggeven.* (Enduring Leadership.) Amsterdam: SWP.

Graaf, A. de, & Levy, J. (2008). *Klimaatverandering in organisaties.* (Climate Change in Organisations.) Amsterdam: SWP.

Hargaden, H., & Sills, C. (2002). *Transactional Analysis: A Relational Perspective.* Hove, UK: Brunner-Routledge.

Hekken, S. M. J. van (1992). *Verwaarlozing: achtergronden, gevolgen en behandeling.* (Neglect: Background, Results and Treatment.) In: H. Baartman & A. van Montfoort (Eds.), *Kindermishandeling: resultaten van multidisciplinair onderzoek* (Child Abuse, Results of a Multidisciplinary Research) (pp. 166–185). Utrecht, Netherlands: Data Medica.

Hellinga, G. (1993). *"Over derdegraads zie-je-wel-isten."* (About third degree 'I-told-you-so-ism-players). Strook, 15(4), pp. 12–25.

Hine, J. (1990). The bilateral and ongoing nature of games. *Transactional Analysis Journal*, 20(1): 28–39.

Johnson, S. (2008). *Hold Me Tight. Seven Conversations for a Lifetime of Love.* New York: Little, Brown.

Karpman, S. (1968). Fairy tales and script drama analysis. *Transactional Analysis Bulletin*, 7(26): 39–43.

Karpman, S. (2014). *A Game Free Life. The Definite Book on the Drama Triangle and Compassion Triangle.* San Francisco, CA: Drama Triangle Publications.

Mineka, S., & Zinbarg, R. (2006). A contemporary learning perspective on the etiology of anxiety disorder. *American Psychologist*, 61: 10–26.

Mountain, A., & Davidson, C. (2011). *Working Together. Organizational TA and Business Performance.* Farnham, UK: Gower.

Newell, S., & Jeffery, D. (2002). *Behaviour Management in the Classroom: a Transactional Analysis Approach* London: David Fulton.

Novellino, M. (2012). *Transactional Analysis in Action: Clinical Seminars.* London: Karnac.

Shadbolt, C. (2012). The place of failure and rupture in psychotherapy. *Transactional Analysis Journal*, 42: 5–16.

Sork, A. (2007). Attachment before engagement. In: *Naomi Simson's Blog* (she the CEO, Red Balloon Days), November.

Steiner, C. (1984). *Games Alcoholics Play.* New York: Ballantine.

Steiner, C. (2009). *The Heart of the Matter. Love, Information & Transactional Analysis.* Pleasanton, TX: TA Press.

Stewart, I., & Joines, V. (1996). *TA Today. A New Introduction to Transactional Analysis.* Melton Mombray, UK: Life Space.

Stuthridge, J. (2012). Traversing the fault lines: Trauma and enactment. *Transactional Analysis Journal*, 42: 238–251.

Thomson, G. (1983). Fear, anger and sadness. *Transactional Analysis Journal*, 13(1): 20–24.

Vandra, A. (2007). The influence of psychological games on mental health in education. *European Journal of Mental Health*, 2(2): 183–204.

Widdowson, M. (2010). *Transactional Analysis: 100 Key Points & Techniques.* London: Routledge.

Woods, K. (1996). Projective identification and game analysis. *Transactional Analysis Journal*, 26: 228–231.

CHAPTER FIVE

Script

5.1 Basic theory
    5.1.1 Introduction
    5.1.2 The unconscious life plan
    5.1.3 How the script is created
    5.1.4 Existential positions
    5.1.5 Script matrix
    5.1.6 Decisions and redecisions
    5.1.7 Miniscript
    5.1.8 Drivers
    5.1.9 Counter injunctions (Drivers) and injunctions (Stoppers)
    5.1.10 The script system
5.2 Further theory
    5.2.1 The body: foundation of the script
    5.2.2 Script protocol
    5.2.3 The script as organisational structure
    5.2.4 Resilience and the script
    5.2.5 Unconscious relational pattern
    5.2.6 Narrative/constructivist model of script
    5.2.7 The script helix
5.3 Furthermore
    5.3.1 Episcript
    5.3.2 Tragic results
    5.3.3 Script circle
    5.3.4 Attachment and the script
    5.3.5 Hybrid script
5.4 Related theories
    5.4.1 Infant research
    5.4.2 Phases of life
    5.4.3 Narrative approach
References

The previous chapters about ego states, strokes, transactions, and games provide the building blocks for personality and interpersonal communication, according to TA. After reading Chapter Four, the question arises as to why people often seem to hold on to fixed patterns, especially when these patterns are unhealthy, unwise, boring, and even dangerous. The force of habit is tremendous. In this chapter on the TA concept "script", it will be made clear that people often draw conclusions and make decisions about life at a young age, to which they remain true to a large degree later in life. The convictions that a child acquires—about himself, about others, and about the world—can prove to be obstinate and tenacious. Healthy convictions can help us to live happily and successfully. Unhealthy decisions lead us again and again to situations in which we endure setbacks and make the wrong choices. But since these convictions were beneficial to the child at one point or another, letting them go is by no means an easy task. On the other hand, they are "only" convictions, beliefs (often with a strong emotional and physical component). Making a new decision—redeciding—is a powerful opportunity to put one's life on a different track.

5.1   Basic theory

5.1.1   Introduction

Why is it that people find themselves caught in patterns that have them make the same choices time and again: mostly healthy decisions that promote their growth, but also unhealthy, unwise, boring, or dangerous decisions? "Habit" is a key driver of behaviour. Habit can also be referred to with the physiological term "homeostasis": the ability of an organism to keep its internal environment constant. Habits often date back to childhood. Things you learn from your parents and educators are not easily forgotten and you often activate them automatically or unwittingly later on in life. This applies to the strokes you give and invite, the way you deploy your ego states, the types of transactions you enter into, and the games you have a preference for. All this can be summarised under the TA term "script". Berne focused attention on how children draw conclusions and make decisions about themselves and others based on their experiences with adults who are meaningful in their lives. Berne first used the term "script" to convey the sense of how these early childhood decisions formed a kind of life plan that represented the child's first efforts to make sense of what he witnessed and experienced.

Richard Erskine (1980, 1993) says of the script: "The script helps you give an answer to the central question in life: what does someone like me do, with people like you, in a world like this?" The first answers to this question, developed in your younger years, often form the guideline, without your being aware of this, for your behaviour later on in life. "Have I learned to see myself as someone who continually has to prove that I am really capable of something …?" "Have I learned to see other people as only trustworthy after great effort?" or "Have I learned to see the world as a place in which you always need to be alert, otherwise …?"

People live their own answers to the question, Erskine mentioned. Without such answers, whether they help or hinder, one would not get far in life. In this chapter, different views on the script are reviewed. Because Berne unexpectedly died at the age of sixty, his book on script, *What Do You Say After You Say Hello?* (1972) was published posthumously and with limited editing, so his description of script remained incomplete and is in some respects even contradictory. Script theory has been a central topic in the *Transactional Analysis Journal*, with many authors challenging and elaborating the original theory and applying it to different client populations (Erskine, 2010). Research in recent decades has further influenced the concept of the script (Cornell, 1988; Erskine, 2009; Massey, 1989; Noriega, 2010).

Points where there are inconsistencies in Berne's writing pertain, for example, to questions such as the following. Does a child choose his own destiny or is the child subjected by the parents to a script? How rigid is the script? Is one's whole life plan established by the third year or does a person continue to develop it throughout life? What is the role of genetic and congenital factors? How large is the impact of the extended social environment, in addition to that of the parents and carers? Is the script only inimical, a threat to autonomy, or does it also make daily life and work possible?

5.1.2 The unconscious life plan

The script is gradually built up by way of a repeated pattern of transactions which can last throughout one's life. Script decisions taken in early childhood are often adjusted during the course of a person's life. Barrow (2014) suggests that adolescence is a period in which major revision of earlier script formation can take place. He even takes the position that "… the impact of adolescence is more important and greater than that of early childhood in terms of determining how a sense of self is maintained in later life" (p. 169).

Script makes you go in search of characters that fit the roles in your own script, and you make compromises, thereby increasing the sophistication in the design of your script. This results in a life plan, based on decisions in childhood, reinforced by parents and confirmed by subsequent events (Berne, 1972). In Berne's view, the script determines the kind of person you will marry, what kind of work you will do, how you will die, and who will be there when you do. It determines whether you are a winner or a loser, whether you will be successful or will fail in your profession, whether you have long-term, satisfying relationships or are repeatedly disappointed by love. It determines whether you will look back with satisfaction at your life or whether you will be chronically unhappy.

In TA theory it is assumed that children devise a specific plan for their lives at an unconscious level at a very young age. The script, in which the main issues are recorded, answers the following questions.

- Will I succeed in the things I want in my life, or will I become chronically unhappy or something in-between (a winner, a loser, or a non-winner)?
- From which life position do I deal with myself, with others, and with the world in which I live and work (+/+, +/−, −/+ or −/−)?
- How and when do I imagine I will die? Early by accident, old and bitter, or old and satisfied? Will I die after an excruciatingly long deathbed or of old age in my sleep? Will I be mourned by many or missed by a few?

Although it is possible to live an autonomous life, many people live some areas of their lives in self-limiting ways so as to follow the (presumed) commands and expectations of their caregivers and other authority figures. If you are an adult, you are usually unaware of your script, unless you take the time to discover what the most important commandments (drivers) and prohibitions (stoppers) in your life script are, which you (unconsciously) continue to listen to and live by. The script also has a somatic component. It is nestled in your body, as it were (see section 5.2.1). Children who grow up in the same family may follow entirely different life plans.

The family is in the room—father, mother, and two children. The phone rings, the mother picks it up and bursts into tears. She puts down the phone, goes to the father and seeks consolation from him. One child "thinks": gosh, that's good, when you're sad, you will be comforted. The other child "thinks": that's not nice, when mother is sad, I'm left out.

Berne tells the story of two young brothers who kicked up a storm in their house with their depressed mother, who regularly called out, "One day you'll both end up in an institution!" And this is precisely what happened: one of them became a chronic psychiatric patient, the other became a psychiatrist.

As mentioned earlier, Berne's thoughts about the script were not fully developed when he died, so we shall describe and explore the evolving theories of script in the fields of psychotherapy, counselling, education, and organisational development.

Much has been thought and written about the extent to which Eric Berne's own life script may have influenced his ideas about TA (Jorgensen & Jorgensen, 1984; Hargaden, 2003; Stewart, 1992). Berne was born in 1910 in Montreal as Eric Lennard Bernstein, the son of a Jewish doctor and a Jewish writer (Berne, 2010). He had a younger sister. The relationship with his father was close. His father died of tuberculosis at the age of thirty-eight. Eric was then eleven years old. He seems to have identified with both parents in the choice of his career. He became a doctor, like his father, and wrote a number of books, just like his mother. He moved to the United States to specialise as a psychiatrist, and changed his name from Bernstein to Berne. He pursued his training to become a psychoanalyst with, among others, Paul Federn and Erik Erikson, but became increasingly critical of analytical theory and practice. When in 1956 he was denied access as a member of the psychoanalytic institute—and took that as a rejection—and was told that he had to return to his own personal training analysis, he decided to develop an alternative theory which was more practical and easier to understand.

These facts also can be used to tell a different story: that of a highly intelligent man, who lost his father at a young age and spent his life in search of recognition and love. A very hard worker, who covered his vulnerability with sarcastic humour and sharp analysis. He was a man who rarely showed his softer side, who could only play and enjoy himself in a structured setting with colleagues who looked up to him. He was a person who found it difficult to be close and preferred to observe from the sideline. He married three times and had four children. He was a therapist who shed a theoretical light on the darker side of human existence—pain, shame, vulnerability—but who made little room for such things during treatment. Berne predominantly sought Adult control instead of an exploration and understanding of early childhood pain. The script of transactional analysis itself is therefore sometimes described as a "I don't belong" script (Hargaden, 2003).

In recent decades, a lot has been published on the script as one of the central TA concepts. The most important development is that it was recognised that the script also has a constructive side. Indeed, without a script, without an answer to the questions that life presents us, nobody gets very far in life. Based on your script, you deliver the quality that people appreciate and acknowledge you for, as well as the mess that people complain about. Newton (2006) proposed the following more descriptive definition: "A script is an explanatory narrative that gives meaning to the past, provides a blueprint to solve problems in the present, and a forecast for the future." Who could do without that?

A boy, whose father is a psychiatrist with a practice at home, sees all kinds of people enter every day into the great room that is forbidden territory for him. His father then talks to these people for hours on end. It's all a mysterious activity of which he understands very little. All he knows is that he is not allowed in any way to interfere. When he is then asked what he wants to become later in life, he says with complete conviction: "Patient!"

5.1.3 How the script is created

From what has been suggested so far, it is evident that the script is a comprehensive concept that has a great impact on people's lives. How does the development of the script take place? It was long thought that children were born into the world as a "tabula rasa", a blank slate. It is now known that genetic predisposition is of great influence. Certain characteristic temperaments—for example, whether one is introverted or extroverted, easily irritated or calm, social or withdrawn—are (in large measure) innate. The child arrives in this world with a certain predisposition and has already been exposed to all kinds of influences since conception during the period in the womb. It matters a lot whether the pregnancy was wanted or unwanted, whether the mother really wanted an abortion yet didn't go through with it, or whether the parents eagerly looked forward to the time of pregnancy and the birth of their child. Is the mother relaxed during pregnancy and can she get enough rest, or do they need to move house during this time and work until the last moment? Are there external events such as an accident, economic pressures, or even war that affect everyone and create anxiety in the parents? And then the child is born. He experiences everything around him from his Child ego state.

- C_1 experiences the smells and sounds, the atmosphere and the emotional tone of the environment.
- P_1 internalises the messages the parents transmit, from the mother who cheerfully smiles at her baby, but is sometimes angry or sad, from the father who cheerfully lifts the baby from his crib, but who may also grumble quite a bit when he is stressed.
- A_1 tries from a very early age to draw conclusions from all the different impressions.

There is a constant interaction between the inherited predisposition of the child and the qualities of the parents. Sometimes the predisposition of the child is such that even great parents are not able to build a good relationship. And then there are children with such resilience and with such a flexible and social attitude that even inadequate parents cannot spoil them. And then there's everyone else in-between. Good parenting can promote a healthy development. Even if the parents' capabilities are not great, growth and development is still possible after puberty. It is also the case that children can draw different conclusions based on the same messages received. In this case, non-verbal messages can make the most impression. The conclusions may take on a form other than the parents intended. The intention of the caregivers and the effect this has on the child can be very different.

> Father arrives home from work swearing, slams the door shut, and sits down at the table with an angry face. Child A thinks, "I must have done something wrong. I'll keep very quiet, or he'll be even angrier at me." Child B thinks, "I'm going to make him laugh to cheer things up around here." Child C thinks, "Dad is angry but that has nothing to do with to me. He loves me anyway."

The young child makes decisions with which he can live and survive in a world that is sometimes incomprehensible and possibly even life-threatening. At the time, the decision the child makes seems to be the best possible decision under the circumstances. But then in later life, script decisions can be limiting and damaging. Every human being creates a coherent internal system. What someone thinks, feels, and does in the here and now can be understandable if you take the time to go back into a person's history. You can then see how this particular child, in a precise situation, chose a certain type of behaviour. It was the best option at the time, even though it now sometimes works counterproductively.

How are we to understand why a small child sometimes experiences the world as dangerous and hostile?

- A child is physically small and vulnerable. The world seems to be populated by giants. Unexpected loud noises may mean that there is danger.
- A child does not think like an adult and does not yet have the language skills of an adult. He does not experience emotions in a balanced way.
- A child lacks the information and the overview that adults have.
- A child does not have the choice to live somewhere else. Growing up in this family leaves no choice but to deal with it.
- A child is not yet able to cope with stress on his own. The younger the child, the more limited and vulnerable he is to dealing with fear and danger.

The eventual development of a person is a complex interaction between genetic predisposition, the experiences acquired from education and the environment, and the factor of chance. Even the genetic predisposition, in combination with the environment, will not be apparent at this time. "Our genes have feet," says psychiatrist and researcher in genetics Kenneth Kendler (Kendler & Prescott, 2006). Genes appear to seek an environment in which they can flourish. Thus, generally speaking, young people will drink quite a lot between the age of fifteen and twenty-five. At that age, drinking is not a sign of an innate predisposition to addiction, as it is for people who can still be found at the pub on a daily basis when they are forty. Such people haven't grown out of it, are evidently addicted to alcohol, and have a genetic predisposition to alcoholism. This does not mean that a genetic predisposition will inevitably lead to addiction. However, it does mean that knowledge of the interaction between genes and the environment can cultivate an understanding of the struggle against addiction for clients, social workers, and bystanders, as well as provide tools for treatment.

5.1.4 Existential positions

As discussed in the introduction to this book, TA presupposes that people are born with a loving heart—a potential source for human value. In TA, we call this position "I'm OK, you're OK", which is also indicated with +/+. The earliest experiences in life are coloured by the answers to many questions. Did you feel welcome? Were you welcome as a boy or were you supposed to be a girl? Were you allowed to cry at night or were you not supposed to be "a nuisance"? There are millions of daily experiences since birth, which form the basic judgement about ourselves, others, and the world.

As mentioned in Chapter Four, the genesis of the concept of existential positions came to Berne by way of looking for a method to categorise games. Later, in discussions in the San Francisco seminars, the OK/not OK concepts as existential positions were connected with the script, a sense of the meaning of oneself in the world. Steiner proposes to define the I'm OK-you're OK position as signifying freedom, equality, democracy, and a level playing field for the pursuit of happiness and human potential (Steiner, 1974, p. 2).

In TA, this is referred to as the existential position or life position: a person's basic beliefs about himself and others. They are used to draw conclusions, to make decisions, and to justify behaviour, the basic attitude that someone has, in relation to the people and things of substantial value in his life.

TA distinguishes between four life positions:

- I'm OK, you're OK.

    You and I are worth the effort. We are valuable people. When you and I have a conflict, I want to solve it, but my concern for the result does not come at the expense of me or you. My concern for us is equally important to my concern for the solution. You are you and I am I, and it's nice when we meet. Change, growth and intimacy are possible.
- I'm not OK, you're OK.

    My life is not worth as much effort as yours. I'm not as important as you. I am worth less; you can do more and are better than me. If we have a conflict, I will concede. The result is less important than what you think of me. I don't take care of myself, because I'm not happy. I feel helpless in comparison with you. I often find myself in the position of Victim, and you can surely rescue me.
- I'm OK, you're not OK.

    Your life is not worth as much effort as mine. I am more important. And if we have a conflict or problem with each other, I will push through my solution because I think the result is most important, even if this is at your expense. That is of no concern to me. I know, Rescuer that I am, what is good for you better than you do.
- I'm not OK, you're not OK.

    Ah, life is not worth the effort. It doesn't really matter. We cannot add or detract anything from it. It is what it is. Why should we make an effort to solve a problem? Our situation is hopeless anyway. I prefer to avoid everything. I don't really need you and you don't want anything to do with me anyway.

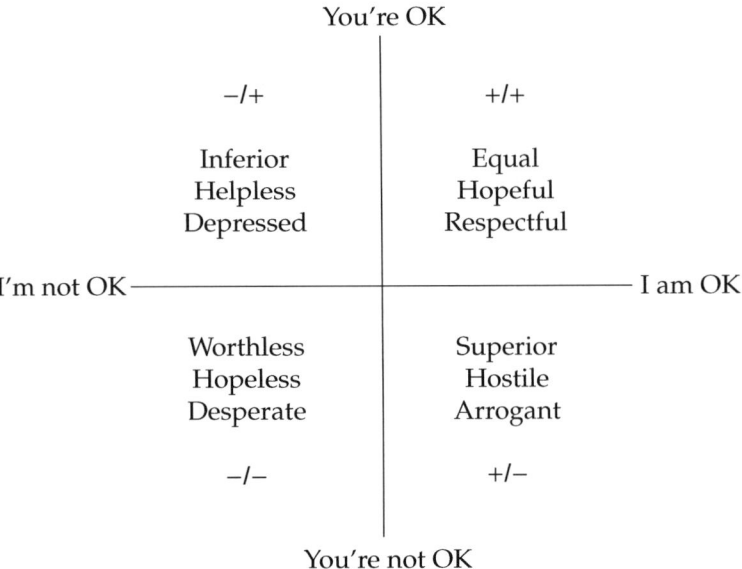

Figure 5.1. Four existential positions: levels of being.

From the beginning of our life, we develop our existential positions, influenced by all of our life experiences. Often, complex self-fulfilling prophecies arise, whereby a child who enters the world full of confidence subsequently meets people who understand, support, and value him, while a child who is suspicious and wary evokes adverse reactions. In this way, script decisions become reaffirmed by the corresponding existential positions.

> Three months before Adrian's birth, his father is killed in an accident. His pregnant mother is left behind with her three-year-old daughter. From the moment of birth, Adrian has a sense that he needs to make up for things. He is named after his dead father, whose picture has a prominent place on the dresser. He needs to make his mother happy—yet he has the feeling that he continues to fail in this task. When she gets angry with him, she includes her deceased husband in the conflict: "If your father were alive, he would have known what to do with you!" Or she sighs sadly: "Your father did that much better." Adrian is placed mainly in the position "I'm not OK, you're OK". Sometimes he gets angry, with his mother, his failed life, and he then shifts to "I'm OK, you're not OK", or he gets bogged down in powerless withdrawal: "I'm not OK, you're not OK". Only rarely is he in the equal, cooperative position "I'm OK, you're OK".

In the book *I'm OK–You're OK* by Thomas Harris (1967), the position is taken, unusual in TA, that babies at birth have the position "I'm not OK, you're OK". They are, says Harris, so completely dependent on their parents that this has to be the conclusion. Within TA, however, the view is generally shared that children retain their core of +/+, unless they come to different conclusions and decisions based on their early childhood experiences.

Eventually, the existential positions of all adults can be recognised in their behaviour and thus in the way they interact with others. Franklin Ernst (1971) called these behaviours "operations" and he designed the diagram in Figure 5.2, the OK corral, by analogy with a ranch where the horses are located in a corral, an outdoor arena. Because it concerns social interaction, he used the phrases "I'm (not) OK with you" and "you're (not) OK with me". From moment to moment, people change position, sometimes as a result of a conscious choice, but often without realising it. If it is a conscious choice, they can invite the other to take a complementary position. Often our social behaviour is a script-based justification for the corresponding life position.

> Tom is driving on a summer evening when the sun is beginning to set on the highway. He is irritated, the meeting went on longer than expected and he still has a long way to go. Suddenly he sees a police car behind him which passes him at high speed and then signals him to stop. Annoyed, he brings the car to the side of the road. He greets the officer with: "So, don't you all have anything better to do? Shouldn't you be catching criminals?"

He reacts from the existential position +/−. It won't help him much in this situation, on the contrary. But it can be different.

> Marlie is driving on a summer evening when the sun is beginning to set on the highway. She is satisfied with her day and is sitting relaxed behind the steering wheel. Suddenly she sees a police car behind her which passes her at high speed and then signals her to stop. She is startled and immediately realises, "I forgot to put my lights on!" She stops, gets out, and immediately says, apologetically: "You are quite right, I forgot to put my lights on! Silly of me!" The officer smiles and says, "Ma'am, this time I won't give you a ticket."

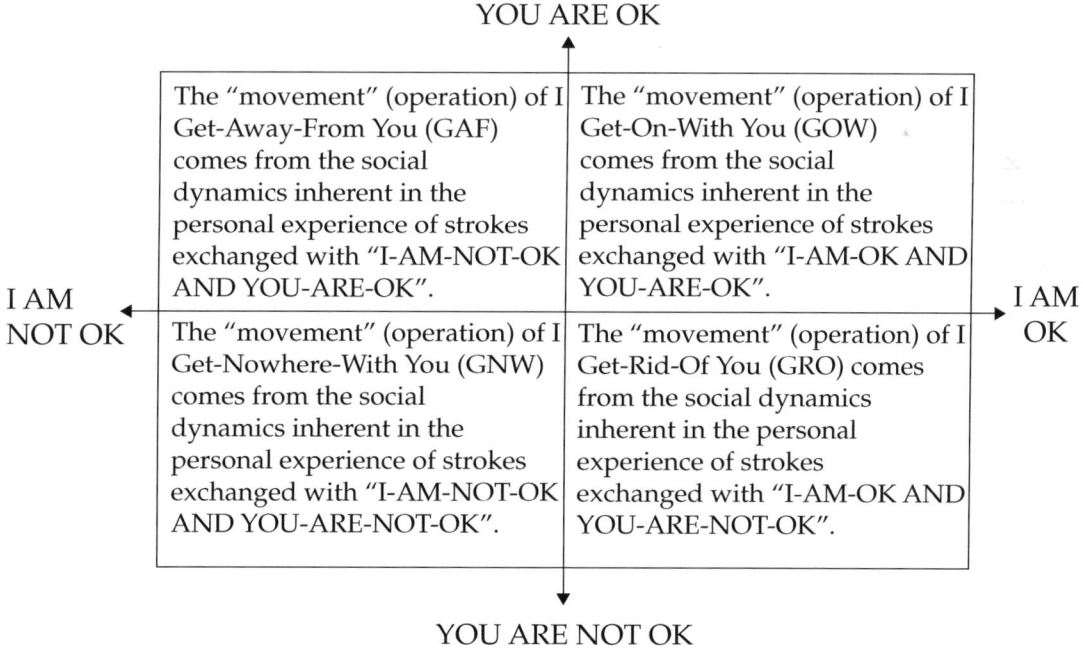

"OK-Corral: Grid for what's Happening"

(F. Ernst, 1971)

Figure 5.2. Four existential positions: levels of behaviour.

Sometimes it has advantages if you can choose the position -/+. Most people know all four positions, but have a preferred position from which they think, act, and feel. This is the position from which they exchange strokes and structure their time. The position occupied says everything about the content of the script. The position "I'm OK, you're OK" is also called the "healthy position" because it makes it most likely to live an enjoyable life. Sometimes people feel secretly superior. In this case, underneath the position "I'm OK, you're OK", they conceal the position "I'm OK, you're not OK". People who view the world from the position "I'm OK, you're not OK" sometimes have a big mouth but are actually timid. Faced with adversity they can fall into the position "I'm not OK, you're OK". Their arrogance then turns into depression.

Julie Hay (2009, p. 21) calls the existential positions "the windows on the world", the spectacles through which you view the world. The window you look through determines your attitude and influences the attitude of the other. She argues that the existential position is a mixture of convictions, behaviours, and feelings that usually correspond with each other, but not always. Convictions determine how people think about themselves and others. Behaviour consists of how people actually express themselves in the presence of others. Feelings are sometimes visible, especially if they match our behaviour. However, it is also possible that we hide our feelings, consciously or unconsciously. Who doesn't know of situations where some people behave superior (+) but feel inferior (–), or a moment when someone might know better (+) but concedes, given the fact that the other person has power (–).

Hay developed (based on an idea by Graham Barnes) the following diagram (the disposition diamond) in which convictions, behaviours, and feelings can be represented as if they are separate (Hay, 2009, p. 27).

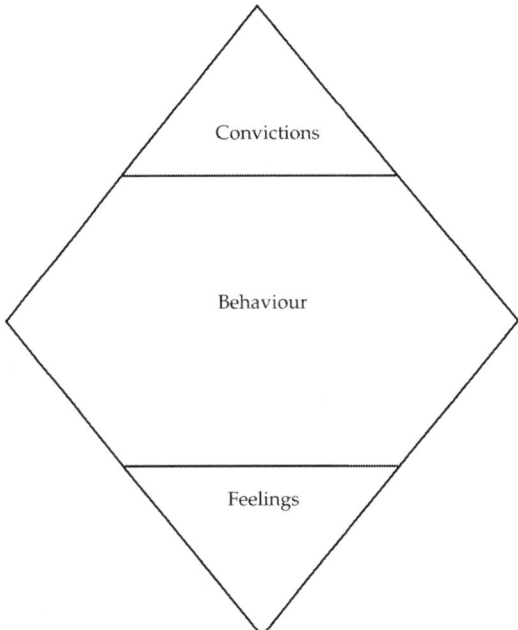

Figure 5.3. Disposition diamond.

With each of the three components—conviction, behaviour, and feelings—you can occupy one of the four existential positions (+/+, −/+, +/− and −/−). According to Hay, this yields twenty-seven possible combinations, though only six occur frequently. She gives these combinations catchy names like: the martyr, the complainant, the bully, the victim, the benefactor, and the pessimist. The bully, for example, feels somehow less capable than other people (the inner conviction is −/+). The bully camouflages these underlying doubts with behaviour by which it seems as if he knows everything (+/−). The bully tells others what to do. But deep down, the bully feels desperate about himself and others (−/−). This brings some extra nuance to the existential positions and, according to Hay, helps understand certain situations much better. The combination of convictions, behaviours, and feelings is picked up by people and in part determines their response.

Often people hardly realise how much their own behaviour evokes certain behaviour in others. How you see yourself colours the glasses with which you perceive the other (De Graaf & Kunst, 2005). If you manage to replace not-OK glasses with OK glasses, your life will change.

5.1.5   Script matrix

Parents and carers convey messages—intentionally or unintentionally, by what they say, but even more by their behaviour—to a child about how life works, how to stand your ground, and how to create your own happiness or unhappiness. In TA, this process is elucidated by means of the script matrix. The script matrix was developed for the first time by one of Berne's early co-workers, Claude Steiner (1966). The script model offered by Steiner emphasised the power of parental injunctions and attributions, resulting in "A script [that] is essentially the blueprint for a life course" (1974, p. 51). Steiner described three basic life scripts: depression, or "no love" script; madness, or "no mind" script; and drug addiction, or "no joy" script.

Some script theorists would argue that it would be more accurate to direct all the arrows in Figure 5.4 towards the Child of the child, since in the earliest stages of life this is the only present ego state. This is where all the early messages are internalised.

Gradually, as the child grows up, some messages pass from A_1 to A_2 and from P_1 to P_2. Because the process of script development continues throughout life, the messages this diagram seeks to convey often change over the course of childhood and the course of life. The parents pass on messages to their children from their ego states (Parent, Adult, and Child). In its original conceptions of script the child was understood to "receive" his script (counter injunctions, permissions, and injunctions) mainly from the parent of the opposite sex and he learns the programme from the parent of the same sex. The boy becomes the man his mother wants him to be, but the father demonstrates the way to achieve this. This model was a reformulation of the psychoanalytic theory of the Oedipal stage of development. From a more contemporary perspective, in which many family systems are no longer the nuclear family of father, mother, and child in clearly gender-defined roles, there are often multiple influences in the development of a child's script.

One other more recent adaptation of the script matrix is the idea that the child also influences the parents, so the vectors are not one-way but directed from parent to child and vice versa (see section 5.2.6). This idea is developed further by Tudor and Summers (2014) in their script helix; we come back to this in section 5.2.7.

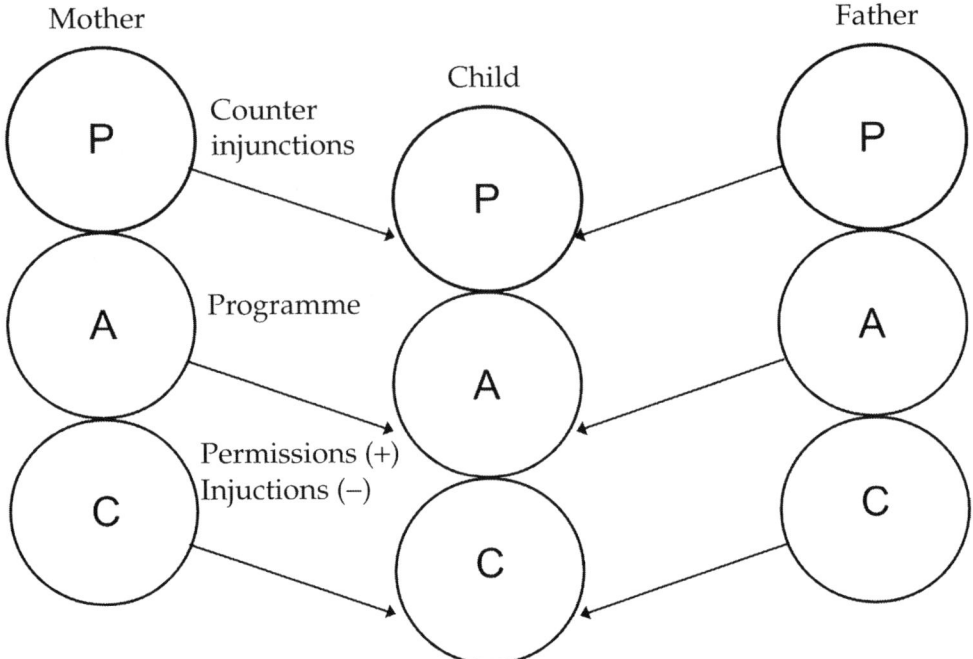

Figure 5.4. Script matrix (Stewart and Joines, 1987, p. 129).

The script matrix consists of the following components.

- The permissions and injunctions, from the Child of the father and mother. Because permissions and injunctions are given from the Child of the parents, they are often non-verbal messages that the child selects from the behaviour of the parents. What makes Daddy happy? When does Mommy sigh and frown? When does Dad lose his temper? Permissions refer to situations or behaviour of the son or daughter which makes the Child of the father or mother happy or which it enjoys. Injunctions are about behaviour or situations in which the jealous, angry, fearful, or neglected Child of the parents is triggered. Often the parents are not aware of this. We deal with this in more detail in section 5.1.6.
- The counter injunctions, from the Parent of the father and mother. This more frequently involves verbal messages of which the parents are aware and which they support. Counter injunctions often have a positive content ("That makes us happy!") or a moral component ("If you are kind to others, they will also be kind to you", "Do your best at what you do, and do it from the heart", "Take responsibility for your actions"). Sometimes they may include resentment or jealousy: "If you were born poor, you'll never become rich", "Acting normal is crazy enough as it is", "People will walk over you if you're too kind".
- The programme, from the Adult of the father and mother. This is what informs you how to arrange a home and how to organise the household. This is how you behave at school, at

work, in front of your friends. This is how you deal with problems. This is what you do when things seem to go against you.

A special form of injunction is the attribution, a message about the qualities of the child, which the child comes to believe: "Our Elly is our little dumbo", or "Of all our children, Alfred is the fastest child at everything. He was able to walk at ten months and started reading when he was four". Attributions are also given from the Child of the caregiver, often when a son or daughter is still very young: "Our Larry is such a temperamental little fellow …". The young child therefore often sees the attribution as unchangeable: "Yes, that's just the way I am". Attributions are often said to others, mostly in the presence of the child.

> Rachid grows up as the eldest son in a family with three children. His mother is often sick and can't handle the housekeeping or take care of the children. His father has a busy job and is often away. As the eldest child, Rachid learns at an early age to look after his mother. He also takes on the role of father with regard to his younger brother and sister. He is a good student and the expectations of him are high. He notes that he gets attention from his father when it comes to his performance at school. When he goes to college, it is hard for him to be away from home or to build a social network. He misses the automatic recognition he received from his mother and finds it hard to approach people. When he is approached by a woman a few years older than himself, who makes an exuberant and worldly-wise impression, he responds eagerly to her advances. After a short time, she falls pregnant. They get married and soon have two children. It then turns out that his wife is not a very caring mother. She still enjoys going out and increasingly expects him to stay home and take care of the children. Despite his busy job, he tries to keep all the plates spinning. When he discovers that his wife has had an extramarital relationship for the past six months, and is now pregnant with this man's child, he finds himself depressed at home.

The following can be said about Rachid's script matrix.

- The injunctions: because, as the eldest son, he had to take over many duties from his sick mother, he developed the injunctions "You cannot be a child and you must grow up quickly and take on responsibilities" and "Others are more important than you". He received little attention from his father, though his father was happy with his responsible son. He therefore developed the permission "You are a strong and powerful person".
- The counter injunctions: if he ever complained, his mother rebuked him, telling him not to be selfish; that he had to be there for others. This led to the counter injunction from this mother "Care for others, erase yourself". He was encouraged by his father to work hard in school, to pursue a good education, and get a good job. The counter injunction is "Work hard".
- The programme: mainly based on the example of his father: "The important thing is for you to take responsibility, both at work and at home". The traditional script matrix positioned the mother and father above the child, with the vectors of the script messages pressing down upon the child, illustrating the power and authority of the parental figures over the developing mind of the young child. In his now classic critique of traditional script theory, Cornell (1988) suggested a flattening or levelling out of the script vectors, placing the parent's ego states on the same plane as those of the child. He further argues that the vectors of influence

are not only from the parents to the child but from the child to the parents, as has been amply demonstrated in the child development literature. Cornell's position was further elaborated in the model of co-creative transactional analysis developed by Graeme Summers and Keith Tudor (Summers & Tudor, 2000, 2014), as shown in figure 5.5.

Ideally, the child receives messages that make him happy and successful in life. Even under optimal conditions, parents can sometimes be grumpy or curt. They have their own (bad) habits, sometimes based on what they missed during their youth. Children will therefore always to a certain extent be neglected, criticised, and misunderstood. The needs of the child will not always be fulfilled, and, to some extent, children will be used in order to satisfy the unmet needs of the parents. This does not necessarily have to have an adverse effect on the development of the child. Daniel Stern, who did research with very young infants, published a lot about this, and we will discuss this in more detail in section 5.4.1. Children also prove to be resilient and they can become strong because of difficult circumstances. Cornell has written about this. See section 5.2.3.

It is said that every person will have at least three opportunities to grow up, to learn the lessons that are needed for a happy and healthy life. You get the first chance in the family home in which you grow up. The lessons you receive from your father, mother, brother(s), sister(s), grandfathers and grandmothers, peers and friends at school, can be used to build a successful life. But you're not "finished" when you leave your parental home. You get a second chance at maturity when you enter into a partner relationship. You choose the partner with whom you can continue writing the script you originally developed in your family home, and from whom you can learn lessons of life you didn't learn before.

Your third chance at maturity comes in your place of work and with your co-workers. Here, too, the script developed at home provides you with qualities which you can make use of. However, work also challenges every person to grow further, and to think, feel, and act more autonomously.

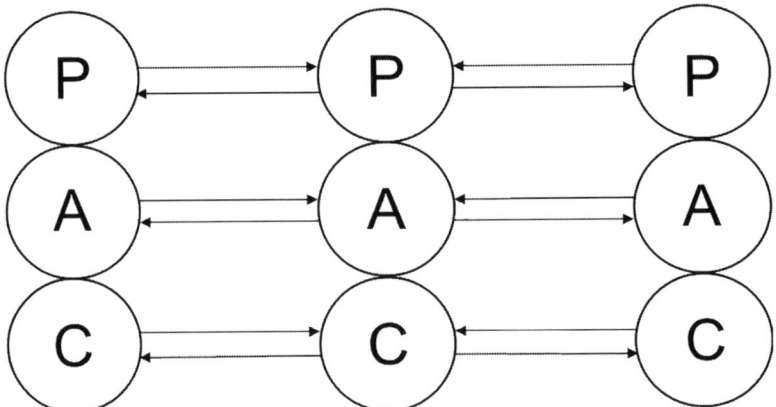

Figure 5.5. Co-creative script matrix.

Everyone has a script, an unconscious plan for life. However, one person's script may contain far fewer restrictions than that of another. The goal of therapy or other forms of TA support is not to become "script free". It is about becoming more autonomous, about becoming a person with a personal conscience, a person with spontaneity and the ability to be authentic, a person who is capable of forming a connection with people and the world around him, from a position of self-respect and respect for others. Part of this process will be about discovering and developing the resources and positive aspects of one's script.

5.1.6 Decisions and redecisions

Bob Goulding and Mary McClure Goulding (1976, 1978, 1979) made an overview of the different themes they encountered in their therapeutic work with early negative decisions of their clients. An essential element in the approach of the Gouldings is that they focus on the decisions that people have made for themselves based on the messages or injunctions of their parents. It's not that the parents' injunctions are imposed upon the weak-willed child, for the child has made a choice. There were also other possibilities for a child to fashion from parental messages and pressures.

In our view, it is not only about the messages of the parents, but about a far broader process: the central themes in the family. The child looks for a way of dealing with those themes (the do's and don'ts). Decisions are the attempts made by the child to best deal with the main themes in his family and to find an answer to the question "Who am I, who are the others, and what am I doing here in this world?"

Bob and Mary Goulding argued that people are capable of making a different decision at any time in their lives, against the grain of the early limiting decisions. They named their therapeutic approach redecision therapy, to distinguish it from other forms of TA practice.

Whether certain messages from the parents lead to injunctions with the child, depends on a number of variables.

Frequency: Is the child repeatedly told that he is not capable of something, or just once? Degree of threat (to life): Is the child looked at angrily when the previous messages are expressed? Is he kicked and beaten and/or put into a dark room? Or does it all take place at the table in a tone of conversation, followed by a positive message?

Timing: Does the mother call out "Don't come near me" when she is grieving intensely after just having had a miscarriage? Such a message can have a much greater impact than when the mother is lying in bed with a headache.

Emotional intensity: A child comes running with a bloody knee. Sometimes a parent may then say something like "be a bit tougher" with far more emotion than intended, perhaps because the parents themselves have difficulty showing their vulnerability and find it easier to be angry than sad.

The term "injunction" can lead to confusion. Although these are messages from the parents from their Child ego state, given at times when they themselves are unhappy, anxious, angry, frustrated, or disappointed, it is ultimately their son or daughter who draws conclusions and makes decisions. The child actually imposes a ban or a restriction on himself based on these injunctions. The Gouldings distinguish between the following twelve injunctions.

1 Don't exist

This is the most basic injunction; a decision made by the child if he is not desired by the parents, or if he has the feeling of being worthless, useless, and unloved from the first. Sometimes this message is openly expressed, as with Anton, whose mother died in childbirth. His father was not able to cope. When his father had a tantrum or had had too much to drink, he would shout at Anton: "Your mother died because of you. I wish you'd never been born." More often, the existence injunction is absorbed by the child in a more subtle manner. Maria knows that her mother almost died giving birth to her, and since then suffers from severe pelvic complaints. Each time her mother complains about the pain, it is a confirmation of Maria's script: "Don't exist".

> Paul has always felt that it would have been better if he didn't exist although his parents have always denied the notion. He was the eldest. His parents were just twenty years old when he was born. In a psychotherapy group, he discusses that his parents had always wanted to emigrate to Australia to build a new life there. Everything was done and dusted: the tickets had been bought, the furniture had been sold—and then it turned out that his mother was pregnant. They found the risk of emigrating in this situation too high and they therefore cancelled everything and remained at home. Although Paul knows this story, he feels the significance of this event when he talks about it in his therapy group. Suddenly he realises, in every fibre in his body, that his birth had made his parents' plans go up in smoke, and that they, secretly and unconsciously, resented him for this.

2 Don't be yourself

A child might take on this injunction if the parents would have preferred to have had a child of the opposite sex. The fourth girl in a row is named "René" and develops into a boyish, sportive child who prefers to play wild games outside. It may also be that the child is repeatedly compared to another child, the older brother, for example, who is a much faster learner and more obedient. Or the child is compared to Uncle Pete who also never wanted to conform or achieve anything.

> Sometimes first names and surnames play a role. For example, a girl called Marian van As, may at times wonder how much of "Marian" and how much "van As" has crept into her script. The quest for individuality, of being allowed to be yourself, can sometimes be at odds with the behaviour of the demands of the system—the family. "You're becoming a real 'van As'," says a proud father to his daughter. But when he is less happy with what Marian has been up to, he says "a real 'van As' doesn't do such things, Marian." In such a context, a child easily picks up the idea that it is forbidden territory to be yourself too much or too much of an individual. The conflict between "I and we" remains a script theme in each new group that Marian becomes part of.

3   Don't be a child

In this case, a parent (or both parents) assumes the position of the child and the young child has to take care of the parent. It may also be that the parents were not able to be children themselves when they were young, and therefore reject the playful or childlike behaviour of their children.

> When John was eight years old, his father suddenly died, leaving the mother behind with three children, of whom John is the eldest. He sees the grief of his mother, who tells him: "Now you're the man of the house." He decides at that moment to take care of his mother and his younger brothers.
> In Berne's memoir of his own childhood, he wrote of being ten years old when his father was dying of tuberculosis. He recalled visiting his father on his deathbed:
>
>> "Hello," said Father, and took my hand. We looked at each other for a few seconds, and then Father said, "A little boy should take good care of his mother and sister." I nodded and Father dropped my hand. "Good-bye, Father," I said. "Good-bye, Lennard," said Father. (2010, p. 95)
>
> A less dramatic example is Martin's family, who never allowed the children to cheerfully mess around, play with paint or glue, or splash through the puddles and the like. All this made too much of a mess. The house had to remain spic and span. Doing "childish things" just didn't fit the picture.

4   Don't grow up

The youngest in the family may take on this injunction. The parents want to continue to take care of a child or keep the child small. The parents' fear of being left alone or remaining alone often lies at the root of their need to keep the child small. The child decides to stay with the parents instead of becoming an adult man or woman with a life of their own.

> Marie is now forty-three years old. She still lives with her parents and considers it her job to care for her parents, now that they are in their seventies. She has resigned herself to the fact that she won't have any children and has decided to look after her parents until their death. Her older siblings are secretly pleased that their sister has taken on this responsibility and give her strokes for her commitment.

5   Don't be close

The child does not learn to enjoy touching and hugging. The parents never learned this themselves. It may also be that a younger sibling is born and the eldest child receives the message when he wants to climb on his parent's lap: "You're too old for that now!" The family or family culture can turn out to be detached. The child never sees the grandparents interact intimately with his own parents. They shake hands, and sometimes not even that. There is also no real eye contact when family members speak to each other. Anyone who admits to the need to get close is averted by the family's game-like patterns.

> When Annette was little, her father often hugged her and she enjoyed sitting on his lap. This happens less now she is about ten years old. She gets the feeling that her father is keeping her at a distance. She questions her self-esteem. She "decides" to mainly focus on her performance at school because she notices that this makes her father happy and proud.

6   Don't belong
    The child learns to not feel at ease with others and to be afraid of strangers, perhaps because the parents are themselves afraid of others or because the child grows up in an isolated family. People living with this injunction often know an immediate answer to the question: "When you were young, what part of yourself did you have to isolate at home in order to fit in?" The double-bind (conflicting message) of this injunction continues to cause trouble in later life. You are part of groups, but your script forbids you to really be a part of them.

> Annemarie's family is the only Catholic family in a neighbourhood of Protestants. Furthermore, the family lives in a fairly affluent area. Her father is not an engineer or a doctor, but a public official. She goes to a different school from the other children in her neighbourhood and she has few girlfriends to play with after school. She "decides" that she prefers to read rather than to play. She isolates herself.

7   Don't be important
    Is the child allowed to find his self and happiness important, or does he primarily learn the importance of modesty and self-effacement? In some religious traditions, this injunction seems to set the tone in many parenting situations; "Just be normal", "Don't live above your means". This can sometimes feel like the collective injunction of society as a whole. "It's not about you!" "It's not about this life!"

> Even in his own wedding photos, Henri usually stands modestly in a corner, smiling shyly at the photographer. He thinks it is all nonsense, all this fuss, and feels uncomfortable to be the centre of attention throughout the day. He still regularly hears his parents telling him that "Acting normal is more than enough" and "This kind of thing is not meant for people like us".

8   Don't be healthy
    Being ill or having certain ailments was the primary way to get attention from the family. Some families are kept active by it. There is a "problem child" who seems to slurp up all the attention from mom and dad. The other children quickly realise how they can make sure that their mother will take a whole day off from work in order to be there for them.

> Margaret's parents are always busy with their work and social activities. At one point, she gets terrible abdominal pains at school and her mother is called in from work. Margaret is rushed to the hospital and is found to have appendicitis. Suddenly she receives a lot of attention and care and both her parents sit by her bedside. After two weeks, she returns to school and everything goes back to normal. However, Margaret regularly has abdominal attacks and each time her father or mother rushes from work to pick her up from school. She enjoys all the attention and "decides" that being ill is an effective way to draw her parents' attention.

9   Don't succeed
    Is the child allowed to be successful in life or does he receive messages from the parents such as "People like us won't succeed at things like that" or "You can't be better at things than me"?

> When Floris is twelve, he beats his father at tennis for the first time. He's very proud, until he realises that his father is not at all content with this. His father is annoyed and walks around grumbling about all sorts of trivial issues. The next time, Floris lets his father win, who then treats him to an ice cream, and says, "Well, your old father still has it in him, doesn't he?" And Floris makes a decision. But which one? Continue to let his father win, give up tennis and take on hockey and make it to the first team, or never play tennis with his father again?

10 Don't think

Does the child learn to think about himself, about others, and the world? Or is any inclination towards (thought) experiments and investigating curtailed? Is debating and discussion between the children or with the parents viewed as enjoyable and interesting? Or is having a different view a threat to the family or to tradition?

> Five-year-old Astrid is full of questions: "Is the moon cold?" "How do they make chocolate sprinkles?" "Where does my poo come from?" "Why do you have so many wrinkles, Mom?" "Who was God's father?" Sometimes it's all too much for the parents and then they say: "All right, little smarty pants, you don't need to know everything", or they get irritated and then Astrid bites her tongue. She "decides" that she receives more strokes when she doesn't ask too many questions.

11 Don't

Can the child go on adventures, explore the world, take initiatives, and undertake activities, or is he largely expected to remain calm and quiet and not touch anything?

> Mo grows up in a small, noisy upper apartment. His parents would like to move and live in the countryside, but don't have the money for this. Mo and his brothers are often told that they make too much noise, if not by their parents then by the downstairs neighbours. Mother becomes gloomy and apathetic by the whole situation. She doesn't want to go outside where the kids would have more space to play. Mo learns to wait, to sit quietly with his PlayStation or a book on the sofa.

12 Don't feel

Was it permitted to have, feel, and express emotions? Or was "being strong" an important motto at home? Sometimes, specific emotions are prohibited, such as sadness or intense anger.

> Wang and Li grow up in a family where expressing emotions is a taboo. When mother becomes seriously ill, father works even harder and shows nothing of his emotions. Mother awkwardly tries to remain jovial. Eventually, mother dies. Father reacts with irritation to Wang's expression of sorrow: "Big boys don't cry", while giving Li strokes for taking on certain household tasks. Both children decide not to show their emotions. Wang devotes himself to school and gets compliments when he comes home with high grades. Li devotes herself to others, trains to be a social worker, and makes caring for others her profession.

13 Don't have needs

The injunction "Don't be a child" can also take the form of "Don't have needs". The child learns to have no needs or to hide them carefully. The decision made after this injunction may be to deny self, or to go crazy in order to get needs met (Goulding & Goulding, 1978, p. 218). The existential position is used to justify decisions. For example, the decision "I won't get too close" can be justified by the existential position +/−, "I'm OK, you're not OK". "You're a bit pathetic if you need others; I can do it alone without others." By contrast, the decision "I won't succeed" is often accompanied by the existential position −/+, "I'm not OK, you're OK". "I can't do what others can do." The injunctions are usually non-verbally transferred from the parents' Child ego state to that of the child. Often, neither the parent nor the child is aware of this. When someone gets stuck later in life, it becomes apparent that this person has been held back by these early "decisions".

5.1.7 Miniscript

The script matrix correlates with the psychodynamic tradition in which the investigation of the genesis of problems and discovering the roots of childhood are important. As TA developed, there arose another way to analyse the script: the miniscript (figure 5.6). The miniscript is the script "in a nutshell" and it makes clear, often in a matter of seconds, how we traverse our script. While the script matrix uses the terms "counter injunction" and "injunction", Taibi Kahler uses the terms "driver" and "stopper" in the miniscript (Kahler & Capers, 1974). The miniscript has four positions, each characterised by one of the four existential positions with corresponding racket feelings (substitute feelings that are experienced in stressful situations, see section 4.2.3 in Chapter Four).

1. Driver: the position of being "conditionally OK": "I'm only OK if I …" If you can no longer satisfy the driver, you arrive in the position of stopper.
2. Stopper: the position "I'm not OK, you're OK" with one of the twelve injunctions from section 5.1.6, including the corresponding substitute feelings such as guilt, depression, or feeling inferior.
3. Blamer: the position "I'm OK, you're not OK" with the corresponding substitute feelings such as triumph, hatred, resentment, or anger.
4. Despairer: the position "I'm not OK, you're not OK" with the corresponding substitute feelings such as despair and worthlessness.

Going through the miniscript always starts with one of the five drivers: "Try hard", "Hurry up", "Please me", "Be strong", and "Be perfect". In driver behaviour, you find yourself—at the social level—in the position "I'm OK, you're OK", but only on the condition that you stick with the driver behaviour. On a psychological level, you are driven by the conviction "I'm OK, if I …". As long as this works, to satisfy the Parent and to achieve results with driver behaviour, you will remain in position 1 and will stop the driver behaviour after a certain period of time. However, if you are under pressure or are tired, driver behaviour may often not suffice. You will no longer find yourself being friendly, you can't maintain your pose, you get stuck in your perfectionism, or you wear yourself out doing your best or hurrying. And then comes

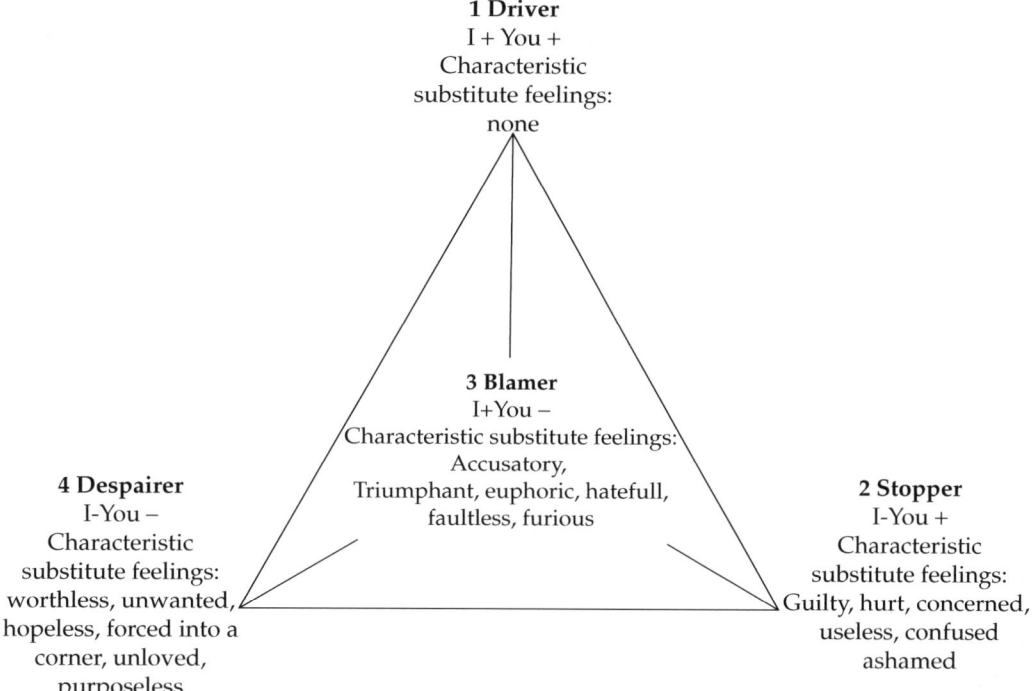

Figure 5.6. Miniscript.

the underlying stopper. The early decision, such as "I don't belong", "Success is not for me", or "I'm not allowed to think", suddenly becomes palpable and can no longer be held at bay by the driver behaviour. Now, even more, you feel guilt, hurt, shame, or confusion. You doubt whether you're good enough for the work you do or whether you are worthy of this friendship or relationship.

You change your life position from conditionally "I'm OK, you're OK" to "I'm not OK, you're OK". After a shorter or longer period, you may move on to the third position, that of the blamer. The uneasy substitute feeling from the second position is replaced by a different substitute feeling. Instead of the Victim you become the Persecutor and the existential position becomes "I'm OK, you're not OK". You might eventually arrive in the fourth position, the despairer, based on the life position "I'm not OK, you're not OK". This is characterised by the conviction that life is worthless, that you will never be able to feel happy or successful.

The miniscript flawlessly brings out "the lie of the script", the false promise that you're OK, if only you … You need not go through all the positions in the miniscript. Sometimes you remain stuck in the first position, and you never get beyond driver behaviour. Some people are more likely to remain in the second position of the stopper and rarely pass into the third or fourth position. Others go from the driver position briefly on to the stopper and then quickly on to the third position of the blamer or the fourth position of the despairer.

This is closely related to the "favourite" life position. If the life position is predominantly +/+, you remain at a distance to the miniscript or you end up at most in the first position. If the life position is often –/+, then you easily slide to the second position and start to feel the stopper. Someone with a life position +/– will quickly move from the driver on to the third position of the blamer; if you can burn the other to the ground, you no longer have to feel the pain of the injunction. Someone with a life position –/– will soon slide into the fourth position, the despairer, and also spend quite a bit of time there. In relationships, the miniscripts of both partners often correspond.

> Jack's drivers are "Be perfect" and "Be strong". If things do not go the way he wants, he gets irritated. He momentarily feels the pain of his stopper (his injunctions are "Don't succeed" and "Don't feel") and then slides straight into his favourite position, the blamer. His girlfriend Karen's drivers are "Please me", and "Try Hard". If things are not going well at home, especially when Jack starts grumbling, she moves to her stopper. Her injunctions are "I'm not important" and "Don't grow up". She feels embarrassed and hurt. Usually they manage to climb back up. Jack makes a qualifying sensible remark or comforts Karen. Or Karen gathers herself together and does something nice for Jack. They find each other again. Sometimes, however, they both land up in the fourth position of the despairer and then it may take days before one of them tries to approach the other.

The way out of the miniscript is to break through "the lies of the script". This starts with the first step: "I'm only OK, if I …". You exit the miniscript if you let go of the conditionality of yourself and others: "I'm OK, and others are too".

5.1.8 Drivers

In the 1970s, Taibi Kahler observed TA therapy groups (Kahler, 1978, 2008; Kahler & Capers, 1974). He observed the content and tone of what people said, as well as their posture, gestures, and facial expressions, just before they fell into script behaviour. He found that their behaviour could be classified according to the five drivers:

- Try hard
- Hurry up
- Please people
- Be strong
- Be perfect

The driver is defined as a characteristic set of words, intonations, gestures, postures, and facial expressions which mirror the inner message: "I'm only OK, if I …" (try hard, hurry up, please people, be strong, be perfect).

> Rezha teaches from the driver "Try hard". He tries to explain things clearly, but often has the feeling that this is not entirely successful, so that he tries to do even better. If a student asks him a question, he often feels criticised, as though he hasn't done well enough. Students often get confused because he then stutters and talks himself into a corner in his effort to explain it even better.

> Sylvia teaches from the driver "Hurry up". She often comes into class a little late and calls out before she sits down "OK everyone, get out your books." She talks fast and sometimes she is unintelligible. If anyone asks something, she often gets annoyed since it's holding back the lesson. When she gives homework, she says it's not that much. The students should have it done within half an hour.
>
> Aïsa teaches from the driver "Please me". She finds the atmosphere in the classroom most important, and takes her role as mentor very seriously. If there are conflicts between pupils, she spends a lot of time resolving them. Students find her insecure and sometimes take advantage of this. They know they can get away with an easy excuse when they haven't done their homework. Sometimes there is an extreme amount of fooling around during her lessons.
>
> Steven teaches from the driver "Be strong". He finds it is important to clearly convey the curriculum and does not tolerate any messing about in the classroom. When he was a mentor a few years ago, neither he nor the class was very pleased about that. He found the mentor lessons a waste of his time and his students preferred to go with their problems to their mentor from the previous year. He put himself forward for scheduling tasks for the following year.
>
> Peter teaches from the driver "Be perfect". He enjoys grading papers and meticulously marking students' errors with a red pen. He takes a long time for grading, because he would hate it if he missed a student's mistake or made one himself. In his explanation, he is sometimes hard to follow because of his long sentences with many nuances and clauses. He is not easily satisfied, with himself or his students.

Table 5.1. Drivers

	Try hard	Hurry up	Please me	Be strong	Be perfect
Words	Often "try", "difficult", "awkward"	Often "quickly", "briefly", "we have to go"	Often "yes, but", and looking for" agreement	Aloof and general, feelings overpower me	Many clauses and nuances
Intonation	Pinched voice	Staccato, fast	High voice, sentences ending on question mark	Flat, monotone	Sounds Adult
Gestures	Hand next to eye, to ear, clenched fists	Tapping, waving feet, looking at watch	Extended hand, much nodding	Few gestures	Lists: firstly, secondlly, etc.
Posture	Bent over forward towards the other, crouched	Impression of being agitated	Shoulders high, bent toward the other	Closed, motionles	Upright, in balance, Adult
Facial expression	Eyebrows together	Frequent and fast changes in eye direction	Looking up to the other, horizontal brow wrinkle, tense smile	No expression, motionless	Eyes directed upwards as if the ceiling has the perfect answer

Petruska Clarkson (1992) suggested that each driver has a strong positive component—enthusiasm, speed, amiability, endurance, excellence.

Julie Hay (2009) proposes calling the sunny side of driver behaviour "working style" and the shadow side "driver". People who show their working style make use of their qualities; people who overshoot their driver expose their pitfalls. "When what can be done, must be done" describes how the compulsive script takes over and changes the working style into driver behaviour. De Graaf and Kunst, in *Einstein and the Art of Sailing* (2005), offer the following summary of the qualities of working styles and pitfalls of the drivers:

Try hard

Quality: People who follow the driver "Try hard" are essentially those who take on tasks enthusiastically. They especially put a lot of energy into new things, by examining all sorts of possibilities. They rarely overlook something. They are highly motivated people who do well getting things off the ground. They are at the front of the row when there are new tasks that need to be done.

Pitfall: "Everything is connected to everything—I can't skip anything. There is so much I have to think about that it takes effort to know where to begin—and certainly to get it done!"

Hurry up

Quality: People who follow the driver "Hurry up" work fast, respond well to deadlines, and are able to do much in little time. This is the main quality of these people. They can get a mountain of work done quickly! Their energy increases as the pressure increases. "Hurry up" differs as a working style from the others. Usually, this working style is an addition to one of the other styles; often to "Please me" or "Try hard".

Pitfall: "I've already done the work, can I go now? OK, it doesn't look very organised, but I think it's good enough."

Please people

Quality: People with the driver "Please people" are excellent team players. In their team, everyone's view of things is considered. They make sure of this. They seek harmony in their work, they are intuitive, and reserve plenty of time and space for the feelings of others. They offer their services and have a cooperative attitude. "Please people" people are pleasant to have around because they are tolerant, empathetic, and understanding.

Pitfall: "I want someone else to tell me what to do. You're the manager here, you tell me if what I'm doing is OK."

Be strong

Quality: Calm and steady, this is how one can best describe "Be strong" people. They deal well with stress and are therefore good crisis managers. They are perseverant and not likely to give up on a whim. They are people with a strong sense of duty, who are not shy of doing some of the dirty work. They keep a logical steady mind when others begin to panic. They don't ask others for help very quickly.

Pitfall: "Who here actually needs a plan? I can do well without. I also don't need any support from others. I'll do it alone."

Be perfect

Quality: People who follow the driver "Be perfect" are those looking for perfection. Everything should be done as carefully as possible, without error. "Be perfect" people are extremely well-organised in their job. They look forward, because they want to avoid problems. They are accurate people who do their work conscientiously and carefully fulfil their commitments.

Pitfall: "I take so long to get my plan exactly right that I certainly won't get it done, let alone get to the point of implementing it."

Attempts to add drivers to this list, such as "Be the best" ("needing to be number one", Harris & Harris, 1985) or "Take it" ("I deserve more than you", Tudor, 2008) never made it into the canon.

With drivers, you push yourself (from the Child ego state: "I always have to") or others (from the Parent ego state: "Others must always"). The drivers are defence mechanisms to keep painful feelings at bay. With the driver "Try hard", for example, the feeling that you might fail is kept at a distance. If the driver fails, you literally fall silent and the underlying feeling emerges (powered by the stopper).

> André is training a team from his driver "Try hard". He notes that the coordinator of the team looks bored so he tries extra hard to come across as fascinating and convincing. When he arrives at the end of his explanation and asks if there are any questions or comments, the coordinator says, with, in André's eyes, a condescending smile: "Well, I think it's all nonsense." At that moment André feels the ground beneath his feet fall away. He stands there motionless without knowing what to say.

The drivers are a way not to feel the (often deep) pain of the stoppers. A stopper can pertain to each of the twelve injunctions the Gouldings described. "As long as I can do others a favour, I feel less sadness from my belief that I really should not exist." "As long as I do my best, I'm less haunted by the disappointment and anger of my sense that I'm not allowed to be successful." "If I succeed in being strong, then no one will see how vulnerable I sometimes feel."

Drivers and stoppers are founded on four myths (Kahler, 1978):

1. I am responsible for your happiness, derived from the negative Nurturing Parent.
2. You are responsible for my happiness, derived from the negative Adapted Child.
3. I am responsible for your unhappiness, derived from the negative Structuring Parent.
4. You are responsible for my unhappiness, derived from the negative Adapted Child.

The word "myth" indicates that these ideas are not in line with reality. After all, responsibility for one's own happiness (and unhappiness) can never be delegated to another. Becoming happy is something you have to do yourself, which does not mean that you have to do it alone.

Many people working in health care, education, or other professions in which they work a lot with other people, believe in myths 1 and 3. Many patients, clients, students, and subordinates believe in myths 2 and 4. Whole systems and organisations are built around these myths. Often it is not easy to let them go.

5.1.9 Counter injunctions (Drivers) and injunctions (Stoppers)

If drivers (counter injunctions) no longer function to keep a person's head above water, then the stopper (injunction) becomes manifest, pulling the person down. Adrienne Lee (in Tilney, 1998) illustrates this with a diagram (Figure 5.7) of someone who is almost drowning under the weight of bricks (stoppers) but is held aloft by balloons (drivers). This image of a drowning person makes it plain that it is risky to encourage someone to simply give up their drivers when they are in a process of change.

As stated earlier, driver behaviour protects someone from the deep pain of his script. Encouraging someone to "do his best" without healing the underlying "don't succeed" is useless and sometimes undesirable. A person who decided as a child that doing someone a favour is a good antidote to the pain of feeling that he really should not exist, will re-experience his "don't exist" injunction if he stops doing others a favour. In such cases, this can be highly dangerous.

5.1.10 The script system

Erskine and Zalcman (1979) and O'Reilly-Knapp and Erskine (2010) have summarised the theory of the script in an orderly manner using the script system. In their first publication it was still called the "racket system". Later they called it the "script system" (Table 5.2). The script system comprises three elements: the script beliefs and associated feelings, the expressions of script with their observable behaviour, and supporting memories. These writers defined the script system as a self-supporting, distorted system of feelings, thoughts, and behaviour that is maintained by persons bound by their script. Using this analysis in a conversation with a client, it can be made clear how this person maintains his frame of reference.

> Hannah is the eldest. She has a younger brother. When her mother was pregnant, her father still lived with his parents. Her mother moved in with him on the farm. Hannah's birth was a desired event, and the memory of her early years is that they were safe and comfortable. However, everything changed when her brother was born. The grandfather considered her brother to be the heir to the farm and he received the natural recognition of her father and grandfather that Hannah longed for. Moreover, she began to see the problems of living with this large family. The grandfather—an ill-mannered, tyrannical, authoritarian man—viewed her parents as having no say in the affairs of the household and on the farm.
>
> She learned from her mother to ignore difficult situations and to efface herself. She saw how her mom was sometimes suffering from the situation and she tried to support her by being the loyal eldest

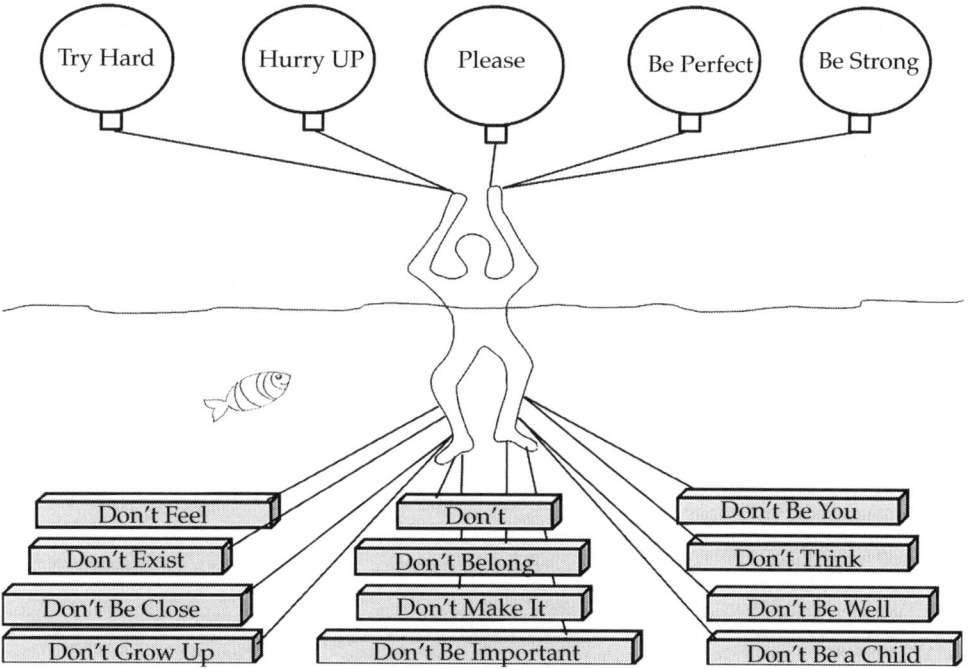

Figure 5.7. The drowning person diagram (adapted from Adrienne Lee, in Tilney 1998, p.30).

> daughter. She didn't express her jealousy of the privileges her brother enjoyed. Instead of getting angry, she would feel sad or she secretly felt sorry for herself. Her low self-esteem led to the conviction that she was too fat. She could not really enjoy herself or relax. She hoped her problems would disappear when she moved in with her boyfriend. However, she remains intensely troubled by feelings of guilt for abandoning her mother and by her frustrations with the state of affairs on the farm.

Supporting memories

- Everyone at the table: grandfather eats a lot and has no shame or table manners; no one listens to her, while there is plenty of attention for her brother's stories
- Father and mother have an argument about how grandfather controls the money and father takes the side of grandfather, not mother.
- Grandfather is proud of her brother and ignores her.
- Mother calls her when she is sad and tells her that she misses her daughter.

The three columns are mutually reinforcing and thus ensure the self-supporting effect of the script system. The trick is to break the vicious cycle. This can be done at any point:

- Reformulating the script convictions into positive terms and making space for repressed, authentic feelings.

Table 5.2. The script system.

A. Script beliefs and feelings	B. Expressions of script	C. Supporting memories
Beliefs about: 1. Oneself; 2. The other; 3. Life and the world.	1. Observable behaviour.	Emotional memories of script-forming moments (at these moments one collects "stamps" which bring the unfolding of the script closer).
Intrapsychic processes: Repressed feelings and needs during script-decisions.	2. Internal consequences, such as somatic disorders and muscle tension.	
	3. Fantasies which maintain the script and which connect you to the pain in the script: 'That will teach them, later they will regret that...'	

- Changing behaviour into positive, powerful, and autonomous behaviour.
- Replacing unpleasant feelings with pleasant and relaxing feelings.
- Changing fantasies into plans and positive visualisations.
- Supporting memories of positive situations.

You can begin to revise your script convictions by entering into conversation from your Adult with people you trust. In this way you can verify if what you consider to be true correlates with reality. You learn to distinguish between then and there and here and now. You can also change your behaviour, which is often easier to revise than your beliefs. Someone who is convinced that he is "not worth the effort" may be instructed to behave for ten days as someone who oozes self-esteem. This person can then experience how the environment reacts to this. Role-playing during training sessions or therapy also works this way. This provides an opportunity to practise with different behaviour and to experience how the feedback from the other changes in such a way that supporting the old behaviour becomes impossible. This is also true in society. The sometimes hard-fought legislation imposed by the government to wear seat belts has changed perceptions of safety in traffic (Hay, 2004). The smoking ban in public places has significantly reduced the number of smokers. If you land up in a positive spiral by these measures, instead of receiving the same negative self-fulfilling prophecies, you build up a large arsenal of positive experiences from which you can draw.

Table 5.3. Hannah's script system.

A. Script beliefs and feelings	B. Expressions of Script	C. Supporting memories
1. My desires and needs are not important. I am fat and ugly. I achieve the most when I am quiet and sad and never angry. 2. Every one in the family is more important than me. I have to remain quiet and adapt, just like mother. 3. Girls don't really count. Autonomy is dangerous. Repressed feelings: anger, shame and fear.	1. Adaptive and friendly behaviour, attention and care for others, effacing oneself. 2. Eating disorders, tense muscles. 3. Fantasies about the death of grandfather and grandmother, so that the family is finally together again. Fantasies that her brother has an accident and that her father finally values her. Or fantasies that she becomes severely ill and then gets attention and recognition, especcially from her father.	– Everyone at the table: grandmother eats a lot and has no shame or table manners; no one listens to her, while there is plenty of attention for her brother's stories. – Father and mother have an argument about how grandfather controls the money and father takes the side of grandfather, not mother. – Grandfather is proud of her brother and ignores her. – Mother calls her when she is sad and tells her that she misses her daughter.

Table 5.4. The autonomy system.

A. Revisited convictions and feelings	B. Autonomous expressions concerning one's life plan	C. Positive supporting memories
Revisited convictions about: 1. Oneself; 2. The other; 3. Life and the world. Intrapsychic: authentic feelings.	1. Observable behaviour. 2. Identifying and accepting internal effects in your body. 3. Developing and stimulating positive fantasies and visualisation.	Collecting positive emotional memories.

Cognitive dissonance

If you give a person who is convinced he is "not worth the effort" the task of behaving like someone "brimming with self-esteem", this person will experience an inner conflict between behaviour and conviction. A cognitive dissonance is created. The non-congruency of acts and convictions causes stress. Often people tend to resolve this stress by returning to their old behaviour. If, however, they have planned to really want to change their behaviour, they will encounter their old limiting script convictions. There is a good chance that they will then be able to replace these with new attitudes, which promote autonomy (see Table 5.4).

5.2   Further theory

5.2.1   The body: foundation of the script

The formation of the script begins from birth and perhaps even in the womb. In the first years of life, the brain undergoes tremendous growth and early experiences are neurobiologically recorded. In particular, the right brain hemisphere, the more associative, non-verbal part of the brain, is active. Caregivers and the child are connected via their right hemispheres. Without words, the child incorporates the intense relationship patterns from this time: the emotions of the parents and the experiences they have with each other and with the baby. These experiences are stored by the young child and contribute to the development of functions like regulating emotions and mentalising: understanding that the other person has a different spirit than you, and thinks, feels, and acts according to a different frame of reference. From all this, we can deduce that the beginning of the formation of the script takes place without words, and especially physically. Berne called this basis of the script the protocol: the original experiences that form the basic pattern of the script. The child feels and sees how the parents behave in all sorts of circumstances, and he incorporates these experiences with their corresponding affective colouring.

This process is preverbal and not conscious and usually only becomes visible during intense moments in adult life, in intimate relationships. Suddenly a wordless memory from a very early relationship is re-enacted in the here and now, often with corresponding bodily experiences (Cornell, 2008a, 2008b; Ligabue, 1991; Steere, 1982; Waldenkranz-Piselli, 1999).

Cornell (2008a, 2010) elaborated and described the concept of the "protocol". He described the therapy process of a young, successful lawyer, struggling for years with her anxiety about being overweight. Now that she had a steady relationship, this anxiety occasionally came out fiercely. At one point, when she had gained a few pounds, she got negative comments from her mother ("Now your boyfriend will surely end it") and her grandfather. She herself said that "my body is unhappy". The therapist asked her to whom her body actually belonged: herself, or to her mother, who suffered from chronic bingeing and who had been chronically unhappy and lonely since her divorce (which happened, according to the mother, because she was too fat)? It appeared that the separation from the mother still had not taken place, which became increasingly evident once she entered into the relationship with the young man.

In psychotherapy, one can work with this kind of early somatic experience if the therapist is receptive to what the client is communicating. Cornell calls this "somatic resonance". Feelings that a client cannot handle, and of which the client is often himself not aware, are nonetheless present in the room and can be absorbed by the therapist and returned to the client in a form that is manageable for him.

5.2.2 Script protocol

Berne wrote at great length about scripts and the young child's efforts to make sense of his family environment, so as to make adaptive decisions to adjust to the world created within that family's system. Script was a form of early childhood narrative that guided (and inhibited) the growing child's developmental arc. The formation of script was dependent upon the child's attainment of some self-reflective and language-based capacities of awareness. Berne made fleeting references to what he called the script protocol as the preverbal and non-verbal incorporations of a family's ways of being and relating that a child internalises unconsciously. But Berne left this idea and any systematic accounting of the preverbal years of life undeveloped.

A series of articles in the *Transactional Analysis Journal* in recent years have taken up Berne's idea of script protocol and elaborated a much fuller accounting of the patterns of non-verbal foundations of script (Caizzi, 2012; Cornell, 2010; Cornell & Landaiche, 2006, 2008; Guglielmotti, 2008; Ligabue, 2007; Pierini, 2008). Cornell and Landaiche elaborated the significance of Berne's brief comments on the protocol that underlay script formation:

> protocol is not a set of adaptive or defensive decisions like a script; it is not remembered in a narrative fashion, but lived/felt in the immediacy of one's body; protocol is the literal embodiment of the repetitive, often affectively intense, patterns of relatedness preceding the infant's capacity of ego function … . (2006, p. 204)

We are suggesting that with this concept of protocol, Berne was trying to capture the sense of the most fundamental, non-verbal aspects of what it means to relate to someone. This deepening understanding of protocol has begun to address the somatic foundations of script. It has provided a theoretical insight that has further linked TA to the clinical theories of Bollas (1987, 1989) and other contemporary psychoanalysts and to recent research in subsymbolic organisation (Bucci, 1997, 2008), implicit and procedural memory, and trauma.

5.2.3 The script as organisational structure

One of the criticisms of the original script theory is that it is too rigid and especially that it is pathologising. Fanita English (1988) found Berne too fatalistic in his view that the games are like small rehearsals for the big show of the script.

According to her, games are failed attempts to retrieve and return strokes, especially when the switch occurs. Many people quickly revert to their familiar substitute feelings after the switch (see section 4.2.4 in Chapter Four). English prefers to speak of the script as an existential pattern that serves to assist in understanding the reality around you. In her view, everyone weaves his own tapestry according to the person's temperament, early experiences, convictions, and fantasies.

The script is an organisational structure in this process, which has its origins in childhood, but is subject to change throughout life. The script is not necessarily pathological, but is mainly a blueprint that is constantly adjusted on the basis of the human need for structuring time, space, and relationships. English developed a "four story exercise", whereby people describe fairy tales or novels that impressed them during different stages in their lives: one story before their fifth year, a story from their time at primary school, a story from their adolescence, and one recent story. From these stories, certain elements and patterns are crystallised. The themes are already visible in the first story from childhood. The story in adolescence is sometimes a tale of protest and sometimes a reconsideration of the potentially harmful or constraining aspects of the script. Eventually, a creative and dynamic story arises about the main themes in everyone's life (English, 2010).

5.2.4 Resilience and the script

Cornell (1988) delivered fundamental criticism of Berne's concept of the script, based on research from developmental psychology. He quotes Thomas and Chess (1980), who did research among "normal" children, children from "high risk" families, blind and deaf children, and children with motor disabilities. They concluded that because of the plasticity of the brain, children, despite a disability or stressful life circumstances, can develop into well-functioning adults. Important to success and satisfaction in later life are the temperament and skills of the child and also whether or not there is a "good fit" between the child and his family and the social environment, particularly in school. It is dangerous to conclude on the basis of psychopathology in adults, that poor childhood necessarily leads to disorders in adulthood (Cornell, 2008). It is much more informative to ask which children do well, and why, despite the setbacks in their lives.

Another study that Cornell cites is that of Vaillant (1977), who followed 256 "promising students" at Harvard University; 95 of them participated in the study for more than thirty years. Vaillant emphasised the importance of adaptation and the development of mature defence mechanisms, such as sublimation, suppression, anticipation, altruism, and humour. One of his conclusions is that a successful career and a fulfilling marriage are relatively independent from whether or not the person had a happy childhood. The lives of the men examined in the study were full of surprises.

Vaillant describes his interview with the fifty-five-year-old Alan, who participated in the study for more than thirty years. As a twenty year old, this man was described as "promising" but also as a rebel in whom it was not yet clear how his life would unfold. In the decades that followed, Alan remained on the sidelines of life. He had an insignificant, poorly paid job and wanted to be a writer, but his manuscripts were not being accepted anywhere. He married and divorced three times and had little contact with his children or friends. When he was fifty-five, he lived in a shabby apartment in a bad neighbourhood. And yet he gave a bright, balanced impression. In the last five years, two important changes had taken place in his life. He had come out to reveal his homosexuality and he had had a few short-term relationships with men. Moreover, over the last few years, some of his short stories and poems had been published in regional magazines and through publishers.

Cornell concludes on the basis of the aforementioned studies:

1. A reconstruction of childhood based on the adult's script is by definition incomplete and inaccurate.

2. Isolated traumas from childhood rarely have a great influence on adulthood.
3. Defensive patterns change, both in childhood and adulthood.
4. Psychological maturation is not linear and smooth, but often discontinuous.
5. Intimate relationships in adulthood (with a partner and friends, at work, or sometimes also in psychotherapy) have a large influence on the improvement in the quality of life.

The aim in life can be to give meaning to one's life experiences, no matter how negative, annoying, or confusing these may be. Cornell defines the script as an ongoing process of self-defining and sometimes self-limiting psychological constructions of reality. People can take important script decisions at any time during their lives. A key concept for the rehabilitation of people faced with adversity is resilience, a mix of cognitive strategies, social support, and self-esteem. Factors such as luck and timing also play a role. This also means, Cornell argues, that it might be more beneficial if a professional, together with the client, carefully maps the effectiveness of the client's current daily functioning, rather than attempting to therapeutically "re-enact" a particular phase of development.

5.2.5 Unconscious relational pattern

Richard Erskine states that the script develops at times when there are deficiencies in meaningful relationships, between the child and the parents, but also in the present between partners, colleagues, or friends. He defines the script as: "a life plan based on survival reactions, implicit conclusions and explicit decisions which may be taken at any time of development, whereby spontaneity is inhibited and the flexibility to solve problems and to engage in relationships with other people is constrained" (2010, p. 1).

In Erskine's view, the script is thus predominantly limiting and psychotherapy is aimed at "script cure": freeing oneself from the script. According to Erskine, it is mainly experiences of "misattunement", of misunderstanding or a lack of attunement, which lead to script decisions (2010). Critical needs or the small daily needs of the child were not met. The parents did not respond optimally because they were tired, stressed out, too busy with other things, or ignorant. The child can perceive such a lack of tuning as "I'm not important", "I'm a bad kid", or "I must do it myself, and I can!" Such unconscious decisions and conclusions lead, later on in life, to a solid sense of self or to feelings of unfulfilled longing, emptiness, unpleasant physical sensations, and the feeling that you have to be wary in relationships.

Cognitive fixations

Script convictions are often difficult to change. They can be understood as "cognitive fixations". Cognitive fixations do not readily change under the influence of cognitive interventions, such as reading a book, speaking, convincing, discussing, debating, and/or being lectured to. A change of cognitive fixations calls for social interventions: new experiences with others. People need new experiences to start to believe that something can be different, experiences that convince them that a different way may be more interesting and effective.

According to Erskine, the best antidote for a limiting script is a healing relationship, a friendship or love relationship, a healthy professional relationship at work, or a form of psychotherapy based on the therapeutic relationship. The therapist uses "inquiry, attunement and involvement" (enquiries, tuning, and being involved) as techniques to establish contact with the client (Erskine, 1993). Next, the therapist offers a relationship style in which the client can experience needs that have been neglected.

Cornell and Bonds-White (2001) offer a different perspective on aspects of the therapeutic relationship that facilitates script change, emphasising the therapeutic relationship's provision of space for "inquiry, disturbance, and creativity" (p. 80) through which clients are able to develop the capacity for self-observation and self-agency. They suggest, "It is the gradual development of the client's capacities for curiosity, self-scrutiny, differentiation, and relational conflict within the therapeutic relationship that is carried outside the office as the basis for structural and interpersonal change" (pp. 81–82).

5.2.6 Narrative/constructivist model of script

The narrative/constructivist perspective on script (Allen, 2010; Allen & Allen, 1995, 1997; Doan, 1997; Parry, 1997; Tosi, 2010) argues for a conceptualisation of the storytelling and meaning-making functions of life scripts, while challenging the more deterministic aspects of traditional script theories. Tosi, for example, writes, "Narratives are not only an expression of the script, but also a way of shaping and reshaping it, finding new meanings and integrating old and new experiences" (p. 35). She places Berne's definition of script as "a sub-set of this more inclusive way of understanding scripts" (p. 35).

From a similar narrative viewpoint, but considering script through learning theory, Newton (2006) links script formation and its ongoing development to the learning cycle; experiences, both early and subsequent, are unconsciously processed (reflected on), partly through the stories we hear, to create personal meanings which are then generalised into script beliefs and decisions. Our resulting actions can reinforce those decisions but can also be changed through relational experiences different from those that influenced our early learning. The "learning cycle" of script formation can become a learning "spiral" of restorative experiences.

In the summary of their efforts to bring a constructivist sensibility to transactional analysis, Allen and Allen (1997) offer a comprehensive, side-by-side comparison of the two models. The aim of the constructivist perspective is to free the client from the dominating, self-defining stories of one's life and capacities, to see script as highly influential, psychological texts "of which he or she may not be totally the author" (p. 97).

5.2.7 The script helix

Summers and Tudor (2000), and Tudor and Summers (2014), agree with Cornell in emphasising the mutuality of the relationship between child and parents. They add a further dimension by stating that script influences are not limited to the relationship parents-child, but also involve other polarities and the continua between them. In their "script helix" they describe the influence of polarities like female-male, heterosexual-gay, black-white, among others (see Figure 5.8). So may the predominant polarity that influences the experiences of a child brought up by gay, lesbian, bisexual, or transsexual parents, depending on their circumstances at certain points in their life, be a gay-straight polarity. Or an important polarity in the identity development of a black child brought up in a predominantly white culture is likely to be the black minority home culture and the white dominant school culture. Such influences are not determined, but constructed: the construction of the script matrix is itself a personal construct. The script matrix becomes a co-created series of matrices, rather like a constantly changing helix of relational atoms, spinning around us, by which we tell, retell, and reformulate the stories of different influences on our continuing development.

5.3 Furthermore

5.3.1 Episcript

Sometimes people pass on their pathological script messages to others. This way they divert their own tragic life and pass it on like a "hot potato" to others, who then later go on to harm themselves or others. English discovered this mechanism (English, 1969) when one of her supervisors reported that another of his clients had "gone and done themselves in". Surprised at the bluntness of this statement, she continued her enquiry. She discovered that this supervisor himself had a destructive script with suicide as the final settlement. Without being aware of it, the supervisor had passed on his suicidal tendencies to his client, who, by committing suicide, had provisionally relieved the supervisor of the need to end his own life.

The episcript plays a role between parents and children, but also with teachers, managers, therapists, religious leaders, and other "donors" who can find a vulnerable "receiver" for their pathological script.

5.3.2 Tragic results

Berne described three endings to the tragic scripts:

- With suicide, from the existential position "I –, you +".
- With murder, from the existential position "I +, you—".
- With going mad, from the existential position "I –, you—".

Holloway (1973) developed this further. The injunctions from childhood are supplemented by these negative "escape clauses": if life really becomes unbearable, I can always kill myself, murder someone, or go mad. To make a script change possible, in this kind of script, it is essential that, first, via an Adult decision, this outcome is reviewed, for example, with the statement "Whatever happens, I will continue to live", or "I will never kill myself or another, either by accident or on purpose", or "I will not go mad" (Goulding & McClure Goulding, 1978; Holloway, 1973).

It is important that—in the long run—this is not a promise that the client makes to the therapist (for then the Child of the client can still get out of it), but an Adult decision of this person. Following the decision not to kill himself or another, a redecision can be made to live. This should be done from the Child ego state.

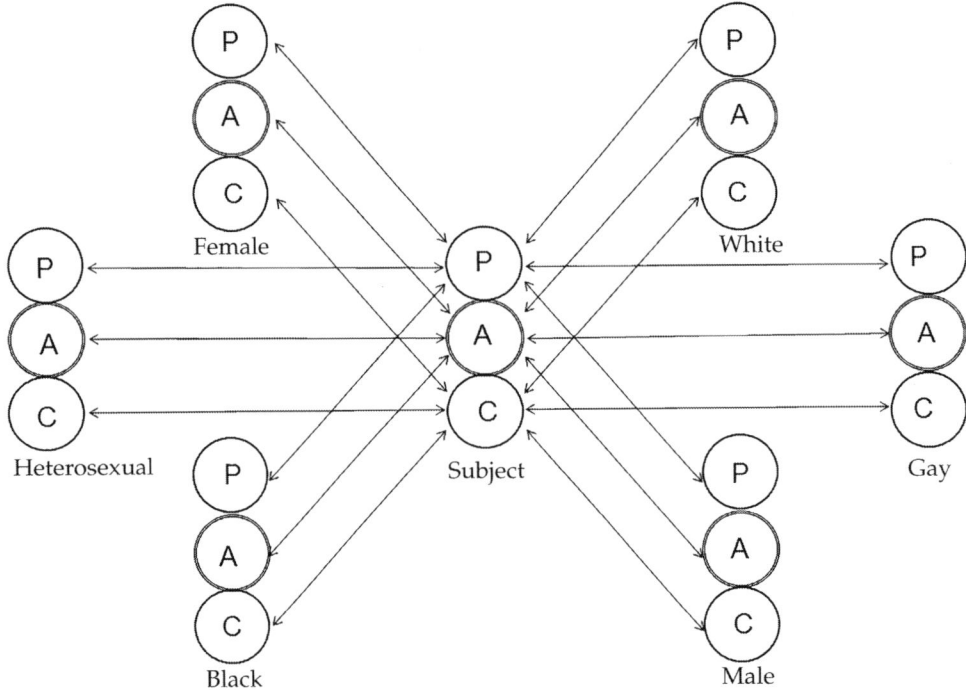

Figure 5.8. A script helix.

In extreme cases it is not possible to make a "no suicide", "no murder", or a "don't go mad" contract. Sometimes someone is acutely suicidal and he does not want to create a "no-suicide contract", even for a short period of time, like until the next session. Sometimes someone is psychotic or has brain damage, or is under the influence of alcohol or drugs, or the person is living in such difficult social and economic conditions that the environment actively supports the decision to commit suicide or murder. In such situations, the client must be very intensively monitored or committed to care, until he is in a position to make such a contract.

If a "no-contract" is agreed to, this may mean that the Child of the client is initially anxious because the familiar escape route has been closed. At the same time, it can be a relief for the Child that the pressure has been taken off and space can emerge for redecision and script change (Stewart, 2010). Destructive scripts can be passed on from one generation to another. Berne (1972) stated that the script should not be traced back to the parents, but the grandparents. Noriega (2004, 2010), who received the Berne Memorial Award in 2008, elaborated on this in her study on the transgenerational transfer of scripts.

5.3.3 Script circle

The script is, properly considered, a closed system. It was originally formed in the life of a child who was looking for ways to get what he needed. But in the here and now, it is often limiting to autonomy. Piet Weisfelt (1996) explains that the script consists of a (continuous) circle: from experience to interpretation, from interpretation to conclusion, from conclusion to conviction, from conviction to decision, from decision to behaviour, from behaviour to reaction, and from reaction to payoff (translated for this edition). The payoff is the confirmation of the original script convictions. Told you so!

> Frits experiences time and again that his father looks at him in a certain (annoyed) way when he tells him about his performance at school (experience). He interprets this look as one of disapproval and concludes that in his father's eyes, he is not trying hard enough at school. Gradually he becomes convinced that he is inadequate in situations where he must perform. He decides to avoid situations as much as possible in which things are required of him. He exhibits hesitant and wait-and-see behaviour as soon as he is expected to perform. The reaction of the world around him, especially at work, is often one of annoyed glances. Those glances appear familiar to Frits. He is, so to speak, back home. The initial experience with his father is reinforced time and again (payoff).

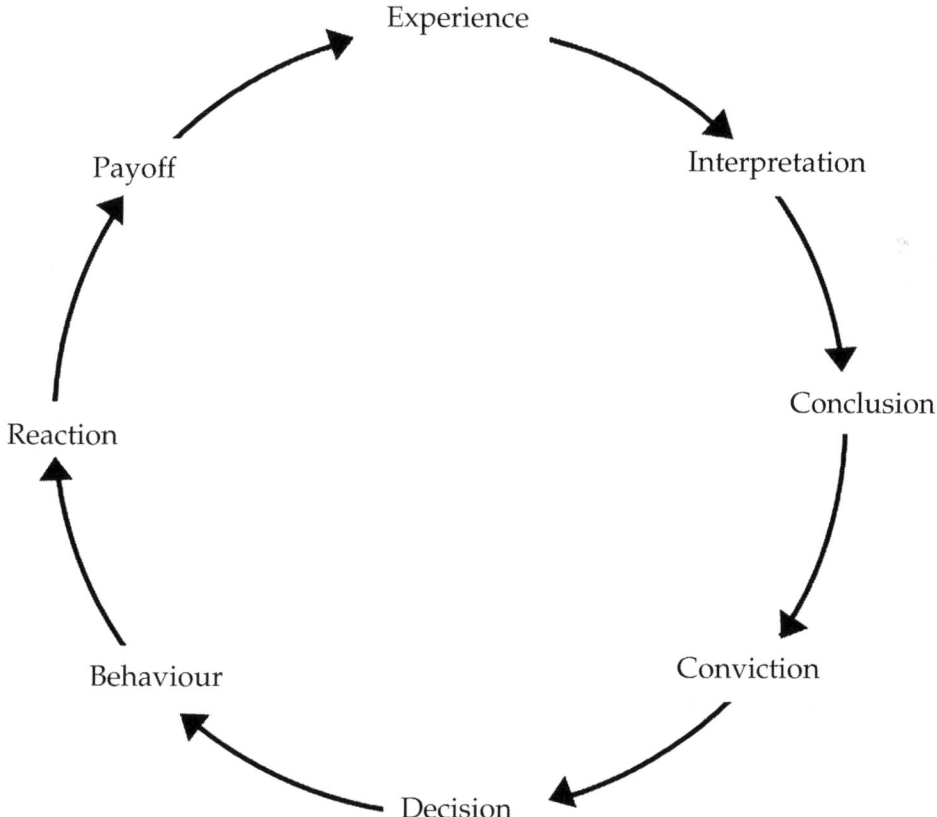

Figure 5.9. Script circle.

The script circle is an extremely effective tool to map script patterns. After all, awareness is the first step towards greater autonomy.

5.3.4 Attachment and the script

Richard Erskine (2009) believes that in the course of years, too little thought has been given to the influence of "primal" dramas on the formation of the script. Especially the influence of very early, preverbal, and physiological survival responses at the protocol level, with corresponding conclusions and decisions of the child, have not received enough consideration within the development of the perception of the script and script formation. The formation of the script, according to Erskine, takes place within a complex network of neural pathways found in thoughts, affections, biochemical and psychological reactions, fantasies, relational patterns, and the capacity for self-regulation. In this regard, Erskine corresponds closely with Cornell's thinking (see section 5.2.3).

It was John Bowlby (1979) who examined insecure attachment and described this as the physical result of a disruption of attachment in early childhood dependency relationships. Ainsworth, Blehar, Waters, & Wall (1978) found that mothers of securely attached children were well tuned to their children. These mothers noticed if the attunement was not quite right, and were able to correct this immediately. In addition to secure attachment, which occurs with around 70% of humans, there are also three insecure attachment patterns: avoidant, preoccupied, and disorganised. These attachment patterns (script patterns), according to Erskine, are noticeable in behaviour, transactions with others, script convictions, fantasies, and everything people make themselves believe about life. The healing of an insecure attachment requires a professional relationship, in which sensitivity, respect, appreciation, consistency, and reliability are paramount.

5.3.5 Hybrid script

Can the behaviour of someone be sufficiently explained if you only examine the personal script? As noted earlier, such an explanation may have too many characteristics of linear causal reasoning: A is caused by B. However, once people are involved, principles of linear causal explanation fall short (see Chapter Three). Individual behaviour can never be completely understood by examining someone's personal history. It seems that Berne (1961) already suspected this when he wrote "The goal of structural analysis is to establish the predominance of reality-testing ego states and free them from contamination by archaic and foreign elements. When this has been accomplished, the patient can proceed to *transactional analysis*: first, the analysis of simple transactions, then the analysis of stereotyped series of transactions, and finally the analysis of long complex operations often involving several people and usually based on rather elaborate fantasies" (p. 22). At least he realised that complexity is a necessary part of a thorough analysis. This complexity comes into view when it is recognised that behaviour always occurs in a context in which that behaviour is always influenced by that context.

No human being is a "standalone". Every individual is part of a network of contexts: the family in which one lives, the family in which a person grew up, the city or area where someone lives, the nationality that a person has, the company or organisation where someone works, and so forth. In social psychology, there is a movement that assumes that human identity is by definition a social identity. What behaviour is considered appropriate and acceptable, is largely determined by the norms of the context in which a person finds themselves. Hogg and Abrams (1998) speak of "the social psychological nature of group membership". The group largely determines the intergroup and intragroup behaviour of group members. Groups to which a person belongs have a profound influence on the identity of the individual. In traditional social psychological approaches, it is often overlooked how groups provide the individual with an identity. Hogg and Abrams call this "the group in the individual" (p. 3). In each answer that someone gives to the question "Who am I?", there are traces of the group of which the person considers himself a member. Whatever a person does, one will always need to consider the extent to which that behaviour is partly controlled by the script characteristics of the group.

After all, whoever says "I am a man", or "I am a woman", hereby categorises him- or herself as a member of this particular social group. That does something to one's behaviour. The same goes for someone who says, "I'm Dutch", "I'm a therapist", "I'm a civil servant", or "I'm a TA professional". At a subconscious level, this identification influences what a person does or does not do, and how someone does something. This becomes very evident as soon as there is a question of stereotyping. A real man! A 100% Dutchman! A true civil servant! An all-out TA professional! Stereotyping is always provoked by self-stereotyping.

The founder of psychodrama, Jacob Levy Moreno (1946), with whose work Berne was acquainted, follows a path down the middle and states that "the individuals themselves and the interrelations between them must be treated as the nuclear structure of every social situation". Moreno believes that if you want to properly understand behaviour, you have to simultaneously study the greater whole and its parts. Within TA, we propose speaking of this in terms of the fundamental hybrid nature of script behaviour. Just as it is not always clear, with a hybrid car, which engine propels the car (gasoline engine or electric motor), one cannot see from the outside what makes a person do what he does. This insight leads to a necessary restraint in assessing the behaviour, for example, of employees in groups and organisations. In section 13.3 of Chapter Thirteen we discuss the influence of the cultural script on behaviour.

5.4 Related theories

5.4.1 Infant research

In recent decades, more and more research has been done among very young children, even with babies only a few days old. One of the first who did this kind of research was Margaret Mahler, who with her colleagues observed toddlers and their mothers while the children played with each other in the nursery and sometimes came to their mothers when they had fallen or needed something. On the basis of this study, she developed her theory of separation-individuation, which concerns the different stages a child goes through from when he psychologically detaches from his caregivers until he reaches a certain degree of individuality around the third year. At this point, "object constancy" is achieved, which is to say that the child forms a constant, positive internal image of the mother (Mahler, Pine, & Bergman, 1975, p. 109).

Daniel Stern (1985, 1990, 1995) and his colleagues examined much younger children: babies of several days to months old. From the experiment of recognising the milk from their own mothers, it was made clear that more than just C_1 is present within an infant of only a few days old (which can only smell stimuli of the external world). There is also an A_1 which can convert sensory stimuli (the smell of the milk) into motor responses (turning the head) and which can choose. At this young age, the roots of the script are formed and physically recorded.

5.4.2 Phases of life

The developmental psychologist Erik Erikson (1902–1994) is generally regarded as one of the most influential thinkers in the field of developmental psychology. He gave a permanent place to the concepts of identity and "basic trust" in theories on the evolution of humans "from the cradle to the grave". The central theme in Erikson's work (1950) is the importance of identity and the role of the social environment. In his work as a child psychoanalyst, he learned to see the psychopathological symptoms of his young patients as characteristics of a crisis that every growing young adult has to go through. The child learns to find his own place in society along a path of conflict and crisis.

In his theory of the life cycle, which has become one of the standard theories within developmental psychology, Erikson relies primarily on Freud's model of psychosexual development. Yet Erikson grants the individual a greater freedom in relation to the drives of life than Freud was prone to do. Erikson especially saw a greater role laid out for the social environment in which the child develops.

The development of the human being, in Erikson's view, proceeds, from the cradle to the grave, in eight phases in which an existential aspect of human existence is central. In each phase, a crisis occurs between the polarities of the corresponding aspect. The developing person is confronted in each stage with the task of taking ownership of the positive end of the polarity, rather than the negative. These are the polarities:

- trust versus mistrust.
- autonomy versus shame and doubt.
- initiative versus guilt.
- industry versus inferiority.
- identity versus role confusion.
- intimacy versus isolation.
- generativity versus stagnation.
- ego integrity versus despair.

A central concept in the psychology of Erikson is "reciprocity". The growing person develops his own identity in relation to the environment and the people around him. This means that mutual influence takes place. In the interaction with children, educators meet themselves. The quest for one's own identity inevitably arises in the contact with small and larger children.

5.4.3 Narrative approach

The narrative approach assumes that people are often trapped in a "dominant" story that restricts them from finding solutions and alternatives. By placing oneself, as therapist, in a "not-knowing" position and considering the client as an expert in his own situation, you can establish a conversation in which the self-respect of the client is enhanced.

By listening to the stories of individual clients or families, you can encourage them to see their identity as separate from their circumstances, a process called externalisation (Fraenkel, Hameline, & Shannon, 2009; White, 2007). Through metaphors, associations, drawings, and other creative approaches, clients are encouraged to reconnect with their expectations, dreams, and plans.

For example, they write a letter to themselves from the imaginative position of what their lives will be like over two years. Moreover, not the vulnerability, but the resilience of clients is given a central position: their own strength, creativity, and assertive ability to survive in sometimes difficult circumstances (Rober, Walravens, & Versteynen, in press). This approach, whereby clients are regarded as the experts of their own situation appears to help them regain their self-respect and their hope for a better future. These authors have elaborated applications of narrative theories in psychotherapy independent of transactional analysis, but they have much in common with the narrative/constructivist model developed within TA.

References

Ainsworth, M., Blehar, M., Waters, E., & Wall, S. (1978). *Patterns of Attachment*. Hillsdale, MI: Erlbaum.

Allen, J. R. (2010). From a child psychiatry practice. In: R. Erskine (Ed.), *Life Scripts: A Transactional Analysis of Unconscious Relational Patterns* (pp. 151–178). London: Karnac.

Allen, J. R., & Allen, B. A. (1995). Narrative theory, redecision therapy, and postmodernism. *Transactional Analysis Journal*, 25(4): 327–334.

Allen, J. R., & Allen, B. A. (1997). A new type of transactional analysis and one version of script work with a constructivist sensibility. *Transactional Analysis Journal*, 27(2): 89–98.

Barrow, G. (2014). "Whatever!" The wonderful possibilities of adolescence. *Transactional Analysis Journal*, 44(2): 167–174.

Berne, E. (1961). *Transactional Analysis in Psychotherapy*. New York: Grove Press.

Berne, E. (1972). *What Do You Say After You Say Hello?* New York: Grove Press.

Berne, E. (2010). *A Montreal Childhood*. Seville, Spain: Editorial Jeder.

Bollas, C. (1987). *The Shadow of the Object: Psychoanalysis of the Unthought Known*. New York: Columbia University Press.

Bollas, C. (1989). *Forces of Destiny: Psychoanalysis and human Idiom*. Northvale, NJ: Jason Aronson.

Bowlby, J. (1979). *The Making and Breaking of Affectional Bonds*. London: Routledge.

Bucci, W. (1997). *Psychoanalysis and Cognitive Science: A Multiple Code Theory*. New York: Guilford Press.

Bucci, W. (2008). The role of bodily experience in emotional organization. In: F. S. Anderson (Ed.), *Bodies in Treatment: The Unspoken Dimension* (51–76). New York: Analytic Press.

Caizzi, C. (2012). Embodied trauma: Using the subsymbolic mode to access and change script protocol in traumatized adults. *Transactional Analysis Journal*, 42: 165–175.

Clarkson, P. (1992). Physis in transactional analysis. *Transactional Analysis Journal*, 22: 202–209.

Cornell, W. F. (1988). Life script theory: A critical review from a developmental perspective. *Transactional Analysis Journal*, 18(4): 270–282.
Cornell, W. F. (2008a). Babies, brains, and bodies: Somatic foundations of the Child ego state. In: *Explorations in Transactional Analysis. The Meech Lake Papers* (pp. 141–158). Pleasanton, CA: TA Press.
Cornell, W. F. (2008b). Body-Centred Psychotherapy. In: *Explorations in Transactional Analysis: The Meech Lake Papers* (pp. 176–198). Pleasanton, CA: TA Press.
Cornell, W. F. (2010). Whose body is it? Somatic relations in script and script protocol. In: R. G. Erskine (Ed.), *Life Scripts. A Transactional Analysis of Unconscious Relational Patterns* (pp. 101–126). London: Karnac.
Cornell, W. F., & Bonds-White, F. (2001). Therapeutic relatedness in transactional analysis: The truth of love or the love of truth. *Transactional Analysis Journal*, 31(1): 71–83.
Cornell, W. F., & Landaiche, N. M. (2006). Impasse and intimacy: Applying Berne's concept of script protocol. *Transactional Analysis Journal*, 36: 196–213.
Cornell, W. F., & Landaiche, N. M. (2008). Nonconscious processes and self-development: Key concepts from Eric Berne and Christopher Bollas. *Transactional Analysis Journal*, 38: 200–217.
Doan, R. E. (1997). Narrative therapy, postmodernism, and constructivism: Discussion and distinctions. *Transactional Analysis Journal*, 27(2): 128–133.
English, F. (1969). Episcript and the hot potato game. *Transactional Analysis Bulletin*, 8(32): 77–81.
English, F. (1988). Whither scripts? *Transactional Analysis Journal*, 18(4): 294–303.
English, F. (2010). It takes a lifetime to play out a script. In: R. G. Erskine (Ed.), *Life Scripts. A Transactional Analysis of Unconscious Relational Patterns* (pp. 217–238). London: Karnac.
Erikson, E. H. (1950). *Childhood and Society*. New York: W. W. Norton, 1993.
Ernst, F. (1971). The OK Corral: The grid for get-on-with. *Transactional Analysis Journal*, 1(4): 33–42.
Erskine, R. G. (1980). Script cure: Behavioural, intrapsychic, and physiological. *Transactional Analysis Journal*, 10(2): 102–106.
Erskine, R. G. (1993). Inquiry, attunement and involvement in the psychotherapy of dissociation. *Transactional Analysis Journal*, 23(3): 184–190.
Erskine, R. G. (2009). Life scripts and attachment patterns: Theoretical integration and therapeutic involvement. *Transactional Analysis Journal*, 39(4): 207–218.
Erskine, R. G. (Ed.) (2010). *Life Scripts. A Transactional Analysis of Unconscious Relational Patterns*. London: Karnac.
Erskine, R. G., & Zalcman, M. (1979). The racket system: A model for racket analysis. *Transactional Analysis Journal*, 9(1): 51–59.
Fraenkel, P., Hameline, T., & Shannon, M. (2009). Narrative and collaborative practices in work with families that are homeless. *Journal of Marital and Family Therapy*, 35: 325–342.
Goulding, R., & McClure Goulding, M. (1976). Injunctions, decisions and redecisions. *Transactional Analysis Journal*, 6(1): 41–48.
Goulding, R., & McClure Goulding, M. (1978). *The Power Is in the Patient*. San Francisco, CA: TA Press.
Goulding, R., & McClure Goulding, M. (1979). *Changing Lives through Redecision Therapy*. New York: Brunner/Mazel.
Graaf, A. de, & Kunst, K. (2005). *Einstein and the Art of Sailing*. Watford, UK: Sherwood.
Guglielmotti, R. L. (2008). The quality of the therapeutic relationship as a factor in helping to change the client's protocol or implicit memory. *Transactional Analysis Journal*, 38: 101–109.
Hargaden, H. (2003). Then We'll Come from the Shadows. *Script*, 33(5): 3–6.
Harris, A. B., & Harris, T. (1985). *Staying OK*. London: Jonathan Cape.

Harris, T. (1967). *I'm OK–You're OK*. London: Pan.
Hay, J. (2009). *Working It Out at Work: Understanding Attitudes and Building Relationships*. Watford, UK: Sherwood.
Hogg, M., & Abrams, D. (1998). *Social Identifications: A Social Psychology of Intergroup Relations and Group Processes*. London: Routledge.
Holloway, W. H. (1973). *Shut the Escape Hatch. Monograph IV*. The Monograph Series. Ohio, OH: Midwest Institute for Human Understanding.
Jorgensen, E. W., & Jorgensen, H. I. (1984). *Eric Berne: Master Gamesman. A Transactional Biography*. New York: Grove Press.
Kahler, T. (1978). *Transactional Analysis Revisited*. Little Rock, AR: Human Development Publications.
Kahler, T. (2008). *The Process Therapy Model. The Six Personality Types with Adaptations*. Little Rock, AR: Taibi Kahler Associates.
Kahler, T., & Capers, H. (1974). The Miniscript. *Transactional Analysis Journal*, 4(1): 26–42.
Kendler, K. S., & Prescott, C. A. (2006). *Genes, Environment and Psychopathology*. New York: Guilford Press.
Ligabue, S. (1991). The somatic component of the script in early development. *Transactional Analysis Journal*, 21(1): 21–30.
Ligabue, S. (2007). Being in relationship: Different languages to understand ego states, script, and the body. *Transactional Analysis Journal*, 37: 294–306.
Mahler, M., Pine, F., & Bergman, A. (1975). *The Psychological Birth of the Human Infant*. New York: Basic Books.
Massey, R. F. (1989). Script theory synthesized systematically. *Transactional Analysis Journal*, 19(1): 14–25.
Moreno, J. L. (1946). *Psychodrama (Vol. 1)*. Beacon, NY: Beacon House.
Newton, T. (2006). Script, Psychological Life Plans, and the Learning Cycle. *Transactional Analysis Journal*, 36(3), 186–195.
Noriega, G. (2004). Codependence: A transgenerational script. *Transactional Analysis Journal*, 34(4): 312–322.
Noriega, G. (2010). Transgenerational scripts: The unknown knowledge. In: R. G. Erskine (Ed.), *Life Scripts. A Transactional Analysis of Unconscious Relational Patterns* (pp. 269–290). London: Karnac.
O'Reilly-Knapp, M., & Erskine, R. G. (2010). The script system: An unconscious organization of experience. In: R. G. Erskine (Ed.), *Life Scripts. A Transactional Analysis of Unconscious Relational Patterns* (pp. 291–308). London: Karnac.
Parry, A. (1997). Why we tell stories: The narrative construction of reality. *Transactional Analysis Journal*, 27(2): 118–127.
Pierini, A. (2008). Has the unconscious moved house? *Transactional Analysis Journal*, 38: 110–118.
Rober, P., Walravens. G., & Versteynen, L. (in press). In search of a tale they can live with. Accepted for publication in *Journal of Marital and Family Therapy*.
Steere, D. A. (1982). *Bodily Expressions in Psychotherapy*. New York: Brunner/Mazel.
Steiner, C. (1966). Script and counterscript. *Transactional Analysis Bulletin*, 5(18): 133–135.
Steiner, C. (1974). *Scripts People Live: Transactional Analysis of Life Scripts*. New York: Grove Press.
Stern, D. (1985). *The Interpersonal World of the Infant*. New York: Basic Books.
Stern, D. (1990). *Diary of a Baby*. New York: Basic Books
Stern, D. (1995). *The Motherhood Constellation*. New York: Basic Books.
Stewart, I. (1992). *Eric Berne*. London: Sage.
Stewart, I. (2010). The "three ways out": escape hatches. In: R. G. Erskine (Ed.), *Life Scripts. A Transactional Analysis of Unconscious Relational Patterns* (pp. 127–150). London: Karnac.

Summers, G., & Tudor, K. (2000). Co-creative transactional analysis. *Transactional Analysis Journal*, *30*: 23–40.

Summers, G., & Tudor, K. (2014). Co-creative transactional analysis/introducing co-creative transactional analysis. In: K. Tudor & G. Summers (Eds.), *Co-creative transactional analysis: Papers, responses, dialogues, and developments* (pp. 1–28/235–250). London: Karnac.

Thomas, A., & Chess, S. (1980). *The Dynamics of Psychological Growth*. New York: Brunner/Mazel.

Tilney, T. (Ed.) (1998). *Dictionary of Transactional Analysis*. London: Whurr.

Tosi, M. T. (2010). The lived and narrated script: an ongoing narrative construction. In: R. G. Erskine (Ed.), *Life Scripts: A Transactional Analysis of Unconscious Relational Patterns* (pp. 29–54). London: Karnac.

Tudor, K. (2008). "Take it": A sixth driver. *Transactional Analysis Journal*, *38*(1): 43–57.

Tudor, K., & Summers, G. (Eds.), *Co-creative transactional analysis: Papers, responses, dialogues, and developments* (pp. 235–250). London: Karnac.

Vaillant, G. E. (1977). *Adaptation to Life*. Boston, MA: Little, Brown.

Waldenkranz-Piselli, K. C. (1999). What do we do before we say hello? The body as the stage setting for the script. *Transactional Analysis Journal*, *29*(1): 31–48.

Weisfelt, P. (1996). *Nestgeuren*. (Nest Odors.) Baarn, Netherlands: Nelissen.

White, M. (2007). *Maps of Narrative Practice*. New York: W. W. Norton.

CHAPTER SIX

Passivity and discounting

6.1 Basic theory
    6.1.1 The Cathexis model
    6.1.2 Symbiotic structures
    6.1.3 Passivity, discounting, and redefining
    6.1.4 Passivity cycle
6.2 Further theory
    6.2.1 Discount matrix
    6.2.2 Steps to success
    6.2.3 Passivity confrontation
    6.2.4 Reparenting
    6.2.5 Parent ego state interview
    6.2.6 Integration of differing approaches in TA
    6.2.7 Parent education
    6.2.8 The cycles applied
6.3 Furthermore
    6.3.1 The Cathexis crisis
    6.3.2 Critique and re-evaluation
    6.3.3 Schema therapy
6.4 Related theories
    6.4.1 The "schizophrenogenic family"
    6.4.2 Anti-psychiatry
    6.4.3 "Primary maternal preoccupation"
    6.4.4 Milieu therapy
    6.4.5 Research
    6.4.6 Defence mechanisms
References

In the previous five chapters we considered the core concepts of TA: ego states, strokes, transactions, games, and the script. In the following five chapters we will elaborate on other aspects of TA theory and practice. We will begin with the theory surrounding symbiosis, passivity, discounting, and redefining. The question here is what mental mechanisms keep the script going. What makes people continue to repeat themselves, even when this yields little to no new results? Why is it that people keep investing energy into activities which they ought to know don't offer them what they need? In this chapter the focus is on the phenomena that foster chronic behavioural and cognitive processes, which in TA are often referred to as "passivity". Central to these issues is the mechanism called "discounting", through which people unconsciously ignore certain aspects of themselves, others, and the world around them. The result is that learning and changing do not take place, for there is no incentive to put things in motion.

6.1   Basic theory

6.1.1   The Cathexis model

The late 1960s and early 1970s were a period of intense creativity and experimentation in transactional analysis. Three primary models of TA theory and practice emerged during this time. The first was what came to be known as the "classical" school, a model focused primary on cognitive/behavioural change following closely on Berne's work. The second was the redecision approach developed by the Gouldings, incorporating Gestalt therapy principles. The third was the Cathexis model that was developed to work with severe thinking disorders and emphasised an intense, pseudo-parental therapeutic relationship. Interestingly, each model tended to focus on a different ego state as the primary mechanism of treatment: the Adult in the classical model, the Child in redecision work, and the Parent in the Cathexis approach.

Jacqui Lee Schiff (1969, 1975, 1977) developed a model of TA-based treatment focused initially on her work with severely disturbed adolescents, who were understood to be suffering from schizophrenia. The central premise of the model was that schizophrenia was a mental disturbance resulting from specific kinds of faulty parenting, which are incorporated in the Parent ego state of the child. According to Schiff, the influence of the patient's "crazy" Parent ego state (1969, p. 53) becomes the source of lifelong thought and behavioural disorders. Schiff described the family system of schizophrenic patients as one in which one or both parents established a chronic, unhealthy symbiosis with the growing child, a symbiosis that was dominated by the "crazy" Parent ego state of the mother and/or father. This symbiotic structure prevented the natural and increasingly independent development of the child. Instead of separating and individuating, the child was forced to develop a set of "passive" behaviours that re-established the symbiotic relationship. Therefore Schiff saw it as an essential treatment goal to interrupt and correct passive behaviours and the symbiotic relations that the passivity sought to maintain.

Berne (1961) understood psychopathology to be rooted in the rigidity of the individual's ego state structure. He emphasised that the establishment of "the flow of cathexis" (p. 38), that is, of psychic energy, from one ego state to another was an essential focus of therapy. Schiff drew upon Berne's emphasis on the cathexis, of shifting of energy and awareness from one ego state to another, in naming her residential treatment centre in Oakland, California, the Cathexis

Institute. Shortly before his death, Berne (1969) lauded the boldness and potential of Schiff's work, thereby establishing her credibility within the nascent TA community.

Although her writing and other Cathexis material never made reference to the work of others who were treating schizophrenics, their accounting of the fundamental parental influence in the genesis of schizophrenic reactions was quite consistent with the work of Lidz and his colleagues (Lidz, 1973; Lidz, Fleck, & Cornelison, 1965) as well as that of Laing and Esterson (1964) and Cooper (1967), in which the genesis of schizophrenia was understood to be within the family.

While the work of Schiff and her colleagues was founded in the treatment of people she considered schizophrenic, many of the ideas developed in the Cathexis theory have had a continuing influence in TA. As will be made clear later in this chapter, the same cannot be said for many of the techniques and treatment structures used within the Cathexis system.

6.1.2 Symbiotic structures

In the development of a human being, it is essential to learn lessons regarding the triad of having needs→ expressing needs→ the response to the expression of needs. The positive and negative experiences that a child gains from this interpersonal sequence form an important part of the view the child develops of self and others. It goes "wrong" if the child picks up messages like "You're not OK, the world is dangerous, or parents come first". If a child's needs are not met, this may lead to a denial of needs or to the replacement of needs with something acceptable within the family system. The formation of the script is deeply affected by these recurrent patterns of acceptance or rejection within the family. Script convictions almost always contribute to people neglecting themselves or others.

Within the TA community people will often read and hear the following permission: "100% of the time you may communicate 100% of what you need and what you want. Needs, desires and concerns may always be expressed." This does not mean that you will always get what you need or want. It also doesn't mean that you will always find a listening ear for your concerns. It does mean that the risk of passive behaviour, with all its adverse consequences, is thereby greatly reduced.

However, a child does not know at birth what is needed or how to get it. When a child is born, there needs to be a healthy symbiosis between the child and his caregivers. The child is not capable of living independently. The caregivers have to take on certain essential tasks. Caregivers assume the—not yet present in the baby—Parent and Adult functions, and thereby look after the Child of the baby, the only ego state the baby has at this time (see Figure 6.1).

While this symbiosis is natural and healthy, there is also the danger that the caregiver may neglect his or her own Child. The mother lacks sleep because her baby is not yet sleeping through the night, or the father can't lie back and relax after work but has to get straight to the business that awaits him at home. It is important that parents of young children find enough time to fulfil their own needs. A weekly babysitter for a night out to have dinner, or to go to the movies or the gym is not a luxury! Over a while, the baby will require less constant care and attention, and the symbiosis can be gradually released—by both parties—to make way for a healthy relationship, whereby the father can say "Not now, I'm just not in the mood to entertain you. Go play by yourself". A child who is raised this way can see his mother when she plops

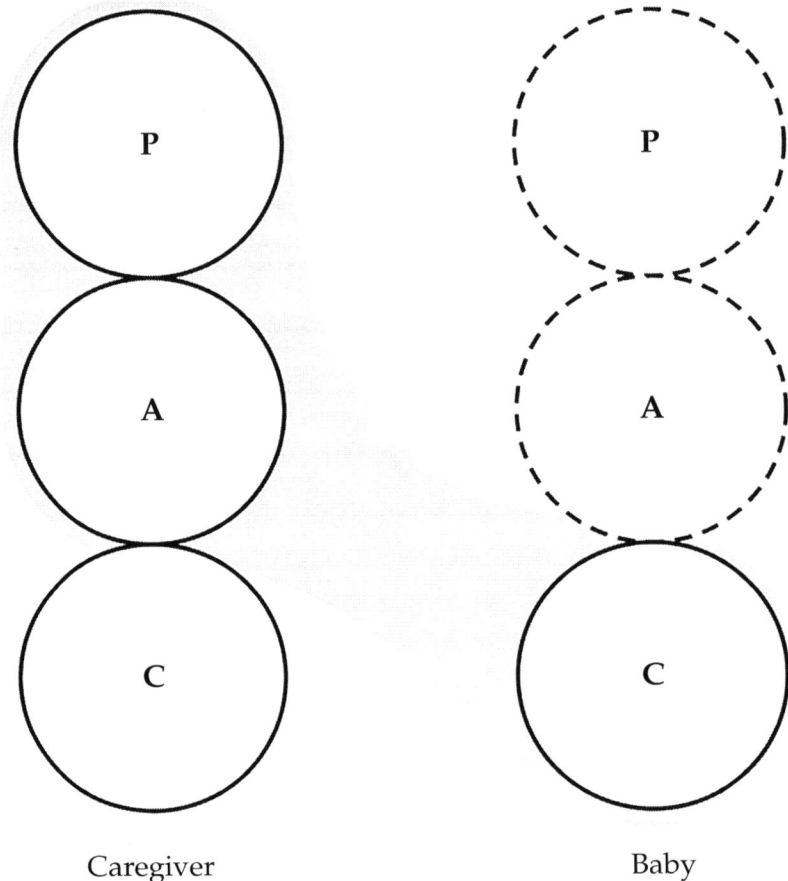

Figure 6.1. Symbiosis between caregiver and baby.

down on the couch after work and he goes over and gives her a hug. If all is well, parents give their children more and more freedom as they grow older and the children themselves break out of the dependency relationship with their parents. The symbiosis is no longer needed and there is an equal relationship.

There are times throughout our development when we tend to re-establish temporary, functional symbiotic relationships. During many periods of significant developmental transition, the structure of a new phase of life (or workplace, as another example) is unfamiliar to us. We are not sure if we have the relevant skills, don't yet have enough information about how things work, and are very likely anxious. So it can be very useful to establish a temporary symbiotic relationship with an experienced or knowledgeable person within the new setting.

However, many people have the tendency, as adults, to occasionally fall back into symbiotic patterns from childhood. They discount the fact that they can ask for the attention they need themselves and … that the other can do the same. If these are not incidental events but form a structural pattern, then an unhealthy symbiosis is created. The person stops thinking as an Adult and either occupies the Child ego state or the Parent ego state.

Often there is a symbiosis at two levels simultaneously: at first glance it seems as if the strong man is caring for his sensitive, dependent wife. Upon closer inspection, however, it is she who is protecting him from having to face up to his own fears. This symbiosis is diagrammed in Figure 6.2.

In the case of the clearly visible symbiosis of the first order, the man mainly uses the Parent and Adult: "I will protect you and will think for you". His wife mainly uses the Child: "Thanks for taking care of me". In the less apparent underlying symbiosis of the second order, the woman uses P_1 and A_1: "I know that you need to see me as weaker and that you are terrified of being left alone". The man uses C_1: "Please take care of me and don't let me fail".

Dysfunctional/disabling symbioses are those that interfere with the capacity of each person within the relationship to develop full autonomy in their own values, competencies, thinking, and expression and satisfaction of needs. Instead there is a severe and chronic imbalance between one person functioning as the controller/provider and the other as the inept/needy one. Often in our professional relationships—such as therapist/client, consultant/customer, or teacher/student—there will be symbiotic tendencies at the start. If these symbiotic tendencies

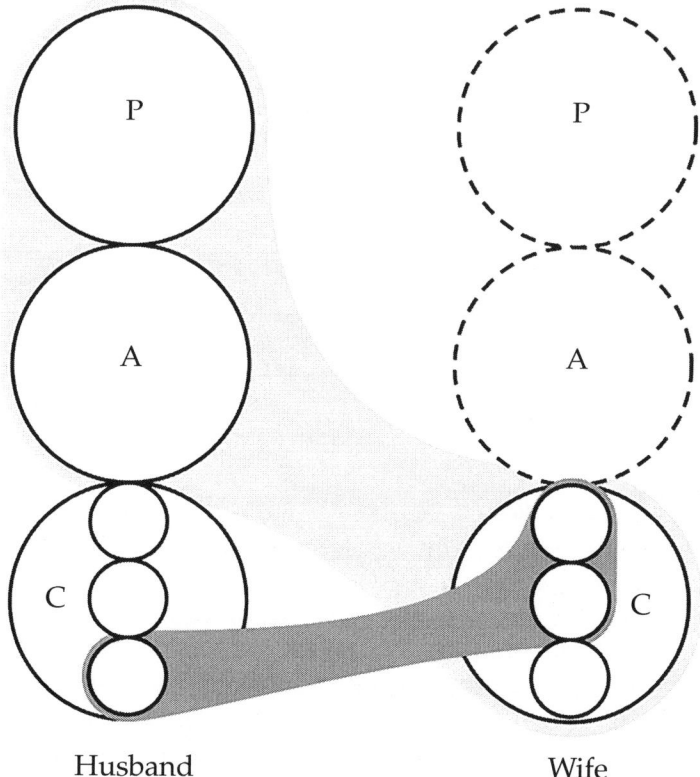

Figure 6.2. First and second order symbiosis.

come to define and structure the relationship, then a disabling symbiosis develops that limits the autonomy and full capacities of both participants in the symbiosis.

> Henry, now in his mid-forties, comes into therapy because he feels depressed and dissatisfied with his life. He says at the beginning of treatment that he never felt appreciated by his parents and that he hopes that the interest and understanding of the therapist will foster his self-esteem and help him feel better. In the first session Henry says that the light on the therapist's desk is too bright, so would he please turn it off. The therapist does, and Henry asks the therapist to please turn it off for every session. For several sessions, Henry arrives and the lamp on the therapist's desk is off. Then one day Henry arrives and the light is still on. Henry gets upset and accuses the therapist of having forgotten him. The therapist replies, "No I haven't forgotten. But I thought this time you could turn it off yourself. I've become curious about what it means that you expect me to do it and what would happen if I didn't. I think your expectations of me have something to do with the difficulties that brought you into therapy." The therapist's comments began to interrupt and identify the symbiosis that was developing between them.

From a Cathexis perspective, games are seen as re-enactments of the symbiotic relationships that children have not resolved with their parents. The source of passivity, according to Schiff, is an unresolved dependency, a dysfunctional symbiosis. She defines symbiosis as "a relationship in which two or more individuals behave as if they constitute one whole person" (Schiff, 1975, p. 5).

Schiff and her colleagues observed that often the symbiotic structure is complementary and each person gets to maintain their favoured relational position. They also observed that some symbiotic relationships are competitive in nature, with both parties competing for the same position, typically the dependent one. In this case there is often an escalation of anger, passivity, ineffectiveness, or demands so as to force the other party into the Parental position. If, on the other hand, the competition is for the position of authority and control (Parent ego state), the effort would be to force the other into the Child position. Typically, symbiotic relationships are highly stable and predictable. However, competitive symbioses are inherently unstable and conflictual. Schiff defined these as symbiotic in that at no time do both members of the dyad (or family or group) utilise all of their ego states.

6.1.3 Passivity, discounting, and redefining

Why do people not do things or do them ineffectively? And how do they maintain this passivity? Schiff argued that healthy organisms respond to stimuli with feelings, thoughts, and behaviours that are effective for their functioning. However, passivity in feeling, thinking, and doing disturbs the balance in social functioning and causes psychological and social problems. Schiff and Schiff (1971) defined the structure and dynamics of the passivity syndrome in terms of symbiosis (pathological), discounting, grandiosity and passive behaviours. They recommend watching "how people don't do tasks and/or do them ineffectively". What they have to say regarding the effectiveness of behaviour is especially interesting. According to this definition, people can be incredibly busy and still be passive. People can be exhausted from all they have done and still achieve nothing. This insight can help those who work in organisations and companies to see how there might be a great deal of activity going on, but that this activity is not necessarily productive.

> Jonathan has the reputation at work that it is better not to ask too much of him because he quickly feels overburdened. His new manager doesn't want to just go along with this and suggests that Jonathan heads a new project. After some hesitation, Jonathan agrees and subsequently fails on all fronts. He forgets to arrange things, forgets to take the minutes at meetings, and doesn't show up at an appointment with the manager. When he is confronted with his passive behaviour, he denies this indignantly and then calls in sick.

A healthy symbiosis is the relationship between parents and young children; in an unhealthy or dysfunctional symbiosis, the development of spontaneity, awareness, and intimacy are hindered. This dysfunctional symbiosis often dates back to early childhood, from the relationship with the child's caregiver(s). The parents continue to treat the growing child as small and dependent, or the child is required to take care of the emotional needs of the parents at a very young age. The result is often that people continue to enter into relationships in which this unresolved dependency plays a role, in the form of a complementary symbiosis where one partner is in the Parent ego state and the other in Child, or of a competitive symbiosis where both partners compete for either Parent or, more frequently for the Child ego state. Through crossed or blocking transactions (see section 3.2.4 in Chapter Three), they avoid confrontations in their contact with others. Their passive behaviour often goes through several stages: from passivity to over-adaptation, to agitation, and finally a violence (explosion) or incapacitation (implosion), after which the person falls back into passivity.

These external behaviours are internally maintained by the mechanism the Schiffs called "discounting" (1971). Discounting is defined as a refusal to acknowledge or consider the information most relevant to the situation. Instead, a person acts from an internal frame of reference about what he thinks, believes, or imagines, ignoring what another person has actually said, done, or felt (p. 36). The outcome of discounting is the exaggeration and distortion of certain aspects of reality, which in turn maintains the belief system underlying the symbiotic structure.

This entire process is summarised under the term "redefining": the maintenance of a previously formed frame of reference by ignoring or distorting all the information that contradicts it.

The various elements of redefining are mapped in Table 6.1.

> Andrew and Mary have been in a difficult relationship for years. If you talk to them individually, it seems as if they are describing two different relationships. Andrew talks about Mary's sloppiness which annoys him terribly. She's never on time, routinely forgets her appointments, and makes a mess of things in the house. Mary says it is almost impossible to live with Andrew. He is so compulsive that even the toothbrushes on the sink have to be placed neatly in a row. Nothing is spontaneous with him; everything has to be planned in advance. Even the holidays preferably need to be determined a year ahead.

In this case, both people discount their own share and exaggerate the other's share in the problems in their relationship. The share of the other is explained in extensive detail, while one's own share is downplayed. The Schiffs (1971) refer to this "thinking disorder"

Table 6.1. Internal processes and external phenomena which establish or maintain a dysfunctional symbiosis (Kouwenhoven, 1983).

Internal processes		
	– Discounting: ignoring stimuli, problems or options; (also see section 6.2.1).	
	– Justification: exaggeration, grandiosity.	
	– Thought disturbances due to over-detailing or over-generalising.	
External phenomena	Two kinds of relations:	– Complementary
		– Competitive
	Two kinds of transactions:	– Tangential
		– Blocking
	Four passive behaviours:	– Doing nothing
		– Over-adaptation
		– Agitation
		– Violence (explosion) or icapacitation (implosion)
	Three roles:	– Rescuer
		– Persecutor
		– Victim

as "grandiosity". Possible exceptions to the other's annoying behaviour are ignored. Many of the external manifestations of redefining were discussed in the chapters on transactions, games, and the script. There are four passive behaviours characteristic of redefining: they make the passivity cycle.

6.1.4 Passivity cycle

> Fay doesn't yet really feel at home in her new team. She needs to get used to the atmosphere, where many of her colleagues gossip about each other while they are very friendly face-to-face. She decides for the moment to just wait and see (do nothing). When a colleague asks her if she likes the team, she says she's really enjoying herself. She says nothing about her difficulty with the atmosphere (over-adaptation). In the period that follows, she notes that her colleagues are not always honest. For instance, a colleague voiced a lot of criticism over another colleague behind her back, but when she confronted this colleague directly about this, the colleague categorically denied having said anything negative. Fay becomes more and more uncomfortable and she begins to feel nervous in the presence of some of her colleagues. She constantly wonders what they might be saying about her behind her back (agitation). At one point she forgets to finish an important piece that she should have sent off. She isn't able to sleep that night because of it. How could she have forgotten something like that? (implosion).
>
> When she arrives at work the next day she expects a scolding, but there is nothing of the sort. Her immediate colleague says with a smile that it wasn't a problem and that everyone sometimes forgets something. And this is when Fay bursts out: crying and yelling, she tells her colleague how she wouldn't say anything now, but that surely she would begin to gossip behind her back. She, Fay, can no longer stand this awful atmosphere (tantrum: explosion).

According to Schiff, dysfunctional symbiotic relationships are not static but pass through different stages, after which a new cycle begins. Central to each phase is a shifting of the responsibility for a problem to the other. As the cycle unfolds, internal tension builds up until this eventually results in a discharge, either as an explosion, often in the form of a tantrum, or an implosion, often in the form of a somatic symptom. Although the tension is released, the problem is not solved, and the symbiosis is maintained.

Within the Cathexis model, it was argued that "to disrupt the symbiosis the passive individual must be made more uncomfortable (responsible for his feelings) than he can make someone else" (Schiff & Schiff, 1971, p. 38). This was done through confrontation of the discounting and the manoeuvres that maintained the symbiosis.

Even in healthy people, passivity can be discerned the moment they engage in an unhealthy symbiosis with another. An everyday example of this is when Frits says "It's really warm in here" and his colleague Matilda jumps to open the window. The passivity cycle is defined as behaviour by which you avoid an autonomous response to stimuli, issues, and options, but by which you try to fulfil your needs or goals by entering into an unhealthy symbiotic relationship (Schiff, 1975, p. 10).

The various phases of the passivity cycle are as follows:

Doing nothing

Instead of reacting to stimuli, issues, and options, the person remains passive and does nothing. Often he is well aware of an uncomfortable feeling, but he does not reflect upon what is going on.

> Berny says to John: "I'm very angry with you because you're too late." John looks startled but says nothing. Waiting for an answer, Berny starts feeling increasingly uncomfortable and gets the urge to Rescue ("Well, it doesn't matter") or to Persecute ("It's always the same with you, you're never on time").

Over-adaptation

The person doesn't consider what he wants but adapts to the goals, desires, and expectations of others. Or he imagines what the goals may be, without thinking about the importance or the meaning of these goals. Because this often makes a helpful, considerate impression, this behaviour earns a lot of strokes. The difference with a healthy adjustment is often difficult to determine. In the case of a healthy adjustment, people do think about their goals in relation to a realistic assessment of the situation. In this phase, the passive person does most of the thinking and is therefore the most accessible for change, through confrontations such as "You can make your own choices", or "You can solve your own problems".

> Andrew wants to go shopping but at that very moment, his wife asks him to mow the lawn. Without a word, he sets about doing what she has asked straight away.

> One day, Janice spent a lot of time cleaning up the office of her husband Hank. Hank had recently spoken about the fact that there are some things he just doesn't get round to doing. Cleaning up his room, including his desk, would surely be one of these things, Janice thought. She was greatly

> disappointed when Hank was mostly angry with her instead of pleased and grateful. "What business is that of yours? My office is my domain. If anything needs to be done there, I'll do it myself!" he had said. And she had even missed her tennis lesson to do this for him.

Agitation

The person falls into repetitive, non-purposeful activities, such as tapping their fingers, pacing back and forth, stuttering, stammering, smoking, drinking, or lying awake worrying. He feels uncomfortable. The inner tension rises and these activities reduce it somewhat. Thinking is confused and unproductive. Agitation distracts him from other feelings (anger, fear, guilt). Calm comments from the Parent of the other can break this behaviour: "Sit down and think for a minute about what is happening now. What are you after?" This brings the person back into the phase of over-adaptation, after which effective thinking and action become more likely.

> Aziz finds the lecture lasting much too long. Also, the speaker is not able to articulate the subject in an interesting manner. The room is becoming more and more restless. People in the audience are starting to shift back and forth in their chairs. If you listen carefully, you can hear a heavy sigh here and there. After doodling on the handout for a while, Aziz begins tapping his pen more loudly against the leg of the chair. Aziz agitates rather than leave the lecture or ask the lecturer a question that might engage him more fully with his audience.

Incapacitation (implosion) or violence (explosion)

The energy which has been building up during the previous three phases is now discharged in this phase. In this context, it is an attempt to restore the symbiosis with force. The person in this phase has now become unreasonable and is no longer able to think clearly. He does not take responsibility for his own behaviour. Powerlessness often manifests itself in physical symptoms: migraine, fainting, vomiting, hyperventilation, low back pain, and so on. Violence can easily take the form of a tantrum in which verbal and non-verbal attacks on people or property can take place.

The other must then provide a sense of security until the escalation has passed, and then help the person to reload his Adult ego state. It is important, however, not to give too many strokes to this powerless or violent behaviour, positive or negative, because both types of strokes affirm and reinforce the behaviour. Having a more neutral attitude and then appealing to the other's Adult position prevents this person from restoring the symbiosis.

> It is becoming increasingly difficult for teacher Michael to maintain order in his high school classroom full of adolescent girls. Some of them seem to have no respect for him at all. Eventually Michael does not know how to respond to the snide remarks which have a downright hostile undertone. His only option seems to be to grit his teeth and bear it and hope that next year's schedule is kind to him. Everyone is surprised when Michael finally hits a student who he thinks is the one setting the tone in the class. The school has no choice but to temporarily suspend Michael.

Any doctor can tell you that over 70% of the complaints heard from patients on a daily basis are related to unresolved issues at home or at work. Passivity appears to be the root of many physical complaints. Stress causes the heart rate to go up, as well as blood pressure. Stress also contributes to an accelerated respiration, rising blood sugar levels, slow digestion, and an "explosion" in the production of adrenaline and cortisol. Prolonged stress can weaken the immune system.

The risk is therefore great that a social issue becomes a medical problem. Medication is quickly prescribed, and, given the often short time available, the general practitioner's consultation room is not the place where patients can learn to deal with the stress in a way other than by passivity.

6.2 Further theory

6.2.1 Discount matrix

The internal process of discounting is the engine that starts redefinition. It is also the case that this mechanism is healthy to a certain extent. To keep yourself afloat in a complex reality full of stimuli, you need to make a selection in order to shield yourself. However, if you systematically ignore stimuli that are relevant in order to accomplish a certain task or to solve a problem, then this constitutes an unhealthy denial or discounting. This is what is meant by the term "discounting". Mellor and Sigmund (1975a, 1975b) summarise the different types and levels of discounting according to the following matrix (Figure 6.3).

This, at first glance complex matrix is an excellent tool to estimate the intensity with which someone discounts. It is also a tool to assess the level at which you must approach this person in order to offer help or guidance. In Figure 6.3, the aspects of "stimuli", "problems", and "options" are combined with the factors "existence", "meaning", "changeability", and "personal capacity". The most serious level of discounting is the denial of the existence of a stimulus. Subsequently, the second worst level is formed by the denial of the meaning of this stimulus and/or the existence of a problem. This creates the following classification of levels:

T1: The highest level of discounting is level T1, the denial of the existence of stimuli.
   The alcoholic who smells of booze in the morning and staggers when he walks, denies that he is surrounded by a haze of alcohol. The schoolgirl who has overslept and arrives at school at half past nine, denies that she is late. The employee who has accumulated three months' sick leave over the past year, denies he is often sick.
T2: Level T2 involves the discounting of the meaning of stimuli and/or the existence of a problem.
   The alcoholic admits that he smells like booze, but says it doesn't mean anything or that it isn't a problem. The schoolgirl plays down arriving too late and doesn't find it a problem. The employee thinks of all sorts of excuses for his sick leave and does not seem to worry much about it.
T3: Level T3 involves the discounting of the changeability of the stimulus, the meaning of the problem, and/or the existence of options.

	ASPECTS		
INTENSITY	Stimuli	Problems	Options
Existence	T1 Existence of stimuli	T2 Existence of problems	T3 Existence of options
Meaning	T2 Meaning of stimuli	T3 Meaning of problems	T4 Meaning of options
Changeability	T3 Changeability of stimuli	T4 Solvability of problems	T5 Changeability of options
Own capacities	T4 Own capacity of change stimuli or to react differently	T5 Own capacity to solve problems	T6 Own capacity to apply options

Figure 6.3. Discount matrix.

The alcoholic says there is nothing to be done about his morning drink. He's been doing it for years, and otherwise his hands tremble all day. The schoolgirl says that school starts far too early, and that the day-and-night rhythm of adolescents is such that they can't perform until ten o'clock and that therefore nothing can really be done to change the situation. The employee attributes his high level of sick leave to the fact that he has a poor constitution and asthmatic symptoms. He emphasises that when he is present, he works for three. So it's all right like this, isn't it?

T4: Level T4 involves the denial of one's own capacity to react differently, the denial of the solvability of the problem, and the denial of the meaning of options.

The alcoholic says that addiction is a disease. His father also suffered from it. The problem can't be solved and all those treatments out there today are ... well, they are really for a very different kind of person than he is. The schoolgirl says she sleeps through every alarm clock. She really can't do anything about it. For a while, her mother would get her out of bed, but this made her cranky, so that didn't work either. The employee responds to all the advice he is given (more exercise, stop smoking, a healthy lifestyle) with a "yes, but" and says that these solutions might work for others but not for him.

T5 : Level T5 involves the denial of one's own capacity to solve problems and the denial of the changeability of options. In this case, the person recognises, in theory, that the problems can be solved. However, the alcoholic says he does not have enough willpower to really stop drinking and that, moreover, all the clinics are too far away or too expensive. The schoolgirl says that laziness is one of her main characteristics. There's not a single approach to remedy that. The employee says he lived a healthy lifestyle for a time, but he was unable to maintain this pattern. Everything he has tried so far has no effect.

T6: Finally, level T6 involves the denial of one's own capacity to apply options.

The alcoholic has lost confidence to be able to stop drinking since he started drinking again after several successful treatments. The schoolgirl has really done her best for a while to arrive on time, but nevertheless gradually lapsed into her old behaviour. The employee is frustrated and feels like a failure because he sees that the company doctor's approach is working with some of his colleagues yet not with him.

If you are unable to solve a problem, it may be that you are not approaching things at the right level of discounting. For example, the coach tries to motivate the client to change his lifestyle while the client thinks it is not a problem that he never does any sport and drinks a bottle of wine per day. The management team has already planned the entire reorganisation, while the employees still have no idea "for what problem this is a solution". The following questions can be a tool to determine whether a person systematically discounts something that is essential for the solution to a problem (Kouwenhoven, 1983).

- Level T1: Identification of the stimuli
  What happened, what do you need, what do you feel, think, do, or want?
- Level T2: Identification of the problem
  Is what you said at T1 important or is it an issue for you or for others?
- Level T3: Identification of the solutions
  Could it be different, how important is the problem for you or for the other, are there solutions to your problem and, if so, what?
- Level T4: Identification of the target
  Do you have the capacity to react differently, is the problem solvable and are the options that you just mentioned relevant for solving your problem?
- Level T5: Identification of barriers
  Are you able to solve problems and to bring about lasting change?
- Level T6: Identification of capacity to act
  Can you apply the solution to the problem in such a way that your problem remains solved?

The higher the level of discounting, the more difficult and longer the process of change will be.

In 2006, Mellor, together with Ritchie Macefield, an information technologist, returned to the idea of the discount matrix and created two new tools for task- and option-oriented functions in business and education. These are the awareness-discount matrix and the awareness action sequence. For use in learning contexts in particular, both tools emphasise a person's awareness rather than the discounts they revert to, and explore possible interventions for each level of awareness/discount: existence and significance of data, significance and viability of options, allocation of and ability to take responsibility, concluding with mutual agreement of tasks (Macefield & Mellor, 2006). A similar "turning around" of the discounting levels is the accounting-empowerment approach in education (Clarke & Dawson, 1998; Napper &

Newton, 2000) where each level—problem, significance, solvability, and personal capacity—is acknowledged in turn, leading to students' empowerment.

6.2.2 Steps to success

Although the Cathexis model was developed for the treatment of severely disturbed individuals, patterns of symbiotic relationships and passive behaviour exist in many of the contexts in which people work and think together. That is why Julie Hay (1995), using the Cathexis theory on discounting and writing from an organisational perspective, outlined the steps to success in order to help managers assess where they are within a process of change. Many changes in organisations stagnate, or are pseudo-changes, because certain steps are skipped.

- Step 1: Situation
  Does everyone who is involved in the change plans have a similar picture of all the facts? If this question is answered in the affirmative, we can proceed to step 2. Otherwise, more research will be needed in order to create awareness of the problem.
  Example: A manager is dissatisfied with the way the team conducts meetings. The team members do not (yet) share his view on the functioning of the team.
- Step 2: Significance
  Does every person give the same meaning to the situation at hand? If not, then first work needs to be done to arrive at a balanced consensus of the seriousness of the situation.
  Example: The team now sees that some things could be different and better here and there, but members still don't have the motivation to think about solutions.
- Step 3: Solution
  Is there agreement on the solutions that are needed to change or improve what has been qualified as a sufficiently problematic situation? This is often where the turning point lies. If steps 1 and 2 have been sufficiently explored, then step 3 marks the beginning of change.
  Example: Now that the whole team is convinced that the meetings can be different and better, it is now able and willing to work with the manager to think about solutions.
- Step 4: Skills
  Do all those who are going to have a role in the realisation of the change also have the skills needed? To create successful change, it is sometimes necessary to acquire the necessary knowledge, skills, and expertise that is not yet present.
  Example: The team decides to attend a number of training and coaching sessions on conducting meetings effectively.
- Step 5: Strategy
  Along which route and with what degree of planning will the change be achieved? Because a change does not occur in a training room, it is desirable to create a plan, including moments of evaluation, to ensure that the improvements are actually put into practice.
  Example: After the training days, the team decides to ask one of the trainers to observe the team meetings, so that team members are guaranteed sufficient feedback on their commitment to improve.

- Step 6: Success
  How is the success of the desired and actual change going to be "celebrated"? The energy to tackle the next development often stems from celebrating a previous success. In TA terminology, celebrating pertains to collecting a sufficient amount of strokes. A result can be transformed into success by celebrating it.
  Example: Now that the team has succeeded in having meetings that are effective (result) and pleasant (relationship), the board arranges for the team to go out for dinner at a top restaurant.

Whoever skips a step, invites others to engage in passive behaviour. In companies and organisations, the management and staff can be very busy with "not changing".

It is important to recognise that while the Cathexis model focuses on thinking and behaviour, these patterns are established in our earliest years of life and are not typically conscious. It can seem strange that something that is so repetitive is not fully conscious. Often it is the task of a consultant to bring these patterns of passive thinking and behaviour to the conscious awareness of the company.

Sometimes there is a complementary symbiosis between managers and employees. A management system may maintain a position of authority to which the employees are all too happy to capitulate their own autonomy and responsibility, simply doing what is expected. Such a complementary symbiosis may be very stable, but is unlikely to produce creative employees or have the flexibility to change when circumstances change. However, this very same management system of top-down authority could also provoke a competitive symbiosis. Passivity then leads to competition, by which managers and employees engage in unconscious battles for control. The manager, for example, thinks of how things could be different and better but spends no time or attention on how to involve the employees in the plans. The employees do not feel involved and they resist the changes. This creates a competitive symbiosis with regard to power and influence: "We want to see just who is in control here". People can be very busy and yet still be very passive, since they do not achieve what they want to achieve.

6.2.3 Passivity confrontation

The Cathexis model of psychotherapy was typically carried out in residential community formats or intensive groups, often meeting for several days. The group was structured to be a highly responsive environment in which all members were expected to identify and confront any and all discounting and passive behaviours among the members. The therapists took actively Parental positions, defining what was considered a healthy perspective on reality: "The concept of intervention, injecting ourselves [the therapists] between the patients and their ineffective operations with their environment in a forceful and caring way, describes what we try to do" (Schiff, 1975, p. 103).

Seen through a contemporary lens, the Cathexis approach was a "one-person" model within which the therapist defined reality and interpreted the client's behaviour. The client's frame of reference and subjective experience was seen to be disturbed, and the therapist was the designated holder of reality. There was no discussion in the Schiffian literature of the therapist's countertransference.

Although contracts were considered to be important, many of the Cathexis clients, at least in the earlier stages of treatment, were seen as so disturbed as to make contracts meaningless. Instead, there was a general contract to confront and be confronted, "in order to insure that the constant level of external feedback is maintained, staff and patients alike are expected to make a commitment to a general confrontation contract" (p. 101). The operating assumption was that the patient's internal world and the resulting patterns of discounting and passivity so consistently and significantly distorted reality that it was the task of the group and the therapists to provide high levels of external feedback and expectations of behavioural change.

6.2.4   Reparenting

Jacqui Schiff was a social worker. She was dissatisfied with the lack of therapeutic perspectives for her severely disturbed patients and with the general attitude of the professionals in her field who thought that chronic patients needed to accept their disabilities. She participated in the seminars with Berne in San Francisco and began to apply TA thinking with her patients. She noted that with the help of TA concepts, her patients became less depressed and that they became motivated to change their lives. Through the work of her husband Moe she came into contact with young people suffering from schizophrenia. They took one of these young people into their home and noted that adopting the parental role was effective at times when psychotic confusion increased. Gradually they began making therapeutic use of the entering into a symbiosis. They applied the theory of ego states in order to investigate the internal structure of their patients and to eliminate the sick ego states (often a destructive P_1 or unrestrained C_1) by not allowing any energy to go into them. They noticed that the youngsters were better able to control themselves using their Parent messages. They called the process "therapeutic regression and reparenting" (Jacobs, 1994; Schiff, 1977).

Schiff advocated the total decathexis of the original Parent ego state. Often one of the requirements of treatment was that the patient terminate all contact with the family of origin and accept the therapist(s) as new parents. It was a premise of Cathexis theory that "the energy removed from the [original] Parent is then available for incorporating the new Parent" (1975, p. 88). The role of the therapist as parent was crucial for providing adequate structure and containment. So too was the structure of the therapeutic family, community, or group seen as essential in providing a Parental structure. With the enforced decathexis of the Parent ego state, patients often entered significant periods of regression, during which the therapists and group members provided more appropriate structure and expectations, which Schiff and her colleagues thought to then be internalised in a new, healthier Parent ego state (1975, pp. 91–97). Regressed patients could be bottle-fed; some wore nappies, which were changed by their therapist.

Schiff believed that psychotic individuals were capable of this total decathexis of the Parent ego state. She did not, however, think that non-psychotic patients (and trainees) needed to undertake this total decathexis.

6.2.5   Parent ego state interview

John McNeel (1976), working within a redecision model, addressed the specific situation in therapy in which clients were not able to establish a reflective distance from and about their

Parent ego state. He developed an intervention he termed the Parent (ego state) interview. His premise, somewhat in contrast to the Cathexis model, was that rather than the Parent ego state of the client being "crazy", it was threatened by the therapy and therefore rigid. With the Parent interview, the client is asked to role-play as fully as possible, his parent, be it mother or father. The intention is for the client to begin to have a visceral appreciation of the dilemma faced by the mother or father that was the genesis of the rigid Parental position that was then internalised by the growing child. The goal here is to achieve a cognitive and emotional decontamination in which the client through Adult and Child awareness can come to understand that his parents were separate individuals with struggles of their own, which sometimes resulted in poor caregiving or rigid parenting. The Parent interview can be a deeply moving experience. The direct intervention within the Parent ego state, rather than the replacement of the Parent, has continued to evolve (Clarkson, 1992; Dashiell, 1978; Guglielmotti, 1996; Loria, 1988; Mellor & Andrewartha, 1980; Oblas, 1981).

Erskine (Erskine & Moursund, 1988; Erskine & Trautmann, 2003) has taken the Parent interview further so as to engage directly with the Parent ego state (the introjected parent figure) as therapist. The effort here is to conduct therapy with the activated Parent ego state in role-play in order for the therapist and the client to understand the dilemmas and vulnerabilities of the mother or father during the client's developmental history. In so doing, Erskine makes a direct challenge to the Cathexis model, "the replacement of a Parent ego state with another introjection is *not therapeutic*" (2003, p. 104, italics in the original). Here the goal is to facilitate the client's awareness and separateness from the historical parent's own conflicts so as to relieve the client's intrapsychic conflict.

6.2.6   Integration of differing approaches in TA

Clarkson (1992) integrates three different TA approaches into her perspective on psychotherapy (and on processes of change in general). She has developed this into three models. In her view, psychosocial disturbances may occur in the following ways:

1. Confusion: affective and cognitive disturbance of the functioning of the integrated ego
2. Conflicts: an internal conflict between parts of the ego
3. Deficiencies: inadequate parenting leading to deficits in the development of the child.

Model 1 is largely inspired by Berne's thinking on the role of the changer. This approach was once called the classical school in TA. The key word here is "decontamination". Berne mainly worked in his therapy practice on strengthening the Adult. The effective functioning of the Adult, this was his reasoning, is often hampered during the process of script development, resulting in the contamination of the Adult by Parent or Child material. The therapeutic goal in model 1 is to make the boundaries between the three ego states healthy. Mental health is the strong functioning of the integrated Adult without the intervention of archaic experiences (Child) or the non-integrated ego states of significant others (Parent).

In model 2, we encounter the work of Bob and Mary Goulding, also referred to as "the redecision school". The Gouldings invited clients to examine script decisions on which their dysfunction was based and to make new decisions. The key word here is "redecision". According to the Gouldings, mental health is to function in daily life without inhibiting needs, values, or emotions. Not functioning properly is mainly caused by what they called "stuck points" between the different ego states; impasses. The work of redecision—which is mainly an emotional, affective process—is aimed at breaking these impasses.

Schiff is given a prominent place in Clarkson's third model. Here, the key word is "reparenting", which is mainly concerned in offering its patients new and healing experiences with "healthy parents". From the perspective of what used to be called the Cathexis school, undesired functioning is partly caused by inadequate, pathological, or neglectful parenting at critical moments in the life of the child. Mental health then means: to be able to function with a (autonomous and integrated) set of supportive and challenging values.

For years it was commonplace within TA to talk of three schools (directions) within TA. Each school represented a significant development in the tremendous growth of TA during the last century. Thanks to the works of Clarkson, who found a unifying principle, there is now less mention of the existence of three more or less separate principles of thought concerning change. For Clarkson, the three schools are not really separate visions of change but different stages in the therapeutic process of change as a whole.

Although no process of change will follow a single model exactly, it is often advisable to first eliminate the confusion so that the client has sufficient access to the Adult ego state. After this, the professional, together with the client, can examine possible internal conflicts in order to then make new decisions that may remove the sting of the conflict. In therapeutic work, it is always the goal, sometimes more explicitly than at other times, to offer the client a (new) healing experience when working with this particular professional. For the client, the professional can represent a "parent" who is reliable, caring, and safe. This corrective experience may be internalised by the client in his internal Parent system.

6.2.7 Parent education

The perspective in the Cathexis school, as Clarkson says, of considering the deficits and potential of parenting ("unhealthy" and "healthy") was to lead to a developmental Parent education approach that focused on "what is good enough parenting?" and "what do children need at different stages?". This derived in part from the work of Pamela Levin-Landheer (1982) who identified six developmental stages, from birth to the age of nineteen, each with its own tasks (for the child) and needs (from the caregivers). Levin's work was in a therapy setting, and her concern was with the gaps or deficits that a client might have experienced in childhood and how these might be repaired. At the same time, she proposed that people continue, throughout life, to recycle through the developmental stages in (hopefully) age-appropriate ways, and that we return, under stress, to stages where we missed out on something we needed. Levin saw this model (cycles of development) as a contribution to script theory but this has been much disputed (see, for instance, Cornell, 1988). The model proposed by Levin-Landheer has found more use as a base for parent education and further applications in schools, adult education, and organisations. This is essentially an optimistic model, valuing growth and development, suggesting that we can reshape ourselves, with help or through our own understanding, in the present.

In part, the cycles of development model identifies affirmations that are essential to each stage of development. These are supportive messages that are taken in by the little person, not necessarily aurally but also by touch and visually. Jean Illsley Clarke used these affirmations, adding to them and putting them all into positive language, to create a system (and programme) of parent education explained in her book Growing Up Again (Clarke & Dawson, 1989). The aim is to share with parents and caregivers "guidelines" for care that will promote healthy psychological and emotional development for children and at the same time enable parents to understand their own reactions to their children's changing needs as they grow up, as well as offering insight into their own developmental history and the possibilities for repairing their own "gaps". The chart shows the stages and ages, the main developmental tasks for each stage, and key developmental/educational affirmations.

Stages of development—summary chart (Adapted from Barrow, Bradshaw & Newton, 2001, p. 92).

	Stages	*Tasks of child*	*Needs, strokes*	*Helpful behaviours and key affirmations*
1	Being 0–6 m	Learn to get needs met; learn to trust; bond emotionally; accept care, touch	Love, care, touch; consistency; you belong here; think for baby	Consistent care; use touch, holding, talking, singing; be reliable; think for child as needed You belong here.
2	Doing 6–18 m	Explore and experience; develop senses, initiative; learn to get help; form secure attachment	Safety, encouragement, variety, protection, support; don't interrupt; OK to be active, quiet	Provide encouragement, safe environment with varied sensory experiences; listen to child; respond and model language You can explore and experiment.
3	Thinking 1½–3 yrs	Learn to think, test reality, solve problems, express feelings; begin to separate; give up being centre	Encourage thinking; give reasons, how-to's; accept feelings; set limits	Give clear directions, information; stroke thinking; accept feelings; be consistent You can think for yourself.
4	Identity 3–6 yrs	Assert separate identity; acquire info about self, place in family; test power; social behaviour; separate fantasy / reality	Both sexes are OK; give info; answer questions; stroke OK behaviour; get own support	Answer questions accurately; connect feeling and thinking; be clear about responsibilities; teach acceptance You can explore who you are.

(*Continued*)

(Continued).

	Stages	Tasks of child	Needs, strokes	Helpful behaviours and key affirmations
5	Skills 6–12 yrs	Learn skills; make mistakes; listen; reason; rules and structure in and out of family; values; disagree; test ideas; co-operate	Lots of strokes; be reliable, clear; offer tools; set rules; allow consequences; challenge behaviour	Teach conflict resolution, problem-solving; support skills development; respect child's opinions You can find ways of doing things that work for you.
6	Integration 13–18 yrs	Separate; be independent, responsible; have own needs, values; integrate sexuality	Understand, encourage, accept, support, discuss, celebrate	Offer support; confront destructive behaviour; encourage independence; negotiate rules and responsibilities You can develop your own interests and causes.

6.2.8 *The cycles applied*

Clarke's intention was to promote healthy parenting for children and young people. Her model has inspired others to broaden its scope into wider fields. One adaptation for early-years, schools, and teachers offers practical help in assessing children's emotional and self-esteem needs and providing appropriate pastoral support as an underpinning requirement for effective cognitive progress (Barrow, Bradshaw, & Newton, 2001).

> At just under four years old Nathan had very little language, a stiff, tense way of holding himself with jerky movement, never smiled and had no apparent awareness of other children in the nursery. The staff were despairing of helping him during his short placement. They had noticed that Nathan had his own ways of playing alone, liking to throw small items and watch them fall, and to play with water. A discussion with the local behaviour support team led to the nursery staff giving Nathan the opportunity to return to earlier stages and experience them more positively—they offered careful and increasing physical contact, lots of visual and sensory affirmation, and opportunities for exploratory play around body sensations with an adult joining in—in short, letting Nathan be an infant and toddler again. After seven months Nathan was able to talk and ask for help, smiled and would play with other children, could understand and respond to instructions, and his body had become supple and active. He was affectionately accepted as a member of the nursery, belonging there with the other children.

This real-life story (summarised from Newton & Wong, 2003) shows the way that each stage builds on the successful outcome of the previous stage. Rather different applications are the use of the stages model to support adult learning (Napper & Newton, 2000) and to identify phases in the process of change (Hay, 2009).

> A huge fast-growing company employs around twenty new employees every month. The management is very much aware that if they ask the newbies to have a go very fast and meet their agreed-on targets, a lot of them will in the long run not be as productive as they can be. The (TA trained) manager in charge of the introduction programme therefore allows the just-arrived colleagues to have a look around for the first week. There is no pressure to do anything. The chairman of the board welcomes them. The office manager takes ample time to show them around all the faculties the office has to offer. They are allowed to take time to find out how the IT-environment operates. Etcetera. The message is: We're happy to have you!

The profound lessons learned from the above-cited thinking—of above all Clarke (Clarke & Dawson, 1989)—are that whoever wants to go fast at the beginning will be slowed down in the long run. Just like with the growing-up process of human beings each stage builds on the successful outcomes of the previous stage. Employees who feel welcome and who are given time to settle themselves will be more effective in activities that require doing and thinking.

6.3   Furthermore

6.3.1   The Cathexis crisis

The work of the Cathexis Institute became an increasing object of controversy by the mid-1970s. Schiff and her colleagues often argued that to work with such deep levels of psychopathology, non-traditional and often extreme measures were necessary. They encouraged patients to sever all ties with their biological parents and sometimes literally adopted their patients. Some of Schiff's adopted, reparented children then worked with her as co-therapists and trainers. Although there was no systematic theory of transference and countertransference, the Cathexis model provided a therapeutic environment that invited intense, idealising transference relationship and created profound countertransferential pressures on the therapists. Frequently, Cathexis-oriented therapists would undertake reparenting relationships with clients, only to find themselves eventually overwhelmed by the demands of these relationships. Ethics charges became common as clients became disappointed or infuriated when the reparenting relationships collapsed. The Cathexis Institute closed down after one of the young people in the institute died after being restrained and submerged in a tub of too hot water. A legal charge followed and one of the staff members was arrested and ultimately pleaded guilty to involuntary manslaughter. There were numerous other legal charges of assault and battery against Schiff and her staff. In 1978, the ITAA Board of Trustees revoked the membership of Jacqui Schiff of ITAA including her right to train within the organisation (McClendon, 1978).

6.3.2   Critique and re-evaluation

As a result of the crisis and collapse of the Cathexis Institute there was no systematic re-evaluation of Schiffian theory and technique. The reparenting model, for the most part, disappeared from the TA landscape, but its disappearance was for many years accompanied by silence rather than discussion and reassessment. The numerous ethical and legal matters that grew around the Cathexis programme and its offshoots in other areas of the

US and the world made it very difficult for the community to examine what happened from more objective clinical and theoretical perspectives. Nearly a decade passed before the complex ethical and clinical issues surrounding the reparenting model began to be discussed in professional conference panels, resulting in the rewriting of the ITAA code of ethics (Weiss, 1994).

Alan Jacobs (1987, 1994) undertook the first systematic critique of the Cathexis model, challenging the TA community to examine its complicity in the ethical questions surrounding the reparenting methodology: "We ignored the significance of or even denied references to violence and power in the reparenting literature; when abuses were alleged, we did nothing for several years" (1994, p. 52). Four years later, the *Transactional Analysis Journal* devoted a full issue to reassessing the use of regression and reparenting in psychotherapy (Novey, 1998).

In summary there are two major theoretical and practical objections against Schiff and her staff: first, the way they tended to work with therapist-defined goals, and second, the total lack of a theory about or even of awareness of transference and countertransference.

While systemic reparenting procedures and therapeutic communities designed in accordance with the operations of the Cathexis Institute are now rarely practised, the Cathexis-based theories of discounting and passivity have proven useful and valid in a variety of therapeutic, counselling, educational, and organisational contexts. A history of Jacqui Schiff and the Cathexis Institute remains to be written. However painful this period has been for everyone involved in TA then and now, the crisis also produced development and growth.

6.3.3 Schema therapy

Outside TA there is increasing interest in "limited reparenting" as a technique, for example, in schema therapy (Young & Klosko, 1994; Young, Klosko, & Weishaar, 2003), a widely used treatment in the Netherlands for patients with personality disorders. Limited reparenting is not based on the Cathexis theory, nor do we find any references to transactional analysis in schema therapy, although many of the concepts use the same phrases as we know from transactional analysis.

In schema therapy they refer to limited reparenting if the therapist, within the boundaries of the therapeutic relationship, offers what the patient needed earlier but did not get from his parents. With patients who have been neglected, mistreated, abused, or were abandoned in their youth, the therapist will provide stability, warmth, empathy, and leadership. With patients who have had less severe experiences or traumas at a later stage in their lives, the therapist's reparenting will especially encourage autonomy, realistic limits, self-expression, reciprocity, and spontaneity. The difference to the Schiff approach is that reparenting does not stimulate regression. Setting healthy boundaries is an important element in limited reparenting.

Much reparenting occurs spontaneously in partnerships such as those between teachers and students, between coaches and those being coached, or between managers and employees. All those who carry responsibility for the growth and development of others can assume the role of "new parent".

6.4 Related theories

6.4.1 The "schizophrenogenic family"

Theodore Lidz (1973; Lidz, Fleck, & Cornelison, 1965) was a psychoanalytically trained psychiatrist who devoted much of his career to the study and treatment of psychosis and schizophrenia. Having trained with Harry Stack Sullivan and Frieda Fromm-Reichmann, both of whom worked intensively with schizophrenic patients, he did not consider schizophrenia to be a disease, but to be a reaction to a disturbed family system. He observed that many creative people could be seen as schizophrenic for some periods of their lives. He argued that the ground for schizophrenic reactions was the child's inability to achieve independence and develop sufficient ego strength to make the transition into an autonomous adult life (and hence the frequency of the onset of schizophrenia for late adolescents and young adults). His observations are quite consistent with the position of Jacqui Schiff, although there is no published evidence that she was familiar with or influenced by his work or that of Sullivan (1962) or Fromm-Reichmann (1960).

Concepts of the schizophrenogenic mother developed within psychoanalytic and family systems models between the 1940s into the early 1970s. This conceptualisation has now been quite thoroughly discredited by subsequent research underscoring the biological factors in schizophrenia (Harrington, 2012; Neill, 1990). The disadvantage of the recent emphasis on neurobiological aspects is that attention to the family dynamics is in danger of being overlooked.

6.4.2 Anti-psychiatry

Another interesting development was the criticism of the anti-psychiatry movement of both psychiatry and psychoanalysis. Laing and his colleagues (Cooper, 1967; Laing, 1960, 1969; Laing & Esterson, 1964), starting from an existential philosophic point of view, situated the "schizophrenic" dilemma as an expression of profound alienation from both self and the normative social structure. From the anti-psychiatry perspective, the depersonalising, reductive perspective, and terminology of psychiatry actively contributed to the profound sense of alienation underlying schizophrenic breakdowns. In Laing's view, schizoid and schizophrenic patients were more sensitive than most and unwilling to compromise to the normative social structure by adapting a false-self. In this regard, the anti-psychiatry movement resonated with many of the critiques embedded in Lidz's critique of the traditional psychiatric attitude towards schizophrenia and psychosis (1971). Also consistent with Schiff and Lidz, Laing and his associates situated the roots of schizoid and schizophrenic disorders within the family system.

In 1965 Laing and his colleagues established the therapeutic community, Kingsley Hall and the Philadelphia Association in London to provide residential refuges for those experiencing psychotic breakdowns, the first of a series of therapeutic households. All were committed to the premise that these breakdowns were an expression of profound existential crises, and the breakdown allowed the possibility of a more authentic way of being (Burston, 1996, 2000; Mullen, 1995). These households eliminated all distinction between the professional and patient roles—the exact opposite of the structure utilised at the Cathexis Institute.

One of the authors of this volume (Cornell) had been working in residential treatment centres for severely disturbed adolescents while at university and was deeply affected by Laing's work. As he approached graduation he wrote Laing asking if he might apply to him as a staff member at Kingsley Hall. Cornell remembers: "The reply was welcoming, but the caveat was that there were no staff positions to apply [for]—I was welcome to come and live in the community and if they all thought I had something to offer, I would be welcome to stay. Of course, I would have to find another job to support myself."

Like the Cathexis Institute, the duration of Kingsley Hall was short-lived, closing down five years later. The work of Laing and his colleagues tended to valorise "madness" and demonise psychiatry (Cooper, 1978). The very term "anti-psychiatry" conveys the frequent polarisation between biological vs. psychosocial models of schizophrenia. It is now abundantly clear that there is no single disorder or illness that constitutes schizophrenia or psychosis (Fujii & Ahmed, 2007, Read, Mosher, & Bentall, 2004; Van Os & Kapur, 2009). Neither is there a single cause. It is not necessary or therapeutic to split the biological and psychosocial models of these deep disturbances of self-coherence (Geekie & Read, 2009; Haykin, 1998). It is, of course, very possible to offer and demonstrate deep interest and respect for the patient's subjective experience in the midst of a psychic crisis without getting lost in it (Bollas, 2013; Garfield, 2009; Geekie & Read, 2009).

6.4.3   "Primary maternal preoccupation"

Central to Winnicott's work was the effort to identify the factors that supported the development of a coherent and vital sense of self. Winnicott (1956, 1971) did not use the language of symbiosis, but his conceptualisations, seen from a TA perspective, were vivid descriptions of functional, transitional forms of symbiosis.

In his concept of primary maternal preoccupation he describes an organised state of hypersensitivity to the infant's bodily and emotional needs, significantly setting aside or dissociating from the mother's own needs during the weeks after birth. This, Winnicott argues, provides the infant with a fundamental, bodily sense of "going-on-being" from which the infant is then able to develop a sense of the mother as a separate person.

Winnicott (1962) saw psychotic breakdowns as "environmental deficiency diseases". Chronic environmental failures within the parenting relationships were understood to increase the likelihood of later disintegrations or disturbances of the coherence of the self, including autism, latent schizophrenia, a rigidly dissociated "false-self", a schizoid personality, or psychotic breakdown. Winnicott's thinking was a major influence in Laing's early formulations of the "divided self".

Winnicott's concept (1954) of "regression to dependence" was central to the working through of psychotic anxieties and schizoid splits (Little, 1990). He understood regression as the revisiting of early, non-verbal experiences that would likely underlie the psychotic disturbance. His approach to working with patients in regressed states offers a startling contrast to the position taken by Schiff and her reparenting colleagues, by emphasising the therapist's vulnerability to intense countertransference reactions (1954, p. 278). Winnicott was keenly aware of the stress that the accompanying of regressed states placed upon the analyst:

The treatment and management of this case has called upon everything I possess as a human being, as a psychoanalyst, and as a paediatrician. I have had to make a personal growth in the course of this treatment which was painful and which I would gladly have avoided. ... and it has always turned out in the dozen or so resistance phases that the cause was in a counter-transference phenomenon which necessitated further self-analysis in the analyst. (p. 280)

One can only wonder, had Jacqui Schiff undertaken this level of self-examination, what might have been the outcome of her work and that of her Cathexis colleagues.

6.4.4 Milieu therapy

Winnicott worked with patients in schizoid and psychotic states in the setting of a one-on-one psychoanalytic practice. Many clinicians seeking to find effective ways to work therapeutically with these deep levels of disturbances to the self-coherence worked in groups, community, and/ or milieu treatment settings (Cumming & Cumming, 1962). Models of milieu treatment are not so concerned with the causes of schizophrenia as with identifying the elements of the therapeutic environment that are most beneficial to the patient. The intention is to provide an actively structuring environment that builds a patient's sense of agency and reconstructive potential rather than focusing on history, memories, and regressive longings. In milieu treatment, all staff who have contact with patients are trained and expected to contribute to the functioning and well-being of the patients. Patients are actively engaged in evaluating the efficacy of their treatment and a patient government process that provides patients with direct input on the functioning of the structure and processes within the treatment setting.

Unlike such therapeutic communities as Kingsley Hall and the Cathexis Institute, milieu therapy has been subjected to rigorous research and debate. One of the consistent findings of the research is that high intensity and confrontations are more often than not overstimulating and detrimental to the stabilisation and resolution of schizophrenic and psychotic difficulties (Drake & Sederer, 1986; Vaglum, Friis, & Karterud, 1985). On the other hand, a well thought-out residential treatment programme can offer a corrective environment, for example for emotionally neglected youngsters (Rose, 1990). A carefully structured programme with formal and informal activities, and with a staff who cooperate in a healthy way, offers opportunities for new relationships for the patients. Here they can learn to integrate these new experiences, which contributes to a growth to normal adulthood.

6.4.5 Research

There is still not much research into the effectiveness of TA psychotherapy. One exception is the research of Mark Widdowson (2012) into the effectiveness of TA for the treatment of depressed patients. Widdowson developed a model for case-research, a "hermeneutic single-case efficacy design" study which potentially can lead to a new research methodology and give data which show the effectiveness of outpatient psychotherapy based on transactional analysis.

Another example is a Dutch multicentre study in which different formats (outpatient, day care and inpatient treatment, short term and long term) for the treatment of patients with personality disorders are compared. One of the programmes participating in this research was a three-month inpatient programme with TA as the method of psychotherapy. The research showed that this TA programme was the most effective of the different programmes in reducing symptom level in patients with a cluster C personality disorder (avoidant, dependent, and obsessive-compulsive); moreover it was also a cost-effective programme (Bartak et al., 2010; Soeteman et al., 2011).

6.4.6 Defence mechanisms

The concepts of "discounting" and "redefining" in psychoanalysis are examples of defence mechanisms. In TA there is little mention of defence mechanisms and the unconscious. This is possibly due to the personal history of Berne. When he became disappointed and turned away from psychoanalysis, he may have needed to position TA as a theory in contrast to the concepts of psychoanalysis. And yet it is certainly not the case that he had no eye for unconscious processes within the individual person or in the transactions between people. But he referred to them in different terms. He talked about the ulterior motive in game transactions and about the script that takes place "outside of Adult consciousness". In his posthumously published book, *What Do You Say After You Say Hello?* (1972), he uses some interesting concepts that he didn't elaborate upon much further: the "death drive" (mortido) in individuals, groups, organisations, and nations, and the "little fascist" that sees other people as prey, a residue of the early development stages of humankind when survival was paramount. He links both of these to the script and says "You can think of the script as the elaboration of the veiled death instinct of the individual" (Clarkson, 1992). A concept like the "joker" in the script, which suddenly pops up when everything seems to be going well and then succeeds in completing the script payoff, is not further explained by Berne, though it certainly seems to have unconscious components.

The concept of "the unconscious" was coined by Sigmund Freud, who was the first to really describe how inner conflicts can lead to all sorts of physical and psychological symptoms—without the person being at all aware of the existence of a conflict. These conflicts can take place between impulses and desires on the one hand (the *Es* or id), and another part of the person on the other (for example, a strong conscience, the *Über-Ich* or superego, or a rational decision by the *Ich*, the ego).

It may be a conflict between different impulses within the id or a conflict with the outside world. This means that of all three agencies within the person, the id, the ego, and the superego, parts are unconscious. In TA terms you could simply say: the unconscious is all that lies outside the Adult consciousness:

- The contaminated parts of the Adult ego state.
- The fixed or excluded parts of the Child ego state.
- The fixed or excluded parts of the Parent ego state.

If you use the concept of "integrated Adult", you could say that everything that is not part of the integrated Adult is unconscious. With fixations, certain parts of an ego state are closed off, for example, repressed traumatic memories in the Child ego state or non-integrated introjections in the Parent ego state.

A defence mechanism is defined as a psychological manoeuvre by which the person strikes a balance or compromise in a conflict between an impulse, a need, or a desire on the one hand and a prohibition on these things from the inside or outside of the person on the other.

In the therapeutic relationship, the defence mechanisms are evident in the transference, especially in the resistance that the client offers to the activities of the therapist. For example, the therapist politely asks how the patient experienced the previous conversation and the patient says hesitantly, "A bit like a police interrogation." If the therapist then asks what the patient means by that and what feelings that brings about, he does not answer this question but begins to tell a sweeping story about the role of the police in this society.

Defence mechanisms inhibit the ability to achieve intimacy, spontaneity, and consciousness, for two reasons. The defence itself (the internal resistance against an impulse or need) costs energy, more energy than the satisfaction of the need would cost. In addition, the resistance restricts the flexibility of response. It acts like a kind of disability around a particular area. This then needs to be compensated for, again which itself takes extra energy.

A definition of defence mechanisms which is more in line with TA concepts is the following: a defence mechanism is any internal tactic that protects script decisions. Because the script is originally created by the Child as the best strategy for the fulfilment of his own needs, you can also describe defence mechanisms as survival mechanisms. Some transactional analysts argue in favour of this designation based on the following considerations.

- To emphasise that it concerns decisions that the person once took himself and which can therefore be changed (Goulding & Goulding, 1979).
- As a name for physis, human creativity, and the aspiration to survive (Clarkson, 1992).
- As one of the three basic human needs, in addition to the need to rest and the need for strokes (English, 1972).
- As an aid in the diagnosis of patients and the formulation of a treatment (Berne, 1964).
- To understand how the patient continually repeats inadequate patterns for reasons of safety and from the hope of a better outcome (Thunnissen, 2007).

The basic pattern that underlies every defence mechanism is the crossed transaction. A child has certain needs that the parent does not satisfy (via a complementary transaction) but actually ignores or rejects (through a crossed transaction). The child finally decides to let go of these needs, desires, and feelings.

This results in fixations within the Child ego state as well as habitual crossed transactions by the child and later the adult person, when later in life situations occur that resemble the original situation. Instead of the original feelings, the person exhibits racket feelings. Instead of complementary transactions, the person internally changes his ego state and engages in parallel and crossed transactions. Thus, contact is broken, internally within the person and externally between two persons.

References

Barrow, G., Bradshaw, E., & Newton, T. (2001). *Improving Behaviour and Raising Self-Esteem in the Classroom: A Practical Guide to Using TA*. London: David Fulton.

Bartak, A., Spreeuwenberg, M., Andrea, H., Holleman, L., Rijnierse, P., Rossum, B., Hamers, E., Meerman, A., Aerts, J., Busschbach, J., Verheul, R., Stijnen, T., & Emmelkamp, P. (2010). Effectiveness of different modalities of psychotherapeutic treatment for patients with Cluster C personality disorder: results of a large prospective multicentre study. *Psychotherapy and Psychosomatics, 79*: 20–30.

Berne, E. (1961). *Transactional Analysis in Psychotherapy*. New York: Grove Press.

Berne, E. (1964). *Games People Play*. New York: Grove Press.

Berne, E. (1969). Reparenting in schizophrenia: Introduction. *Transactional Analysis Bulletin, 8*(3): 45–47.

Berne, E. (1972). *What Do You Say After You Say Hello?* New York: Bantam.

Bollas, C. (2013). *Catch Them Before They Fall: The Psychoanalysis of Breakdown*. London: Routledge.

Burston, D. (1996). *The Wing of Madness: The Life and Work of R. D. Laing*. Cambridge, MA: Harvard University Press.

Burston, D. (2000). *The Crucible of Experience: R. D. Laing and the Crisis of Psychotherapy*. Cambridge, MA: Harvard University Press.

Clarke, J. I., & Dawson, C. (1989). *Growing Up Again (2nd edition)*. Center City, MI: Hazelden, 1998.

Clarkson, P. (1992). *Transactional Analysis Psychotherapy. An Integrated Approach*. London: Tavistock/Routledge.

Cooper, D. (1967). *Psychiatry and Anti-Psychiatry*. London: Tavistock.

Cooper, D. (1978). *The Language of Madness*. London: Penguin.

Cornell, W. F. (1988). Life script theory: A critical review from a developmental perspective. *Transactional Analysis Journal, 18*(4): 270–282.

Cumming, J., & Cumming, E. (1962). *Ego and Milieu: Theory and Practice of Environmental Therapy*. New York: Atherton Press.

Dashiell, S. (1978). The Parent resolution process: Reprogramming the psychic incorporations in the Parent. *Transactional Analysis Journal, 8*(4): 289–294.

Drake, R. E., & Sederer, L. I. (1986). The adverse effects of intensive treatment of chronic schizophrenia. *Comprehensive Psychiatry, 27*: 313–326.

English, F. (1972). Sleepy, Spunky and Spooky. *Transactional Analysis Journal, 2*(2): 64–67.

Erskine, R. G., & Moursund, J. P. (1988). *Integrative Psychotherapy in Action*. Newbury Park, CA: Sage.

Erskine, R. G., & Trautmann, R. (2003). Resolving intrapsychic conflict: Psychotherapy of Parent ego states. In: C. Sills & H. Hargaden (Eds.), *Key Concepts in Transactional Analysis: Contemporary Views, Ego States* (pp. 83–108). London: Worth.

Fromm-Reichmann, F. (1960). *Principles of Intensive Psychotherapy*. Chicago, IL: University of Chicago Press.

Fujii, D., & Ahmed, I. (Eds.) (2007). *The Spectrum of Psychotic Disorders: Neurobiology, Etiology, and Pathogenesis*. Cambridge: Cambridge University Press.

Garfield, D. A. S. (2009). *Unbearable Affect: A Guide to the Psychotherapy of Psychosis*. London: Karnac.

Geekie, J., & Read, J. (2009). *Making Sense of Madness: Contesting the Meaning of Schizophrenia*. Hove, UK: Routledge.

Goulding, R., & Goulding, M. (1979). *Changing Lives through Redecision*. New York: Brunner/Mazel.

Guglielmotti, R. L. (1996). Parents who are orphans: Implications for second-generation scripts and eating disorders. *Transactional Analysis Journal, 26*: 132–137.

Harrington, A. (2012). The fall of the schizophrenogenic mother. *The Lancet, 379*: 1292–1293.

Hay, J. (1995). *Donkey Bridges for Developmental TA. Making Transactional Analysis Memorable and Accessible*. Watford, UK: Sherwood.

Hay, J. (1996). *Transactional Analysis for Trainers. Your Guide to Potent & Competent Applications of TA in Organisations*. Watford, UK: Sherwood.

Hay, J. (2009). *Working It Out at Work: Understanding Attitudes and Building Relationships*. Watford, UK: Sherwood.

Haykin, M. D. (1998). Fifty years—a perspective. *Transactional Analysis Journal, 28*(1): 35–44.

Jacobs, A. (1987). Autocratic power. *Transactional Analysis Journal, 17*(1): 59–71.

Jacobs, A. (1994). Theory as ideology: Reparenting and thought reform. *Transactional Analysis Journal, 24*(1): 39–55.

Kouwenhoven, M. (1983). *TA in Nederland*. (TA in the Netherlands.) *Part I*. Zwolle, Netherlands: Tulp.

Laing, R. D. (1960). *The Divided Self*. London: Tavistock.

Laing, R. D. (1969). *The Politics of the Family and Other Essays*. New York: Pantheon.

Laing, R. D., & Esterson, A. (1964). *Sanity, Madness and the Family*. London: Tavistock.

Levin-Landheer, P. (1982). The cycle of development. *Transactional Analysis Journal, 12*(2): 129–139.

Lidz, T. (1971). Schizophrenia, R. D. Laing, and the contemporary treatment of psychosis: An interview with Dr. Theodore Lidz. In: R. Boyers & R. Orrill (Eds.), *R. D. Laing & Anti-Psychiatry* (pp. 151–199). New York: Perennial Library.

Lidz, T. (1973). *The Origin and Treatment of Schizophrenic Disorders*. New York: Basic Books.

Lidz., T., Fleck, S., & Cornelison, A. (1965). *Schizophrenia and the Family*. New York: International Universities Press.

Little, M. I. (1990). *Psychotic Anxieties and Containment: A Personal Record of an Analysis with Winnicott*. Northvale, NJ: Jason Aronson.

Loria, B. R. (1988). The Parent ego state—theoretical foundations and alterations. *Transactional Analysis Journal, 18*(1): 39–46.

Macefield, R., & Mellor, K. (2006). Awareness and discounting. *Transactional Analysis Journal, 36*(1): 44–58.

McClendon, R. (1978). Board reaches decision on thics matter. *The Script, 8*(10).

McNeel, J. (1976). The Parent interview. *Transactional Analysis Journal, 6*(1): 61–68.

Mellor, K. & Andrewartha, G. (1980). Reparenting the Parent in support of redecisions. *Transactional Analysis Journal, 10*(3): 197–203.

Mellor, K., & Sigmund, E. (1975a). Discounting. *Transactional Analysis Journal, 5*(3): 295–302.

Mellor, K., & Sigmund, E. (1975b). Redefining. *Transactional Analysis Journal, 5*(3): 303–311.

Mullen, B. (1995). *Mad to be Normal: Conversations with R. D. Laing*. London: Free Association.

Napper, R., & Newton, T. (2000) *Tactics*. Ipswich, UK: TA Resources.

Neill, J. (1990). Whatever became of the schizophrenogenic mother? *American Journal of Psychotherapy, 64*: 499–505.

Newton, T., & Wong, G. (2003). A chance to thrive: Enabling change in a nursery school. *Transactional Analysis Journal, 33*(1): 79–88.

Novey, T. B. (1998). Letter from the editor: Regression in psychotherapy. *Transactional Analysis Journal, 28*(1): 2–3.

Oblas, A. S. (1981). The Parent interview and indirect suggestion. *Transactional Analysis Journal*, 11(2): 126–129.

Os, J. van, & Kapur, S. (2009). Schizophrenia. *The Lancet*, 374(9690): 635–645.

Read, J., Mosher, L. R., & Bentall, R. P. (2004). *Models of Madness: Psychological, Social, and Biological Approaches to Schizophrenia*. Hove, UK: Brunner-Routledge.

Rose, M. (1990). *Healing Hurt Minds. The Peper Harow Experience*. London: Routledge.

Schiff, A., & Schiff, J. L. (1971). Passivity. *Transactional Analysis Journal*, 1(1): 71–78.

Schiff, J. L. (1969). Reparenting schizophrenics. *Transactional Analysis Bulletin*, 8(31): 47–63.

Schiff, J. L. (Ed.) (1975). *Transactional Analysis Treatment of Psychosis. Cathexis Reader*. New York: Harper & Row.

Schiff, J. L. (1977). One hundred children generate a lot of TA: History, development, and activities of the Schiff family. In: G. Barnes (Ed.), *Transactional Analysis after Eric Berne: Teachings and Practices of Three TA Schools* (pp. 53–76). New York: Harper's College Press.

Soeteman, D., Verheul, R., Meerman, A., Ziegler, U., Rossum, B., Delimon, J., Rijnierse, P., Thunnissen, M., Busschbach, J., & Kim, J. (2011). Cost-effectiveness of psychotherapy for Cluster C personality disorders: A decision-analytic model in The Netherlands. *Journal of Clinical Psychiatry*, 72(1): 51–59.

Sullivan, H. S. (1962). *Schizophrenia as a Human Process*. New York: W. W. Norton, 1974.

Thunnissen, M. (2007). *Begrijpen en veranderen. Theorie en toepassingen van de transactionele analyse.* (To Understand and to Change. Theory and Practice of Transactional Analysis.) Halsteren, Netherlands: DWG.

Vaglum, P., Friis, S., & Karterud, S. (1985). Why are the results of milieu therapy for schizophrenic patients contradictory? An analysis based on four empirical studies. *Yale Journal of Biology and Medicine*, 58: 349–361.

Weiss, L. (1994). The ethics of parenting and reparenting in psychotherapy. *Transactional Analysis Journal*, 24(1): 57–59.

Widdowson, M. (2012). TA treatment of depression: a hermeneutic single-case efficacy design study—case two: "Denise". *International Journal of Transactional Analysis Research*, 3(2): 3–14.

Winnicott, D. W. (1954). Metaphysical and clinical aspects of regression within the psycho-analytical set-up. In: *Through Paediatrics to Psychoanalysis* (pp. 278–294). London: Karnac.

Winnicott, D. W. (1956). Primary maternal preoccupation. In: *Through Paediatrics to Psychoanalysis* (pp. 300–305). London: Karnac.

Winnicott, D. W. (1962). Ego integration in child development. In: The Maturational Processes and the Facilitating Environment (pp. 56–63). Madison, CT: International Universities Press.

Winnicott, D. W. (1971). Mirror-role of mother and family in child development. In: *Playing and Reality* (pp. 111–118). London: Tavistock.

Young, J., & Klosko, J. (1994). *Reinventing Your Life*. New York: Plume.

Young, J., Klosko, J., & Weishaar, M. (2003). *Schema Therapy. A Practitioner's Guide*. New York: Guilford Press.

CHAPTER SEVEN

Contracts

7.1 Basic theory
    7.1.1 The contract in TA
    7.1.2 Requirements of contracts
    7.1.3 Contract and script
    7.1.4 Multi-cornered contracts
7.2 Further theory
    7.2.1 The pentagon of changes
    7.2.2 "Not" contracts and problem-solving sanctions
    7.2.3 Effective vs. ineffective contracts
    7.2.4 Contracting in psychotherapy
    7.2.5 Contracts with organisations
    7.2.6 Co-creative TA
    7.2.7 The therapeutic process and the therapeutic frame
    7.2.8 Contracts and context in relational work
7.3 Furthermore
    7.3.1 Psychological distance
    7.3.2 The conversation contract
    7.3.3 Learning contracts
7.4 Related theories
    7.4.1 Visitor, plaintiff, or customer
    7.4.2 Socratic motivation
    7.4.3 Learned helplessness
    7.4.4 Collaborative diagnosis
References

Eric Berne worked with "contracts" in his therapy practice, which clearly defined the role (tasks and responsibilities) of the caregiver and the role (tasks and responsibilities) of the client. This emphasises the equality of both parties and the fact that therapy, counselling, education, or coaching has a purpose that is stated at the beginning of the process. This chapter provides information on the theory and practice of working with contracts.

7.1   Basic theory

7.1.1   The contract in TA

The concept of contracts is fundamental to the practice of transactional analysis in all fields of application. According to Eric Berne (1966), it is always about achieving clarity with the client about what will be done together. "A contract is an explicit bilateral commitment to a well-defined course of action," as Berne put it. While Berne focused on therapeutic contracts in individual and group therapy, TA practitioners apply the use of contracts in a broad range of settings: families, students, supervisees, organisations, etc., with the goal being that of establishing a mutual working relationship. Berne emphasised the direct engagement with the client's intelligence and investment in learning and change. Berne distinguished between three different aspects of the contract.

1. The procedural contract. This level of the contract between the professional and the client (organisation) contains agreements on the reasons for intervention, the course of events, and the cost of the intervention. What legal requirements do the client and the professional have to adhere to? What are the duties and responsibilities of both the client and the professional? What facilities and other support are offered by the organisation?
2. The professional contract. This is to determine the agreements made between the professional and the client (organisation) with regard to the goals of the intervention. In the case of interim management, for example, there will need to be an agreement as to whether there is also a desire for change on the part of the client. With coaching, there will need to be a discussion about whether there is wish for change or improvement on the part of both the coachee and client (more on the importance of such a triangular contract later). In psychotherapy, the contract will—in terms of the therapist—be more focused on structural rather than symptomatic change within the Child ego state, where the therapeutic relationship is an important component within this change. Incidentally, the distinction between symptomatic and structural change is artificial. The various change processes usually overlap.
3. In the psychological contract the motives at a psychological (hidden) level between the client (organisation) and the professional play a crucial, and often disruptive, role. The key question here is: "What could stand in the way of a successful outcome?" According to Berne, many clients who seek therapy are unconsciously aiming to learn how to play their games more efficiently rather than change. They quickly realise whether they can include the therapist in this aim and avoid changing (Berne, 1961). However strange this may seem, there is always a certain degree of ambivalence when people seek treatment or change. On the one hand they want genuine change, but on the other hand (often unconsciously) they want to

maintain their script, although perhaps in a more pleasant way. So too, the hardworking, overburdened manager wants to work fewer hours, but is then startled when his overly responsible behaviour and the conditional strokes he seeks in this way are questioned by a consultant: how much do you need your conditional strokes for your hard work, and what happens if you just do nothing for a while? In another context the overly involved teacher wants to fret less about her troubled students when she is at home, but does not actually want to let go of the pattern of being there for others, which she learned at an early age. The ardent smoker wants to get rid of his cough and improve his health, but would prefer to do so without quitting.

Julie Hay (2007) suggests adding two further levels, linked to the psychological level, when contracting with an organisation, particularly relevant when working cross-culturally or in any situation where frames of reference are likely to differ between those involved:

4. The perceptual level, which refers to the way relationships are perceived. There may be a perception, for instance, that coaching is only made available to "favourites", or to those under threat of demotion. This might be addressed through careful questioning in the contracting process.
5. The political level, which is about the unavoidable socio-political context, takes account of the way that power is expressed in an organisation. There may be someone else (a psychological leader), apart from the one who seems to be in charge, who pulls the strings. This also might be addressed through careful questioning in the contracting process.

> Thirty-year-old Hanno is looking for coaching because, as a teacher, he sometimes has no authority in the classroom. The contract that is drawn up during this first session is therefore about the goal of acquiring more authority in the classroom. In addition, the contract includes the way in which this goal is to be achieved: "To use more assertive behaviour and to get behind myself more". During the initial session it is noted that he absolutely does not want to have children himself, to the dismay of his wife. During the third coaching session he talks about his deceased father; Hanno was eight years old when his father died suddenly of a heart attack. From that moment on he, as the eldest of three children, took on the father's role in the family. When the coach replies that this must have been a very difficult task for an eight-year-old boy, Hanno breaks down. The coach carefully asks what he decided at this time. In tears, Hanno said that "I would never do this to my children." The only sure way of upholding this decision seemed to be to not have any children. Suddenly all this became crystal clear to Hanno. It became clear that underneath the contract (of acquiring more assertiveness and authority) lay an entirely different theme. Deep inside there is still an eight-year-old boy who misses his father who is doing his utter best to replace him. The coach now proposes to also include this in the contract—"getting behind myself" also means making contact with the eight-year-old Hanno. Slightly confused, he goes home, and in the remaining coaching sessions he tells how he is now suddenly speaking with his wife in an entirely different way about the possibility of having children. He feels his never-expressed grief over the death of his father, and talks to his mother about this. To his surprise, things start going better at school. There is more calm in the classroom and he has more pleasure in teaching. In the follow-up session, six months later, he says, embarrassed and proud, that his wife is now pregnant.

A common misunderstanding among many professionals is that the contract precedes the work, when in actual practice the professional and the client may meet for several sessions before establishing a treatment or consultative contract. Setting up a good contract is an essential part of the overall work of the professional. Research (Van der Waals, 2007) into ineffective change management—processes about which the clients were not or were less satisfied—shows that the cause of this dissatisfaction is in all cases due to insufficient "expectation management" by the professional during the initial contact. An intervention not going according to plan can always be traced to insufficient contracting between the professional involved and the client. The result of inadequate or poor contracting is that a change process becomes stranded in good intentions and a fake change or no change at all is the result. This also often leads to antipathy on the part of the client with regard to change processes in general.

The first question that Bob and Mary Goulding (1978) ask of those who participate in a workshop with them is "What do you want to change?" The use of contracts in which the purpose of the therapy, counselling, or coaching is established, was already common in TA long before working with treatment protocols and written arrangements came into vogue.

Organisations have their own scripts, which create unconscious resistances to change. Examples of organisational scripts can be seen in a mental health institution in which the notion prevails that patients are capable of only bearing a small degree of personal responsibility, the school which tries to ensure safety with ever more rules, or the business in which profit is more important than the working climate and the atmosphere among the staff.

What is the place of the client in the force field of the organisation? How will the power and influence that he has ensure a successful intervention or actually hinder its success? Some council members in governmental organisations want to have full control of all the levers and strings when it comes to processes of change implemented by interim managers. In this case, the client/team leader, but also the hired manager, will need to have a clear view of all these things.

7.1.2 Requirements of contracts

The basic TA philosophy, "I'm OK, you're OK", makes it a matter of course that the equivalence between the contracting parties is emphasised in the contract. The fact that one party requests a service or seeks help from the other party does not need to imply that one's right to self-determination is put into question, or that the professional thereby acquires power. This is an essential feature of the work of TA professionals and it applies to all three contracts: the procedural, the professional, and the psychological.

Steiner (1974) took the drafting of contracts in legal matters as an example and suggested that contracts within TA should meet the following four requirements.

1. Mutual consent. Both parties must agree on the contract. The contract is drawn up in negotiation by both parties.

    A good example of the complexity of this is the "advanced directive" that is used in current psychiatry in the Netherlands: the patient states in the contract that if he again becomes manic, psychotic, or otherwise "less accountable", he gives the therapist permission to intervene with medication, extra supervision, and possibly an emergency admission. This is done in the knowledge that once someone is psychotic, he is no longer reachable and in hindsight may have regrets about the damage that is often caused by the psychosis.

2. Valid considerations. A form of reasonable compensation in exchange for the work of the professional. What is reasonable can partly be seen as a matter of market supply and demand. What is the client willing to pay for the quality delivered by the professional? What is it worth to him? What do other professionals ask who provide a similar service? Since Steiner first drafted these considerations, we have seen the rise of third party payers, such as governmental agencies and insurance companies, which often dictate remuneration. Steiner also suggested that the consideration may be other that monetary, for instance barter, or a skills exchange such as a client providing clerical services in return for coaching.
3. Competency. Both the professional and the client must be competent to perform that which has been agreed upon in the contract. For the professional this means possessing and maintaining professional competence in order to enable the client to work towards achieving the desired change. The client must be able to understand the contract, have an overview of the consequences, and possess the physical and mental faculties to fulfil the contract.
4. Lawful object. The objectives and conditions of the contract must be in accordance with the law. For the TA professional this also means following the ethical principles of the professional group to which she belongs.

In the illustrative book *Contracts in Counselling & Psychotherapy* (editor Charlotte Sills, 2006) several TA authors and practitioners give their view and conceptualisations of contracts. They describe the utilisation and applicability of contracts in a broad range of modalities and settings.

Contact before contract?

By making a contract (too) quickly, professionals, before they realise it, may place the unconscious at a distance. The unconscious elements of the therapeutic process may then later emerge in the work in a positive or (more often) a negative way. The unconscious is the realm of feelings, thoughts, desires, and memories that people find unacceptable, unpleasant, or dangerous. Taking the time to get to know your client and make contact with each other before drawing up a contract is therefore not just a matter of politeness or decency. Take your time and see if you can understand something of the manifestations of the unconscious. Don't fixate it (too quickly) in a contract. This is also true in education and consultancy, where exploratory time with the client will allow important needs and issues to emerge which the resulting contract can then account for.

7.1.3   Contract and script

As we saw in Chapter Five, the script is a complex mix of positive/stimulating and negative/destructive elements (Thunnissen, 2007). From this perspective, the script can also be seen as an early contract between a child and his parents about important issues in life, such as what he will always do (drivers) and never do (stoppers), how he will live (programme), how does he behave towards others and how does he feel in the world (life position), and how and when will he die (script payoff). An organisational script can be seen as a contract with the founder of the company or organisation on how employees should behave, what they will always and never do, and how to deal with the environment, the market, and customers.

The difference between the script and a contract, as it is defined in this chapter, is that the script is an unconscious agreement while the procedural and professional layer of the contract is a conscious, explicit agreement. The contract is often at odds with (certain parts of) the script: it gives the client permission to change the (psychological) script contract or at least to disobey certain parts of it. Drawing up a contract is thus often an exciting adventure for the client because it means he loses the approval of the parents or of the founders. Changing the original contract will therefore also have a direct impact on the client's stroke maintenance: not only does he let go of old, familiar internal strokes that originally came from the parents or of the founders, but there is also a chance that the internal Parent may react with negative strokes or punishment.

Making a redecision disturbs the internal equilibrium and the internal Parent tries to restore the old equilibrium. Things that are usually plain sailing, now suddenly go wrong.

Clients who apply for coaching or therapy mainly require an easing of their symptoms during the initial phase, but they will often try to use the contract to make a compromise in order to keep their script intact. With this compromise, they can reassure their internal Parent so as not to have to face the fear of re-experiencing conflicts from their childhood or the early years of the company or organisation. Obviously, such a "deception" by the client is not intentional but an unconscious manoeuvre, an attempt at a psychological contract, as a defence against anxiety, and as a way to ensure safety. During the process of agreeing upon a working contract, it is important to become aware of these manoeuvres (the psychological contract), so that there is room for the real needs of the Child of the client. The client can then accept the professional as an ally, as an alternative, positive Parent, and he will then feel hope: a major factor in the healing process.

Often, during a change process in an organisation or company, the degree of games is discussed, by which management and staff keep the old organisation script going. Letting go of the "old contract" in favour of the "new contract" is frequently accompanied by a period in which everyone experiences a stroke deficit. The source of (often negative) strokes, the game behaviour fuelled by the old script, dries up, while the new script is still in its infancy. An important task of the specialist in charge of change management is to guide all those involved through this period of limbo. Often this can be done by the specialist—temporarily—being the source of positive strokes.

7.1.4 Multi-cornered contracts

Fanita English (1975) elaborated on the ideas of Berne and suggested that most contracts are not bilateral, as Berne described them, but "three-cornered contracts". In addition to the contract between the professional and the client, there is the contract between the professional and the organisation, the system. This contract also has an influence on the development and outcome of the intervention. The same applies to the contract between the client and the organisation or system.

It is important to take full account of this factor to ensure a successful intervention. The TA concept of the triangle contract helps professionals manage expectations at the start as well as later during the intervention as effectively as possible. All three levels of the contract must therefore be examined by all three parties. The figure below shows what this looks like.

Julie Hay (1992), who specialises in contracting from an organisational standpoint, believes that a contract is neither bilateral nor three-cornered, but multi-cornered. For the professional, there is always a question as to all those who have an interest in the work that she will be doing. In psychotherapy, it is important to establish whether there are family members or friends who have high or low expectations of the therapy. Who is watching over the client's shoulder? When working in organisations or companies, it is important to have a clear picture of all the stakeholders inside and (often also) outside the company or organisation (as in Figure 7.2). In schools, these stakeholders extend from parents and school governors to local and national policymakers. Whether working in psychotherapy, counselling, teaching, or organisational work, those standing in the corners may be explicit participants in the change process or may be hidden, peripheral characters who have not necessarily participated in the contracting process.

7.2. Further theory

7.2.1. The pentagon of changes

The subject of "change" is a hot topic in many theories of management, coaching, and therapy. When has a person, a team, or an organisation really changed? And how can you ensure that

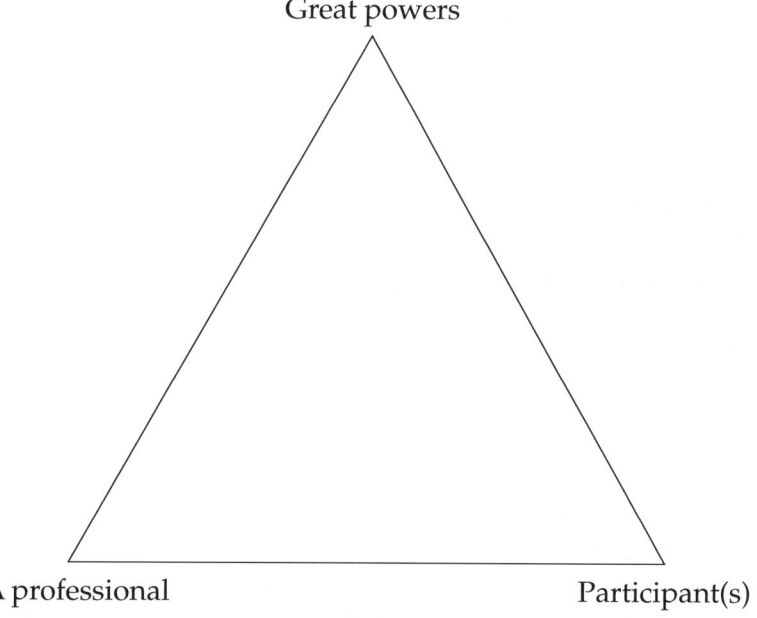

Figure 7.1. The three-cornered contract.

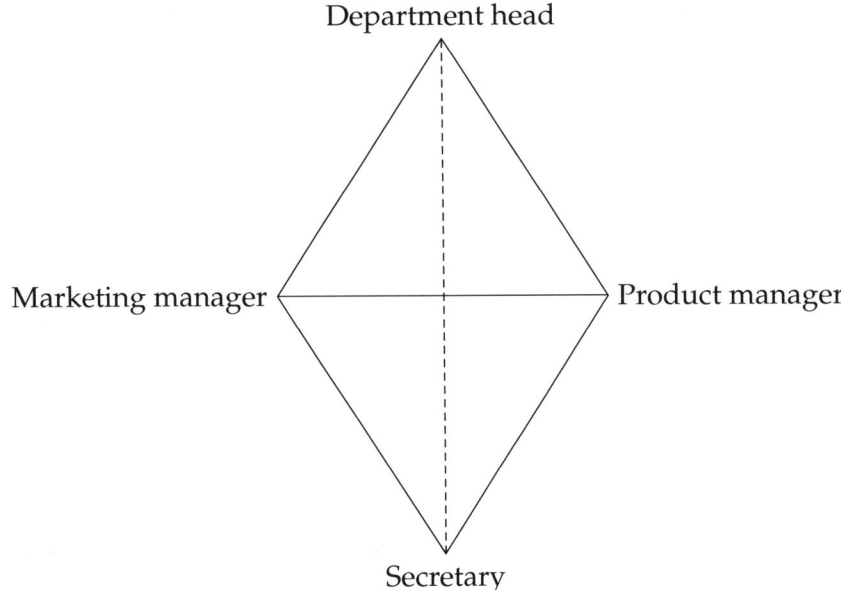

Figure 7.2. The parties of the contract.

once change has been achieved, it is maintained and the client doesn't fall back into old patterns? Often, after a while, clients recognise their preferred position in the drama triangle and certain games they regularly play. They then realise how often they do this and how it relates to their script. At this point, people can continue their path of change. It is also possible that they then drop out. When the therapist or coach does not want to confirm her role as Victim or does not want to entertain her Persecutor lamentations about all that is wrong with others, she stops the therapy or counselling and remains unhappy or she finds another professional who does want to enter into the drama triangle.

According to Berne, people can change from a frog into a prince, and thus reclaim their membership in the human race. But sometimes they are satisfied with becoming a nicer frog (1966).

Clarkson (1988) distinguishes between five possible "changes" which she links to classical Greek mythology:

- Script change is like the arduous journey of Odysseus, who, after the Trojan War, undergoes a difficult journey full of dangers yet ultimately arrives home healthy. Through trial and error, the client achieves a better balance and a happier and healthier life.
- Instead, one can also make many small steps of progress, while not changing in essence, as in the myth of Echo, the nymph who was deprived of her voice by Hera, the wife of Zeus. Echo falls in love with the beautiful young Narcissus, but can only repeat his words and not talk herself. When he rejects her, she mourns incessantly. She retreats into a cave where she can only repeat what is said. The client, for example, has learned to avoid stress—which is progress, but not a radical change.
- Clients may also take flight into the counter-script: the messages of the script are replaced by the messages of the therapist or counsellor. This creates an illusion of autonomy, but

eventually allows the evil prophecy to come true, as in the myth of Oedipus (see section 4.3.1 in Chapter Four).
- Instead of changing, one may end up in the myth of Icarus, who escaped from captivity with wings of feathers and wax. Despite warnings he flies too high. The sun melts the wax and Icarus falls to his death. After enthusiasm and commitment in the beginning, the client fails to implement the change and ends with disillusionment and despair.

7.2.2. "Non"-contracts and problem-solving sanctions

In the contract, both parties record their commitment—from their own role—towards reaching the goals formulated in the contract. The client will hereby comply with the rules, such as being on time, using his energy positively, and providing for payment of the costs. Specific services and responsibilities of the professional are: providing permission, protection, and potency, the three Ps (Crossman, 1966; Kouwenhoven, 1985; Steiner 1974). In working with clients towards change, protection entails providing adequate security and safety against the fear that change evokes.

Berne puts it as follows in his script questions: "Am I—as TA professional—able to stand up to your Parent ego state?" This also has to do with potency. Does the TA professional have enough professional expertise and experience as well as enough personal power and energy to help someone over his important (emotional) barriers? What is also essential in order to change is the permission to stop dysfunctional behaviour and to choose healthy behaviour. The professional can perform as an auxiliary Parent, like a bridge, until the client has incorporated the healthy messages into his own Parent.

To avoid tragic script outcomes it is sometimes necessary to explicitly close certain loopholes or escape hatches (Kouwenhoven, 1985; Stewart, 2007). Precisely in order to bring about lasting change, it is desirable to exclude such outcomes. The professional can become aware of these with the question: "And if it gets really bad, if you're terribly gloomy, angry, confused, or sad, what do you then say to yourself, 'I can always …'?" Often the client will then tell you about thinking of taking impulsive decisions, such as quitting his job, ending a relationship, going on a drinking spree, admitting himself to a (psychiatric) hospital, or possibly even thoughts of suicide. Especially if the client has attempted such self-destructive exit plans in the past, or is considering them now, it is important to explicitly state in the contract that the client will not do these things again. While the client looks at the professional, the client declares: "I will not hurt myself or another, I will not commit suicide or attempt to do so, even if I have the urge to do so." Or "I will not allow myself to become confused or psychotic, I will not use alcohol or drugs, even if I have the urge to do so." Sometimes a client may not be able to agree on these terms indefinitely, but agrees to them for a specific period of time, such as for the duration of the treatment or perhaps only until the next session.

Because the "non"-contract deprives the client of a certain escape route, it is also important that something replaces this destructive behaviour. The "non"-contract is then supplemented with: "Instead of this, I will …" and then it will be discussed what options he has; maybe, call a friend, do something distracting or caring such as performing a household task (like doing the dishes), take a bath, or put on his favourite music. It has become common now for many psychiatric patients to carry an emergency card that includes a list of a number of these alternative activities.

If someone inadvertently fails to adhere to the contract, it is important to confront the client with this at the level of his Adult ego state, so as to engage his thinking about what is going on that interferes with the stated contract. But often, more is needed. For the question is why he failed to adhere to it, even though the client was convinced of the usefulness and necessity of the contract. The client often expects punishment or rejection, in compliance with his expectations from his own script. To break this pattern, a problem-solving sanction which "opens a front door" can also be a good idea. This may be a sanction which gives permission to no longer obey the script, whereby the person allows the flow of (un)conditional strokes, thereby strengthening the relationship between the client and the professional (Kouwenhoven, 1985).

> Ella has social anxiety and would like to learn how to allow people into her life more. Her stated goal in the treatment contract is: "I am not a wallflower; I am a colourful woman." Because in the past she sometimes drank too much alcohol to forget her loneliness, she also makes a no-alcohol contract: "I will not consume more than one glass of alcohol per day while in the therapy." After two months of treatment, when a friend of hers cancels an appointment, she finishes off a bottle of wine by herself and arrives the next day at therapy, filled with guilt and shame. In consultation with the therapist it is decided to implement a problem-solving sanction: she calls the friend in question and proposes that they go to an open salsa dance together, something they both really like doing but which Ella dreads doing on her own.

Clarke (1996) proposed adding two additional Ps, practice and perception, besides protection, potency, and permission, when it comes to taking on leadership responsibilities and tasks in an educational setting. Educators provide protection, working with a broad set of behaviour working agreements. They guard the boundaries of their own role (especially in terms of space and time). Potent leaders and teachers hold themselves and others accountable to the contract and know what they are talking about. They give students and staff permission to think and make decisions for themselves, appropriate to the "task in hand". They also create a space in which staff and students are invited to practise new learning and, further, to investigate their own (script) convictions.

7.2.3. Effective vs. ineffective contracts

Within TA there is a great deal of experience with, as well as thinking about, what makes contracts effective. Morris and Natalie Haimowitz believe that it is paramount that a contract is drawn up with all three ego states. The Parent keeps an eye on whether the desired new behaviour is moral, legal, and ethical. The Adult examines whether the desired new behaviour is possible and safe. The Child wonders whether the desired new behaviour is enjoyable and interesting (Haimowitz & Haimowitz, 1976). Stewart and Joines (1987) list the following seven characteristics of effective contracts.

- Effective contracts are stated in positive terms. Often clients will initially be especially aware of what they do not want in their lives: "I no longer want to be afraid of 'bosses'." A valuable question is then: "What is it that you do want?" From a TA perspective, someone with

a "not"-contract runs the risk of stopping behaviour that has been necessary for survival without having a healthier alternative (the Child) in its place. Another possibility is to have the contract consist of two sentences: "I will come down from my ivory tower and I will make friends."
- The goals are achievable. In short, this feature means that any contract that is physically feasible, is also possible. You can only change "yourself". Bringing about a change in another is (physically) not possible.
- Goals are specific and observable. Achieving a goal is more likely if the goal is not expressed in general terms. "I want to be a more sociable human being" is too general. A question that demands more specification is "What will you do when you've become a more sociable person?" Others, in the environment of the client, should also be able to experience the change. Change, it is sometimes said, is not a goal but a consequence!
- The goals are safe. Make sure the Adult always assesses whether the target is physically safe and socially acceptable.
- The contract is agreed upon from the Adult, with the cooperation of the Natural Child. The point is that the goal fits within the current social context, and that the result of the change will help the Child to (finally) be fulfilled in his needs. The contract is therefore preferably formulated in the language of an eight year old.

  If a contract is made by the client from the Adapted Child, it will almost always confirm the script. Not infrequently, the initial request for help is steeped in script convictions. The decision to ask for coaching or to go into therapy is often influenced by the script conviction: "I will (only) be OK if I ..." A client tells in the first session how much she suffers daily from anxiety, fear, and (sometimes) panic attacks. She wants to get rid of this. The coach or therapist who doesn't first show this client that the frightened Child is asking to be accepted, or the supervisor who is too quick to suggest or mainly offers advice or techniques for relaxing, can actually be sending, on a psychological level, the (script-confirming) message: "You're only OK if you're no longer afraid (and learn to be strong)." It is the client's experience that he is OK in the eyes of the coach or therapist no matter what he brings to the consulting room, that often works wonders. Only then can real change take place, like letting go of fear or seeking relaxation.

- Achieving one's goals always costs something. Change has a price that the client needs to be willing to pay. The client hereby adds value to the desired change. Is the client willing to spend his time and money on the coaching or therapy? Is the client willing to tolerate the changes in and resistance from his social system? In addition to a personal level, change always also has an interpersonal and system level. Does the client want to face the fear of change?

  Hay (1993) is of the opinion that much change goes wrong because it is always said that you will "mourn" during a change. Change is mainly seen as a loss within that paradigm. Mourning theory, like that of Kübler-Ross (1969), seems commonplace in the theory and practice of many change experts. Within TA, change is seen more from the perspective of child development. Whoever observes children will note that they are always wanting to learn something different and something new. A child that is walking does not mourn the time when crawling was the only option.

- There is commitment to do the work. There is often literally work to be done for those who go into coaching or therapy: practising new options for behaviour, performing tasks in order to further investigate the script, and more …

Bob and Mary Goulding (1978) suggest that, when drawing up a contract, special attention be given to the language and behaviour that denies autonomy. The Gouldings speak of "con-words", misleading terms or phrases such as "I want to try to …", "I do not think I'm going to be able to", or "That always makes me furious", or instead of using "I", using the words "it", "you", or "we" and "that just might work". These words harbour the first game invitation and it is important to challenge them from the very beginning. This gives the Child of the client confidence that the therapist is indeed more powerful than his parents.

In a workshop for therapists, one of the participants says that she just got a new job and still finds it very exciting. In passing, she casually mentions that she took a bet with one of her colleagues: if she's still working there after a year, she will treat the colleague to a dinner and if she is fired within the year, her colleague will have to buy her dinner. "What a load of nonsense," Bob Goulding responds; "so you made a bet on your loss?" And then he suggests: "Are you ready within two weeks after you get back from the workshop, to offer your colleague that dinner?" The implicit message is: of course you'll be working there after a year, and if you were to leave within the year, then that's your own autonomous decision and not something done to you.

Some clients tell with relish the story of their umpteenth failure or setback. It may even be so contagious that the therapist will chuckle along with them. The Gouldings were very strict about this gallows laughter. They had a large cowbell standing beside them that they would strike if they sensed a con-word or any gallows humour. The body language of clients can reveal whether they are telling their story from the Adapted Child (head tilted, a little hunched) or from the Structuring Parent (upright, pointing finger). The Gouldings paid very close attention to which ego states were involved in making contracts, so as to anticipate contracts that would prove unworkable. Eventually the therapist seeks to make the contract with the Adult, with the agreement of the Natural Child and the Nurturing Parent.

7.2.4. Contracting in psychotherapy

In TA psychotherapy (Thunnissen, 2007) the contract is formulated in such a way that it provides an alternative to the script. In the first phase of drawing up the contract, the therapist and the client will examine the exact form of the script, how it repeats itself in the client's present life and in the here and now with the psychotherapist and possibly the psychotherapy group. A clear contract often emerges only after a period of work that may be dominated by script and game-based behaviours. The following example involves clinical psychotherapy for which people were admitted for a period of three months.

> Forty-six-year-old Anton registered for short-term inpatient psychotherapy associated with fears, doubts, and depression. He also regularly consumes too much alcohol. For years he has had problems

> with work and relationships. Anton is a middle child, with a five-year older brother and a five-year younger sister. Their father was a career officer in the army and left shortly after Anton's birth to go to Indonesia. Anton only saw him again four years later. The family used to relocate a lot in the past, due to the father's job, who also was often absent and sometimes had temper tantrums. Anton describes his mother both as a cold woman who formed a single front with his brother and gave him the feeling that he couldn't do anything. On the other hand, he also had an erotically tinged relationship with her, whereby the mother used him as a substitute for his often absent father. Drinking and eroticism have played a role in his life since childhood.
>
> Compared to his peers, he used to feel like an outsider. He fought a lot and was himself beaten regularly, also by his brother. In his student days he went drinking a lot and found it easier to make contact with people using his bravura. He married a woman who was attractive, but with whom he actually had no real contact. They had a son together. After six years they divorced, but—eight years later—they still have a fairly intense and sometimes sexual relationship.
>
> The therapist notes in communication with Anton that he quickly chooses to battle with him. In the group, Anton remains on the sidelines and keeps people at bay with his cynical humour, which is often at the expense of himself or others.
>
> In the group therapy session, during which Anton drew up his therapeutic contract, he tells his story with some bravado, as if making the contract is a piece of cake. The therapist decides to ask the group members how they have experienced Anton over the last few days. With some hesitation, they say that they mainly find Anton to be distant and angry; some members are a little afraid of him. Other members feel challenged, and especially those who have been in the group for some time also feel somewhat indignant: Anton continually comments on the rules and agreements and he does not really seem to want to conform to the group. Initially, Anton is resentful: do they really think they already know him after only a few days? He tries to discuss a number of examples which the group mentioned. When the therapist asks whether this situation is familiar to him, and how he feels now, he becomes silent. He recognises that he has become an outsider in this group within a matter of days—a position that has been a recurring theme throughout his life. When the therapist says he seems to be in a trench, like his father in Indonesia, he bursts into tears and says he never had a good relationship with his father. Anton eventually decides with the therapist and the group upon the following therapeutic contract: "I will come out of my foxhole. I want to be a companion with others."

7.2.5. *Contracts with organisations*

A contract in the context of an organisation aims for script-breaking results. From the beginning, it is important to take the complexities of any organisation into account. Contracts in organisations are always multi-cornered and multi-layered. They are multi-cornered in the sense that it is advisable to always ask the question whose interests are at stake when designing the intervention. They are multi-layered in the sense that it is always advisable to examine the psychological level. This can be done by regularly asking the question: "If this intervention does not produce the result that has been agreed upon, what are the causes of this?" The causes can lie in the script of the consultant, in the script of the client, in the script of the organisation, or in the interaction among these script-based psychological and behavioural pressures. In an organisation it is important to start with a first phase contract in which the consultant will have time to do some research into the nature of the organisational structure and dynamics. Only after this phase can a plan and a cooperation contract be drafted, in which the clear professional contractual agreements can be developed.

> When he drove on to the neatly raked terrain in which the new office of the Water Authorities had been built, he immediately began to collect information in order to investigate the script of this potential client. He looked carefully at his surroundings and absorbed the atmosphere of the building. He noted that it had a very polished appearance. His welcoming was done smoothly as well. He was expected, the receptionist told him, and offered him a cup of coffee and asked him to take a seat in the waiting room. After a few minutes he was approached by the secretary of the director with whom he had an appointment. He noticed that it was quiet in the building. The doors of the many rooms he passed were all closed, apart from a few exceptions. The consultant recorded his thoughts: people are working hard behind those doors. In the interview, which took place right on time, the director said that "A new and attractive building required a new corporate culture."
>
> The organisation, which was facing more cuts in the near future, needed to achieve a high degree of efficiency. More work had to be done with fewer people and fewer resources. "And because I, as a former water district chairman, have more knowledge of dykes than of people—ha, ha, ha—I'm wondering just how you will be able—ha, ha, ha—to get the job done?" The consultant noted that he himself shifted slightly backward in his chair after this whirlwind opening from the client. During the interview, he examined, via a series of questions posed to the director, what the characteristics were of the current business culture, and what the director wished to have changed. He was curious to know what this change, in addition to efficiency gains, would yield. Of course, he was also curious about what the director, as one of the bearers of the business culture, was willing to do in order to make the change possible. Together they investigated what could possibly form an obstacle to achieving the stated goal of change. In the tender offer, the consultant was able to make a tentative analysis of the issue and the provisional approach he wanted to choose. Whatever the case, the consultant first proposed a period "of observation and research" in the organisation, before making a final proposal. A half-day working with a mixed group of staff (including management as well as employees from the work floor) was part of this investigative phase.
>
> In his own logbook, the consultant noted a number of remarkable facts and experiences. His preliminary diagnosis contained TA reflections on the "Be-perfect" appearance of buildings (neatly cleaned and organised) and procedures (a reception which was more than decent) and the "Hurry-up" style of the director (get the job done), the firm Structuring Parent in the egogram of the director (he briefly shifted backwards), the potential gallows humour of the director (I have more understanding of dykes than of people—ha, ha, ha), and more. He was interested in moving ahead with the assignment, but was very aware of the possible pitfalls and obstacles he may still encounter. The psychological level of the potential contract would demand a lot of attention.

7.2.6. Co-creative TA

While the recent model of co-creative TA, developed by Keith Tudor and Graeme Summers (2014), does not explicitly address contracts, the co-creative perspective is very consistent with Berne's emphasis on the establishment and valuing of a mutual working relationship. The primary focus in the contracts fostered by both Berne and the Gouldings was for behavioural change. Within the co-creative model, primary attention is to the relational process between the therapist and client (or consultant and organisation). Grounded in the person-centred and humanistic traditions, the central principles of co-creative TA include:

- The principle of "we-ness" in which the Adult-Adult relationship is stressed over that of the Parent–Child dynamics.

- The principle of shared responsibility in which the responsibility of the therapist is seen as "co-equal" to that of the client.
- The principle of present-centred development in which therapy is seen as an Adult-Adult learning process, in contrast to the more past-centred perspectives of more psychoanalytic, transferentially oriented models of psychotherapy.

7.2.7. The therapeutic process and the therapeutic frame

Michele Novellino (2012) has introduced a renewed psychoanalytic perspective of TA treatment and supervision in his model of psychoanalytic transactional analysis. Novellino emphasises that contracts are two-fold in nature, addressing both content and process. The process contract attends to the "how" of the therapeutic work and relationship. A process contract seeks to foster the development of a therapeutic alliance, while including an agreement for either party to address anything that may interfere with or weaken the alliance. Part of the process contract is to explicitly address and work with the transferential/countertransferential relationship.

Novellino equally stresses the importance of the establishment of an explicit therapeutic setting and frame, that is, the working environment that is mutually agreed upon. In psychoanalytic TA the clarity and consistency of the frame is essential to providing a holding environment and atmosphere of security. Within this perspective, it is understood that a client (be it an individual, a group, a student, or an organisation) may bring game and script behaviours to the therapeutic frame as well as the person of therapist (or consultant). Therefore, any violation or agitation in relation to the frame needs to be given as close attention and meaning as the direct, interpersonal dynamics.

7.2.8. Contracts and context in relational work

Relational TA (Fowlie & Sills, 2011) takes a new perspective on contracting in therapy. An important aspect of relational work is uncertainty, or "bounded instability", and a firm contract for outcomes early in the relationship is potentially a limit on the therapeutic process. If a goal can be articulated it must be part of the present mindset and so leaves no room for new meanings and new directions to emerge (p. 136). Sills proposes a contracting matrix with axes from hard (observable and verifiable) to soft (subjective and phenomenological) and from known to unknown. The four types of contract are thus behavioural (hard/known), clarifying (hard/unknown), discovery (soft/known), and exploratory (soft/unknown). This framework allows client and therapist to make flexible, dynamic contracts according to the client's perceived and emerging needs.

All practitioners and all clients exist in a social and cultural context which forms a background, not always acknowledged, to the work and therefore the contract. Tudor (1997) suggests that we need to be "socially intentioned" and make contracts which account for and include the impact that a client's change(s) will make on his social world and make specific social contracts about what he will do differently. This was developed into the idea of "two-person plus" psychology,

Table 7.1. Types of contracts (Fowlie & Sills, 2011).

	Soft	*Hard*
Known	Discovery	Behavioural
Unknown	Exploratory	Clarifying

giving attention to the client's sense of connection/disconnection to, for instance, faith, history, and the natural environment (Tudor, 2011).

7.3. Furthermore

7.3.1. Psychological distance

The three-cornered contract works well to examine the expectations of the client (higher power) in relation to the expectations of the subject of the intervention as well as the expectations of the professional who will perform the intervention. The intervention can take the form of training, interim management, coaching, and more.

Micholt (1992) supplements the model of the three-cornered contract, as first proposed by English, with the concept of psychological distance. In this way, the TA professional can better estimate the consequences and possible risks of the almost signed or already signed contract. Micholt defines psychological distance as "the perceived proximity (and distance) and clarity in the relationship between the three parties of the three-cornered contract". It thus concerns the subjective experience of the contracting parties. She then distinguishes between healthy and unhealthy psychological distance. The psychological distance is healthy if the three sides of the triangle are seen to be equal. The expectations of all parties are clear and everyone's role and duties are clearly defined. If the distance is unhealthy, then it will be experienced as unequal by one of the parties. This holds certain risks for the success of the intervention. It is not uncommon for game behaviour to be both cause and effect of an unhealthy psychological distance between the parties. By having the commissioning client (usually the one who pays the bill) continuously "in mind" and sometimes "in the room", the professional can help ensure that the psychological distance between all parties involved in the intervention doesn't become too great. Micholt suggests several problem solving interventions when the perceived psychological distance becomes too great.

She proposes making the process of change transparent and examining the implications and options together. Many trainers start their training with a team or department in an organisation with a short meeting attended by all parties. The client explains what has been agreed with the trainer. The team or department can ask questions about this or engage in conversation. The trainer hereby gives himself a chance to determine whether there are issues at play on a psychological level that need to be addressed before getting started on the intervention. English has already recommended always explaining the concept of the three-cornered contract. In addition, the concept of "psychological distance" is very suitable for a drawing on a flipchart.

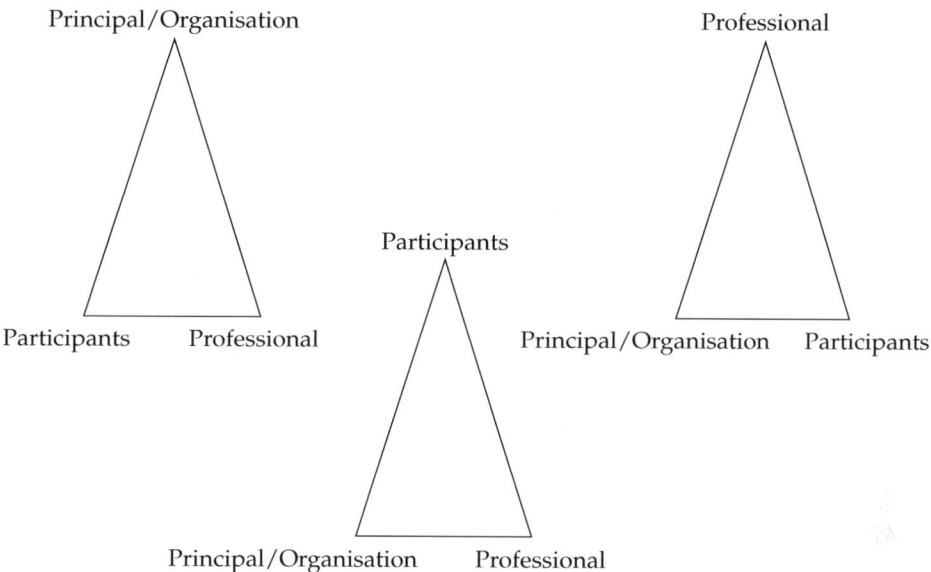

Figure 7.3. Three-cornered contracts and psychological distance.

7.3.2. The conversation contract

As De Graaf and Kunst describe in their book, *Einstein and the Art of Sailing* (2010), it is beneficial to start every conversation with a clear contract. The hallmark of a contract is that it is drawn up with mutual consent. This makes both interlocutors responsible for the "what" and "how" of a conversation. This contract includes the following mutually agreed components:

- Theme: "What do you mainly want to talk about during the next three quarters of an hour? What do you think should be on the agenda for this meeting? I myself would like to talk to you about...."
- Goal: "What should have taken place by the end of our conversation? Would you then like to move on with a good feeling? You want to talk to me about ... [theme]. Can you specify what you aim to achieve with that? Where should this conversation, in your opinion, lead to? What would make you satisfied? I myself would at least like to achieve...."
- Mutual expectations: "Could you specify exactly what you expect from me? What do you—in this conversation—mainly want me to do? What I expect from you is that you are honest and talk openly about ... [theme]."
- (Pre)conditions: "We have three quarters of an hour for this progress discussion." And: "I want to ask you to make a short appointment list afterwards."

Working with a conversation contract helps to get to the core of what will be discussed. It provides structure and spurs the right questions. Afterwards, the content and quality of the conversation can be evaluated.

7.3.3. Learning contracts

Contracting has a special, and very specific, place in the educational field. Most people's perception of school, and therefore often of learning, is of something imposed—and this may be carried into adult life so that later learning experiences become marred by transferential relationships with teachers and institutes. TA educators include "learning contracts" in every situation, from short one-off events to longer courses and school curricula. These contracts will be multi-cornered to account for the school or college system, education authorities, parents, as well as students—and they are always openly negotiated. This sometimes comes as a surprise to learners, but even five year olds in primary school can discuss what is acceptable interpersonal behaviour in class and, later, what they want to learn and how. Adult learners are stimulated by gaining autonomy and responsibility for their own learning. Using the three-cornered contract with adult learners (individuals and groups) addresses unconscious assumptions about, for instance, assessment and evaluation and "What are we here for?" The contract around the process, the role of the teacher, the methods to be used, and how teachers and learners are perceived will be determined by the underpinning educational philosophy (Napper & Newton, 2000; Newton, 2003). These "learning imagos" will be discussed in more detail in Chapter Eight on groups.

In school, contracts in class can be a vital addition to a teacher's toolkit for effectiveness in enabling students' autonomy and liberation. For example, research by music professor Howard Rovics (1981) found that students studied better and enjoyed their projects more when they contracted for the grade they wanted/needed to achieve. Pierre (2002) describes how, in a high school, she negotiates contracts with students for the year and for each session, with individual pupils, with parents, and as a strategy in resolving conflict and problems, all of them based on discussing the underpinning values that she and her students share. All these contracts have the possibility of renegotiation written in. A specialised use of in-school contracts is in behaviour support where TA-literate practitioners include the psychological level in their contracting process, not simply looking for behavioural change but at what goes on in the school culture that prompts the difficulty in the first place (Barrow, Bradshaw, & Newton, 2001).

7.4. Related theories

7.4.1. Visitor, plaintiff, or customer

At the beginning of treatment or counselling, and when drafting the contract, it is essential to estimate the client's motives for seeking treatment or counselling. In the solution-focused approach (Bannink, 2006), three types of motives are distinguished (translated for this edition):

- The visitor has been referred by someone else (the courts, the partner, the supervisor, the school, an insurance company) and does not himself have a problem to be dealt with. There is usually no request for help. In such situations, it is important that the professional does not judge but asks what the client wants and accepts the answers. The professional gives

recognition to the fact that the client would rather not be in these sessions, with questions such as: "How can we ensure that your time here is as short as possible?"
- The plaintiff is under pressure and has a request for help, but does not see himself as part of the problem and/or the solution. There is no motivation to change his own behaviour. The plaintiff would like to see others change, or may wish that there were some magic pill or miracle, or that the intervention of the therapist might decrease the suffering. The therapist gives recognition to the suffering via questions such as "How are you holding up?" The therapist can encourage the client to stop thinking about the problem and focus more on goals and solutions via questions such as "Are there times when the problem is momentarily not a problem?"
- The customer sees himself as part of the problem and/or solution, has a request for help, and is motivated to change his own behaviour. These clients are the icing on the cake for professionals, and often become a positive reinforcement for the therapist.

Seen from a TA perspective, neither the visitor nor the plaintiff is likely to succeed in establishing valid, working contracts so long as he maintains these positions.

The challenge for the professional lies in increasing the motivation for behavioural change especially among "visitors" and "plaintiffs".

7.4.2. Socratic motivation

People only really change if they are driven internally to do so (Appelo, 2007), often by a consideration of (relative) advantages and disadvantages and using as little mental energy as possible.

> Marlie is afraid of the dentist. She hasn't been for a check-up in ten years and now has toothache. However, she is so afraid of anaesthesia and drilling that she's postponing a visit to the dentist. Albert is in a rehabilitation programme, but is likely to fail because he regularly drinks too much and then doesn't fulfil his commitments. Abe comes to therapy because his wife is threatening to leave him. He often drinks too much and sometimes beats her. If she wouldn't moan, he wouldn't have to use violence.

In these situations, Appelo suggests using the technique of Socratic motivation. The premise of this technique is that people do not ask for therapy because they have complaints, but mainly because they have lost control of their symptoms or receive insufficient social support in handling them. Essential to Socratic motivation is the question: what exactly is the request for help and from whom does it stem? The Socratic method allows a balance between directive and permissive styles and facilitates self-directed problem-solving (Overholser, 1991). This is derived using the following steps:

1. What is the problem according to the client? If the problem, in the view of the client, mainly lies with someone else (e.g., it is the partner or manager of an organisation who needs to change), then no therapy or counselling will be started and the parties are informed of this decision.

2. In the introductory phase, the therapist or counsellor asks the client about what motivates him in life: what does his life look like? What goals, wishes, and desires does he have, and what has come of this so far? On the basis of this information, the therapist formulates a hypothesis of the problem.
3. What are the pros and cons of the problem in the short and long term?
4. Does anything need to change according to the client or is it maybe better, after all that's said and done, to leave the situation as it is?

The consequences of step 4 are: do nothing if the client does not really want to change, offer more options if the client has doubts, or take action if the client wants to change.

7.4.3. Learned helplessness

The term "learned helplessness" comes from Martin Seligman. In animal experiments, he discovered that when animals failed to escape from an unpleasant or painful situation, they would (eventually) give up the effort, even when they could escape a little later. Seligman applied his observations to the development of a theory of depression. If people have the feeling of having no control over a situation, they lapse into apathy and passivity. Later he developed his theory as "positive psychology" (2002a), including his theory of "learned optimism". His research showed that both children and adults can learn to challenge negative beliefs and so prevent depression and anxiety. Building a strength, such as optimism, and teaching people when to use it, rather than repairing damage, is an effective preventative (Seligman, 2002b). Seligman believes that the field of psychology has been deformed through its emphasis on damage. The implication for contracting, in any application, is to change the emphasis to resource building.

7.4.4. Collaborative diagnosis

The principles of collaboration and mutuality in psychiatry are gaining prominence. Traditional psychiatry has long cast the client in the role of the "ill" person and the doctor in the role of the skilled observer and assessor of the nature of the client's disturbance. The traditional place of the psychiatrist is the ultimate in the "one-person" model of professional relationships. However, research has increasingly demonstrated that clients are much more likely to follow treatment plans and continue to take medications when decisions are collaborative. Two recent books by Francis Allen (2013a, 2013b) that offer important challenges to the new DSM-5 diagnostic manual emphasise diagnostic collaboration. Allen, who was involved in the development of the DSM-3 and the DSM-3R and was then the chairman of the DSM-4 Task Force, has given prolonged and careful thought to the problems and limits of traditional psychiatric diagnosis. Allen has come to question the pervasive influence of the DSM diagnostic structure beyond the practice of psychiatry into the overall practices of mental health disciplines, heavily promoted by the pharmaceutical industry's pursuit of profit and the insurance companies' pursuit of control.

Writing to professionals, Allen (2013a) writes, "… make the search for the diagnosis a joint project that displays your empathy, not a dry affair that feels invasive—and always provide information and education. The patient should walk out feeling both understood and enlightened" (p. 7).

Writing to clients, Allen (2013b) urges, "Psychiatric diagnosis requires collaboration between you and your mental health clinician. … There are no objective laboratory tests in psychiatry, and therefore there is no way for anyone to diagnose your problems without your help. … The key to psychiatric diagnosis is self-report, and this is impossible without careful and persistent self-observation" (pp. 229–230).

References

Allen, F. (2013a). *The Essentials of psychiatric Diagnosis: Responding to the Challenge of DSM-5*. New York: Guilford Press.

Allen, F. (2013b). *Saving Normal: An Insider's Revolt against Out-of-control Psychiatric Diagnosis, DSM-5, Big Pharma, and the Medicalization of Ordinary Life*. New York: William Morrow.

Appelo, M. (2007). *Socratisch motiveren*. (Socratic Motivating.) Amsterdam: Boom.

Bannink, F. (2006). *Handboek oplossingsgerichte gespreksvoering. Oplossingsgerichte vragen*. (Solution-focused questions. Comprehensive Textbook of Solution-focused Therapy.) Amsterdam: Pearson.

Barrow, G., Bradshaw, E., & Newton, T. (2001). *Improving Behaviour and Raising Self-Esteem in the Classroom: A Practical Guide to Using TA*. London: David Fulton.

Berne, E. (1961). *Transactional Analysis in Psychotherapy*. New York: Grove Press.

Berne, E. (1966). *Principles in Group Treatment*. New York: Oxford University Press.

Clarke, J. I. (1996). The synergistic use of five transactional analysis concepts by educators. *Transactional Analysis Journal*, 26(3): 214–219.

Clarkson, P. (1988). Script cure? A diagnostic pentagon of types of therapeutic change. *Transactional Analysis Journal*, 18(3): 211–219.

Crossman, P. (1966). Permission and protection. *Transactional Analysis Bulletin*, 5(19): 152–154. San Francisco, CA: TA Press.

English, F. (1975). The three-cornered contract. *Transactional Analysis Journal*, 5(4): 383–384.

Fowlie, H., & Sills, C. (Eds.) (2011). *Relational Transactional Analysis: Principles in Practice*. London: Karnac.

Goulding, B., & Goulding, M. (1978). *The Power is in the Patient*. San Francisco, CA: TA Press.

Graaf, A. de, & Kunst, K. (2010). *Einstein and the Art of Sailing*. Watford, UK: Sherwood.

Haimowitz, M. L., & Haimowitz, N. R. (1976). *Suffering is Optional: The Myth of the Innocent Bystander*. Evanston, IL: Haimowoods Press.

Hay, J. (1992). *TA for Trainers*. Maidenhead, UK: McGraw-Hill.

Hay, J. (1993). *Working It Out at Work: Understanding Attitudes and Building Relationships*. Watford, UK: Sherwood.

Hay, J. (2007). *Reflective Practice and Supervision for Coaches*. Maidenhead, UK: Open University Press.

Kouwenhoven, M. (1985). *Probleemoplossende sancties*. (Problem-solving sanctions.) In: M. Kouwenhoven (Ed.), *TA in Nederland*. (TA in the Netherlands.) Part 2 (pp. 43–61). Ermelo, Netherlands: Administratief Centrum.

Kübler-Ross, E. (1969). *On Death and Dying*. London: Tavistock/Routledge.

Micholt, N. (1992). Psychological distance and group interventions. *Transactional Analysis Journal*, 22(4): 228–233.

Napper, R., & Newton, T. (2000). *TACTICS: Transactional Analysis Concepts for Teachers, Tutors and Trainers (second, revised, edition)*. Ipswich, UK: TA Resources, 2014.

Newton, T. (2003). Identifying educational philosophy and practice through imagos in TA training groups. *Transactional Analysis Journal*, 33(4): 321–331.

Novellino, M. (2012). *The Transactional Analyst in Action: Clinical Seminars*. London: Karnac.

Overholser, J. C. (1991). The Socratic method as a technique in psychotherapy supervision. *Professional Psychology: Research and Practice*, 22(1): 68–74.

Pierre, N. (2002). *Pratique de l'Analyse Transactionnelle dans la classe avec des jeunes et dans les groupe*. Issy les Moulineaux, France: ED ESF.

Rovics, H. (1981). Contract grading in the college classroom. *Transactional Analysis Journal*, 11(3): 254–255.

Seligman, M. E. (1975). *Helplessness. On Depression, Development and Death*. San Francisco, CA: W. H. Freeman.

Seligman, M. E. (2002a). *Authentic Happiness: Using the New Positive Psychology to Realize Your Potential for Lasting Fulfilment*. New York: Free Press.

Seligman, M. E. (2002b). Positive psychology, positive prevention and positive therapy. In: C. R. Snyder & S. J. Lopez (Eds.), *Handbook of Positive Psychology*. New York: Oxford University Press.

Sills, C. (Ed.) (2006). *Contracts in Counselling & Psychotherapy*. London: Sage.

Steiner, C. (1974). *Scripts People Live. Transactional Analysis of Life Scripts*. New York: Grove Press.

Stewart, I. (2007). *Transactional Analysis Counselling in Action*. London: Sage.

Stewart, I., & Joines, V. (1987). *TA Today (2nd edition)*. Melton Mowbray: Lifespace, 2012.

Thunnissen, M. (2007). *Begrijpen en veranderen. Theorie en toepassingen van de transactionele analyse.* (To Understand and to Change. Theory and Applications of Transactional Analysis.) Halsteren, Netherlands: DGW.

Tudor, K. (1997). Social contracts: contracting for social change. In: C. Sills (Ed.), *Contracts in Counselling* (pp. 157–172). London: Sage.

Tudor, K. (2011). Understanding empathy. *Transactional Analysis Journal*, 41(1): 39–57.

Tudor, K., & Summers, G. (2104). *Co-creative Transactional Analysis: Papers, Responses, Dialogues, and Developments*. London: Karnac.

Waals, J. van der (2007). *Als het mis gaat, gaat het mis aan het begin. Evaluatie van complexe opdrachten.* (If It Goes Wrong, It Goes Wrong at the Start. Evaluation of Complex Tasks.) Amersfoort, Netherlands: intern onderzoeksrapport advies- en managementbureau BMC.

CHAPTER EIGHT

Groups and organisations

8.1 Basic theory
    8.1.1 Group theory in TA
    8.1.2 Authority
    8.1.3 Structure (public and private)
    8.1.4 The work of a group
8.2 Further theory
    8.2.1 Working with large groups and organisations
    8.2.2 Organisational script
    8.2.3 Group development
    8.2.4 Learning imagos
8.3 Furthermore
    8.3.1 Psychotherapy, counselling, and consultative groups
    8.3.2 The group in the individual
8.4 Related theories
    8.4.1 Group phases of Levine
    8.4.2 Healing factors of Yalom
    8.4.3 Group-focused conflicts
    8.4.4 The escalation ladder
    8.4.5 Family constellations
    8.4.6 Standards and roles
    8.4.7 Group relations
References

Transactions seldom take place in an isolated one-on-one context. From the very beginning of TA, it was clear that the greater whole—the family, team, company, or organisation—cannot be ignored when making a (transactional) analysis. Because TA analyses transactions between people in groups as a means to identify ego state patterns and the script of each of the participants, TA can be used both interpersonally and intra-psychically. Eric Berne devoted one of his first books (Berne, 1963) entirely to thinking through the structure and dynamics of groups and organisations. Over the past fifty years, TA has grown into a fully-fledged theory on the functioning of systems. Central to this theory is the concept of boundaries, which are seen as essential to the understanding and facilitation of healthy and productive groups.

8.1   Basic theory

8.1.1   Group theory in TA

Groups fill our lives—the family group, the team at the office, a management group, a therapy group, classroom groups, social groups. The recognition of the place of groups in our lives was central to Berne's development of transactional analysis. One of the most significant innovations that Berne made was his inclusion of work in groups as part of the ongoing treatment process. While Berne's book *Games People Play* (1964) became a worldwide bestseller and was read by a popular audience, two of his most important books, *The Structure and Dynamics of Organizations and Groups* (1963) and *Principles of Group Treatment* (1966) were written for fellow professionals. Berne would typically see a new patient for a few individual sessions and then work with the person in a group setting, which Berne found to be the most efficient and effective way to reveal and analyse transactions and games. When Berne saw that a patient was able to understand and change some of his repetitive interpersonal patterns through Adult ego state awareness, he would then return to individual therapy for work with the script within the more archaic experience of the Child ego state. Over the years since Berne's death, transactional analysts have continued to develop the theories and techniques of working in groups, so that now script analysis is as likely to be carried out in groups as in individual sessions (Stuthridge, 2013).

When a person joins a new group, he will inevitably become involved with and influenced by the "rules" by which the group works. Some of the rules about how this group functions are explicit, but many are unwritten, only to be discovered as the process of the group and the expectations of the members unfold. Think of the new employee in a team, the four-year-old child on the first day of school, the prisoner at the beginning of a three-year term in prison, or a patient who has to spend six weeks at a rehabilitation department to recover from a complex fracture. Each will find to what degree his frame of reference and his script relate to the context and the script of the group. Each new person may have a lot or perhaps little trouble adapting. He will probably be challenged to either change his script or to try to change the group so that it better suits his own script.

Patterns of typical ego state functioning, effective and ineffective ways of transacting, games, and script beliefs can be derived from the behaviour among the group members. In a seemingly trivial event, someone may act out the story of his life (his script) within seconds (according to Berne, in three seconds!). The notorious latecomer provokes increasing irritation within the group when he arrives five minutes late for the umpteenth time, wearing a guilty smile. He may play "Kick me" from the existential position "I'm not OK, you're OK" or "I'm not OK, you're not OK".

There may be a therapy group member who demands a lot of direct attention, making sure that he gets the most attention from the leader (often in the form of negative strokes). He often assumes the position of Victim and draws out Rescuers and Persecutors from the group members. In a business context there is often the character of the inconspicuous team member—after the meeting no one really knows if this member was present or not. He has perhaps incorporated the injunction "Don't be important" which he repeats in any situation when there are more people present. And, of course, families provide our first group experiences so that even if when the siblings are fully grown, there are times the scripts within the family group are performed "in a nutshell". At Christmas, the elder sister arrives first and helps mother with the coffee; the middle brother sits down, allows himself to be served and tells a funny story, while the youngest brother arrives late and immediately draws all the attention to himself. The interpersonal dynamics of our behaviour within group settings is often out of conscious awareness, such that working within group contexts has become a central tenet in TA practices in psychotherapy, counselling, supervision, training, and organisational consultation.

8.1.2 Authority

The authority within the group consists of two parts, according to Berne: leadership and the group canon.

Fox (1975) succinctly summarises Berne's theory in the following table.

Table 8.1. Analysis of groups in TA terms.

Group authority	Group structure	Group work
Leadership: – responsible – effective – psychological	Public aspect: the structure of the group	Task of the group
Group canon: – constitution – laws – culture	Private aspect: group imago	Group process

Leadership

- The responsible leader is the person to whom authority has been formally granted, the person whose acts are performed without veto and thus the one with the power to reward and punish.

- The effective leader is the one who has the most influence in practice. The effective leader ensures that the tasks are carried out. In a group or organisation, any group member can, in principle, take on an effective leadership role.
- The psychological leader has the most influence on a subconscious or psychological level. Berne, as an example, observed that besides the "village chief", there is often a "medicine man" who determines whether and how work will be done and whether a change will take place or not.

Berne, as a product of his time, mostly considered top-down, hierarchically driven organisations, where the responsible leader was primarily meant to be the effective leader. In recent decades, much has changed in the world of business and organisations as well as in education and child rearing. However, the kinds of leadership Berne defined are nonetheless still useful for making a leadership analysis. For example, in many organisations today, you find that the responsible leader is one who encourages employees to take on effective leadership roles. To ensure effective leadership throughout an organisation, at its heart we might say, then employees will need to be given the opportunity and responsibility to assume leadership in the areas within which they have specific knowledge and/or skills. The psychological leader may be an "invisible" leader, in the sense of not having an official leadership position but is one who exerts powerful, subconscious influence within a group. Psychological leaders can provide important vision or momentum to the life of a group or they may bring an organisation into lockdown and dysfunction.

> Martin is a young enthusiastic executive who has now been head of a team of teachers for two years. Usually he is good at consulting with the employees. Together they carry out what has been agreed upon. In some discussions, however, he notes that if a decision needs to be taken, colleagues surreptitiously watch Pete. You see, Pete has been working at the school for twenty-five years, and has earned the place of the psychological leader among his colleagues. Martin soon discovers that if he has Pete on his side, the rest will follow naturally.

Euhemerus

Every organisation has a history that begins with an individual or group of individuals who are the founders of that organisation. Berne calls this long-dead, prime leader(s) the "Euhemerus". The Greek thinker Euhemerus saw the Greek myths as stories about recent events that repeatedly get their current form because they are retold. The founders of a company often come to life through the (idealised) stories told about them. The late Steve Jobs, one of the founders of Apple, is a powerful example of such a Euhemerus. His influence will be felt for years because stories (myths) continue to be told about him both inside and outside the company.

Group canon

Berne observed that the stories and myths about the Euhemerus that are passed on in the life of a group acquire a kind of sacred quality that is embedded in the culture of the group, which he called the group canon. The psychological function of the canon is to regulate the internal group process and to provide a sense of identity and belonging among the group members. Included in the group canon is the constitution of the group, which defines such elements of life within the group as:

- What is the purpose of the group?
- What are the laws of the group? Through which written rules and agreements is this purpose regulated?
- What is the group culture? By which unwritten rules and agreements is work conducted?

Each group has its own culture that consists of several aspects. The technical skills and scientific knowledge needed to perform a group activity are found in the (rational) Adult aspect. In addition, the culture contains a (traditional) Parent aspect in which etiquette and the norms and values that are closely linked to the survival of the group are located. Finally, each group has its own character in which behaviour has its place, with which group members can express their individuality without being considered rude. This is the (emotional) Child aspect.

Most of Berne's writings on groups were limited to psychotherapy groups and such institutional settings as hospitals. Now his theories of groups are applied in a broad spectrum of institutional and organisational settings. Early in his career, Berne was very interested in cross-cultural studies, but this interest was not represented in his TA writings. More recently, Pearl Drego (1996, 2005, 2009) has applied Berne's observations within a sociocultural perspective.

Group cultures can be too weak, soft, and lax, with insufficient Adult and a lack of targeted and structured activity, resulting in decay and impending failure. Or they can be too rigid: overstructured and severe, with the possible result of passive resistance or open rebellion. In groups which are too soft, cohesion is weak and the members slowly but surely choose their own way; in both too soft or too rigid groups, there will be intensive game-playing.

8.1.3 Structure (public and private)

The group structure has a public aspect: how is the group organised, arranged, and equipped? What are the roles of individuals in the group? In addition, each group has a private aspect: what does the group look like "in the minds" of each individual in the group?

In Berne's thinking on groups and organisations, the concept of boundaries is particularly significant. A boundary defines who participates and how. The public structure is shown in Figure 8.1. Berne summarises a group as an organism with internal boundaries and an external boundary, with separate regions for the members, for possible subgroups between members, and with a separate region for the leader (Berne, 1966).

Lee (2014) suggests that the structural diagram (of a process group) needs to be studied in relation to five aspects of group process and development: containment, leadership, responsiveness, interaction, and expansion. For a healthy development, the boundaries need to be permeable. Containment of the group activity is the leader's first concern: inviting feelings of inclusion and acceptance or exclusion and rejection. This is about the primary contracts for the group concerning its activity and purpose. Around the question of leadership, issues of trust and safety will emerge. Members will replay childhood developmental struggles. The task of the leader is to allow the group to establish its own culture without losing his robustness. Next, members of the group may wonder whether or not they are individuated for the leader. They

216   INTO TA

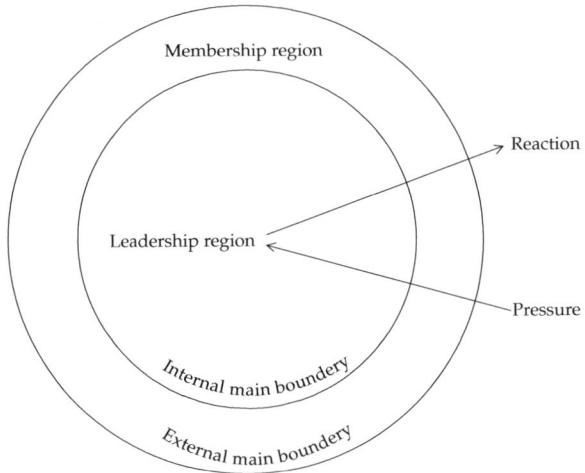

Figure 8.1. Public structure of groups.

re-evaluate the question "Do I matter here?" (often related to their experience in their family of origin) in relation to his responsiveness. The leader then encourages a dialogue that is meaningful and contact-full. Permeable boundaries give permission for intimacy and open relationships. Finally the question will be how the (learning) experience in the group can be taken outside into other group processes. Although Lee obviously has a therapy group in mind while writing this, the issues at hand are as important to teachers, managers, and other professionals working with and in groups.

The private structure of groups is given shape by the group imago, which changes over time under the influence of the development of each group member. Each individual group member has his own picture of the relationships in the group, especially his own relationship to the leader. Some aspects of a group member's picture will be conscious, but important elements will be unconscious, which Berne considered to be the basis of the group imago. The imago largely determines each member's behaviour in the group. In a new group, for example, a group member may have the following group imago:

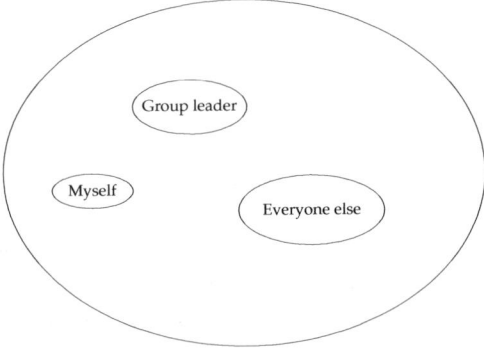

Figure 8.2a. Beginning group imago.

Over time, this imago changes to a partially differentiated group imago:

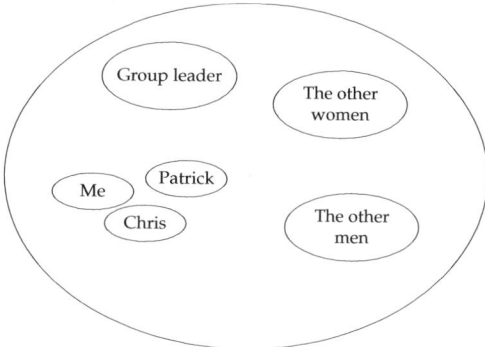

Figure 8.2b. Partially differented group imago.

Eventually, a differentiated group imago emerges:

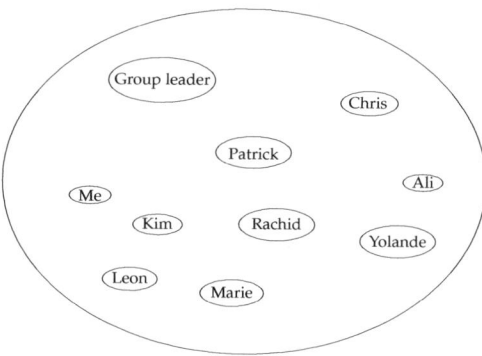

Figure 8.2c. Differented group imago.

Moreover, the ideas about the group and the group's experiences develop. In a "successful group process", the group imago changes as follows.

- Provisional group imago. A beginning group member forms a provisional group imago based on preconceived ideas about the group.
- Adapted imago. When someone really joins the group, an adapted imago emerges, whereby this person lets go of certain expectations and fantasies and adjusts his preliminary group imago to the reality of the group.
- Operative imago. In the third phase, an operational imago is formed, whereby differentiation is made between the different group members and themes like power, control, rivalry, and the forming of subgroups become apparent. Each group member is mainly concerned with the question: "How do I make myself count in this group? What kind of place do I have or do I want to take within this group?"

- Intimacy and autonomy. Finally, a phase of intimacy and autonomy may take place. Now the group members each have their own role in which they come into their own in relation to the group task.

The imago within the group of the person who is in charge at a certain time (whether this is the responsible, effective, or psychological leader) has great influence on what makes the group effective or not and how the group continues to function in situations of adversity and resistance.

8.1.4 The work of a group

Working groups, such as a therapy group, AA meetings, a business, a management team, or a classroom, have an identified task that is supposed to be shared by the group's members. There are, however, often tensions within the group created by the dynamics among individual group members that may interfere or conflict with the overt tasks and purpose of the group. Berne observed: "There are various forces which determine group membership, and the individual is not necessarily attracted mainly by the activity of a group" (1963, p. 161). Individual members of a group may have all sorts of wishes, motivations, and fantasies about being in a group that do not necessarily correspond to the stated purpose of the group. One of the challenges to a group leader is to help the group attend both to the stated working tasks of the group and to the internal processes within the group that may facilitate or interfere with the work of the group.

In a well-functioning group the leader is imbued with sufficient authority by the members of the group so that he or she is able to define and maintain a consistent structure within the group and attention to the tasks of the group, facilitating the thinking and contributions of each member to the work at hand. The group leader is able to define an external boundary for the group that allows the group to attend to its task. In a well functioning group the group members perceive and value the leader's skills and authority, thereby allowing a congruence of the psychological, effective, and responsible psychological leadership functions.

Again, Berne (1963, p. 140) divides leadership into three categories: 1. Psychological leadership: the person who, though not always with the title, has the most power. 2. Effective leadership: the person whose answers and solutions to problems are often followed. 3. Responsible leadership: the person who is officially in charge, to be called to account. Berne seems to suggest that at best all these three categories are to be found in the same person. Modern management theory and practice points out that for a team to be as effective as can be, effective leadership roles need to be taken up by a variety of group members. It is said that bad leaders create followers, while good leaders create (effective) leaders.

In a well functioning group, the group imago and the scripts (of both the individual members and the group itself) become increasingly open to Adult observation and reflection. Group members are able to differentiate one from another and to find a place from which to contribute to the work of the group. The group leader is able to give primary attention to the work of the group.

However, it is not uncommon for the internal dynamics among the group members and between the group members and the leader to undercut the work of the group. Berne referred to these groups as "ailing" groups in which the primary focus needed to shift to the internal group process until the group re-established its capacity for self-observation.

For example, a long-term psychotherapy group had functioned effectively for more than two years, when three of the members decided to leave the group at the summer break, each having fulfilled the treatment contracts that had brought them into the group. In saying goodbye, the group leader and members celebrated the accomplishments of their work in the group. Resuming in the autumn, the group members informed the leader that they were not ready for new members. The group meetings slipped into "pastiming", and attendance, which had been highly regular for all members, began to slip. Then a couple of the members said they were thinking about leaving because they were no longer finding the group useful. The therapist asked each member to think about and describe what seemed to have changed in the group. She asked, "What is troubling this group?" She was inviting the members to begin to speak to the process within the group. What began to emerge was the recognition of unexpressed feelings about the group members who had left at the start of summer. Some group members felt that they should have stayed, to contribute what they had learned about themselves to the work of others in the group—that their decision to leave was "selfish". Other members expressed anger at the leader for not having taken the time to recognise the loss to the group of members leaving. There was "celebration" but no grieving. As the group leader facilitated the group's reflection on its internal process, the group became a working group again. Attendance became consistent again, and the group decided it was ready to welcome new members.

The survival and effectiveness of a group can be threatened from pressures within the group as we have just seen, or from outside the group like noisy renovations in the building.

For example, when a community mental health centre lost a significant part of its public funding, it became much more dependent on payment through insurance companies. One of the requirements of the insurance companies was the provision of an immediate diagnosis on the first session. Psychiatric diagnoses had not been part of the centre's professional culture. The director, anxious that he might have to fire staff due to the loss of funding, became very demanding of the therapists providing immediate diagnoses. Suddenly there was a significant decline in patients continuing after the first interview. The staff began to undercut the director, turning instead to one of the eldest members of the staff who was deeply invested in the humanistic traditions of TA and critical about the superficiality of this way of classifying patients. The staff no longer imbued their director with the credibility and respect of the responsible and effective leader, turning instead to a competitive psychological leader. With a serious threat of the collapse of the centre, the director called in an outside consultant. The consultant was able to hear the hostile and conflictual feelings of the individual staff members with empathy and objectivity. She was then able to lead the staff through a series of group process sessions in which they were able to re-establish more trust in one another, engage in a reflective capacity on the impact on the centre's culture of these unwanted changes, and create strategies to ensure the service to their patients and to secure the payment of the insurance companies.

In every group there is a conflict between the ideal representation that every member has of the group and reality. This tension can lead to agitation between the members themselves and, in a developed group, mostly between the individual members and the leader. If the group is to survive, the group imago of the (responsible, effective, or psychological) leader must be consistent with reality (substantiated by data verified by the Adult) and the cohesive forces in the group need to match up against the destructive forces.

8.2 Further theory

8.2.1 Working with large groups and organisations

The healthy functioning of groups and organisations has a large influence on their effectiveness. To understand a group or organisation that has trouble functioning, specific information is necessary, namely about the history, structure, and purpose of the group, as well as the motivations of its leaders and members. On this basis, an analysis can be made of the source of the problems and proposals can be made to improve the situation. A change in the group's imago of the leader often has a significant impact on the structure, cohesion, and decisiveness of the group.

In many organisations, games are played, making them function less efficiently and effectively. Employees (and employers) will sometimes get stuck between forces. The kind of games often differs between for-profit and not-for-profit organisations (Berne, Birnbaum, Poindexter, & Rosenfeld, 1962).

- In not-for-profit organisations, such as an outpatient clinic of a psychiatric hospital, the work is focused on caring for patients. However, it is not the intention to eliminate the waiting list completely whereby the therapists come to sit around with nothing to do. If too many patients are helped, the individual employees are jeopardised, particularly those who do their job effectively. The game "I'm just trying to help you, without curing you entirely" can no longer be played.

  It is also the case that schools nowadays benefit from a large number of students without consideration of the effect this has on the quality of education. If teachers stick to their quality standards and fail or reject students on this basis, then this can threaten to have a negative effect on the school. The reputation and grading of the school, and consequently available funding is often contingent upon the number of graduating students.
- In for-profit organisations, the games look slightly different and often involve the balance between permanent and temporary staff. As long as there is a shortage of staff, the manager of the department can complain to her superior that there is not enough staff to get the job done. However, if there are enough staff and work is being done efficiently, the manager can no longer play this game. She may then complain, for example, about the quality of the temporary staff, who are then fired, so there is again a shortage of staff and the old situation is restored.

For the individual employee, these games revolve around the question "How effective can or should I be without getting fired?"

Although organisations, at an open or social level, have the aim of serving as many clients as possible, or educating as many students as possible and making as much profit as possible, there may be entirely different issues at play at the unconscious, psychological level. For example: take it easy. It's good that we have a waiting list. We spend a lot of money on luxuries and economise on some of the content and quality of the work. Prevention is not important and modest goals are good enough. In such an organisation, an efficient employee is a threat who will be edged out after a while, whether by promotion to a safe location or by being dismissed.

8.2.2 Organisational script

Rosa Krausz, who received the Berne Memorial Award in 2012 for two articles on organisational scripts (1986, 1993), describes how the script (the culture) of organisations strongly affects the individual and collective behaviour. In order to properly understand this, she suggests that you must be especially attentive to how organisations deal with four central themes in the daily life of the organisation:

- work
- time
- people
- money

Each of these themes has its own set of (script) convictions related to how the world of organisations and businesses function. The four themes can be linked to the four existential or life positions (see the Introduction to this book and section 5.1.4 in Chapter Five).

Work

Roughly speaking, you can look at the role of work in organisations in four different ways:

- Work is focused on results. It is about effectiveness, from the life position +/+
- Work is task oriented. Doing your best is enough, from the life position +/−
- Work is survival oriented. The status quo should be maintained, from the life position −/+
- Work is focused on failure. Destructive actions, risks, illegal procedures, from the life position −/−

Time

Time is a resource that can be used to the advantage or disadvantage of the organisation. Here, again based on the four existential positions, you can observe four convictions about time:

- Time is a valuable resource, from the life position +/+
- Time is a means to maintain power relations, from the life position +/−

- Time is something to tolerate, from the life position −/+
- Time is of no importance at all, from the life position −/−

People

The convictions about people have much influence on recruitment and selection and the working climate within the organisation. Franklin Ernst (1971) used short strong terms in order to characterise people based on the four windows on the world:

- Get-On-With! (GOW). Focused on cooperation, mutual respect, openness, and trust, from the life position +/+
- Get-Rid-Of! (GRO). Focused on exploitation, manipulation, lack of trust, and personal involvement, from the life position +/−
- Get-Away-From! (GAF). Characterised by dependency relations, lack of influence, poor problem-solving ability, from the life position −/+
- Get-Nowhere-With! (GNW). Characterised by passive and alienating relationships, apathy, and disinterest, from the life position −/−

Money

The way money is viewed within an organisation determines to a large extent the strategic position developed by an organisation. You can only spend money once and this has a huge impact on investments in things like technology, resources, training, and development. Generally speaking, you find four types of beliefs about money in organisations:

- Money is a means to an end and not an end in itself. Earning money is the logical consequence of delivering quality, from the life position +/+
- Money is an end in itself and not a means to an end. It's all about making money, from the life position +/−
- Money is sometimes a means to an end, and sometimes an end in itself. Ambiguous: money is as easily earned as it is lost, from the life position −/+
- Money is neither a means nor a purpose. There is demoralisation, nothing matters now, the survival of the organisation is at stake, from the life position −/−

8.2.3 Group development

The moment a group member first participates in a group, he has a number of "hungers" (see Chapter Two):

- The biological need for stimulation
- The psychological need for structuring time
- The social need for intimacy

- The nostalgic need for familiar transactions
- Expectations based on previous experiences

The task of any group member is to adapt these needs and expectations to the reality that he is confronted with (Berne, 1963; Clarkson, 1992).

- In the first phase of the development of a group, the group members form a provisional group imago with which they can structure time by "retreating" and with rituals. Often, the group member initially focuses on the leader: "What does the leader think of me? Where do I stand and who am I in the eyes of the leader?" Usually, the member projects the imago of his parents (sometimes grandparents or parental figures such as teachers) onto the leader. The imago of siblings and early playmates is projected onto the fellow group members. After all, you acquire your first team experiences in the family in which you grew up. In this phase, which Tuckman calls forming, group members are concerned with orientation, testing the limits of interpersonal behaviour and the task of the group. In this way they find their appropriate relationship with the leader, with other group members and with the canon of the group (Tuckman, 1965). In this phase it is important that the leader defines and safeguards the external and internal borders of the group, including by making a clear agreement about who does and does not belong to the group and who is in charge. The leader must, just as a parent, have the courage to be loved by the group, knowing that the ultimate goal is to lose this love (Clarkson, 1992).
- In the second phase of group development, the group members form an adapted group imago and they structure time via pastime. Conflicts arise between group members and the leader. Tuckman calls this storming. The group members oppose the influence of the group and the demands that participating in the group presents. Sometimes there is overt or covert criticism of the leader. It is also possible that members of the group exhibit passive, over-adjusted, or withdrawn behaviour, so that there is little energy in the group. An effective group leader then gives members the opportunity to test him, while remaining strong and not reverting to punishing the group members or excusing himself.
- In the third phase, the group members form an operative group imago. They mainly structure the time with games. It is the stage of norming, whereby group cohesion arises with new norms and roles. The leader facilitates interpersonal skills and exhibits constructive behaviour as an example of emotional literacy: this is the ability to understand one's own emotions and to express them productively, to listen to others, and to sympathise with them (Steiner, 2003). In this way the leader helps the group members with individuation and self-actualisation.
- In the fourth phase, the group members exhibit a secondary adjusted group imago. It is the phase of performing, in which the roles of the group members are flexible and functional and the energy of the group is focused on the work that needs to be done, namely, to gain insight into personal behaviour, changing this behaviour, and actively solving problems. The time structuring of "intimacy" becomes more visible, the group members take personal responsibility for their task, and the group leader moves more into the background.

- Finally, in the fifth phase, the group members have a clarified group imago, no longer constrained by earlier projections. The structuring of time by means of "retreat" becomes more common, in preparation for the farewell and the mourning thereof. According to Tuckman, this is the phase of mourning or adjourning (pausing), in which members sometimes experience old, unresolved grief that is actualised by quitting the group. The group leader keeps the members focused by helping them to accept the reality of the loss, experience the pain, and adapt to the changed environment. He also helps them to withdraw their emotional energy away from the group and invest it in other relationships.

The stages described above apply to any group, whatever its purpose. In their writings, both Berne and Clarkson were thinking of psychotherapy groups but in fact the same process happens in other groups too. In learning groups for example, the development of the group, and the individual members, through these stages can be part of the learning process. The leader—tutor, trainer, or whoever—will have an imago based partly on his previous experiences in groups, maybe including a fantasised or remembered teacher on his own learning journey. Awareness of this provisional imago and any associated anxieties or excitement can help the leader to ground himself and contract clearly with the group at all levels for the learning experience they are embarking on together.

As the group moves into the adapted stage the tutor will find himself being tested and needing to respond to challenges to his competency or to his teaching methods from an OK position while affirming individuals' ideas, maintaining flexibility, and resourcing the learning. Flexibility and positive modelling are also important in the operative stage to help the group develop healthy norms, for relating and for studying, maybe drawing on personal experience of seeing others demonstrate containment while encouraging learners. As the fourth stage begins, the sense of closeness in the group, and the leader being seen as a real person, leads to "letting the group happen" as people take on more self-directed learning and share responsibility. As a course comes to an end, and the group begins to anticipate a sense of loss, the tutor will give time for the "group story" and time to grieve, but also be clear about assessment requirements and the reality of the ending.

8.2.4 Learning imagos

When a learning group has met for a while and become a familiar place, Clarke (1996) suggests that a "group's group imago" develops (in addition to personal imagos). This is a shared picture of how things are in the group, what happens when something changes such as someone joining or leaving, how participants relate to the tutor or leader. This joint imago is related to the operative stage of the group and its moving into the secondarily adjusted stage. By combining this idea with that of diverse underpinning philosophies of adult education, Napper & Newton created imago diagrams to picture how the contract, stroking and discounting patterns, relationships in the group, and metaphors of teaching and learning differ between groups (Napper & Newton, 2000; Newton, 2003). The imagos are briefly described and illustrated in Chapter Fourteen in Part II.

8.3 Furthermore

8.3.1 Psychotherapy, counselling, and consultative groups

Richard Erskine (2013) has developed a relational model of group psychotherapy that is grounded in the group's provision of positive regard, empathy, respect for each member's phenomenological experience, and validation of each individual's perspective. In this model it is a fundamental function of the group and the group leader to create an interpersonal environment of security and dependability so as to allow maximum safety in which members can come to more clearly understand "how implicit memories and archaic ways of relating may be re-enacted within the group, in families, and in everyday life" (p. 271). The group then affords an atmosphere within which individuals can experiment with new behaviours, attitudes, and relationships. When addressing conflict and confrontation in the group process, Erskine stresses the risk for shame and retraumatisation and argues for sensitivity and a high level of personal regard. Without this, "the result may be resistance, resentment, and an interruption in the working alliance within the group" (p. 270).

There is a similar emphasis on the establishment of a secure base, from an organisational perspective, in the work of George Kohlrieser. In *Hostage at the Table* (2006), Kohlrieser argues, "The fact is that people do not kill people; they kill things or objects." To kill another human being, a person needs to first "deprive the other of his or her humanity" (p. 106). He has made it his life's work to challenge executives to provide a secure basis for their employees. The employees as real people with personal values and goals are all aspects of a secure base. "The heart of any healthy group lies in the intensity of the bonding between people and to the organisation's goals" (2006, p. 15). If people continue to see each other as people, they are significantly less likely to want to hit each other, literally or figuratively, over the head. Conflicts in Kohlrieser's approach are necessary for the development of groups and organisations and are examined and used from a basic OK-view of others and of one's self.

Other transactional analysts have developed models of group work based in object relations and Bionian theories that describe the power of unconscious factors in group dynamics as expressed through projection, splitting, transference, and countertransference among the group members and towards the group leader. These models draw much more attention to the ongoing group processes as the primary means of exploring the meanings of behaviour within the group. This approach also emphasises the inevitability of conflict and anxiety in groups and the rich learning potential afforded by the group's thoughtful attention to areas of discord and difference among group members and with the leadership (Cornell, 2013). Writing from the position of organisational consultants, De Graaf (2013), Petriglieri and Wood (2003), and Van Beekum (2006, 2012) bring a Bionian perspective to group work. Writing from clinical and counselling positions, Deaconu (2013), Hopping and Hurst (2011), and Landaiche (2012, 2013) articulate perspectives which significantly shift the therapeutic group process from the traditional TA model of working with the individual in the group to work with the group-as-a-whole. For these authors, conflict within the group is a central focus of the therapeutic process. Here conflict and disturbance are to be welcomed and explored rather than soothed or avoided, as we can see in the perspective put forward by Landaiche, "I bother with groups and with my discomfort because I am keenly interested in their potential for learning, for collective struggle and elaboration in relation to certain key problems" (2012, p. 194).

Another difference in working with groups is the choice whether to work on the one hand with group processes and the group as a whole, and on the other hand with the individuals in the group. For a well-functioning group therapy, a therapeutic environment within the group is essential: a good communication network in which the group members can stay close to their feelings. Moreover, an optimal level of regression is essential. People must be willing to expose themselves and must also retain an adequate observing ego in order to share the attention for each other. The therapist may choose to use interventions to address the group as a whole or to address one or more group members individually. Each of these approaches may be given preference at certain moments.

In working with a group TA concepts can be used, such as the stroking climate in the group, the egogram of the group as a whole, the transactions between different group members, the time structuring within the group, and the presence of the drama triangle.

8.3.2. The group in the individual

De Graaf (2013) calls for a shift from relying on individual psychology to understand behaviour in groups, to an appreciation of systemic influences and unconscious dynamics within the group as a whole. He argues that there are multiple forces driving observable behaviour in groups. He encourages us to be alert to the group(s) in the individual. The moment the individual enters a group, the group enters that individual.

He suggests that it is hardly possible to make a statement about the self without categorising oneself. Hogg and Abrams (1998) suggested that each person is born into a cluster of conversations (scripts): family, community, political, economic, and cultural. When working with or in groups it is wise to be aware that such conversations are governed by norms and agreements concerning appropriate or acceptable ways to behave and opinions to hold under certain circumstances. Spot the group in the individual. People are never in one conversation at a time. Each act they perform is at the nexus of many conversations. It takes time to disentangle interwoven contexts.

Zimbardo (2008) puts into words the most profound lesson to be learned in this area: "The traditional [dispositional] approach [to understanding behaviour] has been to identify inherent personal qualities that lead to action. ... This makes one ask 'who-questions' like: Who is responsible? Who caused it? Who gets the blame? Who gets the credit?" (p. 7). Zimbardo encourages all who work with or in groups to start asking "what-questions" with a more social orientation, such as: "What conditions could be contributing to certain reactions? What was the situation like from the perspective of the actors? What are the situational variables and environmental processes that influenced the actors?" The driving forces (plural) behind observed behaviour in any group come from various scripts of systems of which the person is part. This requires a shift from personal script orientation to working with the idea that all behaviour has, by definition, a complex hybrid character.

Identifying with a group is the basic mechanism by which people evaluate themselves. The way we see ourselves is heavily influenced by the script of any organisation or group of which we are (and were) a part. As Hogg and Abrams (1998) wrote, "The process of self-categorizing produces a so-called enhancement effect" (p. 68). That is, we tend to inflate our self-image through the process of self-categorising, and self-categorising occurs, in part, by identifying with groups to which we belong. De Graaf concludes that being a transactional analyst and thus part of the TA community requires holding certain views and opinions, and pursuing practices, which have a profound impact on an individual transactional analyst's identity.

8.4 Related theories

8.4.1 Group phases of Levine

Processes at the level of a group can be described according to the successive phases of development in a group and according to the tasks of the leader in each phase (Levine, 1979). Levine describes how a therapeutic group goes through four phases: the parallel phase, the integration phase, the reciprocity phase, and the final phase.

In the parallel phase (in accordance with the undifferentiated group imago), the members are mainly focused on the leader and have little differentiation with respect to each other. They fluctuate between distrust/avoidance and trust/rapprochement. The therapist is the one who sets the standards. In the integration phase, the group engages in contact and confrontation with each other. Behaviour, such as described by Bion (1961), becomes visible: fight or flight, dependency and pairing. The standards set by the therapist are challenged and the group sets its own new standards. In the reciprocity phase, the group really begins to get to work together. Intimacy and personal exchanges become possible; the therapist is more in the background. In the final phase, the group members detach themselves from the group, which can be accompanied by feelings of guilt, hostility, and abandonment, but also with greater autonomy. The phases can last for weeks to months. Sometimes an impasse is reached and the group "remains stuck in one phase" for a long period of time.

8.4.2 Healing factors of Yalom

Yalom (1975) has drawn up a list of healing factors in group psychotherapy. This overview can be put to good use in groups in general. Yalom describes the following factors:

- Awakening hope: I can get something from this and be encouraged!
- The experience of universality: there are more people like me; I'm not "crazy"!
- The experience of altruism: others may get something from me!
- Gaining corrective experiences: I am actually being listened to!
- Developing social skills, learning from each other, experiencing group cohesion: I belong, this is my group!
- The experience of catharsis: dare to cry in the group and notice that this feels better!

Finally, existential factors:

- Recognising that life is unjust and unfair at times.
- Accepting that you have to face life alone.

- Facing the basic problems of one's life and death and therefore becoming less taken up with trivialities.
- Understanding that you are responsible for the way you live your life.

These healing factors have been investigated extensively by Yalom and others (Yalom & Leszcz, 2005). Feedback, advice and suggestions, universality, insight and cohesion, interpersonal learning, and catharsis are highly valued as primary therapeutic factors in group treatment. In a well-known study (Lieberman, Yalom, & Miles, 1973), therapists from different schools of thought were compared. The research revealed remarkably few significant differences in efficacy of the different group models utilised by the therapists in the study. One significant difference was that laissez-faire therapists were found to achieve poorer results, while Bob Goulding, a therapist who participated in the study representing TA methodology, was one of the highest scoring therapists (Berk, 2005; Kapur & Miller, 1987)!

8.4.3 Group-focused conflicts

In the focal conflict theory (Whitaker & Lieberman, 1964), processes are described that occur within a single session or within a few sessions, in which each group member plays a specific role in the matrix of the conflict. Whitaker and Lieberman posed the following question: "Is it possible that everything that manifests itself in a group can be regarded as the result of a power play between, on the one hand, the desires, wishes and impulses from group members, and fears, inhibitions and prohibitions, which are precisely activated by those desires, on the other?"

After ten years of analysis of audio tapes of different therapy groups, they were able to give a positive answer. In every group, there was the formation of a constant tension between a disturbing motif and a reactive motif, which together form the group focal conflict. Eventually, the group finds, in synthesis, a successful solution to the focal conflict. Subsequently, a new disturbing motif emerges.

A group member is angry with the therapist because he feels that the therapist is offering insufficient help to another group member. Several of the other group members agree. In the next session, some members want to continue to talk about their anger (they represent the disturbing motif), while others believe that there's been enough talking about it. They want to continue with other matters (the reactive motif). Ultimately, they end up talking about the anger after all. It becomes evident, from the background of the various group members, precisely why some did and others did not want to talk further about the anger. One member of the group discovers how afraid he is of authorities: criticism of a leader is not possible in his frame of reference. Another group member discovers her rebellious position, and thereby her avoidance of taking responsibility. The therapist remains somewhat in the background and then asks, at the end of the session, how they feel with regard to their anger at him. This appears to have vanished into thin air (synthesis).

8.4.4 The escalation ladder

The process of the escalation of conflict, which in groups and organisations often goes unnoticed, has been investigated and described by conflict expert Friedrich Glasl. In *Confronting*

Conflict (1999), Glasl explains how this gradual escalation process works. He maintains that many groups and organisations either avoid conflict or allow it to escalate to such an extent that it can no longer be stopped.

His insightful view of the escalation ladder provides pointers to discover in which stage of escalation a conflict is situated, so that the appropriate interventions can be made.

Glasl describes three phases in the escalation, whereby, after phase 1, a threshold is crossed that excludes certain interventions from being successful.

- Phase 1: win-win. In phase 1, there is a win-win possibility in which all stakeholders can benefit from the conflict.
- Phase 2: win-loss. Phase 2 has winners and losers, so that only one of the parties leaves the arena unscathed.
- Phase 3: lose-lose. Phase 3 only has losers. At a certain point, a good conversation no longer works. Mediation is then offered. In the case of further escalation, there is also no room for mediation, but arbitration remains a possibility. An outside intervention into a conflict in phase 3 is sometimes the only option.

A careful analysis is required of the phase in which a conflict is situated in order to choose the appropriate intervention.

> In a large university medical centre, an intense clash had been going on among several of the specialists working there. By the time the "quarrel" came out and became public, the conflict had already escalated such that only an intervention from outside could offer some solace. The situation was worsened by the fact that the conflict drew the attention of the media. The board of directors proposed to sit down with all stakeholders yet again. "We're all adults. We are sure to find some kind of solution, right?" At least, this is what the chairman, who had an incomplete picture of the level of escalation of this conflict, thought. The inspector, who was more skilled with dealing with conflicts, knew that only an intervention from outside would work. The inspector's motto was: "Protect the patients and limit any further damage!"

Glasl suggests investigating initial tensions immediately. Moreover, the energy that is released thereby can even have a favourable influence on the development of the group or organisation. It is important to be well aware of signals that a conflict is escalating. In the various stages of an escalating conflict, those involved exhibit different behaviour. Anyone who has an eye and ear for this can inhibit further escalation and utilise the released energy to the benefit of healthy development.

After the first few weeks of teaching in the new class, the mentor hears some students complain to each other about that "jerk from English". The students are talking about his very capable colleague Newman. The mentor understands that something is wrong in the relationship between the class and his colleague. If it is no longer about "Mr. Newman" or "Newman" but "that jerk from English", then it's time for a thorough conversation to find out how the escalation in the conflict needs to be handled.

Viewed from a TA perspective, one can determine that a conflict may yield fruit as long as all those involved can still see themselves and the others as OK. In phase 1, the ones involved in the conflict can be challenged and lured into opting for a +/+ approach. In phase 2, in the

1	2	3	4	5	6	7	8	9
Discussions harden								
Mutual impasse	Intellectual violence							
Understanding is no longer obvious	Competition	No words but actions						
Shielding	Feeling superior	Non-verbal communication	Stereotypical characterisations					
Cooperative solution of the conflict	Polarisation	Matter of prestige	Self-fulfilling prophecy	In your face attacks and loss of face				
Providing help	Style of the debate	Refusal to step back from position taken	Expansion of conflict	Dirty games	Strategies of threats			
Pro: distinction	Scoring	Ability to empathise is significantly reduced	Desire for sympathy	Unmasking	Hard demands	Opponent is purely an object/enemy		
Contra: connection	Provoking irritation	Mutual responsibility is gone	Getting people to choose your side	Not seeing each other, declaring other as dead	Panic reactions	Violence	Systematic destruction	Together into the abyss
Selective attention	Laughing response	Cancel solution	Forming coalitions	Immoral behaviour	Sanctions	Damaging the other	Dividing the opposition	
			Black and white dichotomy		Stress			
Phase 1 Win-Win			**Phase 2 Win-Lose**			**Phase 3 Lose-Lose**		

Source: NPI, Zeist.

Figure 8.3. Escalation ladder (translated for this edition).

Glasl view, those involved have left the +/+ field. They are now looking at each other through a +/− window, or a −/+ window. That leads to winners and losers. Once they have arrived in the −/− field, the situation is hopeless. Then there are only losers.

8.4.5 Family constellations

Bert Hellinger was introduced to transactional analysis by Fanita English (Hellinger, 1998). Hellinger's development of his therapeutic work with family constellations is deeply influenced by TA. It can be seen as an approach that works directly with what Berne called "the private structure" of groups and organisations (see section 8.1.3. in this chapter).

The core of Hellinger's work is formed by "constellations": family constellations and organisational constellations. A constellation is a group process, where participants, with the help of a facilitator, can explore their personal issues. The client presents his issue and asks members of the group to represent himself and others (family members, colleagues) and places them somewhere in the room. Then the client sits down and observes. Several minutes elapse while the representatives stand still and silent in their places, using their perceptive intuition. The aim is to tune into what Hellinger describes as the Knowing Field. The Knowing Field is claimed to guide participants to perceive and articulate feelings and sensations that mirror those of the real family members they represent. The representatives have little or no factual knowledge about those they represent. Nevertheless, the representatives usually experience feelings or physical sensations that are thought to inform the process.

The facilitator may ask each representative to briefly report how he feels being placed in relation to the others. Often, by configuring multiple generations in a family, it is revealed that certain traumas continue to unconsciously affect the living, long after the original victims or perpetrators have died.

This might consider stillborn or children who died young, war experiences of grandfather or father, betrayal or distrust within the family. A healing resolution for the issue generally is achieved after the facilitator repositions the representatives or adds key members of the system who have been forgotten or written out of the family history. When every representative feels right in his place and the other representatives agree, the facilitator may suggest one or two sentences to be spoken aloud. If the representatives do not feel at peace with their new position or sentences, they can move again or try a different sentence. When the facilitator feels that the healing resolution has taken hold among the representatives, the client is invited to replace his representative in the constellation. This allows the client to perceive how it feels to be part of a reconfigured system. When everyone feels comfortable in their place, the constellation concludes.

Constellations offer the ability to investigate what is happening on an unconscious level in families and organisations: patterns of ineffective cooperation, repetitive conflicts, or stagnation. Examining and experiencing a constellation can bring new, profound insights. These insights can be the starting point for interventions in order to address what has sometimes remained dormant for a long time.

In assessing an organisation constellation (Hellinger, 2011), a number of concepts are central (translated for this edition):

- Binding: everyone within a system has an equal right to a place.
- Planning: based on seniority, hierarchy, commitment, and qualities.
- Balance: there must be a balance between giving and taking.

To function effectively and efficiently, it is important that all three principles are secured. Just like a living organism, there are—through unconscious processes in which existing themes play a role—patterns in an organisation that promote or hinder a positive state of affairs. In a constellation, a number of components (teams, individuals, or major themes) of an organisation can be spatially charted, so that patterns literally become visible. By doing this, those elements can be better understood as well as provided with an appropriate next step. Drawing a group imago and the developments of that imago, as is customary within TA, entails an applied and limited form of working with a constellation.

8.4.6 Standards and roles

Hoijtink (2009) described the different norms and values that develop in every group, such as standards on desirable, task-related behaviour. He defines a group standard as "the shared view of group members on which behaviour in a certain situation is appropriate or not". In a team, for example, this may be drinking a cup of coffee together before starting work or having lunch together on Thursdays. In a therapy group, this means telling each other about personal experiences, listening to others, giving feedback, and expressing emotions. Groups that manage to bring these standards into practice have the best chance of success.

Unwittingly, however, standards that sabotage tasks may nevertheless emerge. The fifteen-minute coffee break becomes a half hour in which some team members gossip about a certain colleague who does not drink coffee and immediately goes to work, or it may be about the supervisor who reigns over the team like a slave driver. In the therapy group, a certain member of the group would never be addressed concerning irritating behaviour. There is no mention of sexuality and also the repeated lateness of certain group members is not discussed.

There may be rigid roles and interaction patterns that have emerged: everyone knows that you needn't ask Karel to do an extra task because you'll get a whole sermon, while Annie is always willing to take up the slack and take over your tasks. In therapy groups, spontaneous communication can be limited by a rotation system or by devoting an entire session to making one person central instead of opting for free interaction.

In addition, in each group here are norms about "forbidden" behaviour. For example, you do not challenge each other in front of the manager, or you do not act like a show-off. In therapy groups, there are often strong norms about not violating the confidentiality and non-use of physical violence.

These standards should be mandatory, as they relate to conduct which may threaten the survival of the group. In addition to the formal roles, such as that of the manager, the assistant, and the team member, each group has informal roles—usually as a result of an agreement between a person's personality and a certain need of the team or group.

Several of these roles are (translated for this edition):

- The invisible leader, a team member to whom authority is granted by the team members.
- The dominant team member, who often talks above the others out of fear and uncertainty and in this way tries to keep the team under control.
- The silent team member, who is often actively invited to participate at first, but who after some time risks ending up in a social vacuum.
- The "team thermostat", who regulates the emotional tension in a team.
- The helper, who helps others in order to indirectly collect strokes for himself.
- The mascot: the nice, accommodating team member who brings in many positive strokes (until the group begins to get annoyed with him after a while).
- The scapegoat is the opposite of the mascot and incurs the collective rejection of the team (Hoijtink, 2009).

8.4.7 Group relations

Bion, a British psychoanalyst, has had a major influence on the thinking about group dynamics (1961) in psychoanalysis, transactional analysis, and organisational training and consultation. He suggested that a well-functioning group behaves as a "working group" in which members are engaged in the task of the group. If the working group is not functioning properly, regressive processes will come to the forefront and a "basic assumptions group" will be formed. An inadequately functioning group, as Bion observed, then oscillates between a state of productivity and one in which primarily defensive positions are taken.

Often, both types of functioning are simultaneously present in a group. In the basic assumptions group, the group loses its differentiated character and the group members react as if they are being driven by primitive, intense emotions. Unconscious fantasies, convictions, or assumptions then define and determine the atmosphere and the processes of the group. Bion distinguishes three basic assumptions:

- Dependent basic assumptions group.

   The group members behave as if the therapist is omniscient and omnipotent and could give them anything they crave. It goes without saying that this idealisation leads to disillusionment, after which the group members feel helpless, unprotected, and worthless. In the group, this pattern can lead to one group member, who is not doing well, being pushed forward while the group waits expectantly for the therapist to help this group member. If the therapist accepts this offer, the group becomes dependent instead of autonomous problem-solving. The therapist will endeavour to identify the idealising and omniscient pressures within the group and work with the group to understand that it has unrealistic expectations.
- Fight-flight basic assumptions group.

   The group members behave as if they have to fight an enemy or should avoid the problem. The group joins together and projects the aggression onto objects outside the group, or primitive subgroups or divisions may emerge within the group to unconsciously represent the threat experienced in the group. When this defensive splitting and subgrouping develops within the group it is very likely that some members will be cast into the position of scapegoat. Sometimes an invisible—psychological—leader takes over the leadership from the therapist.
- Pairing basic assumptions group.

   The group members behave as if in the future an event will take place that will solve all problems. The atmosphere is one of hopeful expectation, whereby often something beautiful happens between two group members that the other group members expectantly follow as a solution to the difficulties within the group. This assumptions group often develops at the end of a group therapy, as a defence against the reality of the end of the group (Berk, 2005).

Although Bion's theories and observations developed in his work as a psychoanalyst, his work has come to have important implications in organisational development and training. Not only in therapy groups, but also in teams and organisations, basic assumptions groups can arise, which, if not recognised, can seriously impair the atmosphere and the effectiveness of the team or organisation.

A well-functioning group may, according Turquet (1974), be recognised, for example, by how such a group uses the leadership and the various qualities of the group members. In successful teams, leadership is shared on the basis of the quality present among group members in relation to completing the diverse tasks to be undertaken by the group members. Successful teams do not continually look expectantly at the responsible leader. Successful teams are also always curious about their own performance. Such a team is always doing ongoing research to test hypotheses about its own functioning.

References

Beekum, S. van (2006). The relational consultant. *Transactional Analysis Journal*, 36(4): 318–329.
Beekum, S. van (2012). Connecting with the undertow: The methodology of the relational consultant. *Transactional Analysis Journal*, 42(2): 126–133.
Berk, T. J. C. (2005). *Leerboek groepspsychotherapie*. Utrecht, Netherlands: De Tijdstroom.

Berne, E. (1963). *The Structure and Dynamics of Organizations and Groups*. Philadelphia, PA: J. B. Lippincott.
Berne, E. (1964). *Games People Play*. New York: Grove Press.
Berne, E. (1966). *Principles of Group Treatment*. New York: Oxford University Press.
Berne, E., Birnbaum, R., Poindexter, R., & Rosenfeld, B. (1962). Institutional games. *Transactional Analysis Bulletin*, 1(2): 12–13.
Bion, W. (1961). *Experiences in Groups*. New York: Basic Books.
Clarke, J. I. (1996). The synergistic use of five transactional analysis concepts by educators. *Transactional Analysis Journal*, 26(3): 214–219.
Clarkson, P. (1992). *Transactional Analysis Psychotherapy. An Integrated Approach*. London: Tavistock/Routledge.
Cornell, W. (2013). Relational group process: A discussion of Richard Erskine's model of group psychotherapy from the perspective of Eric Berne's theories of group treatment. *Transactional Analysis Journal*, 43(4): 276–283.
Deaconu, D. (2013). The group quest: Searching for the group inside me, inside you, and inside the community. *Transactional Analysis Journal*, 43(4): 291–295.
Drego, P. (1996). Cultural Parent oppression and regeneration. *Transactional Analysis Journal*, 26(1): 58–77.
Drego, P. (2005). Acceptance speech on receiving the 2004 Eric Berne Memorial Award.
Drego, P. (2009). Bonding the Ethnic Child with the Universal Parent: Strategies and ethos of a transactional analysis ecocommunity activist. *Transactional Analysis Journal*, 39(3): 193–206.
Ernst, F. (1971). The OK-corral: The grid for get-on-with. *Transactional Analysis Journal*, 12(1): 231–240.
Erskine, R. (2013). Relational group process: Developments in a transactional analysis model of group psychotherapy. *Transactional Analysis Journal*, 43(4): 262–275.
Fox, E. M. (1975). Eric Berne's theory of organisations. *Transactional Analysis Journal*, 5(4): 345–353.
Glasl, F. (1999). *Confronting Conflict. A First Aid Kit for Handling Conflict*. Trowbridge, UK: Hawthorn Press.
Graaf, A. de (2013). The group in the individual: Lessons learned from working with and in organizations and groups. *Transactional Analysis Journal*, 43(4): 311–320.
Hellinger, B. (1998). *Love's Hidden Symmetry. What Makes Love Work in Relationships*. Phoenix, AZ: Zeig, Tucker.
Hellinger, B. (2011). *De kunst van het helpen*. Groningen, Netherlands: Uitgeverij Het Noorderlicht.
Hogg, M., & Abrams, D. (1998). *Social Identifications: A Psychology of Intergroup Relations and Group Process*. New York: Routledge.
Hoijtink, T. (2009). *Diagnostiek van het groepsfunctioneren*. (Assessment of group functioning.) In: S. Colijn, H. Snijders, M. Thunnissen, S. Bögels, & W. Trijsburg, *Leerboek Psychotherapie* (Comprehensive Textbook of Psychotherapy) (pp. 369–381). Utrecht, Netherlands: De Tijdstroom.
Hopping, G., & Hurst, G. I. (2011). Relational transactional analysis and group work. In: H. Fowlie & C. Sills (Eds.), *Relational Transactional Analysis: Principles in Practice* (pp. 249–258). London: Karnac.
Kapur, R., & Miller, K. (1987). A comparison between therapeutic factors in TA and psychodynamic therapy groups. *Transactional Analysis Journal*, 17(1): 294–300.
Kohlrieser, G. (2006). *Hostage at the Table. How Leaders can Overcome Conflict, Influence Others and Raise Performance*. San Francisco, CA: Jossey-Bass.
Krausz, R. (1986). Power and leadership in organizations. *Transactional Analysis Journal*, 16(2): 85–94.
Krausz, R. (1993). Organizational scripts. *Transactional Analysis Journal*, 23(2): 77–86.
Landaiche, N. M. (2012). Learning and hating in groups. *Transactional Analysis Journal*, 42(4): 186–198.

Landaiche, N. M. (2013). Looking for trouble in groups developing the professional's capacity. *Transactional Analysis Journal*, 43(4): 296–310.

Lee, A. (2014). The development of a process group. *Transactional Analysis Journal*, 44(1): 41–52.

Levine, B. (1979). *Group Psychotherapy*. Englewood Cliffs, NJ: Prentice Hall.

Lieberman, M. A., Yalom, I. D., & Miles, M. B. (1973). *Encounter Groups: First Facts*. New York: Basic Books.

Napper, R., & Newton, T. (2000). *Tactics—Transactional Analysis Concepts for All Trainers, Teachers and Tutors + Insight into Collaborative Learning Strategies*. Ipswich, UK: TA Resources.

Newton, T. (2003). Identifying educational philosophy and practice through imagoes in transactional analysis training groups. *Transactional Analysis Journal*, 33(4): 321–331.

Petriglieri, G., & Wood, J. D. (2003). The invisible revealed: Collusion as an entry to the group unconscious. *Transactional Analysis Journal*, 33(4): 332–343.

Steiner, C. (2003). *Emotional Literacy. Intelligence with a Heart*. Fawnskin, CA: Personhood Press.

Stuthridge, J. (Ed.) (2013). Perspectives on working with groups. Theme issue of *Transactional Analysis Journal*, 43(4).

Tuckman, B. W. (1965). Developmental sequence in small groups. *Psychological Bulletin*, 63(6): 384–399.

Turquet, P. M. (1974). Leadership: The individual and the group. In: G. S. Gibbard, J. J. Hartman, & R. D. Mann (Eds.), *Analysis of Groups* (pp. 349–386). San Francisco, CA: Jossey-Bass.

Whitaker, D. S., & Lieberman, M. (1964). *Psychotherapy through the Group Process*. Chicago, IL: Aldine.

Yalom, I. D. (1975). *Group Psychotherapy in Theory and Practice*. New York: Basic Books.

Yalom, I. D., & Leszcz, M. (2005). *The Theory and Practice of Group Psychotherapy*. New York: Basic Books.

Zimbardo, P. (2008). *The Lucifer Effect: Understanding How Good People Turn Evil*. New York: Random House.

CHAPTER NINE

Ethics

9.1 Basic theory
    9.1.1 Introduction
    9.1.2 Moral development
    9.1.3 Ethics in practice
    9.1.4 TA codes of ethics (EATA & ITAA)
9.2 Further theory
    9.2.1 The integrated Parent
    9.2.2 "Dual relationships"
    9.2.3 Ethical dilemmas
9.3 Furthermore
    9.3.1 Autonomy
    9.3.2 Risk, trust, and "minding the gap"
    9.3.3 Bystanding
9.4 Related theories
    9.4.1 Kohlberg and moral development
    9.4.2 Crossing boundaries
    9.4.3 Statistics are in
    9.4.4 Virtues
    9.4.5 Self-disclosure
    9.4.6 "Ethicability"
    9.4.7 Ethical maturity?
References

In Chapter Eight, we discussed, among other things, how "boundaries" can be handled respectfully. This is fundamentally an ethical question. This chapter focuses entirely on how TA deals with ethical issues. We could also claim, with equal ease, that actually all the previous chapters were also about ethics. The central ethical question within TA is, after all, how TA professionals can make a "valuable" contribution to the growth and development of their clients. Not a single (communicative) situation can be seen separately from ethical questions. This chapter provides an overview of how ethics have been and are viewed within the (international) TA community, both in the past and present.

9.1 Basic theory

9.1.1 Introduction

Ethics is not an easy term to define. Many people are convinced that they are "doing the right thing", but that does not necessarily mean that they think about their behaviour from an ethical perspective (De Graaf & Levy, 2011). When people reflect on the ethics of their actions, for example in their work and relationships, it is not so easy to clearly define ethical criteria. People often have contrasting ideas that all seem ethical. It is then difficult to determine the right course of action. De Graaf and Levy make use of two important principles for thinking and talking about ethics.

1. A debate about ethics never ends, but lingers on. It is about the ongoing quest for what is appropriate.
2. The purpose of a debate on ethics is not to find out what is right or wrong. The aim is to create awareness about the choices people make.

Sometimes it seems easier not to enter into a discussion on ethics. Many people—including politicians, captains of industry, and managers—avoid ethical discussions, even if they are badly needed in order to address such global problems as the financial crisis, the distribution of wealth, global warming, globalisation, and problems of security and privacy with regard to the rapid growth of the internet. New values are needed. But it sometimes seems as if a conspiracy of silence is in progress. People would rather choose to remain on the sidelines as spectators (Bystanders) rather than becoming actively engaged. As described in Chapter Four, this can be seen as a fourth role within the drama triangle. In *The Bystander* (1996), Petruska Clarkson devotes many pages to the ethical questions surrounding Bystander behaviour. She says, quite sharply: "The point of this book is not to posit a final answer to the intricate human dilemmas, but to question the lie (or the inauthenticity) that people can truly claim to be uninvolved, or that there is, in fact, such a position as that of innocent bystander" (p. 33).

In addition, it is a political reality that people in the higher echelons of power can often afford to act unethically, while people at the bottom of the social ladder are forced, by rules and authorities, to behave in ways that are considered acceptable and ethical (Suriyaprakash, 2011).

Cultural differences regarding what is or is not ethical may be related to differing worldviews and values. Ethics are like the practical living out of our beliefs and frame of reference, partly derived from our family and culture and partly consciously decided. One currently prevalent and influential worldview is that of market-led capitalism, combined with an individuated view of society. With the impact of the global village this view, of gaining control over the world's resources, challenges other philosophies such as, in India, *dharma*—control over oneself and one's own being, and of bringing one's actions in line with principles of justice, religion, and ethics (Suriyaprakash, 2011) or, from southern Africa, *ubuntu*, the idea that a person is a person through other people—community, and our common humanity, as building blocks of society. In Europe, in the last twenty-five years since the fall of the Berlin Wall and the ending of the tension between capitalism and communism, national cultures, values, and ethics are being constantly explored in the project of "living together" in the EU, while at the same time defining a place that is both separate from and together with the USA. Again, the most hopeful path, like that of dharma, is one of maintaining a constant dialogue, without expectation of one day establishing that one is better than the other.

9.1.2 Moral development

Moral development is not the least important task of a person's growth towards adulthood. The ability to think and act with regard to questions about what is and is not appropriate is a prerequisite for working and living together in society. Every child learns at a very young age that there are rules that must be followed. These rules are usually provided by the parents and are initially stored in the Parent of the child (P_1). The child does not yet have the ability to reflect on the logic or sense of these rules.

Only when the capacity for reflective thinking (the Adult, A_2) has developed sufficiently, can a person think about why he should comply with the regulations. Only then is one able to create one's own system of values and standards in the Parent, and then begin to think and act from a set of values rather than from standards. The way in which the internal Parent (and internal Adult) develops may provide more insight into the development of moral reasoning.

Eric Berne wrote little about ethics. He did, however, develop a model of the integrated Adult, using the term "ethos" for the Parent, "logos" for the Adult, and "pathos" for the Child (Figure 1.5 in Chapter One). The ethical principles are located in the Parent ego state. These principles evolve through the following phases.

1. Learning and instilling rules (standards). The development of P_1, between the ages of three and six.
2. Learning and instilling values. The development of P_2, between the ages of six and twelve.
3. Learning and evaluating general principles. Integration phase, between the ages of twelve and eighteen.

Woollams and Brown (1978) provide a detailed description of the development of P_1. They argue that the Somatic Child (C_1, see section 1.2.1 in Chapter One) gets upset when parents react negatively to the spontaneous way in which the child expresses himself. In response to these strong feelings, the Little Professor (A_1) attempts to find out exactly what parents expect. Through a process of experimentation, the child discovers what behaviours and feelings will evoke approval. The set of all these behaviours and feelings can be seen as the Parent in the child, P_1.

The established "arguments" within a family often reflect a magical image of reality. "If I do not finish my plate, Mommy will go away and never come back." "If I smile, everybody will like me." P_1 is therefore sometimes called the Magical Parent. At the same time, issues are magnified in the Magical Parent. "If I hit my brother, my parents will get so angry that I might get sent away and won't be allowed to live with them any more." The P_1 may also contain very negative, destructive messages. In the Sixties of the last century—a period in history in which all kinds of parental systems came under fire—it was referred to as pig Parent or Witch parent. TA professionals don't use these outdated words any more.

It's all about the very first frame of reference that is used to understand and respond to the world. P_1 thus has the important function of "holding the reins" of the other parts of the Child: the unwanted eruptions of one's own C_1 and A_1. Whatever takes place within the Child during its early development can also be seen as the first steps in the moral development of a person. Berne also called P_1 the "electrode", so as to emphasise the often automatic response to stimuli from the environment.

While the child reacts from P_1 to what the parents do, the child simultaneously stores his own version of what the parents do in the Parent (P_2). Woollams and Brown argue that the child does this on the basis of three criteria:

- The degree of vulnerability of the child. The very young child, very dependent on the parents, stores almost everything.
- The power of the parental figure. The somewhat older child (depending on the pressure exerted on him) is more selective in what he stores and what he does not.
- The credibility of the parent figure. The maturing child makes judgements based on reliability and authority.

While the reasoning from A_1, the Little Professor, is still highly intuitive and creative, when the Adult ego state, A_2, begins to develop, the child begins to use more logical and linear reasoning. The latter develops from the time that language development gets going (towards the end of the first year of life). This continues to develop well into adolescence when logical, analytical, and abstract thinking becomes available.

The development and crystallisation of the various ego states and associated competences will largely determine from which stage of the moral development an ethical argument develops. If the internal Parent (P_2) did not get a chance to develop into a fully-fledged helmsman/helmswoman when it comes to control or support, the Parent in the child (P_1) continues to pull the strings. If the internal Adult (A_2) was not stimulated into action, this will result in insufficient reflective moments between impulse (C_1), judgement (P_1), and action (A_1).

Those who pay close attention to the basic philosophy of TA will see that the values expressed in TA inevitably lead to a number of ethical codes for TA professionals. Those who think that people are OK will never write off the whole person, but will only assess the behaviour of that person. Those who think that people can think will be extremely reluctant to offer unsolicited suggestions or give advice. Those who believe that people can change will never give up hope.

It is not surprising that the ethical codes and guidelines within TA are based on key elements such as dignity, autonomy, awareness, responsibility, and the life position "I'm OK, you're OK". In addition, the contractual relationship is an important principle in TA. Elements of this are: properly informing the client, causing no damage, and no exploitation of any kind whatsoever with respect to colleagues and clients.

The foregoing raises a number of dilemmas. To what extent will the professional completely respect the autonomy of the client, even if he shows unhealthy behaviour such as addiction or self-neglect? Or, what if the client does not adhere to agreements made? Is it not inevitable that professionals consciously or unconsciously try to transfer their own system of values—which, after all, is tested, well thought-out, and ethical—to their client? Don't professionals always manipulate the mental structure of the client into a configuration which they consider healthier or more desirable? The stroke pattern of the professional affects the clients.

> Alfie notes the approval of his coach when he says that he has been to the gym twice in the last week. Maria feels that the therapist has trouble with her secret extramarital relationship. Annie, a single mother, says that she is pregnant with her second child, again by a man who does not want to take responsibility as the father.

How do you react in these different situations as a professional? It is important for you as a professional to be aware of the contents of your own ego states and stroke pattern. Furthermore, it is important to regularly receive peer feedback and/or supervision to discuss your frame of reference and the feelings that clients evoke, as well as your feelings of sympathy and antipathy with regard to your clients.

9.1.3 Ethics in practice

The core of most ethical questions revolves around the dilemma of how reciprocity can be maintained within an asymmetrical power relationship (Eusden, 2011). The intention to act ethically and not to damage or abuse the client does not automatically mean that one's actions are ethical. The intention behind actions, the behaviour that is the result of that intention, and the effect of that behaviour on the other are three clearly distinguishable categories. All three, even when they are outside the consciousness of the parties involved, are in need of ethical scrutiny.

Tailgating?

> John enters the therapy session in an agitated state. He was almost hit from behind by a woman who was tailgating and driving recklessly, and with her children in the back seat no less! The therapist lets him blow off some steam and is surprised by the vehemence of his anger which does not seem to be in proportion to the event. She connects the event to the subject of the therapy session. John is considering re-establishing contact with his adult children, whom he has not seen for years since his marriage break-up. The therapist realises that she is rather insisting on this encounter, stemming from her own experience that it can be healing to reconnect with your parents after years of estrangement. With John, she explores the meaning of his experience for their therapeutic relationship. John admits that he sometimes also sees the therapist as a "tailgater" who wants him to go faster than he wants.

A good intention can be clouded by misjudgements and may have unintended effects on the environment.

I'm not married to you

> After one of the two trainers briefly explains the significance of the psychological (hidden) layer in a contract, it emerges that two participants in the training group are married to each other. They had decided to keep this to themselves and not to tell the trainers or the other participants. "I'm here as a participant and not as the wife of …" as one of them explains. The trainers decide to go round the group to examine what the (hidden) relationship network in the training group looks like and what the meaning is of "loyalties beneath the surface". Many of the participants appear to share some kind of bond with other participants, either from their recent past or further back. One used to work with another participant in the same company. For another, it is not the first time that he has been in a training group with two others. A third turns out to be a family member of a trainer who is known by many of the participants.

And so on. The "secret" of the couple leads to intense reflection on how unobservable ("under the surface") issues in a group can determine the observable behaviour on the surface. The trainers may also question what "secrets" in their relationship can still be examined. Could it be that "the secret of the couple" reflects something that is still hidden?

It is inevitable that professionals make mistakes and fail—in a certain sense, they regularly act "unethically". Ethical behaviour also means that this is a topic of conversation. Where and when do the professional or the client experience, for example, that the trust and sincerity in the contract is being breached? In such a conversation, the subtlety of what a code of ethics can provide can be discussed. A code of ethics then functions as a platform and not a defence shield.

The paradox regarding ethics is that the code of ethics elicits best practice. And specifically this best practice means daring to make mistakes, taking risks, causing fractures in the contact and re-establishing them, or falling into patterns of repetition and discussing them with the client. Therefore, it might be better to look at the characteristics of a good enough practice. Talking about best practice can lead to the closing of the ethical debate. After all, there can be no better than best.

Placing too much emphasis on safety in the workplace can stifle the need to take risks, thereby leading to a defensive mode of working. In order to learn and change, it is necessary for the professional to take risks. It may also be desirable that the professional temporarily does not know about something. If you do not dare to be considered unethical, this can be unethical in itself. If the professional acts as an authentic person instead of as a neutral "self-less" object, the client may have the chance to engage in corrective experiences instead of falling into repetitions of negative experiences from the past.

9.1.4 TA codes of ethics (EATA & ITAA)

Both the EATA (European Association for Transactional Analysis) and the ITAA (International Transactional Analysis Association) have an ethical code. In recent years, the code of the EATA has been revised and adapted in significant ways. In the following, we restrict ourselves to the EATA code (EATA, 2008), which applies to all national TA associations in Europe.

Instead of a code with a set of rules for ethical behaviour, the EATA opted to apply the following basic values:

- Dignity, as described in the Universal Declaration of Human Rights (1948): each person is valuable.
- Self-determination. Everyone is free to decide on his or her own future, within the limits of the law of his or her country, and taking into account the needs of themselves and others. Everyone can learn from experience and take responsibility for themselves without damaging the world or the freedom of others.
- Health. Every individual has the right to physical and mental stability, and this right should be actively protected.
- Security. Everyone should be able to develop in a safe environment.
- Mutuality. Every person lives in a world with other people, and is thus mutually involved in the welfare of others. He or she is mutually dependent on others in the development of reciprocal security.

These values have been further formulated as ethical principles which provide guidelines for behaviour in professional practice. This practice extends to clients, professionals, students, colleagues, and the community. The ethical principles are:

- Respect for every person, whatever characteristics or qualities they may have.
- Empowerment. Encouraging everyone to take responsibility for their own destiny and to develop themselves.
- Protection. Caring for oneself and others, both physically and mentally, based on the uniqueness and value of every living being.
- Responsibility. Being aware of the consequences of your actions as a client, trainer, therapist, supervisor, counsellor, or other practitioner.
- Commitment. A genuine interest in the well-being of the other.

These values and principles are further elaborated into ethical standards with concrete examples, such as: EATA members will not participate in discrimination, oppression, or exploitation within their professional relationships. They shall refrain from disparaging remarks about other EATA members. They will also treat any oral and written information from and about clients confidentially. They will abide by the laws of the country where they work. The latter pertains, for example, to the fact that in some countries, TA is not a recognised therapeutic method.

There are also developments aimed at increasing and guaranteeing quality of care in the free market. There are growing efforts in national legislations relating to health care by which psychotherapy is seen as a medical treatment, and laws are drafted for the protection of the client against low-quality care. For example, in the free market there are quality systems that have emerged from the question "How can a client know that a certain professional delivers quality?" In many countries there are initiatives on ethics in the field of coaching, training, and organisational consulting.

The procedures for addressing ethical complaints are described in the ethical codes of the EATA and the ITAA. These codes of ethics can be found at www.eatanews.org/ethics.htm and

244   INTO TA

www.itaaworld.org. As we have seen in the discussion of the crisis with the Cathexis Institute, ethics codes need to be periodically reviewed and updated.

Certified transactional analyst (CTA)

Reasonably soon after TA boomed in the 1960s, the ITAA decided, under the direction of Eric Berne and Dave Kupfer, that it was undesirable that "anyone who had read a book about TA" would be able to present themselves as a transactional analyst. Since then, thousands of professionals enjoyed participating in the international certified transactional analyst exam. They did this and do it still so that clients all over the world will know that if they consult a professional with "CTA" on their business card, then the services provided will be of high quality. Ethics are an integral part of the examination for qualification as a transactional analyst. Those who want to know more about the possibility of becoming TA-certified can consult the aforementioned sites of the EATA or the ITAA.

9.2   Further theory

9.2.1   The integrated Parent

Kouwenhoven (2011) developed a fascinating model of the integrated Parent that promotes safety and integrity. He distinguishes four relevant areas in the Parent:

The Structuring Parent uses standards, the Nurturing Parent uses values. The stimulating Structuring Parent (SPstim) and the stimulating Nurturing Parent (NPstim) are aimed at promoting positive behaviour. The inhibitory Structuring Parent and the inhibitory Nurturing

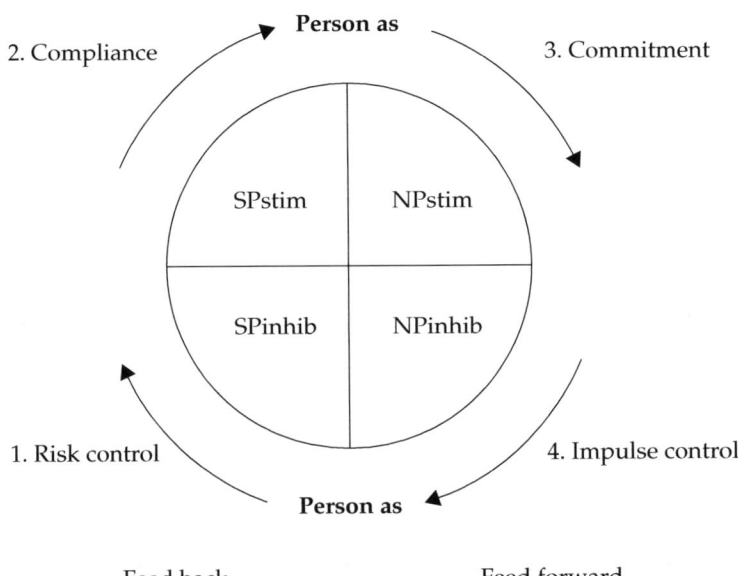

Figure 9.1. The integrated parent.

Parent (NPinhib) are, in the opinion of Kouwenhoven, aimed at reducing negative behaviour. In practice, this looks like:

- NPstim promotes positive values through commitment. People connect with each other or with a task.
- SPstim promotes positive intent by "compliance", enforcing pre-established standards. A danger with the latter can be that the number of rules keeps increasing. This plays into the hands of infringement, leading to more control and less effect. Rules can inhibit until you finally stop: you do nothing wrong, but also then do nothing good. This is why the values of NPstim and the standards of SPstim should complement each other in a cybernetic system whereby commitment and compliance go hand in hand.
- NPinhib inhibits impulsiveness and helps in managing internal desires.
- SPinhib reduces risk by managing external inducements such as locking your car and leaving your wallet in sight.

If these four aspects of the Parent work together in an integrated manner, they form a system that seeks to ensure safety and encourages integrity. Ultimately, this can contribute to an honest, civilised society. For further elaboration, see section 13.2 in Chapter Thirteen.

9.2.2 "Dual relationships"

An important issue in the practice of TA is that of the so-called dual relationships. Can you develop, during or after the conclusion of treatment, consultation, or training, a friendly relationship or a working relationship with a former client or former trainee? Psychotherapist Bader (1994) defines a dual relationship as one in which the therapist and the client enter into an additional relationship with each other, with a purpose that is clearly other than giving and receiving therapy. Most TA theorists advocate for a guideline on how to deal with these relationships, which can be quite complex, rather than imposing strict prohibitions.

Cornell (1994) described his experiences with dual relationships in his own therapy process. One of his therapists later became a good friend, while another of his therapists maintained a strict code of analytic anonymity. He learned a lot from both of them, though sometimes he felt awkward and uncomfortable with the carefully distant therapist. For example, there was a period of time when this therapist's home and property were severely damaged by a tornado. The therapist came to sessions often exhausted and distracted. Although he explained the impact of the storm, he declined offers of help. As a person, Cornell felt the need to offer the therapist some concrete help in the extensive repairs to his property, or at least sympathy. As a client, he felt that there was not the space for the expression of more personal concern, so the therapist/client boundary felt overly rigid and depersonalising.

Clarkson (1994) also addressed this issue. Sometimes it turns out, according to her experience, that clients benefit a lot from casual contact with the therapist, as for example, if they run into each other at the theatre or in the street. When there is inadvertent contact outside sessions, this contact cannot be taken simply as casual but will need to be discussed thoughtfully in the professional session. Sometimes clients "pay" for their treatment or counselling by providing such services as administrative assistance, cleaning, or garden work. Besides the question of whether the client is then entering too much into the private life of the professional, these arrangements can lead to undesirable conflicts of interest. The treatment may then become extended because the therapist has come to depend on the client's services.

How much distance and how much proximity is necessary or desirable in order to work together effectively is a question the professional must ask herself continuously. In educational and training relationships no matter how flattering it may be for the self-esteem of the teacher, she will have to review the excessive interest of pupils in her private life with a fitting amount of restraint and not accept her students as Facebook friends. So, too, in management relations the manager will need to ask herself whether it is better to politely decline the invitation to the annual Christmas dinner at her client's house.

Discussions are regularly held in psychotherapy journals on the boundaries of the therapeutic relationship. Some people choose a safe position: every contact, every encounter outside the therapy hour is prohibited. However, the damage that you bring about with such a formal position is less visible than the damage caused by the crossing of boundaries. The question is whether you possibly deprive your clients by exclusively presenting yourself as a "professional". Others therefore choose an individual assessment in different situations and, if they think the interest of the client is served by this, may decide, for example, to share with a client that they have experienced a similar problem with their children or to have a chat with a client whom they happen to bump into in the city.

Our professional relationships—be they educational, consultative, counselling, or psychotherapeutic—often do not occur in a vacuum. In organisational and academic environments there will often be overlapping roles such as student/teacher, assistant/employer, supervisee/supervisor, applicant (for a promotion, grant, graduation, certification)/evaluator, or colleague and co-worker. In psychotherapy and counselling someone who began as a client may become a supervisee or a peer as a member in a workplace or professional association. In some professional associations these overlapping or sequential professional relationships may be deemed unethical. In other professional structures these changes in relational roles are seen as acceptable, even as evidence of accomplishment and maturation. These transitions can be complex and filled with transferential pressures from both sides of the relationship. Careful, mutual attention during these role transitions is needed, and supervision or consultation may well be wise and useful.

At the core of the ethical codes of transactional analysts is the contract. The ITAA code of ethics, for example, stipulates that the professional relationship ends with the completion of the contract, but that there are certain professional responsibilities that continue beyond the termination of the professional contract. These include the continuation of confidentiality, the avoidance of any exploitation of the previous relationship, and the provision of follow-up care if needed (which could include supervision for role transitions).

9.2.3 Ethical dilemmas

In many professional relationships, ethical dilemmas come into play. It is not just about large, complicated problems, but rather the small daily disconnections in contact and so-called "misattunements". Inherent in working with people is that unconscious psychological dynamics come into play, which may have a healing effect or may cause additional damage. In psychotherapy, where injured people seek treatment, it is essential to be able to work with these dynamics. The ethical code often does not deal with the subtlety and depth of such processes. Nevertheless, it is still necessary to reflect on the possible breaks in the therapeutic relationship, preferably before an ethical complaint can be filed (Eusden, 2011).

Teachers too encounter similar ethical dilemmas when their beliefs about the best interest of the pupils in their care have to be balanced with the context of other "interested parties"—parents, school authorities—while recognising that children can often only express their feelings through their behaviour. "What am I doing in this situation and by what right?" is a constant ethical question for educators (Newton, 2011).

In the different fields, different kinds of dilemmas can arise. You can examine them using the following questions:

- Which ethical considerations bring this dilemma to the surface?
- Which values, and their related standards, are at stake?
- In what form do we find those values and standards represented in the EATA and ITAA codes of ethics?
- What would your advice be? What is the basis for this advice?

Here are some examples of the dilemmas:

1. You are coaching the CEO of a company. He tells you that he sometimes has sexual contact with female employees, who he believes want this. He knows that this is wrong, but he finds it exciting. His wife is unaware.
2. The wife of a client calls you. She is very anxious because her husband is threatening to commit suicide. She does not dare to leave the house and she does not want you to tell him that she called you.
3. You work on behalf of the executive board as an interim manager in a large organisation. You notice that the other members of the management team are "choosing" to be selective in what they tell the executive board. "These board members are too far from the practical side of the business," so goes the argument.
4. You work as an interim professional in a company. Your "boss" (and client) is getting married and asks you to her wedding dinner. The job that you are doing for her is not finished yet.
5. You start a new relationship and you discover that one of your clients is a close colleague of your new partner. Your partner tells you about cooperation problems with this colleague. Do you tell your partner that this colleague is in therapy with you?

There are no "right" or "wrong" answers to these questions. It's about the dialogue within one's self, with others, and within one's professional communities.

9.3 Furthermore

9.3.1 Autonomy

The question every TA professional asks herself, again and again, is "How does the intervention that I wish to make contribute to the development of the other's autonomy?" Autonomy is one of the most important values in TA. Yet not much has been written about it. In his bestseller

Games People Play (1964, p. 178), Berne explores the concept of "autonomy". Autonomy manifests itself by the release or recovery of:

- Awareness: the ability to observe in a purely sensory manner, as a newborn child, without interpretation.
- Intimacy: a game-free exchange of emotional expression without exploitation.
- Spontaneity: the ability to choose from a wide range of options when it comes to thinking, feeling, or acting.

Stewart and Joines (2012) believe that autonomous thinking, feeling, or acting is a response to the here and now (rather than in response to script convictions). This definition is similar to what Berne says about autonomy in *What Do You Say after You Say Hello?* (1972, p. 183): "Real autonomy is if the Adult is free from 'bias' (Parent) and free from wishful thinking (Child). Autonomous behaviour is the opposite of script behaviour." The more a person realises his autonomy, the less the script has a grip on him.

In the past decade there has been a growing debate as to whether people have a free and autonomous will. Some neuroscientists argue that free will does not exist. They argue that, at their deepest level, people have no control over their decisions. What are we to think of books such as *Wij zijn ons brein* (We Are Our Brains) (Swaab, 2010) and *De vrije wil bestaat niet* (Free Will Does Not Exist) (Lamme, 2010)? These books argue that unconscious brain activity is the boss over free will. Autonomy, from this perspective, is seen as an illusion. The brain has been active for seconds before you even notice it. The Belgian philosopher Jan Verplaetse, also a neuroscientist, believes in *Zonder vrije wil* (Without Free Will, 2011):

> One of the biggest misconceptions in the free will debate is that this debate is actually about free will. That is not the case. The free will debate is not about free will, that mysterious ability to make free decisions. The question is not whether this ability exists. If only it were that simple. The question is what the consequences are of a non-existent free will. What if free will does not exist? Is responsibility still possible? Can you be guilty? Does it make sense to blame people? (p. 14; translated for this edition)

The explosion of new technologies that have allowed much more detailed studies of the brain and mind in action has been illuminating on the one hand and blinding on the other. In the US the National Institute of Health declared the 1990s the "decade of the brain", and expectations of this new scientific exploration have run very high. We are at risk of over-generalising what this new research actually means. We are at risk of conflating the brain and the mind. Burton (2013), Rose (2005), and Rose and Abi-Rached (2013) are among recent authors who have urged caution in what we think we "know" from the new "brain sciences", and these cautions carry substantial ethical implications.

Rose, for example, in his discussion of "Ethics in a Neurocentric World" (2005, pp. 297–305), observes that "the claims of my colleagues have become ever more ambitious and comprehensive," as though "… humans are simply somewhat more complex thermostats, fabricated out of carbon chemistry" (p. 297). Rose argues that all of this neuronal activity occurs and is constantly shaped within biosocial organisms, and as such, "… we retain responsibility for our actions, that we, as humans, possess the agency to create and recreate our worlds" (p. 305). He concludes: "Our ethical understandings may be enriched by neuroscientific knowledge, but cannot be replaced, and it will be through agency, socially expressed, that we will be able, if at all, to manage the ethical, legal and social aspects of the emerging neurotechnologies" (p. 305).

The question of free will is essentially not a medical-neurological or philosophical debate, but an ethically loaded question. Can people rely on their script if they morally lose control? Insanity? Can people use their poorly developed autonomous capabilities as a plea for innocence? "What can I do about it?"

The American neuroscientist Michael Gazzaniga discusses in *The Ethical Brain* (2005) the ease with which the debate on the role of the brain enters into a black and white dichotomy. He raises the question "Where do the hard-and-fast facts of neuroscience end and where does ethics begin?" Later Gazzaniga introduces the concept of "emergence": "When it comes to responsibility and freedom, we are dealing with emergent properties that arise when multiple brains interact with each other." Emergence (Gazzaniga, 2011) is the development of complex organised systems that exhibit certain characteristics that are not visible by the reduction of their parts. An emergent property is a property that occurs or is observed when you change levels, for example, from the atomic level to the human visual level. An example of emergence is colour. Individual atoms have no colour, but when a (large) number of atoms are arranged in a particular manner, they are able to absorb or emit light of certain wavelengths, creating a visible colour. Colour is, in this case, an emergent property. The mind is sometimes called an emergent property. The mind arises from physical processes, but cannot be reduced to these physical processes. The emerging quality has its own character, but cannot exist without the underlying material elements. A brain is a machine that follows a particular decision route. But the analysis of an individual brain cannot explain where the ability to "take responsibility" comes from.

"Responsibility is", so believes Gazzaniga (2005), "a dimension of life that comes from social interaction and social interaction requires multiple brains." In the world of transactions, co-organised by our brain, ethical questions retain their legitimacy. In this perspective, the reductionist view of authors like Swaab and Lamme does injustice to the infinite complexity that humans represent.

9.3.2 Risks, trust, and "minding the gap"

Tim Bond (2006), an ethics expert and consultant in the UK, addressed the unavoidable interrelationships of the intimacy, risks, and uncertainties that are inherent in counselling and psychotherapeutic work. Bond articulates what he names as "an ethic of trust … that supports the development of reciprocal relationships of sufficient strength to withstand the relational challenges of difference and inequality and the existential challenges of risk and uncertainty" (p. 82). He challenges the "risk-avoidant culture" (p. 83) that has come to permeate many professional and legal cultures, which he argues "is fundamentally dishonest and existentially infantilizing" (p. 83). Echoing the concerns of Grace McGrath (1994) expressed a decade earlier, Bond argues, "… professionally, it may lead to dysfunctionally defensive practice that prioritizes the therapist's self-protection over being therapeutically effective" (p. 83). Bond's paper was written in the context of his participation in a world TA conference focused on the theme of "Freedom and Responsibility", which resulted in a series of papers exploring clinical and cultural aspects of ethics (Cornell, 2006; Drego, 2006; Naughton & Tudor, 2006; Salters, 2006).

Building on the work of McGrath and Bond and drawing upon her experience serving on an ethics committee, Sue Eusden (2011) observes that "therapists often act unethically in their practices, not through gross misconduct but through inattention, going for the easy option (e.g., soothing rather than disturbing), or making poor interventions" (p. 102) and suggests that such errors themselves are not unethical so much as the professional's lack of attention to the gap or disturbance created for the client by the professional's actions. She describes the intense shame that therapists may feel when their ethics are called into question, which may then aggravate the disturbance rather than facilitate problem solving and resolution. She argues that "Our present professional codes do not account for the subtlety and depth of unconscious, two-person psychological dynamics inherent in working the edges of disturbance central in many psychotherapeutic practices" (p. 104). She then offers clinical examples of how a therapist can mind the gaps of disturbances and errors so that the therapy continues rather than the gap widening into an ethical breach. Her article is the lead article in a special issue of the *Transactional Analysis Journal* that addresses ethical concerns in all four fields of TA practice.

Writing a year later from clinical and training perspectives, Cook (2012), Mazzetti (2012), and Shadbolt (2012) offer further illustrations of addressing ("minding") therapeutic errors in ways that support the ongoing therapeutic work.

9.3.3 Bystanding

Although all TA concepts have the more or less implicit invitation to use them in ethical reasoning, there is one TA concept that is ethical by nature. Petruska Clarkson (1996) introduced the Bystander as a fourth role to Karpman's drama triangle. She is aware that "Karpman's Drama Triangle does not allow for the fact that the drama almost always has an audience. The audience is both affected by the play and has a profound effect on what transpires" (p. 42). Part I of her book is all about the moral complexity of playing games. Keyword here is "responsibility". "Bystanding is predicated upon the denial of obligation and responsibility for others," Clarkson writes (p. 15). In Chapter Four more is to be found on the role of the Bystander.

9.4 Related theories

9.4.1 Kohlberg and moral development

One of the most well-known theories of human moral development was put forward by the psychologist Lawrence Kohlberg. He built on Jean Piaget's work on the development of human cognitive ability. Kohlberg based his model on qualitative research he conducted among groups of children and young adults. He presented them with a series of moral dilemmas. He was not primarily interested in the choices they made but in the reasoning they employed in order to arrive at their choice.

A famous dilemma

A woman is suffering from a particular form of cancer. There is one drug which her doctors think might save her: a certain form of radium, recently discovered by a pharmacist who lives in the same city. The production of this drug is very expensive. In addition, the pharmacist is charging ten times the amount it costs to produce it. It costs him 200 euros per dose to make it and he's selling it for 2000 euros per dose.

The woman's husband goes to everyone he knows to borrow money. He gets no further than half of what is needed to save his wife's life. He tells the pharmacist that his wife is dying and asks him to sell it for a lower amount or to defer payment of the full amount. However, the pharmacist refuses, saying "No, I discovered the drug and I intend to make a profit from it." The husband becomes desperate and breaks into the shop of the pharmacist to steal the drug. Question: What is your opinion on the ethical behaviour of the spouse? (Kohlberg, 1973).

Kohlberg classified the reasoning at different stages in people's moral development. Briefly these are as follows:

- Pre-conventional morality.
  Moral judgements are dependent on physical and external stimuli, aimed at avoiding hurt feelings ("How do I avoid getting punished?") and on self-interest ("How do I benefit from this?").
- Conventional morality.
  Moral judgements are tailored to the approval or rejection of authority figures (often parents), aimed at avoiding social disapproval and avoiding judgement. Law and order morality.
- Post-conventional morality.
  Moral judgements are based on self-evaluated principles, aimed at countering condemnation and functioning as part of society. Conscientious.

All three stages follow a different logic in response to the question whether the man from the dilemma above is justified in breaking in to save his wife's life. In stage 1, the argument may be that he should not do that because he runs the risk of ending up in prison. Or he may do so, because ultimately it comes down to stealing something that costs only 200 euros. In stage 2, it can be argued that every man who really cares about his wife would do this for her. After all, he first tried to do everything he could without breaking the law. However, he must accept the consequences if he is arrested. In stage 3, the following reasoning may apply: he may steal the drug because the right to life takes precedence over the right to property. Or he may not steal it because the pharmacist is entitled to fair compensation for all the research he has done. And besides, he is not only stealing the medicine from the pharmacist but also from another potential patient who may need the drug just as much as his wife.

9.4.2 Crossing boundaries

When things go wrong and professionals cross a certain boundary, it usually concerns relationships involving exploitation, or situations in which reduced judgement plays a role or when interests clash. Often it is a gradual process of which neither the professional nor the client is initially aware.

While most professionals agree that they sometimes experience sexual or erotic feelings towards their clients, it is far from common practice to discuss this during training, supervision, or intervision (peer-supervision).

In the second year of therapy, a patient remains silent for a large portion of the session and seems to be having trouble talking. Eventually, the patient says, "There's something I just need to know. Do you think I look nice? Are you attracted to me?"

You are having a conversation with a new client. When you see the client, you instantly become a supporter of the concept that you have often ridiculed: love at first sight. You invite the person to your consultation room, and during the conversation the feeling only becomes stronger that this is the one, this is the only person with whom you want to spend the rest of your life. You think to yourself, "I need to interrupt this, I have to say that I cannot engage with this person in a therapeutic relationship. I need to see if we can have a coffee together somewhere. I will give this patient the names of some other therapists."

The examples just given are taken from the book *Sexual Feelings in Psychotherapy: Explorations for Therapists and Therapists-in-training* by Pope, Sonne, and Holroyd (1993), in which the authors provide a clear framework for exploring and discovering sexual feelings and reactions. They provide seven basic rules:

1. Exploring the sexual feelings and reactions of the therapist is an important part of training and professional development.
2. A clear distinction should be made between having these feelings and actual sexual intimacies with clients.
3. No therapist should ever engage in the sexual misuse of a client.
4. Most therapists have at one time or another been sexually attracted to or have been sexually aroused by a client.
5. When it comes to sexual attraction or sexual feelings, it is very important to recognise and accept these feelings; avoiding them may have a counterproductive or even harmful influence on the therapy and the patient.
6. These feelings can best be explored and discovered in a safe, non-judgemental, and supportive environment.
7. A "recipe book" approach to the nature, meaning, and implications of individual sexual feelings and reactions does not exist.

The descriptions and recommendations in their book are more broadly applicable than just the sexual domain.

9.4.3 Statistics are in

It seems to be breaking news when the Dow Jones or the CAC40 are going up or down. Managers seem to use the daily ratings to manage. Politicians receive the weekly polls with trembling hands. Quantity defeats quality, so it seems. The preoccupation with figures might be questioned ethically. It might hide a deeper fear! Paul Verhaeghe (2009), professor of clinical psychology and psychoanalysis, argues that it hides a fear of thinking. Using common sense seems to frighten people more and more. Numbers are supposed to produce the truth about reality. Figures, he states, caused the financial crisis. The banking world stopped thinking. Figures, however, are best used within a nuanced ethically based thinking process. "Outside such a process they are nothing more than arguments in the hands of those who manipulate the naive majority." Who only has words is suspect. "Statistics are in, rhetoric is out," Verhaeghe seems to say (p. 223; translated for this edition). An over-reliance on figures threatens to deprive us of more poetic ways of communicating about what is the most difficult to say, the ineffable.

Verhaeghe (2004) also undertook a stunning critique of the applications of the DSM diagnostic model. While it is outside the scope of this book, seen from a perspective of ethics, Verhaeghe's book offers a powerful example of the ways in which our capacities for critical thinking ensure ethical practices. In a similar vein of critical thinking about social, professional, and legal trends and pressures that carry serious ethical implications, Bond and Mitchels (2014) and Bollas and Sundelson (1995) provide challenging reflections on the erosion of confidentiality and the fundamental ethical responsibilities to maintain confidentiality in our professional relationships, especially those with counselling and psychotherapeutic contracts.

9.4.4 Virtues

In *The Virtuous Psychiatrist* (2010), philosopher Jennifer Radden and psychiatrist John Sadler describe the virtues psychiatrists must have when providing care to people with serious psychiatric problems. Their vision is applicable to a broad group of professionals and not only psychiatrists. They argue that character traits, or virtues as Aristotle called them, should be guiding the ethical behaviour of professionals. From these virtues, ethical values and standards can be deduced.

Radden and Sadler provide an outline sketch of a kind of hierarchy of virtues. Every professional must possess the virtues of reliability and moral integrity. In addition, professionals who work with people must also possess decency, respect, benevolence, kindness, empathy, compassion, perseverance, warmth, self-knowledge, and realism. They need to monitor their boundaries, show moral leadership, be gender-sensitive, determined, respectful, and patient.

They further describe some particular virtues, such as "unselfing", a special quality of proper listening and focusing on the other within the limits of the therapeutic relationship, in which the professional effaces herself to a certain extent. Another virtue is "phronesis" or practical wisdom. Phronesis, which is also a term coined by Aristotle, involves, for example, translating scientific evidence to the situation of unique clients, packing multiple objectives into a few interventions, or making decisions in complex situations with little available information.

In Radden and Sadler's view, professionals should be humble and recognise that their ideas and attitudes may also be biased or prejudiced. This creates an area of tension between professional knowledge, on the one hand, and the open-mindedness needed to be receptive to new situations on the other. Virtues are often seen as a matter of personal character, but professional values and ethics can also be learned.

9.4.5 Self-disclosure

When does the disclosure of personal information on the part of the professional benefit the professional relationship and/or growth of the client? Weiner (1978) suggests that this is the most important criterion when it comes to self-disclosure by the professional. He argues that in many cases, a therapist revealing personal matters is more a matter of satisfying either the need for transference, acting out of countertransference, or a lapse into narcissism. In some cases, during short-term therapies for example, self-disclosure can have a useful function in validating certain feelings of the client, promoting identification with the therapist, or by offering an example of a learning experience in which the therapist is the model.

Weiner illustrates how self-disclosure can be useful to increase the reality awareness and self-esteem of the client. He suggests that self-disclosure can act as feedback for the client. Self-disclosure may be appropriate if therapy is interrupted by personal elements of the therapist's life. Self-disclosure can be a corrective emotional experience in which one experiences the human relationship.

The pitfalls of self-disclosure, according to Weiner, can be great, however, because both the therapist and the client are more likely to give information unconsciously that neither is aware of. Weiner therefore calls for restraint and self-reflection. Therapists in particular need to ask whether their self-disclosure can be manipulative or interpreted as seductive, or whether it actually serves the needs of the therapist more than those of the client. Or, the therapist may go along with the resistance of the client, by making the latter dependent, for instance. Weiner's main recommendation is thus: if you're in doubt as to whether you should tell something about yourself, don't!

Our professional relationships, whether we are working as psychotherapists, counsellors, educators, supervisors, or organisational consultants, are asymmetrical in authority and responsibility. It is perhaps in the psychotherapeutic literature that we find the most thorough discussions of the potential meanings, advantages, and problems of self-disclosure (Aron, 1996; Bass, 2007; Cornell, 2014; Maroda, 1999; Skolnikoff, 2011). These discussions and reflections make it clear that no single hard and fast rule can adequately guide decisions with regard to self-disclosure.

Discussing the tensions between asymmetry and mutuality within a professional relationship, Lew Aron (1996) suggests that we cannot know in advance the consequence of self-disclosure but need to pay attention to what happens afterwards. "The critical issue seems to be whether the analyst's interventions invite or discourage further elaboration, correction, observation, and associations from the patient" (p. 98). Karen Maroda (1999) stresses the therapist's willingness to be open about her emotions in relation to a patient, arguing that "It is the therapist's willingness to be forthcoming and to show emotion that is *curative* and stimulates emotional honesty" (p. 103, italics in the original), going on to say that we must not present our self-disclosures as a final word but to allow space for the patient to say if the therapist's self-disclosure does not match the patient's experience. One of the risks of too much or too personal self-disclosure on the part of the professional is that of the erasure of the asymmetry and foreclosure of the patient's own experience. Skolnikoff and Cornell each offer clinical vignettes of decisions to self-disclose and not self-disclose, illustrating that there are consequences for decisions in either direction.

9.4.6 *"Ethicability"*

A practical approach to the (ethical) challenges facing businesses is "ethicability" (Steare, 2008). In his book of the same title Roger Steare says that ethicability helps us decide what's right and find the courage to do it. Although based on insights from moral philosophy and human psychology the aim is to encourage people to think through dilemmas for themselves with the aid of a straightforward schema of preparation, decision, and testing.

Preparation:

How do we feel? Who's involved? What are the facts? What sort of dilemma is this? What are our intentions? What are our options? Have we thought creatively?

Decide what's RIGHT:

What are the Rules? Are we acting with Integrity? Who is this Good for? Who could we Harm? What's the Truth?

Testing our decision:

How would we feel in their shoes? What would be fair and reasonable? What would be the adult thing to do? What would build trust and respect? What would stand the test of time? Have we the courage to do what's right? What can we learn from this dilemma?

9.4.7 *Ethical maturity?*

How can we recognise ethical maturity? This is the question posed by Michael Carroll (2013). He suggests that the term itself involves a movement, from immaturity to maturity. Just as we grow up physically we develop our ethical thinking from childhood through adolescence to adulthood, making decisions in different ways at different stages. Ethical maturity is: having the reflective, rational, intuitive, and emotional capacity to decide actions are right and wrong, having the courage and resilience to implement those decisions, being accountable for ethical decisions made (publicly or privately), and being able to learn from and live with the experiences involved.

It therefore comprises six components, each of which plays a part in thinking and decision-making for people working in any helping profession.

1. Ethical sensitivity and thoughtfulness.
2. Ethical discernment and decision-making.
3. Ethical conversations (accountability).
4. Ethical implementation (capability).
5. Ethical sustainability and peace (living with decisions).
6. Learning from the experience of making ethical decisions (critical reflection).

References

Aron, L. (1996). *A Meeting of the Minds: Mutuality in Psychoanalysis*. Hillsdale, NJ: Analytic Press.

Bader, E. (1994). Dual relationships, legal and ethical trends. *Transactional Analysis Journal*, 24(1): 64–66.

Bass, A. (2007). When the frame doesn't fit the picture. *Psychoanalytic Dialogues*, 17: 1–27.

Berne, E. (1964). *Games People Play*. New York: Grove Press.

Berne, E. (1972). *What Do You Say after You Say Hello?* New York: Grove Press.

Bollas, C., & Sundelson, D. (1995). *The New Informants: The Betrayal of Confidentiality in Psychoanalysis and Psychotherapy*. Northvale, NJ: Jason Aronson.

Bond, T. (2006). Intimacy, risk, and reciprocity in psychotherapy: Intricate ethical challenges. *Transactional Analysis Journal*, 36: 77–89.

Bond, T., & Mitchels, B. (2014). *Confidentiality and Record Keeping in Counselling and Psychotherapy*. London: Sage.

Burton, R. A. (2013). *A Skeptic's Guide to the Mind: What Neuroscience Can and Cannot Tell Us about Ourselves*. New York: St. Martin's Press.

Carroll, M. (2013). *Ethical Maturity in the Helping Professions* London: Jessica Kingsley.

Clarkson, P. (1994). In recognition of dual relationships. *Transactional Analysis Journal*, 24(1): 32–38.

Clarkson, P. (1996). *The Bystander (an End to Innocence in Human Relationships?)*. London: Whurr.

Cook, R. (2012). Triumph or disaster?: A relational view of therapeutic mistakes. *Transactional Analysis Journal*, 42: 34–42.

Cornell, W. F. (1994). Dual relationships in transactional analysis training, supervision and therapy. *Transactional Analysis Journal*, 24(1): 21–29.

Cornell, W. F. (2006). Letter from the editor. *Transactional Analysis Journal*, 36(2): 74–76.

Cornell, W. F. (2014). The intricate intimacies of psychotherapy and questions of self-disclosure. In: D. Loewenthal & A. Samuels (Eds.), *Relational Psychotherapy, Psychoanalysis and Counselling: Appraisals and Reappraisals* (pp. 54–64). London: Routledge.

Drego, P. (2006). Freedom and responsibility: Social empowerment and the altruistic model of ego states. *Transactional Analysis Journal*, 36(2): 90–104.

EATA (2008). *Ethical Code* (www.eatanews.org).

Eusden, S. (2011). Minding the gap: Ethical considerations for therapeutic engagement. *Transactional Analysis Journal*, 41(2): 101–113.

Gazzaniga, M. (2005). *The Ethical Brain*. New York: HarperCollins.

Gazziniga, M. (2011). *Who's in Charge? Free Will and the Science of the Brain*. New York: Ecco (HarperCollins).

Graaf, A. de, & Levy, J. (2011). Business as usual? Ethics in the fast-changing and complex world of organizations. *Transactional Analysis Journal*, 41(2): 123–128.

Kohlberg, L. (1973). The claim to moral adequacy of a highest stage of moral judgment. *Journal of Philosophy*, 70(18): 630–646.

Kouwenhoven, M. (2011). Bouwen aan een integere samenleving. Integriteitzorg vanuit een geïntegreerd Oudersysteem. (Building an ethical society. Integrity management from an Integrated Parent system.) *Strook, theme number Ethiek*, December: 20–33.

Lamme, V. (2010). *De vrije wil bestaat niet*. (Free Will Does Not Exist.) Amsterdam, Netherlands: Bert Bakker.

Maroda, K. (1999). *Seduction, Surrender, and Transformation*. Hillsdale, NJ: Analytic Press.

Mazzetti, M. (2012). Teaching trainees to make mistakes. *Transactional Analysis Journal*, 42: 43–52.

McGrath, G. (1994). Ethics, boundaries and contracts: Applying moral principles. *Transactional Analysis Journal*, 24: 6–14.

Naughton, M., & Tudor, K. (2006). Being white. *Transactional Analysis Journal*, 36(2): 159–171.

Newton, T. (2011). The nature and necessity of risk: Minding the gap in education. *Transactional Analysis Journal*, 41(2): 114–117.

Pope, K., Sonne, J., & Holroyd, J. (1993). *Sexual Feelings in Psychotherapy: Explorations for Therapists and Therapists-in-training*. Washington, DC: American Psychological Association.

Radden, J., & Sadler, J. (2010). *The Virtuous Psychiatrist*. Oxford: Oxford University Press.

Rose, S. (2005). *The Future of the Brain: The Promise and Perils of Tomorrow's Neuroscience*. Oxford: Oxford University Press.

Rose, N., & Abi-Rached, J. M. (2013). *Neuro: The New Brain Sciences and the Management of the Mind*. Princeton, NJ: Princeton University Press.

Salters, D. (2006). Simunye—Sibaningi: We are one—we are many. *Transactional Analysis Journal*, 36(2): 152–158.

Shadbolt, C. (2012). The place of rupture and failure in psychotherapy. *Transactional Analysis Journal*, 42: 5–16.

Skolnikoff, A. (2011). Talking about onself. In: S. Akhtar (Ed.), *Unusual Interventions: Alterations of the Frame, Method, and Relationship in Psychotherapy and Psychoanalysis* (pp. 141–164). London: Karnac.

Steare, R. (2008). *Ethicability: How to Decide What's Right and Find the Courage to Do It*. Sevenoaks, UK: Roger Steare Consulting (self-published).

Stewart, I., & Joines, V. (2012). *TA Today: A New Introduction to Transactional Analysis. Second Edition*. Melton Mowbray, UK: Lifespace.

Suriyaprakash, C. (2011). Ethics in organizations: My Eastern philosophical perspective. *Transactional Analysis Journal*, 41(2): 123–128.

Swaab, D. (2010). *Wij zijn ons brein*. (We Are Our Brains.) Amsterdam: Contact.

Verhaeghe, P. (2004). *On Being Normal and Other Disorders: A Manual for Clinical Psychodiagnostics*. New York: Other Press.

Verhaeghe, P. (2009). *Het Einde van de Psychotherapie*. (The End of Psychotherapy.) Amsterdam: De Bezige Bij.

Verplaetse, J. (2011). *Zonder vrije wil*. (Without Free Will.) Amsterdam: Nieuwezijds.

Weiner, M. (1978). *Therapist Disclosure. The Use of Self in Psychotherapy*. Baltimore, MD: University Park Press.

Woollams, S., & Brown, M. (1978). *Transactional Analysis*. Ann Arbor, MI: Huron Valley Institute.

CHAPTER TEN

Supervision

10.1 Basic theory
    10.1.1 A mutual learning process
    10.1.2 A contractual relationship
    10.1.3 Focus of supervision
    10.1.4 An example
    10.1.5 Checklist
    10.1.6 Supervision and therapy
10.2 Further theory
    10.2.1 Integrating supervision model
    10.2.2 Parallel processes
    10.2.3 The comparative script system
10.3 Furthermore
    10.3.1 From unconsciously incompetent to unconsciously competent
    10.3.2 Supervision as meta-modality
10.4 Related theories
    10.4.1 Phases in training and supervision
    10.4.2 Situational leadership as a model for supervision
References

The professional who works with and carries responsibility for people will have to deal with the question of whether and how these people will grow as individuals, and how they will develop as professionals. In order to handle this situation properly, it is an (ethical) necessity that these professionals constantly manage their own growth and development. Though this is the last chapter of Part I, supervision should not come at the bottom of the list for the TA professional. Thinking about the why and the how of supervision and formulating ideas for the practice of supervision are the theme of Chapter Ten.

10.1 Basic theory

10.1.1 A mutual learning process

Eric Berne (1968) experimented with the concept of staff-patient conferences in the 1960s. In the hospital where he worked, he involved patients directly in staff deliberations. He first let the staff talk about the patients in their presence. Then he asked the patients to reflect on what they had heard the staff members say. His experience was that most patients appreciated this model and that they had sufficient strength of ego to handle these conferences. The staff often had more difficulty with this set-up. But over time they too came to appreciate the process (p. 164).

Cornell also applied this model (Cornell, Shadbolt, & Norton, 2007). In the clinic for severely mentally challenged children where he worked, every child and the parents were involved in the discussion of the treatment plan.

Later, as a TA supervisor, he organised supervisory groups called "bring the client day". Each therapist brought along a client who was present in the group for the entire day. Each client chose a therapist (not his own therapist) and worked with this therapist in the presence of the supervisor (Cornell), his own therapist, other therapists, and other clients. In the discussion afterwards, all participants talked about their thoughts and observations. The supervisor, therapists, and clients were all involved in a process of mutual learning. The clients typically reported that they learned a lot from this. The process of therapy had become less mystical, and the capacities of their Adult were strengthened.

10.1.2 A contractual relationship

Supervision is an important tool in learning to work with TA. It is one of the cornerstones of TA training (Tudor, 2002; Zalcman & Cornell, 1983). In 2012, the Italian psychiatrist Marco Mazzetti was honoured with the Eric Berne Memorial Award for his article on supervision (Mazzetti, 2007). Numerous other authors within TA have also written about supervision. This chapter has been drawn from these writings. Berne himself was a teacher par excellence, and he saw supervision as an important part of the learning process. His weekly seminars had a strong supervision component (Mazzetti, 2007).

If we consider the components of the word "supervision" separately ("super" and "vision"), we get a picture of the aim of supervision. It is a process that invites one (metaphorically) to take a step back to get a meta-perspective: a broad view on one's working practice. Supervision can be defined as a contractual relationship between supervisor and supervisee aimed at improving the professional relationships and efficacy of the supervisee. In transactional analysis, supervision is usually carried out in both group and individual formats. Over time, aspects of the professional's personality may be addressed within the supervisory process, creating an opportunity for personal as well as professional development. The supervisory relationship also provides a forum in which ethical issues can be addressed.

Supervision is a process through which the supervisee develops her identity as a professional. The safety to be able to show one's fears, uncertainties, and potential errors is essential to this learning process. The supervisor must respect and encourage the personal style of the supervisee. In the interpersonal relationship with the supervisor, the supervisee may examine the interpersonal relationship with the client and make use of this parallel process.

Whether supervision lasts for a long or short time, a supervision contract is an essential part of the supervisory process. Attention to the contractual aspects of supervision focuses the tasks of the supervisor and supervisee, while providing an ongoing modelling of the contractual process itself. For short-term supervision this may be a contract per session. "I want to explore why this client/patient/student irritates me." If the supervision takes longer, then this may be a more comprehensive contract for a period of several months. "I would like to learn how to improve my boundaries as a coach, which is to say, not to let sessions run late and not to put too much on my plate. I want to find out why I tend to go beyond my limits." Using the contract, the boundaries of supervision can become clear, and whether the needs of the supervisee can be fulfilled by the supervisor can be assessed.

Supervision is not an instrument that is only used during a professional's initial learning phase. Erskine (1982) describes how supervision with novice professionals is first aimed at developing skills and confidence and later at the formation of a professional identity. Eventually, supervision is mainly focused on the integration of the different approaches, so that the supervisee can apply these flexibly depending on the needs of the client. Clarkson (1992) indicates that supervision is a method of continuous learning and growth during one's professional career. There is always an opportunity for further growth and development, whereby supervision offers senior professionals the opportunities, challenges, and support to broaden their horizons.

The naturalness with which professionals from the world of psychotherapy seek supervision is still lacking in many other professionals who work daily with people's growth and change. Recent years have seen more and more interest in maintaining the quality of professionals in educational settings. The number of trainers and teachers who regularly seek supervision in order to continue their development has been growing. Few (interim) consultants and managers consider it natural to seek supervision to hold up a mirror to their daily actions. Coaching, on the other hand, has expanded enormously in recent years. However, coaching is often deployed when things are going wrong. The mindset of supervision holds to the adage "You do not have to be sick to get better". More and more coaches, and coaching associations, are realising the value of supervision for their work.

10.1.3 Focus of supervision

Stewart (1992) presents a clear supervision model, based on the "seven-eyed" model (Shohet & Hawkins, 1989), in which he distinguishes the different areas in which supervision takes place: the supervision matrix, the therapeutic matrix, and an area of overlap (Figure 10.1). The supervision matrix is where the contact between the supervisor and the supervisee is located. The supervisee discusses facts from the therapeutic matrix, matters that relate to the client and the therapy. Supervision also considers the interventions and countertransference of the supervisee as a therapist. Finally, supervision also considers the countertransference of the supervisor and the process between the supervisor and the supervisee, the area of overlap.

1. Facts concerning the client. How long has the client been in counselling or therapy? What is the problem, the request for help, or the diagnosis? And the contract? What has happened so far during counselling or treatment? Sometimes it becomes evident that a professional has not enquired about certain essential facts about the client which can shed new light on the problem and its solution.
2. The process of the session, the factual analysis of the transactions. Using a transcript or an audio or DVD recording of the session, much can be made clear about the actual interaction between the client and the professional, both socially and psychologically. An audio and possibly a visual report can give the supervisor a representation of the session that is as objective as possible. Moreover, listening to his own supervision conversation can offer the supervisee the opportunity to take a more objective, more Adult position with regard to his own work.
3. Analysis of the interventions of the professional/supervisee. Which interventions has the supervisee used? What was the intended goal and what was the effect? Do the interventions fit within the contract?
4. Countertransference. Which role should the professional/supervisee play within the script of the client, or the client within the script of the professional/supervisee?
5. Parallel process. To what extent is what happens between the supervisor and the supervisee a parallel of the process between the professional/supervisee and the client?
6. Countertransference of the supervisor. What happens to the supervisor? To what extent does this have anything to do with the relationship with the supervisee or with the background and experiences of the supervisor?

Obviously, there is an interaction between these six elements. Because the supervisee submits his questions about the supervision to the supervisor (1, 2, and 3), the supervisor sometimes

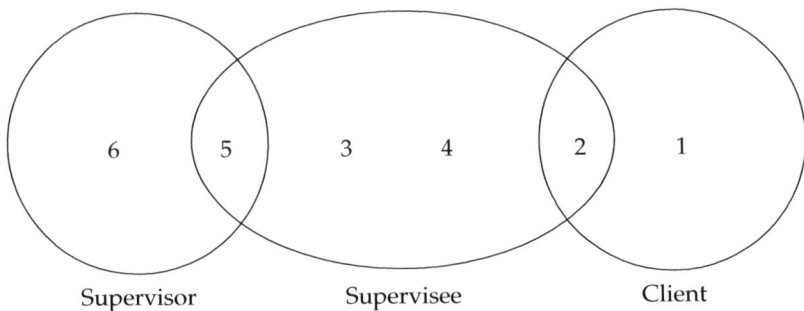

Figure 10.1. Supervision-matrix and therapeutic-matrix.

helps in the growth of the client via "remote control". Alternatively, it may become apparent during the parallel process between the supervisor and the supervisee (5) what is blocking the supervisee during the supervision of his client. Sometimes the client says exactly those things during therapy which the supervisor can use for the benefit of the supervisee—as if the client is listening in the position of the supervisor whereby it almost seems as if the supervisor is being supervised by the client.

Often, the supervisor uses the feelings of the supervisee with regard to the client as information about the problem of the client. The assumption is that the supervisee is reasonably transparent and not overly influenced by feelings in the countertransference relationship. After all, the supervisor only knows the client from the supervisee's stories! The purpose and the contract of supervision are to promote the professional skills of the supervisee, but sometimes this may include some personal therapy of the supervisee. In this personal therapy, the psychotherapist engages in her own personal explorations and changes as a part of her professional/personal learning process, in order to identify blind spots, to gain experience with the role of client, and to experience the method of therapy first hand.

Although Stewart's model is focused specifically on the training and supervision of psychotherapists, most aspects of the process he describes are typical of the supervisory process in all fields of application in transactional analysis. While a coaching or teacher supervisee may not be instructed specifically in the language of countertransference, for example, he would be expected to develop the capacity to identify and reflect upon his emotional reactions, beliefs, and expectations that may interfere with his working relationships.

10.1.4 An example

During a supervision session, which can last between twenty and sixty minutes, emphasis is gradually placed on different elements. (In the TA training, supervision often takes place in a group and lasts about twenty minutes per supervisee; the same format is used in the examination to become a TA supervisor). First, the contract between the supervisor and the supervisee is drawn up and a discussion is held on which theoretical or practical question will be addressed during the supervision.

Next, an hypothesis is made regarding the problem and possible parallel processes. Then, ethical and strategic issues can be discussed. Finally, the question as to whether the contract has been fulfilled and whether the question of the supervisee has been answered will be addressed. An important question within each supervision is "What can you learn from this client?" (Clarkson & Leigh, 1992). Reflection on this question helps the supervisee in his own professional development.

A supervisee, working as a trainer in a company that develops and produces high-quality technical products, seeks supervision because she has noted that during training groups, the participants are becoming more and more cautious in response to the request to contribute practical issues. The supervisee experiences herself as safe, approachable, and accessible. She very rarely experiences this problem. "I just can't seem to get a firm grip on this," she tells her supervisor.

> With the supervision she hopes to investigate what is possibly at play. What role does she play in the training group and which intervention might provide for a breakthrough? The supervisor starts the supervision by analysing the supervisee's contractual phase at the beginning of her assignment to give training, together with her, bearing in mind the TA motto "If something goes wrong, it is often at the beginning!".
>
> As it turns out, during the few times she visited the company prior to getting the job, the owner-manager showed her around his company. Together they walked through the laboratory and the production departments, visible to every employee she would later meet during the training. When asked by the supervisor about her feelings towards the client, she says (sighing and after a long hesitation, as if she has difficulty sharing this with her supervisor) "He is an impressive man … quite the boss … somewhat old school … I believe I'm a bit afraid of him! He's also a very dominant and strict man. It's as if his (negative) Structuring Parent is always present." The supervisor remains silent for some time and gives the supervisee time to think about the significance of this revelation and what light this sheds on the issue at hand within the current supervision. The supervisor has also taken note of the hesitation of the supervisee in sharing this story. This too may have meaning (parallel process).
>
> The supervisor invites her to reflect on the following hypothesis together. "Because you and 'the boss' were regularly seen together, the psychological distance between you and the staff has developed unfavourably. You're too much seen as 'belonging with him'. The reluctance to speak freely with management has therefore entered the training space." Later in the discussion, the apparent hesitation of the supervisee to share her feelings with her supervisor is used to deepen the analysis and to develop options for an intervention. The supervisee makes the commitment to have a conversation with her client. "If I have the courage, I will definitely say that I feel intimidated by him. I now see very clearly how the process went and what I have overlooked at the beginning." By the end of the session, the supervisor and supervisee decide to investigate what is going on between them that made the supervisee very reluctant to speak about her feelings regarding her client.

10.1.5 Checklist

To evaluate whether the supervision has been effective, Clarkson (1992) developed the following checklist, which is also used for the TA supervision exam:

- Has the contract been fulfilled?
- Have the core themes been identified?
- Has the likelihood that harm might be inflicted on the client or to others been reduced?
- Has the potential for development of the client and the supervisee been magnified by the supervision?
- Does the supervisor provide a model of a healthy therapeutic relationship?
- Is there equality in the relationship?

Supervisors in transactional analysis are required to undergo several years of formal training, supervision, and ultimately examinations to develop competencies as a supervisor. The supervision model developed by Clarkson has been incorporated within the TA oral examination for certification as a TA supervisor. Mazzetti (2007) proposed adding another item to the list—emotional empathy, the capacity of the supervisor to make contact with the supervisee and pay attention to the importance of feelings in the process.

The contract is the overt agreement between the supervisee and supervisor. The core themes are the themes that play out on a more unconscious level. Often, it only becomes clear by the end of the supervision what the core themes were and what their relationship is with the contract. In the earlier example, the contract is as follows: to understand why the group participants did not want to contribute practical examples. The core themes are: fear of the dominant critical director, and the perception that the trainer has a bond with this director. Ethical themes, such as reducing possible harm to the client or others, are of great importance in supervision. The supervisor is not only a trainer and educator, but also a representative of a professional organisation. This brings with it obligations with respect to the client of the supervisee and with respect to the quality of the application of the method. In a conflict between the interests of the supervisee and those of the client—fortunately something that does not happen often—the interests of the client will be paramount.

Landy Gobes (1993) offers a focused checklist of the four C's and four P's that are important functions in supervision.

- The C's: the *contact* between supervisor and supervisee, the *contract* for the supervision, the *context* in which the supervision takes place, and the *content* of supervision all need to be considered. Sometimes the context that needs to be addressed can include complex aspects of the supervisory relationship, such as, the supervisor also being the boss of the supervisee, or a dual relationship (e.g., if the supervisor is a colleague or friend of the supervisee).
- The P's: the *process* of supervision, possible *parallel* processes, the *professional* level of the supervisee's experience, to which the supervision needs to be adapted, and the *plan* for the future that requires attention over the course of supervision.

10.1.6 Supervision and therapy

Even though supervision, coaching, and therapy often resemble each other closely, there are still significant differences. Supervision and coaching focus on the present (here and now), therapy is also about the past (then and there). In supervision and coaching, personal themes can be identified whereby the client/supervisee can become aware of painful feelings. However, typically in transactional analysis the working through of these feelings and script-based issues is done in therapy. In supervision and coaching, professional development is primarily the focus, whereas in therapy it is personal development. Julie Hay (2007) places emphasis on two questions: what world model informs your work, and to what extent are you working in the here and now? Without making the boundaries between the types of work too rigid, the following picture emerges. In supervision the supervisor works in the here and now with the world model of the professional practice in which the supervisor and supervisee work. In therapy the therapist also works with her "own" world model (of a healthy life and the therapeutic approach to which the therapist adheres). She also makes use of regression. Coaching and counselling work in the here and now, using the world model of the supervisee, which may be questioned by the supervisor if there is a possibility of discounting and contamination.

10.2 Further theory

10.2.1 Integrating supervision model

Newton and Napper (2007) integrated a number of methodological models for supervision in a dynamic schema. The classic functions of supervision are: management, support, and development (Kadushin, 1992). In the field of management, supervisees can learn the procedures and working methods of the institutions to which they are attached, or how to structure their practice effectively. They can also learn how to deliver quality work according to the ethical, professional standards of the organisation and occupational group. Through the supervisor's support, supervisees can develop personally, and pay attention to the emotional impact of their practice. The supervisor stimulates, offers strokes, challenges, broadens perspectives and thereby, if necessary, restores the overview and mental peace of supervisees.

In the area of development the supervisees can further develop their professional knowledge, individual creativity, expertise, and skills. Newton (2012) translates this into the following figure (see Figure 10.2), in which she captures the content and the process of supervision as a stool with three legs. If one of the corners is given too much emphasis, the stool becomes unbalanced.

The trick is to deploy this model flexibly, adapted to the needs of the supervisee and based on the personal style of the supervisor.

10.2.2 Parallel processes

To the surprise of many beginning supervisees, the process that takes place in a supervision often resembles that which takes place between the supervisee and the client. For example, the supervisee mentions a client with whom he feels annoyed or bored, and to his surprise, the supervisor or members of the supervision group subsequently feel annoyed or bored during the supervision. This is called the parallel process in a supervision relationship.

> Eusden (2011) describes the following case: Maria is in supervision with Sue and mentions a client who is seriously suicidal. Sue is worried and she suggests a weekly supervision. The therapy becomes increasingly difficult. Maria feels overloaded. She eventually goes to her doctor, who prescribes that she reduces her workload. Maria realises how stopping treatment, especially for this client, would mean a repetition of the client's sense of abandonment. But at the same time this is precisely what she wants to do. Then the supervisor realises the parallel process. She too has considered stopping this difficult supervision. She too is too much "on top" of Maria, placing high demands on her, just as Maria does to herself, and the client does to himself, and in the same way that the client and Maria demand too much of each other during the therapeutic process. By discussing this during supervision, a sense of relief and space is created in Maria, so that she can continue with the supervision and therapy.

> Another example: the group of trainers developing and executing a large-scale training programme for a large company notes that one trainer after another returns home unsatisfied after the training session. The energy in the groups of employees is low. It seems that the participants do not want (or dare?) to talk openly about what really concerns them. For most trainers this means a day of pushing, pulling, hanging, and strangling. Only then does the session have value. But the balance has been

Risk: too structured
↑

Accounting/management:
Contracts, ethics, organisation and context
Boundaries and responsibilities
Competences, standards, criteria
SP+; protection; focused on thinking; learning philosophy; behaviour and technique

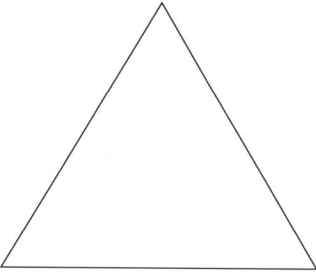

Support/nurturing:
Supervision relationship; process and dynamics
Script and rackets; (counter)transference
NP+; permission
Philosophy; humanistic
Focused on feelings and person
Reflection, supervision of supervision

↙
Risk: too comfortable

Transformative/development:
Action, research
Learning cycle: experiencing, reflecting, analysing, doing
Exploring methods, models and philosophy,
Personal experiences and yourself as an instrument;
Adult, potency, doing
Developing competences, narrative

↘
Risk: too challenging

Figure 10.2. Supervision triangle.

---

lost. The participants rarely evaluate the training with more than a six or a seven (out of ten), which is below standard for most of the trainers. Although they are not used to this, they seek out supervision as a group. After two sessions, the supervisor notes that she too is beginning to build a sense of dissatisfaction with the group of trainers. There seems to be little room for an open discussion. Suddenly she realises that the trainer who is the group's leader was not part of the contract phase. One of the other trainers had approached her for this role after the group had established its contract. When this fact emerges during the third session, then everything falls into place. Suddenly the parallel process becomes crystal clear. The supervisor finds her energy leaking and experiences dissatisfaction in the group of trainers and realises she contracted only with some of the trainers instead of with the whole group. The same seems true for the employees with whom the trainers are working. Where are the leaders of all those employees who diligently turn up for the training?

The first description of the concept of "parallel process" dates back to the 1980s. The term refers to an unconscious shift in behaviours and feelings that may take place during therapeutic and supervision relationships and is an unconscious repetition of relational patterns from meaningful primary relationships (Cassoni, 2007). These patterns provide a blueprint that is unconsciously transferred from former to current relationships.

Moreover, such a pattern can influence the other in the relationship to such an extent that he becomes involved in the repetition. This also applies to the (counter)transference in a therapy situation, but is much broader than that and plays a role in any meaningful relationship, including supervision relationships.

Searles (1956) first used the term "reflexive process" for supervision, where a correlation arises between two relational systems so that the supervisor becomes for the supervisee what the supervisee/therapist is for the client. Thus a situation can arise whereby during supervision a supervisee plays out the helpless, dependent, or demanding behaviour of the client and the supervisor feels tempted to either "save" or "persecute".

Doehrman (1976) found in her research that there is always a form of parallel process between a supervisor and a supervisee because of the subtlety of transference and countertransference. It is important that the supervisor is very attentive to the way the supervisee presents the client's issues and his relationship with the client. If the parallel process is not clearly identified and worked through, both the relationship between the supervisee and client as well as the relationship between the supervisor and the supervisee are endangered.

10.2.3 The comparative script system

The comparative script system provides a framework for organising the large amount of facts and the diverse and extensive data that emerge in the supervisory process. Initial experiences and events from the past and the meaning that the person has given to them continue to work in current patterns of thinking, feeling, and behaviour (Lapworth, Sills, & Fish, 2001; Sills & Salters, 1991; Sills & Mazzetti, 2009). Thus, the dynamics of the script can be mapped and it becomes clear how past and present interlock.

> For example, as a child, Ben was often read to by his father who taught him how to read when they were together on the couch (A). This early experience led to the conclusion that learning is fun, that the world is a fascinating place in which to explore all sorts of things and that others can help him in this (B). He loves studying and derives pleasure from it (C). He becomes a teacher and passes his knowledge on to others (D).

> Another example: During therapy, Heidi speaks with a monotonous and flat tone (D), and describes her life as empty, boring, and not worth bothering about (C). Susan, the therapist, begins to feel flat, empty, and lifeless. From Heidi's background story it is revealed that her mother was depressed after childbirth and would sit motionless for hours or would lie in bed and barely gave Heidi any attention or care (A). From childhood, Heidi experienced life as a desert, empty and flat (B).

In a professional relationship, the script systems of the client and the professional meet. This becomes clear by slightly rotating and mirroring the diagram of the comparative script system.

In the therapeutic relationship, patterns of behaviour (D) and thinking/feeling (C) of both the client and professional/supervisee become clear. The background of the behaviour, thoughts, and feelings of the client (initial experiences (A) and attributing meaning (B)) is part of the therapy of the client and relevant to the supervision. Initial experiences (A) and meaning attribution (B) of the therapist/supervisee are mainly discussed during the professional therapy of the supervisee, and only in a limited amount during supervision.

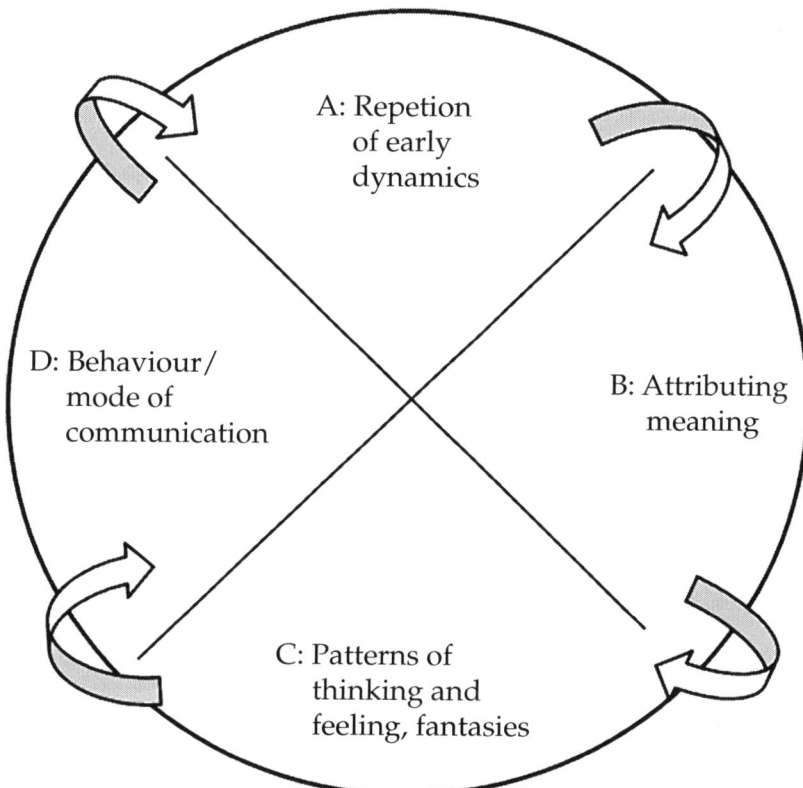

Figure 10.3. The comparative script system.

A beginning therapist who is just entering into supervision is often primarily engaged in asking the client questions (DD) and in her own internal dialogue "Am I doing this right?" A more experienced therapist may realise, to her surprise, that a particular new client makes her anxious and that this has to do with the question of the client "Doctor, will I get better with this treatment?" (D), and the underlying plea "Look after me!" (C). As the supervision progresses it may become clear that the client has an underlying symbiotic need, based on early experiences (A) with injunctions such as "Don't grow up", "Don't be healthy", and "Don't think" (B). At the same time, the supervisee's anxiety at the symbiotic need of the client also references her own early experiences (A) and decisions (B). The supervisee can discuss these past experiences in a limited manner during supervision, or, if it concerns a more elaborate script theme of the supervisee, during her own personal therapy.

> Heidi's therapist, who is beginning to feel flat and lifeless during the therapy sessions, explains the situation to her supervision group. The supervisor asks the other supervisees from the group to share the feelings and images that are evoked by this story with each other. Gradually the therapist feels a great sorrow for her client, which she will discuss with her client in the following therapy session. She also realises that this touches on her own history with a sick, absent mother.

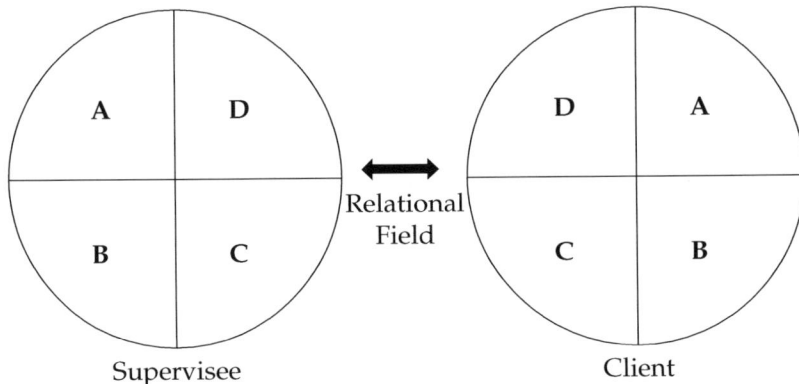

Figure 10.4. The comparative script systems of the client and supervisee.

Thus, the comparative script system is a tool that can be used to chart the relational field between the supervisee and client as well as between the supervisor and supervisee. It helps in making the boundary between supervision and therapy clear, as well as clarifying which themes belong in supervision and which are better to be dealt with during the supervisee's personal therapy.

10.3 Furthermore

10.3.1 From unconsciously incompetent to unconsciously competent

Newton and Napper (2007) describe the process of unconscious incompetence to unconscious competence. If you start in a specific work setting, you're often not aware of what you cannot do and cannot know (unconsciously incompetent). Subsequently, as you become more aware of the complexities of the tasks, you begin to feel insecure and uncertain (consciously incompetent). Then you start to apply your knowledge and to do the work according to the given rules and agreements (consciously competent). Finally, you are able to do the work using creativity and knowledge without constantly wondering what you're doing or how it should be done (unconsciously competent).

Newton and Napper's description is consistent with the competency curve with which Hay (1993) visualised the learning process that a learner goes through. Hay states that every learner needs a (short) period to experience what happens in a new situation before being able to proceed to action. Supervision offers this reflection space in order to become aware of what is required in new situations and how this aligns with the insights and behaviours gained so far.

In a process of learning and development, such as supervision, which is intended to stimulate, people go through a number of recognisable phases (Hay, 1993).

1. *Rigidity*. People need time to become aware of a change. The discovery of falling short in one or more fields and not yet being able to satisfy the requirements of the job is often quite

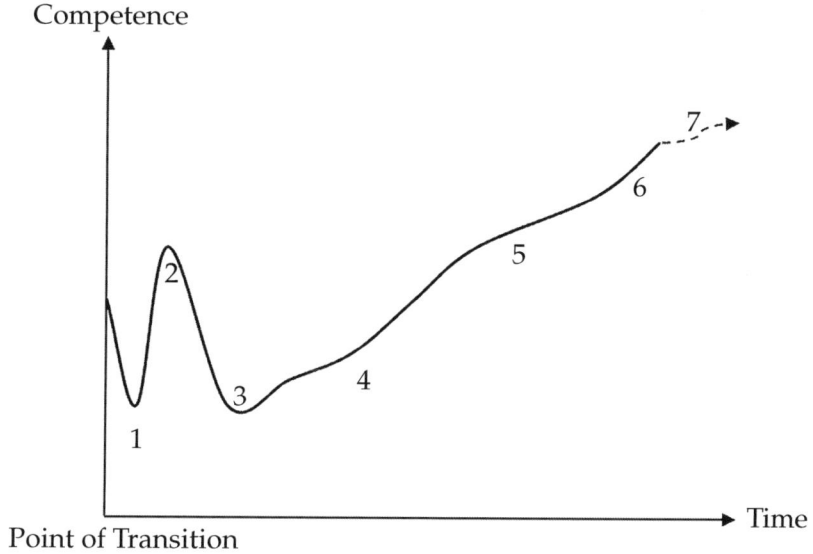

Figure 10.5. Competence curve.

confronting. Simmering for a while in the position of not knowing what and how and being aware of one's fear of an unfamiliar area of knowledge or skill-set can make you stay still for quite some time, as if you are in parking mode.
2. *Denial.* Once in motion again, you work as if the moment before awareness is still applicable. You often cling on to the (script-based) approach that used to work so well for you in the past. This somewhat defensive attitude, while allowing you to carefully experiment with new insights, eventually lets you down slowly but surely.
3. *Frustration.* In every process of change and development there is a phase of frustration. You understand that things should be different, but you're not yet able to practice this at an adequately competent level. This contributes to a growing feeling that you're falling short. The fear that others, including clients, will not accept your new approach, often adds to the frustration.
4. *Acceptance.* By continuing to practise you will dare to let go of old (script) convictions and their associated behaviour. You derive pleasure from experimentation and its results. You experience that the current way of working is more successful than that of the past. A new framework is in the making.
5. *Development.* Now you're in momentum. You focus on acquired knowledge and the new skills that are required. The experience of being competent in your "new world" feeds your self-confidence.
6. *Application.* In this phase, you do everything to consolidate your identity in the new role. Your role and task have become clear in relation to those of others. You get your own insight into new possibilities within the whole of the reality in which you work.
7. *Completion.* Once again you feel competent and at ease. The "pain" of change is forgotten. Life and work are now good.

10.3.2 Supervision as meta-modality

Van Beekum (2007) notes that a shift is visible within the theory and practice of supervision. Previously, the emphasis in supervision was more on what he calls (self)research. Supervision was primarily a means to make the growth and development of the supervisee possible. This concerned traditional supervision questions such as "Do you work with and adhere to a contract?" and "Have the core themes been adequately identified and examined?" or "Has the possibility of damage been reduced?". Van Beekum seems—by emphasising the difference between supervision of individual/personal work and supervision of working in and with organisations/systems—to be searching for ways to use supervision as an intervention. Supervision is then not a tool for further professional development but a necessity for working effectively within broader social contexts. In Chapter Five, we investigated the relationship between the personal and the organisational script. We stated that those who enter an organisation need to take into account that the organisation also enters into them, influenced both consciously and unconsciously by the canon and scripts of the organisation. With supervision, the significance of this is examined and brought back to the organisation in question.

Van Beekum (2007) outlines an historical perspective on the evolution of supervision practices. When Freud presented a new approach to "mental instability" at the beginning of the last century, he did so from his professional context (Freud was a doctor) and as a child of his time. Freud's approach was centred in the idea that the doctor knows what is good for you. The more humanistic approaches, around the middle of the last century, including people like Rogers and Maslow, seemed at odds with this more authoritarian model. In TA the notion that "the power is in the patient" (Goulding & Goulding, 1978) became popular. By the end of the last century and to this day, a more systemic and psychodynamic approach has come to the forefront (Senge, 1990). This approach revolves around two central ideas: "Everything is related to everything" and "No one is to blame, everyone is responsible". Here we have a more holistic relational approach according to which the development of the supervisee is part of the systemic context in which she works. It is also precisely about the development and growth of the client system in which he works.

Van Beekum sees, on the basis of this historical survey and analysis, that the practice of supervision allows for four approaches. Each approach is founded on a personal view of the helping relationship between the professional and client.

1. *Contractual approach*. This concerns the result of the supervision itself. The supervisor and the supervisee work together on the agreed learning goal of the supervisee. The development of the supervisee is central.
2. *"Open space" approach*. A contract is seen as a potential obstacle in the way of new or unexpected discoveries. The supervisor and the supervisee use supervision as a (open) research area. What comes to the surface during this research? What is the significance of this for the supervisee and her client (system)?
3. *Role-analysis approach*. This concerns the role that the client selects within the specific social context. The interaction between the role, the person, and the system is focus in this approach. The more clarity the supervisee has about how she as a person can assume a specific role within the system in which she intervenes, the more the client benefits from the interventions.

4. *Relational approach.* Here, the transference from the supervisee to the supervisor is an important phenomenon, as well as the countertransference on the part of the supervisor. It is this approach, in Van Beekum's opinion, that challenges supervisors to come down from their ivory tower and to not only examine their countertransference and its significance within their own supervision but also within the supervision-relationship with their supervisee.

10.4   Related theories

10.4.1 Phases in training and supervision

In the following overview (Table 10.1) the different phases in the learning process in training and supervision have been summarised, whereby the supervisor or trainer assumes a different role in each phase, until finally an amicable, cooperative relationship develops (Loria, 1983; Watkins, 1994).

Table 10.1. Phases in training and supervision.

	Learning process	*Training*	*Supervision*	*Role of supervisor/ trainer*
1	Role shock: knowledge	Development of skills in the areas of concepts and interventions; development of trust in the skills one already has.	Openness to listen to the struggles of the trainee; avoiding deep analysis and strong confrontations; permission to be and to belong (in the group).	Keeping it together, stabilising, supporting as a guide, teacher, and leader.
2	Role recovery: transition; insight and understanding	Stimulating independent thoughts and performing own interventions; practice and presentation of theory; permission to do research and to think.	Deeper research of the feelings of the trainee; learning to better recognise process themes and learning how to deal with them.	Stimulating awareness, facilitating mild confrontations.
3	Role consolidation: applying and demonstrating	Using a combination of concepts, cognitive skills, interventions and ethical values; starting with the case study, situation presentation and treatment planning.	Analysis of (counter) transference & parallel processes; how do these influence efficiency? Permission to be different and important.	Amicable consultant, focus on the exchange between personal and professional themes.
4	Role mastery: integration and separation	Offering alternative concepts: challenging all aspects of concepts and interventions of the supervisee; working with other trainers and exam preparation.	More intensive process-analysis; high level of confrontation is possible, the supervisee develops her own professional support system; permission to be separate and different.	Working together, amicable, supporting, and challenging.

274   INTO TA

10.4.2 Situational leadership as a model for supervision

Hersey and Blanchard (1969) presented their model of situational leadership. Within this view, it is the main task of managers to influence others in such a way that their ability to tackle independent tasks increases. The manager in this model has two lines along which she achieves this goal. She can (and will) be task-oriented and relationship-oriented in her work with the employees.

Characteristic of more task-oriented or directing leadership is the focus on the end goal and the execution of the task. The manager sets the goals and objectives, plans and organises the work, prioritises, determines which working methods are to be followed, how monitoring and evaluation will take place, and closely monitors the progress.

If the manager works more in terms of relationships or support, then the emphasis is on the interrelationship. The manager encourages, affirms, praises, listens actively, asks for suggestions and ideas, encourages independent problem solving, makes information accessible, encourages teamwork, and dares to be vulnerable. You could say that it is the same in the working relationship between a supervisor and supervisee.

Just as for the manager, the supervisor's goal is to influence his supervisee in such a way that she is able to take on tasks independently. Hersey and Blanchard show that in order to

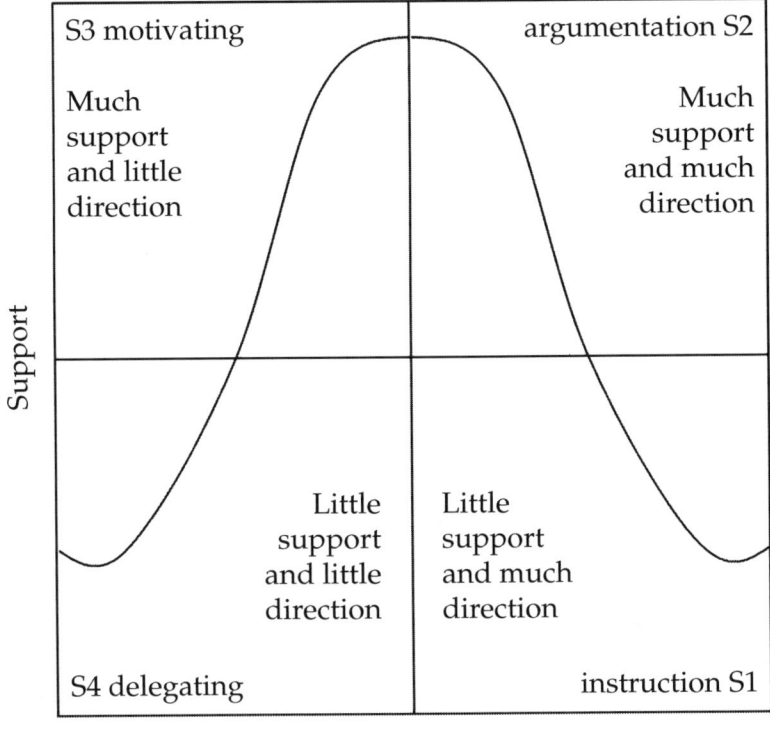

Figure 10.6. Situational leadership.

achieve this goal, a manager will have to always select a different style of leadership, based on an accurate assessment of what is necessary for a particular employee. Figure 10.6 shows the four styles (phases) of leadership (Nijs, 2007).

This corresponds with the growing competence of the supervisee.

- In phase 1, the supervisee is incompetent as well as unmotivated or uncertain. The supervisee stands at the beginning of a professional career and is in need of knowledge and skills from the instructional role of the supervisor.
- In phase 2, the supervisee is incompetent but motivated and confident. The supervisee still does not have much knowledge but she does have enthusiasm. The danger is that the supervisee may run too fast. The supervisor sometimes needs to slow down and steer the supervisee.
- In phase 3, the supervisee is competent but unmotivated or uncertain. The supervisee has already learned a lot but is therefore more aware of all that she does not yet know. This can lead to uncertainty. In this phase, the supervisor must not react with directions, but rather with support towards the independent functioning of the supervisee.
- In phase 4, the supervisee is skilled and also motivated and confident. The supervisor takes on the role of the more experienced colleague and may delegate duties from this position.

The work of the supervisor, who has the independence (autonomy) of the supervisee in mind, may also develop along this line. The supervision of the beginning professional will still have a strong advisory nature. But by the time the supervision can be terminated, the supervisor will leave more of the work to the supervisee.

References

Beekum, S. van (2007). Supervision as metamodality and a multiarea activity. *Transactional Analysis Journal*, 27(2): 140–149.
Berne, E. (1968). Staff-patient staff conferences. In: M. James (Ed.), *Techniques in Transactional Analysis for Psychotherapists and Counsellors* (pp. 153–164). Reading, PA: Addison-Wesley, 1977.
Cassoni, E. (2007). Parallel process in supervision and therapy: An opportunity for reciprocity. *Transactional Analysis Journal*, 37(2): 130–139.
Clarkson, P. (1992). Training, supervision and work. In: *Transactional Analysis Psychotherapy. An Integrated Approach*. London: Tavistock/Routledge.
Clarkson, P., & Leigh, E. (1992). Integrating intuitive functioning with treatment planning in supervision. *Transactional Analysis Journal*, 23(4): 222–227.
Cornell, W. F., Shadbolt, C., & Norton, R. (2007). Live and in limbo: A case study of an in-person transactional analysis consultation. *Transactional Analysis Journal*, 27(2): 159–171.
Doehrman, M. J. (1976). Parallel processes in supervision and psychotherapy. *Bulletin of the Menninger Clinic*, 40: 3–104.
Erskine, R. (1982). Supervision of psychotherapy. *Transactional Analysis Journal*, 12(4): 314–321.
Eusden, S. (2011). Minding the gap: Ethical considerations for therapeutic engagement. *Transactional Analysis Journal*, 41(2): 101–113.
Gobes, L. (1993). C4 P4: A consultation checklist. *Transactional Analysis Journal*, 23(1): 42–44.
Goulding, R., & Goulding, M. (1978). *The Power Is in the Patient*. San Francisco, CA: TA Press.

Hay, J. (1993). *Working It Out at Work. Understanding Attitudes and Building Relationships*. Watford, UK: Sherwood.

Hay, J. (2007). *Reflective Practice and Supervision for Coaches*. London: Open University Press.

Hersey, P., & Blanchard, K. H. (1969). *Management of Organizational Behavior: Utilizing Human Resources*. Upper Saddle River, NJ: Prentice Hall.

Kadushin, A. (1992). *Supervision in Social Work (3rd edition)*. New York: Columbia University Press.

Lapworth, P., Sills, C., & Fish, S. (2001). *Integration in Counselling and Psychotherapy. Finding a Personal Approach*. London: Sage.

Loria, B. (1983). Beyond training: The education of transactional analysts. *Transactional Analysis Journal*, 13(3): 134–141.

Mazzetti, M. (2007). Supervision in transactional analysis: An operational model. *Transactional Analysis Journal*, 37(2): 93–103.

Newton, T. (2012). The supervision triangle: An integrating model. *Transactional Analysis Journal*, 42(2): 103–109.

Newton, T., & Napper, R. (2007). The bigger picture: Supervision as an educational framework for all fields. *Transactional Analysis Journal*, 37(3): 150–158.

Nijs, M. (2007). *Situationeel leidinggeven; gedrag van de leider—competentie van de medewerker*. (Situational Leadership: Behaviour of the Leader—Competency of the Employee.) [Workshop, GGZ Westelijk Noord-Brabant, Netherlands.]

Searles, H. (1979). *Countertransference and Related Subjects*. Madison, WI: International Universities Press.

Senge, P. M. (1990). *The Fifth Discipline: The Art and Practice of the Learning Organisation*. New York: Doubleday Currency.

Shohet, R., & Hawkins, P. (1989). *Supervision in the Helping Professions*. Maidenhead, UK: Open University Press.

Sills, C., & Mazzetti, M. (2009). The comparative script system. A tool for developing supervisors. *Transactional Analysis Journal*, 19(4): 305–314.

Sills, C., & Salters, D. (1991). The comparative script system. *ITA News*, 31: 1–15.

Stewart, I. (1992). *Supervision Models*. Training Endorsement Workshop, Brighton (unpublished).

Tudor, K. (2002). Transactional analysis supervision or supervision analyzed transactionally? *Transactional Analysis Journal*, 32(1): 39–55.

Watkins, C. E. (1994). The supervision of psychotherapy supervisor trainees. *American Journal of Psychotherapy*, 48(3): 417–431.

Zalcman, M. J., & Cornell, W. F. (1983). A bilateral model for clinical supervision. *Transactional Analysis Journal*, 13(2): 112–123.

PART II

PRACTICE

CHAPTER ELEVEN

Psychotherapy

11.1. How do we get there from here? Modes of intervention in TA
11.2. Countertransference as a pathway to understanding script
11.3. Depression
11.4. The redecision analysis of transference formula: combining a transactional analysis and a psychoanalytic perspective
11.5. Transactional analysis in a hospital setting with patients with personality disorders

Professionals working in the field of psychotherapy help their clients to (re)gain their capacity for self-actualisation, healing, and change. The aim is to work together with the client to detect old (self-)limiting patterns and foster change. The goal is that clients understand themselves and their relationship patterns and create options to live more autonomous and satisfying lives.

The *Handbook for TA Training and TA Certification* describes the core competencies for this field. See www.itaaworld.org/itaa-training-examinations-handbook.

Clients may choose (or be referred to) psychotherapy because they have become troubled and are suffering from fears, depression, personality problems, addictions, phobias, and/or compulsions, which interfere with the quality of life, and their problem solving capacities.

11.1. How do we get there from here? Modes of intervention in TA

William Cornell

11.1.1. Introduction

Central to the work of a TA psychotherapist are the techniques and procedures to facilitate self-awareness and change in the enactment of games and scripts.

In Berne's theory of games (1964), he made distinctions between what he called "first, second, and third degree" games, which can also be applied to the understanding of the enactments of script-based beliefs and behaviours. By "first degree" Berne was referring to defensive patterns that were reasonably available to conscious awareness and cognitive change. Berne characterised therapy at this level as serving a "social" function, which is to say, to make relationships more predictable. "Second degree" games and scripts serve defensive purposes that are often outside conscious awareness and control. Here, as we have described earlier in this book, Berne saw a split between one level of communication that is conscious and another, more psychologically significant level, that is unconscious. "Second degree" games are seen as serving a more fundamental psychological rather than social function. "Third degree" games and script were characterised by Berne as held and lived at the "tissue" level, by which he meant at the level of the body rather than the mind. Berne himself was rather pessimistic about the potential of psychotherapy to make a significant difference in defence at the third degree, tissue level. One of the main advances in transactional analysis psychotherapy and counselling in recent decades is to develop effective treatment styles for third degree games and scripts.

11.1.2. Different interventions for different degrees of games

With his model of delineating the degrees and levels of defensive functioning, Berne gave transactional analytic practitioners a structure for differentiating the appropriate styles of intervention.

First degree defences are typically worked with through cognitive and behavioural interventions designed to assist clients in developing a broader and more flexible set of problem solving skills.

The primary focus of therapeutic work with second degree defences is to identify the unconscious psychological aims of the ulterior transactions and bring them into conscious awareness and choice. This focus is quite consistent with the fundamental psychoanalytic process of making the unconscious conscious. Berne was an innovator of a model for group treatment, seeing work in groups as the ideal means to address games and scripts that were enacted at a second degree level. In the group interactions, the therapist was able to observe and describe the repeated, typically unconscious patterns of interaction. Berne thought that the diversity among group members increased anxiety and the likelihood of a more rapid emergence of game and script patterns. In Berne's model the therapist was an outside observer to the actions and interactions that were played out among the group members. Whether or not the treatment was carried out in a group, the focus of the therapist's attention was on developing a more conscious understanding of the motivations for one's games. In Berne's time, this was seen as strengthening the Adult ego state's capacity for objectivity and more conscious decision-making. In contemporary language, we would describe work at the second degree level as developing the capacity for self-reflection and mentalisation. Today much of this therapeutic work is likely to be done in individual psychotherapy with the second degree dynamics addressed through the understanding of internal object relations and the analysis of transference and countertransference.

Berne never elaborated treatment styles for psychological problems held and enacted at the third degree, "tissue" level that are fundamentally unconscious. Since Berne's death, coming to understand and work effectively with these issues has been at the leading edge of developments in TA theory and techniques. While Freud (and Berne) saw the work of therapy as that of making unconscious experience conscious, therapeutic work at the third degree level probably comes closer to what Christopher Bollas (1992) has described as the work of the therapist opening conscious awareness to the depth and vitality of unconscious realms of experience. In efforts to work more successfully at the "tissue" level of psychic organisation, defence, and pain, some transactional analysts have developed much more systematic models of working within the transference/countertransference matrix.

Some have developed models of working with trauma at both the interpersonal and bodily levels (Cornell & Landaiche, 2007; Goodman, 2007; Ligabue, 2007). Others have addressed working with bodily trauma and dissociative defences (Novak, 2013; Stuthridge, 2006, 2012). The past decade has witnessed the evolution of a relational model of transactional analysis (Fowlie & Sills, 2011; Hargaden & Sills, 2002; Zvelc, 2010), and there has been growing interest in incorporating therapeutic interventions at a somatic level (Banks, 2013; Caizzi, 2012; Cornell, 2010; Joseph, 2010).

11.1.3. Different games at different stages

11.1.4. First degree games; exploration

Since Berne's death, clinical theory in TA has come to understand that different aspects of one's games and scripts may be formed, consolidated, and then enacted at these distinct levels of psychic organisation. It is not unusual for a client to enter treatment to address difficulties at the conscious, first degree level. As therapy proceeds many clients become aware of more underlying, unconscious and entrenched patterns of belief and behaviour, organised at second and third degree levels. As a result of this awareness, TA psychotherapists are trained in a range of skills from cognitive/behavioural and psychodynamic to relational and somatic.

I will offer here an example of a somewhat fictional client, case material that is an amalgam of issues unfolding across the flow of a day and over the years. Sean, as he is presented here is fictional, but the course of this treatment is not.

Sean entered psychotherapy for the first time in his late thirties. Although successful in his career, he had been troubled for quite some time by his difficulty in sustaining close, personal relationships. He had read a number of "self-help" books in an effort to figure things out by himself. In his search he came across a popular introduction to transactional analysis, *TA Today* (Stewart & Joines, 1987). In it he found a way to begin thinking about himself more clearly, and a practical model that appealed to him. He sought me out as a TA therapist.

The initial focus of his attention, and our contract, was to learn to talk more openly to his girlfriend of several years and decide if he wanted to marry her (she wanted to marry him). There was little direct conflict within their relationship; when difficulties arose, they were typically managed through quiet withdrawal by both of them. Sean found talking openly with me difficult as well and it was the source of considerable anxiety. It was not unusual for him to suggest separating sessions by two or three weeks. I saw here the beginnings of a transference relationship that I was sure mirrored his difficulties in many of his personal relationships, but I thought it premature to draw attention to this. So we continued with the stated contract, working at the first degree level by exploring how he could begin to broach difficult topics with his partner more effectively. He wanted to talk to his girlfriend; we would plan and strategise how he could begin saying all that he wanted to say, but somehow he never got his mouth open. As we pursued it, Sean became increasingly aware of how incredibly anxious it made him. It became clear that we needed to shift the focus of our attention and our working contract.

11.1.5. Second degree games, avoidance, and ambivalence

I began to enquire about his childhood and his experience of life in his family of origin. While he was quite close to his siblings, he had virtually cut off his parents. His cutting off was not hostile, but it was avoidant and thorough. Other than the Christmas holiday, he always had convincing excuses readily at hand as to why he could not make it to other family gatherings. He described his mother as passive and beleaguered by life. He said his father was distant, rather critical, and could be downright mean—focusing his nasty outbursts on his wife rather than his children. As Sean talked about his parents, he got his first glimpse into a childhood script-based fear that if he married, "I might turn into my Dad." By staying "just a boyfriend", Sean felt he could give his partner her independence but if he became her husband, he feared he would become "a controlling prick". With this recognition, Sean and I both accepted that his emotional waters were more troubled and turbulent than he had realised. As a teenager, often flying into adolescent rages himself, he feared that he was becoming a version of his father. His quiet but persistent distance from the people in his life was unconsciously designed to protect them from him and the qualities he feared in himself.

He wanted very much to be a father, but he feared the kind of father he might become. Time was running out. As my own father had been very distant, I felt a certain identification with Sean and recalled when as a younger man myself how much I wanted to be a father and how ill-equipped I felt for the task. I kept this identification to myself, but it keenly informed me about Sean's ambivalence and avoidance. In contrast to his fears of becoming some kind of intolerant, demanding monster to those he loved, I felt a deep regard for his integrity and his willingness to examine himself. He had come into therapy taking account for his problems, not blaming them on his girlfriend or others. Sean and I were now squarely in the terrain of the transference/countertransference matrix. I decided to speak directly to Sean about the contradiction I experienced between his projected image of himself as turning into a controlling bastard and my own experience of his being thoughtful, caring, and responsible towards those around him. This observation brought tears of relief, followed by fury at his father.

11.1.6. Second degree games, working in the (counter)transference relationship

As we continued working, I felt deepening paternal feelings towards Sean and a growing affection for him. I kept these feelings to myself, but I knew they were in the room with us and that they registered in Sean. One day he quietly said to me, "Ya know, I think you actually look forward to seeing me, like you might even like me." I needed only to smile in response. It became more and more real and reliable to Sean that as he talked with me more and more openly, he felt better about himself, and we became closer. He could now see that talking more openly to his girlfriend and friends could actually draw them closer. The gradual changes he was making in how he was bringing himself towards his girlfriend and friends were welcomed by those around him.

He wrestled with the distance he kept from his parents, but as he grew more aware of how angry he was towards them, especially his father, he felt a need to maintain the distance. I made the mistake of suggesting that he didn't need to keep such distance, that perhaps his parents would also welcome his new openness. Sean fell silent. He went cold. I knew I had made a mistake. I had forgotten his childhood decision to use distance as a way of protecting those around him—which, of course, included his parents. I knew I had made a mistake, but in the moment I couldn't find a way to recover from it and speak to it. As I anticipated the next session, I thought I would start with an apology for my error in the previous session. But Sean walked in and began talking as though there was absolutely nothing wrong. In my confusion, I fell silent. As I listened to Sean, I began to realise that his talking was empty. He was carefully holding me at a distance. Here we were living out the script together. I took a deep breath and said that it seemed to me that he was talking to me in a different way this session than we had been able to talk together for quite some time. I wondered if he noticed this and wondered if it might have some connection to the previous session. Sean stopped. And then he blew up, "You were out of your fucking mind last week. What a stupid fucking thing you said. Don't you get it, you stupid fuck! If I talked openly to my parents, my Dad would blow. And he wouldn't blow at me. *Were you listening?!* He'd blow at my Mom. She'd suffer, not me, and he wouldn't learn a thing. All this time, and you just don't fucking get it." His fury went on for quite some time.

To my surprise, I felt neither frightened nor ashamed. I felt excited and touched by his rage. I could literally see the struggle in his body—his voice breaking, his throat tightening, his shoulders freezing. I listened, and I waited. Gradually he became quiet again, and then he apologised.

"The last thing I need from you is an apology, Sean. You're right. I did forget and I fucked up last week." He began to reach towards me, and then he froze. He pulled back. Now we were at the "tissue" level—the struggle was alive in his body in this moment. Of course, I wasn't thinking this at the time, but my own body was stirred and alive in the moment as well. *I* moved towards *him* and placed my hand on his tense shoulder. It was not my intention to offer comfort but rather to use touch to bring attention to the tension and holding back in his shoulders. I was offering a form of non-verbal communication.

Sean's shoulders relaxed a bit, and he reached his hand to mine, clasping his hand over mine. Looking at me, he began to weep and fold into my arms. He wept the tears he could never bring to his father. He stayed in my arms and talked of his lifelong yearning for his father's company and interest. And he spoke, tears flowing, of his determination to become a father himself. If he got into trouble, he now knew how to ask for help.

11.1.7. Conclusion

This story of Sean illustrates the range of therapeutic interventions that are possible over the course of psychotherapy within a transactional analysis model. The theoretical differentiation of different levels of psychological and interpersonal organisation provides a structure within which the professional can observe and assess patterns of a client's way of being and then find the most appropriate style of intervention. In my work as a psychotherapist and as a trainer and supervisor of psychotherapists and counsellors, this is one of the greatest assets of transactional analysis theory and practice.

11.2. Countertransference as a pathway to understanding script

Jo Stuthridge

11.2.1. Introduction

Erin was a woman in her mid-thirties who lived alone and struggled with depression and overeating. Her face was screwed up in an expression of anguish and she seemed sunk in a feeling of irritable hopelessness. She scowled at the carpet as she told me about the day's events. In a familiar whining tone, she complained about her manager's lack of support for her, "She could have said something … anything … like 'Well done Erin,' that wouldn't be so difficult. Oh … it's just the same … nothing changes … ." Erin's high-pitched whine trailed off into tears. There was a long sigh, then she said, "I feel like leaving … I just want to go …"

This was the place we arrived at over and over—a state of helpless frustration and despair. I wanted to block my ears, to shut out the relentless wailing sound. Thoughts like, "I wish the session was over too" flirted at the edge of my awareness, marginally fenced off by guilt. My mind drifted towards plans for dinner … I was hungry.

In the past these thoughts would not have been allowed in. They would have been stopped at the gates of consciousness by my own script and my early TA training. I might have moved swiftly in a moment like this to relieve Erin's suffering (but mostly my own) by pulling up another chair and cajoling redecisions from her Child ego state; or maybe I would sit up straight and launch rational appeals to her Adult ego state; or perhaps confront her critical Parent messages. I was taught to look within the client for answers, while today I often look within myself, relying on my countertransference experience to understand what is going on. My focus has shifted from enquiry into the client's intrapsychic world and past experience to the immediacy of the relational dynamics between us. I have learned to listen for unconscious patterns as well as conscious. I feel less urgency to make clients feel better and more willingness to bear pain.

My thinking is still grounded in classical script theory, however my methods diverge from Berne's (1961) objective analysis of games and script. Transactional analysis provides me with a theory that is both intrapsychic and profoundly interpersonal. The model sits easily alongside a contemporary relational style of therapy that sees the therapist as a player in the action, rather than an onlooker. Relational methods within TA have developed in various ways (Fowlie & Sills, 2011; Hargaden & Sills, 2002). I use the term "relational" to refer to an approach that views the mind as continually constructed from transactional experience, in which the therapist uses her participation in enacted game and script patterns to understand the client. Berne's (1961) notion of script provides an excellent metaphor for thinking about therapy as a live interactive performance involving two subjects in the theatre of the consulting room.

11.2.2. Script: a transference drama

Script theory describes how we unconsciously repeat unresolved issues through transference, turning our lives into dramas with predestined endings: "Scripts belong in the realm of transference phenomena, that is, they are derivatives, or more precisely adaptations, of infantile reactions and experiences" (Berne, 1961, p. 117). Berne depicted script as "an ongoing drama that is actually taking place right now, divided into scenes and acts (1972, p. 58). He had a feel for dramatic irony, and his theory drew on Aristotelian principles of Greek tragedy. Script decisions are defensive attempts to avoid wounds from childhood but inevitably lead us to repeat the old trauma. In a therapy relationship, most clients begin consciously wanting change but unconsciously organise the relationship to replay the script. The client who expects betrayal will eventually feel betrayed. The client who expects to be exploited will invariably feel used.

Berne, in keeping with mainstream thinking at the time, believed it was possible to remain outside the transference by detecting the client's provocations to games. He analysed scripts by observing from the audience seats, rather than accepting an invitation to join the stage, which he would have viewed as a countertransference error (1972, p. 352). This approach works well in the analysis of conscious or preconscious cognitive process but is less effective for analysing unconscious script processes.

Relational analysts (Harris, 2009; Mitchell, 1997; Stern, 2010) argue that we are never outside transference but that transferences are always present in shifting forms. Mitchell (1997, p. 182) compared countertransference to "weather" since it is a constant presence, not something that occurs on occasions like rain. From this perspective the therapist's involvement in the drama is considered inevitable and perhaps necessary to understanding the client's unconscious communication.

I find myself recruited to play shifting character roles, but always on the stage, not off. From the hundreds of possible relational configurations within me, the client will inevitably evoke the precise emotional nuance needed for the role in his or her script. These feelings belong to me, with origins in my script but are uniquely elicited by each client. In my work with Erin my emotional experience or countertransference eventually offered clues to the drama being replayed between us and her underlying script.

Erin

The scene I described above had occurred many times in our work, often with an implied threat that she might walk out of a session at any moment, quit the therapy, or even quit life in suicidal moods. These scenes might be understood as escalating degrees of the same underlying game pattern (Berne, 1964, p. 64). She often ended sessions angrily, leaving me feeling inept. In this particular session something different happened.

Once I noticed my reactions I became curious. What was going on between us? I began to think of Erin's complaint about her manager as a transferential transaction (Novellino, 1990). I imagined it was me she was angry with and me whom she wanted something from, in the same way she had desperately begged her mother to notice her feelings as a child.

JO: "Do you recognise that feeling with Ann (her manager)—maybe it feels the same with me?

ERIN: "Yes … I know that feeling … I know it's the running race and the laundry and the story of my whole life!"

Erin was referring to moments when her mother harshly refused to acknowledge her presence, either her successes or her tears.

ERIN: "Why can't I get past this? Arrgh … ." (She wrung her hands and her voice rose in pitch.) "So it's all over to me again … I have to figure it out on my own … that's the same as it always is … It's no different here than everywhere else …" (the angry whine rose to a crescendo, imploring me to do something, make it better …).

I felt that Erin understood my comment but ignored it somehow. My irritation climbed in unison with Erin's lament, "If only she would stop the whining …"

Instead of dismissing this thought I began to wonder what it might mean. Did her mother feel exasperated with this clamouring baby?

I noticed how much Erin's voice grated and it occurred to me that my escape fantasies might be an unconscious attempt to avoid the sound of my own detested needy-baby-self. I knew this feeling of contempt and I wondered if Erin hated or feared this part of herself? Was she trying to get away from the hungry baby? There was a shift in my state of mind as irritation gave way to curiosity and compassion. I think Erin picked up on the shift between us although no words were spoken.

Erin paused, "I'm doing it here now, aren't I?"

J: "Yes, I think you are. I think you might be feeling 'Jo never gives me anything—why can't she just tell me how well I'm doing?'"

E: "I do! Why can't you just throw me a bone?"

J: "Because you deserve more than bones. I won't feed you scraps."

E: "I know you don't do that and I know it doesn't work when anyone does say something nice …. It's like a drop in the ocean … it goes nowhere. (Pause) Oh I think I'm finally getting it … It's like I keep trying to get something from you and everyone else and I just get stuck in the same old bitter feeling. It's like with mum, trying to get blood from a stone. (Pause) … You must wish you had never agreed to start with me." (Berne might have considered this last line a con and confronted the client whereas I stayed within the transference.)

J: "Perhaps you're afraid of being too much for me, like you felt too much for mum?"

E: (In a small voice) "I am always afraid you'll leave, because you've had enough of me."

J: "Maybe you were a little kid that scavenged for scraps of human warmth … and there is something unbearably sad about that. Perhaps you didn't get enough. (These words emerge slowly as I begin to sit with the sadness.) I wonder if you are still scavenging, trying to get what you can, to stop me leaving?"

Erin shifted gears quite suddenly and told me about the auditor's visit to her work that day, as if I had said nothing.

J: "Hold on, you just changed the subject. It's like you moved away from me."
E: "I can't stay with that ... I have to get rid of it ... it's too much."
J: "You mean the sadness is too much?"

Erin nodded and a quiet calm enveloped the room while tears began to spill down her face, falling softly between us. Her sorrow was palpable and painful but it seemed we both could bear it.

After a time, we talked about her recurrent attempts to extract caring from others, including me, which typically left her feeling lonely, resentful and rejected, repeating the script, instead of grieving for the little girl who was emotionally starved.

At the end of the session, Erin noted how different she felt and recognised how close she came to going down the same old path of sulky hurt and anger, "... like going down the path to eat worms. I could have opened a big can and scoffed the lot!" We shared a laugh and there was a tender feel to our parting. I was reminded of Berne's comments about laughter as a signal of insight (1972, p. 338).

11.2.3. Countertransference as a pathway to understanding script

I think of script analysis involving two primary tasks: first I have to discover what role I'm playing in a client's script; then I have to find a way out of the drama. The first part involves listening to countertransference feelings and finding links with the client's story. This usually comes as a surprise as it did with Erin and often involves feelings that are difficult to own such as shame, sadness, or hostility. Ogden (1994) described in vivid detail how unconscious elements of countertransference can be accessed through the therapist's free floating associations and bodily sensations. I've learned that seemingly irrelevant thoughts can provide precious clues and my countertransference is often the most accurate way I have of understanding unconscious script processes.

The second part, finding a way out of the role, means freeing oneself from the impasses that inevitably arise when client and therapist become entangled in a mutual drama. Often the therapist needs to integrate something within herself in order to foster the client's capacity to link incongruent affect (Stern, 2010). In my work with Erin, as I began to tolerate the feeling of intense neediness, Erin developed a capacity to contain her distress and think about it rather than simply enact it with me, over and over in the game episodes that reinforced her life script.

These ideas assume that the therapist brings her own script to the consulting room, and with a commitment to ongoing self-analysis her script can become an asset in the work rather than an impediment (Harris, 2009; Slavin, 2010). In contrast, the therapist's attempts to maintain neutrality can foster repression or dissociation in both participants.

11.2.4. Conclusion: a more coherent script

The following week Erin related a dream in which she was at her parents' house. Her home was further away. She was pregnant and feeling at peace. Her family was all present and there was a calm between them. Erin told her family that the baby was a girl and her sister said, "That means she won't eat you out of house and home."

In discussing the dream, Erin said, "It's my baby, not my mother's." These words fell out of her mouth without forethought and struck us both as odd, yet significant.

ERIN: "I guess that means it's up to me to take care of the baby—and I know that baby girl is me … and I think I'm OK with that."

I noticed her self-assurance in this session and the absence of the familiar demands on me as "mother". We talked about the pregnancy as an image of containment for Erin's starving baby self and also a wonderful metaphor for new possibilities. Previously Erin had alternately detested this needy part, enacted it with me and others, or projected it through her work caring for neglected children. We agreed that the hungry baby was no longer threatening to dismantle the therapy, or endanger her psychological stability, that is, "eat her out of house and home". Erin's eating patterns began to settle in the months that followed.

Our conversation, like the dream, seemed to bring together parts of Erin to create a more complex coherent script, a story capable of containing unwanted characters, thwarted needs, loss, and hope. This vignette illustrates the way internal script change can occur as a result of shifts in the interpersonal relationship, or as Stern put it, "The new story, then, is not the engine of change, but the mark change leaves behind" (2010, p. 117). In this instance, work within the countertransference provided the engine.

11.3. Depression

Mark Widdowson

11.3.1. Introduction

Depression is one of the most common psychological disorders and is estimated to affect around 6% of adults in any one year, and around 15% of all adults during their lifetime (Kessler, Berglund, & Demler, 2003; Kessler, Chiu, Demler, & Walters, 2005). Depression has two main features—low mood (feeling down, hopeless etc.) and loss of interest or pleasure in activities (anhedonia). Other possible symptoms include; deep feelings of sadness, irritability, guilt and/ or shame, difficulty sleeping, changes in appetite, poor concentration, indecisiveness, feelings of inadequacy and intense self-criticism. Essentially, depression is a negative, pervasive and persistent frame of reference which affects the individual's sense of self, thought processes, memory, emotions, physiology, behaviours, interpersonal relationships and way of experiencing, interpreting and interacting with the world.[1] TA has demonstrated its effectiveness as a therapy for depression in a series of research studies (Van Rijn & Wild, 2013; Van Rijn, Wild, & Moran, 2011; Widdowson, 2012a, 2012b, 2012c, 2014a).

11.3.2. Client case example

Vicky was a forty-two-year-old woman who self-referred for therapy. She was a solicitor and described her working conditions as "… just horrendous. The amount of work we are expected to do is unrealistic and I'm certainly not paid enough." She had not had a relationship for many years, stating "I am useless at relationships. I just don't know how relationships work and it's safer on my own and also I won't end up hurting someone with my baggage." She described many years of persistent low mood. She felt she had no or little worth, was "bad" and "useless" as a person, and described an inability to make even basic decisions, difficulty sleeping, and loss of appetite. She described having had several periods of depression through her adult life and had been prescribed antidepressants in the past, but had decided to opt for talking therapy this time. I conducted a brief diagnostic and history taking interview, which included completion of outcome measures. Her scores indicated severe depression and moderate-severe anxiety. I explained that the prognosis was positive, and that there was a good chance she would improve in therapy, and that I would ask her to complete outcome measures every few sessions to monitor her progress.

Following this, I explained about how I understand therapy to work and about the tasks and processes involved in therapy. This role induction process effectively teaches the client how to be a client and therefore get the most out of therapy. I also emphasised that the more "active" she was in her recovery process, the greater chance there was of her getting better quickly.

11.3.3. Principles of TA psychotherapy for depression

Part of the therapeutic process involves facilitating the client's interest in and positive engagement with others, life, and the world in ways that enhance well-being. Behavioural contracting for between-session homework and self-care can be helpful. Fortunately, clients with depression often do well in therapy and many will recover with fairly short-term therapy (Cuijpers et al., 2013). As a sense of hopelessness and despondency is often a feature of depression, it can be helpful to let new clients who present with depression know that there is good reason for them to be optimistic about their chances for improvement. The use of outcome measures such as CORE-OM (Evans et al., 2002) and/or PHQ-9 (Kroenke, Spitzer, & Williams, 2001) is particularly recommended, as this will not only provide a benchmark for the severity of the client's symptoms at the start of therapy, but will give a good indicator as to the magnitude of his change. Discussing positive improvement with the client can be helpful and can be very encouraging. Where there is deterioration or no improvement, this can be used to indicate that the therapist needs some additional supervision and may need to adjust her way of working with this client.

11.3.4. Vicky's outcome measure data

	Session 1	Session 4	Session 8	Session 12	Session 16	Session 20
CORE-OM	22 Moderate	13.5 Sub-clinical	12.3 Sub-clinical	9.4 Normal	8.5 Normal	8.2 Normal
PHQ-9	20 Severe	8 Mild	7 Mild	4 Normal	3 Normal	3 Normal
GAD-7	11 Moderate-severe	5 Mild	5 Mild	5 Mild	6 Mild	1 Normal

From the table above, it is clear that Vicky experienced rapid and large improvement within the first four sessions. Such early gains are known to be a very positive prognostic indicator (Tang & DeRubeis, 1999). The outcome measures demonstrate clinically significant change for Vicky by the end of therapy.

Despite how down she felt at the outset, Vicky put in great effort to make changes in her life. She made a point of seeing friends every week and started to go swimming twice a week, even though she didn't feel like doing anything. Her thinking and outlook also changed during therapy. Her outcome measure scores plummeted and this inspired her to continue making changes in her life.

Avoidance is a common symptom and maintaining factor in depression (Widdowson, 2014b). People who are depressed often feel demotivated and experience little pleasure from activities. Consequently, they end up doing less and less, which creates a self-perpetuating system where they are effectively starved of positive strokes, stimulation, structure, and recognition. This then reinforces script beliefs that they are "inadequate" and may activate a harsh, Critical Parent driven internal dialogue. The reduction in activity caused by avoidance:

> ... deepens the depression and can trap the person with depression into a profound passivity—hoping that things will improve, and waiting to act and do things until such a time as they feel motivated and energised. However, this approach is flawed. If they wait until they want to do something, then the change process will likely be slow and laborious and the client is at risk of the depression worsening. The therapist needs to carefully and sensitively promote an increase in the client's levels of activity and engagement with others and the world ... The process of gradual re-engagement is best done from a position of collaboration, as opposed to one where the therapist is Parental and inviting the client into compliance. (Widdowson, 2011, p. 7)

Effective TA therapy is based on creating an "I'm OK, you're OK" therapeutic relationship (Stewart & Joines, 1987). This can be difficult and requires constant monitoring: clients who are depressed can be negative and the therapist's countertransference to this can trigger unhelpful, negative, and critical ways of relating. Ensuring that the therapy is characterised by an atmosphere of permission and protection (Crossman, 1966) and that the therapist is experienced by the client as having potency (Steiner, 1968) is helpful. Research has repeatedly demonstrated that a climate of empathy, warmth, genuineness, and acceptance has a positive impact on the outcome of therapy (Norcross, 2002).

> A crucial aspect of the recovery process is interpersonal engagement. A sense of isolation and alienation is a central aspect of the experience of depression for many people. Because they feel isolated and alienated, they pull back from interpersonal contact. By providing an empathic and accepting environment, by helping the client to understand their depression and by being willing to really hear and understand the depth of the client's pain, the therapist can help the client to feel less isolated. (Widdowson, 2011, p. 6)

Vicky stated in her third session: "This is great. I can say whatever I want and you won't be offended. I don't need to take care of you in any way—I can just say how I feel and you understand. I don't think I've experienced that before."

The clients who have participated in my research have all stated that the therapist's sensitive use of challenge and caring confrontation has been beneficial. Confrontation of contaminations, discounting, and grandiosity can be extremely helpful in the therapy of depression, but also must be done carefully. It is common for people with depression to get angry with themselves and heavy confrontation can feed this process.

In one session, Vicky was giving herself a really hard time about something. I challenged her about this and in response she said: "See, I told you I was stupid! I keep doing it. What's wrong with me? Why can't I stop?" and so continued her self-critical dialogue. I realised that my confrontation had probably been too abrupt and that she had taken it and incorporated it into her inner dialogue. Recognising this, I said: "You know, I think I was a bit heavy on you there. What I'm wondering is if you'd be willing to say something out loud, just to see how it feels." She was intrigued and wanted to know what it was. I said: "'How about you say 'I made a mistake, but that's only human. Nothing terrible happened, so I can learn from the experience and relax about it now.' Say it out loud and see how it feels." She did, and started gently crying. Her anger with herself dissipated and we spent the rest of the session identifying self-critical internal dialogue and replacing it with self-nurturing statements. These were written down, so that she could take them with her to remind herself how to self-nurture.

At the heart of depression is a complex series of script beliefs about the self, others, and the world. In TA therapy, we understand that an individual's script beliefs colour the lens through which they see, experience, interact with, and make sense of the world (Berne, 1972; Stewart & Joines, 1987). People with depression tend to have a negative attributional style of interpreting events which feed into their contaminations and script beliefs and which are also maintained by the mechanisms of discounting and grandiosity. It is well known that depressed people often experience things going wrong as catastrophic and largely their fault, thereby reinforcing feelings of hopelessness and generating further self-criticism (Strauman & Kolden, 1997).

In therapy, we seek to identify and change these patterns of interpreting experience through examining them and their origins and through reappraising these automatic attribution and interpretation systems by inviting the client to use his Adult ego state and develop a more realistic and self-compassionate position. Indeed, the development of a self-compassionate, self-nurturing stance and internal dialogue is perhaps the most important task in TA therapy for depression.

In each session I focused on helping Vicky to change her negative self-beliefs and develop her ability to appraise herself and situations using her Adult ego state. I encouraged her to see her shortcomings as just part of being human. She had always been so hard on herself for making mistakes, and over time had stopped doing anything new in order to avoid feeling disappointed when she inevitably made mistakes. She came to view mistakes as part of the learning process, and to let go of her perfectionistic and unrealistic expectations.

Working through layers of emotions, through racket feelings (Erskine & Zalcman, 1979) and into the process of deconfusion (Hargaden & Sills, 2002; Widdowson, 2010) is often a major part of the therapy of depression. The client is encouraged to explore and express his emotions in each successive layer. The therapeutic approach is to remain empathic and validating, and to normalise the client's repressed emotions to facilitate the process (Erskine, Moursund, & Trautmann, 1999).

In our sessions Vicky expressed how bleak her childhood was. She cried tears of loss for the love and caring she never received from her alcoholic parents and for the childhood that was gone forever. She became aware of the injustice of this, and started to feel angry with her parents for how they treated her and her siblings. Over the course of six sessions, this anger moved to acceptance as she realised that the only thing she could change was her life in the here and now.

There are many TA methods and models which the therapist can use to assist the client to improve the quality of relationships and the effectiveness of communication. People who are depressed are often compliant and unassertive and/or hostile and irritable with other people—both of which are interpersonally problematic. Encouraging the client to experiment with new ways of relating to others and increasing the frequency and amount of positive stroking and the level of intimacy he experiences in relationships is likely to be beneficial.

In one session, I taught Vicky about the drama triangle (Karpman, 1968). This had a profound effect as over the coming weeks she reflected on it and decided to set boundaries in relationships with family members. Vicky recognised her mother was stuck in a Victim role, and would repeatedly invite Vicky to Rescue her, and then switch to Persecutor. Vicky challenged her mother and made it clear she would not be Rescuing in future. Her mother retaliated from a Persecutor position. Vicky told her mother that she was not prepared to be emotionally blackmailed and that she would not tolerate such discussions in future. This significantly changed the dynamic in their relationship.

11.3.5. Conclusion: key points in TA therapy for depression

- Therapists are encouraged to pay attention to the "role induction process" and the development of a collaborative relationship with the client as an active agent in his change process.
- Facilitate development of a new, more adaptive interpretative framework.
- Support the client in changing a self-critical internal dialogue to one which is based on self-compassion/self-nurturing.
- Normalise the client's reactions and emotions to reduce the sense of shame.
- Address any tendencies towards avoidance or perfectionism.

11.4. The redecision analysis of transference formula: combining a transactional analysis and a psychoanalytic perspective

Michele Novellino

11.4.1. Introduction

Maria is a forty-three-year-old psychologist, referred to me by a female colleague who suggested to her that she see a male therapist, given her problems, but telling me that the real reason was the immediate aversion that Maria had awakened in her.

In this chapter I will discuss this first emotional reaction (pre-established countertransference) with my model of the redecision analysis of transference formula (RATF) (Novellino, 2003a, 2003b). The germ of this model was planted by Carlo Moiso (1985) and myself and subsequently developed by various authors, in particular by the British school (Clarkson, 1992; Hargaden & Sills, 2001). In this model we work with the ego states in different ways in successive phases of therapy. Before going to the clinical case, I will give an overview of the model.

11.4.2. The methodology of transactional psychoanalysis

In transactional analysis, working with the ego states has always taken a prominent place. Many authors have described different modes of interventions, summarised in the following table.

In transactional psychoanalysis, working with the ego states finds its place mainly in the therapeutic alliance that expresses and renews itself continuously. We distinguish the following processes:

- Decontamination with the objective of making an observing ego develop in the patient; an Adult ego state capable of identifying and understanding his transference projections onto the therapist and onto the rest of his interpersonal world.
- Deconfusion as a redecisional re-elaboration of the transference impasses and the making of new decisions outside the constraints of the script.
- Re-learning as a consolidation phase of the new decisions and an elaboration of the separation from the therapist.

The transference alliance develops through the following strategic phases:
   The redecision analysis of transference formula (RATF) presents the methodological phases of the transactional psychoanalysis approach to individual psychotherapy in a sequential process:

Table 11.4.1. Classification of ego state interventions (Novellino, *Didactic Dictionary of TA*, in press).

Parent	Adult	Child
1. Schiff's reparenting (1975)	1. Berne's therapeutic operations (1966)	1. Berne's regression analysis (1961)
2. James's self-reparenting (1974)	2. Stuntz's multiple chairs technique (1973)	2. Goulding & Goulding's redecision work (1979)
3. Osnes's spot-reparenting (1974)	3. Karpman's options (1971)	3. Kupfer & Haimowitz's rubberband work (1971)
4. Dashiell's Parent resolution process (1978)	4. Berne's game analysis (1964, 1972)	4. Erskine's disconnecting rubber bands (1974)
5. McNeel's Parent interview (1976)	5. Kahler & Capers's miniscript analysis (1974)	5. Novellino's redecision analysis of transference (1985, 1987)
6. Erskine & Trautmann's psychotherapy of the Parent ego state (2003)	6. Erskine & Zalcman's racket system analysis (1979)	6. Clark's empathic transactions (1991)
	7. Summers & Tudor's partial transferential transactions (2000)	7. Hargaden & Sills's relational deconfusion (2001)
	8. Allen & Allen's co-creative narrativism (1995)	8. Clarkson & Fish's re-childing (1988)
		9. Cornell's body-relational work (2003)

Table 11.4.2. Strategic phases of transactional psychoanalysis.

Strategic phases	Strategic objectives
1. Alliance + setting	1. Contract + transference alliance
2. Decontamination	2. Social control + observing ego
3. Deconfusion	3. Protocol insight + transference impasse redecision
4. Relearning	4. Behaviour options + separation from therapist

$$S + A \rightarrow T + CT \rightarrow TI \rightarrow In \rightarrow R$$

1. *S*etting + *a*lliance in the contractual phase.
2. Awareness and cognitive analysis of *t*ransference and of *c*ounter*t*ransference in the decontamination phase.

3. Reliving of the *t*ransference *i*mpasse.
4. *I*nterpretation of the unsatisfied need and of the redecision of the script at the base of the impasse.
5. *R*edecision.

11.4.3. A clinical case

Maria graduated at the age of thirty-three. She took a long time for her degree thesis, since she was in an intimate relationship with the professor. In the end she left very disillusioned because the professor had not kept his promise either to leave his wife or to give her a job in his faculty. After one year, she married a man whom her family liked, but with whom she was not in love. After a few years, she found the strength to divorce, but was not able to find another relationship or work.

Maria is depressed and inactive, but is most worried about her long obsessive rituals related to personal hygiene. Her therapeutic objective is to get rid of the rituals.

During adolescence she underwent a long cognitive-behavioural therapy with a female therapist to cure phobias marked by panic attacks, with a beneficial result for several years. I ask her how she felt by the referral from the colleague, and she replies that she felt very disillusioned and thought she was "unliked". She adds that she was curious, but also a little worried, about working with a man because her father abandoned the family when she was five years old.

I establish the alliance and the setting: 1. the validity of her reasons for freeing herself from her symptoms; 2. the opportunity to consider together a liberation from a past full of disillusions; 3. a setting of two sessions a week; 4. paying attention to her experiences with regard to the therapist, her curiosity and initial worry towards me. Maria understands and accepts, relieved to be able to not be talking only about her obsessive symptoms.

We spend the first months on a decontamination of the obsessive symptoms and soon a significant symbol emerges: spending a long time on personal hygiene represents a substitution of a sexuality, now absent in her life and a source of frustration in the past. She confesses that she never had full intercourse, not even with her husband. It emerges that she experiences her femininity in an infantile way, composed mainly of fairy-tale dreams and deep fears regarding virility, felt as dangerously aggressive. The rituals disappear quickly, and we shift attention to her depressive state. Maria starts to experience two new things: she remembers many dreams, which had not happened since she was a child, and she feels that it is literally difficult to end the sessions. She is not able to get up from the couch where she went, at my suggestion, after the first months of therapy.

Her dreams reveal a great anger towards feminine types, while she soon realises that "not being able to get up" corresponds to "not wanting to leave". I suggest that the relaxation she feels on the couch is helping her to relive the efforts she went through to separate from her father who had abandoned her (interpretation). Maria confirms this, remembering how she was in bed, with different illnesses, for a long time after her father left. It becomes clear how she took refuge in "impossible" relationships: first with the married professor, then with a husband who revealed himself to be homosexual. Her sexuality was fuelled by masturbation with fantasies about unattainable men. Maria realises, painfully but clearly, that her real problem is that she is still waiting for her father to return and love her, to prefer her to other women.

During this phase, Maria takes up some sports again, and she decides to sign up for a specialisation course for a work project. She often feels very deferential towards me, like a "student" with the "professor", words which she herself states with surprise and caution. She expresses the fear of repeating with me the experience that she had with the university professor (transference impasse). We analyse her fantasy for several sessions. Maria comes to understand that in reality her fear expresses and covers a desire of having an amorous relationship, which she describes as never-ending conversations and innocent physical caresses.

I feel strangely bothered by these fantasies. I analyse them (self-analysis of countertransference, Novellino, 1984), remembering my adolescent experiences of attraction and fear towards the opposite sex. I realise that my worry is an identification with the bother Maria feels, both towards herself for having to tell me about her childhood dreams and towards me for being too much of a "coward" for hiding behind the rules of the setting (transference impasse). Working on these reciprocal experiences, we conclude that probably Maria is repeating a known script: the fear of finding in me a father who left her alone.

Through the verbalisation and explanation of my countertransference, Maria understands how she felt like a "sister" to the men who are really attractive to her. In her transference she sees again the temptation to be seductive to her father to make him return. The few times that she saw him as a child, she was always very careful to be cute and graceful, but her father, the "coward", left every time. Maria realises that she is not only depressed, but is really sad to accept that she has waited for her father all her life, blocking herself into a sort of chronic adolescence. In the following period, Maria begins to feel a growing anger towards the male staff of the specialisation course, because they seem to note the other students, but not her. This would appear to be an unconscious communication (Novellino, 1990) actually directed towards me, which I propose as an interpretative hypothesis. Maria first denies it angrily. After a while, she relaxes and asks me what this possibility means to me. Listening to my internal reactions, I understand that it is important to give her an answer that is not only rational. I explain to her that emotionally I feel honoured to be so important to her, and that I think that she is trying to face with me what was interrupted with her father. Maria cries and is relieved. She thanks me for not having answered as if she was a child and states decidedly that she wants to close that "thing" (interpretation of unsatisfied need).

A difficult and complex phase of the therapy begins, during which we alternate direct work with the father figure, sometimes with the Gestalt two-chairs technique, while working with her evolving emotional relationship with me. Maria arrives at two fundamental conclusions: she feels that the impossibility to seduce the therapist, the university professor, and the professors of the specialisation course is a repetition of her incapability to make her father return; and she imagines that, had she succeeded, it would demonstrate that she, a child, was stronger than her mother and therefore a "real woman". This refers to her script belief: "I am not capable to make myself loved, I am only a girl," and script decision, "I will fight until my father returns." Her racket was that of depression and disillusionment, her psychological game, "Do me something". The transference impasse was a conflict between a very young part of C_1 looking for reassurances from an idealised paternal Parent ($=P_1+$) projected onto me (a second degree emotional transference impasse).

In the therapeutic relationship Maria finally finds the permission to relive the early emotional relationships for which she has felt ashamed. She sees in the therapist the welcoming

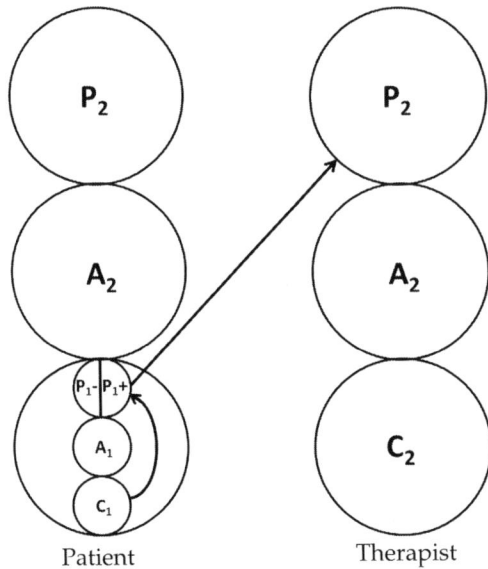

Figure 1.

and respectful father whom she missed. This helps her to internally reconstruct a trust towards herself and towards men (redecision: "I am worthy of attention and love").

Maria becomes involved with a person of her age who seems sincerely interested in her and who says that he will have sexual relations with her when she feels ready. The specialisation course ends ,and she decides to start working in a medical practice. In the last phase of the therapy, Maria accepts the separation from the therapist, with serenity and respect, sad about the ending of a relationship in which, for first time, she felt listened to and respected as a woman and relieved to finally experience her femininity with a partner who is so different from the men in her past.

11.4.4. Conclusion

In this chapter, we presented a combined transactional analytic and psychoanalytic approach.

My hope is that, on the one hand, cognitive-oriented transactional analysts can think about this methodology without preconceptions and without considering the Bernean therapeutic model to be the definitive and radical eclipse of psychoanalysis. On the other hand, I hope that more psychodynamically-oriented transactional analysts can consider in a more balanced way that every methodology has its strengths and weaknesses.

11.5. Transactional analysis in a hospital setting with patients with personality disorders

Moniek Thunnissen

11.5.1. Introduction

For more than thirty-five years transactional analysis has been used in a short-term inpatient psychotherapy programme in de Viersprong, a psychiatric institute in the Netherlands.

In this programme, which has a fixed duration of three months, insight-oriented elements from psychoanalysis and transactional analysis are combined with principles of cognitive therapy (Thunnissen, Duivenvoorden, & Trijsburg, 2001). The programme includes group psychotherapy, non-verbal therapies (e.g., movement and art therapy), and sociotherapy (e.g., discussions with nurses regarding here and now issues) in a therapeutic milieu. In the clinic, the language of transactional analysis is used to describe interpersonal and intrapsychic processes. In the group psychotherapy, the redecision model of transactional analysis (Goulding & Goulding, 1976, 1978, 1979) is used extensively.

Most patients in this programme suffer from cluster C PD's: avoidant, obsessive-compulsive, or dependent PD (54.4%), although there are also patients with a cluster B PD (most often borderline PD) (16.8%) or PD NOS (a combination of at least ten traits of different PD's) (17.6%) (Thunnissen, 2006).

11.5.2. A case vignette

Harry, forty-two, is admitted to the Psychotherapeutic Centre de Viersprong because of increasing work problems over the last three years due to crippling fear in many situations. During his twenties, he also received psychotherapy because of loneliness and difficulties in social relationships. The result of that treatment was positive: he finished school and built a social life. Now, twenty-three years later, Harry wants to change his negative self-image, stop continuously asking for affirmation, and quit his habit of escaping responsibilities and choices.

In the first session Harry came across as shy and terrified. It seemed as if, from a young age, he had adopted the identity of a failure. His mother was overprotective, and his father was an outsider in the family. Harry never succeeded in meeting his father's high expectations and kept symbiotically tied to his mother. Because of this symbiosis, he had to repress both his aggressive and sexual impulses and developed an avoidant, passive-aggressive style of functioning. Harry preferred an isolated existence in which fantasies about relationships were more important than real relationships. Only a year previously—at the age of forty-one—he had had his first sexual contact, with a prostitute. To compensate for his strong feelings of inferiority, he developed grandiose ideas. His affective life was seen as rather primitive and immature, although he functioned well at a cognitive level. In terms of the *Diagnostic and Statistical Manual (DSM-5)* (American Psychiatric Association, 2013) we diagnosed Harry with the personality disorder "not otherwise specified" with avoidant, dependent, and passive-aggressive traits.

Central in our transactional analysis diagnosis was his need to have symbiotic relationships with others, excluding his Adult and Parent and using the Parent of the other person. His dominant ego state was Adapted Child, with strong injunctions of "Don't grow up", "Don't be a man", "Don't feel" (especially aggression and sexuality), and "Don't succeed". Most of his games started from the Victim position: "Stupid", "Poor Me", "Schlemiel", and "Look What They Are Doing to Me".

11.5.3. Treatment

The central aim in Harry's treatment was to grow up and become a man, symbolised by his no longer taking the patient role and starting to use his own strength, and to make direct contact instead of using passive-aggressive and avoidant manoeuvres. At the start of treatment, he made a slack and soft impression, though he acknowledged that, in fact, he was much more powerful. He still seemed to seek intimacy with his mother or a mother-figure. Despite his previous treatment twenty years before, his life seemed to be characterised by quiet suffering. He, the group, and the therapists agreed on the following contract: *"I stop waiting in the 'mother ship'; I am a guy with potency."* He particularly liked the word "potency".

In the first half of his treatment, Harry persisted in his old behaviour: waiting awkwardly, trying hard in a pitiful manner. The secondary advantage of his acting like a patient/victim became clear, and he realised how empty his social life was. To increase the inner conflict between the shy little boy and the man he wanted to become, he was given a large, plastic toy sword. Instead of experiencing this as an offence, he saw this as recognition and paraded proudly with the sword around his waist. Gradually, his aggression came to the surface more, and he began disliking his position in the group—and in life.

Halfway through the treatment, when all the patients went home one week, Harry discovered how uninhabitable his house actually was, and he started to make it more of a home. He then developed an outbreak of eczema, which seemed to make visible his fear of intimacy. The group therapist asked him whether this was the way he showed his aggression: with red, itching spots on his skin that hurt him and kept others at a distance.

When four new members were introduced into the group, Harry took the position of controller and organiser and wanted to keep them "little"—just as his mother had done with him. He declared that he wanted to get rid of the toy sword but could not articulate what had changed by wearing the sword. He discussed in a group session the link between the sword and his relationship with his mother. He realised how much security he got from clinging to the past and how he was comfortably nestled into a regressive Child position. Harry experienced this conflict over the next week in the various therapies and a week later he formulated clearly what he would gain if he let go of the sword: he wanted to be independent and to use both his feelings of aggression and sexuality in contacts with others. He wanted to stop waiting passively for his life to evolve and he wanted to really love other people. For the first time in his treatment, firmness and strength in his statements were clearly visible and the therapist proposed that a male group member—like the knights in medieval times—use the sword to dub Harry into a man. This happened, and it was a solemn moment. Afterwards, a procession followed to the trash container, where Harry broke the sword into pieces.

This group session was a turning point in Harry's treatment. His attitude became firmer, he found a distinct place in the group, and he became important to others, using humour and confrontation. He began to dress differently and bought new glasses. Stimulated by the staff, he went into the solarium a few times and enjoyed, for the first time, warmth on his skin. His growth continued steadily, and eventually he left with his contract fulfilled. He acquired sufficient skills so that he could leave his existence-at-the-sideline and go into the world; he became a robust man with a good sense of humour. Harry decided to pursue further education and to take more responsibility and initiative at work. He also considered eventually taking another job and moving to a new house. He decided he wanted to obtain his driver's licence and made plans to develop his social contacts.

11.5.4. Link to redecision theory

The names of Robert and Mary Goulding (Goulding & Goulding, 1976, 1978, 1979) have been linked inextricably with redecision theory. By combining elements of transactional analysis, Gestalt, and behaviour therapy, they developed a unique and dynamic mode of group treatment quite distinct from that utilised by Berne. One of the core elements of their conceptualisation of the nature of script was to make a distinction between the script messages children get, particularly from their parents (e.g., "Don't exist", "Don't be important", "Don't be close", etc.), and the decisions they make for themselves based on such messages. Berne elaborated a theory of script *injunctions*, while the Gouldings emphasised the child's early script *decisions*. At the most primitive level, this concerns decisions from the primitive Adult (A_1). These self-limiting Child decisions exert a powerful, sometimes unconscious influence on later life decisions. Once these early decisions become more conscious, they can be reconsidered in Adult awareness and "redecided" in the Child ego state. The Gouldings argued that if in this redecision process the Child ego state is involved, it is possible to alter the early Child decision.

Important concepts within the Gouldings' approach include "child magic" and the importance of strokes. Many people suffer from magical ideas, such as, "If I remain angry or sad long enough and hard enough, it is possible to change the past." This applies, for example, to a woman who continues to lament her deceased mother, but also to Harry, who refused to grow up out of the hope of getting the attention he missed from his parents. Such a magical idea can underlie such games as "Psychiatry" or "If it weren't for him" that shift one's own responsibility to somebody else. The therapist can start to raise question marks after such racket patterns with questions like, "And how long do you plan to remain angry/sad/small, etc.?" The real redecision needs a respectful attitude from the therapist towards the power of the survival decision and a shift of energy into the more healthy ego states resulting in the patient taking a new decision and letting go of the old patterns.

As we have seen in the earlier discussions of game theory, people can maintain their games by means of their time structuring and stroke patterns. Hence, redecisions must be paired with intensive strokes from the therapist and group members and a change in the patient's ways of structuring time. In Harry's treatment we see one of the advantages of a clinical setting: patients can practise within and outside the structured therapies with strokes and time structuring and significantly change their stroke profile and ways of structuring time.

The Gouldings emphasised the patient's own strength and responsibility, so they immediately interfered if a patient said, for example, "You make me angry" or "This happens to me all the time." They would ask the person to reframe the sentence into the active voice: "I get angry." In addition to the techniques of decontamination and reinforcing the Adult, the Gouldings also used many techniques to reach the Child. They would ask patients to fantasise what they would do without a certain injunction or to imagine how it was at the dinner table when they were young. They worked with patients' dreams, had them talk to a dead father in his coffin or to a former schoolteacher in the classroom, or had them project an annoying headache onto another chair. They clearly distinguished between humour and what Berne labelled "gallows" laughter, although the latter is sometimes very contagious; that is, if patients tell tales concerning their misfortunes and bad luck, it is sometimes hard for the therapist not to laugh. A powerful counter-message from the therapist might be, "I don't think that is funny." The toy sword that Harry received in his treatment was a way to reach first his Adapted Child, later his Rebellious Child, and finally his Free Child.

In their redecision workshops and groups, the Gouldings used a number of specific techniques, including countering symbiotic invitations from clients, such as "You know …" or "I don't know" or "What did you say?" Bob Goulding used to reply to such comments with "No, I don't know any either"—or he would clang a big cowbell the moment a client used symbiotic language.

McNeel (1977), in a captivating overview of the different techniques or types of intervention in redecision therapy, divides them into seven categories:

1. Emphasis on personal power and responsibility of client and therapist.
2. Fostering a nurturing environment.
3. The leader's modelling behaviour.
4. Separating myth from reality.
5. Confrontation of incongruity.
6. Particular techniques, such as letting go of the past and talking to parental projections in two-chair dialogues.
7. Procedural rules, such as don't gossip (don't talk about people who are not in the room), stick to the time limit, no violence, no alcohol, have sex only with your own partner during the workshop, and stay on the property during a three-day marathon.

11.5.5. Research

The strength of the redecison approach has been confirmed in a number of studies. The first is a study by McNeel (1982) into the impact of the Gouldings' weekend workshops. In a second research study (Thunnissen, 2006; Thunnissen et al., 2008), 128 patients with personality disorders underwent the three-month inpatient redecision psychotherapy described earlier in this section. After the inpatient programme they were randomised to either a reintegration training programme aimed at improving general functioning and work resumption or to booster sessions with the same method and therapists as the primary treatment. Outcome measures used were symptom level, work status, and absence from and impediments at work. The results showed that symptomatic change at follow-up were considerable (effect size of 2.00 in the reintegration training programme and 2.01 in the booster sessions; an effect size of more than 0.4 is large). This effect size indicates an exceptional effect of treatment, generated mainly in the three-month inpatient programme, which then stabilised during the aftercare and follow-up period.

In a multicentre study the positive results of the above-mentioned studies were repeated: the short-term inpatient TA programme proved to be the best treatment for patients with cluster C PD's (Bartak et al., 2010) and for patients with PD NOS (Horn et al., 2014).

References

Allen, J. R., & Allen, B. A. (1995). *Narrative theory, redecision therapy, and post-modernism. Transactional Analysis Journal, 25*(4): 327–334.
American Psychiatric Association (2013). *Diagnostic and Statistical Manual of Mental Disorders-5*. Arlington, VA: American Psychiatric Association.
Banks, K. (2013). Skin as a container mediating primary self-other relationships: An exploration of the psychological function of skin disorders. *Transactional Analysis Journal, 43*(2): 164–173.
Bartak, A., Spreeuwenberg, M. D., Andrea, H. A., Holleman, L., Rijnierse, P., Rossum, B. van, Hamers, E. F. M., Meerman, A. M., Aerts, J., Busschbach, J. J. van, Verheul, R., Stijnen, T., & Emmelkamp, P. M. G. (2010). Effectiveness of different modalities of psychotherapeutic treatment for patients with Cluster C personality disorders: Results of a large prospective multicentre study. *Psychotherapy and Psychosomatics, 79*: 20–30.
Beekum, S. van (2006). The relational consultant. *Transactional Analysis Journal, 36*(4): 318–329.
Berne, E. (1961). *Transactional Analysis in Psychotherapy*. New York: Grove Press.
Berne, E. (1964). *Games People Play: The Psychology of Human Relationships*. New York: Ballantine, 1996.
Berne, E. (1966). *Principles of Group Treatment*. New York: Grove Press.
Berne, E. (1972). *What Do You Say after You Say Hello? The Psychology of Human Destiny*. New York: Grove Press.
Berne, E. (1972). *What Do You Say after You Say Hello? The Psychology of Human Destiny*. New York: Corgi, 1975.
Bollas, C. (1992). *Being a Character: Psychoanalysis & Self Experience*. New York: Hill & Wang.
Caizzi, C. (2012). Embodied trauma: Using the sub symbolic mode to access and change script protocol in traumatized adults. *Transactional Analysis Journal, 42*(2): 165–175.
Clark, B. D. (1991). Emphatic transaction in the deconfusion of the Child ego states. *Transactional Analysis Journal 21*(2): 92–98.
Clarkson, P. (1992). *Transactional Analysis Psychotherapy: an Integrated Approach*. London: Tavistock/Routledge.
Clarkson, P., & Fish, S. (1988). Rechilding: Creating a new past in the present as a support for the future. *Transactional Analysis Journal, 18*(1): 51–59.
Cornell, W. F. (2003). Babies, brains and bodies. In: H. Hargaden & C. Sills (Eds.), *Ego States* (pp. 28–54). London: Worth.

Cornell, W. F. (2010). Whose body is it? Somatic relations in script and script protocol. In: R. G. Erskine (Ed.), *Life Scripts: A Transactional Analysis of Unconscious Relational Patterns* (pp. 101–126). London: Karnac.

Cornell, W. F., & Landaiche, N. M. (2007). Why body psychotherapy: A conversation. *Transactional Analysis Journal*, 37(4): 256–262.

Crossman, P. (1966). Permission and protection. *Transactional Analysis Bulletin*, 5(19): 152–154.

Cuijpers, P., Sijbrandji, M., Koole, S. L., Andersson, G., Beekman, A. T., & Reynolds, C. F. (2013). The efficacy of psychotherapy and pharmacotherapy in treating depressive and anxiety disorders: A meta-analysis of direct comparisons. *World Psychiatry*, 12(2): 137–148.

Dashiell, S. R. (1978). The Parent resolution process: Reprogramming psychic incorporation in the Parent. *Transactional Analysis Journal*, 8(4): 289–294.

Erskine, R. G. (1974). Therapeutic interventions: Disconnecting rubber bands. *Transactional Analysis Journal*, 4(1): 7–8.

Erskine, R. G., Moursund, J., & Trautmann, R. (1999). *Beyond Empathy: A Therapy of Contact-in-relationships*. New York: Routledge.

Erskine, R. G., & Trautmann, R. (2003). Resolving intrapsychic conflict: psychotherapy of Parent ego states. In: H. Hargaden & C. Sills (Eds.), *Ego States* (pp. 109–134). London: Worth.

Erskine, R. G., & Zalcman, M. (1979). The racket system: A model for racket analysis. *Transactional Analysis Journal*, 9(1): 51–59.

Evans, C., Connell, J., Barkham, M., Margison, R., McGrath, G., Mellor-Clark, J., & Audin, K. (2002). Towards a standardised brief outcome measure: psychometric properties and utility of the CORE-OM. *British Journal of Psychiatry*, 180(1): 51–50.

Fowlie, H., & Sills, C. (Eds.) (2011). *Relational Transactional Analysis: Principles in Practice*. London: Karnac.

Goodman, M. (2007). Focusing on the "bodily felt sense": A tool for transactional analysts. *Transactional Analysis Journal*, 37(4): 278–285.

Goulding, M. M., & Goulding, R. L. (1979). *Changing Lives through Redecision Therapy*. New York: Brunner/Mazel.

Goulding, R. L., & Goulding, M. M. (1976). Injunctions, decisions and redecisions. *Transactional Analysis Journal*, 6(1): 41–48.

Goulding, R. L., & Goulding, M. M. (1978). *The Power Is in the Patient: A TA/Gestalt Approach to Psychotherapy*. (P. McCormick, Ed.). San Francisco, CA: TA Press.

Hargaden, H., & Sills, C. (2001). Deconfusion of the Child ego state: A relational perspective. *Transactional Analysis Journal*, 31(1): 55–70.

Hargaden, H., & Sills, C. (2002). *Transactional Analysis: A Relational Perspective*. Hove, UK: Brunner-Routledge.

Harris, A. (2009). You must remember this. *Psychoanalytic Dialogues*, 19(1): 2–21.

Horn, E. K., Bartak, A., Meerman, A. M., Rossum, B. van, Ziegler, U. M., Thunnissen, M. M., Soons, M., Andrea, H., Hamers, E. F. M., Emmelkamp, P. M. G., Stijnen, T., Busschbach, J. J. van, & Verheul, R. (2014). Effectiveness of psychotherapy in personality disorders not otherwise specified (PDNOS): A comparison of different treatment modalities. *Clinical Psychology and Psychotherapy* (in press).

James, M. (1974). Self reparenting. Theory and process. *Transactional Analysis Journal*, 4(3): 32–39.

Joseph, M. R. (2010). The psychic-somatic continuum: Pathology, cure, and prevention. *Transactional Analysis Journal*, 40(1): 43–53.

Kahler, T., & Capers, H. (1974). The miniscript. *Transactional Analysis Journal*, 4(1): 26–42.

Karpman, S. (1968). Fairy tales and script drama analysis. *Transactional Analysis Bulletin*, 7(26): 39–43.

Kessler, R. C., Berglund, P., & Demler, O. (2003). The epidemiology of major depressive disorder: Results from the National Comorbidity Survey Replication (NCS-R). *Journal of the American Medical Association*, 289(203): 3095–3105.

Kessler, R. C., Chiu, W. T., Demler, O., & Walters, E. E. (2005). Prevalence, severity, and comorbidity of twelve-month DSM-IV disorders in the National Comorbidity Survey Replication (NCS-R). *Archives of General Psychiatry*, 62(6): 617–627.

Kroenke, K., Spitzer, R. L., & Williams, J. B. (2001). The PHQ-9: Validity of a brief depression severity measure. *Journal of General Internal Medicine*, 16(9): 606–613.

Kupfer, D., & Haimowitz, H. (1971). Therapeutic interventions. Part I. Rubber bands now. *Transactional Analysis Journal*, 1(2): 10–16.

Ligabue, S. (2007). Being in relationship: Different languages to understand ego states, script, and the body. *Transactional Analysis Journal*, 37(4): 294–306.

McNeel, J. (1976). The Parent interview. *Transactional Analysis Journal*, 6(1): 61–68.

McNeel, J. (1977). The seven components of redecision therapy. In: G. Barnes (Ed.), *Transactional Analysis after Eric Berne: Teachings and Practices of Three TA Schools* (pp. 425–441). New York: Harper's College Press.

McNeel, J. (1982). Research in redecision therapy. *Transactional Analysis Journal*, 12(1): 10–26.

Mitchell, S. (1997). *Influence and Autonomy in Psychoanalysis*. London: Psychology Press, 2008.

Moiso, C. M. (1985). Ego states and transference. *Transactional Analysis Journal*, 15(3): 194–201.

Norcross, J. C. (2002). *Psychotherapy Relationships that Work: Therapist Contributions and Responsiveness to Patients*. New York: Oxford University Press.

Novak, E. (2013). Combining traditional ego state theory and relational approaches to transactional analysis in working with trauma and dissociation. *Transactional Analysis Journal*, 43(3): 186–196.

Novellino, M. (1984). Self-analysis of countertransference in integrative transactional analysis. *Transactional Analysis Journal*, 14(1): 63–67.

Novellino, M. (1985). Redecision analysis of transference: A TA approach to transference neurosis. *Transactional Analysis Journal*, 15(3): 202–206.

Novellino, M. (1987). Redecision analysis of transference: The unconscious dimension. *Transactional Analysis Journal*, 17(1): 271–276.

Novellino, M. (1990). Unconscious communication and interpretation in transactional analysis. *Transactional Analysis Journal*, 20(3): 168–172.

Novellino, M. (2003a). Transactional psychoanalysis. *Transactional Analysis Journal*, 33(3): 223–230.

Novellino, M. (2003b). On closer analysis: Unconscious communication in the Adult ego state and a revision of the rules of communication within the framework of transactional psychoanalysis. In: H. Hargaden & C. Sills (Eds.), *Ego States* (pp. 149–168). London: Worth.

Novellino, M. (in press). *Dizionario didattico di analisi transazionale*. (Didactic Dictionary of Transactional Analysis.) Rome: Astrolabio.

Ogden, T. (1994). *Subjects of Analysis*. Lanham, MD: Rowman & Littlefield, 2004.

Osnes, R. (1974). Spot-reparenting. *Transactional Analysis Journal*, 4(1): 40–46.

Rijn, B. van, & Wild, C. (2013). Humanistic and integrative therapies for anxiety and depression: practice-based evaluation of transactional analysis, gestalt, integrative psychotherapies and person-centred counselling. *Transactional Analysis Journal*, 43(2): 150–163.

Rijn, B. van, Wild, C., & Moran, P. (2011). Evaluating the outcomes of transactional analysis and integrative counselling psychology within UK primary care settings. *International Journal of Transactional Analysis Research*, 2(1): 36–46.

Schiff, J. L., Mellor, K., Schiff, E., Schiff, S., Richman, D., Fishman, J., Wolz, L., Fishman, C., & Momb, D. (1975). *Cathexis Reader. Transactional Analysis Treatment of Psychosis*. New York: Harper & Row.

Slavin, J. (2010). Becoming an individual: technically subversive thoughts on the role of the analyst's influence. *Psychoanalytic Dialogues*, 20(3): 308–324.

Steiner, C. (1968). Transactional analysis as a treatment philosophy. *Transactional Analysis Bulletin*, 7(27): 63.

Stern, D. B. (2010). *Partners in Thought: Working with Unformulated Experience, Dissociation and Enactment*. London: Routledge.

Stewart, I., & Joines, V. (1987). *TA Today: A New Introduction to Transactional Analysis*. Nottingham, UK: Lifespace.

Strauman, T. J., & Kolden, G. G. (1997). The self in depression: Research trends and clinical implications. *In Session: Psychotherapy in Practice*, 3(3): 5–21.

Stuntz, E. C. (1973). Multiple chairs technique. *Transactional Analysis Journal*, 3(2): 29–32.

Stuthridge, J. (2006). Inside out: A transactional analysis model of trauma. *Transactional Analysis Journal*, 36(4): 270–283.

Stuthridge, J. (2012). Traversing the fault lines: Trauma and enactment. *Transactional Analysis Journal*, 42(4): 238–251.

Summers, G., & Tudor, K. (2000). Co-creative transactional analysis. *Transactional Analysis Journal*, 30(1): 23–40.

Tang, T. Z., & DeRubeis, R. J. (1999). Sudden gains and critical sessions in cognitive-behavioral therapy for depression. *Journal of Consulting and Clinical Psychology*, 67: 894–904. doi:10.1037/0022–006X.67.6.894

Thunnissen, M. M. (2006). *Long-term Prognosis and Aftercare in Short-term Inpatient Psychotherapy of Personality Disorders. A Randomized Clinical Trial of Two Methods of Aftercare*. Halsteren, Netherlands: DWG Marketing Communicatie.

Thunnissen, M. M., Duivenvoorden, H. J., Bussbach, J., Hakkaart-van Roijen, L., Tilburg, W. van, Verheul, R., & Trijsburg, R. W. (2008). A randomized clinical trial on the effectiveness of a re-integration training program versus booster sessions after short-term inpatient psychotherapy. *Journal of Personality Disorders*, 22(5): 483–495.

Thunnissen, M. M., Duivenvoorden, H. J., & Trijsburg, R. W. (2001). Experiences of patients after short-term inpatient transactional analysis. *Transactional Analysis Journal*, 31(2): 122–128.

Widdowson, M. (2010). *Transactional Analysis: 100 Key Points and Techniques*. Hove, UK: Routledge.

Widdowson, M. (2012a). TA treatment of depression: A hermeneutic single-case efficacy design study—"Peter". *International Journal of Transactional Analysis Research*, 3(1): 3–13.

Widdowson, M. (2012b). TA treatment of depression: A hermeneutic single-case efficacy design study—case two: "Denise". *International Journal of Transactional Analysis Research*, 3(2): 3–14.

Widdowson, M. (2012c). TA treatment of depression: A hermeneutic single-case efficacy design study—case three: "Tom". *International Journal of Transactional Analysis Research*, 3(2): 15–27.

Widdowson, M. (2014a). Transactional analysis psychotherapy for a case of mixed anxiety and depression: A pragmatic adjudicated case study—Alastair. *International Journal of Transactional Analysis Research*, 5(2): 66–76.

Widdowson, M. (2014b). Avoidance, vicious cycles, and experiential disconfirmation of script: Two new theoretical concepts and one mechanism of change in the psychotherapy of depression and anxiety. *Transactional Analysis Journal*, 44(3): 194–207.

Zvelc, G. (2010). Relational schemas theory and transactional analysis. *Transactional Analysis Journal*, 40(1): 8–22.

Note

1. The reader who would like to learn more about depression is advised to read: Widdowson, M. (2011). "Depression: Diagnosis, Sub-types, Patterns of Recovery and Psychotherapeutic Models—a Literature Review." *Transactional Analysis Journal*, vol. 41, issue 3.

CHAPTER TWELVE

Counselling and coaching

12.1. Transactional analysis counselling groups
12.2. Long-term counselling in transactional analysis
12.3. Learning as a counsellor for university students
12.4. Counselling, excerpts from a case
12.5. Coming to terms with multiple sclerosis

Counselling is a professional activity aimed at supporting clients by increasing their capacity for managing life problems through achieving greater self-awareness. The idea is to challenge clients to develop their own capacities and resources and help them find a renewed sense of self-agency. The goal is to increase clients' autonomy and social integration within the personal, social, professional, and cultural environment in which they live and work.

The *Handbook for TA Training and TA Certification* describes the core competencies for this field. See www.itaaworld.org/itaa-training-examinations-handbook.

Clients may turn to counselling or coaching when they have questions about how they can deal more effectively with the challenges and the difficulties in daily life and work, to seek help and support when faced with a life crisis, to find meaning, to learn to better manage emotions, and to develop tools for conflict management.

12.1. Transactional analysis counselling groups

Patrizia Vinella

12.1.1. Introduction

The group setting is widely used in transactional analysis counselling, which is oriented to different social and cultural contexts and is more allied with attention to supporting wellness rather than treating sickness. The power of the group facilitates the achievement of the basic goals established in the counselling contract—acquiring self-awareness, improving interpersonal communication, and focusing on personal and interpersonal resources—which can be more easily attained in the context of the dynamic and creative help that a group can provide. Transactional analysis counselling groups have specific characteristics that differentiate them from transactional analysis therapy groups, as well as from other types of groups (encounter, discussion, consciousness-raising, and so on) (Tudor, 1999, p. 41).

12.1.2. Care rather than cure

The main objectives of a counselling group are those of improving communication among group members, developing awareness of communication styles (stroke economy, transactions, games, drivers), facilitating the expression and management of emotions (Cornell & Hine, 1999), developing clients' resources, and preventing distress. What emerges from such exchanges, in accordance with the counselling contract, is shared with the others in an Adult-oriented process. This aspect is easier when the contract has been clearly defined and involves common goals. The change process is thus delineated around a central problem shared by all group members. The group focus, therefore, becomes "care rather than cure" (Loomis, 1982, p. 52). This is in contrast to Berne's premise that the therapist's main objective was to "cure". The concept of "cure" (1961, p. 162) was considered as a process whose aim was to reorient the patient's confused Child so as to attain Adult autonomy. The objective for a counselling group is mainly to "care", by which we mean listening, supporting, facilitating, and enhancing awareness and change through the Adult ego state.

For example, in a counselling session with a group of parents of children in kindergarten, I introduced a reflection on the Parent ego state through a stimulus question: "What kind of Parent am I for myself, and what sort of parent am I for my children?" One of the group members, Francina, began to get upset and said, "I just can't be a good mother. My son never listens to me. If I ask him to put his toys back into place, he laughs and keeps playing. My mother, on the other hand, shouted, hit me, and she terrified me [she cries and fidgets] … I just couldn't laugh the way he does …"

From a "cure" perspective, the group leader's strategy would likely be to look into Francina's relationship with her mother in order to deal with the script elements that have emerged in the work. My choice, in contrast from a "care" perspective, was to not analyse the regressive experience and her script but to acknowledge and accept her sadness.

COUNSELLOR: I see that this makes you very sad, is there something you need in this moment?
FRANCINA: No, I'm sorry, I didn't mean to cry!
COUNSELLOR: Expressing your feeling is good. You don't have to apologise. Does anyone want to say something that can help F in her role as a mom?
MARIA (OTHER GROUP MEMBER): What I've found relevant is that your son laughs. He is not afraid of you, and he keeps playing!
FRANCINA: That's true, my son is quite a cheerful kid, but he doesn't listen to me!
COUNSELLOR: F, would you like to hear about other parents' experiences about rules respecting with their children?

The following step of this process is to place Francina's experience in a here and now context and focus on her role as a mother today. The group facilitates the activation of Francina's Adult through listening and protective and friendly participation, so as to increase awareness which can prove helpful today for Francina in her role as a parent. The aim is to use difficult experiences from the past in a future-oriented perspective, in a change-oriented perspective, so as to "care" rather than "cure".

12.1.3. The counselling contract

The counselling group addresses an increasingly widespread social and cultural need for structured spaces for sharing, in which a professional group leader facilitates, through the appropriate tools and stimuli, new experiences of learning and relationships. How, where, when, and with what goal are fundamental elements in order to build an effective group process aiming at change and growth for each participant.

The most important step is to define the counselling contract together with the group.

I believe it is essential that the contract be the result of the work of the group, that is, participants are invited to define together the objectives and goals of the group's work. The role of the leader is to help group members identify a common path to be followed. In this way, the objective of the contract will be shared by all members. Following a common path implies focusing more on relational aspects among group members than on individual problems. However, as previously stated, the group counsellor takes into account life experiences from the past of the group members (which may even emerge spontaneously during the work) and uses her competent strategies to connect these episodes with the here and now and in accordance with the counselling contract. The focus of the work is to activate the Adult. This aspect is one of the most important differences between a counselling group and a therapy group (Vinella, 2013).

As an example, in a community of elderly people, the contract might be defined through a mutual commitment (leader and group) to common goals, for example, improving communication between members and staff or time management inside the structure. On the other hand, with a group of parents, the common goals might be attaining greater awareness on their own communicative style in their relationships with their sons and daughters.

I have observed that the elements that enhance the definition of a group contract are having a group that is homogeneous, closed, and time limited. The term homogeneous refers to the clients themselves and not to the problems they may have (e.g., they are all parents, elderly people, adolescents, teachers, etc.). In counselling groups, homogeneity makes it easier to establish a group contract and facilitates communication among group members. In a closed group the participants remain together from the beginning to the end, which enhances the cohesion among members and the growth of the group as a whole. A limit to the duration of the group (e.g., six to ten meetings of two to three hours each) leads to a clearer definition of the group boundaries and the development of a counselling work plan.

12.1.4. A change-oriented relationship

Having defined the main elements of the transactional analysis group, I will focus on the aspects of process that facilitate the change-oriented relationship. Before beginning a counselling group, I usually organise one or more introductory meetings on a topic that is of common interest and concern to all the participants. For example, in a kindergarten school, I had two introductory meetings for parents on the topic of strokes. In a wellness centre I conducted a meeting on the relation between emotions and diet with people who took part in a weight loss project. At the end of these introductory meetings, I usually describe the transactional analysis group, which the participants may be interested in, whose goal is to enhance helpful awareness for a change in the specific area of their interest. In these cases, the groups are formed as homogeneous, closed, and time limited, as previously stated.

The group counselling can begin with a series of exercises whose goal is to enhance reciprocal knowledge and straightforward communication on personal expectations and sharing the goals of the group work.

As an example, in beginning a group in which the members are adults and don't know each other, I may present them with an exercise such as this:

COUNSELLOR: I want you to choose another member of the group and introduce yourself to him or her for five minutes, telling him/her who you are and what you expect from this experience. After five minutes please exchange positions, so the one who has just spoken will listen to the other's presentation. In ten minutes, we all get back in the group; each one of us will introduce to the group the person he or she has just met without giving personal opinions, just retelling only the story that he or she has listened to.

An objective of this approach is to enhance communication starting from a very intimate space, pair work, and then get back into the whole group. One intention of this process is to protect those who might have difficulties in talking about themselves in front of a full group of strangers. Another objective is to start a reflection on the emotions aroused by a second person's telling the first person's story.

The speaking sequence in the large group is not completely free; it is facilitated by the group leader who invites members to create connections starting from either common or completely diverging experiences. Examples of facilitating remarks:

COUNSELLOR: Marco, thanks for introducing Ugo; Ugo, anything you would like to add? Do you think Marco left out something that you would like us to know, that you consider important? Who wants to introduce someone who has similar experiences?

These interventions aim at enhancing a more and more dynamic relationship within the whole group through transactions among the participants themselves rather than with the group leader.

A very helpful option with groups of adolescents is to ask the group members to introduce themselves to others by choosing an object or an animal that represents them, and describe themselves as if they were that object. This approach enhances a more emotional and symbolic presentation. It is important that the group is extremely careful, avoids attempts of interpretations from the group, and facilitates a non-judgemental listening of an individual's image described through the symbol chosen.

12.1.5. Focus on wellness

From the very first moments, it is fundamental that the work be focused both on wellness—rather than pathology—and on straightforward communication of emotions, and that any regressive experience or personal paths which could lead astray from the counselling contract be contained by the leader. In my view, script aspects are not the focus of a counselling contract when they are primarily used for intrapsychic work and lead patients into emotional contact with the past. Likewise, working on protocol-level decisions and archaic injunctions is not consistent with the objective and nature of counselling. Instead, script aspects that emerge in a counselling group can be used as a stimulus to facilitate clients' awareness of their own way of "conferring meaning" to things in life (Cornell, 1988, p. 280).

I usually use stimulus exercises carefully chosen to be consistent with the group contract, group climate, and/or group expectations. The purpose is to provide stimuli that lead group members to reflect on communication styles, emotions, and strategies for alternative behaviors. An example of stimulus exercises is "The desert island", where the group members are invited, within a limited amount of time, to choose an object that can help the whole group to survive. The choice must be one and unanimous: the skill is to convince the others, as well as to communicate what they felt during the exercise.

These exercises are merely a tool leading to the central moment of group feedback wherein the leader has an active role as the facilitator of communication. In managing the group process, my aim is to facilitate the construction of a serene and friendly atmosphere using an empathic approach, focusing on active listening, and facilitating communication among group members. The group planning comprises some moments of analysis of functional ego states, transactions, the stroke economy, and psychological games. Each meeting can be enriched by the use of different materials (sheets of paper, cards, colours) to stimulate creativity, or by the use of a video camera, which helps participants identify ego states, both their own and others', and transactions through structured simulation (simulations of dialogues at the bus stop, in a restaurant, at school, and so on) which we tape. The goal is to facilitate observation and awareness of their communication styles. Watching themselves gives participants an opportunity to become conscious of their own image and to verify their relational styles as well as to increase awareness of the communicative methods they used. In a group of adolescents for instance, after watching a film, the feedback revealed interesting realisations: Simon had thought he was being funnier than what he saw in the film, Peter had perceived himself more aggressive than what the video showed, Eddy got upset when he realised he was speaking exactly like his father and saying just the same things he hates to hear. The group reflected on these for a long time, and identified the differences between the inner world experiences and what emerged on video.

12.1.6. Enhancing Adult awareness

As far as feedback is concerned, Berne's (1966) therapeutic operations (interrogation, specification, explanation, confrontation, illustration, and confirmation) prove very helpful. The purpose of these interventions as described by Berne is to clarify and reinforce Adult ego state boundaries (p. 242), to enhance a level of Adult awareness about one's own communicative style and emotional competence, and to allow the group to follow the counselling plan. Sometimes in the group process it is helpful to use some Parental interventions (support, reassurance, persuasion, exhortation) that Berne (p. 248) defined as "other approaches" to be used in special situations. In counselling, they can actually prove quite helpful in supporting cohesion and safety in the group.

12.1.7. Referral and ending

There are times during the meetings when some personal experiences emerge which go beyond the counselling contract. I consider it important to give clear information on the possibility, to handle such emotional issues emerging during group work in a more personal path. I then make a referral, inviting those who may be interested to continue their process in an individual or group therapy setting. For example, during an exercise of symbolic self-representation, one girl gave herself permission to express the serious eating disorder she had been suffering from for a while, and she was able to recognise the necessity to ask for help from a specialist. My role then is to facilitate the referral for psychotherapy.

One last aspect not to be underestimated is the final phase of the group at the end of the six or ten sessions, since this represents an important moment for defining clear boundaries for the group experience. The group leader's central task is to accompany the group to a serene closure, as much as possible without significant questions remaining unresolved, and to make sure that everyone can leave the group with positive feelings.

12.1.8. Conclusion

Transactional analysis group counselling can be a great resource in helping relationships whose aim is to facilitate communication, and improve relationships among participants. The need to communicate in a healthy, constructive, and straightforward way is a stronger and stronger necessity in a world characterised by great connections and lots of networks but by deep incommunicability as well.

The group, carefully structured and competently conducted with a transactional analysis methodology, facilitates the building of a healthy, protective space, enhancing the change established in the counselling contract.

12.2. Long-term counselling in transactional analysis

Sylvie Monin

12.2.1. Introduction

When people seek counselling, they are usually going through a harsh time and want to find support, relief, and answers. Shipton and Smith observe that clients "may not have in mind the idea that it may take a long time to work towards a satisfactory resolution of their difficulties" (1998, p. 76). This article addresses the reality that a significant number of clients, who often come into consultation with a first request for short-term counselling, discover that they need more long-term work.

12.2.2. Beginning the counselling work

In my practice, after the first session and if we decide to work together, I always start with a short-term contract of five sessions. This is for several reasons:

- Security: The client does not know me, or me the client. This will allow us both to get to know each other and for the client to find out more about counselling and the way I work. The five sessions provide me with time to evaluate the client and the situation so as to determine that I may need to refer the client to a specialist if I conclude that his situation is outside my field of competencies (Monin, 2011).
- Structure: Most of the time clients who come into counselling do not have a clear idea what counselling is all about. They consult "someone around a problem in living—a conflict or dilemma that is getting in the way" (McLeod & McLeod, 2011, pp. 1–2). A five session contract provides a holding space in which to take the time to explore and evaluate the distress that has led them to seek counselling. A secure and clearly defined holding space can provide a solid ground for further work.
- Decontamination: At the start, clients are often in the midst of sometimes profound upheavals. So the level of stress is often intense, creating a period when script manifestations are most acute and observable, and the Adult ego state is not so readily available. Once a client's Adult ego state is less overwhelmed and contaminated by Parent judgements and/or flooded with Child distress and affect, the client can better assess the nature of the problems and the work required to address them.
- Trust: These initial sessions can offer a space in which the client builds a sufficient sense of security with me to make an informed choice to eventually go for longer-term counselling if

needed. As Shipton and Smith write (1998, p. 99) "Research shows that the first three sessions are critical in terms of how the counsellor is perceived and whether or not the client feels any hostility from the counsellor, the experience of which is associated with low success rate." These initial sessions are the foundation for the therapeutic alliance that is an essential element of the work.

At the end of this short-term contract, about two in three of my clients decide to end there, as they have got the help and the answers they were looking for and reached their initial goal, while some prolong the contract for a few more clearly defined sessions, typically of up to six months or one year. About one in three chose to move into long-term, open-ended contracts of two to five of more years. The number and rhythm of sessions may vary, often due to economic concerns.

12.2.3. Moving into a long-term counselling contract

Traditionally TA contracts for social control and interpersonal changes were seen as being the core of the counselling work, whereas contracts for structural and script changes were the ground of psychotherapy. I tend to disagree with this classification as in my experience, even in a contract for social control and/or interpersonal changes, working with and through the Adult ego states will have an impact on both the Child and the Parent ego states, thus allowing for a change at the structural and script levels. Furthermore, if the clients' requests are often at the level of social control and/or interpersonal change when they first seek counselling, after an initial short-term contract and with better self-awareness they may come to realise that they want to make a change at the structural and script level and decide on a new contract. It is then important for the counsellor to clearly assess a client's situation to see if the work is within his own competencies. An essential indicator for me is the client's ability to mobilise his Adult ego state, which is in my point of view a mandatory factor to get into longer-term counselling. An Adult ego state not easily available would be a clear indication for me to refer the client to a psychotherapist colleague.

In my practice I have come to work with three additional types of contracts that fit well within the counselling work and contribute to activating and strengthening the Adult ego state while having a deep impact at the structural and script levels:

1. Narrative contract: This is a contract in which the client wants to tell his personal story in a secure, private, and personal space. There is no specific request for change, just a need to confide in an interested and engaged witness.

    Anna came to me a few years ago. She had just recently lost her job. She began the session by saying, "I am forty-eight and I feel the need to tell my story to someone. I never told it before." This is how we entered into a narrative contract. I like McLeod & McLeod's definition of counselling as "making a space to talk it through" (2011). This is exactly what Anna and I did. At this time in her life she needed a space, a special space for herself, a space to talk. By contracting we created that space. She started to tell her story, which was the "it", at times like a broken record, going over and over the same events, but each time with a new detail, a new light, a new awareness. As her story unfolded, many "its" were talked through. Five years later she is still telling me her story, with each memory, each picture, getting more and more self insight and more deeply in touch with herself and her needs. For the first four years we met every other week and moved to one monthly session over the past year. Through her narration, Anna developed a stronger sense of self-awareness and potency, she found a new job and financial security, and got closer to her mother and siblings from whom she had been estranged for many years. We are now working towards ending the counselling work.

2. Contract for understanding: This is a contract in which the client is seeking to understand what is happening, to give meaning to an experience. Like with the narrative contract there might not be a request for change, even though with a better understanding and awareness change often spontaneously occurs.

    Kate approached me just coming out of alcohol detoxification. She had a very clear request: "I want to understand how I got there." This was a contract for understanding. Like a puzzle, she explored the many facets of her life, as a child and as a young adult woman, the image of the puzzle getting clearer and clearer. More awareness brought more understanding. More understanding brought deep changes, mainly at an emotional level, where she could now stop blaming herself and feeling deep shame. Parallel to our counselling work Kate has been seeing a psychiatrist from the detoxification clinic about every three months.

3. Contract for exploration: This is a contract in which the client is aware that something is not going well but is unaware of the ins and outs, the why and the how. For the client, exploring the many aspects of his situation and experience, both internally and externally, can help bring light to and make sense of an experience that can be the first step towards a contract for change. George came into consultation as he was going through an important crisis within the relationship with his wife. He wanted to explore how he came to that stage and to understand the dynamics in his couple, in order to make a thought-out choice to stay or to leave. There was a contract for exploration, both of his own internal process and of the process within the couple and family. Through exploration came a better understanding, and he slowly got in touch with his emotions, which we explored. We paid particular attention to his anger, which he started to recognise as a racket feeling, allowing himself to feel his sadness, which the anger often masked.

"Just talking," writes Landaiche (2013), going on to explain how "each conversation becomes part of a larger story in which I can begin to find the meaning of this particular client's life" (p. 20). In this offered space of counselling, with all the needed time to talk it through and to explore, the client will slowly get a clearer picture, a better understanding of the issues he is struggling with, that are the roots for new self-agency. The client may then enter into a specific contract for change, be it for social control or relational change. However, in my experience the contract for change often remains implicit. While gaining a more thorough understanding of self, others, and the world, the client starts to make changes, feeling new needs, changing opinions and principles, allowing emotions, opening his frame of reference, starting to feel the forceful pull towards something new with new permission and protection to explore and move into yet unknown territories, thus revising his script (English, 2010).

12.2.4. An activated Adult

Narration, exploration, and understanding all satisfy the hunger for structure, more specifically for psychological structure. People need to make sense of an experience. As a counsellor, working in the here and now, through and with the Adult ego state, I am constantly working on that edge, between the pull of the well known, the past, the script, and the hope for a new experience, a new quality of life. As Cornell writes (2008a, p. 75), "The therapist's curiosity about the meaning the client has made of his or her lived experience can awaken the client's curiosity and lead to an examination of and reflection on underlying basic assumptions." This will help the client strengthen his Adult ego state and gain a new capacity for observation, both of self, others, and the situation, shedding a new light on his own experience, developing a different perspective from that of the Child. As Grégoire (2007) writes (I translate here from the French), "The Adult system is sensitive to the way reality works, independently at the same time of our own experience or subjective desires, and of others' reactions and judgements" (p. 123).

It is then my task, as a counsellor, to hold that tension, working on that fine edge between the fear and the hope, the old and the new, the known and the unknown. The client's strengthened, more active Adult is "the entry door to both reflexion that allows for change and to a lucid conscience, one of the aspects of autonomy" (Grégoire, 2007). The Adult, with a lucid perception, can facilitate mediation between the Parent and the Child ego states when internal conflicts arise, helping the client through an impasse and towards the desired change.

12.2.5. Working within transferential and counter-transferential dynamics

Working in a long-term setting allows for a careful observation of what emerges in the meaning, fantasies, and projections about the counselling relationship as experienced in the here and now.

Returning to McLeod and McLeod's "making a space to talk it through", in long-term counselling it is also the counsellor's task to make a space to talk about what is happening within the counselling relationship. This requires the willingness for the counsellor "to explore and use delicately and with sensitivity what is enacted within the relationship with both oneself and the other" (Monin, 2011, p. 120). This keeps the work in the here and now, in the present experience, and can prove to be profoundly healing.

I recently ended a four-year counselling relationship with a client. She wanted to explore her sensorial experiences by the use of body work and deep breathing techniques and move into a new direction. When she made that choice, in reflecting and exploring my own countertransference in supervision, I could feel fear and anger for her decision. I made the hypothesis that these feelings might have been the ones that her own mother experienced when her young daughter, my client, went to live with an aunt, as her mother could not take care of her herself. I made the choice to disclose what was happening for me and to offer my hypothesis to my client (Cornell, 2008b). Sharing my own personal countertransference from my Adult allowed for a space where my client, with her Adult, could look at her archaic experience of feeling abandoned through different eyes. This proved to be a turning point in her renewed relationship with her mother and a new reading and understanding of her script beliefs. This new awareness allowed for a smooth ending of the counselling work and gave her the freedom to affirm herself in her choices.

12.2.6. Conclusion

If the client repeatedly asks for short-term counselling in the midst of crises, both the client and counsellor may at some point consider the need for longer-term counselling. If the request comes from the client, this involves for the counsellor a careful analysis of the counselling situation, which is one of the core competencies of counselling (EATA, 2008) and will require for the counsellor to be clearly aware of her own strengths, vulnerabilities, and limits (Monin, 2011, p. 120). It is this careful assessment that will allow the counsellor to evaluate the potential benefit of longer-term work and analyse it with the client, resulting in a new contract.

Focusing on resources is another core competency in counselling as identified by EATA (2008). In assessing the counselling situation, the counsellor will take into consideration the "local resources in the community which could be of support to the client or to which the client could be referred, including medical, psychiatric, psychotherapeutic and other services", that will provide a holding environment for the client when engaging in long-term and in-depth work.

Fassbind-Kech (2013) explains how she regards the major task of counsellors as to help "their clients develop their awareness and abilities and to use and enhance their own resources and capacities to this end" (p. 25), which is another of the core competencies of counselling. In long-term counselling, "making a space to talk it through" can then become a resource in itself, a space in which the various facets of the personality of the client can emerge, a space that "supports and promotes [his] own movement towards authenticity" (Erskine & Moursund, 2004, p. 64).

12.3. Learning as a counsellor for university students

Mick Landaiche

12.3.1. Introduction

My colleagues in counselling are working in settings nearly too numerous to name: schools, prisons, job sites, military bases, religious institutions, medical facilities, social service agencies, elderly care homes, hospices, public health offices, community centres, drug and alcohol treatment centres, women's shelters, methadone maintenance clinics, birth control clinics, shelters for the homeless, residential treatment homes for adolescents or the chronically mentally ill, crisis hotlines, and private practices. We bring our skills and commitment to bear in countless "special fields" (Clarke, 1981). More than just an acknowledgement, this long list suggests why any definition of counselling will likely fail to capture the extraordinary diversity of the profession.

In this chapter, I look at two aspects that seem particularly important to my own practice and ongoing learning as a counsellor working with university students: 1) the not-always-straightforward process of contracting (Sills, 1997); and 2) the seemingly ordinary process of talking and listening that can lead to such important change, the fundamentally human communicative process that Monin (2011) characterised as one of common interest in all areas of counselling.

12.3.2. One professional's field experience

Like many in the international transactional analysis community, I have a complicated work history. Before training in mental health, I studied visual arts (drawing, photography, printmaking). I worked in corporate communications (slides, video, print production). I taught myself to program software for small business bookkeeping applications. I consulted with organisations and wrote strategic plans, grant applications, research summaries, and operations manuals. Then, after starting work in the mental health field, over twenty-five years ago, I earned a doctorate in the humanities. All of this, including many personal experiences, informs my understanding of the human condition and operates in my function as a counsellor.

For the past eight years, I have worked in a university-based counselling centre, a type of mental health clinic for undergraduate and graduate students of the university that employs me. Most US universities and colleges offer some kind of counselling or mental health service to their students, usually limited in terms of sessions and intensiveness of care. At our centre, we provide basic assessment and referrals (to community mental health resources); brief, twelve-session "counselling" (in quotes because, in practice, our interactions with students are complex and varied); limited psychiatric evaluation and medication management; crisis management (in the event of suicidal impulses or a psychotic break); and case management for students whose access to community and campus resources requires some coordination. Occasionally we work with student couples.

Our student clients range in age from seventeen to the early thirties. They present with an array of symptoms, from mild to severe: unbearable anxiety and panic, sleep disturbance, disordered eating, substance use, depression, suicidal impulses, self-harm, psychosis, academic failure, cultural adjustment, romantic and family relationship problems, social isolation, substance abuse, compulsive internet use, sexual concerns, sexual assault, and so on.

Our university is academically rigorous, with its strongest programmes at seemingly opposite ends of the spectrum. At one end, we are well known for computer science, robotics, and other high tech fields. At the other, we have distinguished schools of drama, music, visual arts, design, and architecture. In between are the other sciences and a smattering of studies in the humanities. The higher-profile areas of study attract very bright, talented, driven, hyper- (and hypo-) mature individuals. We also draw students from all over the world, many pressured by parental and family expectations for success, many struggling to bridge the differences between their home cultures and that of the US.

During one week last spring, the students I saw at the counselling centre were roughly 45% east Asian (Chinese, Korean, Japanese, and Vietnamese), 22% Latino (Chilean, Dominican, and Mexican), 22% Caucasian/European American (from every corner of the US), and 11% Indian.

Every day when I go to work, I have the sense of arriving in another country.

12.3.3. Contracts clear or convoluted

At times, contracting with my clients is fairly straightforward. They say what they want, and I can provide it: "I have been so angry with friends—I need a place to vent"; "I've been depressed—I think I need to talk with someone"; "My drinking [alcohol] is out of control—I want to look at that"; "I keep getting into relationships that end badly—what am I doing?"; or "I need to talk about something that I've never told anyone".

These straightforward contracts can change from week to week as we determine how many times to meet (within the twelve-session limit), what to talk about, or how to talk. Our focus can shift as new awareness develops, which Maquet (2012) described as key to the contracting process. Some clients find talking to be more upsetting than they imagined and so choose to stop, saving self-exploration for a later, less tumultuous time in their lives.

At times my clients cannot articulate why they came to the counselling centre. Their sense of something being wrong may be vague, even if they have given me a list of what would seem obviously problematic behaviours, troubled emotions, disturbed eating or sleeping, even bizarre thoughts. Some clients do not believe talking will help or that they have any role in their own troubles. They just want me to take it (whatever "it" is) away, like a magical doctor. They may be hostile to my enquiries. They may be contemptuous of my interest or my wondering if "A" might be connected to "B". Some refuse to talk, even if they return for additional sessions.

Some give no clear indication that they will keep the next appointment they have made with me. Some seem clearly engaged and then vanish without a word of explanation.

But unless a client presents with a medical or severe enough psychiatric condition (warranting referral to a more appropriate resource), and he is a threat to self or others (in which case I call campus police), or asks for help better secured, for example, from the university career counselling service or an academic advisor, I do not have the freedom to say, "I'm sorry. I don't think I can be of help." This is due to the contract I have with my employer, the university, which expects the counselling centre staff to meet with every student who requests services. Yet I also agree to meet with students when we cannot arrive at a clear contract because I do not believe someone has to have a functioning Adult in order to request or receive help of the kind I can offer.

In such cases, I work with an as-if contract in which I assume that each individual wants to grow and thrive, to be free of as much pain as possible, and to live as if living felt more like a blessing than a curse. In this spirit, "The heart of the counselling contract is facilitating the client's self-awareness and innate maturational forces" (Cornell & Hine, 1999, p. 184).

During the time that I meet with clients, some never achieve a functioning Adult. Some remain quite symptomatic. Still, I am watching carefully all the while for their signs of growth and life, however small or fragile. I am adjusting my interventions (my speaking, listening, being, goading, showing emotion) to their specific developmental needs and rhythm, to the best of my understanding and ability. I am contracting with a future potential I am likely never to see.

12.3.4. Multicornered contracts

Sometimes my clients come to the counselling centre voluntarily; sometimes they are pressured to do so by parents, teachers, or university staff. They may be legally mandated due to involvement in a theft, interpersonal violence, substance abuse, a suicide attempt, or a psychotic episode. I have mentioned already the pre-existing contract with my employer, which can be further complicated by contracts, overt or implicit, with other university personnel, the client's family, outside mental health care providers, and so forth.

Working in the context of multicornered contracts (see English, 1975; Sichem, 1991) is common for counsellors. Even if the client has voluntarily asked for help, there is often at least a third party invested in the client's behavioural change. That third (or fourth or fifth) party might be child protective services, law enforcement, family members, an educational institution, the military, a medical facility, a religious organisation, a government office, a corporation, and so on. The pressure from these other parties is often intense, certainly a constant presence, often impossible to satisfy, though their wishes may be understandable.

As counsellors, we may owe something to these other parties that may directly or indirectly pay our salaries. This tension is a limit on the freedom we might want to offer our clients and their work with us. I work within this tension and area of conflict first by prioritising the welfare of my client, to the best of my ability to define that. I will not do something requested by another party if I think it will harm my client, which is consistent with Grégoire's (1998) priority of protection. At the same time, I keep in mind that my client operates within a larger system, whether of family, university, or the greater community. Unless the outside party is making the client the whole problem (versus concerned about the problem the client may be having), I usually consider there to be something useful in the pressures that those outsiders bring to bear on the counselling and that those pressures represent something the client must live realistically within.

For example, I work with many clients from India, China, and Korea whose families have high expectations of and for them, both academically and professionally. These clients, as university students, may be encountering the American culture of self-determination for the first time and may find it attractive if intensely conflicting with their families' cultures of hard work and social accountability. As students studying abroad, they may be discovering they do not want the lives their families have mapped out for them. So, they may begin to perform poorly, become psychologically symptomatic, and/or engage in high-risk behaviours. Their families may then contact the university to mobilise more local pressure on their children to study harder, stay on track, snap out of it, and so on. The counselling centre is often brought in as a resource for the student. The expectation is that we will help return that student to optimal, pre-symptomatic functioning as defined by the family.

Such situations are highly complicated. However, I am careful not to make the family the problem. After all, they are promoting what they know or believe to be best. There is often some wisdom in their beliefs. More so, their values around work and community are woven into many facets of each family's life.

So, though I do not have to agree with the agendas or goals of the many parties that affect the therapeutic work of my counselling clients, I take seriously the fact that these outside parties likely represent something of the world and context to which my clients will, in some manner, eventually return.

12.3.5. Just talking

A client walks into my office and sits down. From there we find some way to talk together. What could be more ordinary?

As I described earlier, clients arrive in varied states and stages of knowing what they do or do not want to say, expecting or tolerating sometimes very particular, restricted responses from me. So I engage in conversation (or silence) in any manner that seems most comfortable for my clients. All the while, and in parallel, I am registering the flow of this conversation in my own body, perhaps like a traditional Chinese healer or Indian Ayurvedic practitioner who listens to the rhythm and interaction of multiple bodily pulses in the person who has come for help. I ask: what is the effect of this talking—the client's as well as my own—on the flow of sensations and meaning in my body? Does it begin to settle? Does it become more organised? Does it develop in capacity to bear the difficulties of life? I thus register the meaning of our exchange.

This sensing and evaluating is my guide for conversation, whether we are problem solving, commiserating, or apparently just discussing the weather. Each conversation becomes part of a larger story in which I can begin to find the meaning of this particular client's life. All the while, I may be drawing on multiple frames of reference from many sources of training and life experiences.

I have learned to trust that in following this natural human process of interaction, something productive can come of it. I have learned to pay minute attention to the ways in which my part in the process can and must be adjusted to facilitate movement in the direction of maturation and development as those are defined by each client's way of being, history, and current life context.

It may look like ordinary chatter, but it is constrained by my particular way of listening. For no matter how natural or familiar it may appear, I do not talk (or listen) in this way when I am engaged with family, friends, or even colleagues. Yet I also refer to my practice as "just talking" as a way of acknowledging and valuing its everyday, human qualities.

Mazzetti (2012a, 2012b) has discussed how different laws in different countries can affect counsellors' practices, which may include restrictions on the practice of talking to facilitate change. Yet however constrained we may be in terms of our conversations in counselling, I believe that learning to talk in some useful way with the people who come to us for help is a lifelong project that we continually fulfil with more or less success. And in that process, "We learn all the time from our experiences" (Newton & Napper, 2007, p. 150).

12.3.6. The steady flow of pain

For most of the working week, I am locked, as it were, in my office, engaged in some form of conversation. On the few occasions when I get out and walk across our university campus, I am always surprised to see students who are smiling, appear energetic and hopeful, engaged with others. I then realise the skewed view I have of our student body. I only see things going wrong. In some cases, I see students whose lives were not going well before coming to university and whose lives after, given family histories, are not likely to get much better. Every day of work, this kind of unhappiness and pain is what comes to me and my colleagues. And once there is some sign of amelioration, that person is free to move on and make room for the next distraught soul.

12.3.7. The limit and gift of time

Fassbind-Kech (2011) has asked, "What if the first interview is also the last?" (p. 291). At the counselling centre where I work, with clients constantly coming and going, this has become an ever-present question for me, with no clear answer. So I work with the assumption that each time I meet with a client in this counselling context, it may be our last session, even if it is also our first.

I may have this one chance with this particular client, who in some manner has called for help. Existentially, working within the frame of a single session means a radical embodiment in the present, however much I may imagine the past or hope for a better future. This present-centred discipline is echoed for me in Verzaal's (2012) discussion of "the spiritual core of counselling", a practice of helping clients reconnect to their inner cores or "spirits within". Verzaal's reframing of counselling's here and now focus acknowledges that we may have "but a short time with a client whose challenges may seem overwhelming and not realistically resolved quickly, but we may discover how to be with and accept, thus demonstrating a capacity of suffering with that is a mercy in its own right" (Landaiche, 2012, p. 9).

12.4. Counselling, excerpts from a case

Liselotte Fassbind-Kech

12.4.1. Introduction: defining TA counselling

My understanding of TA-counselling is very much based on the following EATA definition as expressed by the EATA Professional Training and Standard Committee (2008):

> Transactional analysis counselling is a professional activity within a contractual relationship. The counselling process enables clients or client systems to develop awareness, options and skills for problem management and personal development in daily life through the enhancement of their strengths and resources. Its aim is to increase autonomy in relation to their social, professional and cultural environment.

EATA specifies this task in the core competencies of the counselling field, of which my own personal favourite is core competency number 8:

"Focusing on resources"

a. [the counsellor] is able to utilize and build on the client's strengths, as the agent for change.
b. identifies existing resources in the client and client's system and integrates them into the counselling process.
c. has working knowledge of other local resources in the community which could be of support to the client or to which the client could be referred, including medical, psychiatric, psychotherapeutic, and other services.

What I especially like in this definition is the implicit presumption that our clients have all the necessary strength and the resources to overcome their difficulties and that our task as counsellors consists mainly in assisting them in the discovery, the validation, and the use of them in the service of a successful resolution of the problem. I find it particularly interesting to consider the client's entire life as a history and repository of potential resources, and I consider the client's body as the first resource. To attend to the client's bodily reactions is a very efficient way to invite the client into the "here and now", thus stimulating the Adult ego state (Berne, 1966, p. 220).

In presenting abstracts of the fifteen session counselling process of Mrs. A, I focus on the situations in which this search for resources was essential. The beginning of a counselling process sets the standards, models the way in which the counsellor and the client will shape their relationship, and thus is essential also in the way of considering the client's resources.

12.4.2. A case example: Mrs. A

Mrs. A is a woman of fifty-four years with three children of nineteen, eighteen, and fifteen years. Her husband has been in a care institution for seven years. He suffers from multiple sclerosis, and his condition is so unstable that recently she was called several times to say goodbye.

The children are in the process of choosing their careers. Mrs. A works 60% in a children's day care centre.

Mrs. A comes ten minutes late for her first interview and is out of breath. "I am sorry," she says, "I am so chaotic that I never manage to be on time." Thus she invites me to be sorry for her or to correct her. Ignoring this offer to engage in a psychological game, I invite her to sit down and to choose the position of her chair. Allowing her the opportunity to arrange her sitting position and thus to control the setting gives her autonomic nervous system the possibility to orient and so to differentiate between reality and thought or felt dangers and to activate her Adult ego state (Berne, 1966, p. 220).

When Mrs. A sits in her chosen position I welcome her again and start to gather her personal data. She knows these procedures from her job where she has to gather personal data from the parents when they register their children. So this "ritual" is another resource which helps in calming her down some more.

After this first structured part of the session Mrs. A. starts in a frenzy to describe her situation and her distress. She feels under constant pressure. She is afraid to fail with her children, their teachers, her husband, the doctors, her boss, her job, and all the people she means to have to satisfy. She realises that her sleeping problems and her frequent headaches are worsening her perception of being driven and not being able to cope with all her duties.

This explosive outpouring of her pain enables me to use another resource and I invite her again to activate her Adult ego state (Berne, 1966, p. 220). I show her my dismay for her difficulties and express my appreciation for the fact that she obviously managed to cope for many years with this challenging situation. She reacts with an immediate discount: "I made a lot of effort, but I mostly just reacted instead of being able to master the situation."

Instead of confronting her with the discount, I use a method as a resource. I invite her to change chairs and to sit on the chair of a best friend. From this best friend's perspective she is able to express appreciation and also to perceive a decrease in muscular tension. Returning to her original chair she recognises an instant increase of tension. She relates her tension to the year-long strain, and in recognising her capacity to stay the course for so many years she notices again a decrease of tension.

Mrs. A is amazed to realise that she asserts a clear difference of tension changing chairs, and changing roles. Thus she has just discovered a new resource, the possibility to observe her body and to give its signals importance. In the course of the sessions she learns how to use these signals in order to relax.

12.4.3. Establishing the contract

Mrs. A is now able to engage in a first contract. She feels relaxed enough to be able to reflect the actual problems with her son in order to start to understand the dynamics between them. She thinks that understanding will help her to react more calmly.

In the long term she wants to get rid of the feeling of being driven and to enhance her self-confidence. Mrs. A is convinced that her sleeping problems and her headaches, for which the physicians could not find a reason, will diminish if she is able to develop a self-assured and calm attitude.

The contracting itself, which is for transactional analysis counsellors a matter of course, is another great resource. In formulating the contract, the client already starts to envisage a future solution of her actual problem. "The brain is stimulated to a neuronal stabilization of the conscious or unconscious information" (Hüther, 2006, p. 87).

Mrs. A starts to talk about her perception of herself as the mother of a fifteen-year-old son. She describes herself as a shouting mother who often loses her temper. She has never beaten her children, but she is upset about her behaviour. She believes that she must make up for the father who, because of his illness, could not assume a classical father role during the last years. Intellectually she knows that she can't assume both roles, but she "feels driven to raise my son to be a valuable man". With her contaminated beliefs about her role as her son's parent (both father *and* mother), each time he does not behave like she wants him to she feels guilty.

Her double contamination is both from her Parent ego state: "If I can't substitute the father, I have to be a perfect mother" and from her Child ego state: "It is my fault if my son does not behave well."

12.4.4. Activating resources

In the search of resources, Mrs. A finds that her son has a good relationship with his uncle, the brother of her husband. She will ask him to spend some "time between men" with her son and thus give herself the permission not to have to do it all by herself but to share the responsibility. She describes that this feels as if she has been able to unload some of the weight she has been carrying. She also realises that her husband is not the only male person in the family, so she does not have to bother too much about her son not having a male model. This brother-in-law is not only a resource for herself, but also a resource for her son.

At the beginning I had asked Mrs. A about hobbies, and she had briefly mentioned her love for horses, emphasising that she had no time to bother with hobbies. This love is still a powerful resource. Mrs. A compares a horse's flight reaction with her own nerves. The horses break loose and flee when they get frightened, whereas she shouts and loses control. When I ask her what a good rider does after a horse has broken loose, she immediately answers that it has to be calmed down, groomed, and finally given some food. Laughing she says, "I see, that's what I should do, when my nerves have let me down. And at night, instead of demoralising myself with all the things I do not manage to do I could plan how to groom myself." Images are a powerful resource, and the more the images are connoted with positive emotions the more effective they can be.

Mrs. A's creativity, her humour, and her spontaneity are resources which help her to engage in the image of the horse. This will probably support her to maintain a position "I'm OK/you're OK, realistic" (English, 1976, p. 29), even if she does not always succeed in being the loving tender mother she expects to be.

12.4.5. Fears emerge

A few sessions later Mrs. A arrives in a state of irritation and nervousness. She wants to calm down in order to be able to find possible solutions for her current problem. After a few moments of noticing her physical sensations Mrs. A. realises that her breath is deepening and her heartbeat calms down. She notices that her feet move involuntarily and seem to express some agitation. "They seem to want to run away," she says, and I stroke this impulse as natural flight impulse, which is an archaic resource of the autonomic nervous system. She imagines walking or running until she says with a smirk, "Now it is time to rest." She notices with astonishment that she feels much more relaxed.

When I ask her for her thoughts about the impulse to run away she answers spontaneously, "The reason is obvious, because I am criticising myself constantly. The more the requirements from the outside are, the more I criticise myself, and the more I criticise myself the less I am able to structure my tasks in order to deal with one after the other." Suddenly she talks about the fears she experienced during childhood, fear of not succeeding in school, fear of being a burden for the parents, fear of being laughed at. At this moment I keep to the principles of counselling I am illustrating here. I do not engage in an exploration of these fears, but look for resources by asking her what kind of pupil she was. She answers that she was rather a good pupil and that she was not laughed at. And when I express my astonishment that notwithstanding her fears she managed to be a good pupil and a good colleague she sits silent for a moment and says, "I never saw it this way." After a while I repeat in a slightly different way, "So you never saw yourself this way." We spend some time to count the accomplishments of this child, during which Mrs. A is able to create a new attitude of self-esteem and to experience a feeling of love which she perceives as warmth in the heart and in her belly. I correlate Mrs. A's work to an aspect of self-reparenting (James, 2002, p. 47).

To use the new love and respect that Mrs. A is experiencing as a resource for the brave girl, I ask her to reflect what this experience could signify for her daily life.

She concludes that it would be sufficient to recognise her actual performances instead of still being afraid not to succeed, not being good enough, or not being accepted by others. She begins to list what realistically she is achieving, and with amazement she realises how easily she is able to list a lot of achievements and particularly how good it feels to name them. As a resource to have on hand if she feels not to be able to achieve anything and not to be good enough, she will start to open a stroke book that can remind her of the respect and the feelings for the brave girl from her childhood and of the courageous, competent, and efficient woman she actually is.

12.4.6. In conclusion: resources and autonomy

In my further work with Mrs. A I saw my task mainly as enhancing the awareness of her own capacities in Berne's definition of autonomy, "Autonomy is manifested by the release or recovery of three capacities: awareness, spontaneity and intimacy" (1964, p. 158).

At the conclusion of her counselling process, Mrs. A. makes a statement which matches my own understanding of counselling and which is also the conclusion of my work with this client. She says: "To see my resources, to experience that someone appreciates them, and finally to be able to appreciate them myself changed very much my self-concept. I experience myself as clearer, more structured, and hopeful."

12.5. Coming to terms with multiple sclerosis

Jan Grant

12.5.1. Introduction

I am a counsellor in private practice in Sydney, Australia, seeing both individuals and couples within a transactional analysis frame. Here I present my work with a woman I saw earlier this year for eight sessions. Written with her permission, she also contributes her experience of our work.

12.5.2. Case example

Sophie (not her real name) presented for counselling looking for support and a place to express her feelings. Six months earlier she had been diagnosed with multiple sclerosis (MS) and was gradually coming to terms with the diagnosis and what it meant for her life.

She is forty-six and a manager in human resources for a large company, quite a demanding job. There are internal politics and some challenging personalities at work that she finds stressful. She had been bullied by a previous manager, who has since left the organisation.

She is single and lives alone with her pets: a cat and a dog. She has a close relationship with her sister and her husband. Her sister is her chief source of support. Although she has some good friends, she has felt upset that some close friends had not "really been there" for her during this difficult period. Her mother died two and a half years ago, which has remained a further stress to Sophie. They had been very close, and she missed her mother's support through this difficult time of her life. Her father is still alive, but their relationship has been a difficult one. Since her mother's death, her father has kept away from her and her sister and has gone into a new relationship. She has a younger brother, but they have little contact, and in the past he had been abusive.

Sophie is very bright, articulate, and competent at her job. I sensed that it was not easy for her to be vulnerable, typically operating from Be Strong and Be Perfect drivers. Nevertheless, she was very emotional in the first few sessions. My initial impression was that it was important for her to have a safe place where she could express whatever was going on for her. In the first session I asked her to draw the MS. She drew herself with lightning bolts going through her brain and stomach. We talked about the "heat" in this image, and during the next week she visualised the wind and rain cooling her down. I have art materials in my consultation room and find it useful to ask clients to draw something that they are experiencing but finding challenging to speak about. Drawing can provide clients with the opportunity to externalise what they are experiencing on the inside. It also helps me to see how they are experiencing their internal world. For Sophie, this helped her express what she was feeling and the fear she had of what was going on in her body—something that she seemed to have no control over.

Sophie was aware that she was still coming to terms with the diagnosis of MS. It was challenging her sense of self: she was not used to asking for help and being vulnerable. She worried about losing her independence. She was very distressed at the thought of not being able to take care of her pets. She was questioning whether she should look for a less stressful job and move closer to her sister, but something was telling her not to rush into any big changes. I thought it was important to support Sophie's trusting of what was right for her, even if she did not quite understand it rationally.

An added dimension to the difficulties Sophie was experiencing was that she had a phobia about needles, and treatment for MS meant that she frequently had to have injections. Not knowing what to do about her job and her house were ongoing stresses for her—she liked to be proactive and taking time to make these decisions was not her normal way of handling things. I saw that her sense of self was being challenged.

12.5.3. Past or present

In the third and fourth session Sophie talked more about her father and what a jerk he had been since her mother's death. She talked more about her brother and how he had been violent and abusive towards her when a teenager. While this was significant history, she seemed resolved about these issues and had done therapeutic work around her brother before. There was a choice point for me here: whether to delve into the past or stay focused on the present. I did not see these areas as needing further work at this stage. More important to Sophie was her distress about her religious beliefs. She is a Christian and was struggling with things she had not liked in the church she attended. She had stopped going to church. I encouraged her to look for a congregation that felt right to her, as she needed spiritual support through this difficult time in her life. Again, I thought it was important to support Sophie's intuition about what was right for her.

12.5.4. Dealing with MS and work

There had been an "episode, symptomatic of the MS", which had thrown Sophie just before the next session. She had not felt great that day at work, still went to Pilates that night, but felt very tired and "odd". She stopped and went home. Sophie was very upset while describing this episode to me. She found the unpredictability of having MS a difficult thing to manage. In the past she had been very healthy and to feel out of control in this way was a new and unwanted experience, challenging her Be Strong driver. She clarified that her goal was to accept MS. I checked how she was feeling about what we had discussed about her father and brother in the last session, to make sure my hypothesis was correct: that she did not need to delve into her past at this stage. She confirmed that she hadn't thought about this during the week and had done a lot of work on it in the past. I felt comfortable with her focus.

At session six she came in and said that she needed to offload about something that had happened at work when she had reacted to a colleague with anger and felt bad about it. This connected back to the earlier situation where she had been bullied by a manager. I have a variety of cushions in my room and various toy objects. I asked Sophie to pick a cushion from the pile in the room to represent the workplace and an object to represent her. The cushion she picked for the workplace was elaborate, "looked nice on the outside but was nasty on the inside". For herself she picked a small lioness, sitting down. The lioness looked vulnerable. At one stage she said: "But I am good at my job," acknowledging how she has lost confidence in her abilities since the MS diagnosis. I asked her to pick another animal to represent her strengths. She picked another lioness—this time standing up and with darker markings. She felt good about this and took a photo of it with her phone.

12.5.5. New ways

At the next session Sophie reported that work had been quite stressful, but she had been managing well. There had been a serious harassment case between a member of staff and a manager. In her experience as an HR manager she had had to deal with similar situations in the past and found them very stressful and draining. She had also been bullied in the workplace (see her perspective), so this was quite triggering for her. She would normally handle such issues herself even though she found them very difficult, accessing her Be Strong driver to do so. This time she had delegated the case to someone else. I saw this as a good example of her making active choices based on a realistic assessment of what she could handle and the skills of her team mates. She had not expected herself to handle this alone. She had also made a big decision to go on an MS Walkathon—a fund-raising event for the MS Society. She had enlisted friends' support for this event. She was quite teary when talking about this and saw it as the next step in acceptance of her illness. The fact that she was talking to friends about her MS was a very big step for her.

In all I had eight sessions with Sophie and I left the door open for her to come back if she wanted to further down the track.

12.5.6. The client's perspective

Here is how Sophie described her side of the experience:

I needed a safe place to talk about what I was going through. Over a three year period:

- I had lost my mother due to a stroke. She was unwell for four months before dying of complications of the stroke.
- My father had lost interest in having a relationship with me and my sister.
- I was diagnosed with MS.
- I had been severely bullied at work by my manager and had the stress of making a complaint about what she had done. Needless to say this working relationship was an extremely abusive relationship. Further, it created an environment where I was not confident of my ongoing employment and being single, being able to support myself.

My first session was concentrating on my response to MS. I was asked to create a drawing of my relationship to MS. I was surprised at how accurate the drawing was. I do not believe I would have been able to articulate how I was feeling and the drawing was a great assistance. I still have the drawing on my fridge, and it is still of use. If I feel a little overwhelmed at the thought of the MS, it reminds me of the value of meditating that a soft wind and rain is easing the system of MS. It also serves to remind me of how far I have come in accepting my diagnosis. It makes me smile!

I was not aware that my self-removal from my church was impacting me. Having a safe space allowed me to explore this and make decisions which included going back to a church. As such I was able to build up the resourcing around me.

With regards to the issues I face at my work, if I feel like some of my colleagues are getting the better of me, I pull up the picture I have on my phone regarding "the cushion and the animals I picked". It takes me back to the session I had with Jan and reminds me of the power and integrity I have and it helps me to put things in perspective and manage the relationship at work more constructively.

I did not have the luxury of time and needed tools and resources to face the issues I was facing in a timely manner. I was so appreciated of the caring and practical approach of the sessions. This did not diminish facing my issues in that there was no skimming over the hard topics.

I still have some fears about life with MS. Life does throw us curve balls at times. I now have the confidence to know that I am able to deal with those fears. For this I will always be grateful.

12.5.7. Conclusion

In conclusion, I see this as a good example of short-term work, using transactional analysis. The counsellor needs to make active choices about what seems important to the client, particularly when it is necessary to work with past issues and when to keep the work focused on the present. The counsellor and client need to identify the client's strengths and build on these. A crisis like a serious illness being diagnosed both pushes people back into script and provides an opportunity to face life differently. Personally, I prefer to keep the work brief when clients have the resources to deal with their situation. The door is left open for them to return if and when they want to.

12.5.8. Postscript

Three months later Sophie contacted me again and came back for another four sessions. Overall, she was stable and coping well most of the time. Work had continued to be stressful and she had a new boss whom she found quite difficult to work with. She had had moments of feeling quite down, but connecting with a new church community had helped her. She felt like she was now accepting MS in her life.

References

Berne, E. (1961). *Transactional Analysis in Psychotherapy: A Systematic Individual and Social Psychiatry.* New York: Grove Press.

Berne, E. (1964) Trading stamps. *Transactional Analysis Bulletin*, 3: 127.

Berne, E. (1966). *Principles of Group Treatment*. New York: Grove Press.

Clarke, J. I. (1981). Differences between special fields and clinical groups. *Transactional Analysis Journal*, 11(2): 169–170.

Cornell, W. F. (1988). Life script theory: A critical review from a developmental perspective. *Transactional Analysis Journal*, 18(4): 270–282.

Cornell, W. F. (2008a). Therapeutic relatedness in transactional analysis: The truth of love or the love of truth. In: *Explorations in Transactional Analysis, the Meech Lake Papers* (pp. 66–77). Pleasanton, CA: TA Press.

Cornell, W. F. (2008b). The intricate intimacies of psychotherapy and questions of self-disclosure. In: *Explorations in Transactional Analysis, the Meech Lake Papers* (pp. 40–47). Pleasanton, CA: TA Press.

Cornell, W. F., & Hine, J. (1999). Cognitive and social functions of emotions: A model for transactional analysis counsellor training. *Transactional Analysis Journal*, 29(3): 175–185.

EATA (2008). *EATA Training and Examination Handbook*, section 5.3.1., p. 5. Extracted from http://www.eatanews.org/wp-content/uploads/2012/09/Section-5-The-Four-Fields2.pdf.

EATA (2008). Professional Training and Standards Committee. *Training and examinations handbook, 5th Edition*. EATA website.

English, F. (1975). Three-cornered contracts. *Transactional Analysis Journal*, 5(4): 383–384.

English, F. (1976). The fifth position. In: H. Grayson (Ed.), *New Directions in Psychotherapy*. New York: Human Sciences Press. (Also (1976) in: *Voices, Journal of the American Academy of Psychotherapists*, 1(43): 29–35).

English, F. (2010). It takes a lifetime to play out a script. In: R. Erskine (Ed.). *Life Scripts: A Transactional Analysis of Unconscious Relational Patterns* (pp. 217–238). London: Karnac.

Erskine, R. G., & Moursund, J. P. (2004). *Integrative Psychotherapy: The Art and Science of Relationship*. Pacific Grove, CA: Thomson, Brooks/Cole.

Fassbind-Kech, L. (2011). The first interview from a counsellor's perspective: What if the first interview is also the last? *Transactional Analysis Journal*, 41(3): 291–295.

Fassbind-Kech, L. (2013). Counselling as a treasure hunt. *Transactional Analysis Journal*, 43(1): 24–37.

Grant, J. (2013). Short term counselling and transactional analysis. *Transactional Analysis Journal*, 43(1): 58–67.

Grégoire, G. (2007). *Les états du moi, trois systèmes interactifs* (The Ego States, Three Interactive Systems.) Lyon, France: Les Editions d'Analyse Transactionnelle.

Grégoire, J. (1998). Criteria for defining the boundaries of transactional analysis fields of application. *Transactional Analysis Journal*, 28(4): 311–320.

Hüther, G. (2006). *Die Macht der inneren Bilder*. (The Potency of Inner Images.) Göttingen, Germany: Vandenhoeck & Ruprecht.

James, M. (2002). *It's Never Too Late to Be Happy*. Sanger, CA: Quill Driver Books Word Dancer Press.

Landaiche, M. (2012). Unsettled gifts from the Chennai conference. *The Script*, 42(10): 8–10.

Landaiche, M. (2013). Working within limits. *Transactional Analysis Journal*, 43(1): 14–23.

Loomis, M. (1982). Contracting for change. *Transactional Analysis Journal*, 12(1): 51–54.

Maquet, J. (2012). From psychological contract to frame dynamics: Between light and shadow. *Transactional Analysis Journal*, 42(1): 17–27.

Mazzetti, M. (2012a, July). *Les frontières de la guidance en analyse transactionnelle*. (Frontiers and borders in transactional analysis counselling, Part I.) *Métamorphose*, 63: 14–16. [Originally published 2010 as *I confini del counselling in analisi transazionale*. (Counselling boundaries in transactional analysis.) In: A. Bondi & E. Lo Re (Eds.), *Luoghi e modi del counselling* (pp. 179–194). Milan, Italy: La Vita Felice].

Mazzetti, M. (2012b, December). *Les frontières de la guidance en analyse transactionnelle.* (Frontiers and borders in transactional analysis counselling, Part II.) *Métamorphose,* 64: 14–16. [Originally published 2010 as *I confini del counselling in analisi transazionale.* (Counselling boundaries in transactional analysis.) In: A. Bondi & E. Lo Re (Eds.), *Luoghi e modi del counselling* (pp. 179–194). Milan, Italy: La Vita Felice.]

McLeod, J., & McLeod, J. (2011). *Counselling Skills, a Practical Guide for Counsellors and Helping Professionals (2nd edition).* Maidenhead, UK: Open University Press.

Monin, S. (2011). The art of minding the gap: A counselor's ethical challenge. *Transactional Analysis Journal,* 41(2): 118–122.

Newton, T., & Napper, R. (2007). The bigger picture: Supervision as an educational framework for all fields. *Transactional Analysis Journal,* 37(2): 150–158.

Shipton, G., & Smith, E. (1998). *Long-term counselling.* London: Sage.

Sichem, V. (1991). *Le multicontrat en thérapie d'enfants.* (The multicontract in child therapy.) *Actualités en Analyse Transactionnelle,* 15(84): 125–129.

Sills, C. (Ed.) (1997). *Contracts in Counselling.* London: Sage.

Tudor, K. (1999). *Group Counselling.* London: Sage.

Verzaal, B. (2012, 10 August). The spiritual core of counselling. [Presentation at the 2012 International Transactional Analysis Conference, Chennai, India.]

Vinella, P. (2013). Transactional analysis counselling groups: theory, practice, and how they differ from other TA groups. *Transactional Analysis Journal,* 43(1): 68–79.

CHAPTER THIRTEEN

Management and organisational development

13.1. Working climate: the influence of the weather on the workplace
13.2. How to build an organisational Parent system
13.3. Developing trust and responsibility
13.4. Transactional analysis for organisation development
13.5. The business of redecision work

The TA field of organisations is for professionals working in or with organisations and/or businesses. They are concerned with the (further) development and growth of those organisations and/or companies for whom they provide consultation, training, and management expertise. The focus is on increasing the effectiveness of the (groups of) people whom they work with or for.

The *Handbook for TA Training and TA Certification* describes the core competencies for this field. See www.itaaworld.org/itaa-training-examinations-handbook.

Clients in this field are often leaders of organisations and businesses who are intrigued by, or worry about the productivity and/or quality of the systems within which they work.

13.1. Working climate: the influence of the weather on the workplace

Anne de Graaf

13.1.1. Introduction

"What's it like working here?" the applicant asks. Nine times out of ten, the answer given by the HR management member or the manager will include an impression as to what "working climate" means. In everyday terms, "working climate" describes how it feels to work in an organisation: it refers to something similar to the atmosphere. The notion of the working climate comes originally from social psychology. In this context, working climate is defined as "the prevailing atmosphere in the workplace, the department, or the team as it is experienced by the employees". It's like the office weather system—sunny or rainy, warm or cold. In contrast to the weather outside, it's possible to exert a favourable influence over the weather indoors: this is the focus of this chapter. In this article, working climate elements are associated with an explanation from transactional analysis.

13.1.2. 30%

It is quite a statement to say that the working climate is 30% responsible for the results achieved by a group or organisation. Nevertheless this is what Daniel Goleman (2000), brought to our attention in a recent article. "And that's simply too much of an impact to ignore," he declares. A positive working climate has a beneficial impact on employees and contributes to a good or even outstanding performance.

13.1.3. Dimensions

The climate within an organisation can be measured and managed, according to McClelland (1987). Once it became clear that there was a measurable relationship between the working climate in an organisation, motivation, and results, his work attracted a lot of attention. Climate = motivation = behaviour = result! Since then, there have been indications that the climate can exert an influence in areas such as innovation, stress reduction, trust, reduction in staff turnover, team cohesion, dealing with conflict, professionalisation, etc. In this chapter, the following six dimensions, based primarily on McClelland's work, will be explored: clarity, standards, responsibility, rewards, support, and (team) commitment. First of all, the respective dimension will be described with brief examples of how a high and low performance level in this dimension can be recognised in an organisation. The content of the dimensions will then be further explained by means of one or more concepts from transactional analysis.

13.1.4. Clarity

Employees work with a clear definition of their role and the tasks that go with it. A low level of clarity creates confusion concerning who is authorized to make what decision.

13.1.5. TA concept: contract

Making contracts is a central activity within the TA approach. Effective management of expectations increases the chance of success for everyone involved. It's worth taking the time to make a clear contract for every role and task. In one of his books (1966a), the founder of TA, Eric Berne, defined a contract as follows: "A contract is an explicit bilateral commitment to a well-defined course of action." At the start of a collaborative relationship (as well as a working agreement), a minimum number of matters are clarified in a contract:

- Who are the two parties involved?
- What are they going to do together?
- How long is this going to take?
- What is the intended outcome of this process?
- How will both parties know if the result has been achieved?
- How is this result going to benefit the organisation?

This not only relates to the examination and creation of the factual and formal side of a contract: it's more about examining and revealing the unconscious, informal side. Even unspoken matters, while they are still unconscious, mutual expectations, contribute in the long run to ambiguity regarding roles and tasks. Even if something is not written down in black and white, it is still regarded as a contract: there are always (hidden) expectations when people work together. An open contract has a great many advantages:

- It is a mutual agreement.
- It determines the minimum expectation.
- It provides opportunities to speak with one another.
- Common responsibilities are created.
- Differences in responsibilities become clear.
- Work can be evaluated.

The English organisational consultant Julie Hay (1995b) states that the closing of a contract always involves the management of three things: result, relation, and responsibility.

13.1.6. Standards

Employees know when they are working according to the ruling expectations. High expectations concerning the level of performance to be delivered mean that everyone searches for opportunities to improve personal performance. When there are few or no expectations regarding this level, people are quickly satisfied with the performance that is achieved.

13.1.7. TA concept: windows on the world

The TA concept of "life positions" received worldwide recognition through the successful book *I'm OK–You're OK* by Thomas Harris (1969). The fact that this book, written in the 1960s, is still being printed shows that the author struck a chord with readers. It doesn't deal with everything that a person does to be OK: it's more fundamental than that. It is about the question whether you're ready to accept and treasure another person, unconditionally. Julie Hay later (1993) reworded the term "life positions" as "windows on the world". The four different windows refer to a view of the world, which always has a deep impact on your behaviour in your daily life and work. The leader who predominantly looks through the "I'm OK, you're not OK" (+/−) window makes his employees feel inadequate, incompetent, and sometimes stupid, and then they behave accordingly. The level of performance often sinks dramatically. The leader window "I'm not OK, you're OK" (−/+) causes employees to feel uncertain and, in the long term, to lose their trust in the management. People are quickly satisfied with the performance that is achieved. Finally, the leader who looks through the "I'm not OK, you're not OK" (−/−) window will probably see any energy within his team disappear: the spark is completely extinguished. There are no expectations any more.

High expectations concerning the level of performance to be delivered, whereby every person searches for opportunities for improvement, are experienced by the leader who views the reality of the organisation through the "I'm OK, you're OK" (+/+) window. An OK organisation is one which takes into account people's feelings and needs—employees, managers, customers, members of staff, etc. An OK organisation creates as healthy and pleasant an atmosphere as possible for everyone, both physically and emotionally. An OK organisation focuses on more than competition; it focuses on the collaboration between its employees. An OK organisation's target is learning and development, with a spotlight on improving employee and customer satisfaction: energy flows within the organization!

13.1.8. Responsibility

Above everything else, employees are "their own bosses". Where there is a high level of responsibility employees are encouraged to solve problems themselves. If the level is low, taking risks and exploring new methods is discouraged.

13.1.9. TA concept: autonomy

Autonomy is another core term in TA. Eric Berne never defined this term, but wrote that autonomous people can be recognised by three characteristics (1964):

- They have a high level of awareness. They take notice of what is going on in and around them. They are very discerning.
- As they are so aware they always have a number of options when it comes to making decisions. They know more about the facts surrounding a situation and thus have a better overview.
- They are not too concerned with how others perceive them: they don't spend all day thinking about what other people think of them. This makes them authentic!

The concept of options is a core concept in TA. People often find themselves at a dead end as they only have a single option when it comes to solving a problem at work. If this option isn't successful, they'll often continue in the same way, thereby conforming to Albert Einstein's definition of a fool: "A fool is someone who continues to do the same thing and expects a different outcome!" The effectiveness within organisations increases if employees have at least three options before tackling a problem. It is of great importance that their leader grants them permission to take risks and go down different paths: this heightens autonomy!

13.1.10. Rewards

Employees are rewarded when they work well. A high degree of recognition creates a good balance between compliments and advice, positive and negative feedback. When there is a low degree of recognition of achievements, rewards are incoherent.

13.1.11. TA concept: strokes

People need to feel that others take notice of them, recognise them, both at work and in other areas. This means that, as a leader, you see, hear, and acknowledge the effort they make. Withdrawal, frustration, and cynicism can often trace their origins to a feeling of not being noticed, not being recognised for who they are and/or what they do. The secret of dealing effectively with recognition can be found within the TA concept of "strokes". Eric Berne (1972) used the word to describe a unit of recognition. "Stroke" means both stroking in the sense of gentle contact, but also a strike or a blow. People need strokes to live. If they receive no positive attention (stroke in the gentle sense: compliments, interest, care), it seems that they go and look for negative attention (stroke in the sense of a strike: negative comments, arguments, conflict, punishment) rather than no attention at all. To put it bluntly: people want rather be "struck" than ignored. Those who are continuously ignored gradually lose their spark.

Everyone needs attention, some more, some less. The kind of attention that is needed also varies from person to person. Every human being has an internal thermometer with which to maintain the correct "attention temperature". A lack of interest, recognition, and attention threatens personal and professional development and growth.

13.1.12. Support

Employees experience an atmosphere of trust and support. A high level of support gives employees the feeling that they belong to an effective team which can provide help when they need it. In contrast to this, when the level of support is low, employees feel isolated and alone.

13.1.13. TA concept: permission, protection, and power

Anyone who works with TA does so hopefully on a basis of permission, protection, and power (Crossman, 1966): three essential elements in the relationship between leader and employee.

Permission to do things differently, to change undesired behaviour, to grow and develop. Protection against overly critical treatment and other negative influences that limit change. Power—the way in which the leader uses his own knowledge, skill, and expertise—supports employees' growth and development. A powerful leader strengthens the growth and development of employees.

A leader who provides sufficient permission, protection, and power is in the position to tackle and address matters (and indeed conflicts) that are hidden beneath the surface. This keeps the communication within a team open and clear.

13.1.14. Commitment

Employees are proud to work for this organisation, this team. Employees are particularly loyal to the organisation and its objectives if there is a high level of commitment. A low level of commitment means that they are apathetic towards the organisation and its objectives.

13.1.15. TA concept: Bystanders

The large majority of a group is made up of what is known within the TA game theory as (potential) Bystanders (Clarkson, 1996). If the working climate is OK, all members can exercise their qualities and exert the maximum influence on how things work. However, during "bad weather", employees are more reserved. They withdraw and don't, or no longer, dare to use their qualities. By doing this, they turn themselves into Bystanders in the development of the team or organisation of which they are a functional part and for which they bear responsibility. They don't comprehend that by not intervening, they silently and unintentionally agree with the way things work: they let it happen. They lose their understanding of influence, their level of frustration increases, and there is a risk of them jumping ship and bad-mouthing the organisation.

Of course, Bystanders always have seemingly plausible arguments. They make it possible for themselves not to assume their role and to remain on the sidelines. They are able to talk themselves into believing that they play no part in the organisation. If Bystanders alter their behaviour and attitude and actively apply their influence, they can really get things moving within the system that they're a part of. Those who don't try to change anything in a problematic situation will ultimately be changed by the problem at hand.

13.1.16. Influence?

A not unimportant question, knowing about the dimensions of organisational climate, is of course that of how the working climate can be influenced, above all by leaders. What can they do to maintain a certain level of motivation, thereby guaranteeing productivity? If it is indeed true that 30% of the results are down to the working climate, finding an answer to this question is rather important. The influence of the values, attitudes, and beliefs at work within the company should not be underestimated: in other words, the culture of the organisation.

13.1.17. TA concept: script

The culture of an organisation determines the habits and behaviour that is typical of the employees of that organisation. The concept of "script", as it was developed within transactional analysis, helps the organisation to analyse the culture within it. Each organisation has a legend, a story, explaining its origins, core beliefs, and purpose. The Brazilian organisational consultant Rosa Kraus believes that the script (the culture, the story) of an organisation has a significant impact on the individual and the collective. In order to understand this better, you have to pay particular attention to how organisations handle four central issues in their everyday life: work, time, people, and money. In an organisation that "focuses on the effectiveness of the work", where "time is seen as a valuable resource", where values such as "collaboration, mutual respect, openness, and trust" are present, and where "money is nothing more than a means to an end", there is a large chance that the working climate will contribute significantly to the result in the organisation. In this kind of organisational culture, the six elements described above (clarity, level of presentation, responsibility, recognition, support, and commitment) have a great opportunity to score very highly.

13.1.18. Conclusion

The most important influence on a working climate stems from the leader's behaviour. Goleman (2000) suggests that "… 50 to 70 percent of employees' perceptions of a working climate is linked to the characteristics of the leader." Good leaders are above all "climate managers": they ensure that employees develop, feel good about themselves, are productive, and feel appreciated! A change in the leadership style of leaders therefore changes the working climate. The leader has a major influence on all six elements that determine the working climate. Anyone who, during an exit meeting, which is carried out when an employee leaves an organisation prematurely, asks: "How was it working here?" will, nine times out of ten, be given an answer by the respective employee that includes an impression of the predominant "working climate". In the large majority of cases the leader will be cited as the person responsible for the employee's exit. And that's simply too much of an impact to ignore.

13.2. How to build an organisational Parent system

Maarten Kouwenhoven

13.2.1. Introduction

An organisational Parent system (OPS) is the conscience system of an organisation. It will lead to higher productivity, a positive reputation, and to employees who are proud of their work. In this article I will describe how an organisational Parent system can be developed, what the pitfalls are, and which actions are needed in order to build a positive corporate reputation.

13.2.2. Organisational structure

Every organisation has a personality structure, just like a person. This personality structure consists of three subsystems which are called ego states (Berne, 1963).

- The Parent system, necessary to raise awareness of moral values.
- The Adult system, necessary to develop strategic behaviour, based on logical thinking in the here and now.
- The Child system, necessary for cooperation and inspiration.

Most organisations invest in programmes based on the Adult system, for instance product and service development programmes, and the Child system, for instance employee development programmes. But investments in programmes based on the Parent system, such as developing common moral value programmes, are mostly neglected.

According to my experience, only 2% of humanity deliberately intends not to act with integrity; they come to work in order to violate moral values for their own benefit. For about 18% of humanity, circumstances determine how they conduct themselves. The remaining 80% are affected in a negative way by the actions of these 20%.

A lack of a clear organisational conscience system can damage the reputation of the organisation, as was the case in recent years with the banks, in construction, the food processing industry, in public institutions, in the church, and on the football field.

13.2.3. What is an OPS?

An organisational Parent system (OPS), or organisational conscience system, is a set of written and unwritten values, norms, and rules which are shared by all people in an organisation as a standard to guide behaviour in all situations. Norms and rules only have significance if the underlying values are clearly communicated. This needs to done from a "Why though" and not from a "Why not" attitude.

Why not: "If you arrive late you disrupt the organisation for others and you get a penalty."
Why though: "If you are on time, you contribute to the effectiveness of the workforce which is pleasant for everyone."

13.2.4. How does an organisational Parent system develop?

In our youth, the development of a value system generally takes place between the fourth and sixth year. In that period the value system is still external. The child says, "This is forbidden by my father or mother." The child adapts to these norms either by being obedient or rebellious.

This receiver of norms and standards is called P_1 or "electrode" (Berne, 1972) as shown in Figure 13.1.

In organisations a P_1 system is visible in the form of external rules that are imposed on employees.

An excess of external rules can lead to an anxiety culture. Employees know what is forbidden but not what is allowed. As a consequence they can decide: "As long as I do nothing, I will not violate a rule." From a didactic and from an organisational standpoint this is not very effective. Too many rules may even provoke integrity violations, not by violating a rule but by not following the rules. In that case "rules are made by fools".

During education the external norm system is internalised to an internal value system between the sixth and twelfth year.

In a company, employees will search for the underlying values of expectations, rules, and instructions of their executives. When employees have discovered these values, they are able to predict the reactions of their executives in advance. By then they are part of the OPS.

In a healthy OPS we see a form of didactical leadership. This kind of leadership not only focuses on the transfer of knowledge and the organisation of the work process, but also on transferring corporate values.

Developing an internal value system requires a functioning Adult (A_2) with which you can think logically in the here and now. Employees with only a partially developed Adult have trouble in recognising and finding out the underlying values of expectations, rules, and instructions of the executives. Because of that, they often feel let down and part of an incomprehensible, unpredictable, and threatening organisation. So, explanation, discussion, instruction, and training are the base of a healthy OPS. Managers are the key persons to do that in a didactic way, like parents and teachers do with children. In bigger organisations they can be supervised by specially trained compliance officers (Kouwenhoven, 2014). This will lead to higher productivity, to employees who are proud of their work, and to a positive organisational reputation.

13.2.5. OPS disorders

An OPS can, just like the personality of people, show different disorders.
The OPS can be:

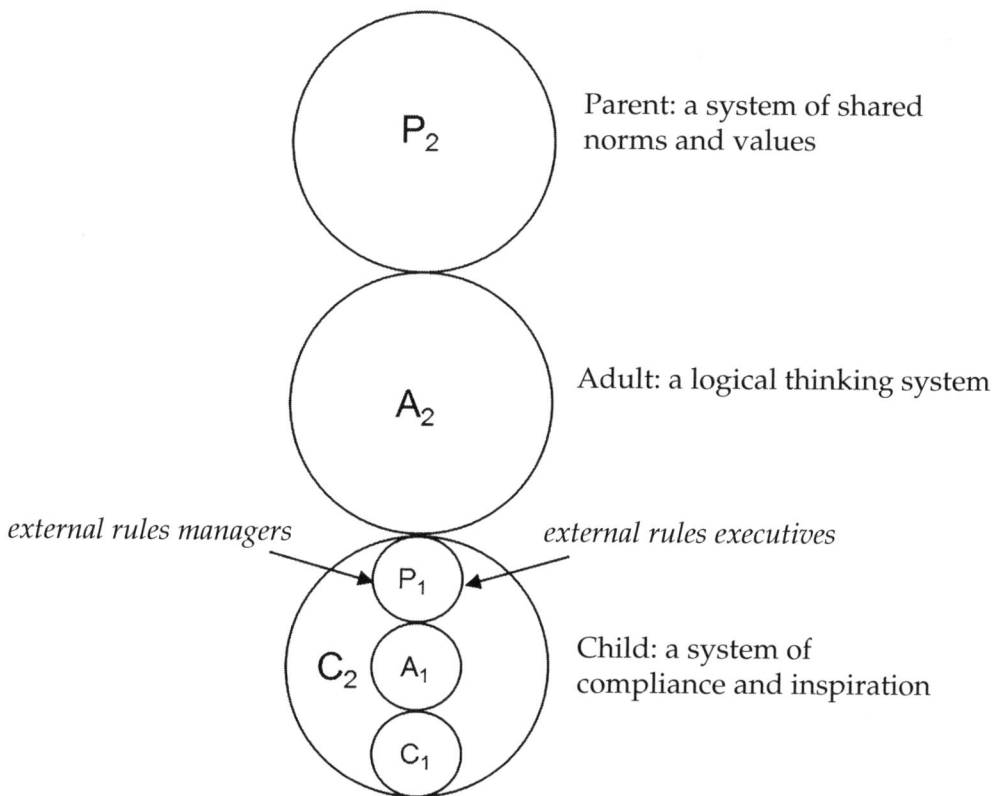

Figure 13.1. P_1 or electrode as the receiver of external rules.

- Non existing (NOPS).
- Big (BOPS).
- Small (SOPS).
- Contaminated and crazy (COPS).
- Deviant (DOPS).

In the following I will explore the most common OPS disorder: the No-organisational Parent system (NOPS).

13.2.6. The development of a NOPS

A NOPS is characterised by inconsistent, contradictory, and unpredictable behaviour of the executives. As a result, employees will feel insecurely attached (Bowlby, 1969). This will lead to stress reactions like fight, flight, and freeze and psychological games (Karpman, 1968).

There is no sharing and caring: executives look after themselves and as a consequence employees do not want to be dependent on them. The internalisation of organisational values stops. Employees will receive the instructions and regulations of the executives in P_1 and then

352   INTO TA

in a clever way, try to get around them. This can lead to asocial or antisocial behaviour. If things go wrong employees will blame their managers and vice versa.

In this disorder the Parent system is not completed. There is no clear communication of shared organisational values. There are only single values, but they are contradictory, they change in time, and are often used to for personal goals. Organisations with a NOPS act from two instead of three ego states. In fact this is not a disorder but a defect.

13.2.7. Characteristics of the Parent system in NOPS

The behaviour of executives, managers, and employees in a NOPS is often described as uninhibited: self-centred, focused on gratification of their own needs, without commitment to other associates, and without understanding their own defects.

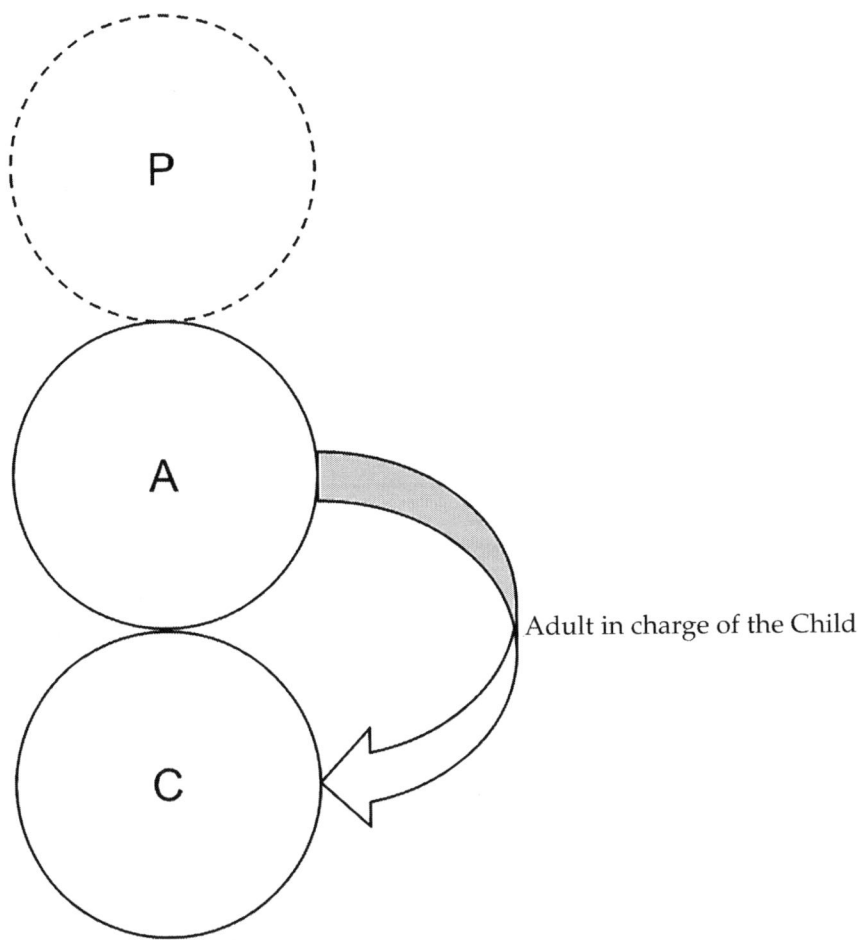

Figure 13.2. No organizational Parent system (NOPS).

Often they are not committed to laws and customs of an ordered society. They behave greedily and think they stand above the law. They benefit from, manipulate, lie, or do not share relevant information with each other. Their behaviour is unpredictable and is based on contradictions and not on the understanding of social rules. This concerns everybody except the persons in question. A negative reputation is the result.

Organisations with a NOPS often penetrate to a high altitude in society. Their executives are smart, strong, and quick and have a radar for money and opportunities. This radar system is in service of their own interests, "more, more and even more", like a "greedy little pig". They seem to be very successful, until the NOPS collapses. Then the organisation goes bankrupt and nobody feels responsible. The creditors, the shareholders, and the taxpayers will pay for the loss.

13.2.8. Characteristics of the Adult system in NOPS

The Adult in the Child system (A_1), also known as the Little Professor, is well developed and is aimed at compensating for the lack of parenting by manipulating the environment in such a way that it gets what it want. The Adult (A_2) is built on this A_1 and as a consequence people in organisations with a NOPS make thinking errors, based on discounting the reality (Schiff, 1975). This is not the same as a thinking disorder, which is a more severe, psychiatric symptom. Thinking errors are based on conclusions that are inconsistent with the reality in the here and now.

A comprehensive inventory of thinking errors is collected by Yogelson and Samenow (1976, 1977).

Examples of thinking errors are:

- I am the centre of the world.
- If you're not for me, you are against me.
- Authorities are there to punish me.
- Beautiful women are there to be caught by me.
- Rules apply to others, not for me.

Most people recognise this kind of thinking in part, but they know it is, in most cases, not true. People with thinking errors really think that their way of thinking is right because their thoughts were never corrected by educators, trainers, or managers.

13.2.9. Characteristics of the Child system in NOPS

The Child system within a NOPS consists of three parts (Schiff, 1975):

1. The powerless part.
    In a NOPS, people are afraid of being humiliated because of their negative self image, based on a lack of positive approval. They think that they are "a big zero and everyone can see this".

354   INTO TA

2. The powerful part.
   People avoid this dreadful powerless position as much as possible by strengthening and extending their omnipotence position. A big house, a big car, and a big mouth are their weapons. In this position they are often angry and have a high opinion of themselves.
   The powerful position is expressed in arrogance, pride, ownership, disobedience, and looking for kicks, with sayings like: "If I want something which belongs to another, then it's actually already mine," and finding excitement in doing things which are prohibited.
3. The hurt part.
   The emotional development of people in an organisation with a NOPS is retarded or blocked. As a result, it is difficult for these people to respond adequately to their own emotions or those of others. They will disguise their authentic feelings of pain and sorrow, which are the result of disregard, abuse, or neglect and show substitute (racket) feelings instead.

"If I am afraid of other people I react angrily. Then others are afraid of me. Then I do not need to be afraid for them any more."

13.2.10. A programme to build a healthy OPS

In a NOPS, people find it difficult to recall problems, to analyse them, to generalise them, and to reflect on them. That is why people do not learn from their mistakes, have a lack of self-control, have limited meta cognitive skills and a lack of impulse control.

With this in mind we developed an OPS programme for executives and managers.

This programme is given in the form of e-learning modules, and face to face courses led by teachers and supervisors. The programme focuses on three dimensions:

1. The Parent system: to raise the awareness of values.
   Awareness of values takes place by asking the question: "What is important for you in your work, in this meeting, in this conversation?"
   Employees and managers reflect on their personal and organisational values, write them on name tags, and order them. So they construct a hierarchic frame of reference of

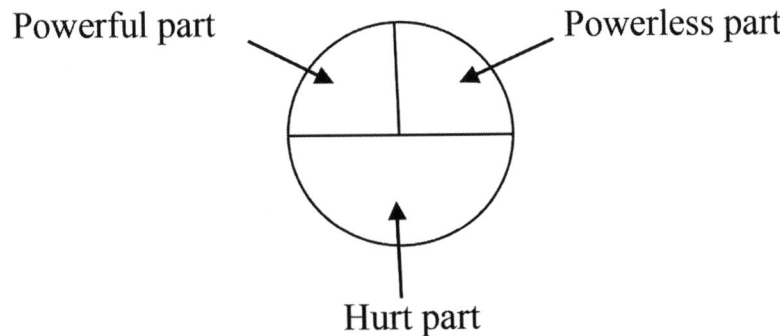

Figure 13.3. Three parts of the Child system.

values. If this exploration and checking of values is successfully achieved, the external values on the name tags (P_1) become an internal, shared organisational value system on P_2 level.

Managers can stimulate this process during all meetings and conversations.
2. The Adult system: to detect and correct errors of thinking.

In order to detect and correct thinking errors we use the coaching matrix (Kouwenhoven, 2007). The coaching matrix starts with an exploration of the subject or question and consists of four chronological steps.

1. What are the relevant facts?
2. What is your problem?
3. What is your goal?
4. What action do you choose to reach your goal?

The coaching matrix is written out on a large sheet of paper on which the person who raised the question writes down the answers.

Thinking errors about facts will be visible in step 1. Thinking errors about managing emotions will be visible in step 2. Thinking errors about moral values will be visible in step 3. And thinking errors about behaviour will be visible in step 4. The strategic coach instructs, supervises, and coaches the employee through these steps.

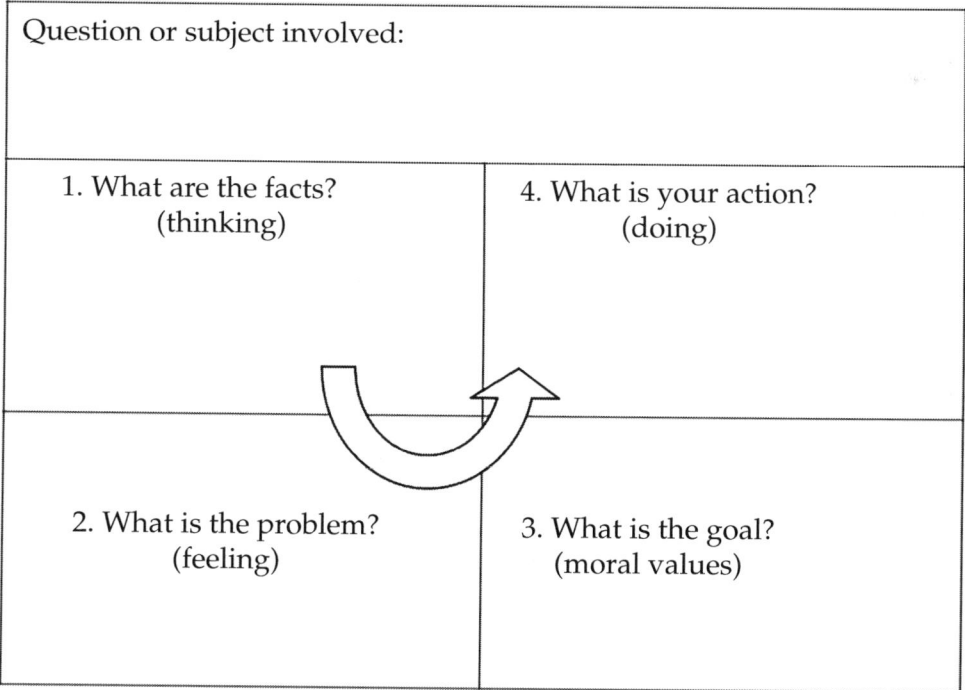

Figure 13.4. The coaching matrix.

3. The Child system: to achieve cooperation and inspiration.

   Inspiring is achieved by training the actions from box 4 in a micro simulation, for example by using symbolic objects and play out situations. Micro simulations are very realistic. This is because our brain does not distinguish between a simulation and reality. In this way a new neurological path is created in the brain. This path can be chosen if the situation really occurs. There is a lot of permission, protection, and it is a powerful way to develop new behaviour.

13.2.11. Conclusion

The model of OPS is helpful to analyse problems in organisations and to restore a healthy functioning moral value system in organisations. The strategic coaching matrix can be used as a tool in order to create an organisation where people trust each other and work effectively together.

13.3. Developing trust and responsibility

Anita Mountain

13.3.1. Introduction

In this chapter I describe a consultation with a management team in a large organisation. In this process, the importance of clarity of assessment, detailed contracting with specified outcomes, and the development of trusting relationships were highlighted. All of these were underpinned by skills development. The outcomes included:

- the workforce, including the senior management team (SMT), taking responsibility for their actions and how they communicated with each other;
- the resolution of differences;
- a friendly atmosphere and culture within the department.

13.3.2. The commission

A not-for-profit countywide organisation approached me to undertake a commission to develop a service within it. The total number of employees was over 57,000 and this department of sixty was responsible for a customer-facing service. The newly appointed head of service (HoS) wanted to develop and expand the service. There had been an investigative report which outlined concerns about relationships within the department. While targets were being met, the issues centred upon the need to develop a healthy culture. To this end the SMT wished to see certain changes which became the outcome contract:

- the ability and willingness of employees to resolve disagreements;
- for the workforce to understand how their behaviour impacts on others and develop the skills to relate effectively.

These would be evaluated by a 1–10 numbering system at the beginning of the commission and again at the end (e.g., questions such as how they experienced their conflict resolving skills and their ability to relate with others, 10 being the highest). Emotional Intelligence is a social as well as individual phenomenon, so raising the awareness and skills in the department was crucial.

13.3.3. Addressing the issues

I interviewed everyone in the department in order to ensure that individuals experienced being heard. I then analysed these interviews and designed the programme based on the needs of the department. Individuals felt discounted by management in terms of their skills and competencies; simple courtesies such as saying "Good morning" were often omitted and people felt alienated. Based on the analysis of the interviews the administrative contract was agreed as two-day programmes for each of the six teams, including the SMT, with an overall day for the whole department. This was followed up with a further day for the SMT to ensure they were able to continue and reinforce the outcomes. Analysis of the standardised interviews showed that:

- benefits of the job outweighed the disadvantages;
- pay was good and on the whole people enjoyed their work;
- the greatest issues appeared to be the organisational culture:
- the culture was one of "I" and/or "we" are OK but "they" are not OK. There were divisions within the whole service both laterally and horizontally.
- close monitoring created an individualistic and hostile culture.
- the experience of being treated like children by the HoS who was seen as autocratic and restrictive in her practices.

In relation to the psychological contract it became clear that the HoS wanted the team to comply to her frame of reference and for me as the consultant to sort out the staff to make this happen.

The analysis led to the development of a five-phase process agreed with the SMT and discussed with staff. This was based on the basic tenets of TA, namely contractual process and OKness. Given the culture of discounting I needed to ensure that people and situations were taken account of, which is why the staff were involved as much as possible in the process.

13.3.4. The programme

Work was done with each team with an identical structure for each of these two-day events, namely: contracting, the TA concepts of OKness, including 3D OKness (Mountain & Davidson, 2011), Structural ego states, OK Modes (Mountain & Davidson, 2011), as well as the Concepts for Thriving model. The training involved a range of exercises.

13.3.5. Concepts for Thriving

The Concepts for Thriving model (Mountain & Davidson, 2011) was used as one of the assessment tools because the interviews showed that communication was dysfunctional and the workforce did not feel emotionally safe. This model was adapted from Roberts's Hierarchy of Functionality (1992). While not directly TA, the model fits with TA philosophy and the belief that safety and security are of paramount importance for a productive and harmonious workforce.

There are seven basic components that promote thriving (see below). These components are built upon each other and when they are established and applied in the organisation, and the relationships within it, are likely to be effective.

MANAGEMENT AND ORGANISATIONAL DEVELOPMENT   359

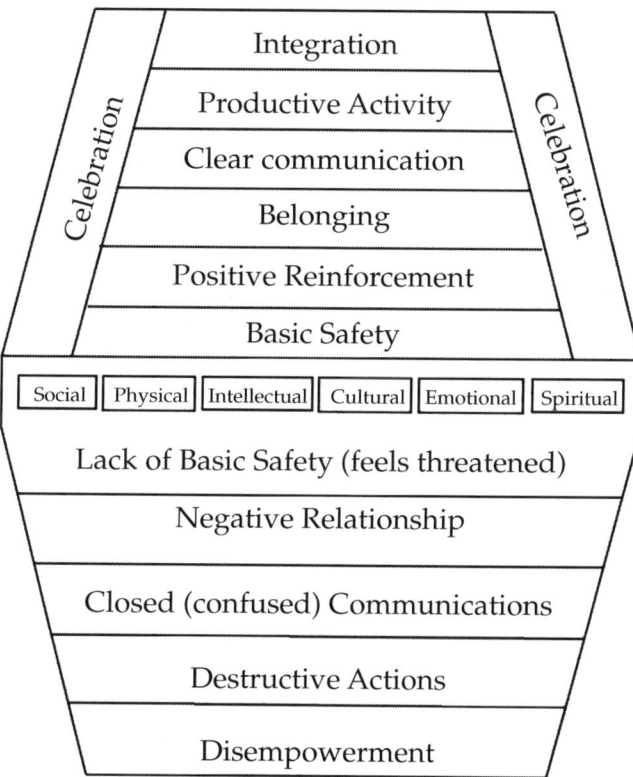

Figure 13.5. The Concepts for Thriving model.

The model was shared with each team and they assess where they thought the difficulties lay. All of them believed there was a lack of a sense of safety and they then decided what needed to be done to address this. Once the internal dynamics were addressed they looked at the inter-team issues.

To show the application of this model after each definition I have put an example, in italics, from this commission.

Table 13.1. Concepts for Thriving Definitions.

Safety	When I have this, my primary needs are taken care of, I am comfortable with myself, and boundaries are maintained. *The workforce experienced being over-monitored and watched by the HoS and never getting anything right.*
Positive reinforcement	I am given positive strokes and there is mutual exchange. *A negative stroking culture was experienced. Few people acknowledged each other in the mornings and there was a lack of empathy between people.*

(*Continued*)

Table 13.1. (Continued).

Belonging	I start to develop a positive sense of who I am in this team or this particular situation. *The workforce experienced a disconnection with the HoS. The structural separation of sections had, to the general workforce, created divisions and greater difficulties in communication. This was added to by the aforementioned sense of over-monitoring and the belief that to get up from their desks to talk to each other would be frowned upon.*
Clear communication	I know I am being heard and I am therefore more willing to hear others. *General communication regarding work issues was effective but individuals did not experience being heard.*
Productive activity	I am in the present moment and collaboratively solve problems. I recognise and am recognised for my competence, and I have a sense of who I am. I am able to balance giving and receiving. *Because the workforce did not feel heard it was difficult to experience working collaboratively.*
Integration	I can be spontaneous. I make positive things happen in my life. I recognise my achievements. I learn from mistakes and continually improve. I enjoy who I am and what I do. *Spontaneity was lacking in this department for fear of being reprimanded. As this was a culture with few positive strokes recognition for achievements was limited. Culture change through trust was a priority.*
Celebration	My achievements are acknowledged. I accept myself, who I am, what I do, and who I am in relation to others and the world. I acknowledge my own, and others' achievements (this runs through every level). *The staff did not experience celebration.*

All teams agreed that they would value talking with management, and in particular the HoS. The concerns included projections onto the HoS about how she viewed them. For this reason the HoS and deputy were invited on the morning of the second day. To ensure the managers also felt emotionally safe, I met with the HoS and deputy without Rescuing the teams, which was a delicate and fine line to tread.

By attending each team's event on the morning of day two, the HoS and deputy developed their own awareness of the issues and their part in these and were willing and able to respond appropriately.

The OK Modes model

Because of the lack of effective communication leading to distrust and animosity I decided to share the concept of OK-ness followed by Mountain and Davidson's (2011) OK Modes model (see below). The OK Modes model provides a visual way of representing how we behave and interact with other people. It has ten different communication behaviour "modes"—four of which are effective and prompted by the process of mindfulness, that is, taking account of current reality and acting accordingly, with the other six being ineffective. With both the OK Corral (Ernst, 1971) and the OK Modes model we use green for the effective and red for the ineffective relationships, just like traffic lights. (In Figure 13.6 the bold black text and grey italic text represent the effective and ineffective areas respectively). Adopting this approach makes it easy to visualise the stop and go (or flow) to each exchange in a conversation and therefore to track and understand what went on.

We then moved on to look at three-dimensional OK-ness so that they could apply this concept between teams in the department.

This model relates to observable behaviour and is therefore appropriate for work in organisations as it requires only social and behavioural assessment of what goes on between people. It also helps us to consider where we need to come from when relating with others.

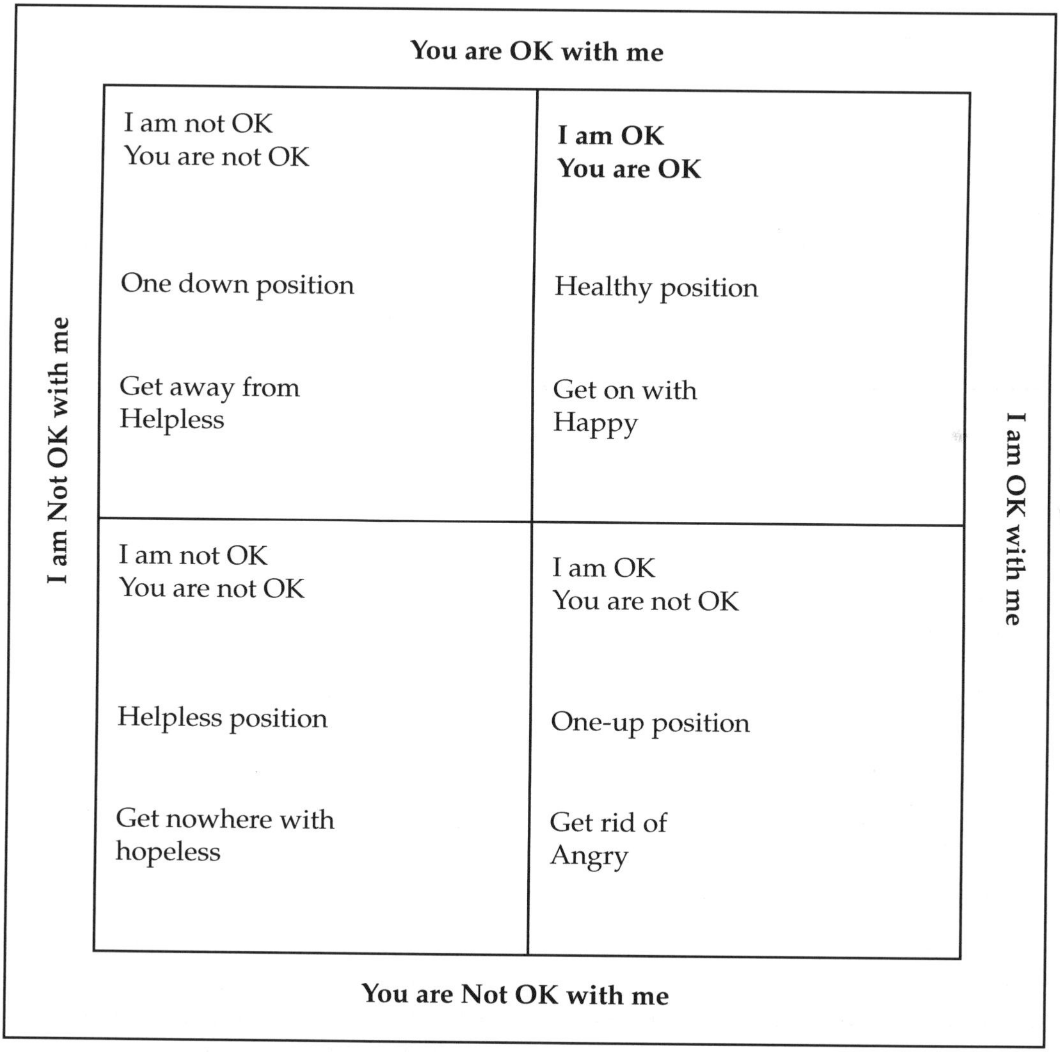

	You are OK with me	
I am Not OK with me	I am not OK You are not OK One down position Get away from Helpless	**I am OK** **You are OK** Healthy position Get on with Happy
	I am not OK You are not OK Helpless position Get nowhere with hopeless	I am OK You are not OK One-up position Get rid of Angry
	You are Not OK with me	

(Right side label: I am OK with me)

Figure 13.6. The OK Corral (F. Ernst, 1971).

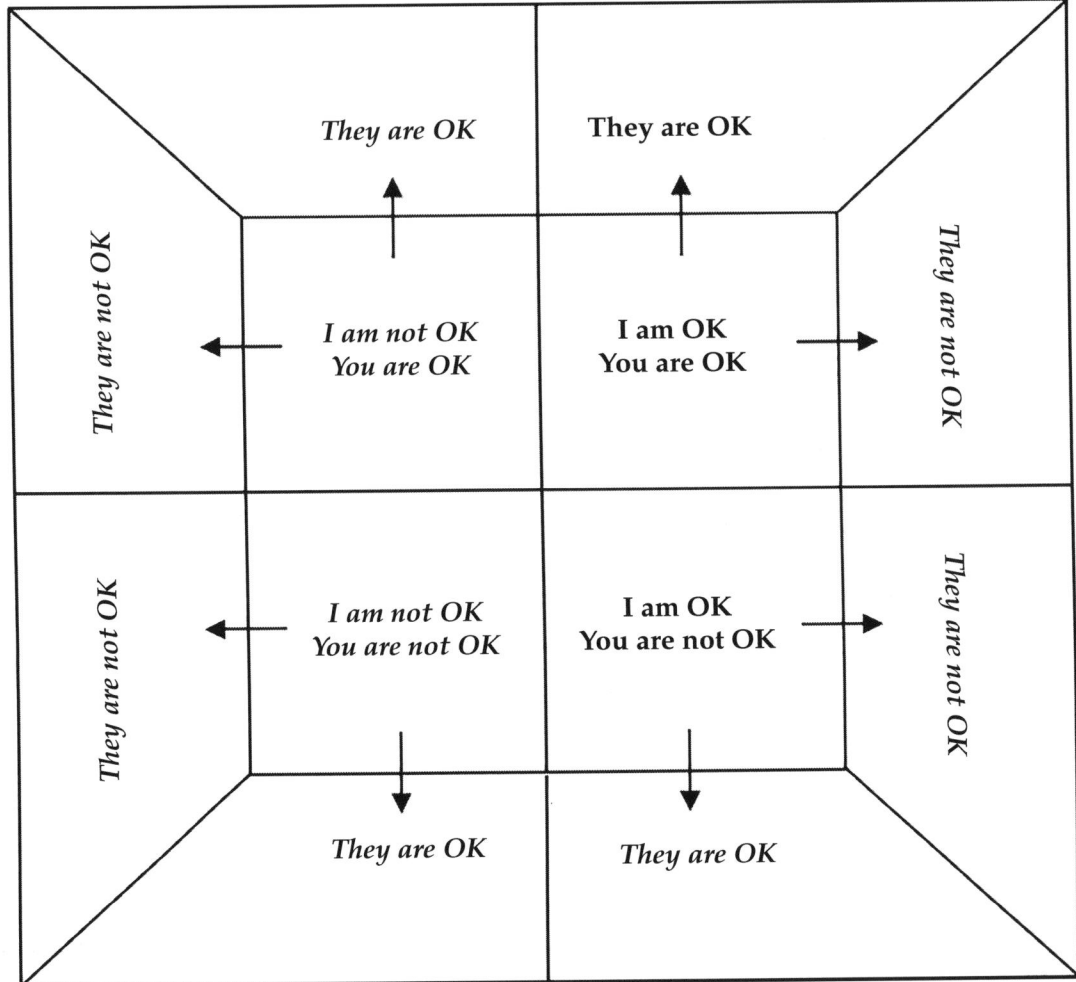

Figure 13.7. The Three-Dimensional OKness.

13.3.6. The diagram

Effective communication

When we are in one of the effective Modes we are responsive to the present situation. Generally when something is said from an effective mode the response from the other person is likely to be from an effective mode, and vice versa.

Effective Modes

The Mindful process

As human beings we respond, react, and initiate. How we behave in any particular moment will depend upon whether we transact in an automatic way, rooted in the past, or are in the

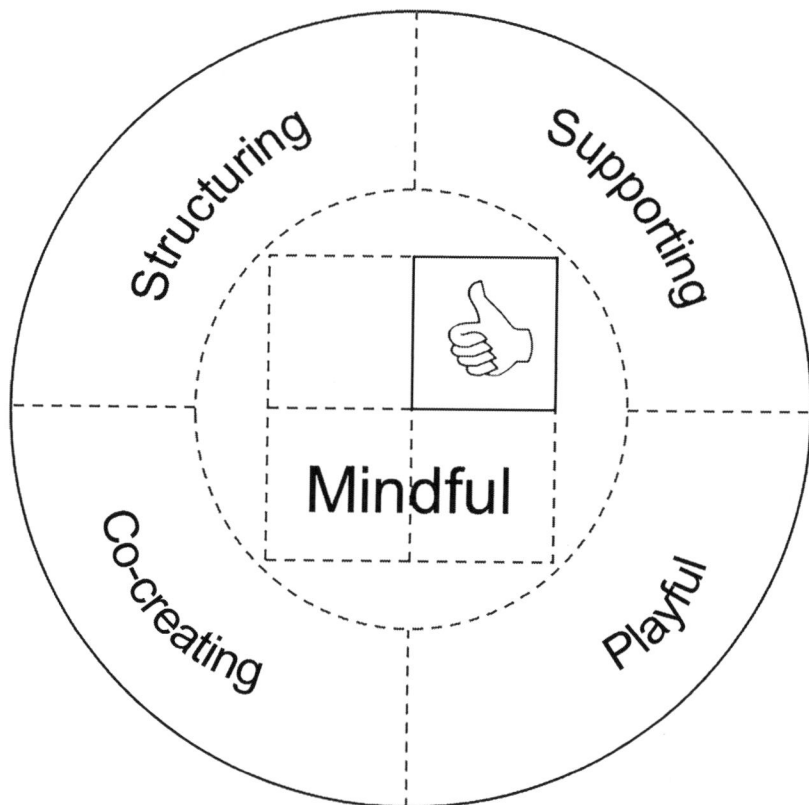

Figure 13.8. The effective OK Modes.

present dealing with current reality. The central area of the diagram is called *mindful* as we need to bear in mind the totality of the situation and possible consequences of any actions and taking account of the present. It is not a mode of behaviour as we cannot see mindfulness, but we will see any subsequent actions, which reflect a *mindful* process. The effective modes are placed within mindful process. There are also times when we need to stand back and observe a situation before deciding what to do next which is why *mindful* is in the centre. All of the effective modes communicate *I'm OK, You're OK, and They're OK*. An example of this being when the HoS decided to call in outside assistance to help address the organisational cultural issues, including how the teams related to each as well as to the SMT. This was a mindful process.

Supportive Mode

In this mode we are appropriately caring, affirming, consistent, and reliable and our support fits with what is needed. Generally the deputey HoS effectively transacted from the Supportive Mode as did most of the team leaders, which explains why productivity levels were relatively high despite the difficulties with communication.

Structuring Mode

When in this mode we are boundary setting, offering constructive criticism, and being caring while firm. Generally the HoS transacted from this boundary-setting mode. However, because there was a lack of balance with the other mindful modes, she tended to be seen as overdoing the structuring and moving into Criticising Mode (see below). The teams therefore tended to feel that they had to be perfect for her.

Co-creative Mode

Co-creativity in this model means being willing to join with others to develop and create something different. From this mode we are able to recognise that we can create something together with others that is greater than the sum of the parts. This was particularly present intra-team.

Playful Mode

This creativity, fun loving, curious, and energetic mode was lacking in the department as a whole.

When in the mindful process it is possible to choose which of the effective modes to use—depending on the situation. If someone is invited to go into an *ineffective mode* they have a choice. They can accept the invitation, and move to a subservient or domineering position in the conversation, or resist this invitation by staying in an OK–OK stance and responding from one of the effective modes—thus remaining mindful.

The ineffective modes are now added to the previous diagram:

The ineffective modes are diagrammed as the three Not OK boxes of the OK Corral. These ineffective zones all reflect outdated and non-integrated experiences from our past. We don't seem to be in control of these responses—which could more accurately be described as reactions. They are the "overdone" counterparts of the positive ones within the mindful process circle and are likely to be "hooked" by a trigger.

Criticising Mode

This mode can be recognised as "overdone" Structuring mode. When here we are authoritarian, persecutory, or patronising. Thus creating a lack of loyalty in a team or department.

The HoS was experienced as coming from this mode. This was an overdone aspect of her structuring mode. Being new and ambitious she increased her Be Perfect driver as she went into first level stress.

Inconsistent Mode

This mode is recognised over time and relates to being first one way and then another so that others are unsure about how to be in relation to us. Leaders in this mode tend to change their behaviour in unpredictable and apparently random ways.

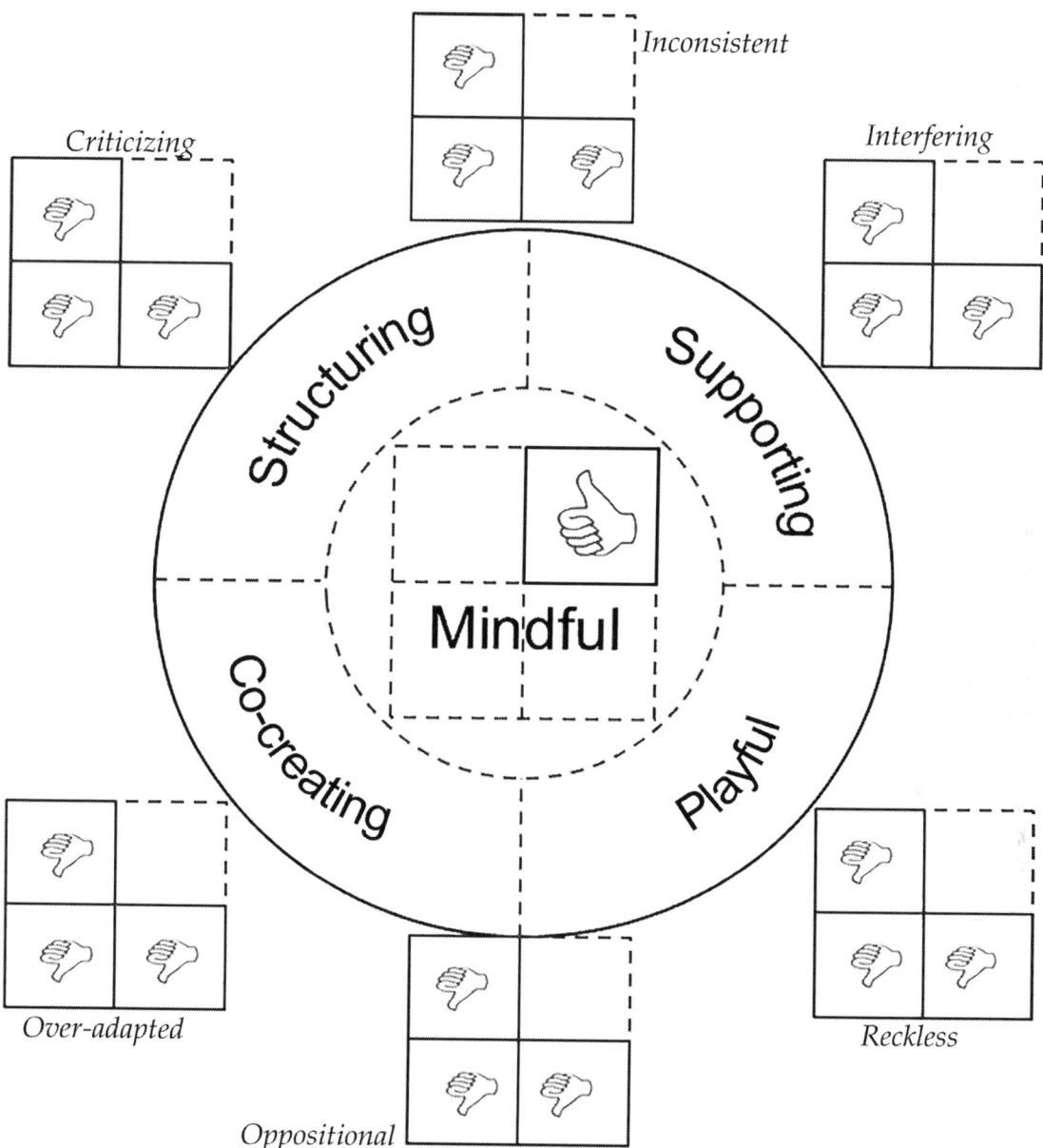

Figure 13.9. The Complete OK Modes diagram.

Interfering Mode

When in this mode, our behaviour is of "Rescuing", that is, doing things for others which they are capable of doing for themselves. We could also be overindulgent or fussing. This can be seen as "overdone" Supportive mode.

Over-adapted Mode

When in this mode we over-adapt to others, that is, we try to please without asking them what they want and tend to be passive and compliant.

Many members of staff were in this mode in relation to the HoS and each other, not expressing their needs.

Oppositional Mode

When in this mode we will be resisting and opposing without any objective or consistent basis for doing so. Employees who do this earn a reputation for being obstructive. When in this mode we are unlikely to be willing to hear others and consider their perspective. Like the inconsistent mode the oppositional mode is only likely to become noticeable over time.

Many of the staff were resisting and opposing in relation to the HoS.

Reckless Mode

At work we will tend to behave in ways which indicate unwillingness to take responsibility for our actions. Our energy appears unfocused; we fail to keep to agreed time boundaries. This mode is different from the Oppositional Mode in that the actions will not be a response to another person, but more doing our own thing, regardless of the people around or the situation.

Areas of difficulty

Initially, the HoS showed little awareness of her involvement in the lack of emotional safety within the department and this was a delicate issue to address. If I raised it with her it could be experienced as Rescuing the teams and Persecuting her. Instead I supported the teams to use the concepts and rehearse how they would share their thoughts and feelings with her and the rest of the SMT. I also prepared the HoS and the deputy for the meetings including how to remain open and OK/OK and look for the grain of truth in what was being said. This meant that all the team members involved had the opportunity to apply the theory in reality.

How this helped the organisation

This model was helpful to all teams when considering their behaviours with each other and in preparing for the meeting with the managers. It offered a non-judgemental way of exploring their actions. By using the philosophy of OK-ness and The OK Modes model they developed communication skills, which developed trust. The distrust had developed through a lack of awareness and the concept of mindfulness was helpful to them in changing this.

The HoS was open to feedback and offered thoughtful responses to the teams. She volunteered vulnerability and took responsibility for her actions, whilst encouraging team members to take responsibility for theirs. The staff subsequently softened their attitude towards her. The outcomes of all conversations between management and the teams promoted emotional safety and diminished the psychological distance between teams and management (Micholt, 1992).

In summary

The department moved from conflict avoiding to conflict resolving, putting down their assumptions and prejudices developed over time (Berne, 1972). They learnt how to maintain their own sense of OKness and keep others OK; subsequently the unhealthy competitiveness diminished. Individuals experienced an increase in positive strokes, which led to a greater sense of attachment and belonging. As honesty developed so too did the levels of trust, and productivity increased. The HoS was willing to ease up on some of the demands she placed on the staff. Her sharing of her own vulnerabilities led the staff to see her in a new, positive light and relationships improved. They were then able to feel stimulated by her vision for the future and to take their own responsibility for their actions.

13.4. Transactional analysis for organisation development

C. Suriyaprakash

13.4.1. Introduction

The purpose of this contribution is to illustrate the application of transactional analysis (TA) as a potent frame of reference for an organisation development (OD) consultant. A composite case study format is used to highlight how TA can be used for interventions at various levels of an organisation. In this case study of a typical small and medium manufacturing industry based in India, TA is used for contracting, diagnosis, and interventions to bring change at the individual, group, and organisation levels. TA models are integrated seamlessly along with non-TA organisational models to facilitate change. Berne's (1963) theory on organisations forms the basis of the frame of reference. It also includes later contributions to organisational TA by Hay (1995a), Krausz (1993), and Schmid (2008).

13.4.2. Client system

Millennium Garments was a small garment export unit situated in a textile cluster town in southern India. It was founded by two friends, Kumar and Raghav, capitalising on the industrial renaissance fuelled by the liberalisation of the Indian economy during the early 1990s. Kumar and Raghav were working in a leading garment manufacturer in that region for over a decade before they decided to start their own business. They started their operations in a humble shed with about fifteen employees and within ten years they grew to a workforce of 100. During the early 2000s they ventured into a major growth strategy of expanding their operations six fold, moving into a new state-of-the-art manufacturing facility with over 600 employees.

The workforce at Millennium Garments was constituted mainly of immigrant workers from the southern districts of the state and a sizeable number of immigrants from northern Indian states. When they were small, all roads led to the cabins of Kumar or Raghav for all day-to-day decisions. Everybody reported directly to them and both of them had full knowledge of all the happenings in the company and every order. There was no formal organisational structure, especially at the managerial level. Everyone did everything, chipping in whenever or whatever was needed. When there was a problem employees turned to either Kumar or Raghav for a solution. They prided themselves on having a family-like culture and employees had a high sense of belonging.

When the organisation grew exponentially, all of a sudden taking wind from the growing economic prospects of globalisation and liberalisation, Kumar and Raghav were taken by surprise.

They were not able to cope with the increased business and size of the organisation. Without a formal organisation structure and reporting systems in place business was falling apart. Orders were not delivered on time and even one day of delayed shipment resulted in huge losses since orders had to be airlifted in those cases. Loyal customers started turning towards other suppliers with many south Asian countries offering much more attractive price advantages. It was at this juncture we were contacted to "do something" to improve the scenario.

13.4.3. Consultants

I am part of a team of three certified transactional analysts. Our consultancy services are primarily based on a TA frame of reference, integrating with complementary approaches of organisational theories and behavioural sciences.

13.4.4. Consultancy

OD is defined as "a long-term effort led and supported by top management to improve an organisation's visioning, empowerment, learning, and problem-solving processes through an ongoing, collaborative management of organisation culture with special emphasis on the culture of intact work teams and other team configurations using the consultant-facilitator role and the theory and technology of applied behavioural science including action research" (French, Bell, & Vohra, 2006). From a TA perspective, OD is defined as "an evolving set of specific activities designed and implemented to achieve the following: to maximise Adult-Adult transactions between individuals; to identify and untangle quickly crossed transactions between people; to minimise destructive game playing among people and between work groups; to maximise authentic encounters (intimacy) between individuals; to develop administrative systems, policies, and work climate that support the preceding objectives" (Randall, 1973). To this we add "in order to improve organisational effectiveness".

We adapt the treatment triangle (Stewart, 1989) to OD consultancy: accordingly an OD project has three major stages, namely contract, diagnosis, and intervention. To this we explicitly add evaluation and feedback for a TA based participatory action research approach to OD.

13.4.5. Contract

The initial problem presented by the client based on the obvious symptoms of an ailing organisation were:

1. Delayed delivery.
2. High rate of product rejection due to poor quality.

Based on these, the contract was to do the required interventions that would result in:

1. On-time delivery of orders.
2. Product quality within permissible limits of rejection.

The time frame initially agreed was six months. Later the project was expanded to three years based on emerging needs and to sustain the changes accomplished.

To fulfil this contract the project was divided into two phases: diagnosis and intervention. Inputs from the diagnosis stage will decide the specific contract for the interventions.

13.4.6. Diagnosis

The organisational script grid (Krausz, 1993) and Berne's six group diagrams (1963) were used as frameworks for diagnosis. A select sample of individual employees were interviewed for the purpose of the project. Interpersonal and inter-group dynamics were assessed through observation of meetings and real-time transactions. Focus group discussions were also held with the top management and other employees separately.

Organisational script analysis of Millennium Garments showed that it had a "non-winner" script. It was characterised by a lifeline of survival, mediocrity, and compassion; an ambiguous, inconsistent management style; low productivity/quality with high costs; the organisational climate was rife with anxiety, insecurity, and confusion; an unclear organisational structure; decision-making concentrated at the top; reactive, fire-fighting problem-solving processes; accommodative inter-group relations; the work ideology was "task oriented"; the time ideology was "to be spent without clear objectives/priorities"; the money ideology was "money was sometimes a means and sometimes an end in itself"; the people ideology was either "get rid of" I+Y- or "get away from" I-Y+. Overall, the organisation's life position vis-à-vis its members was "I'm not OK, you're OK".

Regarding Berne's group diagrams:

The layout diagram and seating diagram showed a clear discrimination among management and factory employees. While the management staff received luxurious and sophisticated work spaces, the factory employees had very basic, primitive facilities at their work space.

The formal authority diagram showed there was no clarity in the roles and responsibilities at all levels.

The group structure diagram showed complex leadership with both Kumar and Raghav occupying the space without clarity of boundaries. Both of them were looking after all the operations which often resulted in confusion and uncertainty in the minds of members not knowing whom to follow or approach.

The group dynamics diagram revealed that a lot of time was wasted in the minor internal processes in the form of game playing among the members, which resulted in delays and poor quality. Major psychological processes between Kumar and Raghav were also surfaced at the top management focus group interview. This resulted in less cohesion for the major external process to combat the pressure from customers and competition.

The complex leadership structure and the resultant confusion and uncertainty were revealed in the group imagos of the leadership and membership. The leadership slot in the group imagos of members lacked consistency with each partner occupying that position for some of the members within each functional group. Some members had placed both the partners in the leadership slot.

The transactional diagrams in the meetings and informal conversations showed predominant CP-AC complementary transactions. Ulterior transactions were also widely prevalent as a result of over-adaptation of the employees. Top management often crossed the transactions from the members which left the members no room for voicing their opinions and ideas, thus reinforcing further adaptation.

As a result of the diagnosis, the following interventions were planned:

1. Clarify the values, mission, and policies of the organisation.
2. Restructure the organisation.
3. Role analysis for all the positions.
4. Training of staff to build awareness about self, communication, motivation, and organisation culture.
5. Team building exercise to foster team spirit and to commit to the organisation's cause.
6. Team coaching to improve functional effectiveness of work teams.
7. Process consultancy to improve intergroup collaboration between functions.
8. Executive coaching to clarify the boundaries between the two partners.
9. Employee assistance programmes to improve employee engagement.

This expanded the scope of the project beyond what was conceived initially and so the project contract was expanded to two years.

13.4.7. Intervention

A business system consultant was brought in to facilitate the first three interventions: to clarify values, mission, and policies, to put in place a formal structure with clear functional departments and authority structures, and to clarify roles and responsibilities of all the positions in the organisation. While the other consultant brought in technical expertise we provided people and process skills in developing these systems. They went on to put in place systems and structures according to the ISO process quality standards. This expanded the scope of our intervention to include "changing the attitude of the members to actively contribute to the development of the system and implement the same".

While the above was going on, staff members also participated in a series of training modules based on corresponding TA concepts:

- Personal styles (ego states).
- Communication, relationship, and motivation (transactions, strokes, time structuring).
- Working styles (drivers).
- Conflict management (psychological games).
- Problem solving (discounting).
- Emotional literacy (stroke economy).

The goal of the training modules was to increase awareness of self, relationships, and organisational culture. It was also intended to provide a common language for the members to facilitate clear and open communication.

Each module was of three hours' duration held at an interval of two weeks. The six modules were followed by a monthly review session of one hour's duration for three months.

Once the new system and its corresponding structures were put in place, the top management team underwent a three day outbound team-building workshop. In this workshop the nine team roles by Belbin (1993) were used along with the drivers as working styles. Members were able to identify what their team roles were and their predominant working style and that of others in their team. This awareness was used to build synergy through strategic collaboration.

The factory workers were also exposed to a three hour module on team effort on the shop floor. These were conducted in groups of fifty to highlight the significance of working as a team. The emphasis was to bring to workers' awareness how their work was intricately connected with that of others in that they all receive from the processes before them and feed into the next process.

All these were preparations towards the actual goal of delivering orders on time and minimising costs by reducing rejection due to poor quality of product. Each newly formed department team underwent weekly team coaching sessions for six weeks. The frequency was reduced to fortnightly for four subsequent sessions and eventually reduced to once a month for the rest of the duration of the project. These team coaching sessions were the main forum for eventually working out individual and team contracts for change. All that they learnt in the training and team building processes was put into action through the team coaching sessions. Emphasis was on engaging in Adult-Adult transactions; quickly converting crossed transactions into complementary transactions by exercising options (Karpman, 1971); fostering intimacy through open communication; identifying game patterns and exercising strategies to minimise game playing. Drawing the transactional imago of the team exercises (Suriyaprakash & Mohanraj, 2006) helped the team members identify their mutual perceptions and to plan changes at the individual level to improve group communication. These sessions helped to identify what changes needed to be made within the department to improve the effectiveness of their operations. Teams developed new formats and procedures or modified existing systems for this purpose. This reinforced the team spirit and camaraderie among team members.

Lack of inter-departmental coordination was identified as the main reason for bottlenecks in the production process which resulted in delayed shipments and poor quality. Inter-departmental coordination meetings were held monthly in the presence of a consultant. The meetings provided the opportunity for the teams to express the discontent and appreciations to each other and also ask for support they needed to perform their function in an effective (quality) and efficient (timely) manner. These turned out to be fertile grounds for conflicts to surface. The process consultancy skills of the facilitators were put to use in these meetings. Group dynamics diagrams, ego states, strokes, games, and discounting were the key concepts that were used to observe the dynamics and provide feedback to the teams. This helped teams to clarify expectations and also freely and openly share their own limitations and possibilities with each other. Group imago work played a vital role in helping teams understand their mutual perceptions and the underlying dynamics and to change attitudes.

A major breakthrough for the project was achieved when the members freely expressed at the team building workshop how the dual leadership caused confusion and anxiety in them. It was a major shift in the culture of the organisation for the members to openly communicate their problem to the top management. The two partners agreed to undertake weekly executive coaching to iron out their differences and underlying dynamics. While two consultants worked with the teams in team coaching, the third member of the consultant team worked with the partners as executive coach. Contract, group-structure, and dynamics diagrams, and game and script theories were used in the executive coaching sessions to bring to their awareness how unresolved personal issues between them resulted in ambiguity and anxiety among the members. Social roles (Schmid, 2008) were used to help clarify the boundaries between the partners. As a result of this process, which lasted for over three months, the partners demarcated their functional territories of the business based on their strengths. Kumar took charge of production and finance while Raghav chose to lead the HR and marketing functions.

13.4.8. Evaluation

Eighteen months after the commencement of the project on-time delivery improved to 80%. It was a meagre 30% when the project was started. Rejection rate of product reduced to 5% from 18% at the beginning of the project. The project continued for three years in order to stabilise the new structure and also to put in place an employee assistance programme.

A counselling centre, with counsellors trained in TA, was contracted to provide group counselling to the employees. Exclusive group counselling sessions were held once a fortnight for immigrant women employees. Employees were also encouraged to approach counsellors for one-on-one sessions if the need was felt.

13.4.9. Conclusion

Transactional analysis is used explicitly and also implicitly in organisational development consultancy. Explicit application includes teaching TA theory to provide a new language and also to bring change. Implicitly, TA works as a frame of reference in the mind of the consultant in all that he is undertaking. The explicit approach is reflected in the TA based training part of OD interventions. The implicit approach is the cornerstone of all facilitative processes like coaching, process consultancy, contracting, evaluation, and feedback.

13.5. The business of redecision work

Mil Rosseau & Rik Rosseau

13.5.1. Introduction

Imagine a beautiful English garden during a sunny Indian summer day. Bright colours, liveliness, delicate fragrances, birds singing. The view invites you into awareness with all your senses. How can you describe this unique, ever-changing picture with words that mainly describe shapes, planting and harvesting methods; the tools you used, the fertilising planning?

What people accomplish during the workshops described below: the intensity of their development process, the sustainability of personal change, is hard to catch in words. The small illustrative stories in the boxes give a glimpse of the importance and the beauty of the results people get out of the training sessions.

In this chapter the authors reflect on the work they do with and for a big retailer in Belgium. Robert and Mary Goulding, first generation TA developers, trained one of them. They like to quote Bob and Mary Goulding: "There is no magic in changing lives!"

13.5.2. Care for people

Measured by profit compared to total turnover, the company we work for and with is the most profitable retailer in the world. The company is a soft discounter. It offers consumers own label products and A-brands at guaranteed lowest price. From 1985 till now, it grew eleven-fold, now being the biggest private employer in Belgium. The key to this all? Genuine care for people! TA has played a central role in the company for almost thirty years now. One important reason for this success is that everybody contributes to process improvements. Bystanding (Clarkson, 1994) is not appreciated! This employee loyalty to the company is also reflected—according to the Belgian Consumer Organisation—in the highest customer friendly approach in the country. At the same time, this company operates with a very detailed hierarchy. Management make sure to give every employee a lot of opportunities to grow a career. They care!

13.5.3. A contract for survival

It is 1985. The company is ranked number five in its business in Belgium and is in trouble. For the first time since its conception, it had to lay off people. The CEO keeps on being a strong believer in his people. Even when the times are tough now, he wants to invest in them. They will enable the company to turn around. His standard expression was and still is: "If people feel good about themselves, you don't have to teach them to act customer-friendly. They will do so from their hearts!" Those were the days he started up a number of personal development courses for all employees. "Assertiveness training" is the working title for the start-up course. We as trainers contract with the CEO that "respectful communication towards customers and towards each other as colleagues" is the ultimate goal (content) and that we will use TA to get there (process).

Since employees will also benefit from the course in their private lives, we agree that, apart from the investment the company makes, they also invest personally. They do so by "handing in" overtime hours. The company pays for the accommodation and the trainer's fee. We also agree that both professional and private topics can be dealt with. There is full confidentiality, which means that nobody in the organisation will ask the trainer for details about participants or about the individual training course outcomes. We also agree that participants send in an evaluation sheet right after the training and another one after six months. In this way we can monitor the outcome and re-contract if necessary.

13.5.4. Growing the organisation through growing people

Our start is very cautious. We are aware that dealing with personal growth in a business environment is not common practice. The first two years of offering this TA training are about exploring boundaries. We teach the basic TA concepts and introduce exercises for participants to explore and have fun with. Keyword is the TA concept of "options" (Karpman, 1971). TA concepts we use are: functional analysis, transactions, hungers, games and drama triangle, functional versus dysfunctional emotions, script, and, last but not least, redecisions. As soon as we start explaining the TA concept of script, we notice that participants get curious. The biggest challenge is to translate the script concept into easy to understand metaphors and language for people who do not have a psychological background. We developed several inspirational lines of thinking:

- If you want to learn a second language, do you have to forget the first one? Do you remember exactly when and how you learned certain words like cheese and bread? We put learning a language as a childhood "decision" under the same flag as script decisions. It is the best possible way available to adjust to your family of origin. This de-pathologises script and puts it in a different context.
- Do you trash defective products at the end of the production or are you looking for the causes of the defects? One of the prerequisites for a sustainable solution is to understand the root cause of a problem. Thinking, feeling, behaving that is intuitively felt as not effective in the here and now, can only be solved by making the link with (one of) the root cause(s). We ask participants: "Where and when was this an intelligent solution for the challenge you had to face then and there?" This puts the script decision again in a context of positive reaction to a (sometimes threatening) challenge that is no longer there.
- How come emotions sometimes seem to hijack thinking? We explain "operating rules" between the different parts of our brain. Brain research offers us a number of insights into what otherwise is perceived as pathological. Taking script decisions out of a pathology

context opens the door for new permissions. This seems also in line with one of the Gouldings' catchphrases: "Be aggressively healthy".
- The entire TA frame of reference offers an almost inexhaustible source of easy to understand insights and tools for people who want to increase the pace and direction of their personal development. Eric Berne wrote (1947): "The object of this book is to make the dynamics of the human mind tangible to those who are more interested in understanding nature than in using big words or memorizing definitions."

From the start we got excellent feedback to our approach, given at the end of the course and also six months later. People documented their feedback with examples of—mostly quite moving, at times spectacular—changes they had brought about in both their professional and private lives. Managers from all over the company started to recommend this—TA based—course to their employees.

JANE: I was fighting all the time. I felt like left out. Why? The answer that made sense was when looking back at my childhood. I was child number five of five. My mother wished not to have more than three kids. Five was too much to handle. I learned to manage this situation by finding my way in everything. I was getting good in organising/arranging things to make sure I wasn't overlooked. That resulted in a good career and even entering World Championships. But that was not what I was looking for.

Discovering the "root cause" of my feelings and behaviours was shocking at first. But I felt it was spot-on. Soon, I made peace with my history. It helped me to be more reflective and more relaxed. My leadership style changed into a participating one. I don't have the urge to "be right" any more. I listen more to ideas of others and get a lot more support.

13.5.5. The work: creating opportunities

What does a typical workshop for this company look like? It can be split into the five stages of genuine TA redecision work: contact, contract negotiation, impasse clarification, redecision, and future pacing.

The initial stages of the workshop are key to a successful outcome. It is important to value each participant. We show genuine interest in whom they are and in what is going on with them and their department. The process of setting the tone of the workshop starts at the coffee machine as soon as participants arrive.

During the "official introduction", we emphasise the fact that participants are "in the lead"—that is, they are in charge of their own change process. Right from the start we use metaphors that "de-psychologise". During contracting we introduce the difference between red and green barriers. Red means: this is an objective limit; green means: this is a self-imposed limit. We stop people at red barriers. We invite them to challenge the green ones. Participants learn that achieving their goals is their own responsibility. "Working rules" are the final part of this introduction.

We use the Goulding standards for good contracts (1997). We don't accept:

- *Parent contracts.*

  A minority of participants come to the course because of some elements in their performance appraisal or because their boss has sent them without checking with them. Even then, the participants will quickly identify their own areas for personal change that are meaningful. It is not unusual that the way they relate with the boss will be part of their contract.

- *Contracts to change others.*

  Bob Goulding states that the majority of his clients start from a Victim position. This is very similar to the situation in the business we work with. It is important to confront Victim behaviour from the start. Every word in the central question in redecision work is a keyword: "What Do You Want to Change Today". Especially the "You" referring to the basic TA value that everyone is responsible for his thinking, feeling, behaving.

- *Forever contracts.*

  For Eric Berne (1972) making progress was not an option in working with his patients. Contracts like "I want to learn how to be more assertive" are not accepted. An absolute key factor for future success is whether or not a contract goal is specific and measurable. This allows participants to experience how much they sometimes sabotage their own success by putting in words like: more, less, better, try. We notice that even though we are still only in the initial phase of the workshop, participants are already positively challenging each other. They support a caring and confronting group culture.

Theo was very silent during the entire contracting stage. When helping him to make his contract specific and measurable, it was clear that he stopped himself in that process. During the break, he came to talk to one of us. He shared that he had lost his wife about two months before and he did not feel comfortable dealing with his feelings in a new group. After clarifying that the way he participates in the course was entirely up to him, he asked if it was OK to not participate in the rest of the course at all. We confirmed that that was OK too. We suggested he would clarify his decision to the training group members, his direct manager, and the department that organises the development courses. He later wrote a thank you letter to the department head, stating that the permission to leave had been very helpful in his grief process.

Refusing and correcting unacceptable contracts helpful for the individuals and the group: as TA professionals we strongly belief that contracting is not something that precedes the work we do; it is an integral part of it. Contracting can take up the entire morning of the first day. As facilitators, we then organise the contracts around themes like: feedback, leadership, resisting manipulation, difficult customers and handling criticism.

13.5.6. Script

The introduction to the TA concept of script is done through a highly energetic, funny exercise about the memory functions of the brain. Based on a first analysis of the contracts, we tell stories about kids growing up, being labelled in a specific way. We also tell stories about how injunctions are transmitted in families. Through these stories, we can clarify how important the script learning process is for survival. In an open round, participants make a first reflection on the connection between their contract and possible script decisions. We then connect the contracts with TA tools, and wherever applicable and helpful, we explore the underlying script decisions. Participants learn in, from, and through the group.

Steve works in a warehouse. The first two days of the training he is silent. The morning of the third day, our opening question is: "What is it that you want to put on your programme today?" Steve starts telling that he is bullied. In the beginning he discounts the seriousness of it. Helped by the silences and the gentle support of the group, he reveals more and more details. He tells the group that he even considered killing himself.

Here we touch upon the core and the power of our multi-cornered contract. We re-contract with Steve, the group, and the "higher powers" in the company. Steve recovered well. Occasionally, he sends a catch-up note to the facilitator.

13.5.7. Future pacing: a result only deserves that name when it is sustainable

"Practice makes perfect." We ask participants to transform their redecisions into an action plan. Participants are able to confront each other in a caring and helping way and the quality of the contracts-for-the-future is usually very high. Six weeks later, we plan a follow-up session. There, participants give examples of what they changed in their lives and in what area they want to do some extra work.

Erica is a very ambitious woman. She is on a career fast track. During role practices on leadership flexibility, she realises that emotionally speaking, taking up her next leadership responsibilities is too much of a stretch for her.

During the interval between the first session and the follow-up, she discussed that with a number of people in the organisation. Her decision is to postpone her promotion by at least two years and set some criteria for her "readiness". In the meantime, she applied for a job with fewer people leadership responsibilities.

13.5.8. Conclusion: Eric Berne talking

TA and specifically the redecision school offer wonderful opportunities to help people develop themselves, also in a business context. Teaching our participants to "behave" in a way that both they and their organisation benefit is our passion for many years. The results of the work we do are multiple: the company benefits, the employees benefit, and to a certain extent, also the private environment of the employees benefits. We'd like to end with a reflection of Eric Berne during a 1966 videotaped interview:

> My feeling is that Freud has set the foundation. I think that we've built something on the foundation. Sometime in the future, someone will build the third story. And I think the answer is in script ... If we can get in there and break that up, than we can really change a person's

life course. Not only for the person, but also for his children … [and] future generations. (Interview at a party in his Carmel house, 1966b)

References

Belbin, R. M., (1993). *Team Roles at Work*. Burlington, MA: Butterworth-Heinemann, 2010.
Berne, E. (1947). *The Mind in Action*. New York: Simon & Schuster.
Berne, E. (1961). *Transactional Analysis in Psychotherapy*. New York: Grove Press.
Berne, E. (1963). *The Structure and dynamics of organizations and Groups*. Philadelphia, PA: J. B. Lippincott.
Berne, E. (1964). *Games People Play. The Basic Handbook of Transactional Analysis*. New York: Ballantine.
Berne, E. (1966a). *Principles of Group Treatment*. New York: Oxford University Press.
Berne, E. (1966b). Close-up: Dr. Eric Berne, the hip-talking California psychiatrist whose best-selling book Games People Play has made him a jet-age folk hero. Keys to a happy life. By Jack Fincher. *Life* magazine, August 12.
Berne, E. (1972). *What Do You Say After You Say Hello? The Psychology of Human Destiny*. New York: Grove Press.
Bowlby, J. (1969). *Attachment and Loss (vol. 1) (2nd edition)*. New York: Basic Books.
Clarkson, P. (1994). Bystander games. *Transactional Analysis Journal*, 23(3): 158–172.
Clarkson, P. (1996). *The Bystander. An End to Innocence in Human Relationships?* London: Whurr.
Crossman, P. (1966). Permission and protection. *Transactional Analysis Bulletin*, 5(9): 152–154.
Ernst, F. (1971). OK Corral, The grid to get-on-with. *Transactional Analysis Journal*, 1(4): 231–240.
French, W. L., Bell, C. H., & Vohra, V. (2006). *Organization Development: Behavioral Science Interventions for Organization Improvement*. New Delhi: Pearson.
Goleman, D. (2000). Leadership that gets results. *Harvard Business Review: March-April*: 78–90.
Goulding, R., & Goulding, M. (1997). *Changing Lives through Redecision Therapy*. New York: Grove Press.
Harris, T. (1969). *I'm OK-You're OK*. New York: Harper & Row.
Hay, J. (1993). *Working It Out at Work: Understanding Attitudes and Building Relationships*. Watford, UK: Sherwood.
Hay, J. (1995a). *Transactional Analysis for Trainers*. Minneapolis, MN: Sherwood.
Hay, J. (1995b). *Donkey Bridges for Developmental TA. Making Transactional Analysis Memorable and Accessible*. Watford, UK: Sherwood.
Karpman, S. B. (1968). Fairy tales and script drama analysis. *Transactional Analysis Bulletin*, 7(26): 39–43.
Karpman, S. B. (1971). Options. *Transactional Analysis Journal*, 1(1): 79–87.
Kouwenhoven, M. (2007). *Het Handboek Stratgisch Coachen*. Soest, Netherlands: Uitgeverij Nelissen.
Kouwenhoven, M. (2011). The strategic coaching matrix. *Transactional Analysis Journal*, 41(1): 77–91.
Kouwenhoven, M. (2014). De compliance officer als VIP deskundige. (The compliance officer as a VIP specialist.) *Tijdschrift voor Compliance*, 3: 78–87.
Krausz, R. R. (1993). Organisational scripts. *Transactional Analysis Journal*, 23(2): 77–85.
McClelland, D. (1987). *Human Motivation*. Cambridge, MA: The Press Syndicate.
Micholt, N. (1992). Psychological distance and group interventions. *Transactional Analysis Journal*, 22(4): 228–233.

Mountain, A., & Davidson, C. (2011). *Working Together: Organizational Transactional Analysis and Business Performance*. London: Gower.

Randall, L. K. (1973). Red, white and blue TA at 600 MPH. In: D. Jongeward (Ed.), *Everybody Wins: Transactional Analysis Applied in Organizations* (p. 137). Reading, MA: Addison-Wesley.

Roberts, D. (1992). *Hierarchy of Functionality*. [Workshop notes from ITAA conference, New Zealand.]

Schiff, J. (1975). *Cathexis Reader*. New York: Harper & Row.

Schmid, B. (2008). The role concept of transactional analysis and other approaches to personality, encounter, and cocreativity for all professional fields. *Transactional Analysis Journal*, 38(1): 17–30.

Stewart, I. (1989). *Transactional Analysis Counselling in Action*. London: Sage.

Suriyaprakash, C., & Mohanraj, I. A. (2006). Transactional imago. In: G. Mohr & T. Steinert (Eds.), *Growth and Change for Organizations: Transactional Analysis New Developments 1995 2006* (pp. 164–172). Pleasanton, CA: International Transactional Analysis Association.

Yogelson, S., & Samenow, S. E. (1976). *The Criminal Personality. Volume I*. New York: Jason Aronson.

Yogelson, S., & Samenow, S. E. (1977). *The Criminal Personality. Volume II*. New York: Jason Aronson.

CHAPTER FOURTEEN

Learning and personal development

14.1. Leadership and school culture
14.2. Learning styles and contracts in adult education
14.3. A multi-perspectival view on being an educator for young children
14.4. Using transactional analysis with community care workers in South Africa
14.5. Advanced dancing classes: choosing "I +, U +"

Within the field of education professionals work in places where people teach and learn, from nursery to university and including formal and informal education and in-service training. The focus is on how the growth and development of the child, adolescent, and adult can best be promoted within the social and cultural environment.

The *Handbook for TA Training and TA Certification* describes the core competencies for this field. See www.itaaworld.org/itaa-training-examinations-handbook.

Clients in this field are both learners themselves and professionals who work with the many daily issues of upbringing and education. They seek to promote greater efficacy and maturity in the thinking and learning processes of the people they work for and with.

14.1. Leadership and school culture

Giles Barrow

14.1.1. Introduction

The following case study is based on work carried out in a secondary school in the UK over a period of a year or so. The students at the school are between eleven and sixteen years old and come from a wide range of ethnic, cultural, and faith groups represented in the local community. The interventions I carried out in the school included:

- staff training;
- consultancy regarding leadership and school culture;
- whole school policy development;
- establishing specialist provision for children disengaged with learning.

For the purpose of this account I will focus on the professional development of staff. In doing so I want to explore the difference between educational transactional analysis and transactional analysis in education.

When I was initially invited to work at the school I learned that prior training in TA at this school had focused on the personal application of core models. The team had an understanding of ego states, for example, and had been considering how to best avoid "being in Critical Parent" while thinking about how to invite children "into the Adult". There had also been an awareness about the importance of script and, again, staff had reflected on their own personal script. The implication of this earlier training was that some staff had become interested in exploring how they could use TA in education. By this I mean that TA models can become a "tool" or technique that might be applied to getting the best out of students. By using TA language both staff and students can begin to talk about relationships in the classroom and make improvements. In addition, while school leaders were highly supportive of staff using TA in their practice, models had not been more fully integrated in school policy or ethos. It seemed as if TA was a really useful idea to run alongside the progressive approach common to the school, but not within it.

14.1.2. First encounter

The first opportunity I had to work with the staff team was a first day back from a break, and all staff—teaching and non-teaching professionals—attended the workshop. After a revisiting of TA basic principles, the first session was based on the cycle of development model (Levin, 1980). In my experience this is one of the more robust and comprehensive TA models available to educators. It is multifaceted in the sense that while it can be applied at the level of individual student, or group of students, it's equally illuminating in thinking about professional growth and organisational change. Often professionals working in schools may have only come across conventional, linear models with an emphasis on deficit, pathology, and a "once and only" chance of growing up. I use the educational adaptation of the material (Barrow & Newton, 2004) which emphasises its natural recycling feature and both normalises and illuminates patterns of behaviour that are especially evident when working with children and adolescents.

In the second part of the day I invited the group to create a storyboard of an early memory of being at school. The exercise involves a structured process whereby the individual revisits early decisions and beliefs about the purpose of learning, the experience of being a learner, and the role of the teacher. It is often a powerful exercise and people often reconnect to a time of considerable formative development. Completing the task includes a consideration of how early decisions and beliefs continue to "show up" in their work as present day educators. The exercise finishes with people sharing their stories and connections. Clearly the whole piece requires careful management and protection—while many find it an intriguing experience, sometimes it provokes shame, guilt, and anger. My purpose in using the task is that it provides a gateway into exploring how classrooms are arenas in which script is formed, not just played out (Barrow, 2009).

The group linked script with learning and during this process I became aware of how committed the school was to professional development. This was a team not only well-versed in the method of progressive and radical pedagogy, but its members were also determined to implement these approaches in everyday practice. By the end of the day I was recalibrating my assessment of the situation. The school's senior leaders were also adjusting their understanding of TA and, specifically, were recognising its wider potential. It was clear to both me and the school that there was significant potential for further work.

14.1.3. Reflections on the encounter

I was asked if I would deliver a residential workshop for staff, and the popularity of TA in the school resulted in more than seventy staff opting to join the event. The focus for the two days was left to me to determine, based on my experience of working with the school. I had begun to realise that generally staff had a reductionist understanding of ego states which was generating a significant limitation in their potency with students. In other words, with a simplistic commitment to Adult transactions, most staff were discounting the potential impact of the Parent ego state, which can be fundamental in promoting the development of young people. Crucially, I noticed how staff were determined to "keep in Adult" and avoid Parent ego state transactions. There was a strong mistrust of the Parent ego state to the extent that I noticed how staff were rendered impotent in their work with students because they did not want to risk becoming critical. My assessment was that a reclaiming of the Parent ego state and the introduction of the Integrating Adult might be a valuable piece of updating work.

Secondly, and connected to the observation about a misunderstanding about ego states, I had also picked up significant reservations in staff members with the school's commitment to progressive pedagogy. The self-doubt following a recent critical inspection visit had led a range of staff to wonder whether there were times when children simply needed to be taught content. However, the commitment to progressive methods was so embedded in the school culture that to express dissent risked becoming a strong challenge to this school culture. I also experienced this sense of discomfort about criticising or appearing ambivalent about progressive approaches. My thought was that if *I* was feeling the tendency to over-adapt and keep quiet, then this would be felt more keenly by staff members. So an important element in my planning for the residential event was to give voice to what was rumbling underneath, to surface important psychological matters.

14.1.4. Educational TA through TA in education

After initial introductions I asked the group to work in pairs and share positive experiences of when they could last remember being looked after by another person and to identify the qualities in the other person in terms of behaviour, attitude, gestures, and language. I then asked what was the result of the impact on themselves. I find this is a straightforward way of introducing Temple's functional fluency model which presents an entirely different perspective to making sense of ego states in action, and can be a transformational learning experience (Temple, 2004). Participants readily have an extended, non-pathological language for describing their day-to-day behaviour, and that of others.

I had decided to complete this session with a final image. I talked about the background to Berne's original P-A-C model with its emphasis on the oppressive impact of the Parent ego state. Importantly, I made it clear that in doing so Berne had created a metaphor. I took the opportunity to share the image of an inverted ego state model in which the Parent is at the base supporting the Adult, with the Child, representing the individual's unique sense of self, topmost (Barrow, 2007). In this metaphor the emphasis is on the Parent providing a stable base from which the potential of the Child might be realised. More importantly, this image emphasises the upward thrust of energy that amplifies and accelerates the growth and potency of the Child. The session closed with staff paired up as they did at the outset, and a consideration of the potential growth that comes from the idea of the Parent. Staff reconnected with the earlier experience of being looked after with a new conceptual frame of reference.

When we regrouped the following morning I decided to start straight off by asking the group to talk about their memories of their own school days and in particular their beliefs and decisions about the purpose of learning, the role of the teacher, and their sense of being a learner. I find this exercise a way into presenting Napper and Newton's typology of learning, (2000). I began with a description of the liberal model of learning and in doing so teach the themes of imago, contract, strokes, and discounts in relation to the learning type. On this occasion I had created large copies of each learning type and began to create a display on the main wall of the training room. I went on to present the technological and humanistic models and the display began to cover the wall, presenting the continuum of learning theory which I have described elsewhere (Barrow, 2009).

As each type of teaching and learning was presented the group had opportunities to clarify their understanding and ask questions of each other and me. Eventually I completed the

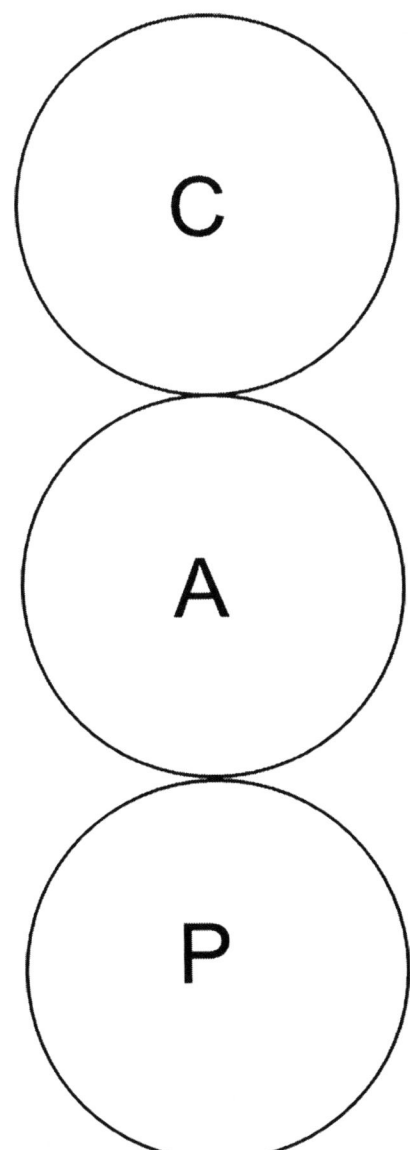

Figure 14.1. Diagram of CAP.

presentation with the progressive and radical types. The crucial learning point in this exercise was to emphasise the importance of the *continuum*, as opposed to reducing discussion simply to types. In other words, if what we seek is an impactful educational experience then the *type* of learning theory is less significant that the awareness and capacity of the educator in *teaching* across different ways of learning. Herein lies what for me is at the heart of educational transactional analysis. How does the educator maintain a sense of himself, moment to moment

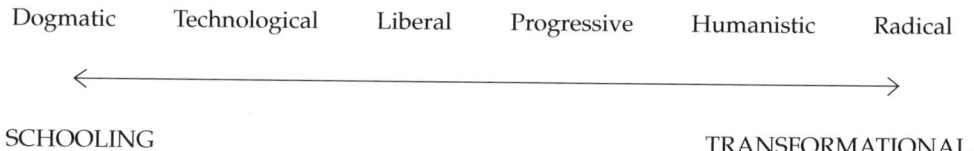

Figure 14.2. The continuum of typology of learning.

in a way that relates powerfully with the learner, while honouring the contract in which the education takes place?

I was aware that by putting the progressive model in a wider pedagogic context I was beginning to surface some of the underlying concerns among staff. I had arranged for groups comprising non-teaching, teaching, and leadership staff to have a set of learning types with which they created their own continuum on the floor. For over an hour staff talked through the implications for staff–student relationship, curriculum challenges, operational dilemmas, frustrations, and enthusiasms for each of the learning types. It was recognised that the progressive model would remain the default position of the school, but with consideration of the value of the other types too.

14.1.5. Permission to teach

By lunchtime we were ready to move into the final piece of work. I wanted to bring together the two themes—pedagogy and Parent—and my vehicle for doing this was through introducing permission. I have been strongly influenced by Jaoui's permission wheel as published by Hawkes (2007) and have used it for the past few years. However, this highly practical tool has been further revised by Papaux (see section 14.3) and has been adapted specifically for educational use and integrates specific permissions with the features of autonomy. The group began to work in pairs using the permission wheel. Some decided to focus on individual students, others took a closer look at themselves.

As the workshop began to draw to a close I wanted to make explicit the shift from TA in education to educational TA. Through a series of question-based discussions, staff groups reflected on what had been impacting them in terms of content and process. During the feedback participants began to connect the concept of Parent ego state with the function of permission. The comprehensive framework of behaviour modes associated with the idea of Integrating Adult complemented a wider and deeper appreciation of how TA might enrich the student–teacher relationship. In most respects the content of the workshop enhanced the staff understanding of TA *in* education.

There was a second group of comments in the feedback which showed an appreciation of how the continuum of learning had been modelled and experienced across the workshop. This was picked up in how I was experienced as holding the group, leading the learning, teaching material, and letting the group go its own way, at different times in the process. This lies at the centre in the work of the educational transactional analyst. The impact of my intervention was always going to be in the enactment of the task, and less so in its content. As with other areas of work, in supervision, therapy, or organisational engagement, the higher level outcome is embedded in the relational dynamic, the space in between practitioner and client. This is what TA educators do in the context of a contract for learning. It involves monitoring the intrapsychic process, utilising helpful, integrating behaviour modes, and, in this instance particularly, stepping into containing and upholding the group from a Parent position. It can also involve assessing when it's time to withdraw from teaching and enabling the process to be taken over by the growing *physis* of the group. And most importantly of all, understanding the relational and pedagogic rationale for the decision-making throughout.

14.1.6. Conclusion

The impact of the workshop is developing at the time of writing. Currently staff have begun to create classroom displays of the pedagogy continuum in order to generate discussion with students about the style of learning contract being used during the lessons. Specialist staff are using Papaux's version of the permission wheel with students struggling at school. Individual teachers are using the language of Temple's behaviour modes to reflect on their relationships with pupils. A second residential event for the school leadership team is planned with a view to furthering the school in how TA informs its practice and in defining its purpose.

For my part, the work with the school has been instrumental in shaping my thoughts about rehabilitating the role of the Parent in TA theory. Increasingly I am drawn to the impact in the relationship when the practitioner is able to uphold and safeguard the learner's capacity to thrive, and I think this can sometimes be discounted in both early accounts of negative Parent in ego state models, and more contemporary writing with an emphasis on co-creative, constructionist methodology (Tudor & Summers, 2014). To some extent this piece of work reconnected me with a deep love for teaching; and in that lies the parallel process. Reclaiming the role of the teacher in a way that does not diminish the learner was the challenge for both myself and the staff team.

14.2. Learning styles and contracts in adult education

Trudi Newton

14.2.1. Introduction

Whatever educational context we work in, what we do—and what we say about what we do—makes apparent our beliefs about ourselves, others, and our world, about the place of learning, its meaning and value. Advertising, curricula, handbooks, the methods we choose, all reveal our underpinning philosophy and tell our students what we think of them. These various philosophies can be the basis of political and social decisions about schools and colleges, local and national education policies. They also, most importantly, impact the *experience* students have and consequently the effectiveness of the learning.

A few years ago I summarised the ideas of Elias and Merriam (1980) and linked them with the contracts, strokes, and discounts, the transactions and ego states evident in adult training/learning groups, to create "learning imagos" (Napper & Newton, 2000; Newton, 2003). These illustrate "what is going on here" in a *group's* group imago—the collective picture we create (Clarke, 1996). To show how the learning imagos model works in practice I will give a brief snapshot of each training style and imago, and explore three practical examples of working with groups with very different expectations.

14.2.2. The learning imagos.

⬭	You will instantly recognise a *liberal* (or traditional) learning group because it so often "fits" with our cultural and actual experience of being taught: an "expert" teacher with novice pupils, and a focus on imparting knowledge and information. This model has existed throughout modern history, alongside a much older way of learning, apprenticeship.
⬭	Today we can call this *technological* education, a behaviourist style where the tutor is also an assessor, teaching according to the criteria and objectives each student must achieve.
⬭	An extreme version of these two is *dogmatic*, a rigid system where students' success is gained through compliance.

	Progressive ideas evolved in the early twentieth century to take account of adult learners' life experience and commitment, using real-life situations as the basis for learning.	
	A little later, *humanistic* learning theorists promoted student-centred learning—the development and nurture of each person's self-actualisation through education. This can, however, appear very individuated.	
	The most recent, more politically and community focused model is the *radical*, which removes the teacher-pupil distinction and proposes that education is the "practice of freedom, the means by which men and women deal critically and creatively with reality and discover how to participate in the transformation of their world" (Freire & Ramos, 1973).	

Barrow (2009) places the six training styles in a continuum, referring to the first three on the left side as "schooling", and on the right of the diagram the three more recently developed, potentially transformative, ways of teaching and learning (see Barrow, section 14.1).

Each of these imagos—ways of seeing education—implies a specific *contract* about the teaching/ learning and the role of the educator in the group.

LIBERAL	I tell you	TEACHER
TECHNOLOGICAL	I assess you	INSTRUCTOR
DOGMATIC	I reward you	GURU
HUMANISTIC	I support you	FACILITATOR
PROGRESSIVE	I guide you	ENABLER
RADICAL	We learn together	ANIMATOR

14.2.3. Relevance of the learning imagos

Why does this matter? By becoming aware of how what we do influences the outcome for learners, we can choose contracts, methods, and metaphors that suit the purpose of any particular learning experience and address the potential transferential relationships between teachers and learners.

For many people learning is inextricably linked to their school experiences—but school is not just about learning, it is one of the major contexts in which we acquire our cultural and social norms. Teachers, as representatives of this system, take responsibility for defining reality for the students. How does this socialisation process affect our beliefs about our own capacities and maybe contaminate our understanding of what it means to be a learner? (Barrow, 2009).

For ordinary grown-up people, wanting to learn, there may be a perception, carried over from childhood, that the teacher knows everything and the learner knows nothing and that therefore the teacher has all the power and the learners are powerless and expect to be "done to" without taking any responsibility—like small children. School experiences of feeling inadequate or inferior get projected onto the teacher-figure who similarly projects low expectations onto the learners. Adult learners get stuck in a "script" place of discounting their own experience and may repeat "old" patterns of "not understanding" or play "stupid"—and similarly the teacher may get stuck in a scripty place of feeling responsible for everything and "doing all the work".

We need to value more traditional forms of education when they are appropriate, when students need clear information and structure, but Barrow suggests the "schooling" models risk maintaining the status quo, while "transformational" learning offers greater opportunity for change.

In these examples, from very different situations, I want to show how choosing and using different styles maximises the learning potential.

14.2.4. Progressive learning

> Serena was, and is, a writer or magazine stories and articles. She already had access to one of humanity's ways of understanding our consciousness—through literature. But it was through her learning in the TA group that she was able to make that real. She came to an informal, community-education funded, personal growth group twenty-five years ago. When Serena arrived the question in her head was "What's so unlovable about me?" She later wrote about her experience in the group: "Suddenly the pain of my early years isn't destructive any more ... it is something to build on, and all through my head the doors of my little prisons are swinging open. The jemmies, wrenches and skeleton keys were laid before me during that first introduction to TA."

When I started these groups participants were accustomed to assertiveness groups (skills in communication) and encounter groups (self-understanding) but what was often missing was *knowledge* and *reasoning*—*why* do we behave the way we do and what can we do *instead*?

I included in the sessions mini-lectures (input)—like a "traditional" style of education. This reassured learners—someone here knows what she is talking about and is willing to share it—as part of the contract: "This is what you are going to learn about." But everything we did and talked about was related directly to participants' own life experience. Group members were invited to connect their new knowledge to personal struggles, gaining insight and awareness—moving to a "progressive" way of learning. A clear educational structure enabled participants to feel secure and gain confidence to apply the ideas themselves.

The power of the learning in that group was in the combination of the security of the familiar structure and the challenge of *using* TA ideas at the same time as hearing *about* them—*doing* TA as well as *knowing* it. Clear, accessible information—not as an instant solution but as something worth thinking about and experimenting with—based on an understandable theory which supported trying out new behaviours, acknowledging that each of us may sometimes act in ways that cause us, and others, problems or distress, but seeing what might be driving that action and opening up the chance of other options.

14.2.5. Humanistic learning

> Hettie believed she "couldn't" write, so when a course she was keen to complete included a written assignment she refused to think about it until the deadline was near and then said she "couldn't" fulfil

> the requirement. She did, however, agree to explore this block with the group. I invited her to think about what she could do. She admitted she had ideas about the topic of the assignment and could explain them verbally. So, after some further exploration, she agreed to be interviewed by a group member and for the dialogue to be recorded. As she later transcribed the recording Hettie discovered that she could write when she did it her own way (not the way she had been expected to do it at school) and passed the assignment. She went on to discover she actually enjoyed writing and wanted to do more.

If one effect of "schooling" is the continuation into adulthood of transferential relationships connected to learning, then forms of passivity such as withdrawal, rebellion, over-adaptation, or incapacitation—silence, arguing, "pleasing teacher", or emphatic self-limitation—may appear in otherwise mature learners.

Looking for where the blocks or disruptions are—in which part of the learning cycle—and what discounts are keeping the script in operation helps learners overcome their scripty beliefs about their capacity to learn.

In Hettie's case she encountered a script decision that she couldn't write (which later transpired in therapy to be linked to her left-handedness and her parents' and teachers' attempts to "correct" that when she was small). She reacted to the perceived demand to complete the assignment by feeling anxious and panicky, stuck in her thinking and unable to see any alternatives, behaving rebelliously towards me and the group ("try and make me"). Her block was not at experience, or reflection—she had taken part in all aspects of the course willingly and discussed everything in the group. It was when the learning needed to become conceptualised in her own ideas, and then assessed, that she went into a script-response. The block was in moving between reflection and theory—and so Hettie became anxious about defining her experience. This led to discounting the solvability of the problem—it had "always been like this" and "there's nothing I can do to change it". What meaning had Hettie made of her struggles to write—literally—when she was small? And how could that change?

First, she was in a supportive environment with the nurture of a humanistic approach where the learner is respected and encouraged to grow, amid the co-creative resources of the group. Second, she could take up her own power within the group, with the opportunity to make a personal contract for her learning. And third, she found authentic encounter with other(s), that moment when something changes through the experience of a different kind of relationship, a chance for a new narrative. Hettie experienced a "disorienting dilemma" (Mezirow, 2000)—the start of a process leading to a change in self-perception at the psychological level, a challenge to some aspect of one's identity that causes a change in the frame of reference. She could have further retreated into her script feelings (maybe used it as an excuse for giving up on the course) or she could accept the empathy and support of others to help her make a script change, and give new meaning and understanding to her experience. Happily, this is what she did.

14.2.6. Radical learning

"Radical" is probably the least well understood of the various styles of teaching and learning because it is based on such different beliefs about education and the way people relate. It overtly addresses the political aspects of education and invites a fundamental change in attitude among learners and teachers.

We can use TA to explore and create new didactic frameworks based on OK-ness. I ask learning groups "What do you want to learn?" instead of telling them what I am going to teach. This leads to negotiated contracts about aims and method, and discussions about ways to get there. Where a truly radical process happens it can be an exhilarating and liberating encounter for everyone—as it was for "the Sutton group".

This group began working together in 2001; all were involved in behaviour or learning support or school improvement services, employed by a local authority or as independent consultants. Some were training towards a qualification in TA; all were using TA in their work with pupils, teachers, managers, parents, and colleagues, and receiving professional supervision. The group worked together, continually changing, for about five years. As I describe how we began working together the TA concepts are "keys" to each example, and the features of radical education in italics.

- Contracting: we began the training in the usual way by making a three-cornered contract (the college as "big powers", the group, and me as tutor). We addressed questions such as "How will we know the learning is effective?" and "Where do we want to get to?" The discussion came alive and there was real excitement as one participant said, "We'll write an article together to show how we use TA in our work to enable kids with difficulties." The contract-making felt open-ended, equal, and authentically *participatory*.
- Symbiosis: in order to *challenge* the potentially symbiotic teacher-student relationship I invited the group to work in pairs, each observing the other as they created a piece of art from materials in the room. I gave no other instructions. Some people became very uncomfortable that they "didn't know what to do" and couldn't respond in their usual way by adapting or rebelling. The offered freedom felt too strange. After the exercise was over we explored how they could each move out of script to decide their own learning goals.
- Accounting: this is the opposite of discounting. The group process was a dialogue—from the moment we all gathered each month we talked about incidents that had prompted people's thinking, ways they had shared TA with pupils or parents, how they had begun to see things differently. There was always a topic as a focus but we ranged widely in exploring it, because the material was *situated* in their lived experience.
- Awareness: the group encouraged each other to bring in what they already knew—either from previous study or from professional life. We reflected together on what they each wanted to add and how they wanted to learn more. We also reflected on the learning process itself—because these people were all in the business of educating others—so the theory-praxis dialogue included learning how to learn. This was *critical reflection* in action.
- Autonomy: the whole group, including me as tutor, were equal in the discussions, negotiating and evaluating the learning. We *democratically* decided that everyone would do some input, choosing a topic each wanted to explore and relate to his work. So each session was led by a different person who structured the process as well as sharing his discoveries in TA and other areas.

- OK-OK relationship: as animator (not teacher) I set aside any idea of being the "big person" and aimed to model an equal relationship. Everyone can think and everyone can change, and we certainly found this to be true as everyone's learning (including mine) became personal as well as professional, *affective*, and holistic.

The results of this group demonstrated the effectiveness of this style of learning. We initiated a research project on the effects of TA in school transition, and wrote, together, not just an article but a whole book (Barrow & Newton, 2004) that "modelled [the] range and potential of TA when applied in a way that promotes the freedom for individuals to engage with, and negotiate, their own learning and development" (Shotton, 2009).

14.2.7. Conclusion

Learning means change, and that change may be expressed in knowledge, skill, or understanding, sometimes in all three. TA offers a frame of reference for didactics in any context and invites lifelong learning and the continuous possibility of change and growth, as we update our Parent, expand our Adult, and value our Child.

14.3. A multi-perspectival view on being an educator for young children

Evelyne Papaux

14.3.1. Introduction

When I first started to apply TA in my practice I was working in a multicultural kindergarten and was in charge of fifteen children aged between two and five years old. I had been trained for three years fifteen years ago and had been working in a kindergarten since then, so I was already well experienced as a professional in education. I was aware of children's needs for play, sleep, and specific food, psychomotor, affective, and cognitive development, attachment theory, and psychopathology. However, discovering and using TA concepts and philosophy has been crucial in the development of further skills, in helping me to make meaning of my work and in keeping my motivation and faith in my job. I know very clearly what has been the added value of TA in my practice: I have been able to explain to others what I was doing and in what ways it was important and valuable for the children's lives and well-being.

Let's use a metaphor to explain the idea further. In the processing of photographic films, the developer is a chemical that makes the latent image on the film or print visible. In the process of my own identity as an educator, TA has had the same effect: it has enabled me to see more clearly what my job is about, to develop a larger view, and at the same time a more specific and closer view of my practice. It has given me new perspectives on what was happening in my relationships with the children and their parents, new options to strengthen potentialities and to cope with difficulties.

14.3.2. Illustration and case study

There are so many stories I could tell, so many examples I could give, to demonstrate how TA made a difference in my own way of being an educator. I will use the story of Matias, a four-year-old boy from Argentina, to present some "pictures" illustrating how TA concepts have informed my practice and how my interventions have helped Matias in settling down in the kindergarten group and have enhanced the development of his autonomy.

14.3.3. A micro-perspective

Mateo and Matias had just arrived from their home countries to spend one year in Switzerland with their families. By chance they both spoke Spanish and were almost the same age; I was really relieved because it made things much easier for them and for me. But soon enough it became a problem as they didn't join the group at all and formed their own group within the group, not wanting to take part in any activity with other children. That group imago wasn't exactly what I was hoping for so I decided to take action. Previously I would have probably interpreted their behaviour as a threat to my authority, or as a sign of my failure to propose interesting activities. Instead of these reactions I decided to take a specific look at what happened in this situation through the lenses of the hungers triangle devised by Clarke and Dawson (1998). I had started by adding a lot of structure, asking them to join, enforcing the rules, and so on, but it had ended up with more rebellion from them and no progress at all. I had thought of stimulation and I had offered many different activities, hoping they would show some interest at least. It didn't really work and I was feeling quite dissatisfied. The only hunger that I had left out in that process was the recognition hunger and funnily it was what was missing for all of us; I wasn't feeling recognised by them and they probably hadn't felt recognised by me on their arrival. Using group imago theory I decided to become part of their group and to gently open it up to all the children. I showed interest in their play, spoke the few words of Spanish that I knew, put on some Argentinian music, stroked them whenever it was appropriate. Soon the group imago was different and I could see them interacting with other children, taking their place in the group and playing a nice role with smaller kids (they were the oldest).

When working with children in a kindergarten, one of the main goals is the promotion of socialisation, that is to say helping children in developing relational and social skills, learning how to live and thrive in a group. The educator can be described both as the secure base and the facilitator of the group; it is up to her to enable each one to feel safe and therefore able to explore all the possibilities offered by the environment. The quality of her presence is therefore paramount: her understanding of the group dynamics can make a huge difference.

14.3.4. A meta-perspective

One day I had decided to divide the group in order to take them in two small groups to the gym. When I told Matias that he would go with the second group, he threw himself on the floor, moaning, his two hands on his face; two tears appeared and he stayed there without moving. However, I could see that he was checking my reaction from time to time, in a furtive way. I thought "Here we go again!" as this kind of episode was happening several times a day. I didn't feel empathetic with him, on the contrary I felt quite angry. I felt invited into a Persecutor role on the drama triangle and it would have been very easy to consider him as a nuisance, ignore him, or give him negative strokes. At that time I really needed to connect my Adult ego state to decide on the interventions I was about to choose in order to help him develop his autonomy and communication skills, and at the same time be an inspiring model for the fourteen other children looking at me with curious eyes. I was also very well aware that my non-verbal communication and my emotional state were much more important than any words I could use at that stage.

In this situation developing a meta-perspective, meaning "viewing self in relation to the other in context" (Gilbert & Evans, 2000, p. 10), being part of the process and at the same time "observing it from a professional stance and with a specific awareness" has been at the core of my intervention. At that age children are actually building up their script and we become part of it, as described by Summers and Tudor in the script helix (2000). So it is worth while thinking about our own behaviours and what we want to be modelling when relating to children and handling puzzling situations, being able to respond more and react less as our actions can be very powerful. The script system (Erskine & Zalcmann, 1979) has been a very helpful tool to deal with this issue, observing the transactions and making hypotheses. I then had the opportunity to notice that Matias's mother had similarly agitated behaviour when dealing with frustrations, and that she had collected a lot of strokes from other mothers. The understanding of the dynamics of the script system and the emotional awareness scale (Steiner, 1996) helped me in promoting Matias's expression of emotions, in order to allow him to connect to any emotions, and avoid if possible the creation of a racket feeling of sadness. I also decided to strengthen the collection of positive memories so I stroked him whenever he was able to express his feeling and needs in a direct way. I also invited him to connect his Adult to ask for what he wanted, instead of crying and looking desperate. These permissions, to acknowledge his needs and to be important, helped him to develop his potency and, little by little, he has been able to change his behaviour and express his needs and feelings much more easily. This enabled him to stop taking the Victim role so often and move to the winner's triangle (Choy, 1990), showing Vulnerability instead of Victim attitudes, but alternatively also Assertiveness or Caring for others.

14.3.5. A systemic perspective

In my initial training the focus was on the children and not much on the parents. I used to be scared of parents' consultations, not knowing how to handle what was taking place in the here and now of the meeting. I learnt to use the time structuring modes as a way to structure the meeting.

When Matias's mother arrived for the meeting I had invited her to, she looked nervous, which didn't surprise me as most parents are nervous in those circumstances. She looked around her, then in her bag, then took out her phone. I asked her if she wanted something to drink and left her for a while, feeling that she needed some time for herself. Coming back with a glass of water I started with some rituals and pastiming about her life in Switzerland and so on. After these necessary stages, I moved to "activity" and came to the actual reason of the meeting: I had noticed that her son aged four couldn't draw. It was not only that he was not interested but at one point he had tried to imitate his peers and soon gave up as he couldn't produce anything other than a scribble. I shared with her my observations in an objective way, asking her if she had seen a difference at home. She seemed very surprised and immediately quite defensive, probably alarmed. She said that nobody in her family enjoyed drawing anyway, that Matias was more interested in physical activities, and so on.

It is never easy to share with parents our concern about their children; previously I would have avoided the activity staying safely in pastiming, talking about other things, or maybe I would have tried to convince the mother ("Why don't you?") and we could easily have ended up in a game. The steps to success, Julie Hay's version of the discounting matrix (1995), is a good way to find out what the person is actually accounting for about the situation, before helping her move gently up the steps. No use in giving options before we can both agree on the stimulus, account for it as a problem, and look for the possibility of change.

I stopped and suggested that she could observe her son as well and that we could talk about it again later on. Some weeks later Matias arrived in the kindergarten wearing glasses and a patch covering one eye. Following our meeting his mother had made some observations, had decided to take her son to the doctor, who advised a visit to the optician. The diagnosis was that Matias had a serious sight problem and needed glasses to correct it as soon as possible.

TA philosophy and concepts also helped me in establishing healthy relationships with parents. The contracting process enabled us to consider our role as different and complementary with the child's well-being in mind. The frame of reference concept allowed me to stay connected when challenged by cultural differences and points of view regarding education. Three-dimensional OK-ness enabled me to consider at the same time parents, children, and myself in the encounter, keeping each of us OK in the process. It enabled me to take what seems to me a good enough distance, not taking the expert role, but acknowledging that the family system is different from the kindergarten system and that the child has to cope with living in both at the same time.

Many studies on resilience show that the primary factor is to have relationships that can provide care and support, create love and trust, and offer encouragement. Additional factors are the capacity to make realistic plans, having self-confidence and a positive self-image, developing communication skills and the capacity to manage strong feelings and impulses. It is important for some children to find adults outside their families who offer inspiring models, becoming "developing tutors" or "resilience tutors" for a time. According to Wright, quoted by Gilbert and Evans (2000), the child is at the beginning of his life "entirely dependent for feeling good or bad on one other person's perspective on himself which inevitably defines and shapes his own view of himself". To start with this will be the primary caregiver, but later the child "can draw on the perspective of third 'persons' to help him develop a multi-perspectival view of reality" (p. 13).

14.3.6. Conclusion

As far as I remember I always wanted to do a job that would be meaningful for me and for others. I chose to become an educator for young children and really enjoyed working with babies, children in kindergarten, children with special needs, children in foster care. Becoming a certified transactional analyst in education gave me even more potency in my interventions and happiness in my professional identity. I know its value and know the impact of early relationships on the future of children. And it also explains why I then decided to become a TSTA and a teacher in the initial training of educators for young children: I wanted to share with other professionals what had been so meaningful in my own way of looking at my job and relating to children and their families. Together with different approaches I present various TA concepts and sometimes I enjoy observing in students' eyes that the developing effect is taking place and that they start to "see" their job in a different way.

14.4. Using transactional analysis with community care workers in South Africa

Karen Pratt

14.4.1 Introduction

I would like to share some of the highlights of using transactional analysis with community care workers (CCWs) in South Africa (SA). The high rate of HIV/AIDS in SA has seen many people trained as CCWs. They play an important role in health care in the country. Many are themselves HIV positive. They experience bereavement of both family members and patients and are often severely traumatised and burnt out and yet feel compelled to continue to do their caring work. Self-care and wellness are often forgotten, despite this aspect of the work being crucial for CCWs and to the sustainability of the service they offer to their communities. I work with an NGO which, ten years ago, saw the need for self-care for CCWs. The organisation developed a range of workshops aimed at self-awareness, building self-esteem and establishing a culture of self-care for these people who give so much to others.

The director describes the work as follows: "Our mission is to mobilise and support individuals, organisations and communities to respond in a caring, creative and sustainable manner to the challenges they face. Our core work is based on a range of self-care workshops and retreats aimed at identifying common responses to stressful events, and then equipping participants with the necessary information, skills and contacts to successfully manage the impact of these stressors" (Roeland, 2013).

Models from transactional analysis form an integral part of these workshops; the following examples show TA in action.

14.4.2 Contracting

The initial step of contracting is one of the most important parts of the work. We usually work as a facilitator pair—this gives an opportunity for both the facilitators to teach, but more importantly to model living the TA principles as the pair works together.

Many CCWs have strong cultural injunctions (Goulding & Goulding, 1976) of "Don't be important", and "Don't be you". As women, they face gender prohibitions and often have a life position of "I'm not OK, you're OK". They have been used to being told what to do in many areas of their lives.

Much of the psychological work is in enabling people to begin to feel a sense of self-worth and to grow in their assertiveness. The most important permissions (or affirmations) that CCWs need are: "I am valuable, my needs are important, and I can appreciate myself." They can hear these affirmations already during the contracting process, and get more of them in the learning activities that follow.

After introducing themselves, people divide into small groups and are invited to discuss and name their expectations. This serves several purposes: people begin to connect with others and build relationships, they can begin to voice their needs within a small group, and they experience solidarity in hearing others with similar wishes. There is often much cheering when the leader shares the expectations of the group with the larger group. This is a way of building self-esteem.

In having a voice right from the start, CCWs begin to experience OK-ness and the right to be heard. The contract is always left open for renegotiation during the workshop. This is a new way of experiencing contracting. In their organisations, the CCWs mostly see a contract as something that is imposed by the person in authority, definitely never negotiable, and mostly used in a punitive way. When experiencing a wellness workshop, it is often the first time that an authority figure has asked them about their expectations for the workshop and how they would like to work together.

Not only do they contract for their learning as a group, they are encouraged to contract with themselves to be open to learn. We do this by inviting each person to set the intention for learning for the day ahead. This is often a new awareness for people—the fact that they can take their power and contract with themselves to do something. It is refreshing for people to be given the opportunity, for example, as to how they would want to be given feedback from others in the group. When the TA models are explored, the participants are reminded of the contract with themselves and are prompted to explore what action they will take.

An example of what can emerge when the contracting is thorough and respectful follows.

Because of the contract of confidentiality, a participant shared about there being lots of corruption in her NGO. Getting the support and encouragement of the group enabled her to take steps to make sure that her own well-being was taken care of. She was finding herself doing many more tasks over and above her role as a caregiver. She decided that she was going to ask for a more precise job description and get a clearer contract so that she could receive the salary that was a fair reward for the extra work that she was doing.

14.4.3 Strokes

In teaching about strokes, the concept of a stroke tank is used (and expanded to include different levels). The CCWs are familiar with the concept of water tanks that will not be able to provide any water if they are empty. This enables the concept of strokes to link with their understanding of stress and its impact. The image of filling their tank with positive strokes reinforces their realisation that they need to find ways of minimising their stress through activities that nurture and support them. The CCWs are given time to reflect on their level of positive strokes, as well as to realise how negative strokes can demoralise them. They are invited to think of how they protect themselves against this and once again there are many creative and symbolic ideas that emerge, for example, imagining that they are wearing a raincoat that enables the negative strokes to "run off" them, as rain does from a raincoat. This is a way of the CCWs claiming back their power and giving themselves permission to refuse to accept negative strokes, especially when they have come from a contamination and an "I'm OK, you're not OK" place in the stroke giver.

After explaining the stroke economy (Steiner, 1966), they divide into small groups of five people each. The task is to write something that they appreciate about each person in the group. They write this on a heart shaped piece of paper as well as writing hearts for themselves. Then follows a ritual where each person in turn is given the verbal appreciation, supported by the paper heart for them to keep. In this way they experience permission to undo some of the stroke myths around giving and receiving of strokes, and especially stroking themselves. This exercise produces strong emotional responses from people and often ends with tears and hugs of appreciation. One woman said: "EVERYONE in my group told me that I was brave and would go far—so maybe it IS true, and I can start to believe it."

14.4.4 The OK-OK communication model

This model (Pratt & Mbaligontsi, 2014, see Figure 14.3) modified from the work of Susannah Temple (2009), enables people to understand that there can be different ways of transacting with people. When in the OK-OK box and using one of the positive modes of communication, they are likely to invite a response from within the OK-OK box. When they are outside the box they are likely to get a less helpful out-of-the-box response.

An aid to understanding is by using two sets of three hula hoops on the floor to represent the Parent, Adult, and Child of two people. The lived experience of the CCWs is used by inviting role plays with people standing in and moving around the different hoops. Thus an invisible intrapsychic shift, resulting in observable behaviour, can be played out on the floor, and the types of transactions easily seen. Participants soon notice that transactions from within the OK-OK box (using the positive modes of Parent and Child) means that both people stay OK. They notice that their underlying attitude of OK or not-OK results in different sorts of transactions. An example of the insight a manager might get from this model is that she will begin to realise that she can be firm and in charge from the assertive mode, rather than the dominating mode, and that this will invite cooperation rather than resistance from the CCW.

14.4.5 Windows on the world

We teach the concept of life-positions as adapted by Julie Hay as windows on the world (1993). The idea of getting a different view looking out of different windows, makes the understanding of this model, being about our inner attitudes, easier to grasp.

Temple (2000) first wrote about colour-coding the parts of a quadrant for ease of reference. We chose different colours to illustrate the emotions associated with different windows, as follows: yellow (positive, present, hopeful) depicted the I'm OK, you're OK window, blue (depressed, feeling "blue") depicted the I'm not OK, you're OK window, red (aggressive, seeing "red") depicted the I'm OK, you're not OK window, and grey (hopeless) depicted the I'm not OK, you're not OK window. These visual cues assist in cementing the learning and in providing a visual association with the emotion they are experiencing. CCWs would speak of being or trying to be in the "yellow window" as an indication of the OK-OK state or in the "blue window"

402 INTO TA

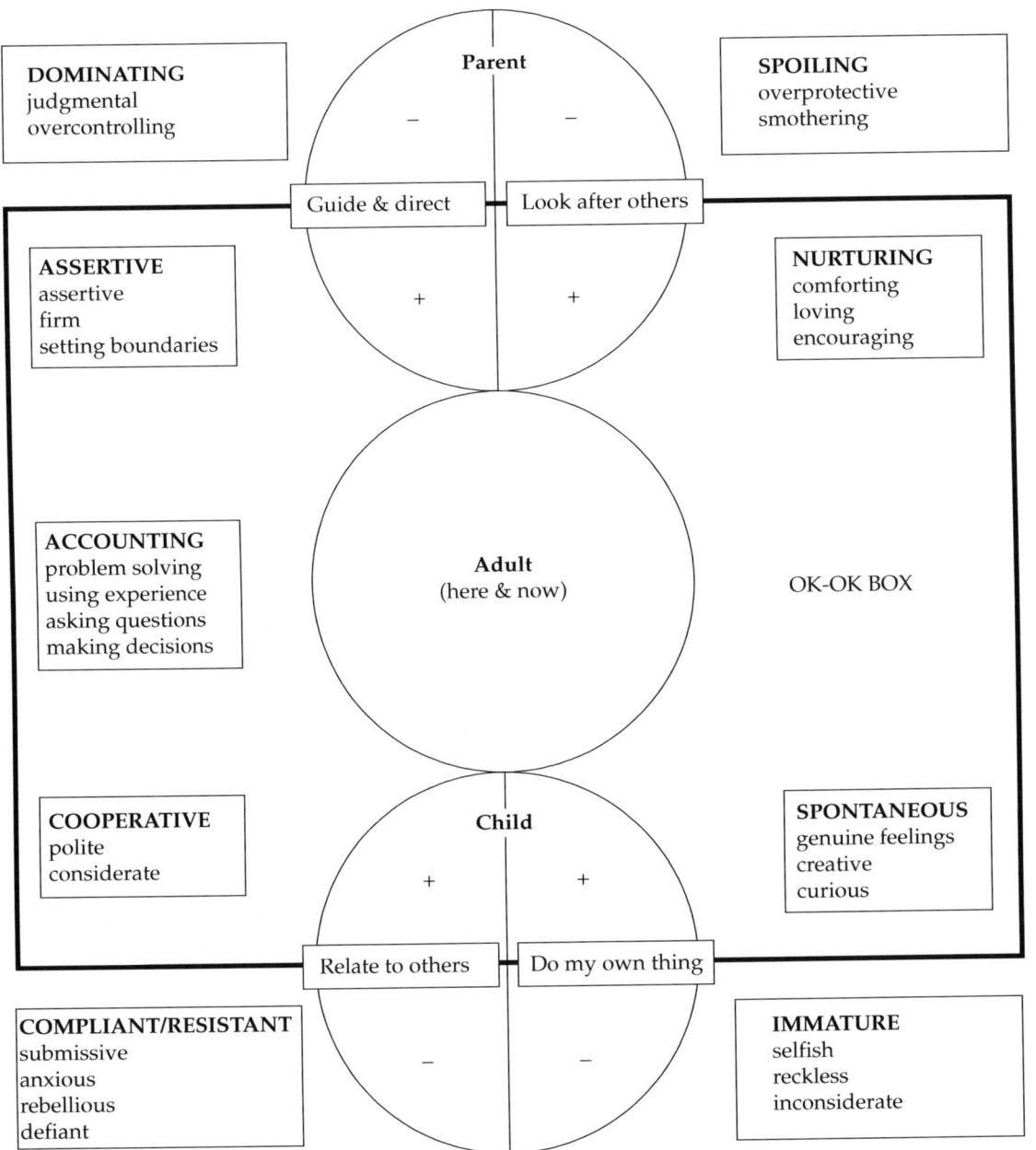

Figure 14.3. The OK-OK communication model.

to indicate their feelings of I'm not OK, you're OK in their relationships. The visual cues are especially important because of the low literacy levels of the majority of CCWs.

Consolidating the learning comes through inviting the CCWs to do role plays of their experiences in the clinics and with their patients. Once a small group has acted out a scenario, the rest of the group analyses which window each person was in and how the outcome was impacted. If there was an unsatisfactory outcome, the group suggests how a more satisfactory outcome can be reached by shifting into the yellow window and the role-players try out a different style of communication.

The CCWs enjoy bringing their experiences into the process. It enables a theoretical model to come alive. All of their senses are engaged as they role-play a situation—they speak, feel, and behave as different role players in a situation. Many of the role plays depict their frustration of being dominated and judged by their managers from an I'm OK, you're not OK position, inviting them to lose their potency and respond from an I'm not OK, you're OK position. In linking this model back to the OK-OK communication model, they can try out using different positive modes to invite an OK-OK response.

14.4.6 Drama triangle and winners' triangle

The drama triangle (Karpman, 1968) is the model with which CCWs have the most affinity as it's easy to identify themselves in these roles. Due to care work being unrecognised and underpaid, most caregivers find themselves in the Victim position from their perspective, both individually and as a part of the culture still present from South Africa's history.

Introducing the winners' triangle (Choy, 1990), and the positive aspects of each drama triangle role, shifts the focus towards options for change. Once again this links back to their understanding of the windows on the world and OK-OK communication models.

We have found that doing creative work and engaging the Child seems to be a powerful way of lessening the influence of the injunctions. Using symbolic language or working creatively with images seems more powerful than Adult factual talk. For instance, the tactile and somatic experience of moulding clay accesses deep preverbal Child states. CCWs become engrossed with their lumps of clay, creating images of finding their voice, or moving to a space of being caring, rather than Rescuing. They create a variety of images which carry significance for them. One woman created a chair and commented "I can now sit on a chair rather than on the floor," indicating that she was claiming her power and breaking the cultural tradition of having to sit on a mat on the floor when she visited her husband's family.

After the creative work, we shift back into more cognitive work such as planning what they would begin to do differently with their new awareness. This work in the Adult seems to consolidate the creative work in the Child and reinforce their new decisions.

14.4.7 Conclusion

Berne and Steiner described TA as a radical psychiatry that has the potential to impact social change. In this work with the CCWs we can see its power as just that. Understanding and embodying TA helps people to find pockets of solidarity and unite to work for a common cause. As people grow in appreciating and believing in themselves, finding their voice, and shifting out of their Victim mentality, some have even become involved in the important work of lobbying for their rights in government.

An exciting communal development has been the birth of the South African Care Workers Forum (SACWF) in 2013, run by CCWs. They sought support in "finding their voices" and the NGO first supported an "Owning our Voices" campaign in 2009. CCWs collectively drafted the CCW Charter and developed key messages to take to government. The membership has grown to over 2000 carers in three provinces.

This is going a long way to fulfilling the advocacy objectives of the NGO:

1. The establishment of community care work as a profession.
2. Ensuring that women and girls can break the cycle of poverty and violence, build economic alternatives, and claim control over their bodies.

Truly the winners' triangle in action!

There are also some inspiring individual success stories, such as that of a young CCW in a workshop, who, when asked to share her dream, said that one day she was going to be a matron of a hospital—a long way from where she was as a volunteer caregiver. I was able to mobilise funding and support for her, and three years later she has graduated as a staff nurse—a few steps closer to realising her dream of running a hospital.

I have been inspired and changed by my interaction with this group of people. I honour their resilience and courage.

14.5. Advanced dancing classes. Choosing "I +, U +"

Jan Ruigrok

14.5.1. Introduction

In this section we discuss how teachers and counsellors can deal with code-red behaviour, behaviour with which people wrong themselves and others, or cause harm. This behaviour includes aggression, extremely risky behaviour, or self-harm. The basic TA-positions "I +, U –", "I –, U –", and "I –, U +" lead to code-red behaviour. In this situation, somebody always loses. Green behaviour takes place in the "I +, U +".

As explained in Chapter Five, the diagram with the four existential positions is also known as the OK Corral (Ernst, 1971), the outdoor arena in which horses can run at a ranch. This corral can be applied to a school, as a building with four doors (see Figure 14.4). Through these doors people can leave the school. There is one front door and three back doors. When the situation escalates, code-red behaviour leads to a back door. Green behaviour leads to the front door.

We turned the OK Corral a quarter compared to the common representation, to let it fit in with the model of "leadership in heart & bones" (*Leiderschap in Hart & Nieren*, Fiddelaers-Jaspers & Ruigrok, 2012), which is discussed later on.

14.5.2. Dancing

The challenge for teachers and counsellors is to keep the front door wide open and the back doors closed. When someone is in danger of pulling out through a back door, he is invited to take the route to the front door. Working with youngsters in pedagogical situations is like dancing in a room with four doors. You dance when you're feeling good and you do it with the people you think are worth it. This means having fun, moving, moving along, challenging, tempting others to go with you in your movement, and being tempted: an encounter with intimacy, but also one where you sometimes stand on each others' toes; fortunately, in the knowledge that when you get tangled, you can work it out together. The pedagogical dance is one where the counsellor leads. The counsellor gives youngsters space, joins in their movements, but within this framework, he determines the dance steps.

Most pedagogical dance masters generally manage to dance with youngsters quite successfully. Pedagogical mastery requires being able to dance with groups of sometimes thirty youngsters who have not always asked for this and who have in common that they are guided by an immature, fickle, and often unpredictable adolescent brain.

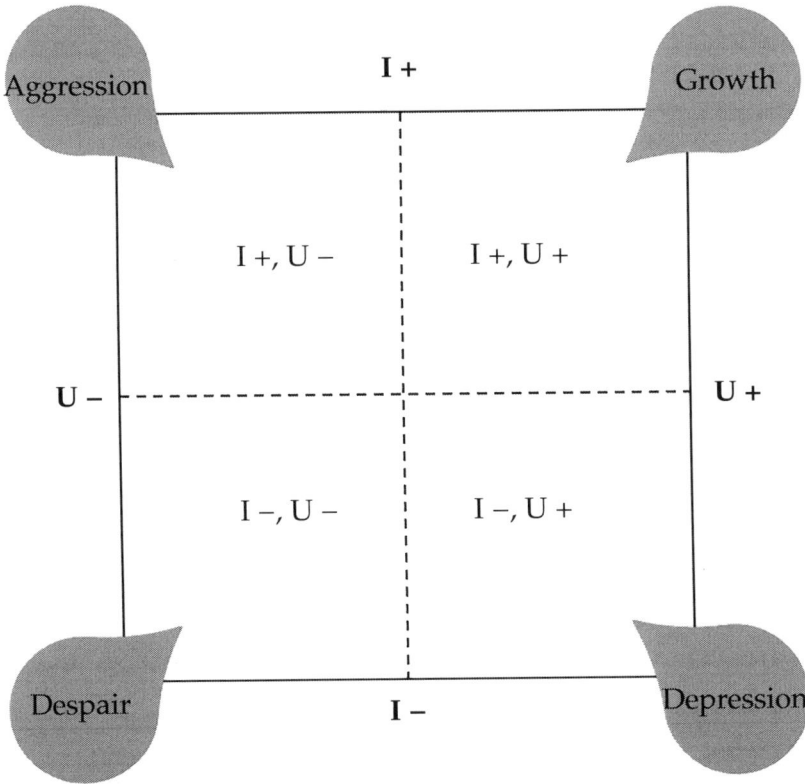

Figure 14.4. The school in the OK- Corral.

There is another major similarity between the youngsters: they all want to feel that they really matter. At their age, they are often very insecure about this. As the differences within the group of youngsters increase, it gets harder to dance in a way youngsters and the counsellor feel good about. Then we talk about advanced dancing classes.

In this section we explore principles from so-called *restorative justice* (Oostrik & Ruigrok, 2007, and Hopkins, 2015) through a TA lens. This is a way of pedagogic action which has its roots with the Maori, the original inhabitants of New Zealand, and which spread from New Zealand across the world.

14.5.3. Teacher in heart and bones

Schools working with restorative justice, do this from the basic model "leadership in heart & bones" (Fiddelaers-Jaspers & Ruigrok, 2012). This model assumes that in a healthy situation, counsellors make proper use of their Structuring (SP) and Nurturing Parent (NP), in addition to their Adult. They are guiding (SP) as well as supporting (NP). When the SP and NP of the counsellor are in balance and guided by the Adult, there is leadership in heart and bones.

The supportive interventions come from the Nurturing Parent. Key words are: atmosphere, cosiness, empathy, understanding, and recognition (NP+). In an exaggerated way they form the

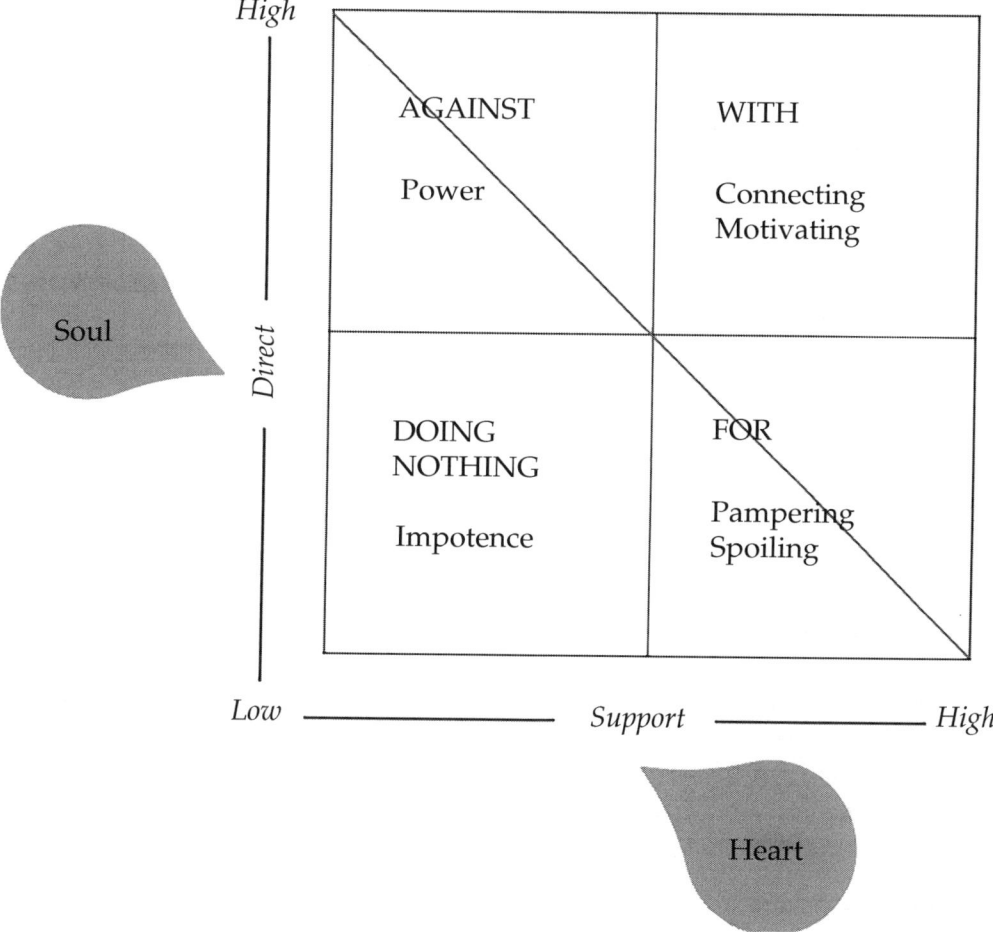

Figure 14.5. Leadership in heart and bones (source: McCold & Wachtel, 2004).

soft side of education (NP-). The image of bones can be linked to guiding interventions: bones give the system strength and keep it upright. Key words are: clarity, achievement-oriented, structure, and setting boundaries. These words resonate in the voice of the Structuring Parent (SP+). The exaggerated variant is the negative Structuring Parent (SP-).

The "connecting and motivating" section is the ideal. Thankfully most teachers and counsellors spend most of their time with their pupils here. When it gets really exciting, you often see them fan out to the sections "against", "doing nothing", and "for". The challenge is to continue working "with", even in cases of disturbing and challenging behaviour. The diagonal in the model goes from "nothing is allowed" (top left) to "everything is allowed" (bottom right).

14.5.4. Contract-based working

The model of "leadership in heart & bones" provides possibilities to draw up and maintain relational contracts and work contracts with pupils. Teachers, using this model, discuss the model with their pupils and state that their intention is to work from the basic position "with". Pupils almost always agree wholeheartedly to this. This isn't strange, as it fits in with their need for being significant.

The next question for teachers is what they need to do to provide guidance and support in the right way. They appeal to the needs of pupils and to their responsibility, or in TA terms: to their Natural Child and their Adult. Because a TA contract is concluded from the Adult, teachers stimulate the autonomy of the pupils with this approach.

It's a good thing to ask pupils what their needs are and how you, as a counsellor, can contribute to these. Equally important is that counsellors bring forward what their rules are. If they don't do this and let the pupils decide how they will treat them as teachers, the counsellors are in the "for" section and relinquish their leadership.

Teachers, who are in "with", also ask their pupils what their own contribution can be, when working from this section. Only when pupils also provide an active contribution to their environment and get recognition for this, can they experience that they have significance. Working on a good atmosphere then becomes a joint responsibility.

The individual relationship contract must be maintained. For example in regular discussions in which all involved assess whether everything is still going all right. A teacher can, if necessary, confront the pupils with the fact that he can't manage to meet the expectations the pupils have of him. This puts pressure on the pupils' needs. The question is then what is necessary to get back to "with". For a relationship contract to be successful, it is important to discuss the atmosphere also when things are going all right. If you only do this when things are going wrong, pupils will soon associate these discussions with arguing and unpleasantness.

14.5.5. Pedagogy of the dance floor

The dance floor has a green part in which you recognise strengths or the winners' triangle: assertiveness, vulnerability, and caring. These are qualities you can expect all counsellors to have plenty of and which you hope they will stimulate in their pupils.

In the red part you recognise the drama triangle with the roles Persecutor, Victim, and Rescuer.

The challenge is to keep your own code-red behaviour and that of others within limits. And when you are confronted with code-red behaviour, to respond with green to this, which results in the other automatically going to green. Not because it's necessary, but because it makes the dancing much more pleasant.

14.5.6. Restorative justice: conflict management and approach from the Adult

Restorative justice is a way of promoting green behaviour from the Adult and responding with green to code-red behaviour. In conflicts and misbehaviour, restorative justice gives the perpetrator or instigator the opportunity to recover the damage he has caused. Pupils who harm themselves or others place themselves more or less outside the community of the classroom or

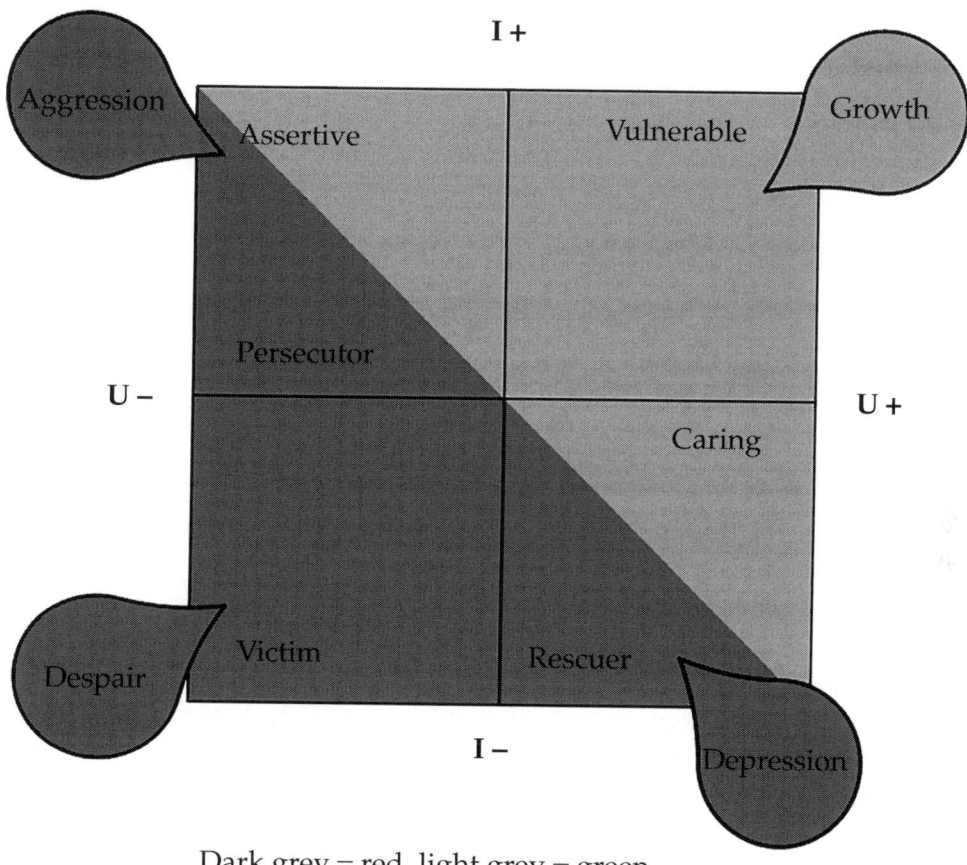

Figure 14.6. Pedagogy of the dance.

school; they are in the red. Restorative justice gives them the right to earn back their green spot (Oostrik, 2010; Oostrik & Ruigrok, 2007).

A restorative justice-based school says to the person who was in the wrong:

> We *have* to do something with what you did. You have no say in *that* something needs to be done. We want to give you influence on *what* is going to happen. You can choose: we either respond from green or from red.
>
> If you go for green, which we would prefer, we look at who was harmed by what you did and together with these others we assess what you can do to restore this. If you choose red, we will respect this and will take a repressive measure. The choice is up to you. (Ruigrok, 2009)

Restorative justice lays the responsibility with the group whose members have to figure out how they can solve this together. The greater the conflict, the more structure the interventions

Table 14.1. Summarises characteristics of conflict management in a green and a red way.

In a red way	In a green way
Often from the Structuring Parent to the perpetrators and causers of damage, and from the Nurturing Parent to the victims.	Mainly from the Adult to all parties concerned ("I +, U +").
The school leaders put on a police cap and ask questions like:	The school leaders take on the role of connecting "village elder" and ask questions like:
• Which rule was violated?	• What happened?
• Who did it?	• Who was harmed by this?
• How are we going to punish him or her?	• What has to happen to recover this harm?
Misconduct is seen as a conflict between the perpetrator and the system (school). The leaders take on the conflict and take decisions.	Misconduct is behaviour under which the community suffers. The responsibility is placed within the group.
There is a "strangle contract": "You have to go along with this or else …" The school is SP, the pupils are AC.	There is a contract in TA terms, which is concluded autonomously from A.
Is geared towards contradictions. The greater you make them, the more chance of victory in the conflict.	Is geared towards common needs that come under pressure. The greater the similarities become, the greater the chance of success.
Results in winners and losers and has the characteristics of a mind game, including the pay-off.	Results in winners only. People are invited to go into dialogue with each other; this takes steps towards intimacy.
Geared towards content.	Geared towards a recovery of disturbed relations.
The back door of Aggression, Depression, and Despair are wide open; the front door of Growth is closed.	The front door of Growth is wide open, the back doors of Aggression, Depression, and Despair are closed.
Carries the core of new conflict within.	Leads to recovery and strengthening of relations.
Teaches perpetrators what they must do or not do to be punished again next time.	Teaches perpetrators what they must do to fulfil their needs in an "I +, U +" way.

have. Sometimes conferences are held in which more than twenty teachers and pupils take part and where the central question is: "Are there possibilities to continue together in an acceptable way?" Minor conflicts can be solved by those involved. For major conflicts, where severe emotions play a role and mutual trust has dropped to a minimum, an external person can be appealed to in the role of "village elder". He or she has enough emotional distance to let those involved protect their own interests. One of the most important qualities of "village elders" is the distant, sometimes cold way of process guidance, showing a lot of Adult. With this, they achieve remaining truly unbiased. The parties are not always willing to go into dialogue. Restorative justice is a right to which both perpetrators and victims can say "Yes" or

"No". Sometimes it doesn't work and it can take a long time before the parties are willing and capable of this.

14.5.7. Conclusion

When no recovery-oriented procedure is reached, this does not always mean that it's a failure. Often the school's invitation to cooperate instead going into a conflict shows so much recognition that those involved feel sufficiently heard.

Practice has also taught us that in situations where disappointed parents make complaints to the board or legal bodies, a school with a recovery-oriented approach has a strong position. This school shows it really focuses on reaching a mutual solution.

References

Barrow, G. (2007). Wonderful world, beautiful people: Re-framing transactional analysis as positive psychology. *Transactional Analysis Journal*, 37(3): 206–209.

Barrow, G. (2009). Teaching, learning, schooling and script. *Transactional Analysis Journal*, 39(4): 298–304.

Barrow, G., & Newton, T. (2004). *Walking the Talk: How TA is Improving Behaviour and Raising Self-Esteem*. London: David Fulton.

Berne, E. (1966). *Principles of Group Treatment*. New York: Grove Press.

Choy, A. (1990). The winners triangle. *Transactional Analysis Journal*, 20(1): 40–47.

Clarke, J. I. (1996). The synergistic use of five transactional analysis concepts by educators. *Transactional Analysis Journal*, 26(3): 214–219.

Clarke, J. I., & Dawson, C. (1998). *Growing Up Again: Parenting Ourselves, Parenting Our Children (2nd edition)*. Center City, MN: Hazelden, 2009.

Elias, J. L., & Merriam, S. B. (1980). *Philosophical Foundations of Adult Education (2nd edition)*. Malabar, FL: Kreiger, 1995.

Ernst, F. (1971). The OK Corral: The grid for get-on-with. *Transactional Analysis Journal*, 1(4): 33–42.

Erskine, R., & Zalcmann, M. (1979). The racket system: A model for racket analysis. *Transactional Analysis Journal*, 9(1): 51–59.

Fiddelaers-Jaspers, R., & Ruigrok, J. (2012). *Leraar in Hart en Nieren*. (Teacher in Heart and Soul.) Heeze, Netherlands: Uitgeverij In de Wolken.

Freire, P., & Ramos, M. (1973). *Pedagogy of the Oppressed (2nd edition)*. London: Penguin Education, 1996.

Gilbert, M., & Evans, K. (2000). *Psychotherapy Supervision: an Integrative Relational Approach to Psychotherapy Supervision*. Maidenhead, UK: Open University Press.

Goulding, R., & Goulding, M. (1976). Injunctions, decisions and redecisions. *Transactional Analysis Journal*, 6(1): 41–48.

Hawkes, L. (2007). The permission wheel. *Transactional Analysis Journal*, 37(3): 210–217.

Hay, J. (1993). *Working It Out at Work*. Watford, UK: Sherwood.

Hay, J. (1995). *Donkey Bridges for Developmental TA*. Watford, UK: Sherwood.

Hopkins, B. (2015). *Restorative Theory into Practice*. London: Jessica Kingsley Publishers.

Karpman, S. (1968). Fairy tales and script drama analysis. *Transactional Analysis Bulletin*, 7(26): 39–43.

Levin, P. (1980). Cycle of development. *Transactional Analysis Journal*, 12(2): 129–139.

McCold, P., & Wachtel, B. (2002). Community is not a place. A new look at community justice initiatives. In: J. G. Perr (Ed.), *Repairing Communities through Restorative Justice* (pp. 39–53). Lanham, MD: American Correctional Association.

Mezirow, J. (2000). *Learning as Transformation*. San Francisco, CA: Jossey Bass.

Napper, R., & Newton, T. (2000). *TACTICS: Transactional Analysis Concepts for All Trainers, Teachers and Tutors Plus Insight into Collaborative Teaching Strategies*. Ipswich, UK: TA Resources.

Newton, T. (2003). Identifying educational philosophy and practice through imagoes in transactional analysis training groups. *Transactional Analysis Journal*, 33(4): 321–331.

Oostrik, H. (2010). *Een basis van respect. Herstelrecht in het primair onderwijs*. (On the Basis of Respect. Restorative Justice at Primary Schools.) Den Bosch, Netherlands: KPC Groep.

Oostrik, H., & Ruigrok, J. (2007). *In plaats van schorsen. Handboek Herstelrecht in het Onderwijs*. (An Alternative for Suspension. Textbook of Restorative Justice in Education.) Den Bosch, Netherlands: KPC Groep/Quirijn.

Pratt, K., & Mbaligontsi, M. (2014). Transactional analysis transforms community care workers in South Africa. *Transactional Analysis Journal*, 44(1): 53–67. (Reprinted with permission of Sage Publications.)

Roeland, B. (2013). *Companion Manual to Train the Trainer Manual—a Guide to Setting Up a Care for Carers Programme*. Cape Town: The Media Chilli.

Ruigrok, J. (2009). *Provocatieve leerlingbegeleiding*. Esch, Netherlands: Quirijn.

Shotton, P. (2009). Transactional analysis training, postmodernism and education. *Transactional Analysis Journal*, 39(4): 293–297.

Steiner, C. (1966). The stroke economy. *Transactional Analysis Journal*, 1(3): 9–15.

Steiner, C. (1996). Emotional literacy training: the application of transactional analysis to the study of emotions. *Transactional Analysis Journal*, 26(1): 31–39.

Summers, G., & Tudor, K. (2000). Co-creative transactional analysis. *Transactional Analysis Journal*, 30(1): 23–40.

Temple, S. (2000). A way of teaching life positions as a foundation for game theory. *Script, Newsletter of the ITAA*, 30(5).

Temple, S. (2004). Update on the functional fluency model in education. *Transactional Analysis Journal*, 29(2): 164–174.

Temple, S. (2009). *Maximising Interpersonal Effectiveness—Functional Fluency*. Bristol, UK: Fleur Temple Publishing.

Tudor, K., & Summers, G. (2014). *Co-creative Transactional Analysis*. London: Karnac.

INDEX

accounting 171–172; mode 24–25
addictions 107–108
Adult 17, 322; in the Child 15; integrated and integrating 17–19, 24, 67, 184–185; Little Professor 13, 15; *see also* ego state, transactions
Adult–Adult, in co-creative transactional analysis 202–203; in organisations 369, 372; *see also* complementary transactions
affirmations, developmental and educational 177–179, 399–400; *see also* permissions
Ainsworth, M., Blehar, M. et al. 152
Allen, F. 208–209
Allen, J. R. 148
Allen, J. R., Allen, B. A. 30, 148
anti-psychiatry 181–182
Appelo, M. 207–208
appreciative inquiry 56–57
Aron, L. 254–255
Assagioli, R. 34
assertive behaviour 94–95
assertive discipline 56–57
attachment theory 32, 111; and script 152; *also* 351
attributions 61, 125, 127, 268, 294
authenticity, movement towards 323

autonomous behaviour 79
autonomy ix, 345–346; system 143–144; the client's 200, 241, 247, 312–313; and counselling 312–313, 329–332; free will emergent 247–249; illusion of 196–197; and integrity 53; in learning contract 206; and organisations 345–346; script 117, 151–152, 248; in social-cognitive school 27–28; and strokes 45, 50; of the supervisee 275; and symbiosis 163–164; and withdrawal 46
avoidance 292–293
awareness, action sequence/discount matrix 171; enhancing Adult awareness 317, 332–333

babies and young children, the world of 15, 55, 128, 154
Bader, E. 245
Banks, K. 282
Bannink, F. 82–83, 206
Barnes, G. 76, 124
Barrow, G. 117, 383–388, 390–391
Barrow, G., Bradshaw, E., Newton, T. 8, 30, 178, 206
Barrow, G., Newton, T. 384, 394

Bartak, A., Spreeuwenberg, M. D. et al. 184, 305
Bass, A. 254
Bastianelli, L., Ceridono, D. 26
Beck, A. 31, 33
Beekum, S. van 23–24, 272–273
behaviour, evoked 125; *see also* autonomous, assertive, bystander, group, virtue, ethical
behavioural modes 388
behaviour, structural analysis of social 26–27
behavioural therapy 31, 33, 45, 110
Belbin, R. M. 372
Benjamin, L. S. 26–27
Berk, T. J. C. 233, 228
Berne, E., development of thought vii, 4–12, 17–22, 28–33; contracts 190; ego states 5; hungers 40–42; games and rackets 86–99, 103–104, 281–282; groups 212–214; own life-script 118; simplicity of transactional analysis 80–81; script 116–118; script-change 378–379; structuring time 46–50; supervision 260; transactions 60–61
Bettelheim, B. 106
Bion, W. 45, 225–233 *passim*
bipolar disorder 22
Bollas, C. 145, 182, 282
Bollas, C., Sundelson, D. 253
Bond, T. 249–250
Bond, T., Mitchels, B. 253
boundaries, group 215–218; in supervision 251–252
Bowlby, J. 32, 111, 152, 351
Bradshaw, E. 15
brain, areas of, *see* neurobiology
Bucci, W. 145
Buda, B. 76
Burger, Y. 109–110
Burgoon, J., Buller, D. et al. 66
burnout, professional 106–107
Burston, D. 181
Burton, R. A. 248
bystander behaviour 97–98, 238, 250, 347

Caizzi, C. 145, 282
Carroll, M. 255
Cassoni, E. 267

cathexis, model 160–164; institute 179–180; decathexis 174
certified transactional analyst (CTA) 244
change, process 190–195, 293–295, 313, 376; in counselling 315; psychotherapeutic 175–176; pentagon of change 195–197
Child *see* ego state; Adapted 5; Free 5; Natural 5; Somatic 13, 15
Child-Adult-Parent (CAP) model 385–386
Choy, A. 94, 397, 403
chronic processes *see* passivity
Clark, B. D. 297
Clarke, J. I. 198, 224, 389; *also* 324
Clarke, J. I., Dawson, C. 53, 171, 177–179, 396
Clarkson, P. professional burnout 106–107; bystander 97–98, 238, 250; psychotherapeutic change 175–176; "pentagon of changes" 196–197; positive components of drivers 138; dual relationships 245; group development 223–224; continuing supervision 261; supervision checklist 264–265; survival mechanisms 184–185
Clarkson, P., Fish, S. 297
Clarkson, P., Leigh, E. 263
classical transactional analysis 160–161
classroom games 108–109
client-centred therapy 34
coaching 78–80; contract in 190–192; matrix 355; relational 80; supervision 261, 265; *see also* counselling and coaching
co-creative transactional analysis 78, 128, 388; and contracting 200–201
co-dependency 23
cognitive behavioural therapy (CBT) 33–34, 110
cognitive dissonance 143–144
cognitive fixations 147–148
cognitive therapy 31, 298, 301
collaboration 208–209, 293–295, 344–348, 360, 369–372, *see also* diagnosis
communication, theory of 11, 61, 75–76, 81–82; meta-communication 82; non-verbal 66, 76, 285, 396
comparative script system *see* supervision
compassion triangle 95–97
competence curve 270–271; unconscious 270

complementary *see* transactions
confidentiality, in group-work 232; in counselling and psychotherapy 253
conflict, escalation 228–230; focal theory 228; in groups 228; in education 408–411; in organisations 225; resolution 31, 178, 206, 357, 367
conscience, personal 129, 184, 322; organisational 349; *see also* Adult, autonomy
constancy 20–21; hypothesis 8
constellations *see* family constellations
contamination 20–22
contracts, chapt 7; viii, 22, 51, 150, 174; aspects of 190–192; and autonomy 200; conversation 205; in counselling groups 314–315; effective 198–200, 331; learning 206; multi-cornered 194, 206, 326–327; no-contract 150; organisational 201–202, 344; power in the 192; for process and frame 203; in psychotherapy 200; requirements 192–193; and script 193–194, 200–201; socially intentioned 203–204; for supervision 260–261; three-cornered 194–195, 204–206, 393; contract based working in education 407–408; *see also* change process, co-creative transactional analysis
contracting matrix 203–204
Cook, R. 250
Cooper, D. 161, 181–182
Cornell, W. 281–285; developing Child 15, 17; games avoiding intimacy 91; conferring meaning 316; relational transactional analysis 79–80; dual relationships 245; ethics 250; avoiding intimacy 91; group processes 225; script change and resilience 17, 146–148; script protocol 144–145, 152; self-disclosure 254–255, 322; somatic interventions 282; critique of traditional theory 127–128, 146; *re* cycles of development 176; *also* 117, 182
Cornell, W. F., Bonds-White, F. 148
Cornell, W. F., Hargaden, H. 33, 78–79
Cornell, W. F., Hine, J. 326, 313
Cornell, W. F., Landaiche, N. M. 145, 282
Cornell, W. F., Shadbolt, C. et al. 260

counselling and coaching, chapt 12; working with Adult 322; contracts 319–321, 325–327; definition 329; groups 313–318; law affects practice 328; long-term 319–323; objectives of 313, 326; focus on resources 329–330; space of 321; working within (counter)transference 322–323; focus on wellness 316–317
counter-injunctions, *see* drivers; and injunctions 139–141
countertransference *see* transference …
Crossman, P. 197, 293, 346
cross-up *see* switch
CTA *see* certified transactional analyst
Cuijpers, P., Sijbrandji, M. et al. 292
Cuilenburg, P. van 34
culture 215, 239, 249, 327
cultural script 153
Cumming, J., Cumming, E. 31, 183
cybernetics 11, 81, 245
cycles of development 176–178, 384

Dashiell, S. R. 175, 297
Deaconu, D. 225
deconfusion 78–79
decontamination 20, 22, 33, 78, 175
defence mechanisms 184–185
depression 291–295, 309; a basic life script 125; and learned helplessness 208; and stroke profiles 51
developmental, affirmations 177–178; phases 154; stages 26, 176–179
diagnosis 10; collaborative 208–209; contextual diagnosis 11; four methods of 10–11; *see also* DSM
Dictionary of Transactional Analysis (*quoted*) 140–141
discounting chapt 6; definition 160; distortion of reality 165; healthy and unhealthy 169; discount matrix 169–172, 397; *see also* defence mechanisms
disposition diamond 124–125
Doan, R. E. 148
Doehrman, M. J. 268
Draaisma, D. 14
Drake, R. E., Sederer, L. I. 183

drama triangle 88–89, 95–96, 104, 294–295, 403; *see also* winners' triangle
Drego, P. 53, 215, 250
drivers 118, 136–140; founding myths of 139–140; further drivers 139; and stoppers 140–141
drowning person diagram 141
DSM (diagnostic and statistical manual) 208, 253, 302
dual relationships 245–246
Dusay, J. 7–8, 92–93

education(al), accounting-empowerment 171–172; affirmations 177–178; appreciative inquiry in 57; games 108–110; nurture and structure 53; parent education 176–177; in school transition 394; stages of development 177–179; teacher potencies 198; for young people *(case study)* 395–398; *see also* learning
educational transactional analysis 383, 385, 387; as a radical pedagogy 384
effectiveness, personal 60
egogram assessment tool (EAT) 30
ego psychology 31; influence on Berne 4–5, 33
ego psychology 31, 33
ego stages 25–26
ego states, chapt 1; the basis of transactional analysis vii; basic theory 4; co-dependency 23; identification of 30–31, 60; within organisations 35, 349; pathology 20; alternative representation of 23–24; *see also* ego stages, structural analysis, functional analysis
egogram 7–10; internal 10; organisational 8; as assessment tool 30
Elias, J. L., Merriam, S. B. 389
Ellis, A. 31, 33
emergence 249
emotional, deprivation 42; literacy 50
emotionally focused therapy 110–111
empathy 34; compassion triangle 95; substitute feelings 104; in group therapy 225; empathic listening 57; in schema therapy 180; in supervision 264; and transference 78; "virtuous psychiatry" 253; *also* 219, 293–294, 359, 393, 406

Emrys-Lamé, M. 111–112 radical
enactment, game 93–94
English, F., episcript 149; four story exercise 146; fourth hunger 52, 185; racketeering 103–104; script revision 321; script is structuring 145; three-cornered contract 194, 204, 326; *also* 230, 332
episcript 149
Erikson, E. 4–5, 118, 154
Ernst, F. 33–34; *see also* OK corral
Erskine, R. G. relationship hunger, relational needs 41; transference 78; script 140–144, 147–148, 152; script system 116–117, 140; supervision 225, 261; therapeutic relationship 147–148
Erskine, R. G., Moursund, J. P. 175, 294, 323
Erskine, R. G., Trautmann, R. 175, 33
Erskine, R. G., Zalcman, M. 140, 294, 397
escalation ladder 228–229
escape clauses 149–150
escape hatch 197–198
ethicability 255
ethics, chapt 9; of care in education 57; codes of 179–180, 242–244; confidentiality 253; and culture 238–239; dilemmas 246–247; ethical maturity 255; and neuroscience 249; dual relationships 245–246; professional 241–242; and social class 238–239; and statistics 253; and therapeutic errors 250; of trust 249–250; and virtue 253
ethos *see* integrated Adult
Euhemerus figure 214
Eusden, S. 241, 247, 250, 266
evaluation 179, 369, 373
Evans, C., Connell, J. et al. 292
exclusion 22
existential positions, life positions, OK corral, windows on the world 121–125; *also* viii, 33, 134, 221–222, 345, 401–403, 405–411; *see also* three-dimensional OKness
externalisation 155

fairy tales 105–106
Fallaci, O. 46

family systems 125, 145, 181, *see also* systems theory
family constellations 230–231
Fassbind-Kech, L. 323, 328–333
Federn, P. 4–5, 31, *also* 118
Fennis, B. 17
Fiddelaers-Jaspers, R., Ruigrok, J. 405–406
Fonagy, P., Bateman, A. W. et al. 32
Fonagy, P., Gergely, G. et al. 56
four story exercise 146
fourth hunger 52
Fowlie, H., Sills, C. 203–204, 282, 286
Fox, E. M. 213
Fraenkel, P., Hameline, T. et al. 155
frame of reference 16, 22, 29, 60, 144, 212
Frankl, V. 98
freedom, individual and social 53; practice of 390
free will 17, 248, *see also* autonomy
French, W. L., Bell, C. H. et al. 369
Freud, S., and ego states 7; experience alters memory 14; "drives" 31; psychosexual development 154; the unconscious 184; mental instability 272; "set the foundation" 379; on therapy 282; transference 71
Freudenberger, H. 106
Freire, P., Ramos, M. 390
Fromm-Reichmann, F. 181
Fujii, D., Ahmed, I. 182
functional analysis 5–6; feelings 103–104
functional ego states 6–7, 69, 317; *see also* ego states
functional fluency 19, 24–25, 385

Gabbard, G. O. 31–32
gallows laughter 200, 304
games, chapt 4; vii, 86; bilateral nature of 88; dealing with 92–93; as enactment 93–94; failed attempts at stroking 145; communication as well as defence 93; degrees of 90, 281; in the classroom 108–109; therapeutic interventions 281–282; recognising invitations 91; in the organisation 111–112, 351; switch 100–102, 105; and symbiosis 164–165; *see also* time-structuring
Games People Play 98–100

Garfield, D. A. S. 182
Gazzaniga, M. 249
Geekie, J., Read, J. 182
Gendlin, E. T. 34
gestalt theory 34, 160
Giessen-Bloo, J., Dyck, R. van et al. 34
Gilbert, M. 29
Gilbert, M., Evans, K. 396, 398
Gilbert, P., Leahy, R. L. 33
Glasl, F. 228–230
Gobes, L. 265
Goleman, D. 343, 348
Goodman, M. 282
Gopnik, A. 15
Gordon, T. 57
Goulding, R. 228
Goulding, R., McClure Goulding, M., contracting 192, 200, 377; cultural injunctions 399; redecision therapy 34, 129–134, 160, 175–176, 185, 301–304; script change from Adult 149; power is in the patient 272; *also* 374
Gowling, D., Agar, J. 93–94
Graaf, A. de 225–227, 343–348
Graaf, A. de, Kunst, K. 94, 125, 138–139, 205
Graaf, A. de, Levy, J. 95, 238
Grant, J. 334–337
Grégoire, J. 322, 326
groups and organisations, chapt 8; authority in 213–215; group behaviour 225–227; boundaries 215; canon 214–215; group-focused conflict 228; counselling groups 313; culture 215, 377; development 222–224; ending 233; identity 227; group imago 216–231 *passim*, 370–372, *see also* learning imagoes; group's group imago 224; group in the individual 152–153, 226–227; phases 227; process 213–226 *passim*, 314–317; structure 215–218; task 218–220; group-work in treatment 212, 225–228
group relations 45–46, 232–233
Guglielmotti, R. L. 145, 175

Haan, E. de 80
Haimowitz, M. L., Haimowitz, N. R. 44, 198

Hargaden, H. 118
Hargaden, H., Sills, C. deconfusion 78, 294; game enactment 93; the self 33; redecision therapy 296; relational transactional analysis 79, 282, 286
Harlow, H. F., Harlow, M. K. 42
Harrington, A. 181
Harris, A. 287–289
Harris, A. B., Harris, T. 139
Harris, T. A. 33, 80, 122, 345
Hawkes, L. 387
Hay, J. accountability 53; change process 142, 172, 178, 199, 270–271, 397; coach supervision 265; contamination 20; contracting 191, 195, 344; development of Child 14; egogram 7, 10; existential positions (windows on the world) 124–125, 345, 401; working styles 138
Haykin, M. D. 182
healthy parenting 176, 178, *see also* parent education
Heathcote, A. 5
Hekken, S. M. J. van 112
Hellinga, G. 90
Hellinger, B. 230–231
Hersey, P., Blanchard, K. H. 274
Hine, J. 29, 88
Hogg, M., Abrams, D. 153, 226–227
Hoijtink, T. 231–232
Holdeman, Q. L. 79
Holloway, W. H. 149
Hopkins, B. 406
Hopping, G., Hurst, G. I. 225
Horn, E. K., Bartak, A. et al. 305
"hot potato" *see* episcript
humanistic approaches 34–35
hunger(s) 40–42, 52–53; to belong 41; recognition 56; stimulus 42; hungers triangle 396
Hüther, G. 331

id-ego-superego 7
identity, individual and group 152–154; mutual influence in development of 154; externalisation of 155; *see also* meta-perspective

I'm OK, you're OK (book) 80; (phrase) viii, 33–34, 121–122, 345; They're OK 53, 363
imago *see* group imago, learning imago
impasses 78, 81, 289, 296
injunctions 125–136, 140; cultural 399, 403
integrated and integrating Adult *see* Adult
integrated Parent 244–245
integrated self 28
integrity 53
interventions, therapeutic 281–285
intimacy scale 49
introject(ion) 13–16, 78; replacement not therapeutic 175
intuition 4, 33

Jacobs, A. 174, 180
James, M. 297, 332
Jaoui, G. 387
Johnson, S. 110–111
Joines, V. 76–77, 91
Jorgensen, E. W., Jorgensen, H. I. 118
Joseph, M. R. 282

Kadushin, A. 266
Kahler, T. 136, 139–140
Kahler, T., Capers, H. 134, 136, 297
Kahn, E. 5
Kapur, R., Miller, K. 228
Karpman, S. intimacy 49; effectiveness 60; exercising options 297, 372, 375; psychological games 351; *see also* compassion triangle, drama triangle
Katzenbach, J. R. 56
Kendler, K. S., Prescott, C. A. 120
Kessler, R. C., Berglund, P. et al. 291
Kessler, R. C., Chiu, W. T. et al. 291
Kets de Vries, M. F. R. 35
Klein, M. 31, 33
Kohlberg, L. 250–251
Kohlrieser, G. 225
Kouwenhoven, M. 166, 171, 197–198, 244–245, 349–356
Krausz, R. 221, 368, 370
Kroenke, K., Spitzer, R. L. et al. 292
Kübler-Ross, E. 199

Kupfer, D. 244
Kupfer, D., Haimowitz, H. 297

Laing, R.D. 181–182
Lamme, V. 248–249
Landaiche, M. 225–226, 321, 324–328
Lapworth, P., Sills, C. et al. 268
leadership, group 213–214; "in heart and bones" 405–407; organisational 35, 109–110; and school culture (*case study*) 383–388; situational 274–275; styles 275
learned helplessness 208
learning, and personal development chapt 14; in counselling relationships 324, 328; contracts 198, 206, 390; cycle and spiral 148; humanistic 391–392; imagos 224, 389–391; progressive 391; radical 392–334; transformational 385, 387, 391
learning styles and types 385–387, 389–394
Lee, A. 140–141, 215–216
Levin-Landheer, P. 176, 384
Levine, B. 227
Lidz, T. 161, 181
Lieberman, M. A., Yalom, I. D. et al. 228
Lietaer, G. Vanaerschot, G. et al. 34
life plan 117–119, 147, *see also* script
life positions *see* existential positions
life-script vii, *see also* script
Ligabue, S. 144–145, 282
Little, M. I. 182
"Little Professor" *see* Adult; also 43, 52, 239–240
logos *see* integrated Adult
Loomis, M. 313
Loria, B. R. 175, 273
Luca, M. L. de, Tosi, M. T. 26, 28

Macefield, R., Mellor, K. 171
Mahler, M., Pine, F. et al. 153–154
management and organisational development, chapt 13; *see also* organisations
Mandela, Nelson 57
Maquet, J. 325
Maroda, K. 254
Maslow, A. 54–55, 272
Massey, R. F. 117

Mazzetti, M., comparative script system 268; legal restrictions to counselling 328; minding therapeutic error 250; supervision 260, 264
McClelland, D. 343
McClendon, R. 179
McClure Goulding, M., Goulding, R. L. 34
McCold, P., Wachtel, B. 407
McCormick, P. 44, 61, 63
McGrath, G. 249–250
McKenna, J. 51
McLeod, J., McLeod, J. 319–320, 322
McNeel, J. 174–175, 304
Mehrabian, A. 66
Mellor, K. 53, 171
Mellor, K., Andrewartha, G. 175
Mellor, K., Sigmund, E. 169
memories, re-enacted 144; rewriting 14; spontaneous 30
mental health 175
mental organs *see* neurobiology
mentalisation theory 31–32, 56
Mezirow, J. 392
metacommunication 75–76, 82, *see also* transactions
meta-perspective, in education 396–397; in supervision 260–261
Micholt, N. 204, 366
milieu therapy 183, 301
"mind the gap" 249–250, *see also* Eusden, S.
mind, theory of, *see* mentalisation
Mineka, S., Zinbarg, R. 110
miniscript 134–136
Minuchin, S. 82
misattunement *see* script: decisions
Mitchell, S. 287
Moiso, C. 296
Monin, S. 319–324
moral development 239–240; reasoning 250–251
Moreno, J. L. 153
motivation 57
Mountain, A. 357–367
Mountain, A., Davidson, C. 41, 111
multiple sclerosis (*case study*) 334–337
Muste, E., Weertman, A. et al. 33

Napper, R., Newton, T. accounting and empowerment in education 171–172; stages of development 178; learning 328, learning contracts 206; learning imagos 224, 389; learning styles 385
narrative approach 148, 155
Naughton, M., Tudor, K. 250
needs, hierarchy of 54–55
Neill, J. 181
neural networks *see* neurobiology
neurobiology 28–30; caution re neuroscience 248; and ethics 249; of free will 248–249; of script formation 144
Newell, S., Jeffery, D. 108
Newton, T. 389–394; educational ethics 247; learning contracts 206; learning imagos 224; script as explanatory narrative 119; learning cycle/spiral 148; supervision triangle 266–267
Newton, T., Napper, R. 266, 270
Newton, T., Wong, G. 178
Nijs, M. 275
Noddings, N. 57
Norcross, J. C. 293
Noriega, G. 117, 150
Novak, E. 282
Novellino, M. 203, 287, 296–300
Novey, T. B. 180
nurture and structure 53

object relations theory 31–33, 225, 282
Oblas, A. S. 175
Ogden, T. 289
OK corral *see* existential positions
OK-ness viii; for care workers 400; in education 393; in management 358; three-dimensional 362, 398
OK-OK communication model 364, 394, 401–403
Oostrik, H. 409
Oostrik, H., & Ruigrok, J. 406, 409
operant conditioning 110
O'Reilly-Knapp, M., Erskine, R. G. 140
organisational development *(case study)* 368–373
organisational Parent system 349–356
organisations, change in 172–174; competencies for 342; critical attachment period for new employees in 112; culture of 8, 11, 35, 348; developing trust within *(case study)* 357–367; games in 109–110; neglected 111–112; neurotic/dysfunctional 35; personality and script in 30, 35, 192, 221–222; redecision work in *(case study)* 374–379; strokes in 54, 56; "working climate" in 343–348; working with 220–221; *see also* management
Os, J. van, Kapur, S. 182
Osnes, R. 297
Overholser, J. C. 207

Papaux, E. 387–388, 395–398
Parent-Adult-Child 32–33; ethos-logos-pathos 18, 239; and the unconscious 184; *see also* Child-Adult-Parent, ego stages, ego state
Parent, *see* ego state; crazy 160; critical 5; magical or electrode 13, 15, 52, 239–240, 350–351; integrated 244–245; in school 384; nurturing 5; structuring 5
parent education 176–179
Parent interview 174–175
parallel processes in supervision 266–268
parenting *see* healthy parenting
Parry, A. 148
passivity and discounting, chapt 6; 160; cycle 166–169; confrontation 173–174
pastimes *see* structuring time
pathology 19–20, 34
pathos *see* integrated Adult
Penfield, W. 5, 30
Perls, F., Hefferline, R. et al. 34
permission, protection and potency 197, 346–347, 397; and practice and perception 198; and injunction 125–126; to teach 387–388
permission wheel 387–388
Petriglieri, G., Wood, J. D. 225
phases, of life 154; in training 273
Pierini, A. 25–26, 145
Pierre, N. 206
Pine, F. 31–32
Pope, K., Sonne, J. et al. 252
positive psychology 208
positive regard 34, 225
Praag, D. van 34

Pratt, K. 399–404
Pratt, K., & Mbaligontsi, M. 401
primary maternal preoccupation 182
professional development, ethics in 252; supervision for 261–265, 272; of school staff *(case study)* 383–388
projection 76–77
psychiatry, anti-psychiatry 181–182; transactional analysis a radical 403; transactional analysis a social 41; *see also* collaboration, diagnosis
psychoanalysis 31–33
psychodynamic approaches 31–32
psychogram *see* egogram
psychological distance 204–205, 264, 366
psychosynthesis 34
psychotherapy, chapt 11; as short as possible 82, 92; collaborative *see* diagnosis; contracting in 190, 200–201; core competencies 280; goal of 78, 129, 190; group and milieu 183, 301–305; interventions 281–285; mutual learning 260; methodologies compared 228; three models of 175–176; four rules of 75

rackets 103–104; feelings 134, 185, 294, 321, 354, 397; patterns 303; system 140; *see* substitute feeling
racketeering 104
Radden, J., Sadler, J. 253
Randall, L. K. 369
rational emotive therapy 31, 33
Read, J., Mosher, L. R. 182
real ego *see* ego stages
re-childing 297
recognition, unit of, *see* stroke
"red and blue" 23–24
redecision therapy 34, 129–134, 175–176, 303–304; case-study 296–300
redefining 165–166, 169, *see also* defence mechanisms
reflexive process *see* parallel process
reinforcement 33
regression 80, 226, 232, 265, *see also* reparenting
relational transactional analysis 79–80, 203–204, 225, 282, 286

relationship, asymmetric 241; breaks in 247; dual 245–246; effective 67–68; hunger 41; inattention to 250
reparenting 34, 174–176, 180, 353
research, on conflict in groups 228; on effectiveness of transactional analysis therapy 183–184, 291; on ego states 26–28; functional fluency 23–25; on healing factors in group therapy 228; infant research 153–154; on milieu therapy 183; on redecision therapy 304–305; on single-case efficacy 183; *see also* evaluation
resilience 17, 146–147, 398
restorative justice 406, 408–410
Rijn, B. van, Wild, C. 291
Rijn, B. van, Wild, C. et al. 291
rituals *see* time-structuring
Rober, P., Walravens. G. et al. 155
Roberts, D. 358
Roeland, B. 399
Rogers, C. 34, 57, 272
Romanini, M. T. 25–26
Rose, M. 183
Rose, N., Abi-Rached, J. M. 248
Rose, S. 248–249
Rosseau, M., Rosseau, R. 374–379
Rovics, H. 206
Ruigrok, J. 405–411

Saint-Exupéry, A. de 57
Salters, D. 250
Satel, S., Lilienfeld, S. O. 14
schema therapy 31–34, 180
Schiff, A., Schiff, J. L. 167
Schiff, J. L. 160–183 *passim*, 164–165, 174–176, 353
Schiff, J. L., Mellor, K. et al. 297
schizophrenia 160–161; no single cause 182; schizophrenogenic family 181
Schmid, B. 368, 373
Schore, A. N. 30
Scilligo, P. 26–28
script, chapt 5; vii, 18, 88; analysis 212, 289, 370; change 148–149, 287–290; comparative system 268–270; as contract 193–194; conviction *see* cognitive fixation 161; cure 147; decisions 34, 147, 303;

episcript 149; formation 144–149, 161; genes and environment 120; script-free 129; hybrid 152–153; miniscript 134–136; narrative model 119, 148; as organisational structure 145–146, 348; patterns 152; protocol 144–145, 152; is structuring 145; and resilience 146–147; revision 117, 321; three-second 212; tragic 149; as transference drama 287; trans-generational transfer of 150; as unconscious relational pattern 147
script circle 150–152
script helix 125, 148–149, 397
script matrix 125–129; diagram 126; co-creative diagram 128
script system 140–144, 397; comparative 268–270
Searles, H. 268
self, awareness 312; -care for care workers 399; in depression 291; -disclosure by professionals 254–255; divided/false 182; -esteem see sense of; integrated 26, 28; origins of 30; -psychology 32; sense of 33, 117; within script 147
Seligman, M. E. 208
Senge, P. M. 272
Shadbolt, C. 93–94, 250
Shazer, S. de 83
Shipton, G., Smith, E. 319–320
Shohet, R., Hawkins, P. 261–262
Shotton, P. 394
Sichem, V. 326
Sills, C. 93, 193, 324
Sills, C., Hargaden, H., viii, 31
Sills, C., Mazzetti, M. 268
Sills, C., Salters, D. 268
Skolnikoff, A. 254–255
Slavin, J. 289
social-cognitive school 26–28
social psychiatry, transactional analysis as a 41
Socratic motivation 207–208
Soeteman, D., Verheul, R. et al. 184
solitary confinement 42
solution focused therapy 82–83, 206–207
somatic, interventions 282; resonance 144
Sork, A. 112
Spitz, R. 42

stages of development 176–179
Steare, R. 255
Steere, D. A. 144
Steiner, C. contracting 192–193, 197; emotional literacy 50, 223, 293, 397; games and addictions 107; I'm OK you're OK 121; OK-ness an interpersonal process 33; script matrix 125; stroke economy 50, 401; transactional analysis as a radical psychiatry 403; also 95
Stern, D. B. 287–290
Stern, D. N. 15, 55, 128, 154
Stewart, I. Berne's script 118, 126; no-contract 150; escape hatch 197–198; supervision model 261–263; treatment triangle 369
Stewart, I., Joines, V. autonomy 248; games 86; script beliefs 294; classification of strokes 43; 2nd-order structural analysis 13, 17; substitute feelings 103, 283; therapeutic relationship 293
stories and storytelling 105–106, 148
stoppers, see injunctions; and drivers 139–141; also 134–136
Strauman, T. J., Kolden, G. G. 294
strokes, chapt 2; classification 43; confusing combinations 44; economy 50, 400–401; in organisations 346; profile 51
structural analysis 4–5; 1st order 9–10; 2nd order 12–17; 3rd order 12–13; see also 23–24
structuring time see time-structuring
Stuntz, E. C. 297
Stuthridge, J. 93–94, 212, 282, 286–290
substitute feeling 102–105
Sullivan, H. S. 181
Summers, G., Tudor, K. 128, 148, 397
supervision, chapt 10; on boundaries 251–252; in coaching 261, 265; comparative script system 268–270; continuing 261; on contract 241, 246; educational 261; functions of 266; integrating model 266; in organisations 272, 274; parallel process 266–268; phases 273; seven-eyed model of 261–262
supervision checklist 264–265
supervision matrix 261–263
supervision triangle 266–267

Suriyaprakash, C. 238–239, 297, 368–373
Suriyaprakash, C., Mohanraj, I. A. 372
survival mechanisms *see* defence mechanisms
Swaab, D. 248–249
symbiosis 160–164; competitive 164; complementary 164; disrupting symbiosis 167; dysfunctional 163–166; healthy and functional 161–162; regression to dependence 182; in teacher-student relationships 393
symbiotic chain 23, 79
systems theory 11, 81–82; *also* 4, 61; *see also* family systems, groups and organisations, script system

talking, "just talking" 327–328
Tang, T. Z., DeRubeis, R. J. 292
Temple, S. 19, 24–25, 385, 388, 401
therapeutic relationship, boundaries of 246–247, 252; in cognitive behavioural and schema therapies 33–34, 180; frame 203; integrated self and 27; metacommunication in 75–76; OK-OK 293; quality of 79–80, 253, 264; facilitates script change 147–148; 293, *also* 160, 190; *see also* relationship, transference
therapy, *see* specific modalities; methodologies compared 228
Thomas, A., Chess, S. 146
Thomson, G. 104
three-cornered contract *see* contract; *see also* psychological distance
three-dimensional OK-ness 53, 361–363, 398
Thunnissen, M. 29, 51, 185, 193, 200, 301–305
Tilney, T. 140–141
time, significance of 328
time-structuring 46–49, 91, 104, 397
Tosi, M. T. 148
training, phases in 273
transactions, chapt 3; vii, 60–61; angular 72–73; blocking 74; bulls-eye 74–75; complementary 23, 61–64, 66, 68–70, 89, 100; crossed 64–65, 67, 70–72, 185; duplex 73–74; exercising options 375; meta-communicative 75–76, 82; and responsibility 249; rules of 66–67; social and psychological levels of 61–64; tangential 74; transferential 287; ulterior 65–67, 72–74, 76
transactional analysis, core statements of viii; interpersonal and intra-psychic 12, 31–33, 41, 60, 77, 81, 212, 301; models, purpose of 81; an over-simplification 80–81; overview vii–ix; philosophy of viii, 192, 240–241, 358, 389, 395, 398; as a radical psychiatry 403; script of 118; *see also* cathexis, classical, co-creative, redecision, relational, social-cognitive
transactional analyst *see* certified transactional analyst; educational 387; identity of 227, 398
transactional psychoanalysis 296–297
transference/countertransference 77–78; in cathexis school 179–180; co-transference 78; in games 93–94; as metacommunication 75; in schooling 392; self-disclosure and narcissism 254; and script change 287–290; in supervision 262–268, 273; transference reaction 71; *also* 293, 296–299, 322
trauma, working with 282
treatment triangle 369
trust viii, 154, 177, 249–250, 343–348, 357
Tuckman, B. 223–224
Tudor, K. 18–19, 139, 203–204, 260, 313
Tudor, K., Summers, G. 78, 125, 128, 148, 388
Turquet, P. M. 233
typology of learning *see* learning styles

ulterior *see* transactions
unconditional positive regard 34, *see also* empathy
unconscious, the 184; competence 270; of therapist and client 33; and contract 193–194

Vaillant, G. E. 146
Vaglum, P., Friis, S. et al. 183
Vandra, A. 76, 109
Verhaeghe, P. 253
Verplaetse, J. 248
Verzaal, B. 328
Vinella, P. 313–318
virtue and ethical behaviour 253

Waals, J. van der 192
Wachtel, T.,
Wagner, A. 23
Waldenkranz-Piselli, K. C. 144
Watkins, C. E. 273
Watzlawick, P., Beavin, J. H. et al. 81
Weiner, M. 254
Weisfelt, P. 151
Weiss, E. 31
Weiss, L. 180
Whitaker, D. S., Lieberman, M. 228
White, M. 155
White, T. 11
Widdowson, M. 75–76, 183, 291–295, 309
Willi, J. 82

windows on the world *see* existential positions
winner's triangle 397, 403–404; *see also* drama triangle
Winnicott, D. W. 31, 182–183
withdrawal *see* time-structuring
Woollams, S., Brown, M. 20, 75, 239–240

Yalom, I. D. 227
Yalom, I. D., Leszcz, M. 228
Yogelson, S., Samenow, S. E. 353
Young, J. E., Klosko, J. S. et al. 33, 180

Zalcman, M. J., Cornell, W. F. 260
Zimbardo, P. 226
Zvelc, G. 282

OVERVIEW OF IMPORTANT WEBSITES

Some TA websites

Find the International Association for Transactional Analysis (ITAA):
www.itaaworld.org

Find information on TA training and TA certification:
www.itaaworld.org/training-and-certification-transactional-analysis

Find regional Transactional Analysis associations:
www.itaaworld.org/ta-associations

Find the European Association for Transactional Analysis (EATA):
www.eatanews.org

Find national Transactional Analysis associations in Europe:
www.eatanews.org/ta-resources-and-links/national-associations

Find out more about the Eric Berne Memorial Award winners:
www.itaaworld.org/itaa-awards